THE JURISPRUDENCE OF SPORT

SPORTS AND GAMES AS LEGAL SYSTEMS

■ ■ ■

Mitchell N. Berman
Leon Meltzer Professor of Law
The University of Pennsylvania Carey Law School

Richard D. Friedman
Alene and Allan F. Smith Professor of Law
The University of Michigan Law School

AMERICAN CASEBOOK SERIES®

American Casebook Series is a trademark registered in the U.S. Patent and Trademark Office.

© 2021 LEG, Inc. d/b/a West Academic
    444 Cedar Street, Suite 700
    St. Paul, MN 55101
    1-877-888-1330

West, West Academic Publishing, and West Academic are trademarks of West Publishing Corporation, used under license.

Printed in the United States of America

ISBN: 978-1-68467-890-7

For my parents—the best sports, always.

MNB

To my children—Rebecca, Danny, and Julia—with overflowing love and pride, and the hope that they will cherish taking their kids to sports events as much as their father and grandfather have. L'dor v'dor.

RDF

PREFACE

We are excited to present this book, which we hope will facilitate and spur the teaching of courses on the jurisprudence of sports, both in law schools and beyond. The simple premise of the book is that competitive games and sports are legal systems, and so they offer as fertile ground for intellectual gain and for exploration of jurisprudential issues as any other area of law. Think how telecasts of some sports events now routinely feature rules experts; the networks realize that rules issues are integral to the sports, and that fans want to understand them. As compared to other legal systems, sports offer at least two substantial and distinct advantages. First, for most sports fans, they are a lot more fun than, say, the law of public utilities or of diversity jurisdiction. And second, they do not demand any prior doctrinal knowledge; that is why we believe this course readily lends itself to use outside of law schools.

A few points of terminology and usage. We have striven for overall gender neutrality. Sometimes, depending on the situation, we have used masculine pronouns, sometime feminine ones, and sometimes, after some hesitation, we have used Merriam-Webster's 2019 Word of the Year, the singular they. One of us (Rich) wishes there were a widely used set of neutral singular pronouns; the other (Mitch) expects that "they" will work just fine. Either way, we have used the singular "they" sparingly and only where the context makes clear that it refers to a single person. We generally use "Black" to refer to persons from sub-Saharan Africa, or with recent origins there, anthropologically speaking. We capitalize "Black," but not "white," for essentially the same reasons that recently led The New York Times to adopt that convention: "white doesn't represent a shared culture and history in the way Black does, and also has long been capitalized by hate groups." Nancy Coleman, *Why We're Capitalizing Black*, N.Y. TIMES, July 5, 2020.

We use "football" to describe the sport known by that name in North America, and "soccer" for the sport generally known as "football," or variations of it, in most of the rest of the world.

We have taken a relatively relaxed approach to citations, largely to avoid clutter. We have used our judgment as to whether we need to offer a citation for a particular proposition. Most of the sources we have cited, other than books, may be readily found on the internet, and we have not presented a url when we thought a good search engine will do the job. Where we have found it useful to provide a website, we have generally given a tinyurl; these, we have found, are easy to use to bring up the source.

When we have included a footnote from a quoted text, the numbering is as in the original. To avoid confusion, all footnotes written by us—whether appended to a quoted text or to our original text—are indicated by letters, consecutive within each chapter.

We have worked hard to make the book current and accurate; given the broad scope of its coverage, however, we suspect that errors have crept in, perhaps many of them. We invite readers to tell us of any, by email to mitchberman@law.upenn.edu or rdfrdman@umich.edu. We will keep a running list of corrections, which you can get by writing either of us.

Of course, we have many people to thank. We will begin with Jody Kraus, our matchmaker. Although the two of us had known each other for years—in fact, Mitch was Rich's student in Evidence long ago—we might never have known that we had a mutual interest in this subject area, and in pursuing it seriously, had it not been for conversations we each had with Jody.

Next, we offer profound thanks to our institutions (the University of Michigan Law School for Rich, and the University of Texas Law School and then the University of Pennsylvania Carey Law School for Mitch), and to our deans (Evan Caminker, Mark West, Bill Powers, Larry Sager, Ward Farnsworth, and Ted Ruger) for their unflagging encouragement and support. We are also grateful to many colleagues, at our institutions and elsewhere, for additional encouragement, advice, and constructive criticism, among them Larry Alexander, Yaron Covo, Paul Gaffney, Scott Hershovitz, Sandy Levinson, Sinclair MacRae, Bill Miller, Bill Morgan, Chad Oldfather, John Pike, and John Russell. Most importantly, we have had enormously helpful staff support and we have been blessed to teach these materials and their predecessors to scores of talented and engaged students whose enthusiasm kept us going, and whose suggestions immeasurably improved this book. For contributions in or out of class, or for research assistance, we especially acknowledge Pratik Agarwal, Kirk Anderson, Matt Behnke, Jamie Bircoll, Sarah Byrne, Ashlynn Dobbs, Devon Donohue, Jonathan Dunn, Jordan Einstein, Jackson Eskay, Kristin Firth, Ondrej Gaiser-Palecek, Daniel Gordon, Kami Groom, Benjamin Harkins, Emily Horwitz, Margaret Klocinski, Nicole Malick, Fadi Mohamed, Kenneth Moreland, Karen Pritula, Nathan Riehl, Cassidy Rowe, Stacey Rzeszut, Brett Schwab, Joseph Skrokov, David Socol De la Osa, and Anthony Vitti. This is surely an incomplete list and we apologize to those whom one or the other of us inadvertently omitted.

Finally, we each thank the other. We are each confident that the book is far better than it would have been if one of us had been foolish enough to try to write it on his own. We came to this project, and we complete it, with different interests and different intellectual orientations, and we believe those differences have strengthened the book and helped it accommodate a wide variety of teaching approaches.

We hope that readers—students, teachers, and anybody else who opens it up—enjoy it as much as we have enjoyed writing it.

Let the Games begin!

MITCH BERMAN
RICH FRIEDMAN

January 2021

ACKNOWLEDGMENTS

The photo on the front cover is from a game played at the Polo Grounds in New York, NY, on September 6, 1952, and is published with the permission of Getty Images. The original caption read as follows: "Jackie Robinson, Dodgers second baseman, doesn't think he was out in the sixth inning when the Giants picked him off second and he didn't waste any time telling Umpire Al Barlick about it. After the fury Robinson walked back to the dugout, just as out as he was before the argument. There were no outs with Pee Wee Reese on third and Robinson on second when the play came. The Giants won the first of two games, 6–4."

We gratefully acknowledge permission from the following authors or their estates, publishers, and organizations to reproduce portions of the works indicated: Ludwig Wittgenstein, *Philosophical Investigations* (Wiley-Blackwell 1953); Aside, *The Common Law Origins of the Infield Fly Rule*, 123 U. Pa. L. Rev. 1474 (1975); United States Golf Association and the Royal & Ancient, *Explanation of Decision to Adopt Rule 14–1b of the Rules of Golf* (May 21, 2013); Major League Baseball, *Comments to Rule 6.01* (2014); Cesar R. Torres & Douglas W. McLaughlin, *Indigestion?: An Apology for Ties*, 30 J. Phil. Sport 144 (2003); Robert L. Simon, *The Ethics of Strategic Fouling: A Reply to Fraleigh*, 32 J. Phil. Sport 87 (2005); Bill Simons, *Common sense vs. the NBA rulebook*, ESPN.com (May 16, 2007, updated May 30, 2007); John Coggon, Natasha Hammond & Søren Holm, *Transsexuals in Sport—Fairness and Freedom, Regulation and Law*, 2 Sport, Ethics & Phil. 4 (2008); NCAA Office of Inclusion, *NCAA Inclusion of Transgender Student-Athletes* (Aug. 2011); Women's Sports Foundation, *Purse Equity in Professional Sports: The Foundation Position* (Sept. 9, 2016); Karen Crouse, *Swimming Bans High-Tech Suits, Ending an Era*, N.Y. Times, July 24, 2009; William J. Morgan, *Athletic Perfection, Performance-Enhancing Drugs, and the Treatment-Enhancement Distinction*, 36 J. Phil. Sport 162 (2009); World Anti-Doping Agency, World Anti-Doping Code (2021); World Anti-Doping Agency, International Standard: Therapeutic Use Exemptions (2021); Aaron Gordon, *The Myth of Competitive Balance*, sportsonearth.com (August 8, 2013); Lee MacPhail, *American League President's Decision on the Pine Tar Game*, N.Y. Times, July 29, 1983; David Pozen, *What Are the Rules of Soccer?*, Balkinization (June 20, 2019); Ronald Dworkin, *Taking Rights Seriously* (The Belknap Press of Harvard University Press, 1977); Bruce Weber, *As They See 'Em: A Fan's Travels in the Land of Umpires* (Scribner 2009); Mark Hamilton, *The Moral Ambiguity of the Makeup Call*, 38 J. Phil. Sport 212 (2011); William T. Pizzi, *"Makeup Calls" in Sports and Courts*, 11 Green Bag 2d 333 (2008); Tobias J. Moskowitz & L. Jon Wertheim, *Scorecasting: The*

Hidden Influences Behind How Sports are Played and Games are Won (Crown Archetype 2011); Stephen Jay Gould, *The Strike That was Low and Outside,* N.Y. Times, Nov. 10, 1984; John Branch, *Rodriguez Keeps Straddling Baseball's Foul Line,* N.Y. Times, June 1, 2007; Bruce Weber, *A Boy Scout Pulls a Fast One,* N.Y. Times, Sept. 18, 2010; Cesar Torres, *On Diving: Soccer's Integrity is at Stake,* The New York Times Soccer Blog, Sept. 17, 2009; Sam Borden, *The Goal is Winning Gold, Not Winning Every Match,* N.Y. Times, Aug. 2, 2012; Edward Wyatt, *BackTalk; Stopping for Armstrong's Spill Draws the Second-Guessers to Ullrich,* N.Y. Times, Aug. 10, 2003; James Corrigan, *When Sport Became More than a Game,* The Independent (U.K.), July 30, 2009; Seth Vannatta, *Calling Your Own: Custom and Law in Sports Officiating* (unpublished manuscript, Sept. 9, 2011); Shayna M. Sigman, *Are We All Dopes? A Behavioral Law and Economics Approach to Legal Regulation of Doping in Sports,* 19 Marq. Sports L. Rev. 125 (2008); Greg Bishop, *N.C.A.A. Penalties Erase Wins but Not Memories,* N.Y. Times, Aug. 1, 2011.

SUMMARY OF CONTENTS

PART V. OUTSIDE THE LINES

TABLE OF CONTENTS

THE JURISPRUDENCE OF SPORT

SPORTS AND GAMES AS LEGAL SYSTEMS

INTRODUCTION

∎ ∎ ∎

Sports play a significant and enduring role in human life. Across the globe, billions of people participate in organized sports regularly, and billions more follow professional and amateur sports as spectators and fans. For example, the NFL Super Bowl now routinely draws over 110 million viewers in the United States alone. That is relatively small potatoes internationally. Over a billion people watched the final game of the 2018 FIFA World Cup, and about the same number (but with a different geographic distribution!) watched India beat Pakistan in the 2015 Cricket World Cup—and that was just a pool-play match. Moreover, fans' interest in spectator sports is not just casual. The notoriously drunken and violent fans of Scottish soccer powerhouse Celtic, for example, once insisted that Celtic is better even than "Drink, Sex, [and] Fighting." Mary Midgley, *The Game Game,* 49 PHILOSOPHY 231, 237 (1974). More encouragingly, sports have a capacity to uplift and unite people rivaled by few other activities. As one commentator observed: "Sport has the power to change the world. It has the power to inspire, the power to unite people that little else has. . . . It is more powerful than governments in breaking down racial barriers." JOHN CARLIN, PLAYING THE ENEMY: NELSON MANDELA AND THE GAME THAT MADE A NATION 4 (2008). The speaker wasn't a sports journalist or league pitchman, from whom breathless praise can be expected. It was Nelson Mandela, who knew a thing or two about breaking down barriers.

Not surprisingly, sport is also big business. In the United States alone, the major sport leagues and associations gross in excess of $30 billion annually. Overall, the sports industry is the eleventh largest industry in the nation, comprising over 2% of GDP. *See* Justin Wolfers, *The Business of Sports,* https://tinyurl.com/y2o4zemg. Prior to the COVID-19 pandemic, the global sports industry was valued at about half a trillion dollars, with further healthy growth expected. Samantha McDonald, *Run the Numbers: Here's How Much the Global Sports Market Could be Worth by 2023,* footwearnews.com (July 17, 2019).

Sports are not only rewarding to play and diverting to watch. They do more than contribute massively to national and world economies. They are also worthy of serious and sustained intellectual attention. They are fit subjects of study.

To start, one simply cannot understand twentieth-century social history, in the U.S. or internationally, without attending to the influence of sport. Mandela issued his paean to sports when explaining why hosting the 1995 Rugby World Cup was integral to his vision for a post-Apartheid

South Africa. Domestically, Jackie Robinson's breaking of the Major League Baseball color line in 1947, and the 1972 passage of Title IX of the Civil Rights Act, which mandates sex equity in every educational program that receives federal funding, were watershed moments in the struggles for racial and gender equality in the United States. In the current day, the story of the Black Lives Matter movement could not be told without a chapter or two devoted to quarterback Colin Kaepernick's silent protest against racial inequality, and the responses and counter-responses it provoked. And Mississippi's decision in 2020 that it would no longer incorporate the Confederate battle flag symbol in its own flag is the latest in a series of significant governmental changes prompted by pressure from the NCAA or other sports organizations.

Increasingly, sports are also being studied by psychologists and economists for the lessons they can teach about human behavior. For example, a study of putting by professional golfers has provided powerful empirical support for the psychological bias called "loss aversion," the phenomenon by which people disvalue losses (bogeys in this case) more than they value gains of equal objective magnitude (birdies). Devin G. Pope & Maurice E. Schweitzer, *Is Tiger Woods Loss Averse? Persistent Bias in the Face of Experience, Competition, and High Stakes*, 101 AMERICAN ECONOMIC REVIEW, 129 (2011). A detailed study of calls by NBA referees demonstrated the presence of racial bias. Devin G. Pope, Joseph Price, & Justin Wolfers, *Awareness Reduces Racial Bias*, 64 MANAGEMENT SCIENCE 4967 (2018). As Nate Silver, the statistician who gained fame for his dead-on predictions of the 2008 and 2012 elections, notes, "Sports and games, because they follow well-defined rules, represent good laboratories for testing our predictive skills." NATE SILVER, THE SIGNAL AND THE NOISE: WHY SO MANY PREDICTIONS FAIL—BUT SOME DON'T 16 (2012).

Silver's comment highlights a reason why sports, and even games that are not considered sports, are an excellent field of inquiry for students of law, as well as of other disciplines: sports and games are, in a clear and recognizable sense, legal systems. The most popular global team sports are all formally governed by "laws," not "rules,"—the "laws of cricket," the "laws of rugby," and so on. Even the major home-grown American team sports (baseball, football, and basketball), which do not formally designate their rules as "laws," do routinely characterize prohibited conduct as "illegal." But the law-ness of sports systems is not merely superficial or semantic. "Every organized sport begins the same way, with the creation of rules." Eric Adelson, *Let 'Em Play*, ESPN THE MAGAZINE, April 21, 2008, at 52. If you begin to play a game with which you are unfamiliar, probably one of your first questions will be, "What are the rules?" Angel Maria Villar Llona, a former soccer midfielder, lawyer, and president of the Spanish Football Federation, has gone so far as to say that "the Laws of the Game" are "the soul of any sport." *See* FIFA, *The IFAB: How it works,* https://tinyurl.com/y395kgl6. Note that the same is not true of, say, going to the beach or a dinner party. Surely there are rules about how one should behave in these contexts, but only rarely would the primary concern of a person newly arriving at either one be, "What are the rules?" And not even a lawyer would say that those rules are "the soul" of a trip to the beach or an evening of companionable dining.

Even informal sports competitions—such as pickup basketball at a local gym—are governed by a type of law, often determined informally and by custom in the way that any community may develop governing norms. But formalized sports systems at every level, from youth leagues to the pros, resemble state governance yet more closely: They are institutions designed to facilitate and regulate complex behaviors, principally by means of formal rules promulgated in advance by rulemaking bodies and enforced by independent adjudicators.

Because this course investigates sports and games as legal systems, it is a study in comparative law or jurisprudence. Comparative law is the study of different legal systems, often with the aim of drawing lessons— both about what works, and about what doesn't—from one system for transplantation or adaptation to another.[a] Representative works by comparative legal scholars have argued, for example, that the American system of adversarial litigation would be improved by incorporating elements of German judicial fact-finding, or that developing nations can better secure individual rights by adopting American-style judicial review.

Comparative Law [handwritten annotation]

This study is doubly comparative, or comparative at two levels. First, we will consider a wide variety of sports, each creating its own legal system. We may find, for example, that some broad principles apply across a wide range of sports. And by examining differences, we may gain a greater insight into the different nature of different sports, leading them to resolve similar problems in divergent ways. Or we may decide that one sport simply handles a given problem better than does another, and that the rulemakers of the second could improve their sport by paying closer attention to the first. Second, we will keep at least one eye on ordinary statist legal systems, drawing occasional lessons for sports from ordinary law, and vice versa.

Because many of the lessons that will interest us are abstract or theoretical, the course is also rightly described as "jurisprudential," a blanket term for theoretical inquiries of and about law. We will be studying principles, concepts, and problems that traditionally occupy legal theorists and philosophers of law—matters like the differences and tradeoffs

Jurisprudential [handwritten annotation]

---

[a] *Cf.* Mathias Reimann, *The End of Comparative Law as an Autonomous Subject*, 11 TUL. EUR. & CIVIL L. FORUM 49, 54 (1996) (listing, among the potential objectives of the comparative study of law, that it "provides foreign models for the improvement of domestic law," "reveal[s] the common core of all law," "provides critical perspectives on [a student's] domestic legal system," and helps students understand law's "contingency on history, society, politics, and economics").

between rules and standards, the nature of the interpretation of legal texts, the scope of legitimate adjudicatory discretion, and the relationship between formal and informal norms.

Our topic—we call it "the jurisprudence of sport"—may be usefully contrasted with "sports law." Sports law is a growing field of law practice. It concerns such matters as the legal regulation of professional and amateur sports leagues, the representation of athletes, the resolution of disputes in national and international athletic competitions, possible liability in tort and criminal law for wrongs committed on the field of play, and much more. It can be an exciting and financially rewarding area of practice, and an engaging subject of study.

But it has nothing to do with this book. This book concerns sports *as* law—not "sports law." Its subject is *not* how ordinary legal systems of a state interact with formal institutionalized sporting systems (entities like Major League Baseball, the Pro Golfers Association, and the NCAA), but rather the sets of rules and standards that these superficially disparate types of systems, and less formal ones as well, establish to create and shape the competitions they oversee. It explores both differences among these systems and ways in which they are alike and can illuminate each other. It is about the surprising and valuable lessons we might learn about sports by thinking hard about law—and about the lessons we can learn about law by investigating sports. And because law and sports are just two of the myriad of complex rule-based systems designed to structure, facilitate, empower, regulate, deter, incentivize, and punish human behavior of varied sorts, attention to sports and law together might even teach us something interesting about human life and institutions more generally.

The book is organized into five parts.

Part I, "Fundamentals," examines some basic issues. We begin by asking, "What is a sport?" together with the related question, "What is a game?" We then use a United States Supreme Court case, *PGA Tour v. Casey Martin,* to explore what (if anything) it means to speak of the essential characteristics of a game. And we canvass some of the most interesting and significant considerations that guide a gamewright when designing, refining, and amending the rules that make up, or constitute, the game or sport. (A gamewright is any entity or person who designs a game or sport or oversees its formal rules. The gamewright can be an individual suggesting to a companion an observation game that they can play while stuck in traffic. Or, at the other pole, it can be a recognized international rulemaking authority.)

Part II, "Structuring the Competition," explores the decisions that gamewrights must make in developing the overall structure of competitions. Topics addressed here include how to determine who wins a contest, how prohibited conduct should be penalized, who should be eligible to compete, what constraints should be imposed on equipment and performance enhancement, and how leagues and tournaments should be organized.

Part III, "Officiating," focuses on the adjudication of sports contests, principally on the role of on-field officials like referees and umpires. Topics examined in this Part include rule interpretation and application, the existence and scope of officiating discretion, the use of instant replay technology as a system of review, and other approaches to correcting officials' errors.

Part IV, "Playing the Game," focuses on various aspects of the often-blurry line between good competitive behavior and misconduct. The topic in this Part is not whether the *formal rules* of a sport should prohibit this or that conduct (an issue addressed in Part II), but on whether, or under what circumstances, players must comply with the rules and whether, or under what circumstances, they may take advantage of competitive opportunities that the formal rules don't foreclose. In short, we examine here the oft-invoked but poorly understood concepts of cheating, gamesmanship, and sportsmanship. (Incidentally, this is one place where we will depart from the gender-neutral language that we favor throughout the book. "Gamespersonship" and "sportspersonship" strike us as just too awkward notwithstanding the considerations that would recommend their use.)

Part V, "Outside the Lines," looks at two clusters of issues external to the design and play of a sport or game: the regulation of athletes' off-field conduct; and the keeping of records and bestowing of athletic honors.

Two icons are sprinkled in the margins through the book. The toolbox icon signals that the text has introduced a concept or analytic device that should be a part of any lawyer's conceptual toolbox. Some of these concepts are, roughly speaking, "internal" to law. The distinction between "rules" and "standards" is an example, as these are frequently understood as different types of legal norms. Other concepts were birthed outside of law, often in economics or psychology, but are of sufficient power and importance for thinking through legal problems that they should be well understood by any successful lawyer or law student. Cognitive biases such as "loss aversion" (already mentioned) are examples, as are agency costs and Arrow's impossibility theorem.

We encourage students to take careful note of the concepts and devices that the toolbox signals. As Ward Farnsworth explains in his wonderful book, *The Legal Analyst,*

> There are, in general, two sorts of things one learns at a law school. First, there are lots of legal rules—principles that tell you whether a contract is valid, for example, or when people have to

pay for accidents they cause, or what the difference is between
murder and manslaughter. Second, there are the tools for
thinking about legal problems—ideas such as the prisoner's
dilemma, or the differences between rules and standards, or the
notion of a baseline problem, or the problem of hindsight bias. . . .
[T]hese tools for thought are by far the more interesting, useful,
and fun part of a legal education. They enable you to see more
deeply into all sorts of questions, old and new, and say better,
more penetrating things about them.

   The problem is that law schools generally don't teach those
tools carefully or systematically. One might imagine it otherwise:
law school courses could be organized around tools rather than
legal subjects. . . . But instead law school is carved up the other
way around: by legal topics, not by tools. . . . Law tends to be
taught, in other words, as if legal rules were the most important
things one could learn, and as if the tools for thinking about them
were valuable but secondary—nice to know if someone happens to
explain them, but nothing urgent.

WARD FARNSWORTH, THE LEGAL ANALYST: A TOOLKIT FOR THINKING
ABOUT THE LAW vii-viii (2007). Farnsworth thinks this a very unfortunate
state of affairs, and we agree. We believe that a principal goal of the type
of course that this book facilitates is to use material that many students
will find familiar, stimulating, and fun as the vehicle for teaching analytic
tools that are at the heart of legal practice and legal reasoning.[b] Given this
book's chief focus (on sports, not on legal tools), it does not introduce all the
analytic devices that will be useful to you as law students and as lawyers.
Furthermore, given this book's length, we cannot always delve deeply into
the concepts that we do deploy; your instructor is likely to explore some of
the concepts further and to skip past others. The toolbox icon is a simple
way to draw attention to concepts and analytic devices with which you
should become familiar if you are not already. They are among the basic
"tools for thought" that can help us resolve problems that arise in law, in
sports, and in life.

   The second icon, the scales of justice, appears when the text raises an
 explicitly legal problem. Because the focus of this book is on
sport, we tend to introduce legal rules, decisions, practices
and the like to shed light on problems or puzzles that arise in
the world of sports. The direction of illumination in these

---

   [b] *New York Times* columnist David Brooks quotes the sociologist Eugen Rosenstock-Huessy:
"The world in which the American student who comes to me at about twenty years of age really
has confidence in is the world of sport. This world encompasses all of his virtues and experiences,
affection and interests; therefore, I have built my entire sociology around the experiences an
American has in athletes and games." David Brooks, *The Sporting Mind*, N.Y. TIMES, Feb. 5, 2010,
at A25. Just as many 20-year-old college students are dedicated sports fans, so are many 25-year-
old law students and middle-aged (or older) law professors.

situations is *from law to sport*. At other times, however, we invite you to harness your knowledge of practices in sport to improve the law. In such cases, the direction of illumination runs *from sport to law*, and we use the scales of justice to signal this inversion.

PART I

FUNDAMENTALS

■ ■ ■

This Part comprises four chapters. Chapters 1 and 2 examine, respectively, what sports and games are, and whether they have an "essence" or nature. Chapter 3 canvasses many of the goals that sports and games, as a class, commonly pursue. Chapter 4 reviews the core levers that a gamewright could deploy to realize the sport's or game's goals. Command of these general matters will aid the student when we turn, in Part II, to basic topics in game design.

CHAPTER 1

WHAT IS (A) SPORT?

■ ■ ■

Consider the following ten activities: baseball, tennis, golf, horse racing, gymnastics, weightlifting, bodybuilding, boxing, chess, and mountaineering. Which are sports?

Seemingly nobody questions whether baseball and tennis are sports. They are paradigmatic cases. If offered a definition of sport that excluded these activities, one would reasonably doubt that the proposed definition is one of sports at all. Yet the sport-ness of each of the other eight activities just mentioned has been contested. Each has been described as a sport by some people and challenged by others. And the list of borderline or contested cases could be expanded greatly. Croquet, poker, auto racing, ultimate, bridge, competitive cheer, League of Legends, darts, diving, ice dancing, ballet, penny-pitching, three-legged races, the egg-and-spoon race, mixed martial arts, fly fishing, deer hunting, long jumping, ski jumping, 100-meter running, 100-meter freestyle swimming, marathon running, and competitive eating—which are sports? Which are games? Which are both? Which are neither?

This chapter addresses these initial definitional or conceptual questions. It also explores why, if at all, they should matter.

———

Let's begin with the definitions of sport offered by two powerful organizations, each of which is periodically called upon to determine whether a particular activity counts as a sport and therefore should be brought within its sphere of administration: the National Collegiate Athletic Association (NCAA), and the International Olympic Committee (IOC). The NCAA defines a sport as "an institutional activity involving physical exertion with the purpose of competition versus other teams or individuals within a collegiate competition structure." NCAA EMERGING SPORTS FOR WOMEN PROCESS GUIDE, https://tinyurl.com/y3dz64fl. And a 2002 report of the IOC's Programme Commission endorsed the "commonly accepted" view that "sport is physical exertion in the conduct of competition." REVIEW OF THE OLYMPIC PROGRAMME AND THE RECOMMENDATIONS ON THE PROGRAMME OF THE GAMES OF THE XXIX OLYMPIAD, BEIJING 2008, Report by the Programme Commission Chairman, Franco Carraro, to the IOC Executive Board, August 2002, § 2.5.

These are strikingly similar definitions, containing two core elements: a sport is an activity that involves (1) physical exertion and (2) competition. But whether or not this is an adequate definition for NCAA and IOC purposes, it is plainly not an acceptable general definition. Take barroom brawling. That's an activity that involves physical exertion and competition, but it's not a sport. Therefore, the NCAA/IOC definition is overinclusive. Even if we add in the NCAA's idea that a sport must be institutionalized, it does not completely solve the problem for, again, not all activities that meet even these conditions are sports. Warfare is a competitive activity involving physical exertion that is also highly institutionalized, subject to an extensive set of rules. But it's not a sport. Auditions for a dance troupe or symphony also satisfy these three conditions but are not sports. So the definition remains overinclusive. The definition may be underinclusive too, for it is not obvious that all sports are institutionalized. (Did, say, snowboarding become a sport only when it became institutionalized and competitive structures developed?)

One possible response is that sports are a special type of *game*. On this common view, sports have three necessary and sufficient conditions. They are: (1) games that involve (2) physical exertion and (3) competition.

This seems to be an improvement. It seems to promise the benefit of excluding from sport the counterexamples (such as warfare and auditions) we have just offered. But in order to evaluate this proposed definition of sport more carefully, we need to know, of course, what games are. And, as it happens, that is the subject of longstanding philosophical controversy, thanks in large part to the eminent twentieth-century philosopher Ludwig Wittgenstein.

At least since Socrates, it has been accepted that a **"true definition"** of a thing consists of the set of necessary and sufficient attributes that the thing possesses. A definition of this sort frequently assumes the form of "genus and differentia," which is to say that it starts by identifying the general category in which the thing falls and then specifies the attributes that,

True Definition vs. Family Resemblance

in combination, differentiate it from all other members of the category. A *chair*, for example, might be defined (to a first approximation) as "a piece of furniture [the genus] designed to be sat upon by one individual at a time [the differentia]." Indeed, the proposed definition of sports under consideration—that sports are games involving physical exertion and competition—fits this model too.

In his posthumous *Philosophical Investigations*, however, Wittgenstein challenged the idea that all concepts have essences, or can be defined by true definitions. Instead, he introduced the notion of *family resemblance* concepts, an idea that he illustrated with the concept of game:

> 66. Consider for example the proceedings that we call "games". I mean board-games, card-games, ball-games, Olympic games, and so on. What is common to them all?—Don't say: "There must be something common, or they would not be called 'games' "—but look and see whether there is anything common to all.—For if you look at them you will not see something that is common to all, but similarities, relationships, and a whole series of them at that. To repeat: don't think, but look!—
>
> Look for example at board-games, with their multifarious relationships.
>
> Now pass to card-games; here you find many correspondences with the first group, but many common features drop out, and others appear.
>
> When we pass next to ball-games, much that is common is retained, but much is lost.—
>
> Are they all 'amusing'? Compare chess with noughts and crosses [i.e., tic-tac-toe]. Or is there always winning and losing, or competition between players? Think of patience [i.e., solitaire]. In ball games there is winning and losing; but when a child throws his ball at the wall and catches it again, this feature has disappeared. Look at the parts played by skill and luck; and at the difference between skill in chess and skill in tennis.
>
> Think now of games like ring-a-ring-a-roses; here is the element of amusement, but how many other characteristic features have disappeared! sometimes similarities of detail.

And we can go through the many, many other groups of games in the same way; can see how similarities crop up and disappear.

And the result of this examination is: we see a complicated network of similarities overlapping and criss-crossing: sometimes overall similarities.

67. I can think of no better expression to characterize these similarities than "family resemblances"; for the various resemblances between members of a family: build, features, colour of eyes, gait, temperament, etc. etc. overlap and criss-cross in the same way. But it is not clear that games can be defined in this fashion.—And I shall say: 'games' form a family.

LUDWIG WITTGENSTEIN, PHILOSOPHICAL INVESTIGATIONS 95 (1953). Wittgenstein's notion of **"family resemblance"** categories, though highly controversial in some circles, won wide acceptance in others. In particular, many scholars accepted that no set of necessary and sufficient conditions could serve as a definition of our concept of a game. A Canadian philosopher, Bernard Suits, challenged that claim in his 1978 book, *The Grasshopper: Games, Life and Utopia*.[a]

On Suits's account, games are rule-governed activities that satisfy four conditions: (a) a participant pursues a goal describable as a state of affairs, (b) using only those means permitted by the rules, (c) where those rules exclude more efficient in favor of less efficient means of realizing the goal, and (d) in which the participant accepts the limitations to make the activity possible. "Playing a game," in Suits's shorthand, "is a voluntary attempt to overcome unnecessary obstacles."[b]

---

[a] Some question whether Suits really did challenge Wittgenstein's claim. They read Suits not as having attempted to define the concept as the community of ordinary users had already employed it, but rather as having proposed a *stipulated* definition of game for certain purposes. And Wittgenstein doesn't deny that we could do *that*.

[b] BERNARD SUITS, THE GRASSHOPPER: GAMES, LIFE AND UTOPIA 55 (1978). For a broadly similar proposal, see KATIE SALEN & ERIC ZIMMERMAN, RULES OF PLAY: GAME DESIGN FUNDAMENTALS 80 (2004) ("A game is a system in which players engage in an artificial conflict, defined by rules, that results in a quantifiable outcome."). And an even earlier analysis that has much in common with Suits's was offered by a pioneering philosopher of sport, S.L. Clemens, who described the success of a boy named Tom in managing to get his peers to perform a task that had been assigned to him:

He had discovered a great law of human action, without knowing it—namely, that in order to make a man or a boy covet a thing, it is only necessary to make the thing difficult to attain. If he had been a great and wise philosopher, like the writer of this book, he would now have comprehended that Work consists of whatever a body is obliged to do, and that Play consists of whatever a body is not obliged to do. And this would help him to understand why constructing artificial flowers or performing on a tread-mill is work, while rolling ten-pins or climbing Mont Blanc is only amusement. There are wealthy gentlemen in England who drive four-horse passenger-coaches twenty or thirty miles on a daily line, in the summer, because the privilege costs them considerable money; but if they were offered wages for the service, that would turn it into work and then they would resign.

MARK TWAIN, THE ADVENTURES OF TOM SAWYER ch. 2 (1876).

An illustration will help. Monopoly is a game, on this account, because each participant aims at the state of affairs in which she alone of the players has money remaining; and each pursues that goal in accordance with rules that issue instructions (such as that players take turns moving tokens around a board, and pay money to other players under specified circumstances) and that confer powers (such as those of purchasing and improving properties), all while proscribing such more efficient means as taking another player's cash when she's not looking.

Sprints are also games, says Suits, because they too employ inefficient means to a goal. The goal, he proposes, is to be the first to pass one's body through a designated vertical plane in space. The inefficiencies imposed by the rules include the following: competitors must start some specified distance from the plane that constitutes the "finish line"; they may not use jet packs or a range of other devices that could speed their movement; they may not cut across the infield; they may not start before an official signal, available to all competitors, announces the start of competition; they may not obstruct the other competitors; etc. Finally, sprinters accept these rules in order to make the activity of competing in a sprint possible and not, say, because they believe they are obligated to do so.

Many sport philosophers have agreed that *games* are as Suits defined them and that *sport* describes the subset of games that involve some more-or-less specified character of physicality. Many others, however, have criticized Suits's account of games as both under- and overinclusive. It is underinclusive, critics say, because it fails to capture paradigmatic games like children's games of role-playing and make-believe. *See, e.g.,* Norman Geras, *Games and Meanings, in* Hillel Steiner and the Anatomy of Justice: Themes and Challenges 185–200 (Stephen de Wijze et al., eds., 2009). And it is claimed to be overinclusive for including some activities—religious rituals, for example—that very few people would deem games, on reflection. *See* Mitchell N. Berman, *Sprints, Sports, and Suits*, 40 J. Phil. Sport 163 (2013).

Let us suppose for the moment that games are as Suits defined them and that all sports are games. That would still not leave us home free, however, for now we must address the additional two conditions that are said to be necessary: competitiveness and "physical exertion."

Do all sports involve competition? Consider "outdoor sports" such as fly fishing, deep sea fishing, and hunting. Consider "adventure sports" such as hang gliding, BASE jumping, and spelunking. Consider parkour, a discipline developed from military obstacle-course training.

Do all sports involve physical exertion? For years, the international chess and bridge federations lobbied the IOC to recognize chess and bridge as sports, a prerequisite (but not a guarantee) under the Olympic Charter for inclusion in the Olympic Games. This wasn't frivolous: the August 14,

1972 cover of *Sports Illustrated* featured the great chess champion Bobby Fischer. In 1999, a committee agreed. But in response to criticisms, the IOC changed course three years later, endorsing the definition quoted earlier and concluding that so-called "mind sports"—a category that it defined as being "sports where the physical elements are not necessarily performed by the player in the conduct of the competition"—should not be eligible for inclusion in the Olympic Games, and that the Charter be amended to that effect.[c]

Was the IOC right to insist that sports require physical exertion? Even if so, is it clear that chess and bridge lack physical exertion? Consider recent research concluding that, due to the demands of mental stress, competitive chess players can burn up to 6,000 calories each day of a multi-day tournament. According to one expert, "Grandmasters sustain elevated blood pressure for hours in the range found in competitive marathon runners." Aishwarya Kumar, *The Grandmaster Diet: How to Lose Weight While Barely Moving,* ESPN.com (Sept. 13, 2019). As Annie Duke, 2004 World Series of Poker Champion, noted: "People don't realize how much you have to take care of your core. . .Poker is very profitable when you play with an edge. When you're tired, you don't have that."[d]

Are chess, bridge, and poker sports? If not, is that because sports must involve "physical exertion," and these games don't? Or is it because sports require a different type of physicality—not physical exertion, exactly, but something else—and that chess and similar games lack the right type of physicality? If that is so, what is the physical ingredient that sports require and that these games lack? Physical "prowess"? The exercise of gross motor skills? Athleticism?

COMMENTS AND QUESTIONS

1.   A problem of method. How do you determine whether a proposed definition of sport—the ones already mentioned, or any other—is satisfactory? Notice how we have proceeded thus far in this chapter. We have tested proposed definitions against specific types of activities, adjudging that a definition is good to the extent it includes activities that are sports and excludes activities that aren't sports, and bad to the extent it includes activities that are not sports and excludes activities that are. For example, we objected

---

[c]   The IOC has not yet taken such definitive action, but neither bridge nor chess has been admitted to the Games. In the meantime, the International Mind Sports Association has initiated what it envisioned as a quadrennial World Mind Sports Games. The inaugural event, held in Beijing shortly after the 2008 Olympics, drew 2,763 competitors from 143 countries in bridge, chess, checkers, go, and Chinese chess; the 2012 Games were not quite so successful, but they still drew about 2,000 competitors from 95 countries. The Games have not been held since. World Mind Sports Games, *2008 WMSG Results,* https://tinyurl.com/yxbsh6tl.

[d]   *Looking Bluff,* SPORTS ILLUSTRATED (Jan. 1, 2007) (noting that "a strong midsection helps improve posture and avoid back pain during hours of sitting"). *But cf.* John L. Jackson, Jr., *New Rules: You Gotta Have Balls, So Poker Is Not a Sport,* THE ROOT (Apr. 25, 2008) ("the activity might take a ton of practice and even stamina, but so does a long calculus exam").

to the definitions offered by the NCAA and IOC by observing that they incorrectly include non-sport activities such as warfare and auditions for the American Ballet Theatre. Is this how you have tried to evaluate whether a proposed definition is satisfactory? (If not, how have you proceeded?) If so, how do you respond to the worry that the approach is circular? That is to say, how can you start with the idea that some activity—warfare, pitching pennies, the javelin throw, musical chairs, the 100m dash—is or is not a sport without first knowing what sports are, or what the correct definition of sport is?

The standard answer invokes the **"method of reflective equilibrium,"** an approach to the management and refinement of one's beliefs predicated on the idea that we best justify our beliefs in a range of domains, not by reasoning forward from premises that we accept as foundational and immune from criticism, but by continually revisiting and adjusting our judgments about diverse propositions in an effort Reflective Equilibrium to produce a coherent and mutually supporting network of beliefs. When applied to ethical judgments, for example, reflective equilibrium counsels that we seek coherence among our considered judgments about the rightness or wrongness of particular acts (e.g., it's permissible to turn the trolley), mid-level rules or principles (e.g., it's wrong to intentionally cause the death of an innocent person), and the even more abstract or general theoretical considerations or commitments that shape, determine, or constitute the rules and principles (e.g., utilitarianism). Of critical importance, no class of judgments is categorically epistemically privileged over another class of judgments: judgments, say, that *"this* is wrongful" and that "one should act only in accordance with a maxim that one wishes would become a universal law" are, in principle, revisable in light of each other, and in light of all other judgments the agent has or may come to have. Reflective equilibrium is a dominant mode of reasoning in law, as it is in moral philosophy. For a careful explanation of the method, and of the criticisms it has attracted, see Norman Daniels, *Reflective Equilibrium,* THE STANFORD ENCYCLOPEDIA OF PHILOSOPHY (Edward N. Zalta ed., Summer 2020 ed.).

2. In or out? Put aside precise definitions for the moment and just consider the following activities, many of which have already been mentioned in this chapter: bridge, chess, poker, baseball, basketball, golf, dressage, auto racing, Ultimate, competitive cheer, League of Legends, darts, mountaineering, diving, gymnastics, ice dancing, ballet, boxing, MMA, fly fishing, deer hunting, long jumping, ski jumping, 100-meter running, 100-meter freestyle swimming, distance running, weight lifting, bodybuilding, competitive eating, competitive chefing, beer pong, arm wrestling, thumb wrestling, foosball. Which of these do you intuitively think of as sports? Which of these do you intuitively think of as games?[e]

---

[e] You might be interested to compare your views on some of these activities, and on others, with those who participated in a *Deadspin* poll, the results of which, and commentary, are available at Barry Petchesky, *Poll Results: What's a Sport and What's Not?*, https://tinyurl.com/yyx5kaqz.

3.   Of sports and games. Are all the activities you would consider sports also games? Consider the short foot races we call "sprints." Do you believe that Suits's account of sprints is accurate? If you asked a sprinter what her goal was, do you think she would say it was to pass her body through the designated vertical plane before the other sprinters? Would she say, as Suits suggests, that she accepts restrictions, such as not being able to start before the official signal or cut across the infield, "solely because there is a rule against it"? Would she more likely say that her goal is to run a designated course faster than other competitors? More generally, consider other competitions that measure time to complete a task or cover a distance, distance thrown or jumped, or weight lifted. Is the athlete's goal to achieve a given state of affairs, or *to achieve it in a certain way*? And if it is the latter, what are the inefficiencies in achieving these goals that athletes accept in these contests?

In assessing the accuracy or usefulness of Suits's definition, does it matter how an athlete herself would characterize her goals, if they *can* be characterized in the way Suits suggests? And if the answer to that question is negative, is Berman right that Suits's definition would include religious rituals as games?

And what follows from all of this? Should sprints be deemed not to be games, but still considered sports, which means that not all sports are games? Or should sprints be deemed to be athletic competitions but not to be sports or games, which preserves the possibility that all sports are games but perhaps at the cost of violating common parlance? Or should we conclude that Suits's definition of games is not cogent—and, if so, that Wittgenstein was right all along?

4.   "Mind sports." Should poker, chess, and bridge, or any of them, be considered sports? Is the IOC Programme Commission's emphasis on whether there is physical exertion "in the conduct of competition" useful? Is dressage, a recognized Olympic sport, truly a sport by this criterion given that, while the horse certainly exerts itself, the rider should be relaxed and appear effort-free while giving minimal aid to the horse?

Is the Programme Commission's use of the term "mind sports" coherent? That is, can mind sports be a subcategory of sports under the Commission's understanding of what a sport is, even though in a mind sport "the physical elements are not necessarily performed by the player in the conduct of the competition"?

Although we have grouped chess, bridge, and poker together, are there any useful distinctions to be drawn within that set? Notice that chess and bridge require no physicality at all, for they do not even require corporality (embodiedness): proverbial "brains in a vat" could compete at these games. In contrast, one might argue that because discerning an opponent's "tells," and hiding or overcoming one's own, are part of the essence of poker, real poker, unlike real chess and bridge, requires an embodied agent. (On this view, internet poker is a degenerate form of that game, whereas internet chess is still ordinary chess.) Do you agree? Is this distinction meaningful for purposes of assessing whether any of these games are sports?

5. *Esports.* In League of Legends, the most popular esport in the world, two teams of five players compete against each other, engaging in virtual combat until one team conquers the other. In 2018, 99.6 million unique viewers tuned in to watch the League of Legends World Championship finals, the culmination of an annual event in which the best teams from all over the world compete for fame, glory, and millions of dollars in prize money. See 2018 EVENTS BY THE NUMBERS, https://tinyurl.com/y34zk9t5. For comparison, an estimated 103.4 million viewers tuned in to watch the 2018 Super Bowl. *Superbowl LII: Ratings for football's biggest game lowest since 2009*, CBSNEWS.COM, (Feb. 5, 2018) https://tinyurl.com/yblrp2bq. To be successful, players in League of Legends must key in complex sequences of buttons and move their mouse quickly, frequently, and on a moment's notice. One way of gauging a player's activity in League of Legends and other similar esports is through their physical "actions per minute" (APM). In some esports, the best professional players routinely take over 300 actions per minute. *See Actions per minute*, WIKIPEDIA, https://tinyurl.com/y6tghdmh. Are esports sports mind sports, or just games? One common reason given for the argument that esports are not true sports is that, similar to mind sports, they lack some physical component actual sports must possess. *See, e.g.*, Eric Johnson, *Video Games on ESPN? It's Time to Stop Pretending eSports Are 'Real' Sports*, VOX, (Apr. 27, 2015) https://tinyurl.com/y65sbgbb (arguing that while esports are "competitions," they should not be considered sports because they lack "easily intelligible physical prowess"). Is this right? Does it matter at all that top esport athletes routinely take over five physical actions per second, often for over 30 minutes at a time? Or are finger speed and hand dexterity simply not the right type of physical actions to properly constitute a sport? Similarly, does it matter at all that almost as many people watch the League of Legends World Championship as watch the Super Bowl? Is an esport that requires a high level of APM and that has a significant fan base "more of a sport" than an esport that is less APM-intensive or that doesn't have a fan base at all?

6. *Objective scoring and simple machines.* Sports economist Rodney Fort maintains that sports must use objective scoring and involve only simple machines, if any at all. Ashlee A. Cassman, *Bring It On! Cheerleading vs. Title IX: Could Cheerleading Ever Be Considered an Athletic Opportunity Under Title IX, and if So, What Implications Would That Have on University Compliance?*, 17 SPORTS L. J. 245 (2010) (citing posting of Howard Wasserman to Sports Law Blog (Dec. 28, 2008)). Is this an improvement? The first condition would rule out barroom brawling and warfare—but also gymnastics, figure skating, diving and most "combat sports" like boxing, among others. Fort's second condition, though embracing baseball bats and tennis racquets, rules out cars and horses, for example; thus, it renders auto racing and horseracing—the latter of which has been dubbed "the sport of kings"—not sports at all.

7. Mutual thwarting. The anthropologist John L. Jackson, Jr., asserts that "in a sport, your opponent has to be able to directly thwart you—by catching a ball, intercepting a pass, blocking a kick, anything. There might be clocks involved, but you can't just be finishing something quicker than a competitor. That is a race, but it isn't a sport." John L. Jackson, Jr., *New Rules: You Gotta Have Balls, So Poker Is Not a Sport,* THE ROOT (Apr. 25, 2008).[f] This definition would not only exclude races of virtually all sorts; like Fort's, it would knock out competitions based on judgments of individual performance, such as gymnastics, figure skating, and diving. And it would also exclude golf. Is this a sound condition?

8. Warranted seriousness. One of this book's authors has proposed that it is a necessary condition of an activity being a sport that it exhibits "warranted seriousness":

> This single condition has two components. First, there exists a recognizable community of participants whose members participate in the activity seriously, in the sense (roughly) of committing significant time and effort both in engaging in the activity and in training for it, as by seeking to improve their skills at it. That is, the activity is taken seriously by enough persons to constitute a community of serious participants. Second, this seriousness of engagement is warranted, not wholly misplaced. At a minimum . . ., an activity warrants being taken seriously if it develops and displays skills or qualities that qualify as human excellences—speed, strength, agility, hand-eye coordination, endurance, resilience, and so forth.

Mitchell N. Berman, *Sport as a Thick Cluster Concept, in* GAMES, SPORTS, AND PLAY: PHILOSOPHICAL ESSAYS 99, 110 (Thomas Hurka ed., 2019). The first component explains why "party games" such as sack racing, egg-and-spoon racing, and pin-the-tail-on-the-donkey are not sports despite being competitive, physical games. It also explains how activities that are not sports can become sports: because a community of committed and serious competitors arises, as is the case with competitive gaming (also called "esports"). The second component explains why the mere fact of serious engagement is insufficient to turn a game or pastime into a sport: we might adjudge that the commitment of significant time and energy to the activity is misguided. Berman invokes competitive eating as an example:

> Even while competitive eating is being treated increasingly seriously by its practitioners—a seriousness of treatment that includes their exploring new speed-eating techniques and their adhering to (at least) moderately demanding training regimens—many observers would refuse to label it a sport. This resistance, I think, stems from

---

[f] Jackson does describe his set of conditions—which also includes requirements that there be "a ball-like object . . . that organizes everyone's attention," and that "there must be a sense of urgency when that ball-like thing is in play"—as tongue-in-cheek. But we have found that the mutual-thwarting condition exerts a pull on some students.

the judgment that, even if competitive eaters take their competitions seriously, such seriousness of commitment is not warranted, but rather absurd or grotesque. . . . And similar things can be said about, for example, cup-stacking or thumb-wrestling: while not absurd or grotesque, they plausibly fail the *warranted seriousness* condition on the ground that the challenges they involve are trivial or silly.

Id. at 112–13. Is this right? Do you agree that the category of *sport* is an "honorific"? Do you agree with those who would dismiss competitive eating as a sport on the ground that serious engagement in competitive eating is not warranted? What standards do you apply in addressing this question? Bottom line, do you think competitive eating is a sport? Note that if the true test of an activity in North America of whether an activity is a sport is, "Does ESPN cover it?," competitive eating qualifies.[g]

9.　*Your favored definition?* Do you accept any of the definitions of sport already discussed? If not, can you propose a definition of games and of sports that corresponds to your intuitive sense of how particular types of activity should be classified? If not, are there judgments about particular activities that you are prepared to abandon?

————

Does it matter what sports or games are? If so, why? As Shakespeare taught, "that which we call a rose by any other name would smell as sweet." Similarly, competitive eating and bridge, basketball and water polo are all what they are regardless of what they are called. Accordingly, one might think it pointless or distracting to focus on definitional or conceptual questions. Judge Richard Posner expressed this objection well with respect to the definition of law. "I have nothing against philosophical speculation," he said. "But one would like it to have some pay-off; *something* ought to turn on the answer to the question 'What is law?' if the question is to be worth asking by people who could use their time in other socially valuable ways. Nothing does turn on it." RICHARD POSNER, LAW AND LEGAL THEORY IN THE UK AND USA 3 (1997).

We agree that conceptual and definitional inquiries can distract us from what really matters; such investigations are sometimes, perhaps frequently, pointless or "arid." Accordingly, we will not place much weight in this book on the bounds of what is a sport or a game. Most of our focus will be on activities that are sports under almost any plausible definition. We will also discuss problems concerning games that are not, or might not be deemed, sports, and occasionally we will take at least sidelong glances at competitions that lie at the fringes of these areas or even well beyond.

———

[g]　*See, e.g., Matt Stonie upsets Joey Chestnut to win Nathan's Hot Dog Eating Contest,* ESPN.com (Jul. 4, 2015) (observing that the contest is broadcast live "like the major sporting event its biggest fans say it has become;" and, in video clip, comparing upset of Chestnut, "a legend in the sport," to others such as Villanova over Georgetown in 1985 NCAA men's basketball final).

Nevertheless, there are at least three reasons that make it worthwhile at least to pose, and pause over, the question of what a sport is. We call these reasons of "rule application," "conduct guidance," and "conceptual analysis."

Rule application. First, the term "sport" is sometimes used as a predicate in a law, regulation, charter or other governing standard, in which case tangible consequences will follow depending on whether some particular activity satisfies a definition of "sport." We have already seen this at the beginning of the chapter: For an activity to be included in the Olympic Games, or to be subject to the oversight and regulation of the NCAA, it must be recognized as a "sport." Tort statutes in many American states provide another example, granting immunity from ordinary negligence actions for persons who cause injury to others when participating in "sports" that involve physical contact.

Cheerleading, or spinoffs from it, provides an illustration. Consider *Noffke v. Bakke,* 760 N.W.2d 156 (Wis. 2009). Brittany Noffke, a high school cheerleader, was injured while performing a stunt before a basketball game. She sued, among others, Kevin Bakke, another member of the squad, claiming that he had negligently failed to spot her. But the court held that he was within the scope of a statute giving immunity from negligence actions to "[a] participant in a recreational activity that includes physical contact between persons in a sport involving amateur teams." The court used a dictionary definition of sport as "[a]n activity involving physical exertion and skill that is governed by a set of rules or customs"; Chief Justice Abramson, writing separately, objected to heavy reliance on the dictionary but did not offer an alternative definition.[h]

Conduct guidance. A second potential value of inquiring into the meaning or nature of sport is that the inquiry might shed light on the proper conduct of participants and officials. Some philosophers of law have argued, contrary to Judge Posner, that the right account of what law *is* does indeed have implications for what people should *do*—like whether ordinary citizens have a moral obligation to obey the law, and how judges should

---

[h] In contrast to *Noffke,* a federal district court held that competitive cheer—also called "acrobatics and tumbling" or "acro"—is not a varsity sport for purposes of Title IX. *Biediger v. Quinnipiac University,* 928 F. Supp. 2d 414 (D. Conn. 2013). But the *Biediger* court did not purport to apply an abstract or general definition or account of sport, relying instead on a multi-factor test of what counts as a sport for purposes of Title IX, developed by the Office of Civil Rights in the U.S. Department of Health and Human Services.

Competitive cheer is, by virtue of legislation signed in 2015, codified at Cal. Education Code § 33353.7, an officially sanctioned high school sport in California. *See* California Interscholastic Sports Federation, *Competitive Cheer,* https://tinyurl.com/yy3c93um. USA Cheer, a sponsoring body for cheerleading, has created STUNT in an attempt to gain recognition as a sport; USA Cheer has applied to the NCAA for STUNT to be given Emerging Sport status. STUNT does away with the crowd-leading element of cheer. It pits teams head to head as they perform various components—partner stunts, pyramids & tosses, jumps & tumbling, and a team routine. About forty colleges (most at the club level) and 200 high schools compete in STUNT. STUNT THE SPORT, https://tinyurl.com/y6x22kyh.

interpret statutes and constitutions. A similar relationship might obtain with respect to sports. It is intuitively plausible that the nature of sport and of games might inform what cheating, gamesmanship, and sportsmanship all involve. (See Part IV.) Possibly, for example, if all sports are games (as some common definitions maintain), that will have implications for what gamesmanship is and whether it's a virtue or a vice. Likewise, a sport official might conclude that the nature of sport shapes or informs how she should interpret the written rules (e.g., in a more purposive or textual manner) or what discretion she should assume and how she should exercise it. (See Chapters 10 & 12.) To be clear, we are not contending that these connections do in fact obtain; at present, we are merely flagging the possibilities.

Conceptual analysis. Finally, even if you will, as law students and lawyers, have little or no occasion to worry about the meaning or nature of *sport,* you will have reason to grapple with *other* complex and abstract concepts, and the current investigation offers practice with this difficult but occasionally important skill.

In saying this, it is worth drawing to the surface a point that we have thus far papered over. We have not been searching for a definition of the **word** "sport," so much as we have been trying to understand the nature and contours of a **concept** that roughly corresponds to that word, or a concept that the word "sport" more or less picks out. While the exact nature of concepts is a matter of controversy, roughly speaking, concepts are ideas; they are the pieces into which we carve up the world. Words are combinations of signs and sounds that refer to concepts (or to other things). In 2020, the English word "dog" corresponds to the concept DOG and so too do the Spanish word "perro" and the French word "chien." (This shows that words and concepts are not the same: different words, same concept.) Because the meaning of a word is determined by the usage patterns of a language community, it is possible that, over time, the English word "dog" will change its meaning. If enough speakers of English come to use "dog" to mean, say, fox, then that will be the meaning of the word. At the same time, people could use another word—maybe "cat," maybe "hippodrome"— to mean what the word "dog" currently means—namely, DOG. But if any or all of this comes to pass, none of it will entail that the concept DOG has changed. Presumably, the concept will remain what it always has been. Lexicographers study the meanings of words; philosophers (or some of them) study the nature of concepts.

But philosophers aren't the only people who are called upon to elucidate abstract concepts. Sometimes lawyers and law students are too. Many legal disputes, especially but not invariably constitutional disputes, involve whether a challenged action promotes or

Words,
Concepts,
and
Conceptions

impairs an abstract value like equality or democracy, and resolution of such disputes often turns upon how a judge understands the relevant concept. For example, much of contemporary sexual harassment law is traceable to the Supreme Court's acceptance of conceptualizations of equality and discrimination urged by feminist legal theorist Catharine MacKinnon. Similarly, attitudes toward the institution of judicial review, and toward the way it should be exercised, often turn on differing concepts of democracy—or, many would prefer to say, different **conceptions** of the same **concept**. The ability to reason productively about the contours of abstract concepts is therefore an important skill for law students to practice, and discussion of any interesting, complex concept can offer that practice.

Exercise 1

You are a sportswriter for your local newspaper. The paper's lead sports editor assigns you to write a feature on the Cigar Smoking World Championships. Held annually since 2010 in Split, Croatia, the event draws forty competitors, selected from nearly three dozen qualifying events staged across the globe, who strive to smoke a cigar for the longest time without allowing it to go out. (The world record, held by Russia's Igor Kovacic, is 3 hours 52 minutes 55 seconds.)

Five years ago, shortly after you were hired, a senior colleague on the sports desk, Alex Williams, was tasked to attend and write about the annual American Fancy Rat & Mouse Show, hosted by the American Fancy Rat & Mouse Association. Complaining that rodent shows are not sports and that writing about them is beneath their dignity as sports journalists, Williams and likeminded colleagues successfully pressured the paper's publisher to pledge in the Staff Handbook that "only articles about 'sports' or 'sport' can appear in the Sports Section."

The paper's "only sports in the 'Sports Section'" policy has not been tested in the intervening years. But Williams, now deputy sports editor, has suggested to you that cigar-smoking competitions don't qualify. Do you agree? If so, write a brief memo to the lead editor explaining why cigar-smoking competitions aren't sporting events. If not, write a brief memo to Williams explaining why they are. The event website is here: http://cswcworld.com/index.html; an article about the 2019 Championships is Andrew Keh, *At Cigar Smoking Worlds, the Best Always Finish Last*, N.Y. TIMES, Oct. 29, 2019, at B11.

CHAPTER 2

"THE ESSENCE OF THE GAME"

■ ■ ■

We begin with a dispute, the Casey Martin case, that not only ended in litigation but that reached the Supreme Court of the United States. Our concern, though, is not with federal anti-discrimination law as interpreted by the Court, but rather with fundamental questions concerning the nature of a sport and the functions of the rules that constitute it.

PGA TOUR, INC. V. MARTIN
532 U.S. 661 (2001)

[Casey Martin was a professional golfer with a degenerative circulatory disorder, Klippel-Trenaunay-Weber Syndrome, that caused him severe leg pain and atrophied his right leg, preventing him from walking golf courses; extensive walking caused him pain, fatigue, and anxiety, and also created a significant risk of hemorrhaging, blood clots, and a tibia fracture so severe that an amputation might be required. The Rules of Golf permit the use of carts. But under the rules of the NCAA, the Nike Tour, the PGA Tour, and the final round of the PGA's qualifying school (Q-School), carts were not allowed. Martin was able to get a waiver from the NCAA, but not from the PGA. Martin sued under the Americans with Disabilities Act of 1990 (ADA), 42 U.S.C. § 12101 *et seq.*, for an injunction allowing him to use a cart. Martin's disorder constitutes a disability under Title III of the ADA, which requires an entity operating "public accommodations" to make "reasonable modifications" in its policies "when . . . necessary to afford such . . . accommodations to individuals with disabilities, unless the entity can demonstrate that making such modifications would fundamentally alter the nature of such . . . accommodations," § 12182(b)(2)(A)(ii). The Court, per Justice Stevens (an avid golfer), held that the PGA's tours and their qualifying rounds fit comfortably within Title III's coverage; among other considerations, golf courses are specifically identified as a public accommodation by the statute. § 12181(7)(L). The principal remaining question was whether allowing Martin to use a cart would be a "fundamental alteration" in the game.] *Issue*

JUSTICE STEVENS delivered the opinion of the Court.

. . . At trial, . . . petitioner asserted that the condition of walking is a substantive rule of competition, and that waiving it as to any individual for any reason would fundamentally alter the nature of the competition. Petitioner's evidence included the testimony of a number of experts, among them some of the greatest golfers in history. Arnold Palmer, Jack Nicklaus, and Ken Venturi explained that fatigue can be a critical factor in a tournament, particularly on the last day when psychological pressure is at a maximum. Their testimony makes it clear that, in their view, permission to use a cart might well give some players a competitive advantage over other players who must walk. They did not, however, express any opinion on whether a cart would give Martin such an advantage.

. . . The judge found that the purpose of the rule was to inject fatigue into the skill of shotmaking, but that the fatigue injected "by walking the course cannot be deemed significant under normal circumstances." Furthermore, Martin presented evidence, and the judge found, that even with the use of a cart, Martin must walk over a mile during an 18-hole round, and that the fatigue he suffers from coping with his disability is "undeniably greater" than the fatigue his able-bodied competitors endure from walking the course. As the judge observed:

"[P]laintiff is in significant pain when he walks, and even when he is getting in and out of the cart. With each step, he is at risk of fracturing his tibia and hemorrhaging. The other golfers have to endure the psychological stress of competition as part of their fatigue; Martin has the same stress plus the added stress of pain and risk of serious injury. As he put it, he would gladly trade the cart for a good leg. To perceive that the cart puts him—with his condition—at a competitive advantage is a gross distortion of reality."

As a result, the judge concluded that it would "not fundamentally alter the nature of the PGA Tour's game to accommodate him with a cart." The judge accordingly entered a permanent injunction requiring petitioner to permit Martin to use a cart in tour and qualifying events. . . .

Like the District Court, the Court of Appeals viewed the issue not as "whether use of carts generally would fundamentally alter the competition, but whether the use of a cart by Martin would do so." That issue turned on "an intensively fact-based inquiry," and, the court concluded, had been correctly resolved by the trial judge. In its words, "[a]ll that the cart does is permit Martin access to a type of competition in which he otherwise could not engage because of his disability."

V

Petitioner does not contest that a golf cart is a reasonable modification that is necessary if Martin is to play in its tournaments. Martin's claim thus differs from one that might be asserted by players with less serious afflictions that make walking the course uncomfortable or difficult, but not beyond their capacity. In such cases, an accommodation might be reasonable but not necessary. In this case, however, the narrow dispute is whether allowing Martin to use a golf cart, despite the walking requirement that applies to the PGA TOUR, the NIKE TOUR, and the third stage of the Q-School, is a modification that would "fundamentally alter the nature" of those events.

In theory, a modification of petitioner's golf tournaments might constitute a fundamental alteration in two different ways. It might alter such an essential aspect of the game of golf that it would be unacceptable even if it affected all competitors equally; changing the diameter of the hole from three to six inches might be such a modification. Alternatively, a less significant change that has only a peripheral impact on the game itself might nevertheless give a disabled player, in addition to access to the competition as required by Title III, an advantage over others and, for that reason, fundamentally alter the character of the competition. We are not persuaded that a waiver of the walking rule for Martin would work a fundamental alteration in either sense.

As an initial matter, we observe that the use of carts is not itself inconsistent with the fundamental character of the game of golf. From early on, the essence of the game has been shotmaking—using clubs to cause a ball to progress from the teeing ground to a hole some distance away with as few strokes as possible.[39] That essential aspect of the game is still reflected in the very first of the Rules of Golf, which declares: "The Game of Golf consists in playing a ball from the *teeing ground* into the hole by a *stroke* or successive strokes in accordance with the rules." Rule 1–1, Rules of Golf, App. 104 (emphasis in original). Over the years, there have been many changes in the players' equipment, in golf course design, in the Rules of Golf, and in the method of transporting clubs from hole to hole. Originally, so few clubs were used that each player could carry them without a bag. Then came golf bags, caddies, carts that were pulled by hand, and eventually motorized carts that carried players as well as clubs. "Golf carts started appearing with increasing regularity on American golf courses in the 1950's. Today they are everywhere. And they are encouraged. For one thing, they often speed up play, and for another, they are great revenue producers."[41] There is nothing in the Rules of Golf that either forbids the use of carts or penalizes a player for using a cart. That set of rules . . . is widely accepted in both the amateur and professional golf world as the rules of the game. The walking rule that is contained in petitioner's hard cards, based on an optional condition buried in an

---

[39] Golf is an ancient game, tracing its ancestry to Scotland, and played by such notables as Mary Queen of Scots and her son James. That shot-making has been the essence of golf since early in its history is reflected in the first recorded rules of golf, published in 1744 for a tournament on the Leith Links in Edinburgh . . . . [Justice Stevens quotes the 1744 *Articles & Laws in Playing at Golf*, one of which is: "4. You are not to remove, Stones, Bones or any Break Club for the sake of playing your Ball, Except upon the fair Green/ & that only/ within a Club's length of your Ball."]

[41] *Olinger v. United States Golf Assn.*, 205 F.3d 1001, 1003 (C.A.7 2000).

appendix to the Rules of Golf, is not an essential attribute of the game itself.

Indeed, the walking rule is not an indispensable feature of tournament golf either. As already mentioned, petitioner permits golf carts to be used in the SENIOR PGA TOUR, the open qualifying events for petitioner's tournaments, the first two stages of the Q-School, and, until 1997, the third stage of the Q-School as well. Moreover, petitioner allows the use of carts during certain tournament rounds in both the PGA TOUR and the NIKE TOUR. In addition, although the USGA enforces a walking rule in most of the tournaments that it sponsors, it permits carts in the Senior Amateur and the Senior Women's Amateur championships.

Petitioner, however, distinguishes the game of golf as it is generally played from the game that it sponsors in the PGA TOUR, NIKE TOUR, and (at least recently) the last stage of the Q-School—golf at the "highest level." According to petitioner, "[t]he goal of the highest-level competitive athletics is to assess and compare the performance of different competitors, a task that is meaningful only if the competitors are subject to identical substantive rules." The waiver of any possibly "outcome-affecting" rule for a contestant would violate this principle and therefore, in petitioner's view, fundamentally alter the nature of the highest level athletic event. The walking rule is one such rule, petitioner submits, because its purpose is "to inject the element of fatigue into the skill of shot-making," and thus its effect may be the critical loss of a stroke. As a consequence, the reasonable modification Martin seeks would fundamentally alter the nature of petitioner's highest level tournaments even if he were the only person in the world who has both the talent to compete in those elite events and a disability sufficiently serious that he cannot do so without using a cart.

The force of petitioner's argument is, first of all, mitigated by the fact that golf is a game in which it is impossible to guarantee that all competitors will play under exactly the same conditions or that an individual's ability will be the sole determinant of the outcome. For example, changes in the weather may produce harder greens and more head winds for the tournament leader than for his closest pursuers. A lucky bounce may save a shot or two. Whether such happenstance events are more or less probable than the likelihood that a golfer afflicted with Klippel-Trenaunay-Weber Syndrome would one day qualify for the NIKE TOUR and PGA TOUR, they at least demonstrate that pure chance may have a greater impact on the outcome of elite golf tournaments than the fatigue resulting from the enforcement of the walking rule.

Further, the factual basis of petitioner's argument is undermined by the District Court's finding that the fatigue from walking during one of petitioner's 4-day tournaments cannot be deemed significant. The District Court credited the testimony of a professor in physiology and expert on fatigue, who calculated the calories expended in walking a golf course (about five miles) to be approximately 500 calories—"nutritionally . . . less than a Big Mac." What is more, that energy is expended over a 5-hour period, during which golfers have numerous intervals for rest and refreshment. In fact, the expert concluded, because golf is a low intensity activity, fatigue from the game is primarily a psychological phenomenon in which stress and motivation are the key ingredients. And even under conditions of severe heat and humidity, the critical factor in fatigue is fluid loss rather than exercise from walking.

Moreover, when given the option of using a cart, the majority of golfers in petitioner's tournaments have chosen to walk, often to relieve stress or for other strategic reasons.[49] As NIKE TOUR member Eric Johnson testified, walking allows him to keep in rhythm, stay warmer when it is chilly, and develop a better sense of the elements and the course than riding a cart. . . .

To be sure, the waiver of an essential rule of competition for anyone would fundamentally alter the nature of petitioner's tournaments. As we have demonstrated, however, the walking rule is at best peripheral to the nature of petitioner's athletic events, and thus it might be waived in individual cases without working a fundamental alteration. . . .

Under the ADA's basic requirement that the need of a disabled person be evaluated on an individual basis, we have no doubt that allowing Martin to use a golf cart would not fundamentally alter the nature of petitioner's tournaments. As we have discussed, the purpose of the walking rule is to subject players to fatigue, which in turn may influence the outcome of tournaments. Even if the rule does serve that purpose, it is an uncontested finding of the District Court that Martin "easily endures greater fatigue even with a cart than his able-bodied competitors do by walking." The purpose of the walking rule is therefore not compromised in the slightest by allowing Martin to use a cart. A modification that provides an exception to a peripheral tournament rule without impairing its purpose cannot be said to "fundamentally alter" the tournament. What it can be said to do, on the other hand, is to allow Martin the chance to qualify for, and compete in, the athletic events petitioner offers to those members of the public who have the skill and desire to enter. That is exactly what the ADA requires. As a result, Martin's request for a waiver of the walking rule should have been granted. . . .

The judgment of the Court of Appeals is affirmed.

It is so ordered.

---

[49]   That has been so not only in the Senior PGA Tour and the first two stages of the Q-School, but also, as Martin himself noticed, in the third stage of the Q-School after petitioner permitted everyone to ride rather than just waiving the walking rule for Martin as required by the District Court's injunction.

JUSTICE SCALIA, with whom JUSTICE THOMAS joins, dissenting.

In my view today's opinion exercises a benevolent compassion that the law does not place it within our power to impose. . . .

I

. . . [E]ven if respondent here is a consumer of the "privilege" of the PGA TOUR competition, I see no basis for considering whether the rules of that competition must be altered. It is as irrelevant to the PGA TOUR's compliance with the statute whether walking is essential to the game of golf as it is to the shoe store's compliance whether "pairness" is essential to the nature of shoes. If a shoe store wishes to sell shoes only in pairs it may; and if a golf tour (or a golf course) wishes to provide only walk-around golf, it may. The PGA TOUR cannot deny respondent *access* to that game because of his disability, but it need not provide him a game different (whether in its essentials or in its details) from that offered to everyone else.

Since it has held (or assumed) professional golfers to be customers "enjoying" the "privilege" that consists of PGA TOUR golf; and since it inexplicably regards the rules of PGA TOUR golf as merely "policies, practices, or procedures" by which access to PGA TOUR golf is provided, the Court must then confront the question whether respondent's requested modification of the supposed policy, practice, or procedure of walking would "fundamentally alter the nature" of the PGA TOUR game, § 12182(b)(2)(A)(ii). The Court attacks this "fundamental alteration" analysis by asking two questions: first, whether the "essence" or an "essential aspect" of the sport of golf has been altered; and second, whether the change, even if not essential to the game, would give the disabled player an advantage over others and thereby "fundamentally alter the character of the competition." It answers no to both.

Before considering the Court's answer to the first question, it is worth pointing out that the assumption which underlies that question is false. Nowhere is it writ that PGA TOUR golf must be classic "essential" golf. Why cannot the PGA TOUR, if it wishes, promote a new game, with distinctive rules (much as the American League promotes a game of baseball in which the pitcher's turn at the plate can be taken by a "designated hitter")? If members of the public do not like the new rules—if they feel that these rules do not truly test the individual's skill at "real golf" (or the team's skill at "real baseball")—they can withdraw their patronage. But the rules are the rules. They are (as in all games) entirely arbitrary, and there is no basis on which anyone—not even the Supreme Court of the United States—can pronounce one or another of them to be "nonessential" if the rulemaker (here the PGA TOUR) deems it to be essential.

If one assumes, however, that the PGA TOUR has some legal obligation to play classic, Platonic golf—and if one assumes the correctness of all the other wrong turns the Court has made to get to this point—then we Justices must confront what is indeed an awesome responsibility. It has been rendered the solemn duty of the Supreme Court of the United States, laid upon it by Congress in pursuance of the Federal Government's power "[t]o regulate Commerce with foreign Nations, and among the several States," U.S. Const., Art. I, § 8, cl. 3, to decide What Is Golf. I am sure that the Framers of the Constitution, aware of the 1457 edict of King James II of Scotland prohibiting golf because it interfered with the practice of archery, fully expected that sooner or later the paths of golf and government, the law and the links, would once again cross, and that the judges of this august Court would some day have to wrestle with that age-old jurisprudential question, for which their years of study in the law have so well prepared them: Is someone riding around a golf course from shot to shot *really* a golfer? The answer, we learn, is yes. The Court ultimately concludes, and it will henceforth be the Law of the Land, that walking is not a "fundamental" aspect of golf.

Either out of humility or out of self-respect (one or the other) the Court should decline to answer this incredibly difficult and incredibly silly question. To say that something is "essential" is ordinarily to say that it is necessary to the achievement of a certain object. But since it is the very nature of a game to have no object except amusement (that is what distinguishes games from productive activity), it is quite impossible to say that any of a game's arbitrary rules is "essential." Eighteen-hole golf courses, 10-foot-high basketball hoops, 90-foot baselines, 100-yard football fields—all are arbitrary and none is essential. The only support for any of them is tradition and (in more modern times) insistence by what has come to be regarded as the ruling body of the sport—both of which factors support the PGA TOUR's position in the present case. (Many, indeed, consider walking to be *the central feature* of the game of golf—hence Mark Twain's classic criticism of the sport: "a good walk spoiled.") I suppose there is some point at which the rules of a well-known game are changed to such a degree that no reasonable person would call it the same game. If the PGA TOUR competitors were required to dribble a large, inflated ball and put it through a round hoop, the game could no longer reasonably be called golf. But this criterion—destroying recognizability as the same generic game—is surely not the test of "essentialness" or "fundamentalness" that the Court applies, since it apparently thinks that merely changing the diameter of the *cup* might "fundamentally alter" the game of golf.

Having concluded that dispensing with the walking rule would not violate federal-Platonic "golf" (and, implicitly, that it is federal-Platonic golf, and no other, that the PGA TOUR can insist upon), the Court moves on to the second part of its test: the competitive effects of waiving this nonessential rule. In this part of its analysis, the Court first finds that the effects of the change are "mitigated" by the fact that in the game of golf weather, a "lucky bounce," and "pure chance" provide different conditions for each competitor and individual ability may not "be the sole determinant of the outcome." I guess that is why those who follow professional golfing consider Jack Nicklaus the *luckiest* golfer of all time, only to be challenged of late by the phenomenal *luck* of Tiger Woods. The Court's empiricism is unpersuasive. "Pure chance" is randomly distributed among the players, but allowing respondent to use a cart gives him a "lucky" break every time he plays. Pure chance also only matters at the margin—a stroke here or there; the cart substantially improves this respondent's competitive prospects beyond a couple of strokes. But even granting that there are significant nonhuman variables affecting competition, that fact does not justify adding another variable that always favors one player.

In an apparent effort to make its opinion as narrow as possible, the Court relies upon the District Court's finding that even with a cart, respondent will be at least as fatigued as everyone else. This, the Court says, *proves* that competition will not be affected. Far from thinking that reliance on this finding cabins the effect of today's opinion, I think it will prove to be its most expansive and destructive feature. Because step one of the Court's two-part inquiry into whether a requested change in a sport will "fundamentally alter [its] nature" consists of an utterly unprincipled ontology of sports (pursuant to which the Court is not even sure whether golf's "essence" requires a 3-inch hole), there is every reason to think that in future cases involving requests for special treatment by would-be athletes the second step of the analysis will be determinative. In resolving that second step—determining whether waiver of the "nonessential" rule will have an impermissible "competitive effect"—by measuring the athletic capacity of the requesting individual, and asking whether the special dispensation would do no more than place him on a par (so to speak) with other competitors, the Court guarantees that future cases of this sort will have to be decided on the basis of individualized factual findings. Which means that future cases of this sort will be numerous, and a rich source of lucrative litigation. One can envision the parents of a Little League player with attention deficit disorder trying to convince a judge that their son's disability makes it at least 25% more difficult to hit a pitched ball. (If they are successful, the only thing that could prevent a court order giving the kid four strikes would be a judicial determination that, in baseball, three strikes are metaphysically necessary, which is quite absurd.)

The statute, of course, provides no basis for this individualized analysis that is the Court's last step on a long and misguided journey. The statute seeks to assure that a disabled person's disability will not deny him *equal access* to (among other things) competitive sporting events—not that his disability will not deny him an *equal chance to win* competitive sporting events. The latter is quite impossible, since the very *nature* of competitive sport is the measurement, by uniform rules, of unevenly distributed excellence. This unequal distribution is precisely what determines the winners and losers—and artificially to "even out" that distribution, by giving one or another player exemption from a rule that emphasizes his particular weakness, is to destroy the game. That is why the "handicaps" that are customary in social games of golf—which, by adding strokes to the scores of the good players and subtracting them from scores of the bad ones, "even out" the varying abilities—are *not* used in professional golf. In the Court's world, there is one set of rules that is "fair with respect to the able-bodied" but "individualized" rules, mandated by the ADA, for "talented but disabled athletes." The ADA mandates no such ridiculous thing. Agility, strength, speed, balance, quickness of mind, steadiness of nerves, intensity of concentration—these talents are not evenly distributed. No wild-eyed dreamer has ever suggested that the managing bodies of the competitive sports that test precisely these qualities should try to take account of the uneven distribution of God-given gifts when writing and enforcing the rules of competition. And I have no doubt Congress did not authorize misty-eyed judicial supervision of such a revolution.

* * *

My belief that today's judgment is clearly in error should not be mistaken for a belief that the PGA TOUR clearly *ought not* allow respondent to use a golf cart. *That* is a close question, on which even those who compete in the PGA TOUR are apparently divided; but it is a *different* question from the one before the Court. Just as it is a different question whether the Little League *ought* to give disabled youngsters a fourth strike, or some other waiver from the rules that makes up for their disabilities. In both cases, whether they *ought* to do so depends upon (1) how central to the game that they have organized (and over whose rules they are the master) they deem the waived provision to be, and (2) how competitive—how strict a test of raw athletic ability in all aspects of the competition—they want their game to be. But whether Congress has said they *must* do so depends upon the answers to the legal questions I have discussed above—not upon what this Court sententiously decrees to be "decent, tolerant, and progressive." [Citation, internal quotation marks, and bracket deleted.]

And it should not be assumed that today's decent, tolerant, and progressive judgment will, in the long run, accrue to the benefit of sports competitors with disabilities. Now that it is clear courts will review the rules of sports for "fundamentalness," organizations that value their autonomy have every incentive to defend vigorously the necessity of every regulation. They may still be second-guessed in the end as to the Platonic requirements of the sport, but they will *assuredly* lose if they have at all wavered in their enforcement. The lesson the PGA TOUR and other sports organizations should take from this case is to make sure that the same written rules are set forth for all levels of play, and never voluntarily to grant any modifications. The second lesson is to end open tryouts. I doubt that, in the long run, even disabled athletes will be well served by these incentives that the Court has created.

Complaints about this case are . . . properly directed [not to Congress but] to this Court's Kafkaesque determination that professional sports organizations, and the fields they rent for their exhibitions, are "places of public accommodation" to the competing athletes, and the athletes themselves "customers" of the organization that pays them; its Alice in Wonderland determination that there are such things as judicially determinable "essential" and "nonessential" rules of a made-up game; and its Animal Farm determination that fairness and the ADA mean that everyone gets to play by individualized rules which will assure that no one's lack of ability (or at least no one's lack of ability so pronounced that it amounts to a disability) will be a handicap. The year was 2001, and "everybody was finally equal." K. Vonnegut, Harrison Bergeron, in Animal Farm and Related Readings 129 (1997).[a]

COMMENTS AND QUESTIONS

1. Test and contest. The Supreme Court majority observes that "a modification of petitioner's golf tournaments might constitute a fundamental alteration in two different ways. It might alter such an essential aspect of the game of golf that it would be unacceptable even if it affected all competitors equally . . . ." Or it might affect a more peripheral aspect of the game but confer an excessive advantage on some competitors. This distinction corresponds to a distinction that philosophers of sport draw between sport "test" and "contest." *See* R. Scott Kretchmar, *From Test to Contest: An Analysis of Two Kinds of Counterpoint in Sport,* 2 J. PHIL. SPORT 23 (1975). In brief, a test is an effort by a single person or entity to attain a prescribed objective, such as to climb a mountain; in a contest, two or more competitors each try to outperform the others in some test. Thus, abrogating the walking rule affects the test of golf, by altering the task to be achieved, and it also potentially alters the contest, by changing the competitive balance. Is one concern more important than the other in this case?

2. Amusement. What do you make of the dissent's assertion that "it is the very nature of a game to have no object except amusement"? If you disagree with this assertion, does it undermine Justice Scalia's basic argument? If the assertion is true, then does it support or undermine the claim that all sports are games? "Amusement" is "the state of being amused, entertained, or pleased," while "amuse" belongs to a set of verbs that "refer to action that provide pleasure, especially as a means of passing time," and particularly "implies directing attention away from serious matters." THE AMERICAN HERITAGE DICTIONARY 62 (4th ed. 2009). War games (i.e., the class of military

---

[a] Harrison Bergeron is a dystopian short story, set in 2081, in which, by virtue of constitutional amendments, all Americans are mandated equal. Those with above-average abilities must bear handicaps to neutralize their advantages.

simulations and exercises, not the video game genre) plainly contradict this claim—if they are genuine games. But perhaps they are not. Still, it surely seems at first glance that many paradigmatic games, possibly most, serve at least *some* goals other than amusement. To take only the most obvious examples, chess, go, bridge, and poker are all claimed to sharpen players' mental acuity and critical thinking, while recreational sports provide many and profound health benefits. Should Justice Scalia really be read as insisting that the *only* object of activities like bridge and basketball is to amuse? Should he be read as denying that these activities are games? Or can his contention be fairly interpreted to mean something else entirely?

If you believe that genuine games can serve ends other than to "amuse" or to furnish "amusement"—and even that they can be designed, and valued, to serve additional ends—is it nonetheless true that amusement must be *among* a game's objects? Is amusement an "object" of the 100-meter dash? Of the marathon or ultramarathons? Boxing? If these or similar athletic competitions do not pursue "amusement" even among their ends, what conclusion would you draw—(a) that not all bona fide games must provide amusement, or (b) that these activities are not games? If you agree that competitive athletic activities such as the foregoing do not pursue amusement, and if you conclude that they are not games, is that because (i) all sports are games, but these activities are not sports, or (ii) they are sports, but not all sports are games?

3. *Arbitrariness.* The dissent also maintains that the rules of all games—including all sports that are games—are "entirely arbitrary." Is this true? What do you take "entirely arbitrary" to mean? One dictionary defines "arbitrary" as "determined by chance, whim, or impulse, and not by necessity, reason, or principle." THE AMERICAN HERITAGE DICTIONARY 91 (4th ed. 2009). But then it seems hard, once again, to take the dissent's claim at face value. For an obvious counterexample, take NFL rules that prohibit helmet-to-helmet hits. They are designed to promote participant safety and therefore must be determined at least in part by "reason or principle," and not "entirely" by "whim or impulse." Even putting aside safety-inspired rules, consider one of the rules that the dissent expressly invokes: the rule that basketball hoops stand 10 feet high. Is this rule "entirely arbitrary"? If so, what sense can be made of the suggestion, pressed by Geno Auriemma, the enormously successful coach of the University of Connecticut's women's basketball team, that the baskets in the women's game should be lowered seven inches?[b] Could you provide *reasons* for or against this proposed rule change? If so, was the dissent's contention that "in all games" the rules are "entirely arbitrary" wholly mistaken, or does it contain a germ (or more) of an important truth? And if it does, what is that truth? Do you suppose that Justice Scalia had in mind a sense of "arbitrary" different from the dictionary definition quoted above, and if so, what do you think it was?

---

      b   *See Geno Auriemma: Lower the rims,* ESPN.com (Oct. 23, 2012). After suggesting a seven-inch differential, Auriemma then proposed that it be 7.2 inches, in honor of Title IX, passed in 1972.

4. Walking and golf: some history. Even if it is not the case that *all* rules of all games are entirely arbitrary, it might nonetheless be true that the rule of PGA golf that requires competitors to walk is.

The requirement of walking the course substantially limited the career of one of history's greatest golfers, Ben Hogan, and also added considerably to his legend. Hogan was terribly injured in a nearly fatal crash with a bus in February 1949. Doctors told him he might never walk again, but eleven months later he returned to competitive golf, and five months after that he won the United States Open—despite having to play the final 36 holes of regulation on one day and then an 18-hole playoff on the next. Hogan continued to have success—he won two major championships the following year and three in 1953—but his difficulty in walking the course limited the number of tournaments he played, and dissuaded him from playing in the PGA Championship, which was then a match play tournament.

In 1964, the U.S. Open still had a 36-hole closing day, and again the walking requirement appeared to play a prominent role in one of the most heroic moments in the history of professional golf, Ken Venturi's victory in brutal heat and humidity. Venturi asked for and received more time than the rules would ordinarily allow because he was suffering so badly. Shirley Povich, *The 1964 U.S. Open: Victory in the Heat of Battle,* WASH. POST, June 11, 1997. After that year, the Open ended the tradition of the 36-hole final day.

The USGA has allowed carts in its Senior Amateur championships since 1969. Its website explains: "Traditionalists who believed walking the course was vital to a valid national title finally allowed carts because the championship is contested in the fall, when fewer caddies are available." *2016 Senior Amateur Fact Sheet*, USGA, https://tinyurl.com/y42m4hs3.

5. Walking and golf: the merits. Keep in mind that, as the *Martin* dissent emphasizes, even if the federal courts didn't intervene there would remain the question of whether, or to what extent, the PGA should retain the walking rule. In focusing on that question, it might help to suppose that you are a member of the PGA's rulemaking committee and that the Supreme Court had come out the other way in the *Martin* case. Is the walking requirement in PGA golf arbitrary? If so, is there any good reason for the PGA not to release *all* competitors from the obligation to walk?

If the walking rule is not entirely arbitrary, what reasons or principles support it? Put another way, given that the Rules of Golf do not require walking, why do you suppose that the PGA requires it on its regular tour? And given that it does, why do you suppose that it does *not* require walking on the Senior Tour or in open qualifying events?

Assuming arguendo that there are good reasons for the PGA not to withdraw the walking rule *wholesale*, should it nonetheless grant an exemption from the rule for Casey Martin and golfers with similar disabilities? If it grants such an exemption, should it also exempt all golfers in competitions in which a disabled golfer has received an exemption?

What factors or considerations are relevant to your decision in answering these questions? Is it significant that a majority of golfers choose to walk even when given the option not to? Are you persuaded by the expert's argument that the fatigue from walking in golf is not competitively significant? Is Justice Stevens right that the impossibility of ensuring equal conditions for all mitigates the PGA's concern about equity? Does it matter that Martin endured greater fatigue even with a cart than his competitors did by walking the entire course?

In thinking about this last question, note that the USGA still generally prohibits carts for most of its championships but—in light of the *Martin* case—it allows golfers (and caddies) to use a cart in cases of "disability as defined by the ADA"; an applicant for a cart must demonstrate "that by providing a golf cart to a player or caddie in that particular circumstances, the USGA would not be fundamentally altering the fairness of the competition by providing a player with an advantage over other players." How should the USGA assess the advantage question? Presumably, given the result of *Martin*, the fact that a golfer can perform better with a cart than without a cart is not itself sufficient to say that the cart gives the golfer an advantage over others. Is the question, then, whether the cart will make fatigue less of a factor for the disabled golfer than for other golfers? If the cart does have this effect, but without the cart the disabled golfer would be unable to compete effectively, what then? And if the cart does not give the disabled golfer an advantage over others in terms of fatigue, but does give some other advantages (more time near the ball to consider the next shot, for example), does that matter?

If Martin were unable to walk the course because of obesity, rather than because of a degenerative circulatory disorder, would your views on any of these questions change? What do you (think you) already know about obesity? What would you want to know? Consider the case of John Daly, who was allowed to use a cart at the 2019 PGA Championship but in the same year was denied one at the British Open, a tournament he had won in 1995. Daly has osteoarthritis, but he is also . . . large. The Championship Committee of the Royal and Ancient Golf Club of St. Andrews (the R&A), the body governing the tournament, asserted that it had "considered all of the relevant factors" in making its decision, and added: "The R&A believe that walking the course is an integral part of the Championship and is central to the tradition of links golf which is synonymous with The Open. We must also ensure that, as far as possible, the challenge is the same for all players in the field." Statement / John Daly, theopen.com (July 6, 2019).

Was Justice Scalia correct in his predictions of the consequences of allowing Martin an exemption from the walking rule?

6. *Essences.* If in considering the previous questions you accepted our invitation to play the role of PGA rulemaker, you might have found yourself reflecting on, among other things, something like the "essentialness" or "fundamentalness" of the walking rule. You might have reasoned that the case for exempting golfers like Martin from the walking rule is strengthened to the

extent that the rule is "peripheral" or "marginal" to the game of golf (or to golf as it is played on the PGA Tour), and weakened to the extent that the rule is "essential" or "fundamental." But perhaps it is not clear that this is even a meaningful question. Indeed, the majority and dissent in *Martin* appear to disagree regarding whether it is sensible, or even intelligible, to inquire into the "essence" of a sport and whether a given rule of sport is "essential."

On one reading of the opinions, Justices Stevens and Scalia agree that whether a given rule is "essential" to a given game or sport is equivalent to whether that rule is "fundamental" to the game or sport, but they disagree over what "essentialness" and "fundamentalness" amount to. Justice Scalia asserts that "it is quite impossible to say that any of a game's arbitrary rules is 'essential.'" But he then suggests that a given rule *is* essential (or fundamental) if eliminating that rule would yield a new game no longer "recognizab[le] as the same generic game." The majority (Scalia says) thinks that a rule could be "fundamental" to a game even if change or repeal of that rule would not render the game no longer recognizable. Do you agree with this characterization of the two views put forth in the *Martin* decision? If so, who has the better of this exchange? Consider the following:

- Is Justice Stevens right that "the essence of the game" is shotmaking—and if so, of what game? Put another way, is he right that "the essence of the game"—again, which game?—does not include walking?

- What is the essence of being a baseball pitcher? Does it include the ability to field bunts? See JASON TURBOW WITH MICHAEL DUCA, THE BASEBALL CODES: BEANBALLS, SIGN STEALING, AND BENCH-CLEARING BRAWLS: THE UNWRITTEN RULES OF AMERICA'S PASTIME 99 (2010) (describing an incident involving Nolan Ryan, then 39: "The entire league knew how Ryan felt about players bunting on him, mostly because the pitcher himself informed them of the fact with a regular pre-game ritual in which he tamped down the grass around home plate with his toe while staring daggers into the opposing dugout. His message: No bunting on me, fellas. And there rarely was.").

- Would it be counter to the essence of basketball to prohibit jumping? Is it counter to the essence of the game to prohibit running with the ball? Does Greco-Roman wrestling, in which it is illegal to grab the opposing wrestler by the legs or to squeeze him with the legs, run counter to the essence of wrestling?

- What do you suppose Justice Scalia means by "the same generic game"? Is that a meaningful phrase? Does Justice Scalia's reference to "how central to the game that [governing bodies] have organized" a given provision is conflict with his assertion that it is impossible to speak of a rule as being "essential" to the game?

- Consider the following sets of games: [baseball, softball] [rugby league, rugby union] [Test cricket, Twenty20] [men's lacrosse, women's lacrosse] [stud poker, draw poker] [NASCAR, Indy car, Formula One] [chess, speed chess] [(court) volleyball, beach volleyball] [stroke play golf, match play golf, miniature golf]. Which of these sets represent different games, and which represent variants of the same game (insofar as you know enough about them to have an opinion)? What considerations drive your judgments?

7. *Big holes*. Take an example about which the majority and dissent disagree: the size of the hole in golf. Regulation golf holes are 4 ¼″ in diameter. Why that odd size? Apparently because that was the diameter of holes cut by the first mechanical hole cutter, which the R&A approved. OK, but why was that the size that the tool cut? No one knows for sure, but it is said that the hole cutter was made from some extra pipe lying around the course where it was developed. Brent Kelley, *Why is the Golf Hole Size 4.25 Inches in Diameter?*, LIVEABOUT.COM (Sept. 18, 2018). In any event, though the majority mistakes the current size of the hole (saying that it is 3″ in diameter; perhaps it just seemed that way to Justice Stevens), it ruminates that a doubling of the diameter of the hole could possibly effect a fundamental change in the game. To double the diameter is, of course, to quadruple the area. (Area $= \pi r^2$.) Would this be a fundamental change? If not, is that because the change is too small, or because *no* change in the diameter of the hole could effectuate a fundamental change? If the latter, is that because the test of fundamentality is the same as the test of recognizableness, and golf would remain recognizably golf no matter the hole size? In the spring of 2014, the PGA proposed a pilot program at approximately 100 courses to increase the diameter from 4.25″ to 15″—roughly the diameter of a pizza. *See* Bill Pennington, *In a Hole, Golf Considers Digging a Wider One*, N.Y. TIMES, Apr. 19, 2014, at A1. (There are occasional big-hole golf tournaments, but the innovation has not taken off.) Would this be a fundamental change to golf? What skills would become more, or less, important? What if the hole were 6′ in diameter? If you feel that you do not know enough about golf to answer these questions, what more would you want to know?

CHAPTER 3

THE GAMEWRIGHT'S GOALS
AND CONSTRAINTS

■ ■ ■

Assuming now—as we think hard to dispute—that sports and games are not, as a class, designed or valued *only* to provide "amusement" for participants and spectators, then it would be possible, and perhaps profitable, to explore in greater depth *all* actual or potential rulemaking desiderata. We do not take on that large task. Here we investigate only some of the most important and interesting considerations—ends to be advanced and constraints to be respected—that face the gamewright. We will consider (1) promoting fairness; (2) facilitating, honing, and rewarding the exercise of skills; (3) presenting optimal challenges; (4) fostering excitement; (5) ensuring uniformity of challenge across time, space, and skill level, or, contrariwise, encouraging diversity of experience; (6) ensuring the health and safety of participants, or, alternatively, providing opportunities for pain and danger; and (7) making the rules readily administrable. Often the gamewright must balance several of these considerations in deciding on a rule.

As we address these various considerations, it might help to bear in mind some important choices gamewrights have made over the years. In baseball, for example, balls and strikes were no part of the earliest known rules, promulgated or codified by Alexander Cartwright in 1845. The rules then in force provided that the batter would instruct the pitcher where he wanted the ball delivered and would remain at bat until, by hitting the ball, he either reached base safely or was put out by a fielder. Balls and strikes were not introduced until 1863, at which point nine balls were required to make out a walk. A base on balls wasn't awarded for four balls until 1889. *See* DAVID NEMEC, THE OFFICIAL RULES OF BASEBALL ILLUSTRATED 22 (1999). What factors properly determine whether baseball is a better sport with walks than without, or how many balls should make a walk and how many strikes should make an out? What considerations bear on whether soccer should eliminate its offsides rule? Or on whether football should eliminate kickoffs or extra points?[a]

---

[a] For a short debate about extra points, *see* Dominic Bonvissuto, *What's the Point?*, SPORTS ILLUSTRATED, Jan. 23, 2014.

A. FAIRNESS

It may strike you right off the bat (sorry) that one of the primary considerations in creating a game is to make it "fair." A "level playing field" is a metaphor often used for fairness, outside as well as in the context of sports. From early-childhood games to professional sports, we expect competitions to be fair; indeed, we may doubt whether a game is worth playing or watching if it is not fair. But as the *Martin* case demonstrates, it is not so simple to say what fairness means or requires: the PGA argued that fairness required that Martin be subject to the same rules as other competitors, while he argued that fairness required an exemption.

1. Systemic asymmetries. Symmetry is one way of minimizing systemic unfairness. For example, in a soccer game, both teams have the same number of players, operate under the same constraints, and have the same objective; furthermore, each team begins with the ball in one half and—to diminish unfairness related to wind or terrain (an *un*level playing field, for example)—each side defends each goal for a half. But not all games are, or can be, symmetrical.

Many war games, for example, are asymmetrical: Each side is given different resources and different goals. Typically, one side is a defender and the other is an invader. What does fairness in such a game mean—that if players of equal skill oppose each other, one side will not win substantially more often than the other? It may be difficult in such a game to devise a useful metric to determine equality of skill. Indeed, in a complex game, we may wind up in a circle, because the most apparent metric of skill may be probability of winning. Perhaps, then we can say that the game is fair if, when two players oppose each other, their respective chances of winning do not depend on which side they take. But games often fail that criterion. *See, e.g.,* McJarvis, *A Thematic Asymmetric Game of Strategy vs Tactics,* BOARDGAMEGEEK, https://tinyurl.com/y3fbya53. ("The epic siege of a doomed defender's castle is well entrenched in the imaginations of gamers everywhere. It is perhaps no surprise, then, that a game like Stronghold would eventually come around in order to capitalize on the idea of doomed defenders facing impossible odds."). Can such a game be considered fair? Does it matter?[b]

Casino blackjack is also asymmetrical: A player has far more choices than the house, but she must complete her hand first, and if she goes over 21 she loses before the house has to draw. Card counting, if done well, gives the player an advantage, so casinos often take aggressive steps to prevent it. Casinos use a multiple-deck "shoe" to minimize the practice. Indeed, they are said to implement a rule under which, at any time the dealer

---

[b] *See* H. RICHARD UVILLER, THE TILTED PLAYING FIELD: IS CRIMINAL LAW UNFAIR? (1999) (arguing that because prosecution and defense are in different positions, fairness requires an uneven allocation of advantages).

believes that the remaining cards in the shoe favor the players—a high proportion of Aces and picture cards—he may reshuffle; such a policy would give the casino an advantage even against counting players. *Doug Grant, Inc. v. Greate Bay Casino Corp.*, 232 F.3d 173, 180 (3d Cir. 2000). Is such a policy fair? Is card counting fair? Is it fair to prohibit card counting? The New Jersey Supreme Court has said that, in crafting regulations of the industry, "[f]airness and the integrity of casino gaming are the touchstones." *Uston v. Resorts Intern. Hotel, Inc.*, 445 A.2d 370, 376 (N.J. 1982). But the odds in roulette are set so that the house has a small but definite advantage. Is it meaningful to speak of fairness in this context? Or is any rule in this context fair so long as players have adequate notice of it beforehand?

2.   *Fairness and asymmetries of schedule and order of play.* Does the order of competition affect the results in a skiing competition? How should spots be allocated in the early rounds? In golf, should all tournaments have a shotgun start—players starting at the same time but from different holes—to equalize weather conditions to the extent possible?

3.   *Fairness and home-field advantage.* Competitions not played at a neutral site contain a built-in asymmetry: In many sports, the home team has a significant advantage. Just why is not certain. Various factors may play a role: comfort with and knowledge of the playing field, the comfort of sleeping at home and not having to travel, a psychological edge given by the cheers of a friendly crowd. But mounting evidence suggests that most of home-field advantage is due to officials' unconscious motivation to conform to the wishes of the home crowd.[c] Whatever the causes of the home-field advantage, the fact of it is well established. Should championship series (or at least ultimate games, such as the seventh game of the World Series) in professional sports be played at neutral sites, as the Super Bowl ordinarily is? If the Super Bowl is scheduled for a site that happens to be the home field of one of the teams playing (as occurred, for the first time, in Tampa Bay in 2021), should it be moved? As of this writing, six of the 22 men's soccer World Cups have been won by the home country. Is that a problem? If so, should anything be done to correct it in the future?

What moves, if any, should a team be allowed to make to increase the home-field advantage? For example, should a baseball team be allowed to change the distances to the outfield fence before the season begins if it believes that doing so will improve its chances of winning? Should it be allowed to do so before a mid-season series? If the other team has better

---

[c]   For a careful econometric analysis that supports this conclusion, see TOBIAS J. MOSKOWITZ & L. JON WERTHEIM, SCORECASTING: THE HIDDEN INFLUENCES BEHIND HOW SPORTS ARE PLAYED AND GAMES ARE WON 110–67 (2011). For supportive evidence from the experience of the German Bundesliga, which played its spring 2020 season in empty stadiums because of the COVID-19 pandemic, see Rory Smith, *How Empty Seats Filled in Gaps About Essence of a Sport*, N.Y. TIMES, July 1, 2020, at B10.

base-stealers, should it be allowed to make the area around first base extra wet? Teams have done so for generations. Playing against the speedy Jose Reyes in 2011, the Atlanta Braves allegedly soaked their infield dirt, causing Reyes to slip and fall repeatedly throughout the game. Brian Costa, *The Curious Case of the Soggy Dirt*, WALL ST. J. (June 16, 2011). Asked to comment on the Braves' tactic, Mets manager Terry Collins said: "We all know a lot of times you alter your field to benefit your home team. It's no big deal." Should a team be allowed to grow the grass to a length that it believes will be optimal for its team? Should the home team in a playoff hockey game be allowed to exclude fans wearing the opposing team's colors from sitting in club seats, close to the action? Should it be allowed to sell tickets only to in-state residents or those who persuade it over the phone that they are friendly? *See* Tom Spousta, *Root for the Home Team, or Else*, N.Y. TIMES, May 21, 2015, at B13. Should the home team in a basketball game be allowed to provide thunder sticks for its fans sitting behind the basket and encourage the fans to use them when an opposing player is shooting a free throw? Should it be allowed to pump up the noise level electronically then? Does your answer depend upon whether, over the course of a season, teams that play each other will play an equal number of games at each team's home venue? If the teams play each other only once each season, is exploitation of home-field advantage okay if each team will host the other an equal number of times over a several-season stretch?

It was said that at the Meadowlands football stadium opening doors behind the goal posts generated wind patterns that made kicking a field goal more difficult. Should the home team be allowed to do so before the visitors attempt a field goal? In answering these questions, to what extent are you applying general considerations or tests, and to what extent are you reaching and reporting highly case-specific judgments that *this* is okay, and *that* isn't?

Since 1979, the walls of the visitors' locker room at Kinnick Stadium, the University of Iowa's home football field, have been pink; now the lockers, showers, and urinals are as well. The university claims that the rationale for this fashion statement is that pink has a calming effect. Some people have protested that the choice is rooted in homophobic and sexist conceptions. Jake New, *The Meaning of Pink*, INSIDE HIGHER ED, Aug. 29, 2014. Would the color choice be an abuse of home-field advantage if those accusations were true? And what if those accusations are incorrect (or can't be proven), but the pink color is nonetheless effective in dampening the competitive intensity of opposing players?

Does home-field advantage create an entitlement? If a baseball game is suspended, it may, depending on the teams' schedules, be completed in the visiting team's home park. (For example, a game suspended in the middle of the 10th inning in Kansas City on August 31, 2014, with Cleveland ahead 4–2, was resumed in Cleveland on September 22.) Is that appropriate? (In considering this question, it might help to bear in mind the caption of a classic New Yorker cartoon, by J.B. Handelsman: "You have a pretty good case, Mr. Pitkin. How much justice can you afford?")

4.   *Earned Advantages.* Tournaments are often seeded based on prior performance: in general, the higher seeded is a competitor, the weaker is its opponent in the early rounds. Is this fair? Some believe that higher seeded teams in the NCAA basketball tournament may get better hotel choices. *See* Eli Saslow, *No Palace for These Cinderellas*, WASH. POST, Mar. 18, 2007. Assuming that the available hotels are not all equal, is seeding an inappropriate way to assign the more desirable options? Is it preferable to assign them randomly, or to schools that pay for the privilege of choosing first, or in some other fashion? When the NBA resumed its pandemic-disrupted 2019–20 season at Walt Disney World in Orlando, Florida, it assigned what would have been the top-seeded teams to the better hotels to compensate them for their loss of home-court advantage in the playoffs. *See, e.g.,* Nick Goss, *Report: NBA assigned teams to these Disney hotels based on seeding*, NBC SPORTS BOSTON (June 16, 2020). Was that a sensible decision?

Should skiers who record the top scores in an early round of a competition get the better spots in later rounds as a reward for their performance? Or should the better spots in later rounds go to the slower skiers to make things more competitive? Or should spots be assigned randomly?

Before 2003, the American League had home-field advantage in the World Series in one year and the National League had it in the next. (The AL had it in odd-numbered years for most of the 20th century, but the pattern switched after cancellation of the 1994 Series.) Thus, the Minnesota Twins won the Series in 1987 and 1991 without winning a single road game, and the Arizona Diamondbacks did the same in 2001. From 2003 through 2016, the advantage went to the team representing the league that won that year's All-Star game. Was that a fair and appropriate resolution? Beginning in 2017, home field advantage has gone instead to the team with the better regular-season won-lost record—the rule in the NBA—even though the teams play very different schedules. Is that a better rule?

5.   *Handicaps.* Many sports and games use handicaps—burdens imposed on more accomplished or advantaged competitors to more nearly equalize participants' probabilities of victory. In the USGA's handicapping system for amateur golfers, for example, the handicap is based on the average of the player's ten best 18-hole rounds of their last 20, adjusted for the difficulty of the courses played. A "scratch" golfer (par average) will have a handicap of zero, and a "bogey" golfer will have a handicap of eighteen. When golfers of differing ability compete in a round, each golfer's

handicap is subtracted from their raw or "gross" score to yield a "net" score that determines the winner. Handicaps in chess, once common but rarely used in serious competitions for over a century, may require the stronger player to play without a pawn or a piece, or may give the weaker player additional moves near the beginning of a match. *Handicap (chess)*, WIKIPEDIA, https://tinyurl.com/y57oh9n3. In principle, do handicaps promote or impair fairness?

In *PGA v. Martin,* Justice Scalia notes that, although handicaps "are customary in social golf," they "are *not* used in professional golf" because using them would "destroy the game." In fact, though, several sports do use handicaps at even the most elite levels of competition. A polo team is assigned a handicap that aggregates the individual handicaps earned by its players. In horse racing, most events are "handicap races" in which the better horses must carry heavier weight in the form of lead plates put in the saddle bag. The races that comprise the Triple Crown are not formally handicap races, but even these events handicap colts and geldings (castrated males) relative to fillies: colts and geldings carry 126 pounds (jockey plus saddle plus lead weights as necessary), while fillies carry 121 pounds. In crew races, by contrast, the weight of the coxswain is not standardized—but the coxswain must carry extra weight if necessary to reach a prescribed minimum. What considerations should determine the circumstances, if any, in which handicaps should apply at elite levels of athletic competition?

———

Exercise 3A

You and some friends are working to establish an intramural student bowling league at your law school. You want the league to be fun and social, but also to take the competition seriously: a trophy and bragging rights are at stake. Most amateur bowling leagues employ handicaps. To encourage broad participation, you plan to as well. But you're also worried that some students might engage in "sandbagging"—the intentional effort to play below one's abilities in early contests for the purpose of securing an overly generous handicap.

What rules and procedures regarding the assignment and use of handicaps should you adopt?

———

The fairness issues we have considered so far have arisen from concern that one competitor will not be treated the same as another. But fairness concerns are sometimes raised even if a rule treats all competitors alike—even if, that is to say, a team operating behind a "veil of ignorance," and so not knowing what will happen in a contest, could not predict with any confidence whether the rule would help or hurt it. The following piece, a famous bit of legal whimsy, ranges far beyond fairness concerns. Nevertheless, we present it in full here, not only because it is a good read but also because it touches on other issues that we will address throughout the book.

ASIDE: THE COMMON LAW ORIGINS
OF THE INFIELD FLY RULE

123 U. PA. L. REV. 1474 (1975)
© 1975 University of Pennsylvania Law Review, reprinted with permission

The[1] Infield Fly Rule[2] is neither a rule of law nor one of equity; it is a rule of baseball.[3] Since the[4] 1890's it has been a part of the body of the

---

[1]   11 OXFORD ENGLISH DICTIONARY 257–60 (1961).

[2]   OFF. R. BASEBALL 2.00 & 6.05(e). Rule 2.00 is definitional in nature and provides that:

An INFIELD FLY is a fair fly ball (not including a line drive nor an attempted bunt) which can be caught by an infielder with ordinary effort, when first and second, or first, second and third bases are occupied, before two are out. The pitcher, catcher, and any outfielder who stations himself in the infield on the play shall be considered infielders for the purpose of this rule.

When it seems apparent that a batted ball will be an Infield Fly, the umpire shall immediately declare "Infield Fly" for the benefit of the runners. If the ball is near the baselines, the umpire shall declare "Infield Fly, if Fair."

The ball is alive and runners may advance at the risk of the ball being caught, or retouch and advance after the ball is touched, the same as on any fly ball. If the hit becomes a foul ball, it is treated the same as any foul.

NOTE: If a declared Infield Fly is allowed to fall untouched to the ground, and bounces foul before passing first or third base, it is a foul ball. If a declared Infield Fly falls untouched to the ground outside the baseline, and bounces fair before passing first or third base, it is an Infield Fly.

Rule 6.05(e) gives operational effect to the definition, by providing that the batter is out when an Infield Fly is declared.

Depending upon the circumstances, other rules which may or may not apply to a particular situation include, inter alia, Fed. R. Civ. P., Rule Against Perpetuities, and Rule of Matthew 7:12 & Luke 6:31 (Golden).

[3]   Although referred to as "Rules" both officially and in common parlance, if the analogy between the conduct-governing strictures of baseball and a jurisprudential entity on the order of a nation-state is to be maintained, the "rules" of baseball should be considered to have the force, effect, and legitimacy of the statutes of a nation-state. The analogy would continue to this end by giving the "ground rules" of a particular baseball park the same status as the judge-made rules of procedure of a particular court.

[4]   Note 1 supra.

official rules of baseball.[5] In its inquiry into the common law origins[6] of the rule, this Aside does not seek to find a predecessor to the rule in seventeenth-century England. The purpose of the Aside is rather to examine whether the same types of forces that shaped the development of the common law[7] also generated the Infield Fly Rule.

As a preliminary matter, it is necessary to emphasize that baseball is a game of English origin, rooted in the same soil from which grew Anglo-American law and justice.[8] In this respect it is like American football and unlike basketball, a game that sprang fully developed from the mind of James Naismith.[9] The story of Abner Doubleday, Cooperstown, and 1839, a pleasant tribute to American ingenuity enshrined in baseball's Hall of Fame, is not true.[10] The myth reflects a combination of economic opportunism,[11] old friendship,[12] and not a small element of anti-British

---

[5] It is only with the greatest hesitation that one hazards a guess as to *the* year of origin of the Infield Fly Rule. Seymour considers it to have been 1893. 1 H. SEYMOUR, BASEBALL 275 (1960). Richter, on the other hand, in an opinion which *The Baseball Encyclopedia* joins, considers the rule to have entered the game in 1895. F. RICHTER, RICHTER'S HISTORY AND RECORDS OF BASEBALL 256 (1914); THE BASEBALL ENCYCLOPEDIA 1526–27 (1974). Finally, Voigt considers 1894 the correct year. 1 D. VOIGHT, AMERICAN BASEBALL 288 (1966).

Although independent investigation of primary sources has led to the belief that the rule first developed in 1894 and 1895, notes 25–35 *infra* & accompanying text, a certain sense of justice would be satisfied if the rule developed as a result of play during the 1894 season. For that season was the first of the championship seasons of the Baltimore Orioles, the team that developed what is now known as "inside baseball," including such plays as the Baltimore chop and the hit-and-run. The Orioles not only played smart baseball; they played dirty baseball. "Although they may not have originated dirty baseball they perfected it to a high degree. In a National League filled with dirty players they were undoubtedly the dirtiest of their time and may have been the dirtiest the game has ever known." D. WALLOP, BASEBALL: AN INFORMAL HISTORY 88 (1969); *accord*, L. ALLEN, THE NATIONAL LEAGUE STORY 68 (1961); *see* R. SMITH, BASEBALL 136–46 (1947). Even if the Infield Fly Rule was not developed as a result of the event of the 1894 season, perhaps it should have been.

[6] For a discussion of origins, *see generally* Scopes v. State, 154 Tenn. 105, 289 S.W. 363 (1927); *Genesis* 1:1–2:9. *But see even more generally* Epperson v. Arkansas, 393 U.S. 97 (1968); R. ARDREY, AFRICAN GENESIS (1961); C. DARWIN, THE DESCENT OF MAN (1871); C. DARWIN, THE ORIGIN OF SPECIES (1859).

[7] For a discussion of common law in a non-baseball context, see W. HOLDSWORTH, A HISTORY OF ENGLISH LAW (1903–1938); O.W. HOLMES, THE COMMON LAW (1881).

[8] *Cf.* Palko v. Connecticut, 302 U.S. 319, 325 (1937).

[9] R. BRASCH, HOW DID SPORTS BEGIN? 41 (1970).

[10] R. HENDERSON, BAT, BALL AND BISHOP 170–94 (1947). The Doubleday theory of origin is outlined in 84 CONG. REC. 1087–89 (1939) (remarks of Congressman Shanley) (*semble*). Congressional approval of the theory, however, was never forthcoming. H.R.J. Res. 148, 76th Cong., 1st Sess. (1939), seeking to designate June 12, 1939, National Baseball Day, was referred to the Committee on the Judiciary, never again to be heard from. 84 CONG. REC. 1096 (1939). Nor did the Supreme Court formally adopt the Doubleday theory. Flood v. Kuhn, 407 U.S. 258, 260–61 (1972) (opinion of Blackmun, J.) (not explicitly rejecting the theory either). An interesting, if unlikely, explanation, offerable as an alternative to both the Doubleday and English theories of origin, is found in J. HART, HEY! B.C. 26 from the back (unpaginated, abridged & undated ed.).

[11] R. BRASCH, *supra* note 9, at 31–32.

[12] R. HENDERSON, *supra* note 10, at 179. The chairman of the commission suggested by A.G. Spalding to investigate the origins of the game was A.G. Mills, who had belonged to the same military post as Abner Doubleday.

feeling.[13] The true birthplace of the game is England; thence it was carried to the western hemisphere, to develop as an American form.[14]

The original attitude toward baseball developed from distinctly English origins as well. The first "organized" games were played in 1845 by the Knickerbocker Base Ball Club of New York City,[15] and the rules which governed their contests clearly indicate that the game was to be played by gentlemen. Winning was not the objective; exercise was.[16] "The New York club players were 'gentlemen in the highest social sense'—that is, they were rich . . . . The earliest clubs were really trying to transfer to our unwilling soil a few of the seeds of the British cricket spirit."[17] This spirit, which has been variously described as the attitude of the amateur, of the gentleman, and of the sportsman,[18] would have kept the rules simple and allowed moral force to govern the game.[19] Such an attitude, however, was unable to prevail.

As baseball grew, so did the influence of values that saw winning, rather than exercise, as the purpose of the game.[20] Victory was to be pursued by any means possible within the language of the rules, regardless of whether the tactic violated the spirit of the rules.[21] The written rules had to be made more and more specific, in order to preserve the spirit of the game.[22]

The Infield Fly Rule is obviously not a core principle of baseball. Unlike the diamond itself or the concepts of "out" and "safe," the Infield Fly Rule is not necessary to the game. Without the Infield Fly Rule, baseball does not degenerate into bladderball[23] the way the collective bargaining process degenerates into economic warfare when good faith is absent.[24] It is a

---

[13] R. SMITH, *supra* note 5, at 31.

[14] *See generally* H. SEYMOUR, *supra* note 5; D. VOIGT, *supra* note 5. The American qualities of the game are also revealed in other than historical or legal contexts. *Cf.* M. GARDNER, THE ANNOTATED CASEY AT THE BAT (1967); B. MALAMUD, THE NATURAL (1952).

[15] R. SMITH, *supra* note 5, at 32–35.

[16] KNICKERBOCKER BASE BALL CLUB R. 1 (1845), *reprinted in* R. HENDERSON, *supra* note 10, at 163–64, *and in* F. RICHTER, *supra* note 5, at 227.

[17] R. SMITH, *supra* note 5, at 37.

[18] Keating, *Sportsmanship as a Moral Category*, 75 ETHICS 25, 33 (1964).

[19] R. SMITH, *supra* note 5, at 68–69.

[20] 1 D. VOIGHT, *supra* note 5, at xvii; *cf. Hearings on S. 3445, Federal Sports Act of 1972, Before the Senate Committee on Commerce*, 92d Cong., 2d Sess. 94–95 (1973) (statement of H. Cosell). *See generally* Keating, *supra* note 18, at 31–34.

[21] Perhaps the most glaring example of this attitude is contained in the career of Mike "King" Kelly. When the rules permitted substitutions on mere notice to the umpire, Kelly inserted himself into the game after the ball was hit in order to catch a ball out of reach of any of his teammates. R. SMITH, *supra* note 5, at 89–90.

[22] *Cf. id.* 68–69; 1 D. VOIGT, *supra* note 5, at 204–05.

[23] *See* Yale Daily News, Oct. 29, 1966, at 1, col. 1.

[24] NLRB v. Insurance Agents Int'l Union, 361 U.S. 477, 488–90 (1960).

technical rule, a legislative response to actions that were previously permissible, though contrary to the spirit of the sport.

Whether because the men who oversaw the rules of baseball during the 1890's were unwilling to make a more radical change than was necessary to remedy a perceived problem in the game, or because they were unable to perceive the need for a broader change than was actually made, three changes in the substantive rules, stretching over a seven-year period, were required to put the Infield Fly Rule in its present form. In each legislative response to playing field conduct, however, the fundamental motive for action remained the same: "To prevent the defense from making a double play by subterfuge, at a time when the offense is helpless to prevent it, rather than by skill and speed."[25]

The need to enforce this policy with legislation first became apparent in the summer of 1893. In a game between New York and Baltimore, with a fast runner on first, a batter with the "speed of an ice wagon"[26] hit a pop fly. The runner stayed on first, expecting the ball to be caught. The fielder, however, let the ball drop to the ground, and made the force out at second.[27] The particular occurrence did not result in a double play, but that possibility was apparent; it would require only that the ball not be hit as high. Although even the Baltimore Sun credited the New York Giant with "excellent judgment,"[28] the incident suggested that something should be done, because by the play the defense obtained an advantage that it did not deserve and that the offense could not have prevented. Umpires could handle the situation by calling the batter out,[29] but this was not a satisfactory solution; it could create as many problems as it solved.[30] The 1894 winter meeting responded with adoption of the "trap ball" rule, putting the batter out if he hit a ball that could be handled by an infielder while first base was occupied with one out.[31]

The trap ball rule of 1894, however, did not solve all problems. First, although the rule declared the batter out, there was no way to know that the rule was in effect for a particular play. The umpire was not required to

---

[25]   1 H. SEYMOUR, *supra* note 5, at 276.

[26]   Baltimore Sun, May 24, 1893, at 6, col. 2. Raised by this statement is the issue of the speed of an ice wagon in both relative and absolute terms. Such inquiry is beyond the scope of this Aside.

[27]   *Id.* The fielder who made the play was Giant shortstop and captain John Montgomery Ward, who became a successful attorney after his playing days ended. 1 D. VOIGT, *supra* note 5, at 285.

[28]   Baltimore Sun, May 24, 1893, at 6, col. 2.

[29]   *E.g.,* the Chicago-Baltimore game of June 8, 1893. "In the second inning . . . Kelley hit a pop fly to short-stop. Dahlen caught the ball, then dropped it and threw to second base, a runner being on first. The muff was so plain that Umpire McLaughlin refused to allow the play and simply called the batsman out." Baltimore Sun, June 9, 1893, at 6, col. 2.

[30]   Text accompanying notes 45–46 *infra*.

[31]   Baltimore Sun, Feb. 27, 1894, at 6, col. 3. The rule stated that "the batsman is out if he hits a fly ball that can be handled by an infielder while first base is occupied and with only one out." *Id.* Apr. 26, 1894, at 6, col. 2.

make his decision until after the play, and, consequently, unnecessary disputes ensued.[32] Second, it became apparent that the feared unjust double play was not one involving the batter and one runner, but one that, when two men were on base, would see two baserunners declared out.[33] The 1895 league meeting ironed out these difficulties through changes in the rules.[34] The third problem with the trap ball rule of 1894, one not perceived until later, was that it applied only when one man was out. The danger of an unfair double play, however, also exists when there are no men out. This situation was corrected in 1901, and the rule has remained relatively unchanged since that time.[35]

The Infield Fly Rule, then, emerged from the interplay of four factors, each of which closely resembles a major force in the development of the common law. First is the sporting approach to baseball. A gentleman, when playing a game, does not act in a manner so unexpected as to constitute trickery;[36] in particular he does not attempt to profit by his own unethical conduct.[37] The gentleman's code provides the moral basis for the rule; it is the focal point of the rule, just as the more general precept of fair play provides a unifying force to the conduct of the game. The principle of Anglo-American law analogous to this gentleman's concept of fair play is the equally amorphous concept of due process, or justice[38] itself.

---

[32] Baltimore Sun, Apr. 26, 1894, at 6n col. 2.

[33] 1 H. SEYMOUR, *supra* note 5, at 275–76. Seymour developed yet another reason for the change in the rule: that "teams got around it by having outfielders come in fast and handle the pop fly." *Id.* 276. This does not appear to be a valid thesis because, from the beginning, the rule referred not to whether an infielder, as opposed to an outfielder, *did* handle the chance, but to whether an infielder *could* handle it. Note 31 *supra.*

[34] Baltimore Sun, Feb. 18, 1895, at 6, col. 4. *Id.* Feb. 28, 1895, at 6, col. 5.

[35] THE BASEBALL ENCYCLOPEDIA 1527 (1974). The current rule is set forth in note 2 *supra.*

[36] *See, e.g.,* Pluck (the wonder chicken).

[37] In the law, this belief is reflected in the clean hands doctrine, which "is rooted in the historical concept of [the] court of equity as a vehicle for affirmatively enforcing the requirements of conscience and good faith." Precision Instrument Mfg. Co. v. Automotive Maintenance Mach. Co., 324 U.S. 806, 814 (1945). For a statutory codification of the clean hands rule, see CAL. HEALTH & SAFETY CODE § 28548, ¶ 2 (West 1967) (requiring food service employees to "clean hands" before leaving restroom). *See generally* Z. CHAFEE, SOME PROBLEMS OF EQUITY, chs. 1–3 (1950).

To be contrasted with the doctrine of "clean hands" is the "sticky fingers" doctrine. The latter embodies the reaction of the baseball world to the excitement caused by the emergence of the home run as a major aspect of the game. Applying to the ball a foreign substance, such as saliva, made the big hit a difficult feat to achieve. As a result, in 1920, the spitball was outlawed. L. ALLEN, *supra* note 5, at 167. The banning of the spitball was not, however, absolute. Seventeen pitchers were given lifetime waivers of the ban, *id.,* possibly because the spitball had become an essential element of their stock-in-trade, and depriving them of the pitch would in effect deny them the right to earn a living. *See* Adams v. Tanner, 244 U.S. 590 (1917); McDermott v. City of Seattle, 4 F. Supp. 855, 857 (W.D. Wash. 1933); Winther v. Village of Weippe, 91 Idaho 798, 803–04, 430 P.2d 689, 694–95 (1967); *cf.* RESTATEMENT (SECOND) OF CONTRACTS § 90 (Tent. Drafts Nos. 1–7, 1973). *But see* Ferguson v. Skrupa, 372 U.S. 726, 730–31 (1963).

[38] *See generally, e.g.,* U.S. CONST. amends. V & XIV and cases citing thereto; Poe v. Ullman, 367 U.S. 497, 539–55 (1961) (Harlan, J., dissenting); J. RAWLS, A THEORY OF JUSTICE (1971); Bentley, *John Rawls: A Theory of Justice,* 121 U. PA. L. REV. 1070 (1973); Michelman, *In Pursuit of Constitutional Welfare Rights: One View of Rawls' Theory of Justice,* 121 U. PA. L. REV. 962 (1973); Scanlon, *Rawls' Theory of Justice,* 121 U. PA. L. REV. 1020 (1973); *cf., e.g.,* Byron R.

Baseball's society, like general human society, includes more than gentlemen, and the forces of competitiveness and professionalism required that the moral principle of fair play be codified so that those who did not subscribe to the principle would nonetheless be required to abide by it.[39] Thus the second factor in the development of the Infield Fly Rule—a formal and legalistic code of rules ensuring proper conduct—was created.[40] In the common law, this development manifested itself in the formalism of the writ system.[41] Conduct was governed by general principles; but to enforce a rule of conduct, it was necessary to find a remedy in a specific writ.[42] The common law plaintiff had no remedy if the existing writs did not encompass the wrong complained of; and the baseball player who had been the victim of a "cute" play could not prevail until the umpire could be shown a rule of baseball squarely on point.

To the generalization set forth in the preceding sentence there is an exception, both at common law and at baseball. At common law, the exception was equity, which was able to aid the plaintiff who could not find a form of action at law.[43] At baseball, the exception was the power of the umpire to make a call that did not fit within a particular rule.[44] The powers of equity and of the umpire, however, were not unlimited. The law courts circumscribed the power of the chancellor to the greatest extent possible, and this process of limitation has been defended.[45] Likewise, the discretionary power of the umpire has been limited: Additions to the written rules have reduced the area within which the umpire has discretion to act. Strong policy reasons favor this limitation upon the umpire's discretionary power. Because finality of decision is as important as correctness of decision, an action that invites appeal, as broad discretion in the umpire does, is not valued. The umpire must have the status of an unchallengeable finder of fact.[46] Allowing challenges to his authority on matters of rules admits the possibility that he may be wrong, and encourages a new generation of challenges to findings of fact.

The fourth element in the development of the Infield Fly Rule is demonstrated by the piecemeal approach that rules committees took to the problem. They responded to problems as they arose; the process of creating the Infield Fly Rule was incremental, with each step in the development of

---

"Whizzer" White (1962–), Hugo L. Black (1937–71), & Horace Gray (1881–1902) (Justices). *But cf.,* *e.g.,* Roger B. Taney (1836–64) (Chief Justice).

[39] Keating, *supra* note 18, at 30. *See also* R. SMITH, *supra* note 5, at 68–69.

[40] Text accompanying notes 25–35 *supra.*

[41] 2 F. MAITLAND, COLLECTED PAPERS 477–83 (1911).

[42] F. POLLOCK, THE GENIUS OF THE COMMON LAW 13 (1912); 2 F. POLLOCK & F. MAITLAND, HISTORY OF ENGLISH LAW 558–65 (2d ed. 1952).

[43] F. MAITLAND, EQUITY 4–5 (1909).

[44] Note 29 *supra.*

[45] 2 F. MAITLAND, *supra* note 41, at 491–94.

[46] OFF. R. BASEBALL 4.19.

the rule merely a refinement of the previous step. Formalism was altered to the extent necessary to achieve justice in the particular case; it was not abandoned and replaced with a new formalism. Anglo-American law has two analogies to this process. The first is the way in which common law precedents are employed to mold existing remedies to new situations. Although the rigid structure of the common law was slow to change, it did change. The substantive change took place not only as a result of judicial decision; it was also caused by legislation, which is the second analogy. The legislation, however, was to a great extent directed at specific defects perceived to exist in the system.[47] Adjustment of the law, not its reform, was the goal of the legislative process. The rules of baseball and of Anglo-American jurisprudence are thus to be contrasted with the continental system of complete codes designed to remedy society's ills with a single stroke of the legislative brush.[48]

The dynamics of the common law and the development of one of the most important technical rules of baseball, although on the surface completely different in outlook and philosophy, share significant elements. Both have been essentially conservative, changing only as often as a need for change is perceived, and then only to the extent necessary to remove the need for further change. Although problems are solved very slowly when this attitude prevails, the solutions that are adopted do not create many new difficulties. If the process reaps few rewards, it also runs few risks.

COMMENTS AND QUESTIONS

1.   A cultural revolution? The *Aside* is, by a wide margin, the most famous contribution to the jurisprudence-of-sport literature. It is also one of the most famous student notes. Its author, William Stevens, went on to an unremarkable career at the American Law Institute and later the American Bar Association. But he earned an obituary in *The New York Times* upon his death in 2008 solely on the strength of the *Aside*, described as "one of the most celebrated and imitated analyses in American legal history." Law professor Robert M. Jarvis explained that Stevens's short piece "encouraged a whole generation of law students, some of whom became law-review editors, to look at subjects previously beyond the pale." According to Professor Jarvis, "[a]fter Stevens, law reviews were never the same. It was a cultural revolution. It cannot be overstated." William Grimes, *William S. Stevens, 60, Dies; Wrote Infield Fly Note,* N.Y. Times, Dec. 11, 2008. Whether or not Professor Jarvis *did* overstate the point, the *Aside* was only the beginning of a surprisingly extensive legal literature on the infield fly rule. *See, e.g.,* Howard M. Wasserman, Infield Fly Rule Is in Effect: The History and Strategy of Baseball's Most (In)Famous Rule (2018); Micro-Symposium, *Infield Fly*

---

[47] F. Pollock, *supra* note 42, at 72.

[48] *Cf.* H. Gutteridge, Comparative Law 77–78 (2d ed. 1949).

Rules Is in Effect: The History and Strategy of Baseball's Most (In)Famous Rule, 13 FIU L. REV. 929 (2019); Neil B. Cohen & Spencer Weber Waller, *Taking Pop-Ups Seriously: The Jurisprudence of the Infield Fly Rule*, 82 WASH. U.L.Q. 453 (2004). Indeed, though Anthony D'Amato had his tongue in his cheek when he wrote that the Rule "is one of the most hotly contested topics in American law today," *The Contribution of the Infield Fly Rule to Western Civilization (and Vice Versa)*, 100 NW. U.L. REV. 189, 189 (2006), he had several citations to back him up.

2. *Revisiting arbitrariness and centrality.* Notice that the infield fly rule does not apply when the only base runner is on first base, or there are runners just on first and third. Why is that? Should that aspect of the rule be changed? Could reasons be given for or against such a change if the rule were "entirely arbitrary"? *Is* the infield fly rule "entirely arbitrary"? Is this particular feature of the rule arbitrary? Note that, as the *Aside* suggests in discussion of the ice-wagon batter, the fielding team may have an incentive to let the fly ball drop and get an easy force play, even if there is just a runner on first, if that runner is significantly faster than the batter.[d] But note that if the fielder intentionally *drops* a fly ball, or even a line drive, after touching it, the Rules prevent the ploy from working in this situation; the batter is declared out and the ball is dead. MLB Rule 5.09(a)(12) and Approved Ruling. Does this combination of rules make sense?

Why, furthermore, does the infield fly rule apply only to a "fly ball," and not to a line drive (which is covered by the intentional-drop rule) or attempted bunt? To *infield* fly balls? To *fair* balls? When there are fewer than two outs? Why does the rule result in the batter being called out whether or not the fielder catches the ball?

According to the *Aside*, the infield fly rule "is obviously not a core principle of baseball." Is this obvious to you? In answering this question, what standards are you appealing to when assessing whether the rule is or is not a "core principle"? How might Justices Stevens and Scalia answer this question?

3. *A matter of fairness?* The *Aside* describes the double play that an infielder could engineer in the absence of the infield fly rule as "unjust" and "unfair." Do you agree? What is unjust or unfair about it? Would it be unfair if the worst thing a batter could do with the bases loaded and no outs was to hit a pop-up to the infield—and if the best thing the pitcher and catcher could do was to induce that pop-up?

Is there any justification for the infield fly rule that is *not* grounded in fairness concerns? That is, could somebody reasonably maintain *both* (a) that, in the absence of an infield fly rule, it would *not* be unfair for an infielder to intentionally let a pop fly fall for the purpose of effecting a double play, and (b)

---

d   This does occasionally happen; Ian Kinsler, second baseman of the Detroit Tigers, did it at least twice in one year. George Sipple, *Tigers' Ian Kinsler fixes swing in time for huge July*, DETROIT FREE PRESS, July 25, 2015 (Xander Bogaerts taken off the bases and replaced by David Ortiz); Andrew Joseph, *Ian Kinsler cunningly missed an easy popup on purpose*, USA TODAY, Apr. 17, 2016 (Colby Rasmus replaced by Tyler White).

that the infield fly rule should not be repealed? In order to answer this question, you might find it helpful to think through how baseball would be different if there were no infield fly rule. Would it be a better or worse sport?

4.   A preventable windfall? Consider an irony of the rule. The rule is intended to prevent cheap double plays, but it does so by giving the defense an automatic out—an out that, as highlighted by the most notorious recent invocation of the rule, *see* p. 99 below, it might fail to earn absent the rule. *Assuming* that it is appropriate to prevent the cheap double play by rule, is there a better way to do it, one that would not involve giving the defense this windfall? *See* Richard D. Friedman, *Just Say No to the Cheap Double Play*, 13 FIU L. REV. 931 (2019).

5.   Dropped third strikes. Ordinarily, if a catcher drops a third strike, the batter is not out if he reaches first base before being thrown or tagged out. But this rule does not apply if (a) there is a runner on first base *and* (b) there are fewer than two outs. Is there a commonality between this rule and the infield fly rule? Absent these rules, what would happen if, say, a batter struck out with the bases loaded and no outs? Would that be unfair or unjust? If you think it would be, is there a way of achieving the goals of the current rule without automatically declaring the batter out when he strikes out and first base is occupied with fewer than two outs? As a segue to the next section, consider whether such a rule would reward skill and luck in a more appropriate way than does the current one.

B. SKILL (AND LUCK)

Sports are, in part, contests of skill. Although some *games* involve no skill at all, and are entirely determined by luck (for example, Chutes and Ladders), this does not appear to be true of any activity that most people would count as a *sport*. Accordingly, it is highly plausible that a core objective of most or even all sports is to hone and reward certain athletic skills or excellences. Some observers, going further, contend that this objective is an essential feature of sport, that an activity that is not designed to test competitors' relative skills can be a game, but not a sport. Do you agree?

If skill is an important feature of sport, what about luck? People often think that skill and luck are opposites, so that if a sport involves a high degree of skill, then it must involve little or no luck, and vice versa. But, at least as put this way, this is a mistake, as is nicely explained in the fascinating book *Characteristics of Games*:

> [W]hen looking at a game as a whole, the two concepts are independent (or, as a mathematician might say, orthogonal): A game can have a large or small amount of skill, and it can have a large or small amount of luck. Knowing the amount of luck there is in a game tells you nothing about the amount of skill, and

knowing the amount of skill in a game tells you nothing about the amount of luck.

GEORGE SKAFF ELIAS, RICHARD GARFIELD & K. ROBERT GUTSCHERA, CHARACTERISTICS OF GAMES 151–52 (2012). The authors note that tic-tac-toe ranks low on both skill and luck, poker ranks high on both dimensions, chess is high skill, low luck, and slot machines are low skill, high luck. Consider too their delightful imagined game of "die-rolling chess":

> Two people play a game of chess (replaying draws). Then a die is rolled: 1–2 means the first player wins, 3–4 means the second player wins, and 5–6 means the winner of the chess game wins. This game has all the skill of regular chess—every book written about regular chess still applies to die-rolling chess—but it certainly has more luck.

The relationship between luck and skill, then, is that "luck decreases, not skill, but the *returns to skill.*" *Id.* (emphasis added).

COMMENTS AND QUESTIONS

1. Luck and returns to skill. What does the distinction between skill and returns to skill mean? If one alters the rules of a competition so that luck is less likely to determine the outcome, will skill be more likely to determine it? One might say that tic-tac-toe involves no luck and little skill. But then what determines the outcome of a game?

Branch Rickey, the great baseball executive, famously said, "Luck is the residue of design." Can we also say that luck is the residue of skill? Suppose that a soccer player takes a difficult shot from thirty yards out. The ball hits the inside of the post and rebounds into the goal. If the ball had hit the post a fraction of an inch to the side, it would have bounced harmlessly back into the field. What can we say about the extent to which luck and skill played a role in the outcome? It is sometimes said that increasing the size of the goal would decrease the role of luck. Why is this so?

Michael Mauboussin, an investment strategist, speaks about the "paradox of skill": "As the overall level of skill rises and becomes more uniform, luck becomes more important." For an example,

> [s]uppose the world's best Scrabble player, which would be a computer, competes against a novice. The computer's skill will routinely ensure victory even if the novice draws better tiles. But if that computer plays an equally skilled opponent, an identical computer running the same program, then the outcome will be determined entirely by the luck of the draw.

John Tierney, *Soccer, a Beautiful Game of Chance,* N.Y. TIMES, July 8, 2014, at D6 (citing MICHAEL J. MAUBOUSSIN, THE SUCCESS EQUATION: UNTANGLING SKILL AND LUCK IN BUSINESS, SPORTS, AND INVESTING (2012)). If the game is between equally skilled human players, rather than between computers, can we say that the outcome will be determined *entirely* by the luck of the draw? Or is it more apt to say that the outcome will be determined by the better performance? If so, does this dissolve the "paradox of skill"? Imagine a scenario in which two competing basketball teams are perfectly equal with regard to skill. Is the team that wins merely lucky? Or did it just play the better match on the day? Can we distinguish usefully between *skill* and *performance*?

One possible implication of a view that treats skill as central to sport is that individual sports should be constructed so as to maximize the returns to skill, and thus to minimize, to the greatest extent possible, the influence of luck on contest outcomes. In contrast to this view, the sport philosopher Robert Simon sees value even with respect to outcomes that are (almost?) entirely attributable to luck and not to skill—what he calls "flukes." Robert Simon, *Deserving to Be Lucky: Reflections on the Role of Luck and Desert in Sports*, 34 J. PHIL. SPORT 13, 15 (2007). "For one thing," he explains,

> the possibility of a fluke's determining an outcome of a contest introduces an element of uncertainty that can make the game more exciting for spectators and participants alike. Moreover, it may promote a desirable degree of humility among even the most successful athletes and create an appreciation for the often arbitrary contingencies that can affect human life.

Id. at 16. Do you agree? On Simon's view, should rulemakers in sports in which flukes make little or no appearance look for opportunities to introduce luck into the competitions? Can you think of any "fluke-free" sports and how they could be made more fluke-friendly?

A more economically oriented take on the problem is offered by Stefan Szymanski. "Of all the major team sports, soccer is the most unequal in the sense that teams with vastly different resources regularly compete against each other at the highest level," he notes. Accordingly, he believes that reducing the importance of luck, which could be done by increasing the size of the goal, would be a bad thing: "If you doubled the size of the goal, then soccer would become like basketball, and in a high-scoring game, the rich teams would almost always win," he says. "Randomness favors the underdog. Would we ever want to reduce the role of luck in soccer? No way." Tierney, *Soccer, a Beautiful Game of Chance*. Do you agree? What does determine the optimal size of the goal in soccer? Should the size be the same for youth soccer and elite adult competitions?

2.   *When absence of skill is an advantage.* Mark Twain once observed that "the best swordsman in the world doesn't need to fear the second best swordsman in the world; no, the person for him to be afraid of is some ignorant antagonist who has never had a sword in his hand before." MARK TWAIN, A CONNECTICUT YANKEE IN KING ARTHUR'S COURT 330 (1889). Why might this be? What, if anything, follows for the design of sporting competitions?

3.   *Net cords.* In a net sport, a ball often touches the net and then goes over it. Sometimes the deflection, by slowing the ball and making it sit up,

makes the shot easy to return. But often, the deflection makes the shot harder to return; indeed, sometimes the ball dribbles over the net, which may make for an essentially unreturnable shot. We can assume that nobody *aims* for net cords; that would require too much precision. Certainly they are at least in part the product of luck, which is probably why many tennis players apologize when they get net cord winners. *Cf.* Howie Abrams, *Stop Apologizing For Net Cord Winners!*, THE BLEACHER REPORT, July 1, 2009. Is an element of skill nevertheless involved in producing net cords? And how should net cords be treated? There are three basic possibilities:

(1) *Treat the shot as no good, giving the point to the other side.* Until 2000, that was the rule with respect to the serve in most volleyball competitions. Todd's Volleyball Rules Page, *The "let" serve—volleyball rules FAQ*, https://tinyurl.com/y5ce68gj.

(2) *Treat the play as a "let"—that is, do it over.* This is the rule with respect to the serve in most tennis competitions.

(3) *Play the point out, without regard to its having touched the net.* This is the rule with respect to shots other than the serve in tennis; it is also the rule with respect to the serve in NCAA men's tennis. It is now the rule with respect to the serve as well as other shots in volleyball.

Are these differences in treatment justified by the different circumstances? What reasons are there *not* to have a rule calling for a let whenever a ball hits the net and goes over? Does it make sense that in tennis a player who is trying to hit the ball clear over the net might hit an unreturnable shot by catching a good deal of the tape (but not enough so that the ball stays on her side of the net)? If you don't like dribbler winners on the serve, but you don't like lets, could you devise a more satisfactory rule?

4. Impediments in golf. If a golfer's ball lands against a tree, that's tough luck for her; she won't be allowed to move the ball—or, for that matter, the tree—without a penalty. The tree is simply part of the course, part of the challenge that the golfer faces; perhaps a more skilled golfer would have hit the ball further away from the tree. The Rules of Golf do not apply the principle generally applied in miniature golf, under which a player may move a ball a putter's length away from an obstruction to allow a full, free swing. Should they? There is a good deal of luck in determining whether a ball lands so close to an obstruction as not to allow a full swing, or in a divot impairing a swing. A player has the option of declaring an unplayable lie and dropping the ball at a spot within two club lengths where they can swing freely—but only with a penalty. (See Chapter 6.)

On the other hand, some courses apply "winter rules" or "preferred lies," not only in the winter but at other times when the course is in bad shape. In general, when winter rules are in effect, a player may improve a lie when the ball lands on the fairway but in an area where the condition of the grass is poor; the rule will typically provide a maximum distance away from where the ball landed (which may be anywhere from six inches to a club length) that she may move the ball, but no closer to the hole. The two leading rule-making bodies, the USGA and the R&A, long refused to endorse the idea of winter rules; they regarded such rules as antithetical to the fundamental principle of the Rules of Golf that one must play the ball as it lies. But in 2004 they adopted an Appendix to the Rules of Golf allowing a course to apply winter rules if it so chooses.[e]

Should preferred lies on the fairway be allowed, without penalty, when a course is in compromised condition? Should they be allowed on other parts of the course then? Should they be allowed more generally? Or, looked at from the other direction, should miniature golf be played according to the Rules of Golf in this respect—that is, tough luck, no moving away from the barrier?

Note also that, although in general a golfer is not allowed to move the ball away from an impediment without penalty, he may move the impediment away from the ball, so long as the ball and the impediment are not in or touching the same hazard and the impediment is deemed to be loose. (He incurs a penalty if in moving the impediment he moves the ball, unless the ball is on the green; then he can restore the ball to its prior position.) If the ball is in motion, however, he may not remove a loose impediment that might alter the motion of the ball. Rule of Golf 11.3. Do these rules make sense? As interpreted by the governing bodies, there is an extensive definition of loose impediment.[f] It is broad enough to cover large objects, such as rocks or felled trees, that can only be moved with great effort, and only with the assistance of other persons, such as caddies and spectators—so long as they (the impediments, that is) are not embedded in the ground. Thus, in a famous incident during the 1999 Phoenix Open, Tiger Woods was allowed to enlist the help of his gallery in moving a boulder that weighed about a ton. Sam Weinman, *Throwback Thursday: That*

---

[e]   The 2019 rewrite of the Rules includes, under a section called "Committee Procedures," a set of Model Local Rules that a Committee—the person or group in charge of a course or competition—may choose to adopt. One of these, Model Local Rule E–3, provides for winter rules or "preferred lies." USGA, RULES AND INTERPRETATIONS.

[f]   Loose impediment: Any unattached natural object such as:
- Stones, loose grass, leaves, branches and sticks,
- Dead animals and animal waste,
- Worms, insects and similar animals that can be removed easily, and the mounds or webs they build (such as worm casts and ant hills), and
- Clumps of compacted soil (including aeration plugs).

Such natural objects are not loose if they are:
- Attached or growing,
- Solidly embedded in the ground (that is, cannot be picked out easily), or
- Sticking to the ball.

Special cases:
- Sand and loose soil are not loose impediments.
- Dew, frost and water are not loose impediments.
- Snow and natural ice (other than frost) are either loose impediments or, when on the ground, temporary water, at your option.
- Spider webs are loose impediments even though they are attached to another object.

Rules of Golf, Definitions.

time Tiger Woods had his gallery perform manual labor and move a boulder,
GOLF DIGEST, Jan. 31, 2019. If, however, Woods had been in a hazard, brushing
his club against a leaf that was also in the hazard would have incurred a
penalty at that time, under then-Rule 13–4. Bob Harig, *Graeme McDowell
penalized 2 shots,* ESPN.com (Sept. 6, 2012) (McDowell noting that he took a
two-shot penalty "[d]espite the fact that nothing moved, the lie hasn't
improved, I just didn't give the branch enough respect."). Carl Pettersson, who
was penalized in the 2012 PGA Championship for brushing a leaf on his
backswing, accepted his penalty without question but griped, "We have a lot of
stupid rules in golf." Jay Busbee, *One wispy leaf could have cost Carl Pettersson
half a million dollars,* YAHOO! SPORTS (Aug. 12, 2012). Was that in fact a stupid
rule? It has since been changed; under new Rule 12.2, a player may move loose
impediments in a bunker. *See* USGA, *Explanation for Each Major Change in
the New Rules of Golf for 2019,* Topic 15.

   5.   Billiards. In some games of pocket billiards, the shooter is credited
with a pocketed ball only if the ball, and the pocket, were as he intended. Rule
1.6 of the Rules of the World Pool-Billiard Association provides:

> In games in which the shooter is required to call shots, the intended
> ball and pocket must be indicated for each shot if they are not obvious.
> Details of the shot, such as cushions struck or other balls contacted
> or pocketed are irrelevant. Only one ball may be called on each shot.
> For a called shot to count, the referee must be satisfied that the
> intended shot was made, so if there is any chance of confusion, e.g.
> with bank, combination and similar shots, the shooter should indicate
> the ball and pocket.

Is this a good rule? Requiring the shooter to call the ball and pocket, unless
they are obvious, clearly increases the return to skill. But if the rule is meant
to reward the skill in planning and executing a shot, rather than the luck of an
unexpected ball dropping into an unanticipated pocket, why does it extend only
to the ball and pocket? Is there any reason why the shooter shouldn't be
required to call, as well, the cushions struck and the other balls contacted?

   6.   Skill at what? Even to the extent that we hope that skill will
determine the outcome of a contest, the question remains: Skill at doing what?
We have already touched on this issue in the *Martin* case, where we considered
whether golf (or at least some forms of it) is supposed to test shot-making alone
or some more complex combination, such as shotmaking-while-walking.

   Some sports do indeed seem designed to measure a single skill; the winner
is generally the competitor who achieves the best measurement in performing
some task that might have meaning even apart from the competition—running
a given distance in the shortest time, for example, or throwing a javelin the
greatest distance. Thus, the man who wins the 100-meter dash at the most
recent Olympics or world championships is often dubbed the fastest human in
the world. But even in sprint competitions, it is not so easy to isolate a single
skill. For example, at the 2011 world championship meet, Yohan Blake of
Jamaica won the 100 meters. What happened to Usain Bolt, widely

acknowledged as the fastest human *ever*? He was disqualified because he committed a false start. And at the 1995 world championships, Gwen Torrence ran an amazing 200-meter race, finishing .34 seconds ahead of her nearest competitor—but she was disqualified for stepping on the line of the lane inside hers. Fred Barbash, *Torrence Disqualified After Winning 200*, WASH. POST, Aug. 11, 1995. So does the 100-meter competition test not only ability to run fast over a short prescribed distance but also ability to react quickly to a starting gun—but without acting before!—and to stay within a lane? And if so is that a (perhaps necessary) bug or a feature? Would it be better to conduct sprint competitions as time trials, each competitor running separately against the clock, with the time measured from when the sprinter leaves the blocks?

By contrast, many sports derive much of their interest from the fact that they demand a combination of diverse skills, mental as well as physical. This is generally true of sports in which the object is to achieve some goal that is defined by the sport itself—scoring the most runs in baseball, for example, or the most points in basketball or football. These sports are, in a sense, unified by the prescribed goal. But consider cases in which that is not true.

One sports philosopher said not long ago that it would not make much sense to have a competition in which the winner was the participant who most quickly ran a prescribed distance and then did a crossword puzzle. Do you agree? And if so, which of the following competitions do you think make sense, and why or why not?

(a) The decathlon, comprising ten common but varied track-and-field events, as disparate as the 100-meter dash and shot-putting.

(b) The biathlon, which combines cross-country skiing and rifle shooting (both skills required for Nordic soldiers?).

(c) The modern pentathlon, like the decathlon and the biathlon an Olympic sport, which comprises five events: fencing, 200-meter freestyle swimming, show jumping, and a combined event of pistol shooting and a 3200-meter cross-country run.

(d) Chess boxing (or chessboxing). A full match consists of six timed rounds of speed chess sandwiched around five rounds of boxing, with a minute break between each round. The most common ways a competitor can win are by achieving a knockout, a technical knockout, or checkmate, or if his opponent resigns or runs out of time (12 minutes total allowed) in making chess moves. *See Chess boxing*, WIKIPEDIA, https://tinyurl.com/lv8s8. (Do you notice an advantage that one player or the other will necessarily have in a single contest?) Is the apparently complete lack of connection between the components of this competition an appealing feature? (Note that the sport was first designed by a comic artist.) Is there in fact a complete lack of connection?

C. CHALLENGE

A touchdown in football is worth six points. After scoring a touchdown, a team is allowed to attempt a "conversion." Traditionally, the ball is placed close to the goal line (on the opponent's two-yard line in the NFL, on the three in the NCAA) and the team that has just scored is allowed to try to kick the ball through the uprights, scoring one point, or to run or pass the ball into the end zone, for two points. Much more frequently, teams attempt the one-point conversion, commonly called a point-after-touchdown (PAT), because they are surer to score: In each year from 2010 through 2014, NFL kickers converted on over 99% of their extra-point tries. In response to this nearly automatic scoring play, the NFL changed the rules starting in the 2015 season. Under the new rules, the ball is placed on the 15-yard-line for one-point conversion kicks, but left at the two-yard line for two-point conversions. Rick Smith, GM of the Houston Texans and a member of the NFL Rules Committee, explained that the principal motivation for the change was "to add some skill to the play." Eric D. Williams, *NFL changes PAT rule for 2015*, ESPN.com (May 19, 2015).

There is something odd about this explanation, for it would seem that, even from the 2-yard line, PATs are a matter of skill. After all, if they are not a test of skill, what are they? Surely they're not a test of luck! Perhaps, then, the more accurate thing to say is that moving the ball back thirteen yards increases the *challenge* or *difficulty* of the task. Indeed, it seems likely that a central objective of sports is to present challenges of optimal difficulty—not too easy, and not too hard. If so, the important tasks for a gamewright are to understand what difficulty is and how it can be measured, and also to determine how much difficulty is optimal.

These questions are themselves surprisingly difficult. Accordingly, the following remarks offer only a start to thinking them through.

First, challenge and difficulty—at least as we will use those terms— are not the same thing. Difficulty is simply a matter of success rate. Compare two games. In the game we call "One Thousand," you think of a number from 1 to 1000 and your friend gets 5 tries to guess it. In "Ten," you think of a number from 1 to 10, and your friend still gets 5 guesses. Obviously, the guesser's success rate will be 100 times greater in Ten than in One Thousand. It seems plausible to conclude that One Thousand is, for the guesser, the more difficult game. But it seems inapt to describe it as a more *challenging* game. That's because both games are entirely games of luck and challenge is in some fashion a measure of return to skill. Ten is easy and One Thousand is difficult, but neither is challenging. Or so it seems to us. There is a more intimate relationship between challenge and skill than between difficulty and skill.

Second, the degree of challenge that a task presents is sensitive to the skill level of the participant. Converting extra points, at least under the old rules, is not challenging for NFL kickers, but may be very challenging for you, or for your six-year-old daughter or nonagenarian grandfather. When course conditions and hole placement for a given golf tournament are described as "easy" or "not challenging," the observation is implicitly indexed to participants in the tournament, and not to the weekend duffer.

Combining these two observations invites the suggestion that degree of challenge for any sport-particular task is a measure of the improvement in performance, given an assumed initial skill level, for any given increase in skill. Picture a graph that plots skill on the x-axis and performance on the y-axis. If the challenge curve is a horizontal line that runs parallel to the x-axis for its entire length, then the task is *entirely* one of luck: *no increase in skill buys an improvement in performance*. And the height of that parallel line determines whether it's an easy test of luck (as in our hypothetical game Ten, or its even easier sibling Six) or a hard test of luck (as in One Thousand). Where the curve is not parallel to the x-axis, it will be upward sloping. The steeper the upward slope, the greater the challenge (for that level of skill); the flatter the slope, the less the challenge. If the slope is constant over its length, the magnitude of challenge does not vary as skill increases. Otherwise, it does. Note that if the assigned task is kicking 90-yard field goals, the graph would be horizontal, within the current range of human skills, and essentially coincide with the x-axis; we might say that it would be an impossibly difficult task but not really a challenge. If the task is kicking field goals from the 2-yard line, the graph would have a flat portion, then a rather steeply rising one, and then another flat one. The task would be virtually impossible but not a challenge for those with insufficient skill or strength, then for those in an intermediate range (some high school kickers, for example), it would be a significant challenge, and then for the most proficient it would be easy and not challenging.

COMMENTS AND QUESTIONS

1.   *The right picture?* Is this the right way to conceptualize degree of challenge? If not, why not? Can you offer a better account?

2.   *Downward slopes?* Why do we assert that the curve will be either level or upward sloping? Can you think of any sports that present challenges that slope downward for any given skill level? If not, can you make up a sport, or a challenge within a sport, that would have a downward sloping challenge curve over any of its range?

3.   *Optimal curves.* Is it preferable that challenges within a sport have constant slope as skill increases or changing slope? Is it preferable that the slope be steep or shallow? In answering these questions, it might be helpful to have in mind two simple patterns: the curve starts steep and then flattens, or the curve starts relatively flat and then steepens. The first curve describes a situation in which beginners will see substantial improvements in performance

as their skill levels increase, but small returns for increases in skill at the expert level. PATs in football (beyond the point on the x-axis that represents no proficiency at all) have this shape. The second curve describes a situation in which the participant will not see significant improvements in performance until she becomes significantly skilled, which is to say that the task is very challenging for experts, but not for beginners. Many events in gymnastics are like this.

 4.   *Test and contest.* Notice that we have been discussing the challenge level of various sport-specific tasks or tests—tasks such as converting a PAT, or sinking a free throw, or reaching par. We have not been looking into the challenge of "winning the contest." So long as a competitive sport remains challenging just in virtue of the fact that the competitors are improving, should we care how difficult the component challenges are? Is there anything illuminating to say about how challenging it should be to, say, "unleash a hard and accurate shot on goal"?

 5.   *The balance of challenge.* When the NFL moved the ball back to the 15-yard line for PATs, it made the job somewhat more challenging for the offense, but it didn't much change the challenge for the defense: Attempting to block a kick when the play starts from the 15-yard line is not very different from attempting to block it from the two-yard line. (It is somewhat different because the trajectory of the kick will be lower and the defense now knows not to expect a two-point attempt). Often, though, increasing the challenge for the defense decreases it for the offense, and vice versa. When baseball lowered the pitching mound after the 1968 season, it increased the difficulty, for pitchers, of getting the batter out and decreased the difficulty, for batters, of getting a base hit. Similarly, when the NFL limited defensive backs' ability to make early contact with wide receivers, it increased the difficulty for the defense and decreased the difficulty for the offense. Did these changes alter the challenge of these tasks as well as the difficulty? What criteria should a gamewright use in determining whether changes of this type are good? As a related matter, pick a sport in which the winner is the side that scores the most points or runs. What's the problem with too little scoring? With too much scoring?

 6.   *A score from anywhere?* In basketball, as it has been played in recent decades, a field goal from behind a prescribed arc counts for three points rather than two. Does that reflect a greater challenge for long shots? Or is it just a different challenge, given that a 3-pointer does not require the offense to work the ball in towards the basket? Note that a touchdown in football counts the same, no matter how long the last play, a run in baseball is a run, whether the scorer hit a homer or was bunted in from third, and a goal in ice hockey is a goal from wherever shot. And shots from beyond an arc in field hockey are *disallowed.* Are these differences justified?

D. EXCITEMENT

 One plausible desideratum in the structuring of a sport is that it should provide "excitement." What is excitement? Is it different for spectators and for competitors? Can it be measured? If not, how would a rulemaker who sets out to make a sport "more exciting" know how to proceed?

First let's think about excitement as it relates to the outcome of the contest as a whole. Consider this suggestion: the excitement of a game depends upon the unpredictability of its outcome, so that "a highly exciting situation" arises "if the winner is undetermined up until the last moment with many swings in the score throughout the game." Jan Vecer, Tomoyuki Ichiba, & Mladen Laudanovic, *On Probabilistic Excitement of Sports Games*, 3 J. QUANT. ANALYSIS IN SPORTS 1, 1 (2007). On this view, "games with closely matched teams with high scoring intensities (expected number of points scored during the game) tend to have higher expected excitement levels." *Id.* The authors—who focus their analysis on soccer—also present a mathematical model. To understand it in simple terms (and putting aside the possibility of draws), think of a graph showing time of the contest on the horizontal axis and the probability that a given side will win, as measured at a given instant, on the vertical. Then excitement as they conceive it is the total vertical distance that the graph moves up and down through the contest; a roller-coaster game would be the epitome of excitement. Does this strike you as a sound way to model and measure the excitement of a contest? Which sports do you think will emerge as especially exciting or unexciting under this account of the ingredients that render a contest exciting? Does this correspond with your intuitive sense of which sports are or are not exciting? If a game has a high expected number of points scored, does it have the potential to be especially *un*exciting? Can dominance be exciting? *See Secretariat—Belmont Stakes 1973*, YOUTUBE, https://tinyurl.com/lvns9jf. Is it important for excitement to have potentially decisive moments relatively *early* in the contest? Could you propose a better account of what makes a sport exciting?

Issues in balancing the desire for excitement against other values arise frequently in designing tie-breaking procedures, which we will consider later on. (Subchapter 5C.)

COMMENTS AND QUESTIONS

1.   Excitement everywhere? Even apart from its bearing on the outcome of a contest as a whole, a particular play may be exciting, perhaps because of the skill required (think, for example, of an alley-oop in basketball) or because there is doubt how it will come out. But some sporting moves or tests are unexciting—for example, a tap-in in golf. Ideally, would all sporting tests be exciting, or does something like a law of conservation of excitement apply, so that unexciting parts of the game make it easier for other parts to be very exciting, and exciting parts entail that other parts will be unexciting?

2.   Excitement and pace. Sometimes, pauses or slow patches may allow excitement to build up. But in baseball, to take a prominent example, slowing pace has come to be seen as a problem, and the rulemakers have begun to take remedial action. Thus, major league baseball has already (a) put a strict and shorter limit on the time allowed for a relief pitcher to come in, warm up, and prepare to throw the first pitch, (b) prescribed that a team that wants to walk a batter intentionally simply gives a signal, rather than throwing four balls, and (c) limited visits to the pitcher's mound, except to change pitchers. Are these good changes? Among other remedies proposed have been (d) using a pitch clock, the penalty for delay being a called ball, and (e) preventing a batter from stepping out of the batter's box between pitches. Would either of these make the game more exciting? What is the relationship between excitement and drama?

3.   *Give a break to the losing side?* As table tennis is sometimes played, if one player reaches game-point the other player serves until such time as the game is tied. By giving an advantage to the player who is behind in the score, this procedure makes the odds that that player will win the game closer to even. Does this promote excitement? Fairness? Amusement?

4.   *The Elam Ending.* The final minutes of close basketball games are often dominated by clock stoppages and free throws caused by tactical fouls made by the team that is behind. In response, Nick Elam, then a middle school principal and now a professor at Ball State University, devised a different ending: The game clock is turned off early, say four minutes before what otherwise would be full time, and a target score is set, perhaps seven points more than the leading team has at that moment. First team to get to the target score wins. Variations on the Elam Ending have been used in some high-profile events, including the NBA All-Star game. In its pure form, it eliminates the possibility of buzzer-beaters—but it also creates "next basket wins" situations. On balance, does it add to excitement?

E. CONTINUITY WITH THE PAST

Many of the questions we have explored thus far can be addressed even with respect to the initial rules of a sport. But as the study of baseball's infield fly rule emphasizes, a striking feature of the rules of sport is that they change. While the initial rules of a sport create a new practice, all subsequent rulemaking activities (enactment of new rules, and repeal or modification of old ones) change an already existing practice. It is worth considering how, if at all, rule-changing differs from initial rule-making. This is a particularly important question given that, while many games have identifiable creators and distinct births, few sports do; rather, most have evolved gradually from distant and hazy origins. James Naismith, the father of basketball, has few counterparts in the sporting world.

Golfers sometimes try new types of club and new ways of striking the ball. Keegan Bradley won the 2011 PGA Championship, Webb Simpson won the 2012 U.S. Open, and Ernie Els won the 2012 British Open, all using long putters, a general term that includes belly putters and "broomstick" models. These victories were part of a broader trend, as more and more golfers of all ages showed interest in the longer putters, some, but not all, of which were used by anchoring them against the body. Karen Crouse, *A Golf Club to Divide Them*, N.Y. TIMES, Nov. 18, 2012, at SP1. Mike Davis, executive director of the USGA, noted that 15 percent of the players on the PGA Tour used an anchored putter in 2012, up from 11 percent the previous year and 6 percent from 2006 to 2010, and that instructors had been increasingly advocating anchored putting. Karen Crouse, *Golf Acts to Ban Anchored Putting*, N.Y. TIMES, Nov. 29, 2012, at B11. In response, the governing bodies of golf, the USGA and the R&A, proposed the following rule:

14–1b   Anchoring the Club

In making a stroke, the player must not anchor the club, either "directly" or by use of an "anchor point."

Note 1:   The club is anchored "directly" when the player intentionally holds the club or a gripping hand in contact with any part of his body, except that the player may hold the club or a gripping hand against a hand or forearm.

Note 2:   An "anchor point" exists when the player intentionally holds a forearm in contact with any part of his body to establish a gripping hand as a stable point around which the other hand may swing the club.

"This is a playing rule," Davis explained, "not an equipment rule." Crouse, *Golf Acts to Ban Anchored Putting*. The governing bodies presented a graphic of grips—in addition to what it designated as the "traditional grip"—that would still be permissible under the new rule, including some using long putters. *See* USGA, *Anchoring the Club—Understanding Rule 14–1b*, 2016, https://tinyurl.com/yxtnx3h8. For example, the golfer may rest the shaft of a long club along one forearm and rest the top of the club against the other hand.

Knowing that the rule would be controversial, the governing bodies did not adopt it immediately, but instead invited public comment. On May 21, 2013, they did adopt it, but with implementation not to be effective until January 1, 2016. (Since then, the Rules of Golf have been rewritten, effective January 1, 2019; the ban on anchored putting is now Rule 10.1(b).) At the same time, they issued a lengthy statement explaining the decision. The statement is excerpted below.

EXPLANATION OF DECISION TO ADOPT
RULE 14–1b OF THE RULES OF GOLF

United States Golf Association and The Royal & Ancient, May 21, 2013
Copyright 2013 United States Golf Association, reprinted with permission

. . .

2. The Underlying Rationale for Rule 14–1b and Its Benefits to the Game

. . .

A. *The Principles on Which the Rules of Golf are Founded*

The playing Rules of Golf are not established on an empirical or scientific assessment of the benefits or consequences of each method or act that might or might not be allowed. Rather, the Rules that govern how golf is played are based on judgments about what is appropriate and best for this unique game of skill and challenge.

The playing Rules are definitional: individually and collectively, they reflect what the game is and how it should be played. For example, a player may not pick up the ball and roll it into the hole. That is not because the rulemakers assessed through statistical or other empirical analysis whether players rolling the ball by hand are more successful than players using a club to strike the ball; rather, it is because rolling the ball with one's hand is simply not "golf." The same is true of making a croquet-style stroke on the putting green (Rule 16–1e), or pushing, spooning or scraping the ball in making a stroke (Rule 14–1). These and similar Rules reflect a judgment that such methods of play are contrary to the essential nature of the game.

Although some Rules are purely definitional, others are also intended to restrict or prohibit practices that *potentially* might enable a player to avoid or diminish the essential challenges of the game. For example:

- The Rules prohibit or regulate many practices that relate to how a stroke may be played, such as by imposing a penalty if a player makes a stroke with someone holding an umbrella over her head (Rule 14–2a); while leaning on another club to steady himself (Decision 14-3/9); with a golf ball held in the hand against the grip (Decision 14-3/6); with a thumb inserted into a bandage (Decision 14-3/7); while a caddie stands directly behind him (Rule 14–2b); or while standing on a golf cart or another piece of equipment being used to build a stance (Rule 13–3).

- The Rules also impose penalties to regulate or prohibit various acts taken in preparation for a stroke, such as using a swing aid to make a practice swing (Decision 14-3/10);

playing a practice stroke from the fairway during the round (Rule 7–2); asking for advice from someone other than one's partner or either of their caddies (Rule 8–1); knocking some leaves off of a tree during a practice swing if such act improves the area of intended swing for the stroke (Decision 13-2/0.5); or testing the condition of a bunker while the ball lies at rest in that bunker (Rule 13–4a).

Such acts are penalized for two interrelated reasons: because they are deemed to diverge from golf's essential character as a game in which the player's basic challenge is to play the ball as it lies and the course as it is found and to do so without assistance of various kinds, and because such acts *might* assist the player in his or her play. The inquiry underlying these types of playing Rules is not whether such acts provide a demonstrable, actual advantage to every player or to the average player or to most players or to a certain minimum percentage of players. . . .

Rather, in evaluating whether a particular act or technique of play should be subject to penalty under the Rules, the focus is on whether such act or technique is inconsistent with the essential nature of golf and, where relevant, on whether it might assist the player in his or her play. What matters is defining the game and assessing the *potential* for advantage. Making such judgments—based on history, tradition, philosophy, experience and prediction—is at the heart of the rulemaking process for the playing Rules of Golf. Empirical analysis of such acts and their potential advantages has never been thought to be a condition for adopting a playing Rule.

B. *Freely Swinging the Entire Club is the Essence of the Traditional Method of Golf Stroke*

In adopting Rule 14–1b, the USGA and The R&A have concluded that freely swinging the entire club is integral to maintaining the traditions of the game and preserving golf as an enjoyable game of skill and challenge. The essence of the traditional method of golf stroke involves the player swinging the club with both the club and the gripping hands being held away from the body. The player's challenge is to direct and control the movement of the entire club in making the stroke.

This traditional form of golf stroke has prevailed throughout the centuries since the game began. It is true to say that one can find isolated or episodic examples of anchored methods of stroke dating back into the early 1900s, just as one can find early examples of almost any method of stroke that creative players might invent or try, such as putting in a croquet style (seen as early as the 1900s or before). But it is only recently that a non-trivial and recurring use of anchoring methods emerged, first with the long putter in the 1980s and then with the belly putter at the turn of the 21st century—an extremely short time in the history of this 600-year old game and not reflective of any established tradition.

The concept of intentionally immobilizing one end of the golf club against the body, in a manner equivalent to creating a physical attachment point to use as a fixed fulcrum or pivot point around which the club can be swung, is a substantial departure from that traditional understanding of the golf swing. Reduced to its most basic elements, golf involves a player swinging a club at a ball to move it toward and ultimately into a hole. The player's most basic challenge is to direct and control the movement of the entire club in making that swing. Anchoring the club while making a stroke also involves a challenge, but it is a different one, in which the player uses the immobilization and stability of one end of the club as an essential component of the method of stroke. It is not the same as freely swinging the club. . . .

C. *Anchored Methods of Stroke Clearly Provide a Player with a Potential Advantage*

In defining the essential nature of an appropriate method of stroke, Rule 14–1b is also based on the related determination that anchoring provides a player with a potential advantage as compared to making a stroke with a free swing of the entire club. This potential advantage is the main reason why golfers use anchoring: intentionally securing one end of the club in place against the body is designed to help to avoid or alleviate some of the inherent obstacles to a successful stroke made with a free swing. . . .

[I]t is essential to understand that the inquiry under the playing Rules of Golf is not whether this method of stroke would necessarily advantage every player, most players, many players, the average player or some other identified set of those who might use it, nor whether it would necessarily provide a benefit on every stroke or in every circumstance or condition of play, nor whether the benefit might be large or small. What matters is that the purpose and inherent nature of this method of stroke create the potential for it to assist an individual player, in some part of his or her play, by reducing variables and alleviating inherent obstacles that otherwise exist in the traditional free swinging method of stroke . . . .

Finally, some comments suggested that anchoring cannot harm the game because, even if it provides an advantage, any golfer can use the method and seek to gain that advantage. But that suggestion cannot be the proper standard for judging whether an act should be prohibited under the Rules of Golf, for it amounts to a view that Rules governing play are not needed at all. This same argument would mean that croquet putting, building a stance, improving a lie, cleaning a ball lying through the green, teeing a ball in the fairway, and countless other acts need not be subject to penalty, because all golfers would be equally free to take such actions. . . .

3.   **The Fact that Some Golfers Will Now be Required to Change a Method of Stroke Does Not Mean that it is Too Late to Adopt Rule 14–1b**

A second major argument heard during our review is that, although it would have been acceptable and perhaps even desirable for the USGA and The R&A to prohibit anchoring as soon as it first arose, it is too late to adopt Rule 14–1b now because too many golfers have come to use and prefer this method of stroke. We understand the view that the current level of controversy and need to adapt might have been mitigated (though certainly not avoided) if anchoring had been prohibited at an earlier time and that, with the benefit of 20-20 hindsight, some might wish that we had done so. But we cannot accept that anchoring must be considered a permanent fixture in golf for the decades and centuries to come, regardless of what experience has revealed or may reveal about its effects on the game. Rules are evaluated on an ongoing basis and revised as necessary to promote the long-term best interests of the game, and players have always adapted as necessary to bring their play into conformance with the evolving Rules. . . .

C.   *It is Not Unfair to Ask Players to Comply with Prospective Changes in the Rules*

* * * Under this new Rule, no act is being retroactively subjected to penalty; only future play will be affected. Moreover, all players are or should be aware that the Rules are subject to revision, that Rule changes occur regularly, and that adapting to those evolving Rules is inherent in the game. No golfer acquires a permanent entitlement to a given set of existing Rules because he or she may have benefited from them in the past or perceives a future benefit from them. It has always been the case that the Rules change, and players adapt. The fact that some golfers must alter their playing methods or strategies cannot prevent the governing bodies from adopting a Rule change that is needed to preserve and enhance the game's long-term interests.

Nor is this approach to prospective rulemaking unique to golf. Countless rule changes in other sports have required participants to abandon or modify techniques that they had developed, practiced and used to their perceived advantage. Examples of this include

- the rule changes in American football that restricted the "bump and run" technique and eliminated or altered many other established techniques of using the head, hands or body in blocking, tackling or running;

- the lowering of the pitching mound and changes in the size of the strike zone in baseball;

- the creation of the three-point shot in basketball and various rule changes limiting the use of hands and altering other defensive techniques;

- the restrictions imposed on underwater swimming after the start and each turn in a swimming competition;

- changes to the Laws of cricket dealing with fast, short-pitched bowling (which the umpire can now determine to be dangerous and unfair);

- changes to the Laws of rugby union allowing players to be lifted in the lineout, and the like.

Such changes were made in the perceived best interests of those sports, even though they may have negatively affected some participants by requiring them to abandon or alter previously successful or preferred techniques—and unlike with regard to Rule 14–1b, participants typically were required to do so the very next year, not more than two and one-half years in the future.

Even beyond sports, it is inherent in any form of rulemaking or legislation that prospective change may upset the status quo. . . . When it is determined that laws and regulations should change going forward, it is understood that the prospective behavior of some or many individuals often will need to change as well.

D. *Rule 14–1b Will Not Cause a Major Dislocation within the Game*

. . . Although we do not believe that the particular number of golfers affected by this decision would be a decisive factor in any event, we believe that any such suggestion substantially overstates the real world effect of the Rule. . . . Overall, although increasing notably in the past two years, use of anchored putting remains at a modest level across the game as a whole. . . . Indeed, far from it being too late to act, this is an appropriate time in which a Rule change can be implemented so as to avoid the possibility that a much larger number of additional golfers might begin to use this stroke on an ongoing basis. . . .

E. *Golfers Can Readily Adapt to Making Strokes Without Anchoring*

. . . [W]ith more than two and one-half years until the January 1, 2016 effective date, all players will have a more than ample opportunity to adopt and practice a putting method that conforms to the new Rule. Golfers often change all or substantial parts of their full or partial swings in less time than that, and they will be able to do the same with regard to the putting stroke. . . .

(i) *Golfers May Continue to Use Long and Belly Putters Without Anchoring*

Rule 14–1b does not change the equipment Rules. A player may use any conforming belly-length or long putter in any manner that does not constitute anchoring the club while making a stroke. This is an entirely feasible option. . . .

. . . A player may use the same long putter, stand in the same upright manner, grip the club in the same split-handed way, and make the same pendulum-style stroke. He or she will only need to move the top gripping hand slightly off the chest rather than locking the club or hand against the chest, and to keep the forearm just clear of the body as well.

Likewise, belly-length putters may continue to be used without anchoring. Golfers throughout the game have done so successfully, as seen most prominently when Angel Cabrera used a non-anchored belly putter to win the 2009 Masters Tournament. . . .

(ii) *Many Other Common and Alternative Putting Methods Remain Available*

Many other methods of putting with standard-length putters also will remain available to all players. The variety of permissible gripping styles, putter types, and swing methods is considerable, including various ways in which a player may seek to lessen the movement of his or her body during the stroke. . . . The difference between putting with the club anchored and putting without it anchored will not require a re-learning of the fundamentals of striking the ball. Many players have used both methods, in practice and/or in play, and have often moved back and forth . . . .

F. *"Grandfathering" is Not a Viable or Fair Solution*

Out of concern for golfers who will need to abandon anchoring as either their preferred method or one of their available options, a few comments suggested that a compromise might be to create a "grandfathering" exception for current players who anchor the club when putting. We understand the spirit underlying this idea, but such an approach seems unworkable and, more important, would itself create unfairness. In the context of a game played by tens of millions of people, at many different levels of play and often over much of a lifetime, any effort to grandfather existing players would be an administrative nightmare. It also would be likely to create a protracted dispute about the fairness of permitting a small set of players to compete, perhaps for decades, using a potentially advantageous method that almost all other players would be prohibited from using. We think that such an approach would indefinitely prolong, and likely exacerbate, the very controversy that helped to prompt this review and that Rule 14–1b can bring to a close after a period of transition.

G. *Rule 14–1b is a Prospective Rule that has No Bearing on Prior Play or Success with Anchoring*

A final concern, heard mainly from a few in the professional ranks, is that Rule 14–1b is unfair to golfers who have used this stroke in the past because an asterisk might, figuratively, be placed next to their prior successes. Our position remains adamant in this regard: Rule changes address the future and not the past. It has been entirely within the Rules for players to anchor the club in making a stroke. There should not be a shred of criticism of such players or any qualification or doubt about their achievements. . . .

The Rules of Golf are continuously revised and updated, meaning that players often have succeeded with equipment or practices that were prohibited by subsequent Rules changes. Prominent examples of this include Bob Jones winning the Grand Slam in 1930 using a concave-faced wedge that was ruled non-conforming the following year, and Sam Snead winning the 1967 Senior PGA Championship using the croquet putting style that subsequently was disallowed. . . .

4.   Rule 14–1b will Promote, Not Hinder, the Health of the Game

A third main concern raised in the comments was that Rule 14–1b may harm participation levels in the game. This argument is based explicitly on the assumption that anchoring does, in fact, provide a significant advantage to those who use it. The concern is that some recreational golfers, if unable to continue to use an anchored stroke, may play less often or, in a few cases, even quit the game altogether.

. . . Although it would be unfortunate if anyone were to play less or stop playing because of this Rule, no one should assume that the only golfers who care about this issue are those who use anchored putting strokes. On the contrary, a great many sentiments were heard and expressed to us in the course of this review from those who believe that anchoring is undermining the game. . . .

B. *"Bifurcation" of the Rules or the Introduction of an Anchoring Condition of Competition Would Be Counterproductive and Harmful to the Game*

Various comments expressing concern about participation levels also raised the question of possible "bifurcation" in implementation of Rule 14–1b. The suggestion is that the Rule should apply only to professionals, and perhaps to elite amateurs, leaving all other golfers free to anchor the club in making a stroke. . . .

We disagree with the underlying premise that more people would play golf if only equipment and playing Rules were relaxed to enable golfers to hit longer, straighter shots, to make more putts, and/or to post lower scores. The need for skill and the challenge of the game are what define golf; they are in fact what have caused so many people to love and play the game for the past 600 years. . . .

The argument that multiple sets of Rules are needed to accommodate players of differing skill levels is refuted by golf's long history and traditions. The history of golf is actually a history of movement toward unification of playing and equipment Rules—and this is more than ever true today, as golfers of different abilities from myriad geographies and cultures seek to play the same sport on a national and international basis, and soon in the Olympics.

Moreover, the game has long used two great innovations—multiple teeing grounds and the USGA Handicap and Course Rating Systems and other handicap systems—to enable golfers to play within their own physical abilities and yet also to compete against one another across ability levels, while playing each shot and each round by the same set of Rules. . . .

Our task as rulemakers is not to make the game easier or to make it harder, but rather to preserve and enhance the game's special and eternal qualities. The USGA and The R&A are committed to the principle that a single set of Rules for all players of the game, irrespective of ability, is one of golf's greatest strengths. An integral part of the game's appeal is that golfers of all levels can play the same courses with the same equipment and under the same Rules, enabling even the casual golfer to compare his or her performance to that of the most elite players and, at times, to play as good a shot as the elite player. . . .

We also disagree with those who suggested that, while a unified set of Rules is generally desirable, there would be no harm in allowing bifurcation solely on the single issue of anchoring. Defining the parameters of how to prepare for and make a permissible stroke is at the core of the game and is reflected in many different Rules. . . .

For the same reasons, we disagree with the suggestion that anchoring be implemented, either permanently or temporarily (e.g., for an extended period such as 10 or 20 years), through an optional condition of competition that could be adopted at the discretion of any individual club or Committee in charge of an individual competition. Conditions of competition are intended to address specific narrow topics that relate to how a particular competition is conducted, not to permit a competition-by-competition variation in core Rules on how to play the game. . . .

COMMENTS AND QUESTIONS

1. Work product. The *Explanation* has an unmistakable lawyerly quality. (Can you describe that quality?) We'd be surprised if it weren't largely drafted by lawyers. Overall, what do you think of it as a piece of legal craft, putting aside the merits of the decision it defends? If you were a member of the drafting team, are there any revisions or additions you might have suggested?

    2.   *Conservatism as a value.* The *Explanation* repeatedly emphasizes "the essence of the traditional method" of a golf stroke. This brings to mind the question asked earlier, in conjunction with the Casey Martin case, concerning whether sports have "essences." If a sport does have an "essence," or if some rules or practices are more central to a sport than others, does this fact have normative significance? That is to say, if some rule is essential, central, or fundamental to a sport, is that itself a reason (even if not a decisive or conclusive reason) not to change it? Notice that when rulemakers contemplate a rule change, critics often object that the proposed new rule "would change the game." To be sure, this is always trivially true: if a game or sport is defined in terms of its rules, in their full particularity, then any change in rules necessarily changes the game. But this can't be what the critics of any particular rule change have in mind, for then their criticism would be tautological and thus uninteresting. More likely, people who object to a proposed rule change on the ground that it would "change the game" mean to suggest that the change would in some sense alter the game's essence or nature, and that its nature should be preserved, not altered. Let's call this view "conservatism." What could be said in favor of conservatism in sport? What, if anything, could be said against conservativism in sport? (Consider Calvinball, from the comic strip *Calvin and Hobbes*, in which the rules are made up as the players go along, and no rule can be used twice—except for that one.)

    3.   *Status quo bias.* In thinking about the costs and benefits of stasis versus change, it is helpful to have grasp of the "status quo bias," a common tendency among people to disfavor change and to attribute greater value to the way things are (the status quo) than its objective merits warrant. Status quo bias is an example of what psychologists call **"cognitive biases"**—systematic errors in human reasoning and judgment. Such biases are close cousins to "heuristics"—mental shortcuts or rules of thumb

Status Quo Bias; Bounded Rationality

that are often-efficient, yet highly fallible, routes to rational decision making. Although there are scores of well-accepted biases, a small sampling of the more familiar ones, in addition to status quo bias, includes:

- *the fundamental attribution error*, people's tendency to over-emphasize personality-based explanations for behavior, while downplaying the influence of situational or contextual factors;

- *hindsight bias*, the tendency to view events, after the fact, as foreseeable or expected even when they would have been very hard to predict based on information available prior to their occurrence;

- *framing effect*, drawing different conclusions from substantively identical information based only on the manner of its presentation;

- *confirmation bias*, the tendency to search for and interpret information in a fashion that confirms one's preconceptions;

- *base rate neglect*, the tendency to overweigh information pertaining to a specific case and to underweigh background frequencies; and

- *just world hypothesis*, an unwarranted belief in the fundamental justness of the world that causes people to rationalize instances of injustice as deserved by the victims.

Biases and heuristics are at the root of such fields as behavioral psychology and behavioral economics, including behavioral law and economics. They inform the **"bounded rationality"** model of human behavior that opposes the idealized model of perfect instrumental rationality that underwrites neoclassical economics. An understanding of the myriad ways in which human decisionmaking and behavior systematically depart from perfect rationality is of fundamental importance to anyone who seeks to influence human behavior. For a brilliant exploration by one of the field's pioneers, see DANIEL KAHNEMAN, THINKING, FAST AND SLOW (2011).

4. *Anchoring and croquet-style putting.* The *Explanation* puts repeated emphasis on the fact that croquet-style putting has been banned for decades; Rule 16–1e provides, with narrow exceptions: "The player must not make a stroke on the putting green from a stance astride, or with either foot touching, the line of putt or an extension of that line behind the ball." But what is wrong with this style of putting? According to one authority, the ban was instituted in response to a complaint by the great former champion Bobby Jones, founder of the Masters tournament. JAMES DODSON, AMERICAN TRIUMVERATE: SAM SNEAD, BYRON NELSON, BEN HOGAN, AND THE MODERN AGE OF GOLF 353 (2012). At the 1967 Masters, Jones told Sam Snead, who had suddenly gained considerable success late in his career with this style of putting, that it "didn't look like golf." Is that a valid concern? Do you think something like it may have motivated the ban on anchoring?

Is the *Explanation* right that "the essence of the traditional method of golf stroke involves the player swinging the club with both the club and the gripping hands being held away from the body"? Is that simply a Procrustean argument—made up to fit the particular problem at hand? (In Greek myth, Procrustes was a figure whose guests fit the size of his bed, by amputation or stretching as necessary.) Why isn't the essence of the traditional method of golf stroke to swing the club in such a way as will likely best move the ball as the golfer desires?

Note also that Rule 16–1e applies only to strokes "on the putting green," but Rule 14–1b applies generally. Is there a good reason why Rule 14–1b should have a broader scope?

5. *The Fosbury Flop, the Solomon Method, and other novel techniques.* Consider also the Fosbury flop, in which a high jumper goes backwards over the bar, head and shoulders before legs and trunk. It is a radically different method from any of the techniques that preceded it. Soon after Dick Fosbury flopped to a gold medal at the 1968 Olympics, the flop became the dominant

method of high jumping, and it remains so to this day. Should it have been banned because it looks so different from prior methods? Could you write a plausible "Explanation" in the style of the one by the USGA and The R&A explaining that the flop was being banned because it "creates an unacceptable risk of changing the nature and reducing the challenge of [jumping over the bar]"? Isn't *any* improvement in technique or equipment in sports meant to "chang[e] the nature and reduc[e] the challenge" of performing some maneuver?

In the finals of the men's 100-meter backstroke event at the 1988 Olympics Daichi Suzuki of Japan won gold, David Berkoff of the United States (a future lawyer) won silver, and Igor Polianski of the USSR won bronze. Using a new technique often referred to as the Berkoff Blastoff, these three stayed underwater, dolphin-kicking, for the first 30 meters, while all the other competitors swam above the surface. After the Olympics, FINA, the governing body of international swimming, imposed a limit, which for some years has stood at 15 meters, for how long a backstroker can stay under water. Even with the limitation, the Blastoff is often considered to have revolutionized the event. Does the 15-meter rule make sense? Should the Blastoff be allowed at all? Should it be limited at all?

In 1999, the world record for consumption of hot dogs with buns in 12 minutes was 20. In 2020, Joey Chestnut ate 75 hot dogs with buns in 10 minutes. How did the record nearly quadruple in just over two decades? The short answer is: technique. For most of recorded history, competitors in hot-dog-eating contests tackled their task the same way the rest of us do: by picking up hot dog in bun and chewing. In 2000, however, the Japanese eater Kazutoyo "the Rabbit" Arai turned the world of competitive eating upside down by introducing a novel technique: he dunked his dogs, dressed in their buns, in water before eating, thus allowing the food to slide down his gullet more easily. Thanks to that slight innovation, the Rabbit won the 2000 Nathan's Famous hot-dog eating competition with 25 franks, besting the previous record by 25%. But that was nothing compared to the revolutionary technique his protégé, Takeru Kobayashi, would unleash the following year: breaking the hot dogs in half, dunking both wiener and bun in water, and eating them separately. On the strength of his novel technique—New York reporters dubbed it "the Solomon Method"—Kobayashi downed an extraordinary 50 dogs, doubling the Rabbit's record, and sending tremors throughout the sport. Steve "The Appetite" Addicks, a contestant that year, pronounced himself "in awe" of the 23-year-old's accomplishment.

> "It was amazing. I was standing next to something that—it's like, ah, I don't know—it was almost a religious experience, you know? Something that I was so close to see, that very few people will ever be able to witness, as far as the magnitude of what it meant to me as an eater. It was just like"—he made a whoosh sound—"whoa ... I'm sitting there watching a miracle."

JASON FAGONE, HORSEMEN OF THE ESOPHAGUS: COMPETITIVE EATING AND THE BIG FAT AMERICAN DREAM 35 (2006).

Not everybody was so favorably impressed. Disagreement over these new-fangled eating methods has divided the sport, leading to the formation of an upstart competitive eating promotion, the Association of Independent Competitive Eaters (AICE), to challenge the older and more established International Federation of Competitive Eating (IFOCE). AICE-sponsored competitions are run under "picnic style" rules, as then-AICE Chairman Arnie "Chowhound" Chapman, explained:

> We don't mutilate the food, we don't mush it, we don't mash it, and we eat the food as is presented in accordance to history, custom, and the culture of that food item. So you have to eat the food as is without it being transformed. When people take food and they pour water on it, and they dunk it in water, what they're doing is transforming the molecular structure of that particular food item and they're really not honestly eating the food. So, 'picnic style' rules is how I like to eat food. I've been in contests before where there wasn't "picnic style" rules. You can eat the food faster when you're allowed to pour water on it and stuff like that, but first of all it's disgusting. Viewers can't see where people are at in the contests, because one guy has got three wieners, and one or another guy has buns all over the place and it's a sloppy mess and it doesn't pay any respect to the food.[g]

Should dunking and splitting be allowed?

The bunt appears to have been introduced in the early years of baseball by shortstop Dickey Pearce; it was often referred to as the "tricky hit." Should it have been forbidden on grounds similar to those cited for prohibiting anchored strokes in golf? If not, is a reason that baseball was not very old when the bunt began?

6.   Change through inaction. Can a sport change by a *failure* to change the rules? Would a failure to ban anchoring have meant that, in time, anchoring would have become an essential, or at least traditional, part of the game? Note the delicate line walked by the drafters of the *Explanation*: They contended that anchoring had not yet become very widespread, but would be if left unchecked. Why did they need to take both positions?

Consider also basketball. The NBA has changed many of its rules since the inception of the league in 1946. For example, it has introduced a shot clock, and a three-point shot, and has routinely revised the rules governing fouls and penalties. But one of the more conspicuous things about the rules is what has remained constant over more than 60 years: the dimensions of the court (94' × 50') and the height of the basket (10'). Over the same period of time, the players have increased substantially in terms of size and athleticism. The average

---

[g]   Regrettably, this excellent explanation is no longer on the web. But we love the quote, and are keeping it! For similar but not identically worded expressions of the sentiment, see Chris Martell, *Competitive eating: It's food for thought*, WISCONSIN STATE JOURNAL, Jan. 31, 2020.

height of an NBA player in the 1950s was 6'4"; for more than a generation, the average height has been over 6'7". Given the increase in competitor size and athleticism, is basketball now a different sport from what it was 50 years ago precisely because the rules governing court size have *not* changed? Should sports conservatives favor increases in court size and basket height? *Cf.* Lawrence Lessig, *Fidelity in Translation,* 71 TEXAS L. REV. 1165 (1993) (arguing that, because meaning is a function of text and context, changes in context can require changed readings of the text precisely to preserve meaning over time).

7.   *Prospectivity and retroactivity.* The *Explanation* emphasizes that the new rule will operate prospectively only, and that not "a shred of criticism" should be leveled against those who have engaged in anchored putting or do so before the rule becomes effective. (Is that entirely true, given the *Explanation*'s argument that anchoring reduces the challenge of golf?) It is widely assumed or accepted that rule changes must be prospective only, which is to say that a rule should not be applied to conduct that already occurred prior to the rule's adoption. For example, in order to reduce injuries, and concussions in particular, the NFL has in recent years tightened restrictions on defensive contact and has enforced those new rules with hefty fines. But it goes without saying that a player could not be fined for having engaged in the now-prohibited practices before the new rules were adopted. Why, exactly, is retroactive application of new rules generally prohibited?

If prospectivity is an important value, how much prospectivity is enough? Was two and a half years too much in the context of anchoring? Too little? Most organized sports have seasons. Rule changes are generally adopted during the off-season and then implemented at the start of the new season. Would it be wrong to adopt and implement rule changes during a season? During a tournament? During a single contest?

Consider the controversy that arose in connection with the 2013 America's Cup. The America's Cup Regatta is a two-boat multi-race competition that pits the Cup defender against a single challenger. In years with multiple challengers, the challengers compete for the right to race against the Cup defender; this multi-race competition, called the Louis Vuitton Cup, takes place shortly before the America's Cup competition itself, over the same course, and under the same rules. The rules for the 2013 America's Cup provided for a new and exceptionally fast class of boat, a wing-sailed catamaran dubbed the AC72. But these new boats proved hard to control when hydrofoiling (lifting out of the water) at their great speeds, and the Swedish challenger crashed during a May practice run, causing the death of a crew member and nearly destroying the boat. In reaction, shortly after the Louis Vuitton Cup competition had begun, Regatta Director Iain Murray proposed a new rule that, by allowing certain modifications to the rudders, would improve boat stability when hydrofoiling. The Italy and New Zealand challengers protested the change, arguing that they had already made other sacrifices and compromises in the design of their boats to improve stability, and the new rules allowed the Cup defender, Oracle, and the Swedish challenger, Artemis, to make improvements to their catamarans to deal with problems that should have been addressed earlier. "You should build the boat for the rule you're under," argued the skipper of the Italian challenger. "We built our boat under the original class rule and I don't understand why there are people who don't respect that." The America's Cup Jury, an arbitration panel established by the Protocol that governed the 2013 competition, rejected the proposed change. What result do you think is appropriate? If the rule change should have been barred is that because it was not sufficiently prospective or because, in some relevant sense, it was not prospective at all?

    8.   Prospectivity and legacy exemptions. As used in the *Explanation,* "grandfathering" refers to a provision exempting certain persons, at least for a time, from a rules change because of some prior status or activity.[h] The *Explanation* rather dismissively rejected the possibility of giving such legacy exemptions to golfers who already engaged in anchoring; it said that this attempt to be fair to those golfers "would itself create unfairness."

    Compare three instances in which major American professional sports have allowed legacy exemptions. (1) In 1920, Major League Baseball prohibited the spitball, but seventeen pitchers who were established spitballers before the ban were allowed to continue throwing it for the rest of their careers; Burleigh Grimes, who eventually reached the Hall of Fame, threw spitters until his retirement in 1934. (2) When, in 1979, the NHL required all players to wear helmets, it exempted players who had already signed professional contracts. Craig MacTavish played without a helmet until his retirement in 1997. (3) That same year, MLB "universally" retired Jackie Robinson's uniform number, 42, but allowed players already wearing it to continue to do so for the rest of their careers. Mariano Rivera (now also a Hall of Famer, and the first unanimous selection, no less) was the last to do so, in 2013.

    Can you rank these four changes—concerning spitballs, hockey helmets, Number 42, and anchored putting—in order of the strength of the case for legacy exemptions? What material differences are there among them? Can you make any general statement of the circumstances under which such exemptions are appropriate? Do you agree that the fact that granting legacy exemptions at least sometimes seems sensible shows that even prospective laws aren't fully prospective because "[i]n the absence of any retroactive effect, grandfathering would be unnecessary"? Jill E. Fisch, *Retroactivity and Legal Change: An Equilibrium Approach,* 110 HARV. L. REV. 1055, 1067 (1997). Should Major League Baseball have attached a transition period to the spitball ban, like that for anchoring, rather than grant lifelong exemptions through legacy exemptions?

---

    [h]   Use of the term "grandfathering" for protecting some group of persons from the adverse impact of a rule change originated with laws enacted in the Jim Crow South that exempted from a literacy test for voting any person who, prior to January 1, 1866, was entitled to vote or was a resident of a foreign nation, or who was a lineal descendant of such a person. Given its historical association with White Supremacy and anti-Black racism, some persons will understandably prefer that the term be retired. One suggested replacement has been "legacy," and though that term might be imprecise, we will use it here, but without altering original texts.

9.   Different rules for different ability levels? The *Explanation* rejects the possibility of allowing anchoring for non-elite amateurs, even while it is prohibited at higher levels of the game. Are you persuaded? The *Explanation* says, "An integral part of the game's appeal is that golfers of all levels can play the same courses with the same equipment and under the same Rules, enabling even the casual golfer to compare his or her performance to that of the most elite players and, at times, to play as good a shot as the elite player." But are they really playing the same course if the non-elite player uses a tee many yards closer to the green than does an elite player—a practice (along with handicapping) explicitly approved by the *Explanation*?

Compare anchoring with the PGA's recently instituted experiment with 15″ holes. (See p. 37). The rationale for the larger holes is that they will make golf easier, less frustrating, and thus more popular. But anchored putting might also serve these ends. Does it make sense to prohibit recreational players from benefiting from anchored putting while allowing them to putt at larger holes?

Note that both the PGA Tour and the PGA of America vigorously opposed the ban on anchoring, but they went along with the rule once it was adopted—though strongly suggesting that implementation for amateurs be delayed until well past 2016. And now consider the reaction of Tom O'Toole, president of the USGA:

> "At the USGA we certainly think anything that would cause somebody to stop and undertake an exercise or endeavour that would ultimately draw them to golf is a good thing . . .

> If it's 15-inch holes or if it's some other aspect that isn't exactly in the game that we have been governing since December 1894 in this country, that's okay.

> What's at issue here is how we drive people to golf. We think the charm of the game is a single set of rules and if we can get people to embrace the charm that we all love about golf, then we have succeeded."

Mark Lamport-Stokes, *Global game responds to cries of 'Fore' with new gimmicks*, REUTERS, May 10, 2014.

Is this position consistent with the *Explanation*? Suppose the USGA were to be shocked—shocked!—to learn that some weekend duffers don't adhere to all the Rules of Golf. What should its attitude be?

Is the USGA's insistence on maintaining a single rule with respect to anchoring consistent with the position it took in the walking controversy? Recall that the Rules of Golf say nothing about walking. But the Rules are supplemented by a set of "Local Rules and Terms of the Competition," which apply to all USGA championships, and a Notice to Competitors, which spells out rules for the particular championship that have been adopted by the USGA Championship Committee. *Olinger v. United States Golf Association*, 205 F.3d 1001, 1003 (7th Cir. 2001); *see also* USGA, *Local Rules and Terms of the*

Competition (2019), https://tinyurl.com/y6yopye9. And that Notice will typically require walking. *See* USGA, HOW TO CONDUCT A COMPETITION App. F, p. 91 (2012). In other respects too, the Rules of Golf spell out options that may or may not apply in a given competition. *See id.* at 90.

F. UNIFORMITY AND DIVERSITY IN PLAYING SPACE AND EQUIPMENT

In the last section, we considered the relative merits of uniformity and diversity across time, and also across playing levels. Now we will consider the same issue with respect to playing space and equipment.

Many sports affirmatively value significant variation in the playing space. Uniform golf courses, for example, would be anathema. Not only do links courses and parkland courses serve up very different challenges and rewards, but the individuality of each course—indeed, of each hole in each course—is close to a defining feature of the sport. Motorsports are much the same. Although strangers to NASCAR often complain that the sport is nothing more than cars traveling fast around an oval, wide variation in track length (from the half-mile short tracks of Bristol and Martinsville to the 2.66-mile superspeedway at Talladega), shape (from perfect ovals to tri-ovals to eggs), and steepness of banking (from 6 degrees at Pocono to 31 degrees at Daytona) combine to reward very different combinations of skills and tactics for each race. And this is all the more true of Formula One races run either on city streets (as in Monaco) or on tracks of vastly different lengths, shapes and configurations.

What considerations or values are at stake in the decision to tolerate, mandate, or prohibit diversity in playing space? Consider baseball parks. As noted by Dan Epstein, in *High and Tight: Our Rock & Roll Baseball Experts Go Balls to the (Outfield) Wall*, "[n]o two major league ballparks ever looked, played or were laid out in exactly the same way." ROLLING STONE, May 30, 2012. Some quirks of early 20th-century parks resulted from them being "shoehorned," as Epstein says, into tight urban spaces. The most famous remaining one of these is Boston's Green Monster, the leftfield wall in Fenway Park. Its 37-foot height seems greater than necessary to keep large numbers of fans from watching games without paying the team, as can still be done from the so-called Wrigley Rooftops in Chicago. But it does compensate, rather unevenly, for the wall being only 310 feet from home plate; some balls that would be routine flies in other parks sail over the Monster, and some line drives that would be extra-base hits, even homers, elsewhere bounce back for loud singles. The original Yankee Stadium, the House That Ruth Built, featured a famous "short porch"—no high wall—in right field, 296′ down the line, not for space limitations but to yield more homers by Babe Ruth himself.

In the mid-20th century, ballparks tended to become more suburban, uniform and symmetrical. And since 1958, MLB has prescribed a minimum distance of 325′ down the foul lines and 400′ to the centerfield fence, Note following MLB Rule 2.01, though existing playing spaces were exempted, and notwithstanding the absolute wording of the rule, further exemptions have been allowed. (Thus, the new Yankee Stadium has dimensions identical to those of its predecessor after a 1970s remodel, 314′ down each line, and asymmetrical in between.) But the Kansas City A's did not get an exemption in 1964 when they tried to replicate the Yankees' porch; after the fence was moved back, owner Charlie Finley had the P.A. announcer inform the crowd, "That would have been a home run at Yankee Stadium" whenever an A's player flied out past a line drawn 296′ from home plate—until he realized that the deeper fence also hurt visiting batters. Chris Landers, *Yankee Stadium's short porch in right field is responsible for some of baseball's biggest moments*, CUT4 BY MLB.COM, Jan. 29, 2019.

In recent years, with more urban building and a retro style of architecture gaining favor, idiosyncrasies have again become common. And the Detroit Tigers, the San Diego Padres, and the New York Mets have all shortened their fences "after their original dimensions were deemed too unfavorable for power hitters." Epstein, *High and Tight*.

COMMENTS AND QUESTIONS

 1. The old ball game. Are diverse dimensions for ballparks a bug or a feature? After briefly sketching some of the variations seen in major league ballparks, the *Rolling Stone* article proceeded to ask its "rock & roll baseball experts"—rock musicians such as Steve Earle, Alice Cooper, and Steve Wynn—for their opinions: "Do you believe that today's ballparks should be more hitter-friendly, or at least more uniform in their dimensions? Or should some ballparks be hitter's parks, some be pitcher's parks, and everyone can just deal with it?" The dominant view opposed uniformity. As Greg Dulli, guitar and vocals for the Twilight Singers and the Afghan Whigs, put it, "Baseball is unique, in that it has no clock and the dimensions of individual parks are left to each team to decide. If I'm an owner or GM, I will put together a team based on what kind of field I'm going to play half my games on. I think it lends to the artistry and imagination of baseball to keep things individual." George Thorogood was the lone dissenter, arguing that if all the parks were uniform, there would "be no more complaints." His motto? "Everything the same, for pitchers and hitters."

 What do you think? Is it relevant to you that baseball tradition appears to pay more attention to individual statistics than most or any other sports? Is it a problem that a player's home stadium might strongly favor pitchers or strongly favor hitters? If you agree with Greg Dulli that stadium diversity is a distinct virtue, then why stop at outfield dimensions? Why shouldn't *infield* dimensions also be allowed to vary, if within specified ranges? We have already noted that teams vary the height of their infield grass, and the condition of their basepaths, for competitive advantage. Do infields vary in other significant ways? Is that good or bad?

2. *Beyond baseball.* Among the major American team sports, baseball is unusual in allowing variation in the size of the playing field. The NFL specifies that all football fields measure 360' × 160', though it allows stadiums to be open or enclosed; NBA courts are 94' × 50', slightly larger than in the international game; NHL rinks are all 200' × 85', but with the corners rounded off by arcs of 28' radius. In contrast to these American sports, the world's most popular sport, soccer, permits some variation in pitch dimensions. While the penalty area must be of uniform size (30m × 16.5m), a field's length and width are allowed to vary. For international matches, the allowed variance is relatively modest (64m to 75m wide, 100m to 110m long). But for domestic matches, the pitch may range between 90 and 120 meters in length and between 45 and 90 meters in width. FIFA Law 1. Is this variability desirable? In cricket and Australian rules football, fields vary considerably in size and shape. The dimensions of the central part of a cricket field, the pitch, are fixed, but pitches differ considerably, particularly in the nature of the grass, and this affects play considerably.

Should the NFL also allow fields to vary, in width if not in length? Consider, for example, a proposed rule change that would allow NFL clubs to establish fields of any width from, say, 145' to 170', or to use somewhat wider or narrower hash marks? (NFL hash marks must be drawn exactly 18' 6" apart, whereas NCAA and high school hash marks are much wider—40' and 53'4" respectively.) Would such changes promote or frustrate fairness? Would it be good or bad, all things considered? The standardization of field dimensions is just one respect in which football values precision more than soccer does; football is also much more precise than soccer about keeping the game clock, and uses many more officials to enforce rules more carefully. For a discussion of these, a suggestion that this difference corresponds to differences between American and European criminal trial systems, and an argument that the American approach is pathological, see WILLIAM T. PIZZI, TRIALS WITHOUT TRUTH: WHY OUR SYSTEM OF CRIMINAL TRIALS HAS BECOME AN EXPENSIVE FAILURE AND WHAT WE NEED TO DO TO REBUILD IT (1998).

3. *Playing high.* Soccer fields do not vary only in width and length. They also vary in altitude. Concerned that high-altitude matches gave home teams that were accustomed to the altitude an unfair advantage over visitors, FIFA issued a set of rulings in 2007 and 2008 that prohibited matches in international competition at high altitude—first, at 2500 meters above sea level and, subsequently, at 3000 meters. In response to protests by Andean countries (Bolivia, Ecuador, and Peru) that have stadiums at higher altitude, FIFA rescinded its ban later in 2008 and announced in 2010 that the issue was off its agenda. Should altitude and other climate conditions be regulated? *See* Cesar R. Torres, *What Is Wrong With Playing High?*, 36 J. PHIL. SPORT 1 (2009).

4. *All or nothing.* For many years, FIFA President Sepp Blatter opposed the introduction of in-ball chip technology that would enable officials to

determine whether a ball has fully crossed the goal mouth in part on the ground that the technology is too expensive to be adopted in all countries. If it cannot be implemented everywhere, he argued, it should not be used. Is this an important consideration in your view? Why or why not?

  5.   Deflategate. As much of the world learned after the 2015 AFC conference championship game, since 2006 the NFL has allowed teams to select the balls they use on offense, but it prescribes a detailed set of specifications:

> The Ball must be a "Wilson," hand selected, bearing the signature of the Commissioner of the League, Roger Goodell.

> The ball shall be made up of an inflated (12 1/2 to 13 1/2 pounds) urethane bladder enclosed in a pebble grained, leather case (natural tan color) without corrugations of any kind. It shall have the form of a prolate spheroid and the size and weight shall be: long axis, 11 to 11 1/4 inches; long circumference, 28 to 28 1/2 inches; short circumference, 21 to 21 1/4 inches; weight, 14 to 15 ounces.

Playing Rule 2, Sec. 1. *Should* the teams each be allowed to pick the balls they use on offense? Is football different from, say, baseball, soccer, or basketball in this respect? Assuming teams are allowed to pick the balls they use on offense, should the degree of inflation be confined? *See* Andy Benoit, *Let Brady Deflate the Ball*, SPORTS ILLUSTRATED, May 8, 2015.

  6.   Tennis. Outdoor tennis is usually played on one of three basic types of surface. Clay is the slowest, yielding high bounces, and it most readily allows players to skid to change directions. Grass is the fastest; the ball tends to stay low and to skid in unpredictable directions. Hard courts stand in between the two. Traditionally, the different surfaces have rewarded different skill sets—to succeed on clay, a player must play the baseline well and know how to skid, but you can't win on grass without a strong serve and excellent volleying skills—and players have had radically different results on them. For example, Gustavo Kuerten of Brazil won three French Opens, played on crushed red clay, between 1997 and 2001, but he never advanced beyond the quarters of any of the other majors. At the other end, Pete Sampras won seven Wimbledons between 1993 and 2000, but only once—interestingly enough, in 1996, the one year in that span when he did *not* win Wimbledon—did he get as far as the semis at the French. The competitions at those two venues operated under essentially the same rules, and they both were called tennis, but one might ask how much of an exaggeration it would be to say they were two different sports; it is interesting to contemplate how dramatic an impact such a wide range of surfaces would have on the way basketball is played.

  To many observers, men's tennis of the Sampras era on the fast services was boring, because it was so dominated by the serve. No less an observer than Rafael Nadal, then a junior player, has said, "Personally, to watch a Pete Sampras versus Goran Ivanisevic match, or one between those kind of players, is not enjoyable. It's not really tennis, it is a few swings of the racquet." Brian

Phillips, *Surface Tension*, GRANTLAND (June 19, 2013). Whether for this reason or not, tournament organizers soon made changes that slowed the faster surfaces. Wimbledon, which previously had used a mix of grass, 70% rye, 30% creeping red fescue, switched to an all-rye formula in 2001, assertedly to make the grass hardier. And, according to Phillips,

> The Australian Open—traditionally the slower of the two hardcourt majors—switched from a surface called "Rebound Ace" to one called "Plexicushion" in 2008. There's disagreement over whether Plexicushion is a higher-bouncing surface than Rebound Ace, but because it's relatively rough, it has the effect of "fluffing up" balls, causing them to fly at slower speeds and increasing the odds of, I don't know, six-hour baseline slugfests that leave both players unable to stand. The U.S. Open—the faster hardcourt major—hasn't officially changed surfaces, but organizers added more sand to its acrylic-paint mix between 2001 and 2003 to slow down play.

And the trend may have continued. In 2019, the veteran player Milos Raonic said he perceived a "gradual decline in the speed of the court" at Wimbledon, adding: "And I don't think it plays any faster than any of the other Slams that's for sure." Kamakshi Tandon, *Raonic Attempts to Explain why Wimbledon's Grasscourts are Slower*, TENNIS.COM (July 5, 2019).

Other factors may have contributed to the lengthening of points and the increased tendency to battle them out from the baseline. Phillips mentions "the rise of the Western forehand grip, which rotates the knuckle of the index finger, making it easier for players to apply topspin but awkward for them to volley," and "the rise of the two-handed backhand, which makes shots more accurate and powerful at the expense of fluid net play." Musab Abid emphasizes improving racquet technology, which makes it easier to hit passing shots, and changing coaching techniques, which emphasize groundstrokes over volleys (though one might wonder whether such changes have any significance independent of other developments in the game). Musab Abid, *The 'slowing down' of Wimbledon is as much myth as reality, and marks a significant step in the evolution of grasscourt tennis*, FIRSTPOST.COM (June 27, 2019) (acknowledging that the 2001 change "has effectively made the Wimbledon courts slower and bouncier").

But the changes in surfaces do appear, as Raonic suggested, to have made the Grand Slam tournaments more similar. Of course, they are still significantly different—Nadal, a great player on all surfaces, is transcendent on clay. But one measure may be that in the 44 years following 1964, only one man, Andre Agassi in 1999, completed a career Grand Slam, winning all four of the major titles. And since 2009, there have been three—in addition to Nadal, the two other dominant players of the era, Roger Federer and Novak Djokovic.

Is the increasing uniformity of tennis playing surfaces—and thus of the playing styles that are most rewarded—good or bad on balance? If you think that it's been a good development, do you also think that what's good for tennis is (presumptively) good for golf? Should the authorities that govern golf try to make the challenges presented by its four major tournaments (the Masters, the British Open, the U.S. Open, and the PGA Championship) less diverse?

G. HEALTH AND SAFETY

Roots of mixed martial arts can be traced back as far as ancient Greece. Pankration, introduced to the Olympic Games in 648 BCE, was an all-out battle in which the contestants were barely restrained by rules: They could, for example, punch, kick, and use headlocks and chokeholds.

The modern history of MMA appears to have begun with Brazilian Jiu-Jitsu (BJJ), a style that grew out of classical judo but diverged from it in various ways, principally by placing greater emphasis on ground fighting and by using chokeholds and joint locks. BJJ was developed by, and became closely associated with, members of the Gracie family; indeed, it is sometimes referred to as Gracie jiu-jitsu. One member of the family, Rorion Gracie, became co-promoter of an eight-man tournament, the first Ultimate Fighting Championship, featuring representatives of various combat disciplines—kickboxers, a boxer, a sumo wrestler, and so forth. There were no holds barred, no weight classes, no time limits, no required gloves, no scoring, and no way of ending a bout other than knockout, tapout (indicating submission), a doctor's intervention, or corner stoppage (throwing in a towel). The bouts took place in an octagonal cage of chain-link fence. The tournament was held in Colorado, which had no state athletic commission. Royce Gracie, a brother of Rorion, won the tournament, winning three successive bouts by submission, two on chokeholds. The event was a surprising success on pay-per-view television. It led to numerous successive UFC tournaments, and to institutionalization of a new sport, termed mixed martial arts by television critic Howard Rosenberg. Although there have been numerous MMA promoters in the United States, even before UFC1, UFC has come to dominate the field.

In the early years, promoters found it useful to emphasize the violence of MMA and its "no holds barred" aspect—"There Are No Rules!" was one slogan (though biting and eye-gouging were not allowed). But this approach generated regulatory resistance. In 1996, Sen. John McCain of Arizona called MMA "human cockfighting," and he began a campaign against it. Most cable companies, afraid to anger McCain, who became chair of the Senate Commerce Committee in January 1997, declined to carry MMA matches. David Plotz, *Fight Clubbed*, SLATE (Nov. 17, 1999). McCain also wrote the governors of every state asking them to ban MMA. And most of the states did so. Of particular importance was New York's law, passed in 1997, which prohibited the conduct of a "combative sport," defined as a professional match or exhibition in which contestants may deliver "kicks, punches or blows of any kind" to their opponents—but exempting boxing, wrestling and designated martial arts, including judo, karate, and tae kwon do. In signing the legislation, Governor George Pataki described MMA as "savage" and "barbaric." One assemblyman asserted that MMA "increase[s] the susceptibility of our youth to violence and also desensitizes those same impressionable minds to needless brutality."

In response, UFC, nearly moribund, modified its rules to make them more palatable to regulators. It introduced weight classes, five-minute rounds, and a scoring system similar to the one most common in boxing. It also prohibited groin strikes, head butts, joint manipulation, kicking of downed opponents (which McCain had found particularly offensive), and striking them in the back of the neck and head. The transformation was effective. States began to permit MMA subject to regulation, or at least ad hoc supervision. Beginning in 2000, the New Jersey State Athletic Control Board (SACB) allowed MMA events upon approval of the promoter's rules and regulations. The next year, the SACB convened a meeting of regulators, promoters, and other interested parties to develop a more systematic framework, which drew on work already done by the California State Athletic Commission. The meeting resulted in development of a uniform set of rules that the SACB formalized in 2002. And those rules quickly swept the nation. By 2012, when a challenge to New York's law—based in part on clear evidence that MMA had become safer than boxing and other combat sports—failed for the first time in federal court, it was the only state not to allow professional MMA. *Jones v. Schneiderman*, 888 F. Supp. 2d 421 (S.D.N.Y. 2012); *see also Jones v. Schneiderman*, 974 F. Supp. 2d 322 (S.D.N.Y. 2013). And in 2016, New York joined the rest of the states. Just before signing a legalization bill, Gov. Andrew Cuomo said, "The economics of the sport are undeniable." Edgar Sandoval & Kenneth Lovett, *New York's first mixed martial arts event slated for Madison Square Garden in November as sport is officially legalized*, N.Y. DAILY NEWS, Apr. 14, 2016.

COMMENTS AND QUESTIONS

1.   Safety in general. All or most sports value the safety of the competitors—at least up to a point. Danger, injury, and pain are prominent, even ineradicable, features of many sports, from contact sports (such as football and rugby), to combat sports (including boxing and mixed martial arts), to "adventure" or "extreme" sports (such as mountaineering, surfing, freediving, and the many sports that make up the X Games). Should such sports be made safer insofar as possible? What would that entail? Alternatively, is significant danger a defining characteristic of sports, properly so-called? Barnaby Conrad, a contemporary of Ernest Hemingway, is reputed to have observed, "There are only three sports: bullfighting, motor racing, and mountaineering; all the rest are merely games." L.J. Burgess, *Open Mic: What's a Sport? Bullfighting, Mountain Climbing, or Auto Racing?*, THE BLEACHER REPORT (July 1, 2008). Is there anything to the view? Consider this view, expressed by Jon Krakauer in his extraordinary first-person account of a disaster on Mount Everest that claimed nine lives:

> I'd always known that climbing mountains was a high-risk pursuit. I accepted danger was an essential component of the game—without it, climbing would be little different from a hundred other trifling diversions. It was titillating to brush up against the enigma of mortality, to steal a glimpse across its forbidden frontier. Climbing was a magnificent activity, I firmly believed, not in spite of the inherent perils, but precisely because of them.

JON KRAKAUER, INTO THIN AIR 282 (1997). *See also* Scott C. Johnson, *Michael Ybarra's Death Underscores the Allure and Dangers of Solo Climbing*, THE DAILY BEAST (July 13, 2017) (quoting Tristan Firman, an experienced South African climber: "Part of the challenge [of free-soloing] is grappling with the mind versus body versus mountain interaction. And because it has consequences, the experience is crystal.").

2.   *Combat sports.* There is no question that combat sports such as boxing and mixed martial arts are more dangerous than most sports. But they account for far fewer serious injuries, adjusted for participation levels, than many other sports. By most measures, the most dangerous sports are extreme or adventure sports like base jumping, cave diving, climbing and surfing. Additionally, rugby, cheerleading, and equestrian events produce more serious head injuries and paralysis than do combat sports. Still, many critics of combat sports find these sports especially objectionable. Are there good reasons to object to combat sports generally, or to MMA particularly, above and beyond any reasons that apply to all dangerous sports? For example, are boxing or MMA a greater "affront to public morals" than comparably dangerous sports? And, if so, why?

Consider the view that combat sports are worse than other sports that produce similar injury and death rates because they require participants to *intend* harm to opponents. As a representative of the Canadian Medical Association noted when explaining the organization's 2010 call that MMA be banned in Canada, "The difference between skiing, hockey and mixed martial arts and boxing . . . is the intent of skiing and hockey is usually not to cause bodily injury to your opponent." *Doctors urge mixed martial arts ban*, THE CANADIAN PRESS, Aug. 25, 2010. Five years earlier, the Jesuit journal *La Civita Cattolica* similarly emphasized the "sinful" intention of its participants when condemning boxing as "a form of legalized murder" that should be prohibited. Mike Pesca, *Catholic Magazine calls Boxing 'Merciless, Inhuman,'* NPR (Oct. 27, 2005). Do you agree that this is a pivotal difference? Is it clearly true that combatants intend to cause their opponents *injury* as opposed to *pain*? Should that make a difference? Should it be okay to intend to *hurt* your opponent but not to *harm* him? If so, what distinguishes the two? Is football distinguishable from MMA in the ways that matter?

Even if there are reasons to disfavor combat sports above and beyond the reasons that apply to all injury-causing sports, should they be banned? If not, why not? Consider these three rationales in favor of legalizing combat sports: (A) Combat sports are worthy of respect because they embody important values or have the capacity to instill significant virtues. (B) Combat sports should be tolerated because people like to participate in them and to watch them, and it is generally good to satisfy people's preferences. (C) Combat sports should be banned "in principle" but in practice should be legalized because banning the sports might send them underground, making them harder to regulate, and possibly leading to more injuries and deaths overall. Do you agree with any of these claims, or would you support legalization of combat sports such as MMA for other reasons?

3. *Paternalism.* Sports leagues regularly require the use of protective equipment, such as helmets and pads. Is this appropriate? Some players prefer to do without some particular device either because they believe they can perform better without it or because they like the experience better. For example, football players might be able to run faster or move more easily without thigh pads, and some hockey players enjoy skating without helmets. Should adult participants be allowed to forgo equipment that is designed for their own protection, as opposed to for the protection of others? Since 2012, the NFL has employed a procedure by which neutral certified athletic trainers ("ATC spotters") hired by the league can, in narrowly specified circumstances, stop a game and require a player to be removed for at least one play or timeout for evaluation by the team's medical personnel—but the system has been criticized as insufficiently vigilant. Ryan Van Bibber, *The NFL's concussion protocol failed Case Keenum. Who do we blame?*, SB NATION (Nov. 23, 2015). Should the NFL instead employ at each game a neutral physician who has the power to remove a player for the balance of the game for medical reasons? (The League does assign an Unaffiliated Neurotrauma Consultant ("UNC"), a qualified physician, to each sideline, but its protocol explicitly provides that "the responsibility for the diagnosis of concussion and the decision to return a player to a game remains exclusively within the professional judgment of" the team's designated physician.) Would such a practice be any different in principle from a boxing referee ending a fight by a technical knockout because one boxer is absorbing too much punishment? What are the limits of justifiable paternalism in sport?

4. *Perverse safety regulations?* It is intuitive that the more protective gear athletes wear, the greater their safety. In fact, though, the relationship is more complex because protective gear also emboldens athletes to engage in more aggressive or dangerous behaviors. For example, many casual observers believe that boxing gloves promote combatant safety by cushioning the force of blows. But they also enable punches to the head that bare-knuckle fighters wouldn't throw for fear of breaking their hands on their opponents' skulls. One proponent of a return to bare-knuckle fighting pointed out: "In 100 years of bare-knuckle fighting in the United States, which terminated around 1897 . . . there wasn't a single ring fatality," whereas recent decades have witnessed three to four every year. Nick Wong, *Why Bare-Knuckle Fighting May Be Safer Than Boxing,* COMPLEX (Nov. 13, 2015). Or consider football helmets. There is

no question that advances in modern football helmet materials and design have substantially improved impact absorption. But when hard-shelled helmets were introduced in the 1950s, "spear tackling" behavior also emerged, leading to catastrophic head and neck injuries soon after. In rugby, helmets remain optional, and, if worn, are usually thin (known as a "scrum cap"). Both sports involve high energy collisions and tackling, putting players at risk for head injury. However, in rugby, players do not typically initiate contact with their head. Indeed, one controlled study concluded that rugby players who used modified head gear with additional padding were at greater risk for injury. Andrew Mcintosh & Paul McCrory, *Effectiveness of Headgear In a Pilot Study of Under 15 Rugby Union Football*, 35 BRIT. J. SPORTS MED. 167, 167–69 (2001). And another found that high school football players who practiced tackling and blocking drills without helmets actually experienced a decrease in head impact during play. Erik Swartz et al., *A Helmetless-Tackling Intervention in American Football for Decreasing Head Impact Exposure*, 22 J. SCI. & MED. SPORT 1102 (2019).

In light of these cases, consider recent debates over the introduction of greater protective gear to women's and girl's lacrosse. Female lacrosse, unlike its male counterpart, is a non-contact sport in which only stick-to-stick contact is permitted. Because of this, official lacrosse rules have required female players to wear a mouth guard and goggles, but no other head protection. However, growing concerns about head injuries have caused several teams and school districts to start requiring headgear for female players. Some argue, however, that wearing more protective equipment will encourage more aggressive and dangerous play. Karin Corbett, the women's coach for the University of Pennsylvania, stated that players "will start to lead with their heads because they feel protected, and that causes more injuries . . . ." Sara Hall, *Will Headgear Make Women's Lacrosse More Aggressive?*, N.Y. MINUTE MAG (Dec. 6, 2017). How should sports authorities act in the face of empirical and predictive uncertainty regarding the likely effects of safety-enhancing reforms?

5. *Sports and COVID-19*. In the summer of 2020, one computer science professor forecast that, if college football games were played in the fall, approximately three to seven football players, out of 13,000 in the NCAA Division I Football Bowl Subdivision (FBS), would die from coronavirus complications. Dennis Dodd, *Coronavirus in college football: Hospitalizations, deaths projected by data analysts if FBS plays in 2020*, CBS SPORTS.COM (June 30, 2020). Putting other adverse health consequences aside just for ease of discussion, should that projection, if deemed credible, be enough to cancel the season? What if experts converge on the lower end of that range? What if the same number of college football players die each season from football-related injuries? *Cf.* Barry P. Boden, et al., *Fatalities in High School and College Football Players*, 41 AM. J. SPORTS MED. 1108 (2013) (finding 12.2 fatalities per year, or 1 per 100,000 high school and college players, from 1990 to 2010).

In 2014, baseball's Playing Rules Committee adopted a new rule, on an experimental basis, in an attempt to limit injuries from collisions at home plate. Many observers believed that the new rule, 7.13, was prompted in large part by the collision that cost catcher Buster Posey of the San Francisco Giants most of the 2011 season. *See 2011/05/25 Posey's injury*, YOUTUBE, https://tinyurl.com/yxoawnl2. Section 1 of Rule 7.13 provided that a runner would be called out if he "deviate[d] from his direct pathway to the plate in order to initiate contact with the catcher." Section 2 provided that if a catcher not in possession of the ball blocked the pathway of the runner to the plate, the runner would be called safe, unless the catcher was trying to field a throw and could not do so without blocking the pathway.

The experimental rule proved very controversial, in part because it resulted in some runners being called safe though they had clearly been tagged, or forced, before they reached home plate. Late in the season, Joe Torre, MLB's Executive Vice President of Baseball Operations (and a former big-league catcher), issued a "clarification" memo, largely in an attempt to prevent confusion during the postseason. As one report summarized, the memo "specifically instructs umpires and replay officials not to find a 'violation' of the rule by the catcher 'unless the catcher's position hindered or impeded the runner from scoring prior to the tag.'" Jayson Stark, *Joe Torre clarifies MLB collision rule*, ESPN.com (Sept. 10, 2014).

After the 2014 season, Rule 7.13 was amended, and renumbered as part of a general recodification of the MLB Rules, as Rule 6.01(i). Changes from Rule 7.13 are indicated in the markup below, where <u>underscoring</u> represents new text, and ~~strike-through~~ is discarded text:

(i)   Collisions at Home Plate

(1)   A runner attempting to score may not deviate from his direct pathway to the plate in order to initiate contact with the catcher (or other player covering home plate), <u>or otherwise initiate an avoidable collision</u>. If, in the judgment of the umpire, a runner attempting to score initiates contact with the catcher (or other player covering home plate) in such a manner, the umpire shall declare the runner out (~~even if~~ <u>regardless of whether</u> the player covering home plate ~~loses~~ <u>maintains</u> possession of the ball). In such circumstances, the umpire shall call the ball dead, and all other base runners shall return to the last base touched at the time of the collision. <u>If the runner slides into the plate in an appropriate manner, he shall not be adjudged to have violated Rule 6.01(i)</u>~~(Rule 7.13)~~.

> ~~*Rule 7.13(1)*~~<u>*Rule 6.01(i)(l) Comment*</u>. The failure by the runner to make an effort to touch the plate, the runner's lowering of the shoulder, or the runner's pushing through with his hands, elbows or arms, would support a determination that the runner deviated from the pathway in order to initiate contact with the catcher in

violation of ~~Rule 7.13. If the runner slides into the plate in an appropriate manner, he shall not be adjudged to have violated Rule 7.13~~ Rule 6.01(i), or otherwise initiated a collision that could have been avoided. A slide shall be deemed appropriate, in the case of a feet first slide, if the runner's buttocks and legs should hit the ground before contact with the catcher. In the case of a head first slide, a runner shall be deemed to have slid appropriately if his body should hit the ground before contact with the catcher. If a catcher blocks the pathway of the runner, the umpire shall not find that the runner initiated an avoidable collision in violation of this Rule 6.01(i)(*l*).

(2)   Unless the catcher is in possession of the ball, the catcher cannot block the pathway of the runner as he is attempting to score. If, in the judgment of the umpire, the catcher without possession of the ball blocks the pathway of the runner, the umpire shall call or signal the runner safe. Notwithstanding the above, it shall not be considered a violation of this Rule 6.01(i)(2) if the catcher blocks the pathway of the runner ~~in order~~ in a legitimate attempt to field ~~a~~ the throw~~, and the umpire determines that the catcher could not have fielded the ball without blocking the pathway of the runner and that contact with the runner was unavoidable.~~ (e.g., in reaction to the direction, trajectory or the hop of the incoming throw, or in reaction to a throw that originates from a pitcher or drawn-in infielder). In addition, a catcher without possession of the ball shall not be adjudged to violate this Rule 6.01 (i)(2) if the runner could have avoided the collision with the catcher (or other player covering home plate) by sliding.

> *Rule 6.01 (i)(2) Comment:* A catcher shall not be deemed to have violated Rule 6.01(i)(2) (Rule 7.13(2)) unless he has both blocked the plate without possession the ball (or when not in a legitimate attempt to field the throw), and also hindered or impeded the progress of the runner attempting to score. A catcher shall not be deemed to have hindered or impeded the progress of the runner if, in the judgment of the umpire, the runner would have been called out notwithstanding the catcher having blocked the plate. In addition, a catcher should use best efforts to avoid unnecessary and forcible contact while tagging a runner attempting to slide. Catchers who routinely make unnecessary and forcible contact with a runner attempting to slide (e.g., by initiating contact using a knee, shin guard, elbow or forearm) may be subject to discipline by the League President.

All references to "the catcher" in this Rule 6.01(i) shall apply equally to other players covering home plate. In addition, Rule 6.01(i)(2) shall not apply to force plays at home plate.

COMMENTS AND QUESTIONS

1.   Section (2). The Torre memo explained that "the intent of the rule was to protect catchers." That explains section (1). But does it also explain section (2)? Why or why not? Would the rule be unfair if it simply scrapped that section? Why shouldn't catchers be allowed to block home plate? Note that, if a catcher does block the plate a runner could barrel into him without violating section (1) because he would not be "deviat[ing] from his direct pathway to the plate."

2.   Coming home. Do you think that collisions at home presented a problem that called for a regulatory response? If so, did the new Rule (in its original form or as amended) take the right general approach? What do you think accounted for the uncertainty in applying it? Were there any inconsistencies in the Rule that might have made application particularly difficult? Did the amendments improve the situation? Do you have other suggestions as to how the Rule might be improved?

H. EASE OF ADMINISTRATION

Ideally, rules are easy to administer. It is highly desirable that persons subject to a rule can reliably predict whether their conduct will be deemed to comply with the rule or not, and that those who enforce the rule can apply it quickly and accurately. This is true in the legal world, but might be even more important in sports, where speed of decision is crucial. Of course, the ideal is not always met. The problem is that, while it is always easy enough to articulate easily administered rules, they will not necessarily be very good ones. And as rules become more complex, to try to fit factual situations better, they may become less administrable.

We begin by discussing the rules-standards distinction, which offers a theoretical overview on part of the problem. We then consider a controversial former rule of football that illustrates how one pervasive issue—determining a player's intent—creates difficulty in crafting rules that are easily administered and yet sensible. And then we examine a basic problem in both football and baseball—how to define a "catch"—and show how attempts to solve it by an easily administrable rule have led to great controversy in both sports.

1. RULES AND STANDARDS

Consider this pair of rules from baseball: A pitcher is entitled to no more than eight preparatory pitches at the start of each inning or when replacing another pitcher, and, when the bases are unoccupied, is required to deliver the

Rules vs. Standards

ball to the batter within 20 seconds after he receives the ball. Rules 8.03 & 8.04. On the other hand, when one or more base is occupied, the pitcher is not required to deliver his pitch within 20 seconds. Instead, he will be penalized (with a balk) only if he "unnecessarily delays the game." Rule 8.05(h).

Rules 8.03 and 8.04 take the *form* of a "rule," whereas Rule 8.05(h) takes the *form* of a "standard." Russell Korobkin explains the difference succinctly:

> Rules establish legal boundaries based on the presence or absence of well-specified triggering facts. Consequently, under a rule it is possible for citizens (with good legal advice) to know the legal status of their actions with reasonable certainty ex ante. Standards, in contrast, require adjudicators (usually judges, juries, or administrators) to incorporate into the legal pronouncement a range of facts that are too broad, too variable, or too unpredictable to be cobbled into a rule. Consequently, under a standard, citizens cannot know with certainty ex ante where a legal boundary would be drawn in the event a set of specified facts come to pass.

Russell Korobkin, *Behavioral Analysis and Legal Form: Rules vs. Standards Revisited*, 79 OR. L. REV. 23 (2000). A "pure rule" is "applied consistently without variation." Examples include the law that makes 18-year-olds eligible to vote (you're out of luck, no matter how mature you are, if your eighteenth birthday falls one day after Election Day), and the 24-second shot-clock. A "pure standard" is "a legal pronouncement that specifies no triggering facts that have defined legal consequences." Examples include the standard in family law that directs child custody to be determined by "the best interests of the child," and the NFL rule that prohibits "excessive celebration." Of course, as Korobkin explains, the distinction is not truly binary, but instead describes endpoints on a spectrum. "The more qualifications and exceptions a rule has, . . . the more likely it will be applied unpredictably," and so it will be more standard-like. Standard-like terms are **vague**; they have fuzzy boundaries.

Admittedly, this nomenclature—which requires us to say that some rules are "rules" while other rules are "standards"—is a little confusing.

 **Vagueness vs. Ambiguity**

Just understand that "rule" is being used at two different places in the taxonomic hierarchy: there's a family of things called rules which consists of two different genera—rules and standards. No doubt it would be nicer not to use the same word at the two different levels, but we confront this **ambiguity** in various areas of life. (A word or phrase is ambiguous if it bears multiple meanings; that a word is vague does not make it ambiguous.)

For example, within the genus of music we call "classical," we recognize a variety of distinct subtypes, including "baroque" (e.g., Bach), "classical" (e.g., Haydn), and "romantic" (e.g., Brahms). Also, while we sometimes use the word "bug" to describe all things within the class *Insecta,* the word also applies more particularly to those insects that are classified in the order *Hemiptera:* flying insects with two pairs of wings, hypodermic-needle-like mouthparts, and various other distinguishing features. The members of this order, which includes ladybugs, bedbugs, stink bugs, and water bugs, are sometimes called "true bugs." Similarly, then, we might think of rules as being either standards or true rules.

Now that the vocabulary is clear, we can ask *why* a rule should be crafted in more rule-like or more standard-like form. Return to MLB Rules 8.03, 8.04, and 8.05(h). It would have been easy to make all of these rules or all of them standards. Why might the rulemakers have crafted the rules as they did? What considerations speak in favor of regulation by rule instead of by standard, or vice versa?

The legal theoretical literature on the tradeoffs between rules and standards is vast. The central insight, though, is that rules are cheaper and easier to apply (because the rule-applier need not make complex or uncertain evaluative judgments), whereas standards are cheaper and easier to craft (because the rule-maker need not convert a potentially large number of relevant factors into a crisp test). Furthermore, whereas rules yield greater predictability and therefore may promote greater compliance, standards (when applied by wise or skilled adjudicators) can sort cases more accurately, as measured by reference to the genuine underlying considerations. There are additional supposed advantages and disadvantages of each form relative to the other. Try to figure out what some of them may be as you read the following materials.

Rules and standards are each optimal in some circumstances; this book touches on the distinction. The incident described in the article below provides a useful introduction to the topic.

WILLIAM C. MARRA, WHAT TROY POLAMALU CAN TEACH US ABOUT THE LAW

Weeklystandard.com, Oct. 30, 2011

When Pittsburgh Steelers safety Troy Polamalu suffered concussion-like symptoms in a recent NFL game, he did what any decent husband might do: He walked to the sideline and called his wife Theodora to tell her he was fine. Polamalu, like so many football players, has a long history of concussions, so surely his wife would have been relieved to hear from her husband.

In response, NFL commissioner Roger Goodell fined Polamalu $10,000 for violating an NFL rule prohibiting "the use of cellular phones . . . and other electronic equipment . . . in club-controlled areas, including . . . sidelines."

Goodell has been almost universally criticized for his decision to fine Polamalu. Steelers head coach Mike Tomlin said Goodell's decision lacked "common sense." AOL columnist David Steele likened Goodell to a "deranged game-show host" for strictly applying the "letter of the law." And Pittsburgh sports columnist Josh Yohe tweeted: "Goodell is a joke."

By calling his wife, Polamalu certainly violated the letter of the NFL's law, which contains a blanket prohibition against in-game cell phone use. Thus the problem, if there is one, with Goodell's decision must be that he allowed the "letter of the law" (its text) to trump the "spirit of the law" (its purpose). Polamalu should not be fined, the argument must go, because the rule *wasn't really intended* to apply to this case.

This tracks an important legal debate that has demanded considerable attention from the Supreme Court: When a statute's text conflicts with its apparent purpose, which should govern?

There is an increasing consensus on the Supreme Court today that when the text of a statute is clear, the text governs, and there is no need to inquire into the statute's purpose. In short, the Supreme Court today would probably side with Goodell.

This was not always the case. In the 1892 case of *Church of the Holy Trinity* v. *United States*, the Supreme Court held that a statute banning contracts to import foreigners "to perform labor or service of any kind" did not proscribe a contract to import a religious minister into the United States. The Court conceded that the contract was prohibited under the letter of the law, because a priest performs "labor or service of any kind." But Justice David Brewer, writing for a unanimous Court, held that the spirit should trump the letter because it "is a familiar rule that a thing may be within the letter of the statute and yet not within the statute, because not within its spirit nor within the intention of its makers." The Court held that the spirit of the statute was to apply only to *manual* labors, and so the Court allowed the religious contract.

But the modern Court is much more likely to apply the clear text of a rule like the NFL's cell phone ban. A century after Justice Brewer wrote his paean to the spirit of the law, Justice Antonin Scalia, also writing for a unanimous Supreme Court, held in the 1998 case *Pennsylvania Department of Corrections* v. *Yeskey* that "in the context of an unambiguous statutory text," arguments related to purpose or spirit are simply "irrelevant."

Two developments in the law have driven this shift. The first is textualism, a mode of statutory interpretation that favors a statute's semantic meaning over the perceived intent of Congress. Textualists argue that because laws are the product of messy legislative compromise, it is incoherent to assert that there is any single or discernable intent of a statute. Courts best respect the legislative compromise by applying a statute according to the terms and level of generality at which it was enacted. When a statute sets forth a rule (a binding directive: "no cell phone use on the sidelines"), it should be treated as a rule; when it sets forth a standard (an invitation to judicial balancing: "no cell phone use unless cell phone use is reasonable considering all the circumstances"), it should be treated as a standard.

Textualism assumes the Constitution's separation of powers and bicameralism and presentment procedures, which are absent from the NFL, where Goodell plays both Moses and Solomon, lawgiver and judge. Yet NFL owners and players presumably request the promulgation of the League's 'statutes' for a reason, namely because they expect those statutes to be followed. Further, the NFL statutes are formulated and vetted by many different individuals within the commissioner's office, so textualism's assumption that there is no single legislative intent could be mapped on to the NFL. Under these assumptions, textualism advises that Goodell will be most faithful to the product of the lawmaking process by adhering to statutory text. Because the NFL's legislative process produced an inflexible rule against cell phone use, Goodell should respect the rulemaking process and adhere to the rule.

The second and related development in the law is a renewed preference for rules over standards—and hence an increased comfort with interpreting provisions like the NFL's cell phone ban as rules, as opposed to converting them to standards. Whereas textualism is rooted in a descriptive assessment of how the legislative process works, the preference for rules over standards is a normative argument for how the *corpus juris* ought to look.

The standards approach has its virtues. A flexible standard allows a judge or NFL commissioner to more effectively dispense justice on a case-by-case basis, perhaps here by not fining Polamalu. Inflexible rules have a hard time accommodating those cases where applying the letter just seems *wrong*. This is "always a problem with trying to have a rule that applies to everybody," Goodell conceded this week.

But in most cases, including with the NFL's cell phone ban, the benefits of rules outweigh their costs. Rules promote equal treatment of like cases, the cardinal virtue of a just legal system. A rule ensures that all cases that fall within the ambit of the text are treated alike—for example, any player who uses a cell phone in-game is fined, whether he uses it to tweet, Google an NFL rule, or chat with his wife.

Standards, by contrast, entrust these matters to the discretion of the judge or commissioner. This leads to a series of difficult questions. If Goodell permits Polamalu's call, must he also permit a player to phone his fiancée, or brother, or friend? What if the player suffered a leg injury rather than a concussion? What if the player texted or emailed rather than called?

And so on. There is no easy way to draw a line between these different situations.

Rules are also more predictable in their application than standards, because rules comprise *ex ante* directives, whereas standards rely on *ex post* evaluations of conduct. Thus rules better allow individuals to structure their conduct to avoid running afoul of the law: A rule clearly tells a player that he may not tweet to his brother that his leg injury is not so bad, whereas a standard can often do no better than, "tweet at your own risk." And rules are more administrable than standards, and do not require difficult and time consuming judicial inquiries, such as into whether an injury was really severe enough to warrant a phone call home.

Finally, rules help check against arbitrary governance. As Justice Scalia has written, "Only by announcing rules do we hedge ourselves in." AP sports columnist Tim Dahlberg complained that by fining Polamalu, Goodell was "enforcing [the law] in such an arbitrary manner." To the contrary, the standards approach is more prone to arbitrary governance because it substantially increases the judge or commissioner's power to enforce the law according to his liking. By binding our decision-makers, rules help ensure that government—be it America's or the NFL's—is "a government of laws and not of men."

COMMENTS AND QUESTIONS

1.   Treating like cases alike. William Marra makes two arguments in defending Commissioner Goodell against criticisms that he mishandled the Polamalu case. First, Marra argues that Goodell was right to interpret the NFL cellphone ban in a "textualist" rather than "purposive" way. Second, he argues that the cellphone ban was properly crafted as a rule rather than as a standard. It is important to see that these two arguments concern very different issues. One could agree with Marra that, given the way the rule was written, Goodell was right to interpret and enforce it in accordance with its literal meaning, while also maintaining—against Marra—that the prohibition should have been written as a standard and not as a rule. Conversely, one could agree with Marra that the prohibition should have been written as a rule, but contend that Goodell should have appealed to the purpose or spirit behind the rule in exercising discretion not to sanction Polamalu. (Interestingly, the rulebook does not specify what the fine will be for violating the cellphone ban, leaving that up to the Commissioner's discretion; as it happens, Polamalu appealed the fine and won.) We will address questions concerning how officials should interpret and enforce rulebooks in Part III of this book. Here we focus only on how the NFL's prohibition on cellphone use should be drafted—in more rule-like or standard-like terms.

On that question, to repeat, Marra endorses the NFL's choice to proceed by rule. What arguments does he supply to defend that choice? Do you find them persuasive? In particular, consider the suggestion that Marra begs the critical question when asserting that "[r]ules promote equal treatment of like cases," for that is to assume that calling one's wife to reassure her after a scary hit and calling one's friend to make plans for post-game drinks are "like cases." Do you think that the existing rule or a well-crafted standard would do a better job of treating like cases alike? Do you think that the existing rule or a well-crafted standard is preferable, all things considered? What, for that matter, would a well-crafted standard for this situation look like?

Given the rule, and the Commissioner's determination to enforce it, does someone in Polamalu's position who wants to promptly reassure his spouse have available any good option?

2. *Rules, standards, and infield flies*. Let's revisit our old (or new) friend, the infield fly rule. Most of the rule is reproduced in footnote 2 of the *Aside*, on p. 45. Recall that for a batted ball to be deemed an infield fly for purposes of the rule it must be catchable by an infielder "with ordinary effort." A comment to the definition of an infield fly in the Official Rules of Baseball provides as follows:

> On the infield fly rule the umpire is to rule whether the ball could ordinarily have been handled by an infielder—not by some arbitrary limitation such as the grass, or the base lines. The umpire must rule also that a ball is an infield fly, even if handled by an outfielder, if, in the umpire's judgment, the ball could have been as easily handled by an infielder. The infield fly is in no sense to be considered an appeal play. The umpire's judgment must govern, and the decision should be made immediately.

> When an infield fly rule is called, runners may advance at their own risk. If on an infield fly rule, the infielder intentionally drops a fair ball, the ball remains in play despite the provisions of Rule 6.05 (L). The infield fly rule takes precedence.

Is "ordinary effort," the critical determination under the rule (or one of them, at least), too standard-like? Would the rule be better if made more rule-like? How?

In thinking about these questions, consider the most notorious call of the infield fly rule in recent decades, in the 2012 National League wildcard game. The Atlanta Braves were three runs behind the St. Louis Cardinals in the bottom of the eighth inning of this loser-go-home game, but they had runners on first and second and one out when Andrelton Simmons hit a fly ball to shallow left field. The Cardinals' shortstop, Pete Kozma, ran back, well onto the outfield grass, and initially called for the ball, but at the last second he moved back towards the infield, apparently thinking that leftfielder Matt Holliday would catch it. Instead, the ball dropped between them, apparently giving the Braves the bases loaded with one out. But at the last minute before the ball hit the ground Umpire Sam Holbrook had signaled for the infield fly rule. So Simmons was out, meaning there were two outs rather than one, and only two runners on the bases (on second and third because they had advanced when the ball dropped) rather than three.

Braves manager Fredi Gonzalez objected immediately that more than "ordinary effort" would have been required to catch the ball: "I thought that the shortstop had to go way out there to make a play on that fly ball," he said later, "and I think we've got to take account of the crowd, 50,000 people yelling, and I thought there was some miscommunication between Holliday and Kozma." Mark Bowman, *Infield Fly Ruling Draws Braves' Ire, Sparks Disruption*, MLB.com (Oct. 5, 2012). Not succeeding in getting the call reversed—surprise, surprise—Gonzalez protested the game. Joe Torre, MLB's Executive Vice President for Baseball Operations, was at the game, and rather than wait he ruled on the spot that Holbrook had made a judgment call that could not be overturned by protest. After the game, Holbrook explained, "I saw the shortstop go back and get underneath the ball where he would have had ordinary effort and would have caught the baseball." Not surprisingly, Kozma thought Holbrook had made the right call: "I went back and I was under it, and I called for and just missed it," he said. "I bailed at the last second." And equally unsurprisingly, some of the Braves—but also some neutral observers—denied that Kozma had been "camped" under the ball, and also thought that Holbrook had made the call too late. Some Braves fans made their displeasure very apparent by throwing trash onto the field, causing a lengthy delay. The next Braves batter was retired, they failed to score in the ninth, and their season (and the career of their illustrious third baseman, Chipper Jones) was done.

You can make your own judgment about the call by watching a video of the play at https://tinyurl.com/y5t4rh2s. Did Holbrook get it right?

3.   *Rules, standards, and corruption.* Fans of NBA basketball, perhaps more than fans of most sports, often complain that the league is biased in favor of big-market teams. Exhibit A in this conspiracy theory was a 1985 change in the draft lottery (from a coin toss between last-place teams to a lottery among all teams that missed the playoffs), which ended up giving the New York Knicks the first pick, and therefore the chance to draft the undisputed top choice, Georgetown's Patrick Ewing. But the supposed bias extends further and is said by some to include instructions to officials to call games in favor of preferred teams. Many fans, and other observers, believe this is just what happened in the 2002 Western Conference Finals, which the Los Angeles Lakers won, 4–3, over the Sacramento Kings. Most suspicious was Game 6 of that series, which the Lakers won 106–102, thanks in part to a staggering 27–9 free throw advantage in the fourth quarter. Indeed, the officiating in that game was so poor that the *Washington Post* columnist Michael Wilbon observed that he had "never seen officiating in a game of consequence as bad as that in Game 6" and David Dupree of *USA Today* agreed that "it's the poorest officiating in an important game I've ever seen." *See* KYLE GARLETT & PATRICK O'NEAL, THE WORST CALL EVER!: THE MOST INFAMOUS CALLS EVER BLOWN BY REFEREES, UMPIRES, AND OTHER BLIND OFFICIALS 46–49 (2007). Does the literature on rules and standards bear at all on widespread concerns about the integrity or competence of NBA officiating? If so, how?

2.   THE PROBLEM OF INTENT: THE TUCK RULE

In sports, as in many other areas of life, a person's intent may be a critical factor in characterizing and assessing her conduct. As Oliver Wendell Holmes, Jr. famously observed, "Even a dog knows the difference between being kicked and being stumbled over." Consistent with the Holmesian aphorism, a hard hit in football or hockey that happens to cause injury is an inevitable and accepted part of the game; a hit intended to cause injury is not, and may be punished severely. A difficult and pervasive problem, though, is that intent—in the sense of purpose, design, or goal—is often difficult to determine. The problem of intent—whether it should matter and, if so, how it should be determined—will recur at various times throughout this book. For now, we will focus on one illustration of how the relevance of a player's intent and the value of administrable rules can come in conflict.

In 1999 the NFL Rulebook added to the definition of "Pass" a note, said to reflect prior practice, providing:

> When [an offensive] player is holding the ball to pass it forward, any intentional forward movement of his arm starts a forward pass, even if the player loses possession of the ball as he is attempting to tuck it back toward his body. Also, if the player has tucked the ball into his body and then loses possession, it is a fumble.

The Note (later amended to replace "arm" by "hand" in the first sentence) incorporated the so-called tuck rule. Under that rule, as explained by a journalist,

> a quarterback's throwing motion begins when he raises the ball in his hand and begins to move his arm forward; that motion doesn't end until the quarterback tucks the ball back against his body, making him a runner. If the ball comes loose any time in between, it's an incomplete pass, not a fumble. Only if the quarterback reloads—and raises the ball again to start a new throwing motion—can he fumble, as long as the ball is knocked loose before his arm begins to move forward again.

Mark Maske, *Tuck Rule Hard to Grasp*, Wash. Post, Oct. 15, 2005.

The rule is best remembered for the critical role it played in the 2002 Divisional Championship game, played in a heavy snowfall, between the New England Patriots and the Oakland Raiders. The Patriots were down 13–10 with under two minutes left in the game when their young quarterback, Tom Brady, lost the ball on a hit by his former Michigan teammate, Charles Woodson of the Raiders. The Raiders recovered the ball and the game appeared to be virtually sealed; the play certainly looked like a fumble, and Brady's reaction showed that he thought it was a fumble.

(You can see the play at https://tinyurl.com/y473ddsc.) But on replay review, the referee ruled that the play was an incomplete pass rather than a fumble. Brady had pulled the ball back, moved it forward in hopes of passing it, and then to his chest; he was holding it with both hands when he lost it, but he had never tucked it into his body. The Patriots tied the game on a 45-yard field goal with 27 seconds left in regulation and went on to win on another field goal in the first possession of overtime. Two weeks later they won Super Bowl XXXVI.

The tuck rule was much criticized. Joe Gibbs, who had won three Super Bowls as coach of the Washington Redskins, said of it, "It says you can pull [the ball] down and do anything you want for the next 10 minutes. It makes no sense to me." But Mike Pereira, who was director of officiating for the NFL at the time of the Tuck Rule game, offered a practical defense of it. "The rule is very specific," he said. ". . . Intent doesn't factor into the rule. Does the ball come out after [the quarterback's] arm is going forward and before he tucks the ball back into his body? If so, then it's an incomplete pass. . . . [I]t makes it an easy rule to call. There's no gray area. It's black and white."

Thus, although the league's Competition Committee frequently considered changing the rule in the years after 2002, it found the task very difficult. "[I]t's one thing to think you need to change it," said Ozzie Newsome, then general manager of the Baltimore Ravens and a member of the Competition Committee, "and another thing entirely to change it in a way that it actually can be officiated." He also said, with Pereira's concurrence, "We tried several different ways to change it. But every time we tried to rewrite it, what we came up with was too difficult to officiate." Maske, *Tuck Rule Hard to Grasp.*

Finally, in 2013 the League did throw out the rule. (Twenty-nine teams voted in favor of the rule, the Washington Redskins voted against, and the Patriots and Raiders abstained.) Here is the new rule, marked up against the old; as before, underscoring represents new text and ~~strikethrough~~ represents discarded text:

> When [an offensive] player is holding the ball to pass it forward, any intentional forward movement of his hand starts a forward pass~~, even if.~~ If the player loses possession of the ball ~~as he is attempting to tuck~~ during an attempt to bring it back toward his body~~. Also, if the player.~~ or if the player loses possession after he has tucked the ball into his body ~~and then loses possession~~, it is a fumble.

Rule 3, Section 23, Article 2, Note 2.

COMMENTS AND QUESTIONS

1. *Intent in principle.* Sometimes intent should matter in principle, and sometimes it shouldn't. For example, under the law of tort, people are generally liable for injuries they cause "negligently" (i.e., through lack of adequate care) even if not intentionally. Newsome seems to have suggested that whether a lost ball should be deemed a fumble or an incompletion should depend *in principle* on whether the quarterback was still intending to pass when he lost control. Why is that? Do you agree? (We revisit this issue briefly in Subchapter 6B2.)

2. *Intent and administrability.* Pereira said that treating intent as a non-factor made this "an easy rule to call." Similarly, after suggesting that whether a lost ball should be deemed a fumble or an incomplete pass should depend, in principle, on the quarterback's intent, Newsome proceeded to explain that the tuck rule as it then stood made intent to pass irrelevant only because the rulemakers had not yet been able to draft an intent-sensitive rule that "can be officiated." Why was that so hard?

3. *The 2013 revision.* Presumably the 2013 rule change was meant to prescribe that a play identical to the notorious one from the 2002 Raiders-Patriots game would now be ruled a fumble. Just what language in the new rule achieves this objective? More generally, is the new rule an improvement over the old one? If so, why did it take so long?

Would the rule be better, in principle or in practice or both, if the words "during an attempt to bring it back toward his body, or if the player loses possession after he has tucked the ball into his body" were replaced by "while bringing it back toward his body or after having done so"?

4. *A crafty QB.* Do you agree with Gibbs that the old rule would let the quarterback immunize himself against a fumble, after moving the ball forward as if to pass, by keeping it down indefinitely without tucking it back into this body? If not, why not? If so, why did quarterbacks not do this before the rule change?

5. *Intent and the* appearance *of intent.* At the start of the 2012 NBA season, the league announced a new rule designed to curb "flopping," generally understood as actions in which a player feigns or exaggerates contact in an effort to fool the referee into calling a foul on an opponent. Under the rule, the league will review video of games and announce violations after the fact. The first violation of the anti-flopping rule draws only a warning, but subsequent violations call forth monetary fines, starting at $5,000 for the first and escalating to $30,000 for the fifth.

It would seem to be in the very nature of flopping that it cannot be committed accidentally or unintentionally, much like "lying" can't be unintentional even though "deceiving" can be. (Do you agree?) One might suspect, then, that flopping would be defined in terms of the player's intent. And it is—in a fashion. Under the rules, "flopping" is defined as "any physical act that appears to have been intended to cause the referees to call a foul on another player." Is this a good solution? What if a player admits after a game that he flopped but he was such a good actor that his flop did not "appear" intended to provoke a foul call on his opponent? Would it be improper for the league to impose a fine?

3. WHAT'S THE CATCH?

Baseball and football have recently confronted difficulties with the rules governing one of the most basic aspects of both games: what constitutes a catch? In both cases, controversies have arisen when a player clearly loses control of the ball after apparently gaining momentary possession of it. A rule making the obvious loss of control determinative is relatively easy to administer, but won't be *accurate* when applied to a player who had perfected a catch *before* losing control.

Here is the definition of a catch from Rule 2.00 of the Official Rules of Baseball:

> A CATCH is the act of a fielder in getting secure possession in his hand or glove of a ball in flight and firmly holding it; providing he does not use his cap, protector, pocket or any other part of his uniform in getting possession. It is not a catch, however, if simultaneously or immediately following his contact with the ball, he collides with a player, or with a wall, or if he falls down, and as a result of such collision or falling, drops the ball. It is not a catch if a fielder touches a fly ball which then hits a member of the offensive team or an umpire and then is caught by another defensive player. In establishing the validity of the catch, the fielder shall hold the ball long enough to prove that he has complete control of the ball and that his release of the ball is voluntary and intentional. If the fielder has made the catch and drops the ball while in the act of making a throw following the catch, the ball shall be adjudged to have been caught.

In spring of 2014, MLB told teams that for a ball to be caught the fielder would have to transfer it securely to his throwing hand. This was a new interpretation of the Rule; apparently, the impetus behind it was the impending expansion of replay review and the belief of umpires that this transfer rule would be easier for them to call, leading to fewer reversals on replay. Early in April, after a challenge by the Tampa Bay Rays, MLB issued a statement saying:

> Umpires and/or replay officials must consider whether the fielder had secured possession of the ball but dropped it during the act of the catch. An example of a catch that would not count is if a fielder loses possession of the ball during the transfer before the ball was secured by his throwing hand.

Baseball analyst Dave Cameron wrote on FanGraphs:

I think there's a reasonable case to be made that, at second base, this interpretation of the rule makes decent sense. There is very little difference in time between when a second baseman or shortstop receives the ball and when they are taking it out of their glove to try and turn a double play; the best middle infielders make this move as close to one action as possible. It is very difficult for an umpire to determine in real time whether a ball was dropped on the catch or on the transfer, and we don't [want] to have every dropped ball at second base reviewed, so drawing a clear line on what is and what is not a catch should help umpires and reduce the need for future replays on dropped transfers at second base.

But Cameron pointed out that applying the rule to catches made elsewhere around the field yielded rulings that flouted common judgments about what a catch is.[i] In one case, for example, right fielder Elliot Johnson

takes multiple steps after the ball enters his glove, crashed into the wall, and still maintains possession. He then spins to make a throw back into the infield but drops the ball while trying to retrieve it from his glove; the ruling is no catch, and on appeal, the ruling is confirmed. The fact that Johnson traveled with the ball in his glove is not enough to make it a catch; the play is ruled a hit because Johnson didn't make the transfer cleanly, even though the transfer occurred after making several steps with the ball in his glove.

Even worse, outfielders could game the rule to "create[ ]the exact play that the infield fly rule was designed to eliminate." Runners, Cameron explains,

are taught to get enough of a lead off the base to maximize their potential advancement in case the ball is not caught while still retaining their ability to return to their previous base if it is. When the ball enters the glove, the runner returns to their prior base in order to avoid a potential double play. Only now, the ball entering the glove is no longer the determining factor of whether or not the catch was made; that is now the ball moving from the glove to the hand.

Consider, he suggests, a situation with runners on first and second, fewer than two outs, and a fly or line drive hit to left field. A savvy left fielder, Cameron observes, should secure the ball and

---

[i]   *See also* Stephanie Katz, *Controversial, but Consistent: The New Secured Possession Rule,* SB NATION (Apr. 10, 2014), https://tinyurl.com/y3hmmh43. Most of the commentary, from teams, fans and other observers, was hostile to the new interpretation, largely because it conflicted with the long-standing understanding of what a catch is.

take a step or two towards the infield with the ball in his glove. The only reasonable decision the runners can make at that point is to return to their prior base, because any further hesitation will result in a sure double play. Once [the left fielder] sees the runners retreating, he should immediately drop the ball on the transfer, pick the ball up, and throw it in to a shortstop positioned close enough to the second base bag to tag the runner on second once he realizes he now has to try and advance, and then easily flip the ball to the second baseman covering the bag to force out the runner from first trying to move up for a second time in the same play.

Dave Cameron, *Baseball's New Strategy: Drop the Ball on Purpose*, FANGRAPHS.COM (Apr. 14, 2019). After Cameron's post (and criticisms raised by others), MLB's Rules Committee weighed in for the first time:

> Beginning with games played tonight, Umpires will enforce the rule according to the standards below.
>
> The Committee has determined that a legal catch has occurred pursuant to OBR 2.00 (Definition of Terms, "Catch"), or a valid force out or tag has occurred pursuant to OBR 2.00 (Definition of Terms, "Tag"),[j] if the fielder had complete control over the ball in his glove, but drops the ball after intentionally opening his glove to make the transfer to his throwing hand. There is no requirement that the fielder successfully remove the ball from his glove in order for it be ruled a catch. If the fielder drops the ball while attempting to remove it to make a throw, the Umpires should rule that the ball had been caught, provided that the fielder had secured it in his glove before attempting the transfer. The Umpires will continue to use their judgment as to whether the fielder had complete control over the ball before the transfer.

COMMENTS AND QUESTIONS

1. Overall. Do ease and certainty of administration justify the interpretation given at the beginning of the 2014 season, under which a catch is not counted if the ball is dropped while transferring it to the throwing hand? If they do not in general, do they, as Cameron suggests, at least with respect to middle infielders? What countervailing considerations are there—tradition? a sense of what the essence of a catch is? Does the availability of replay review affect your answers?

2. The catch rule and the infield fly rule. Is Cameron right that application of the no-catch-without-successful-transfer rule to outfielders

---

[j] The definition of a tag is comparable to that of a catch. It ends with this sentence: "If the fielder has made a tag and drops the ball while in the act of making a throw following the tag, the tag shall be adjudged to have been made."

essentially recreates the same tactical possibility that the infield fly rule is designed to foreclose? Is that a problem if so? If yes, what fix would you suggest?

   3.   *Rules and standards revisited.* Consider the suggestion that the rule that defines a catch as occurring when the fielder "hold[s] the ball long enough to prove that he has complete control of the ball" is fairly standard-like ("complete control" is vague), and that MLB's interpretation sought to displace or administer that standard by means of something more rule-like (not a catch if the fielder loses possession before transfer). Is this an accurate characterization? If so, do Cameron's concerns suggest any more general lessons about the relative costs and benefits of rules versus standards?

––––––––

   In the NFL, dramatic controversy has been generated by what has come to be called the Calvin Johnson rule. In 2010, Johnson, a wide receiver for the Detroit Lions, appeared to make a go-ahead touchdown catch in the final seconds of a game against the Chicago Bears, but he was ruled to have lost possession before completing the process of the catch. *See* https://tinyurl.com/nphehui7. The rule came back to haunt the Dallas Cowboys in a divisional-round playoff game against the Green Bay Packers in 2015. Dez Bryant of the Cowboys appeared to have caught a crucial fourth-down catch, putting the ball within the one-yard line, but like Johnson he was ruled not to have caught the ball because he lost possession as he hit the ground. *See Cowboys vs. Packers: Dez Bryant's Non Catch | 2014 Divisional Round Playoff*, YOUTUBE, https://tinyurl.com/yc7lqcfz.

   NFL Rule 8, Section 1, Article 3, has consistently provided that, for a pass to be complete or intercepted, it is required that a player "who is inbounds"

   (a) secures control of the ball in his hands or arms prior to the ball touching the ground; and

   (b) touches the ground inbounds with both feet or with any part of his body other than his hands . . . .

Until 2015, a further provision, subdivision (c), required that the player "maintains control of the ball long enough . . . to enable him to perform any act common to the game (i.e., maintaining control long enough to pitch it, pass it, advance with it, or avoid or ward off an opponent, etc.)." A Note added:

   Note 1: It is not necessary that he commit such an act, provided that he maintains control of the ball long enough to do so. . . .

The rule further provided:

   If the player loses the ball while simultaneously touching both feet or any part of his body other than his hands to the ground, or if there is any doubt that the acts were simultaneous, it is not a catch.

Item 1: Player Going to the Ground. If a player goes to the ground in the act of catching a pass (with or without contact by an opponent), he must maintain control of the ball throughout the process of contacting the ground, whether in the field of play or the end zone. If he loses control of the ball, and the ball touches the ground before he regains control, the pass is incomplete. If he regains control prior to the ball touching the ground, the pass is complete.

In response to the controversy that the Dez Bryant incident sparked, the NFL rewrote subdivision (c) to require that the player

maintains control of the ball after (a) and (b) have been fulfilled, until he has the ball long enough to clearly become a runner. A player has the ball long enough to become a runner when, after his second foot is on the ground, he is capable of avoiding or warding off impending contact of an opponent, tucking the ball away, turning up field, or taking additional steps (see 3-2-7-Item 2).

Rule 3, Section 2, Article 7, Item 2, to which this Rule cross-referenced, provided in similar, but not identical, terms: "A player becomes a runner when he is capable of avoiding or warding off impending contact of an opponent." The rulemakers eliminated Note 1. And the balance of the quoted portions above was amended as indicated in the markup below:

If the player loses the ball while simultaneously touching both feet or any part of his body ~~other than his hands~~ to the ground, ~~or if there is any doubt that the acts were simultaneous~~ it is not a catch.

Item 1. Player Going to the Ground. <u>A player is considered to be going to the ground if he does not remain upright long enough to demonstrate that he is clearly a runner.</u> If a player goes to the ground in the act of catching a pass (with or without contact by an opponent), he must maintain control of the ball ~~throughout the process of contacting~~ <u>until after his initial contact with</u> the ground, whether in the field of play or the end zone. If he loses control of the ball, and the ball touches the ground before he regains control, the pass is incomplete. If he regains control prior to the ball touching the ground, the pass is complete.

NFL rulemakers were explicit that the rules changes were made for ease of determining when a catch is made. John Keim, *NFL adjusts rule defining catch*, ESPN.com (Mar. 23, 2015). But the change lasted only three years.

In 2018, the rulemakers changed subdivision (c) again, eliminating the "clearly become a runner" test and restoring the "act common to the game" language, so that now it requires that the player,

> after (a) and (b) have been fulfilled, performs any act common to the game (e.g., tuck the ball away, extend it forward, take an additional step, turn upfield, or avoid or ward off an opponent), or he maintains control of the ball long enough to do so.

And the rulemakers added a new Note providing:

> *(2)   If a player, who satisfied (a) and (b), but has not satisfied (c), contacts the ground and loses control of the ball, it is an incomplete pass if the ball hits the ground before he regains control, or if he regains control out of bounds.*[k]

QUESTION

Given subdivisions (a) and (b), what (if anything) is the need for a subdivision (c)? Under the then-prevailing rule, should Johnson have been deemed to have caught the ball? Bryant? How about under an ideal rule? Under the 2015 amendment? Under the 2018 amendment? Did the 2015 amendment improve the rule? The 2018 amendment? If a rule defines a catch more narrowly than an intuitive sense of the term, but yields ready determinations with great regularity, is that a good tradeoff? Did either of the amendments achieve this objective? Can you think of ordinary legal contexts in which a rule that would otherwise be suboptimal may be justified by considerations of administrability?

Exercise 3H

What is the best of all sports? No doubt, any answer to this question will be irreducibly subjective to some degree. But that does not mean that nothing objective can be said on this score, or that no genuine reasons could be adduced to support the relative value of one sport or another.

-----

[k]   In 2018, the rulemakers also eliminated as unnecessary numbered Items that applied to catches at the sideline and in the end zone. Instead they added the language that is underscored below in the prefatory language to the Rule:

> A forward pass is complete (by the offense) or intercepted (by the defense) <u>in the field of play, at the sideline, or in the end zone</u> if a player, who is inbounds:

It seems even the new language is superfluous. At the same time, the rulemakers shortened a Note, which had read:

> *Note: If a player has control of the ball, a slight movement of the ball will not be considered a loss of possession. He must lose control of the ball in order to rule that there has been a loss of possession.*

The new version reads simply:

> *(1) Movement of the ball does not automatically result in loss of control.*

That is certainly terser. So terse as to be cryptic?

The legal scholar Harry Kalven once contended that "baseball is the best of all games," and offered several grounds for this judgment. As the eminent philosopher John Rawls later recalled, Kalven cited six factors:

> First: the rules of the game are in equilibrium . . . . The physical layout of the game is perfectly adjusted to the human skills it is meant to display and to call into graceful exercise.

> Second: the game does not give unusual preference or advantage to special physical types, e.g., to tall men as in basketball. . . .

> Third: the game uses all parts of the body . . .; per contra soccer where you can't touch the ball. It calls upon speed, accuracy of throw, gifts of sight for batting, shrewdness for pitchers and catchers, etc. And there are all kinds of strategies.

> Fourth: all plays of the game are open to view . . . . Per contra football where it is hard to know what is happening in the battlefront along the line . . . .

> Fifth: baseball is the only game where scoring is not done with the ball, and this has the remarkable effect of concentrating the excitement of plays at different points of the field at the same time. Will the runner cross the plate before the fielder gets to the ball and throws it to home plate, and so on.

> Finally, there is the factor of time . . . . Baseball shares with tennis the idea that time never runs out, as it does in basketball and football and soccer.

The Best of All Games, BOSTON REVIEW (March/April 2008). (Were Kalven's factual assertions correct? Do you agree that his criteria are good ones for measuring the value of a particular game or sport? Would you add any criteria to the list? If you were arguing that baseball is the *worst* of all games, what criteria would you cite?) Relying on whatever you take to be the relevant criteria—and anticipating and addressing potential objections and counter-arguments—mount a case for the sport that you deem "the best of all games (or of all sports)."

CHAPTER 4

THE GAMEWRIGHT'S TOOLS

■ ■ ■

Suppose that you are a rulemaker for a sport and that you want to achieve some particular objective. For example, you might want to increase scoring, or keep contests closer, or elevate the importance of this or that skill or complex of skills, or reduce injuries. As Chapter 3 discussed, a reasonable gamewright might be motivated to promote any number of goods, and to avoid or reduce any number of bads. Whatever your regulatory goals might be, you will have a large but finite number of tools at your disposal. What those tools are is the subject of this chapter.

A. CONSTITUTIVE AND REGULATIVE RULES

We have said that rules are the soul of any game. But rules come in a large variety of distinct logical types. There are hortatory rules and mandatory rules, categorical rules, rules of thumb, and many more. (For an excellent survey, see FREDERICK SCHAUER, PLAYING BY THE RULES: A PHILOSOPHICAL EXAMINATION OF RULE-BASED DECISIONMAKING IN LAW AND IN LIFE ch. 1 (1991).) One distinction is particularly prominent in the academic study of sports and games. We gain purchase on the distinction by stepping outside of games for a moment and considering ordinary law.

Many rules issue commands. "Though shalt not kill" and "Honor thy mother and father" are familiar examples. A traditional view of law, associated with the 19th century legal philosopher John Austin, thus viewed law as "the command of the sovereign, backed up by sanctions." This model seems to make sense of the legal rules that probably spring most immediately to mind when one thinks about the law—the rules of the criminal law. Do not take property belonging to another. Do not have sexual relations with another person without their consent. Pay your taxes. These rules impose duties or obligations, and are backed by threat of punishment. They are often called "duty-imposing rules" or "sanction-backed commands."

But not all legal rules work like this. As H.L.A. Hart showed in his celebrated monograph, *The Concept of Law* (1961), the law of wills and contracts, for example, operates very differently from the rules of criminal law. Suppose that the law provides that a will is valid only if (among other things) it is attested by two witnesses. If you make a will and have it signed by only a single witness, the law provides that the will is not valid. But we would not (or at least should not) say that you have "violated" the law. After all, the law governing wills does not purport to command you to secure two witnesses, as the criminal law purports to command you not to kill, rape, rob, or possess contraband. All it does is specify the requirements that must be satisfied for you to effectuate the legal power to make it the case that other actors in the legal system (like probate judges) must follow your instructions. Duty-imposing rules direct what you ought or must do (or not do) regardless of your particular preferences or goals. What Hart termed "power-conferring rules" are indifferent to whether you comply with them. They specify the conditions that must be satisfied in order for specified consequences to be brought about, while adopting an attitude of indifference toward whether they are brought about or not. They provide, said Hart, that "[i]f you wish to do this, this is the way to do it." H.L.A. HART, THE CONCEPT OF LAW 28 (1961).

The distinction drawn by Hart is a close cousin to one often drawn by philosophers between **regulative rules**, which "regulate antecedently or independently existing forms of behaviour," and **constitutive rules**, which "do not merely regulate [but] create or define new forms of behaviour." JOHN R. SEARLE, SPEECH ACTS: AN ESSAY IN THE PHILOSOPHY OF LANGUAGE 33 (1969).[a] Constitutive rules assume the form "*X* counts as *Y* in context *C*." *Id.* at 51–52 (internal quotation marks omitted).

Constitutive
and
Regulative
Rules

Thus, for example, moving the king two squares toward a rook, and moving that rook to the square over which the king has crossed, counts as castling in chess. *See generally* JOHN R. SEARLE, THE CONSTRUCTION OF SOCIAL REALITY (1995). Very probably, most of the rules in most sports specify *how the game is to be played* rather than *what a player is forbidden to do* when playing it. A receiver in football does not violate a directive if he catches a thrown ball with his feet out of bounds; he simply fails in his attempt to perfect his potential power to advance the ball up the field. The rules of balls and strikes in baseball are similar: the pitcher has the power to retire the batter by throwing three strikes before four balls; and the batter has the power to advance to first base by remaining alive at the plate long enough to see four balls. The pitcher isn't commanded not to throw too many balls, and the batter isn't commanded not to allow too many strikes to pass. (That is, these are not directives of the rules of baseball; a player's manager, on the other hand, might issue commands of just this sort.) Contrast rules of this type with the rules that proscribe clipping or horse-collar tackles in football or prohibit a golfer from improving her lie in a

---

[a]   The distinction is related to one drawn by John Rawls, between *summary rules*, which are guides to decisions that are logically prior to the rules themselves, and *practice rules*, which are logically prior to the cases in which they apply. Rawls uses the rules stating what constitutes a walk and a strike-out as examples of the latter type of rule. John Rawls, *Two Concepts of Rules*, 64 PHIL. REV. 3 (1955).

sand trap by removing debris. These seem like commands, or regulative, or duty-imposing rules, not constitutive or power-conferring rules.

To be sure, the distinction between constitutive and regulative rules is subject to criticism. *See, e.g.,* Christopher Cherry, *Regulative Rules and Constitutive Rules*, 23 PHIL. Q. 301, 309 (1973); Frank Hindriks, *Constitutive Rules, Language, and Ontology*, 71 ERKENNTNIS 253, 253 (2009). It is hardly airtight; plainly, there are contestable or borderline cases, as well as rules that at least appear to have dual constitutive and regulative aspects. Accordingly, this book does not place heavy reliance on the distinction. Nonetheless, it is sometimes useful and should find a place in the student's conceptual toolbox. Whether the distinction has deeper significance beyond housekeeping convenience is a matter to which we will occasionally return.

COMMENTS AND QUESTIONS

1. Walking in golf revisited. Recall the Casey Martin case. How would you classify the rule requiring PGA golfers to walk—as constitutive, regulative, or somewhere in between? Is this substantively the same question as whether walking is essential to PGA golf? Are there constitutive rules of a game that are not essential? Are there regulative rules that are essential?

2. Other examples. Given that the rule that a batter gets to go to first base after four balls is constitutive, how about the rule that the batter gets the base after being hit by a pitch: constitutive or regulative? Or the rules of basketball that mandate loss of possession for traveling? Rules of soccer that prohibit handling the ball? The rule of ice hockey that generally prescribes a penalty when a defensive player shoots the puck over the glass, without deflection? Faults in tennis? Can any regulative rule of a game be restated as a constitutive rule?

3. So what? Can you think of any reason why proper classification of a given rule as constitutive or regulative should matter? What, if anything, might plausibly turn on it?

B. ARCHITECTURE, THE MARKET, AND INFORMAL NORMS

Conduct is often regulated—that is, shaped and influenced—by formal rules, such as the rules of a sport or game or the laws of a state or municipality. But many other forces regulate behavior as well. As Larry Lessig has explained, behavior is constrained not only by formal rules but also (1) by social norms, which "constrain because of the enforcement of a community," (2) by markets, which "regulate through the device of price," and (3) by what he calls "architecture," which he defines as "the world as I find it, understanding that as I find it, much of this world has been made." Lawrence Lessig, *The New Chicago School*, 27 J. LEGAL. STUD. 661 (1998).

Obviously, these other regulators of behavior can operate where formal rules are entirely absent, as when social norms encourage tipping though no formal rules require it. And where formal rules do apply, these other forces and constraints can either reinforce or work against what the formal rules require. For example, door and window locks (architecture) work alongside laws that criminalize burglary to deter house break-ins, whereas the vast supply and consequent low price of beer (the market) works against the efforts of lawmakers, wielding regulative rules, to reduce underage drinking.

Perhaps less obvious—and the point of Lessig's article—is that each of these other constraints can *itself* be regulated by law, so that they regulate actors' behaviors differently. Accordingly, he says, lawmakers have a choice: to regulate directly or to do so indirectly, by affecting the other constraints (or to do both). Thus, for example, if the government wants to reduce the consumption of cigarettes, it can: regulate the behavior directly, by enacting and enforcing a ban on smoking; attempt to shape or alter social norms, by running a public ad campaign that depicts smoking as ugly, foolish, and harmful to others; alter the market adversely to consumption, by imposing a high tax on cigarette sales; or change the architecture of cigarettes, by prohibiting nicotine in cigarettes or requiring lower levels, and so reducing their addictiveness.

If Lessig's thesis was news to ordinary lawmakers, it was probably old hat to gamewrights. At a minimum, most gamewrights are acutely aware both that a game's architecture profoundly affects regulatory objectives and that most features of the architecture are at least potentially subject to the gamewright's regulatory control. If, say, rulemakers in basketball, hockey, or soccer wished to facilitate more scoring in their sport, they could proceed either by tightening restrictions on permissible behavior by defenders or by increasing the size of the goal (and by other means as well).

What about social norms? Sportswriters and other journalists have in recent years paid increasing attention to the complex unwritten "codes of conduct" that operate in sports. How should rulemakers respond to these unwritten rules? To what extent should formal rules of sports displace, rely upon, or strengthen these informal norms?

Consider the case of beanballing in baseball. Pitched baseballs are dangerous projectiles. Hurled at speed often exceeding 90 m.p.h., they can break a batter's arm—or worse. While accidentally hitting a batter is part of the game (a batter hit by a pitch is awarded first base but the pitcher is not otherwise penalized), Major League Baseball has long prohibited pitchers from intentionally throwing at the batter, on pain of ejection. For just as long, however, pitchers have occasionally done just that—usually for showing them up in some fashion (as by taking too slow a home-run trot in a prior at-bat), or for violating some other (supposed) informal norm of the game (sliding dangerously, running on the pitcher's mound while returning to a base after a foul ball, being a cocky rookie, and so forth).

Perhaps the most common reason a pitcher will try to hit a batter is to retaliate for the opposing team's pitcher having hit a teammate. Indeed, despite the official rule, for most of baseball's history, the ban on intentionally hitting a batter was policed more by the players themselves than by the umpires. These informal norms are varied and fluid:

> "A lot of teams in the big leagues would throw at the next hitter who came up," said Hall of Famer Billy Williams. "Some teams would wait until the guy that could hurt you, the guy who drove in a hundred or hit thirty home runs, came up and would wait to get him. Other teams would wait until the pitcher was up, and they'd get him. Different ball clubs followed different versions of the rules."

JASON TURBOW WITH MICHAEL DUCA, THE BASEBALL CODES, at 121. But if there's diversity of opinion and practice regarding the whom and the when of retaliation, almost everybody agrees about the where: not at the head. In 1920, the Yankees' Carl Mays killed Cleveland's Ray Chapman with an inadvertent pitch to the head, the only fatality in MLB history. Since then, every generation has seen a star player's career abruptly ended or radically diminished by injuries sustained from an unintentional pitch to the head: Detroit's Mickey Cochrane in 1937, Tony Conigliaro of the Red Sox in 1967, the Astros' Dickie Thon in 1984, Minnesota's Kirby Puckett a decade later. As a result, "[e]ven if a hitter understands that he's about to be drilled, is fully on board with baseball's frontier justice, and is prepared to do nothing more than proceed to first base without issue after the fact, everything changes should the baseball arrive at or above shoulder level." *Id.* at 122. Outfielder Dave Henderson put the position colorfully: "You can drill me all you want. But if you throw at my face, it gets personal. I kill you first, then your grandpa, your grandma—I just go on down the list." *Id.*

In the 1990s, however, an apparent increase in hit batters and resulting bench-clearing brawls provoked MLB to strengthen its enforcement of the formal rule. Currently codified as Rule 6.02(c)(9), the provision prescribes not only that a pitcher and his manager can be ejected ("expelled") for intentionally pitching at a batter, but also that the umpire "may warn the pitcher and the manager of both teams that another such pitch will result in the immediate expulsion of that pitcher (or a replacement) and the manager." The league office instructed umpires to enforce these provisions more strictly, and particularly emphasized that umpires need not wait for a first offense to issue warnings: "If, in the umpire's judgment, circumstances warrant, both teams may be officially 'warned' prior to the game or at any time during the game." As umpire Tim Tschida explained, "Our general feeling on retaliation and fighting used to be one of 'it's over when they decide it's over'. Now it is over when *we* say it is over." ROSS BERNSTEIN, THE CODE: BASEBALL'S UNWRITTEN RULES AND ITS IGNORE-AT-YOUR-OWN-RISK CODE OF CONDUCT 140 (2008).

The new practice has met a mixed reception. Many players and coaches prefer a more robust role for informal enforcement because, they think, it's too hard for the umpires to discern when a pitcher is intentionally throwing at a batter or simply lacks good control. As former pitcher Rob Dibble queried, "How do you get inside the pitcher's head and know what he is really trying to do? Or how do you know if he didn't just let a pitch get away from him? So to have an umpire accuse a guy of throwing at someone intentionally, it is almost laughable." *Id.* at 144. And if umpires can't discern intent reliably, overreliance on formal rules and enforcement produces a variety of bad consequences.

For one thing, the risk that pitchers will be sanctioned when hitting a batter inadvertently might make them too cautious about throwing inside, thereby giving batters an undue advantage at the plate and causing them to no longer develop the important skill of avoiding the tight fastball when necessary. (See the discussion of overdeterrence, in Subchapter 6D.) On the other hand, umpires who are sensitive to the difficulty of discerning intent might be too reluctant to eject a pitcher who deserves it, choosing instead to warn both teams not to do it again. But if the umpire "issues a warning after the first guy gets hit in a game," former Twins' Manager Tom Kelly complained, "well then the other team is stuck. You either have to wait for another day, or another series, or even another season to get back at that guy." *Id.* at 139. Finally, even when an ump does correctly toss the first offender, some players and managers feel that ejection is the wrong sort of justice. As umpire Tschida observed, "Usually, the guy who is most upset at this point is the opposing manager, not the manager of the pitcher you just warned or tossed. The opposing club feels cheated because they didn't get their justice." *Id.* at 140.

Others disagree. Most significantly, many baseball insiders think that the umpires can discern pitcher intent well enough—especially because major league pitchers are skilled enough that they would rarely hit a batter in the head unintentionally. Thanks in part to a league practice of informing umpires before every game of any history between the clubs that might engender bad blood, Tschida believes that "I have enough faith in my judgment and in the judgment of my peers to know when a certain guy has to go." *Id.* Other commentators add that there's no quarreling with success, claiming that "The benefits of this policy are undeniable, because it minimized what seemed in the 1990s to be near-daily incidents of hitters charging the mound, as well as frequent occurrences of overt intimidation." TURBOW, THE BASEBALL CODES, at 122. Still others think that, because ejection is a modest penalty in a 162-game season and because umpires still are reluctant to enforce the rules when intent is at all in doubt, the ballyhooed changes in MLB practice have made little practical difference. Adam Felder, *Battering the Batter*, THE ATLANTIC, MAY 5, 2015.

COMMENTS AND QUESTIONS

1. Beanballing: informal norms versus formal rules. What do you think: Is it better for MLB to police pitcher retaliation by means of formal rules enforced by the umpires or through informal norms policed by the players and coaches? Is there an optimal combination of regulatory devices? Has the league hit upon that optimal combination? Is 6.02(c)(9) good as written? How should it be enforced?

Does your answer depend on the magnitude of the problem? Emphasizing that only a handful of batters have sustained disabling injuries from pitched balls over a century of play, "Black Jack" McDowell, the 1993 American League Cy Young winner, disputed that the incidence of beanings "is out of control and we need to deal with it." TURBOW, THE BASEBALL CODES, at 123. Does it matter that knowledgeable observers agree that, in accord with the informal norms, pitchers rarely do attempt to strike a batter's head? Is the risk of injury from a pitch entirely a bug of baseball or is it partly a feature? (See Subchapter 3G.)

2. Rule interpretation. A comment to Rule 6.02(c)(9) adds: "To pitch at a batter's head is unsportsmanlike and highly dangerous. It should be—and is—condemned by everybody. Umpires should act without hesitation in enforcement of this rule." What is the force or upshot of this comment? The rule itself prohibits "intentionally pitch[ing] at the batter," not "intentionally pitching at the batter's *head*." Does the comment imply that umpires *should* hesitate to expel a pitcher who (in their estimation) intentionally throws at a batter's back? Does it imply that umpires should warn or expel a pitcher for throwing near a batter's head even when unintentional?

3. Architectural solutions? Should MLB make greater use of architectural regulation to address the problem? In 1954, Joe Adcock of the Milwaukee Braves, one day after hitting four home runs against the Brooklyn Dodgers, was beaned by Dodgers pitcher Clem Labine. Although it wasn't required at the time, Adcock was wearing a helmet, and many observers believed it saved him from serious injury. Both leagues soon required protective headgear, and since 1983, MLB has required helmets with ear flaps. Paul Lukas, *Alex Torres and the history of headgear in baseball,* ESPN.com (Apr. 22, 2015). Ear flaps might have prevented serious injury to Conigliaro, for example, but plainly did not adequately protect Thon or Puckett. Should MLB mandate the use of helmet facemasks, as worn in fastpitch softball? Or would that improperly alter the balance of power between pitcher and batter by encouraging the batter to crowd the plate without fear of an inside pitch? (Note that MLB limits the size of hard plastic "body armor" by batters precisely out of concern not to upset the competitive balance between pitcher and batter.)

4. Informal norms generally. Legal scholars and other social scientists have paid increasing attention to social norms in recent years, often concluding that such norms are surprisingly nuanced and that, in some contexts, they affect people's lives more profoundly than does formal law backed by the state. The pathbreaking work is ROBERT ELLICKSON, ORDER WITHOUT LAW: HOW NEIGHBORS SETTLE DISPUTES (1991), a study of norms among farmers and ranchers in Shasta County, California. Ellickson found that these communities tended to resolve disputes without reference to the formal law—about which they were often ignorant—or its agents, such as policemen and judges. Instead, they most often resolved their disputes cooperatively, according to an informal code followed by members of their community and backed by informal sanctions such as shaming and ostracism. Even lawyers representing members of the community tended to be guided more by such norms than by formal law.[b]

In general, what considerations help determine when informal norms are most useful as a means to regulate behavior in sport? Consider the following observation:

> Some rules that could potentially contribute to the attractiveness of a contest are not implemented by the organizer due to prohibitively high enforcement costs. Thus, the gains from implementing these costly rules cannot be realized directly by the contest organizer. It can, however, be beneficial for contest participants with an encompassing interest in the profitability of the contest, to enforce a subset of these rules as norms amongst themselves. When monitoring and sanctioning costs are sufficiently low to leave the individual participant of a contest with a net gain from the norm enforcement, unofficial profit-enhancing norms may be enforced by the contestants.

Alexander Fink & Daniel J. Smith, *Norms in Sports Contests: The Tour de France,* 26 J. SPORT MGMT. 43 (2012). Are Fink and Smith suggesting that whether a sport should directly regulate some behavior or leave its regulation to informal norms turns upon how costly formal enforcement would be? If so, do you find this suggestion persuasive? Complete? What other considerations, if any, might be relevant? For example, are informal norms more likely to prove effective at the professional or amateur levels? In domestic or international competitions?

5. Informal norms and hockey. Another sport with a vibrant code of unwritten enforcement rules is hockey. Consider the following explanation of the role that hockey enforcers serve:

> For the most part, fighters are there to keep the peace and protect their skill players. For teams to have success, they have to put the puck in the net, and that requires talented players who are usually smaller and faster than the other guys. . . .

[b] For other illuminating discussions of informal norms in specialized communities, see, e.g., Lisa Bernstein, *Opting Out of the Legal System: Extralegal Contractual Relations in the Diamond Industry,* 21 J. LEGAL STUD. 115 (1992); Mark D. West, *Legal Rules and Social Norms in Japan's Secret World of Sumo,* 26 J. LEGAL STUD. 165 (1997).

This is where enforcers come in. Enforcers keep a watchful eye on their star players and make sure that the opposition thinks twice before taking any liberties with them. [For example, the Anaheim Mighty Ducks, having lost their two best players, Paul Kariya and Teemu Selanne, for much of the 1997–98 season because of rough injuries,] brought in tough guy Stu Grimson to protect them. The mere presence of the "Grim Reaper" on the bench that year sent a clear message to the opposition: stay away from Kariya and Selanne, or else. Teams couldn't employ dirty tactics to slow the stars down, and it gave the players more space on the ice to do what they did best: score goals. And do you know what? It worked. That next season Kariya and Selanne ranked number two and number three in the scoring race, respectively . . . .

Ross Bernstein, The Code: The Unwritten Rules of Fighting and Retaliation in the NHL 32–33 (2006).

Some observers believe that the norm of retaliation may be diminishing in the NHL, in part because of increased threats of suspension for fighting, increased emphasis on player safety, and the presence of a second referee, giving greater efficacy to official rule enforcement. But the norm clearly retains force. When Milan Lucic of the Boston Bruins put a vicious hit on goalie Ryan Miller of the Buffalo Sabres in 2011, many fans were surprised by the lack of retaliation—for which Sabres players expressed shame. "I'm embarrassed that we didn't respond the way we should have," said center Paul Gaustad. Jeff Z. Klein & Stu Hackel, *Novel Approach in N.H.L.: Turning Other Cheek*, N.Y. Times, Nov. 21, 2011. At the teams' next meeting, Gaustad fought Lucic, and got the worst of it, as the referees stood by. The TV producer was ready, presenting a "Tale of the Tape" with the combatants' heights and weights, as if they were boxers.

Lucic was not suspended for the original hit, on the ground of lack of intent. Should he have been suspended? In general, would hockey be better if the league tried to prohibit all fighting and took on more of the burden of enforcement against misconduct? Or is it better if fighting is tolerated subject primarily to unofficial player-policed norms regarding its use?

6.　*Conduct versus architecture, again.* Recall the decision by the USGA and the R&A regarding anchored putting. (See Subchapter 3E.) The *Explanation* emphasizes that the new rule governs playing rather than equipment; it is a ban on anchored *strokes* (principally but not exclusively putts) rather than on anchored *clubs*. In other words, it is a direct regulation of conduct rather than a regulation of architecture. An alternative regulatory approach—architectural in spirit—might have regulated the length of putters. If you favor a ban on anchored putting, do you think that the governing bodies went about this in the best way? Should the rule have limited the length of putters but allowed them to be used in any which way, or should it have allowed putters of any length but regulated the method of using them? What are the relevant considerations?

Exercise 4B

Baseball provided one famous example of recourse to architectural regulation when, aiming to assist hitters after the unusually low-scoring season of 1968, it ordered that the height of the pitching mound be lowered from 15" to 10." *See generally* William Leggett, *From Mountain to Molehill*, SPORTS ILLUSTRATED, Mar. 24, 1969, https://tinyurl.com/y22 fvss6. If Major League Baseball wanted to increase scoring today, what rule changes, involving both direct and indirect strategies, could it adopt? Try to identify ten distinct possible rule changes and be prepared to discuss the likely advantages and disadvantages of each.

PART II

STRUCTURING THE COMPETITION

■ ■ ■

In the last chapter, we discussed various considerations that might guide development of a game's rules. Now we focus on issues related to the overall structure of a competition. We begin in Chapter 5 with a discussion of various issues related to determination of a contest's winner. We ask questions such as: Must there be a winner? What criteria should determine who wins? If the contest is scored, should the winner be the side with the best total score or the one who has won more of some designated unit of competition? How, if at all, should ties be broken? Chapter 6 explores penalties. Once a gamewright has determined to prohibit this or that conduct, it must also decide whether to enforce that prohibition with a penalty or sanction. What form the penalty should take and what its magnitude should be are the chapter's principal topics. In Chapter 7, we discuss eligibility to compete, including issues related to professionalism, citizenship and residency, sex and gender, and age. Chapter 8 examines questions of performance enhancement, considering the extent to which sports ought to limit competitors' use of drugs, of technologically advanced equipment, and of prosthetics meant to overcome disabilities. Chapter 9 looks at challenges in structuring competition in leagues and tournaments.

CHAPTER 5

WHO WINS?

■ ■ ■

Among their numerous functions, the rules forming and informing sports specify the evaluation system through which value is assigned to goal achievements. Evaluation systems translate goal achievements into uniform, computable, and, therefore, comparable tallies. This is extremely important in competitive sports, in which the addition of these translations is what determines the results of particular contests. Sport-evaluation systems also stipulate the value of the results of particular contests. Such systems help governing bodies manage season-long competitions or tournaments, including round-robin phases in which contestants are ranked. Evaluation systems tend to enjoy a high degree of stability. Nonetheless, because sports are not rigid and closed structures that do not evolve, gamewrights occasionally introduce changes to evaluation systems.

Cesar R. Torres & Peter F. Hager, *Competitive Sport, Evaluation Systems, and Just Results: The Case of Rugby Union's Bonus-Point System*, 32 J. PHIL. SPORT 208, 208 (2005).

When learning about a new game or sport, one of the first questions you are likely to ask is, "How is the winner determined?" This chapter addresses five topics related to that basic question. Subchapter 5A examines contests in which the winner is determined without any type of scoring, usually by which competitor (first) accomplishes a given task. Subchapter 5B introduces the concepts of *measured* and *count* scoring, distinguishes among subtypes of count scoring, and examines tradeoffs among those subtypes. Subchapter 5C concerns ties and draws, focusing on when differences in performance might be so trivial that a tie ought to be declared, on when ties or draws should be allowed to stand, and on how they should be broken. Subchapter 5D discusses mercy rules and other ways of cutting short a contest. Subchapter 5E explores issues arising from *judgmental* scoring—the evaluative scoring systems deployed in many aesthetic sports like figure skating and gymnastics and in many combat sports including boxing and MMA.

A. WINNING WITHOUT A SCORE

In some types of contest, who wins does not depend on any kind of score but on which contestant achieves a given goal, or on who does so first. We could think of head-to-head races this way: Although, in formal competition, the race will be timed, that is for record-keeping purposes only. Of course, we *could* say that the winner is the runner with the lowest time, a form of measured score, but there is no need to do so: The winner can be determined without the clock, simply by determining which runner crossed the tape first.

In some other sports, the criterion could not even be expressed as a score. Chess, as it is usually played, is an example: In a given game, if your opponent does not resign, forfeit, or run out of time, the only way you can win is by achieving checkmate. And in boxing, under the Marquess of Queensbury Rules of 1867, there was no limit on the number of rounds; ordinarily, absent a foul or forfeit, the only way to achieve victory was to knock the opponent out. (The Rules incorporated an earlier set of rules under which, in case of certain interferences, "it shall be in the power of the referee to award the victory to that man who in his honest opinion shall have the best of the contest." *London Prize Ring Rules*, WIKIPEDIA, https://tinyurl.com/y3uawtog.) Fights of more than 20 rounds were rather routine, and in 1893, Andy Bowen and Jack Burke, competing for the vacant lightweight title, fought 110 3-minute rounds over more than seven hours. Neither man answered the bell for the 111th round. The bout was called no contest, though that was later changed to a draw. David Wallechinsky & Irving Wallace, *Boxing Sports Oddities and Trivia*, MINI-ENCYCLOPEDIA OF SPORTS ODDITIES AND TRIVIA, https://tinyurl.com/y4v45spf. Similarly, until the middle years of the twentieth century, there were no time limits on sumo bouts. Nor were there limits on the length of bouts in the early years of Ultimate Fighting Championship (UFC); these were expected to continue until one contestant was knocked out or unable to fight.

Nowadays, most combat sports still provide a goal that, if achieved, gives immediate victory: a knockout in boxing, for example, or a pin in wrestling. But they also provide time limits, and in most cases a secondary method of awarding victory in case neither contestant achieves the primary goal. Thus, professional boxing uses a vote of the judges, a form of judgmental scoring, and wrestling relies on a point system.

Can you think of other sports in which victory is ordinarily awarded without any form of scoring? How could it be scored?

B. TYPES OF OBJECTIVE SCORING

The winner of a high jump competition is the competitor who clears the highest bar. The winner of a baseball game is the team that scores more runs than its opponent. What's the difference between these two methods of evaluation?

One way to capture the difference is by reference to the difference between *measuring* and *counting*. Although often conflated, these are distinct processes. Measuring is continuous or analog; counting is discontinuous or digital. You measure your height or weight, but count your teeth or toes.[a] The high jump uses measured scoring; baseball uses count scoring. As a rough generalization, sports with multiple competitors tend to use measured scoring whereas sports that are played as two-competitor contests tend to use count scoring. (Why? Can you think of exceptions?)

Measured scoring uses a variety of scales: throwing competitions measure distances, lifting competitions measure weight, races measure temporal order, and so on.

---

[a] The distinction corresponds to a linguistic one: "Much" and "less" should be used with continuous variables, and "many" and "few" with countable ones. So, for example, it is appropriate to say that there is "less sand" in one jar than another, but "fewer marbles." Oddly, though, the jars that are filled more fully contain "more sand" and "more marbles." Why this linguistic asymmetry? Should we contrast "less" with "more," but "fewer" with "manier"?

Count scoring depends on discrete, countable scoring elements, called "points" in numerous sports (football, rugby, volleyball, and tennis, for example), and by a variety of different names in other sports—"runs" (baseball, cricket), "goals" (soccer, hockey), "strokes" (golf), "touches" (fencing), and so on. But now notice that sports do the counting in very different ways. In basketball, the winning team is the one that scores more points. In volleyball, by contrast, the winning team is the one that wins more sets, with each set being awarded to the team with more points. Basketball-type scoring may be called *aggregate* scoring, because the winner is the team with the highest aggregate count across the entire contest. And we will refer to volleyball-type scoring as *unit* scoring, because each set is a unit that is won and lost as a whole; however close or wide the margin is for each unit does not affect the count of units. We can think of each point as an atom and units such as sets as molecules. Aggregate scoring counts all the atoms. Unit scoring counts molecules; atoms are worthless to a side unless it wins enough to form a prescribed molecule before the other side does, or it forms a bigger molecule within a given span of competition.[b]

Some sports use one form of scoring or another, depending on the competition. For example, in most golf tournaments, each player competes against the rest of the field, and of necessity medal (aggregate) scoring is used. But in some tournaments, players compete head to head, and then the competition is traditionally by match play: the winner of the match is the one who wins the most holes, a form of unit scoring, rather than the one who complete the course in the fewest number of strokes.

The choice in counting method affects multiple-day or multiple-contest competitions. In fact, the choice may affect whether a given competition is conceived of as a single contest or as a series of contests. Consider Test cricket. Each side has two innings, contested over several days. But in any meaningful sense, the match is one contest, because the scores are aggregated over both innings. But an event like the Ashes, between Australia and England, is best considered a series of contests, usually five, because the scores are not aggregated across the matches; the winner of the series, and the Ashes urn, is the side that wins the greater number of matches, but all matches are played even if one side has clinched the series win.

One could, however, imagine a series like the Ashes being decided by aggregate scoring, notwithstanding a break of more than one day in competition and a shift of venue; soccer frequently uses a "two-legged tie," aggregating scores across matches at each side's home field, to determine advancement in tournaments. By contrast, in North American team sports,

<hr/>

[b]   One coauthor, noting that even "unit scoring" is aggregative, prefers the terms "atomic aggregation" (e.g., basketball) and "molecular aggregation" (e.g., tennis). For the most part, though, we adhere to the aggregate/unit distinction preferred by the other coauthor.

the winner of a competition in a post-season elimination tournament is the team that wins more games than its opponent (often best of three, or best of seven).

And indeed, one of the most dramatic examples of the difference between aggregate and unit scoring occurred in major league baseball. In the 1960 World Series, the New York Yankees outscored, outhit, and outplayed the Pittsburgh Pirates by almost any measure. The Yankees scored a total of 55 runs over seven games to 27 for the Pirates. And the Yankees won three blowout games. But the Pirates won four close games, and with them the championship. The Yankees of another generation wound up on the other side of the double-imbalance. In 1996, they were outscored by the Atlanta Braves 26–18, but they won the Series four games to two.

Simple aggregate scoring and simple unit scoring represent only two of the possible ways that a sport can use count scoring. For example, tennis uses what might be called *tiered unit scoring*—the match goes to the player with the most sets, a set goes to the player who wins the most games, with a game being a lower-tier unit that goes to the player who wins the most points. And note also that various combinations and intermediate choices are possible. For example:

- An overall competition may be scored in the aggregate, but with significance accorded to a unit victory. The most prominent example is probably multi-stage bicycle racing: The yellow jersey in the Tour de France goes to the biker with the best aggregate time, but a victory in each individual stage is highly valued.

- It is possible to have a system of unit scoring in which some units are worth more than others. The skins game, sometimes used for informal golf competitions, is organized that way. (So, more seriously and for better or worse, is the Electoral College, used to select the President of the United States and discussed more fully below.)

- Some sports use aggregate scoring but cap the magnitude of the contribution that any given unit may make to the final score. For example, in some youth baseball and softball games, there is a limit—typically seven—to the number of runs a team may score in a single inning. In miniature golf, there is usually a limit to the number of shots a player may take (and be charged with) on a given hole. And in jurisdictions that use the "10-point must" system for boxing and other fighting matches, there is an informal, non-absolute limit on the importance of a round. One boxer must receive 10 points in a round, and the other receives a number no greater than 10—but absent a knockdown a fighter will rarely receive fewer than nine points in a round, and even if knocked down he will usually receive eight.

What arguments justify use of one system or another? For simplicity, we will focus for now on the simple choice between unit and aggregate scoring.

The case for aggregate scoring is the easier one to make. Once it is determined *how* a contestant scores and *how much* value to accord to a scoring play, then it appears at least presumptively that the side with the greater score should win the contest. Indeed, that simplicity may be a virtue in itself. One way to think about it is that everything we need to know about the value of a scoring play is expressed in the score accorded to that play, and therefore the proper way of determining the winner of the contest is merely to add those values together.

Indeed, one could argue that any departure from aggregate scoring—any rule that allows one side to win the contest even though it loses more points—undermines the integrity of the contest. If the goal of the competition were to determine which is the better side at the particular sport, then aggregate scoring would also be the preferred choice. What better indication could there be of which side is better than that over an extended competition one side has won the most points? In 1960, the Yankees were almost certainly a better team than the Pirates—no knowledgeable fan comparing the rosters would deny that—and their respective performances in the World Series tend to confirm rather than refute that proposition.

There is considerable power in these arguments, and they put the burden on those who favor some form of unit scoring to show why it is justified in a given case. But there are in fact countervailing considerations, explored in the following comments and questions. In some circumstances these may be enough to justify unit scoring.

COMMENTS AND QUESTIONS

1.   Extreme patches. It may be that one competitor fares far better than the other in one rather narrow segment of the competition. If the differential is large enough, that segment alone can be enough to determine the winner under aggregate scoring, even though the loser outperformed the winner through most of the competition. Is that worrisome?

Prof. Michael Herz has argued:

In baseball, overwhelming victories are misleading. Maybe a team is just "on" one day, or it is beating up on the other team's only bad pitcher, or, the game having been lost, the losing manager takes out his best players to avoid injury. Counting a blowout equally with a squeaker avoids overvaluing this isolated and misleading triumph.

> That a team had a particular advantage on a given day does not mean it is a better team altogether.

Michael Herz, *How the Electoral College Imitates the World Series*, 23 CARDOZO L. REV. 1191, 1205 (2002). Are you persuaded? If Team A does slightly better than Team B throughout most of a competition but fails badly in one segment, and the margin of that one segment in favor of B is greater than the aggregate of the margins in favor of A through the rest of the competition, why should B not be the winner? Does the argument raised by Herz have more weight in some kinds of competition than in others? If so, can you identify critical considerations?

If you are persuaded by Herz's arguments, would you apply them *within* a baseball game as well as across games in a series? That is, should the winner of a baseball game be the team that wins the greater number of innings? Note that a game of pesäpallo, or pesis, a sport popular in Finland that resembles baseball in many respects, is by four-inning periods, with a one-inning tiebreaker if necessary. PESÄPALLOLIITTO, OFFICIAL INTERNATIONAL RULES (2003), https://tinyurl.com/yxun87cx. Either of these methods could be transformed into a mixed system by using aggregate score as the next tiebreak; another plausible possibility would reverse the hierarchy, counting aggregate score, as in traditional baseball, but making inning victories a decisive factor if the aggregate score was tied after nine innings. (The next subchapter will address tiebreaking in depth.) Presumably, a change from purely aggregate scoring to any method using unit scoring would provoke changes in team tactics. What changes do you think are most likely? Would they make baseball better or worse? Bottom line: would baseball be improved by adopting one of these changes? If you find Herz's argument persuasive at the level of a series but not at the level of a game, why?

2. *Consistency in format.* When a sport is usually contested in games of a given scope, arguably the same format should be preserved in season-ending or otherwise special competitions, even though those competitions themselves have greater scope or importance. But is there some grandeur in allowing Test cricket to spread over two full innings for each side (to cricketeers, each side's turn batting is called an innings), which requires more time than most competitions would allow? Would postseason baseball series be improved by transforming them into a single contest, spread over several days, of, say, 54 innings? In soccer, does it make sense to determine advancement in tournament play based on the aggregate score of a two-game home-and-home series? If you think that sometimes special competitions should preserve the ordinary format and sometimes not, what criteria do you think should govern?

3. *Guaranteeing a strong finish.* In an aggregate scoring system a contestant can build a big lead and nurse it, hanging on to the end. One might ask, "So what?" Aggregate scoring guarantees that a point near the beginning of the contest is worth as much as a point near the end or anywhere in the middle, and if one side builds an insurmountable lead early on, so be it.

But compare tennis as it is usually played with basketball. To win a tennis match, a player must win the last set, the last game, and the last point. No limping home is possible. As for basketball, note a statistical analysis of the 2005–06 NBA season, *Random Stat: Team Quarter by Quarter Results,* 82GAMES.COM, https://tinyurl.com/y3ary2do, that examined the belief that "NBA games are just back and forth and it all comes down to the last few minutes when the superior teams exert their will." In fact, the analysis contended, better teams tend to get and maintain an early lead; the correlations for that season between net points per quarter and overall winning percentage were: .85 for Q1, .67 for Q2, .75 for Q3, and .38 for Q4. *See* Joseph Skrokov, *Unit Scoring and the NBA* (unpublished manuscript, May 10, 2012).

4.   Crucial junctures. Unit scoring tends to create more crucial junctures in a contest, thus adding excitement to it. For example, suppose two evenly matched tennis players, in a best-of-three-sets match, stand at 6–5 in a first-set tiebreak. If the player with the lead wins the next point, and so the set, she has a 75% chance of winning the match—she need win only one of the next two sets. But if she loses the point, the match is dead even, so her chance is just 50%. That stake of 25% riding on a single point is huge; aggregate scoring cannot produce anything of the sort.[c] At the end of a competition as well, unit scoring is more likely to produce excitement. Consider again the 1960 World Series. It finished with a huge exclamation point, Bill Mazeroski's famous Series-ending home run, that would have been lost had the Series been scored on an aggregate basis. Of course matters could work out the other way; it could happen that, if scored in the aggregate, a contest would end with a thrilling comeback that nearly or completely erases a large lead and makes the outcome unclear to the very end, but if governed by unit scoring the same pattern of scoring would cause the contest to end in an anti-climactic blowout in the final, decisive unit (or perhaps, depending on the particulars, the unit-scored series would have been clinched before the surge even occurred). But that is less likely to happen; over the course of a long contest the more probable outcome is that one side or the other will build an aggregate lead that cannot practically be erased at the very end.

Assuming, for purposes of argument, that unit scoring does tend to increase the number of critical junctures, does that tend to undermine the integrity of the game, by giving some points artificial importance? Why *shouldn't* each point count the same? Consider, for example, the 2019 Wimbledon men's singles final. Roger Federer won more points than Novak Djokovic, 218–204, and more games, 36–32. He won two sets, by scores of 6–1 and 6–4. But three sets went to tiebreaks. Djokovic won them all, and the championship. Is tennis a better sport for being structured so that Djokovic rather than Federer took the trophy? Federer, by the way, has a remarkably

---

[c]   *See* Skrokov, *Unit Scoring and the NBA* (arguing that unit scoring in basketball, by increasing the number of critical junctures, would increase the value of, and therefore incentivize, defensive excellence) (unpublished ms., May 10, 2012); Allen Fox, *The Mental Edge: Keeping Score,* TENNIS.COM (Nov. 25, 2013) ("The tennis scoring system uniquely increases the stress of competition . . . and provides more opportunities to choke than other sports.").

poor won-lost record in matches in which the match loser wins more points. Why do you suppose this is so? Because, given his greatness, other players' best chance of winning is to get lucky in the allocation of winning and losing points? Because he never tanks on his opponent's serve? Because he sometimes tends to choke more often than his opponent on big points? *See* Ryan Rodenberg, *What Every Pro Tennis Player Does Better Than Roger Federer*, THE ATLANTIC, Jan. 13, 2014 (presenting the first two possibilities but not the third).

Also, does unit scoring increase the number of *unimportant* junctures? Suppose, for example, that after eight innings of play in Game 1 of the World Series one team is ahead 8–0. Compare how differently this situation would be treated, depending on whether the Series winner is the team that first wins four games or the team that scores the most runs after 54 innings.

5. *The aim of the competition?* Accepting, again for purposes of argument, that aggregate scoring is better at determining which side is better, is that an important consideration? Should the goal of a competition be to determine which side is better, or simply to test performance on the occasion in question, within an optimal, predetermined set of rules? If the true aim is to determine which team in a league is the best, should postseason tournaments be eliminated, and instead balanced schedules be adopted, with the championship being awarded to the team that has the best record over a season?

6. *Tennis and basketball: historical accident?* Tennis is a classic unit-scoring sport and basketball is a classic aggregate-scoring sport. Is there any reason other than historical accident for this? Would either sport, or both, be improved by adopting, or at least incorporating some form of, the other system?

Suppose, for example, that the whole of a tennis match were scored under the rules now used for tiebreakers. That is, Player A serves one point, Player B serves the next two, Player A serves the next two, and so forth, until one player reaches a prescribed number (say, 100, rather than the seven that is used for most tiebreakers) and is ahead by two. (This resembles the Van Allen Simplified (or Streamlined) Scoring System, VASSS, developed by promoter Jimmy Van Allen in the 1960s. *See, e.g.,* Frank Deford, *Anyone Care to Play Some VASSS?*, SPORTS ILLUSTRATED, July 19, 1965. VASSS did not catch on, but a related Van Allen innovation, the tiebreaker, did.) Would that change to an aggregate system of scoring be an improvement? Why or why not?

Now consider these possibilities for basketball. Would any of them (or some other variation) be an improvement over the simple aggregate system that is now used?

- Count the score by halves: If one team wins both halves, it wins the game. If the teams split halves, they play a short tiebreaker period to determine the winner.

- Divide the game into five periods; the winner is the team that wins three periods.

- Divide the game into quarters; the winner is the team that wins three quarters, with aggregate score used as a tiebreaker.

- Develop a system of tiered unit scoring like the one used in tennis. Thus, the winner of the game is the team that wins the most periods, and the winner of the period is the team that wins the most segments within the period. Segments would be limited by time, but one option could be to make time only a back-up limit: The rules could provide, for example, that a team wins a segment if it scores 20 points first or, neither team having reached 20, has the highest score at the end of eight minutes of play.

7.   *Team tennis tournaments.* Consider the scoring system used in some team tournaments conducted by the United States Tennis Association. Under these alternative rules, each flight plays short sets to four games. If the games are tied at three each in a set, the sides play a tiebreak to decide the set. If sets are tied at one each, then the sides play another tiebreak in place of a third set. Each side contributes to its team's score the number of games it has won, counting each tiebreak as a game. (Note that this is an intermediate form of scoring. A pure form of aggregate scoring would add up the number of points won by each flight. The norm in high school and college tennis is a multi-tiered form of unit scoring in which each match is scored the usual way and the team wins a point for each match won; another immediate possibility would be to give the team one point for winning each set—rather than point, game, or match.)

The aim of these unusual rules, presumably, is to make every game count, so that even a player who is losing badly knows that there is value in winning even a single game. But note an unfortunate consequence, which occurs with some regularity: A player could lose the first set 0–4, then come back and win the second set 4–3 and also take the tiebreak. That player has won the match, or so it seems—she has made an excellent comeback, and won out in a strong, exciting finish—but she has contributed only five points to her team, and the other player has contributed seven. So the winner in reality is the player who fell apart near the end and who lost the supposedly decisive tiebreak.

Is this a problem? If so, why? If you were to be persuaded that this is a problem—if you were to conclude, that is, that the winner of the match (as conventionally scored) should contribute more points to her team than the match loser contributes to hers—how could you fix this scoring system while still preserving an incentive for players who are losing badly?

8.   *Smaller elements in baseball?* Baseball certainly appears to be another aggregate-scoring sport: runs are the atomic scoring element, and the winner is the team that accumulates more runs. But are appearances deceiving? Consider this suggestion:

Runs in baseball are composed of *bases* in much the same way that, in tennis, *sets* are composed of *games,* and that games are composed of *points*. The similarity is obscured by the fact that we don't *say* that a team "scored" a base, as we say that a tennis player or side "scored" a point. But this is just a matter of semantics. The functional reality is that a run in baseball is itself a unit made up of four bases for a given player, just as a game in tennis is a unit made up of at least four points (and two more than the other side). Therefore, the atom in baseball is a base, and baseball employs molecular units, not an aggregate count of atoms.

Is this right? Are bases in baseball analogous to points in tennis, rendering runs roughly analogous to games or sets? (Hint: we think the answer is no, but it takes a little effort to figure out exactly why not.)

9. *Packet scoring.* Football is naturally characterized as a sport of aggregate scoring in which the atom aggregated is the "point."[d] However, unlike many other aggregate scoring sports, such as soccer and baseball, different types of scoring plays in football amass different numbers of these atoms: 6 for a touchdown, 1 for a PAT, 3 for a field goal, and so on. We might say that the points in football come in different sized "packets." The same is true of basketball, with 1-point (free throws), 2-point (field goals), and 3-point packets. What are the benefits of packet scoring? What are the drawbacks? Can you think of ways that a sport that doesn't use packet scoring could be improved by its introduction?

10. *Cancellation scoring.* Cornhole, a sport or game in which players toss fabric bags filled with sixteen ounces of feed corn or plastic pellets onto wooden boards placed twenty-seven feet apart, uses a variation of aggregate scoring called "cancellation scoring." Players each have a total of four bags and toss one bag at a time, alternating with their opponent until all bags have been thrown. The first team to reach twenty-one points wins, where tossing a bag on the board is worth one point and tossing a bag in the hole nets three points. Cancellation scoring provides that the points of one player cancel out the points of the opposing side; as a result, only one side can score in each inning. For example, if side A gets one bag in the hole and two on the board, and side B gets three bags on the board but none in the hole, B's 3 points will be subtracted from A's 5 points, and the inning will be scored 2 points for A and none for B. What is the competitive or tactical significance of cancellation scoring? Would a contest proceed differently if, instead of cancellation scoring, cornhole used ordinary aggregate scoring but increased the total points required for victory from 21 to 31? Note also that bocce uses a somewhat different type of cancellation scoring: Only one side scores in each frame, receiving one point for each bocce ball that is closer to the pallino (the target ball) than are any of the other side's.

---

[d] But is this a mistake? If the atomic scoring component in baseball is "really" a base, notwithstanding that we don't call the base a score, would it follow that football's atomic scoring component is a yard, in which case the count of points to determine a victor is a form of unit scoring?

11. Ordinality and alternatives in measured scoring: the decathlon. How should the decathlon be scored to maximize the chances that the winner will be most deserving of the unofficial title of "world's greatest athlete"?

One obvious possibility would be to rank all finishers in each event from 1 to n (where n is the total number of competitors), add up each competitor's scores from all events, and then designate the person with the lowest total score as the overall winner. This is a wholly *ordinal* approach, which is to say that it takes account only of the *order* of the participants' finish in each event.

A simple ordinal system provides no "winner's premium." For example, a competitor who finishes first in five events and third in the other five would get the same total score as an opponent who finishes second in all ten events; the fact that the first competitor *won* five events would be ignored. Assuming this is a flaw, it could be addressed by making a slight adjustment to an ordinal system, setting the point awards so that they do reflect a winner's premium. That is, the difference between the points awarded for first and second place could be made greater than the difference between the points for second and third, which could be greater than the difference between the points for third and fourth, and so on.

Perhaps a more significant defect of a purely ordinal system is that it entirely disregards magnitudes of differences in competitors' performances. For example, if A and B finish third and fourth, respectively, in the javelin, and fourth and third, respectively, in the hurdles, the two competitors would be tied with 7 points even if there was a very large absolute gap in their performances in one of the events and a tiny gap in the other. Most observers believe that a sound scoring system must be based, at least primarily, on *differences in athletic performances* rather than on *differences in rank order*. But figuring out how best to do this presents a challenge because the scores in the discrete events cannot be simply added together to produce total scores.

First and most obviously, individual events are measured in different types of unit—units of time for the running events (100m, 400m, 110m hurdles, 1500m), and units of distance for jumping (high jump, long jump, pole vault) and throwing events (discus, shot putt, javelin). Not only do the units differ for these types of event, their valences are reversed. In time-scored events, lower numbers are better than higher ones, whereas higher numbers are better than lower numbers for all the distance-scored events. (If that were the only problem, though, it could be solved easily, perhaps by subtracting the time scores from the distance scores.) Finally, a simple additive approach would not work well even *within* event classes: It would not be sensible to add the times in all four running events to produce a single aggregate running score, because differences in short events like the 100m run would be swamped by larger differences in longer events like the 1500m. And the same is true of jumping and throwing events.

How would you solve these difficulties? What standard would you apply for trying to determine how to compare, say, a difference of 0.1 seconds in the 100m run and 1.5 seconds in the 1500m run? And would you incorporate a "winner's premium"? For a clear explanation of actual decathlon scoring, see John Barrow, *Decathlon: the Art of Scoring Points,* THE NRICH PROJECT at UNIVERSITY OF CAMBRIDGE (June 2012).

12. The Electoral College. The President of the United States is elected by a device, the "Electoral College," that uses a form of unit scoring (i.e., "molecular aggregation"). Putting a few complexities aside, each state is assigned a number of electoral votes equal to the sum of Senators and Representatives it is allotted in Congress. For the three presidential elections following the 2010 census, the most populous states, California and Texas, had 55 and 38 electoral votes, respectively, while seven states, and the District of Columbia, were each allotted the fewest possible electoral votes: three. Each state's electoral votes are then awarded to the candidate who won the most popular votes in that state. In consequence, a candidate can win the electoral vote, and thus the presidency, while receiving fewer popular votes than an opponent—an outcome that has occurred five times, most recently in 2016 when the losing candidate, Democrat Hillary Clinton, received nearly 3 million more votes than the victor, Republican Donald Trump. Such an outcome would be impossible under aggregate scoring (i.e., "atomic aggregation").

We observed early in this subchapter that aggregate scoring is the natural default in sports, and that unit scoring is warranted when but only when some special justification can be offered. (Did you agree?) If anything, that posture seems even more compelling in the current context: in a democracy, office holders should, presumably, be the people preferred by the most voters. What, if anything, can be said in favor of unit scoring when it comes to electing the American president?

If you think that unit scoring for the presidential contest is justified, should the units be weighted by population or unweighted? That is, if there are good reasons to abandon aggregate scoring here, why shouldn't the winner of the popular vote in each state be awarded exactly one electoral vote, in much the same way that a tennis player is awarded exactly one set whether she wins that set 7–6 or 6–0, and whether that set is the first out of five or the fifth?

If you think the current system is not defensible, is the principal problem the use of unit over aggregate scoring as such, or the allocation of electoral votes by the total number of a state's Representatives and Senators, rather than by population or, what would approximate that allocation, by the number of Representatives alone. California's 2010 population (37.3 million) was a whopping 66 times as large as Wyoming's (564,000), but it was awarded only 18.33 times as many electoral votes; if Senators were eliminated from the allocation formula, California would have 53 times as many electoral votes as Wyoming—still not quite what the population disparity alone would dictate, but much closer. Wouldn't this be a fairer system?

If so, would it be fairer to scrap the electoral college entirely? Of course, that would require a constitutional amendment, which less populous states would block. So what do you think of the National Popular Vote Interstate

Compact? Every state that joins that plan commits to appoint electors who would vote for whichever candidate wins the nationwide popular vote regardless of how that candidate performs in its own state. The Compact would go into effect when signed by states that collectively represent 270 electoral votes, which is the minimum needed to secure the presidency. *See* NATIONAL POPULAR VOTE, https://www.nationalpopularvote.com/. Should your state join that Compact?

Two states—Maine and Nebraska—eschew the winner-take-all method of awarding their electoral votes that every other state uses. Instead, they provide that the popular winner in each congressional district wins one electoral vote, and that the statewide winner gets the state's two additional electoral votes (those allotted the state in virtue of its two Senators). What are the costs and benefits of this alternative approach?

C. DRAWS, TIES, AND TIEBREAKING

Not infrequently in life, contests and competitions reach their ordinary or expected conclusions without resolution. Juries deadlock, competing candidates for office receive the same number of votes, opposing teams notch equal scores. We often refer to such circumstances as "draws" or "ties." More often than not, we look for ways to *break* a tie, enabling us to declare a winner. What *are* draws and ties? Under what circumstances should they be tolerated as a final result? When a tie should be broken, by what means? These are the principal questions examined in this subchapter.

1. TIES, TIEBREAKERS, AND DRAWS

Suppose you receive offers of post-graduate employment from two law firms. Both offers contain the same financial terms, and the two firms promise equally interesting work and comparably attractive colleagues. It's a hard decision for you. Discovering late in your deliberations that Firm A's building features a well-appointed gym for the use of all tenants, and that Firm B's does not, you accept A's offer. Before you focused on the gym, you might say, the two firms were "tied" in your mind; the gym, as it turned out, was "the tiebreaker."

This is a customary use of the terms. As the U.S. Supreme Court has observed, when decision is governed by multiple factors or considerations, "any one factor will act as a tiebreaker when the other factors are closely balanced." *Metropolitan Life Insurance Co. v. Glenn*, 554 U.S. 105, 117 (2008). Nonetheless, legal scholar Adam Samaha argues, there is a stricter or more restrictive sense of tiebreaker that would not cover cases such as these. *See* Adam M. Samaha, *On Law's Tiebreakers*, 77 U. CHI. L. REV. 1661 (2010). A "tie," suggests Samaha, "means any equality relevant to an observer." *Id.* at 1666. But a tiebreaker is not simply any variable that *turns out* to be decisive. Rather, he proposes, "tiebreaker" refers "to a decision rule that is, at least in part, purposely designed to rank options that would otherwise be considered tied." *Id.* at 1668.

This definition can be made clearer by invoking the concept, introduced by John Rawls, of **"lexical"** (or "lexicographical") **ordering**. *See* JOHN RAWLS, A THEORY OF JUSTICE 42–43 & n.23 (1971). When multiple factors bear on a decision or outcome, those factors need not all be equally important or weighty. How to define when one factor is more important than another is not self-evident, but here is a case in which it is clear: Two options are identical except that (a) option 1 contains good-making factor F to n degree (however that may be measured) more than option 2, (b) option 2 contains good-making factor G to n degree more than option 1, and (c) (for any n greater than zero) option 1 is preferable to option 2. Given these assumptions, factor F is more important than factor G. But we must look further to determine in which of either of two senses—lexical and nonlexical—F is more important. Suppose first that, no matter how much more of G option 2 has, option 1 is preferable if it contains even a very little bit more of F; in other words, *any* degree more of F conclusively resolves the decision in favor of option 1. Then we can say that F has lexical priority over G. Now suppose instead that if option 2 has G to, say, 10 times n degree more than option 1, it is preferable to option 1, though option 1 still has F to n degree more than option 2. Then F does not have lexical priority over G, but we can still say it is more important in a nonlexical sense.

Lexical Ordering

Consider the example above, of the two law firms competing for your services. Suppose that, for you, salary is "the most important factor." What does that mean? Most likely, you mean that you would opt for Firm A if it offers somewhat higher salary than Firm B even if Firm B offers, say, somewhat more interesting and challenging work. In this case, salary has greater importance, in a nonlexical sense, than all other factors. Salary would take "lexical" priority over all other factors only if you would accept an offer from the firm that offers you the most money—even just $1 more than another firm—regardless of any other differences between firms (like the challenge and interestingness of its work or the attractiveness of its environment) that might favor alternatives. That is, as we said, unlikely. Contrast alphabetizing. As Samaha, following Rawls, rightly notes, this "is the paradigmatic form of lexical ordering: ordering indicated by an earlier letter in a word always trumps anything suggested by a later letter." Samaha, *Law's Tiebreakers*, at 1669 n.20. This is why "azure" (a light purplish blue) ranks ahead of "baa" (a bleating sound) in the dictionary. The ranking of hands in poker is also lexical: the hand A, 6, 4, 3, 2 (unsuited) beats K, Q, J, 10, 8 (unsuited), notwithstanding that the total point value of the second hand (48) is significantly higher than of the first

(26), because the highest card in the first hand (Ace) beats the highest card in the second hand (King).

Judo scoring is lexical as well. If either contestant scores an *ippon*—a throw that places the opponent on his back with impetus and control—that earns an immediate victory. Two *waza-ari*—a throw onto the back but with insufficient force to merit an ippon—do so as well. But if one contestant has been awarded a single *waza-ari* and the other none, the first wins the match, no matter how many awards of *yuko*—a throw onto the side—the second may earn. And, as we will explore in depth later, advancement to league post-seasons or to bracket play in tournaments is almost always determined by lexical rules: If one team has a slightly better won-lost record than another, we don't look past that; if those records are the same, we might look next to head-to-head record, and so forth.

Contrast judo scoring with scoring in other combat sports. Take as an illustration professional boxing, in which judges use four criteria to score the outcome of any given round: clean punching, effective aggressiveness, ring generalship, and defense. *See, e.g.*, 19 CRR-NY § 211.42. Though it is sometimes said that a judge should give equal weight (whatever that means) to the four stated criteria, most appear to give greatest weight to clean hitting. *See* Frank Lotierzo, *Clean Punching Counts Most*, THE SWEET SCIENCE (June 2, 2003). But in any event, there is no lexical ordering: A large difference in defense, for example, will outweigh a small difference in clean hitting. Thus, if a judge believes that fighters in a given round are evenly matched in clean hitting, we would not say that the round is tied, nor would we say that the other factors will act as tiebreakers, though they will turn out to be decisive; the judge simply has not yet completed analyzing the factors that contribute, non-lexically, to who should be awarded the round.

With the distinction between lexical and nonlexical ranking in hand, we can return to Samaha's definition: " 'tiebreaker' refers to a lexically inferior decision rule that is designed to rank options if and only if a lexically superior decision rule fails to rank those same options." Samaha, *Law's Tiebreakers,* at 1669. On this definition, a factor that ends up resolving a decision just because the other factors stand in equipoise is not a tiebreaker if those other factors are not given lexical priority over the factor that, in this case, is decisive. In contrast, the rules of sports leagues that decide which teams with equal overall won-loss records go on to the postseason based on such factors as total points scored, or head-to-head play, or strength of schedule *are* tiebreakers. They come into play only if the lexically superior decision rule—choose the team with the better overall win-loss record—fails to discriminate.

So much for ties and tiebreakers. What about draws? We sometimes treat ties and draws as synonyms. But the fact that some games and sports recognize ties and draws as different outcomes suggests that they aren't.

Cricket is perhaps the clearest example. A tie occurs when both sides have the same score at the end of the match. Ties are very uncommon in Test cricket. Draws, by contrast, are very common in cricket Test matches. To win a Test match, a team must score more runs than the opposing side and retire the other side twice. No matter how many runs it is behind, if a team is still batting when time expires, it gains a draw. Accordingly, a team that has reached a high score will often "declare"—that is, end its innings before its batsmen are all out—in order to give it a better chance to get the other side out before time expires.

A celebrated draw occurred in the first Test of the 2009 Ashes, the long-running series between England and Australia. England scored 435 runs in its first innings. After Australia scored 674 for 6 (that is, only six batsmen out—or, put another way, six wickets taken—out of a possible ten), it declared. In the second innings, Australia took England's first five wickets—usually its better batsmen—for only 102. But then the lower ranking batsmen proved hard to get out. At the end, England had scored 252 for 9 (for a total of 677). With unlimited time, Australia surely would have gotten one of England's last two batsmen out for no more than a few additional runs, and then scored the few runs necessary to clinch the match. But time was not unlimited, and the match was drawn. *See* Stephen Brenkley, *Ponting fury as England pull off the great escape*, THE INDEPENDENT (July 13, 2009). Note also the Fourth Test in the Australia-West Indies series in 1960–61, *West Indian cricket team in Australia in 1960–61*, WIKIPEDIA, https://tinyurl.com/y5ghcot9.

Draws are routine in chess, too. In chess, as it is ordinarily played, the only way for a player to win a match—if her opponent does not resign, forfeit, or run out of time—is to checkmate her opponent. Draws occur often when neither party has any discernible advantage, or at least not a significant enough advantage to offer any realistic chance of achieving checkmate. But it is also possible for a match to be drawn even though one player has a significant advantage, in material or position or both. A draw will be declared (or may be claimed) in these circumstances—no matter how great one side's material advantage may be:

(i)   One player is not in check but has no legal moves available.

(ii)   The same position is repeated three times.

(iii) Each player has made 50 moves without a pawn having been moved or any capture having been made.

FÉDÉRATION INTERNATIONALE DES ÉCHECS, LAWS OF CHESS, Art. 9. Furthermore, a game is drawn if a legal move yields a position "from which a checkmate cannot occur by any possible series of legal moves." LAWS OF CHESS, Art. 9.6. And an arbiter may declare that the game is drawn if the arbiter finds that the player with the advantage "is making no effort to win the game by normal means, or that it is not possible to win by normal means." LAWS OF CHESS, Art. 10.2.

In earlier days, there were no decisions in boxing matches: If both boxers were standing and fighting at the end of the match, no matter how badly beaten one was, the match was declared "no contest" or a draw. In 1893, as previously mentioned (p. 123), Andy Bowen and Jack Burke, fighting for the vacant lightweight title, fought 110 3-minute rounds over more than seven hours. Neither man answered the bell for the 111th round. The bout was called no contest, though that was later changed to a draw. Even well into the 20th century, in some places there was a "no-decision" rule under which a champion could lose the title only by a knockout. *See* INTERNATIONAL JEWISH SPORTS HALL OF FAME, *Lew Tendler*, https://tiny url.com/y5fqmdm9 (Tendler "soundly thrashed" Benny Leonard in 1922, but did not take the lightweight title from Leonard because of this rule).

COMMENTS AND QUESTIONS

1.   Ties and draws. Do these examples suggest that a general distinction can be marked between ties and draws? If so, what is the difference?

2.   Why draw? Are the draw rules in cricket and chess sensible? Are they optimal? What if anything can be said in favor of a rule in boxing or other combat sports that a champion can be dethroned only by knockout and not by being out-pointed?

3.   Multiple winners. In the game Cosmic Encounter, the aim of each player is to establish five colonies on alien worlds. The game ends when a player achieves this goal. If as a result of an alliance two (or more) do so on the same encounter, they are both declared winners. *Written Review—Cosmic Encounter,* INITIATIVE: TABLETOP, https://tinyurl.com/y2rgzb5y. Is this conceptually different from the game being drawn?

2.   WHEN SHOULD TIES BE RECOGNIZED?

The most common questions concerning ties are whether they should be allowed to stand, and, if not, how they should be broken. But occasionally a logically prior question arises: whether a tie should even be *recognized* given the possibility of detecting small differences of performance at the lexically highest level of scoring. This is often an issue in sports that use measured scoring, where one could reasonably question how finely the measurements should be made and whether we have sufficient confidence in the measurements to declare a winner.

Consider the case of Dominique Gisin of Switzerland and Tina Maze of Slovenia, who tied for first in the women's downhill skiing event at the

2014 Winter Olympics—each completing the 1.6-mile course, with a vertical drop of 2,600 feet, in 1:41.57. Each was awarded a gold medal. It was a feel-good moment for some, but it provoked an obvious question: why not measure more finely? Skiing, like bobsled and skeleton, reports times to the 100th of a second. But luge and speedskating record and report times to the 1000th of a second. Many wondered why skiing couldn't measure times more finely, as luge does, thereby perhaps preventing the tie. The question gains force from the fact that downhill times are *measured* and even *recorded* to the 10,000th of a second; per Skiing Federation rules, they're just not *reported* to that degree of precision. Though not certain, it's highly probable that, by reference to the measured and recorded times, one of Maze and Gisin was the sole winner that day. So why shouldn't the times be reported as they are measured?

Many thought they should be. The eighth-place finisher, American Julia Mancuso, deemed it "crazy that it comes down to one-hundredths [of a second] and there is not one-thousandths as a tiebreaker." Picabo Street, who sixteen years earlier had won gold in the Super G, by one-hundredth of a second, agreed: "If it's gaugeable, let's gauge it! If it's gaugeable, let me have it. If you've got it, give it to me! They give it to them in speedskating— why not here? Because we're going 80 miles an hour and coming 3,000 feet down a mountain? No, gimme that thousandth! I want it!" Jim Caple, *Skiers tie for downhill win*, ABC NEWS.COM (Feb. 12, 2014).

Mancuso's teammate Stacey Cook thought otherwise. "A hundredth is so close to begin with," she said. "Our sport is pretty amazing that you can cover two miles of distance in less than two minutes and still be that close. Ties are not a bad thing in sport. They both did equally as well. They both deserve the gold medal." Daniel Baumat, vice-president of Swiss Timing, the firm that times the events, defended the decision not to report times finer than to the 100th place. "When you start getting into such small numbers you cannot guarantee the integrity of that number," he explained. "It's an outdoor sport in a winter climate, a piece of flesh could be the difference." Bill Pennington, *First Tie for Alpine Gold, Though Not Precisely*, N.Y. TIMES, Feb. 13, 2014, at B15.

The winners were philosophical. "I don't think you can race for hundredths of a second. Hundredths is always luck," Gisin said. "But luck comes back once in your life. One time you're on one side, one time you're on the other. Maybe just once you're in the middle, like today." Caple, *supra*. "I don't care if there are two happy faces afterward as long as I am one of the happy faces," Maze added. "I guess we will be linked together forever now. We'll become better friends." *Id.*

COMMENTS AND QUESTIONS

1. Tiny increments. What do you think: Should results in downhill skiing be determined by the thousandth of a second as they can be in speedskating? One commentator mocked the defense offered by Baumat, exclaiming, "That answer makes no sense. These aren't rickety old grandfather clocks we're talking about, but expensive and sophisticated machines that can measure with extraordinary precision. The real reason behind the FIS's failure to change the rules is likely inertia." Justin Peters, *There Wasn't Actually a Tie in the Women's Downhill. The Timekeepers Know Who Won.*, SLATE (Feb. 12, 2014). Do you agree?

In thinking through this question, it might help to have to hand the distinction between **precision** and **accuracy**. Although the terms are often treated as synonyms in ordinary usage, they represent distinct ideas. As a Wikipedia article puts the difference, "the accuracy of a measurement system is the degree of closeness of measurements of a quantity to that quantity's actual (true) value. The precision of a measurement system, related to reproducibility and repeatability, is the degree to which repeated measurements under unchanged conditions show the same results." *Accuracy and precision*, WIKIPEDIA, https://tinyurl.com/3aulda. If you throw half a dozen darts at a dartboard, and they all cluster very tightly together, but not near the bull's eye, you're precise but not accurate; if the throws are scattered evenly on around the bull's eye, then a scientist might say that you're imprecise but accurate. Do you think that Baumat would agree that his firm's devices are as precise as Peters claims, but that their precision exceeds their accuracy? Try to elaborate on why that could be. Are you persuaded? Is it helpful to know that, at the speeds top downhill skiers reach, they travel about an inch in a thousandth of a second? Is it more useful to distinguish "fineness"—the number of increments in the unit of measurement—from both precision and accuracy?

2. Fine-tuning vs. lexicality in weightlifting. Consider the following rules for ranking outcomes in Olympic weightlifting:

To calculate the individual ranking in Snatch and in Clean and Jerk the following factors in the following order must be considered:

1.　best result—higher first; if identical, then:

2.　bodyweight—lower first; if identical, then:

3.　best result's attempt number—smaller first; if identical, then:

4.　previous attempt(s)—smaller first; if identical, then:

5.　lot number—smaller first.

INTERNATIONAL WEIGHTLIFTING FEDERATION, Rule 6.7.2.

Notice to start that the rule nicely illustrates the hierarchical or lexical nature of tiebreakers: If competitor A lifts 1 kilogram more than competitor B but outweighs him by 50 kgs (110 pounds), one might reasonably conclude that competitor B's feat was more impressive. Still, competitor A would win because rule 2 is lexically inferior to rule 1. If the tie at level 1 is not broken at level 2, then the next three tiebreakers work like this: Rule 3 gives priority to the competitor who achieved his best result on fewer attempts at that weight; rule 4 gives priority to the competitor whose best result came after making a greater jump in weight from the next greatest weight he had attempted; rule 5 is purely random.

The frequency with which recourse must be made to rule 3 (and therefore to rule 4 or to rule 5) will depend on the fineness with which the weights at issue in rules 1 and 2 are measured. Lifted "weights are set in 1-kilogram increments," Rule 6.5.4, while bodyweight is ordinarily measured in 10-gram increments. See Rules 3.8.1, 6.3.5. Should either of these measurements be made finer? Should competitors, when tied, be allowed to increase their attempts in smaller increments—say, in 100-gram steps? Should bodyweight be measured as precisely as is technologically possible? (Readily available and inexpensive digital floor scales can measure bodyweight accurately to within .01 pounds.)

3.   *From weightlifting to fish weighing.* At the Bassmaster Classic fishing tournament, competitors are ranked by the total weight of the fish caught over three days, with each competitor limited to a maximum of five fish per day. If two or more competitors are tied after three days, they compete in a fish-off the following day. Fish are weighed in pounds and ounces, disregarding fractions of ounces. *2020 Academy Sports + Outdoors Bassmaster Classic presented by Huk—Results,* BASSMASTER.COM (Mar. 2020). Is this a good system? As you would expect, the tournament is held Friday to Sunday. If a fish-off is required it would be held Monday, when the fans will already have returned home. Should the Classic weigh fish to the quarter ounce? Why or why not?

4.   *Weight-adjusting performance.* Should the lexically primary scoring rule in Olympic weightlifting incorporate both weight lifted and body weight in some function? In fact, powerlifting and weightlifting organizations do combine these two numbers—by means of the "Sinclair Formula"—to determine the overall "best lifter" *across* weight classes at a competition. ("Best lifter" is thus like "best pound-for-pound" fighter, an informal or mythical title that fans of combat sports will argue about.) But the Sinclair Formula is not used to determine standings *within* a weight class for the award of medals. Should it be?

And what about indoor rowing? The C.R.A.S.H-B (Charles River All Star Has-Beens) Sprints, held in Boston every March, are the World Indoor Rowing Championships. Participants compete on indoor rowing machines called ergometers, or "ergs," in 2000-meter races, where classes or events are determined by age, sex (or gender), and a variety of physical and intellectual disabilities. As in actual on-water rowing, indoor rowing also recognizes two weight classes: lightweights (165 pounds or less for men, 135 pounds or less for women) and heavyweights. Within each class, competitors are ranked purely by time, where winning times range widely depending on class of competition: in the open men's category, winners will usually break six minutes.

On the water, though, weight matters. Concept 2, the world's leading manufacturer of ergs, explains:

> Generally, a larger, heavier athlete is capable of producing more power than their smaller teammate. In many cases this results in the larger person scoring better on the erg. This does not tell the whole story, because in on water rowing, greater body weight submerges the boat deeper in the water. This creates drag that must be overcome by the power of the rowers. The heavier the rower, the more drag on the boat, and the more power that rower will have to produce to be equal to their lighter teammate. The erg does not penalize the heavier rower in this way, so a heavier rower may appear to have a higher potential than they really have when it is time to get into the boat.

Weight Adjustment Calculator, CONCEPT 2, https://tinyurl.com/yxngl9xb. According to Concept 2's adjustment calculator, a 210-pound competitor who completes the 2k in 6:10 has rowed the same "effective" time as a 170-pounder who takes 6:28. But as is sometimes said, "ergs don't float." To get a more accurate measure of rower ability to help move a boat, should the C.R.A.S.H-B Sprints discount raw erg times by rower weight?

5.   *Tarmoh's torso.* In the Gisin-Maze case, there does not appear to have been any doubt that the times were accurate, to the degree of precision they were reported. But now consider the difficult problem that arose in the race held to determine who would represent the U.S. in the women's 100 meters dash at the 2012 Olympics. Carmelita Jeter and Tianna Madison finished first and second, in 10.92 and 10.96 seconds, respectively. But there were three spots to be won, and it was unclear, even with the use of a photo-finish camera shooting 3,000 frames per second, whether Jeneba Tarmoh had beaten Allyson Felix. Part of the problem, as explained by Roger Jennings, the highly experienced and capable photo-finish judge who made the initial call of that race, is how finishing is defined in track and field:

> In horse racing, . . . it's easy: You go by the horse's nose. In auto racing, the front of the car. In speedskating, by the skate. In cycling, by the wheel. It's the first thing that crosses the line. In track and field, it's the torso. And there is subjectivity in determining where the torso is. That's what we got into in the women's 100 meters.

Jennings had no difficulty determining when Felix's torso crossed the line. But Tarmoh was twisted, and her torso was obscured. Jennings did his best, working from visible data points on Tarmoh's chest and bicep, to "interpolate" when the forward-most spot on her torso crossed the line. The computer then spat out a time of 11.067 for Tarmoh and 11.068 for Felix. But these times were unofficial, and Jennings asked to consult with referees. Ultimately, it was decided that one, Bob Podkaminer, would make the decision. After consultation of more than 20 minutes, Podkaminer, without disputing the interpolation made by Jennings, decided that the race should be declared a dead heat, with both racers being given times of 11.068 seconds. (We will address later the procedures created to break the tie.)

Podkaminer later explained: "In many cases, you can interpolate. But these are the Olympic trials, where there has to be a more exacting standard. An interpolation is not fact. At some point, I might be asked to stand up and justify what I decided." Tim Layden, *Photo finish examiner details how trials race was deemed a dead heat,* SPORTS ILLUSTRATED, June 27, 2012. For images of the finish, see Jonathan Baum, *Allyson Felix-Jeneba Tarmoh tie in 100 meters to be broken by run-off or coin flip,* YAHOO! SPORTS (June 24, 2012). For a discussion of the technology and process for identifying winners, see Sam Borden, *When a Dead Heat Is More Than a Photo Finish,* N.Y. TIMES, June 24, 2012.

Given that the best judgment that could be made was that Tarmoh had crossed the line first, should the place on the Olympic team have been awarded to her? Put another way, should Podkaminer have been more reluctant to award the place to Tarmoh on the basis of the evidence available than to *deny* her that award given that evidence? Was Podkaminer right in being less willing to determine a result on the basis of "interpolation" in this case, given the stakes, than he would have been in a less significant race?

Now suppose the photo evidence had yielded clear evidence that Tarmoh finished a thousandth of a second ahead of Felix. Should a place on the Olympic team be awarded on the basis of such a difference—or should a race that close be deemed a tie, in which some tiebreaking rule would need to be invoked? What if race officials could determine finishing times to an additional significant digit? Suppose, for example, that Tarmoh clocked 11.0682 seconds against Felix's 11.0683 seconds. If you think it would still be better to declare Tarmoh the winner, are you willing to say the same thing no matter how many digits out you have to go to find a difference between the two?

Would your answer to the previous questions be different if runners raced seriatim "against the clock" instead of simultaneously "against each other"? Either way, is measurement by ever-decreasing units a way to *break* ties or rather a way to *avoid* them? Does it matter?

If the difficulty, as suggested by Jennings, is subjectivity and determining where the torso is, should a different, more easily administrable, rule be used? What would that be?

6. *Fine measurements and count scoring.* Ordinarily the problem of whether a close contest should be deemed to be a tie does not arise in count scoring, in which discrete components make up the score: The contest is tied if the sides have exactly the same score, and not otherwise. A difference of one point in a high-scoring basketball game means that the game was close, and probably exciting, but 113 is greater than 112, and the team with 112 goes home the loser. But in some settings a difference might be deemed too small to

determine a winner. Consider a fight that goes the distance with two judges scoring it a draw but the third scoring one fighter ahead. What should the result be: a decision for the fighter who one judge thought won, or a draw on the ground that that's what a majority of judges favored? In boxing and the UFC, the fight will be ruled a majority draw. Does that strike you as the right result? And what if there has to be a winner, because the match is part of an elimination tournament? In that case, the fighter favored by one judge should prevail, no? Not necessarily. In a 2014 bout between Ian Stephens and Roger Zapata on *The Ultimate Fighter*, a majority draw with one judge favoring Stephens turned into a victory for Zapata pursuant to a rule that directed each judge in such circumstances to just "circle the winner."

Occasionally, too, there are contests in which a counterpart to the Gisin-Maze problem might arise: The numbers are so great, and the apparent difference so small, that one might argue that the difference is too small to determine a winner, especially if there is a plausible chance that it is a product of error. Interestingly, the rules governing award of the Oscars previously provided that the two top contestants would each win the award if they were within three votes of each other. Thus, in 1931–32, Fredric March (*Dr. Jekyll and Mr. Hyde*) won one more vote than Wallace Beery (*The Champ*) for the Best Actor award, but they were both given the award. ACADEMY OF MOTION PICTURES ARTS AND SCIENCES, TIES IN ACADEMY AWARD VOTING (Feb. 2020), https://tinyurl.com/y4lobe6x. The rules have since been changed, so that only exact equality in votes will yield a tie. Katharine Hepburn (*The Lion in Winter*) and Barbra Streisand (*Funny Girl*), tied for Best Actress in 1968, and there have been four ties in other categories. *Id.* Was this change for the better? In the 2000 Presidential election, some observers suggested that the result in Florida ought to be declared a statistical tie, because of the difficulty of determining a winner with any confidence.

3. WHEN SHOULD TIES REMAIN UNBROKEN?

In many or most contexts, ties are roundly disfavored. As the common expression has it, ties "are like kissing your sister." Yet it is surely too strong to conclude that ties must be broken. Indeed, ties have often been tolerated as a final result in competitions in which single winners are the norm. We have already seen some examples: the Gisin-Maze tie in the 2014 Olympics women's downhill race, and a few ties for Oscar awards. Here are some others:

- The "World Series" in 1885 and 1890 that pitted the National League champ against the winner of the winner of the American Association ended in 3-3-1 ties.

- In 1969, Denny McClain and Mike Cuellar tied for the American League Cy Young Award. And the National League vote for Most Valuable Player in 1979 was a tie between Keith Hernandez and Willie Stargell.

- The 2002 major league baseball All-Star Game was declared a tie after 11 innings, after the managers reported to the Commissioner that they had no pitchers left. Note that, by contrast, the 1967 and 2008 All-Star Games were each played 15 innings, the National League winning 2–1 in 1967 and the American League winning 4–3 in 2008.

- Elections occasionally are tied. Most often the tie is broken in one manner or another. We will discuss below how such ties might be broken. But for now consider another intriguing possibility—simply letting the result stand as a tie (or a draw). That is essentially what happened in the 1984 Israeli election; neither of the two leading parties could form a government, so they decided to form a national unity government, with the two party leaders each serving two years as prime minister.

- Ties used to be routine in regular-season NHL games; from 1942 until 1983 season, a tie at the end of regulation stood as the final result. The league then introduced a single five-minute overtime. Beginning in 1999, the NHL has given one point in the standings to a team that loses in overtime. And since the 2005–06 season, the league has eliminated ties altogether; a regular-season tie unbroken after one overtime period goes to a shootout.

- Until 1974, a tie after regulation in a regular-season NFL game stood as the final result. In that year, the league introduced overtime, but a tie after one 10-minute overtime period (shortened from 15 minutes in 2017) still stands. Until 1996, college football allowed ties to stand after regulation, with no overtime.

Two philosophers of sport have recently argued in favor of ties:

[L]eaving a contest as a tie is preferable to breaking a tie because breaking ties usually distorts the narrative coherence of the contest. This narrative coherence is made possible through the formal structure of sport that designates how relative abilities of contestants will be measured and compared. Tie-breaking procedures usually deny the validity of the comparison already established, attempt to establish a new and different comparison, and often do so in a way that alters the original means of comparison. It is for this reason that a tie is preferable to forcing a winner and a loser.

Sportspeople, interested in sporting contests properly constituted, understand that a tie is a meaningful resolution to a sporting contest—one indicating that two contestants performed to an equivalent degree. Despite a failure to make a distinction between the relative abilities of two sides, there is an affirmation that the performances of the two sides were fundamentally similar. It is for this reason that ties are so meaningful and must remain a potential end of sporting contests. . . .

A world of sport in which ties are accepted as legitimate measures of athletic excellence not only makes sense but also makes the most sense. Accepting ties tends to eliminate a source of inaccurate measures of athletic merit. . . . [F]orcing a winner and a loser after two sides could not outplay each other during the contest is unfair. A forced outcome does not truly reflect equivalent performances by undeservedly rewarding only one side. Rather than obscuring the internal purpose of competitive sport, letting ties stand serves and honors sport's key distinguishing features.

Cesar R. Torres & Douglas W. McLaughlin, *Indigestion?: An Apology for Ties*, 30 J. PHIL. SPORT 144, 147–48, 153–54 (2003).

COMMENTS AND QUESTIONS

1.   The virtue of ties? Are you persuaded by Torres and McLaughlin? When, if at all, is it necessary or desirable to declare a winner? Do you think views on that question are likely to be socially contingent? Consider whether, in each of the following sports, a regular-season game should be ended as a tie if the teams have the same score at the end of regulation or after a limited period of overtime competition: (1) football; (2) soccer; (3) basketball; (4) baseball; (5) hockey. How do you explain the fact that in recent decades the major North American football and hockey leagues have become less tolerant of ties as a final result, but in baseball a tie was declared in the All-Star Game in 2002 though clearly in an earlier era the game would have gone on? As you read the following material on the various methods for breaking ties, consider whether the Torres & McLaughlin view cuts against all tiebreaking procedures or only some of them.

2.   Incommensurability. Notice that Torres and McLaughlin speak of "equivalent" rather than "equal" performances. What's the difference? Sometimes "equivalent" means something like "not equal, but close enough." Two men, measured at 6′3¼″ and 6′3½″ tall, respectively, can't be "equal" in height given that their heights are measurably different. But they are

Incommensurability

"equivalent" in height if that modest ¼-inch difference doesn't matter for our purposes even when height is relevant (retrieving items from a high shelf, relegating passengers to a car's back seat, assigning players in a friendly pick-up basketball game, etc.). But "equivalent" might also be a near-synonym for "**incommensurable**," a relationship in which two options cannot be assessed by reference to a common metric and therefore are neither unequal (because neither is greater than or less than the other) nor equal (because the two quantities are not the same). Comparing "apples and oranges" presents a special challenge precisely because the items are not commensurable. Francisco J. Urbina, *Incommensurability and Balancing*, 35 OXFORD J. LEG. STUD. 575 (2015). Incommensurability is a deep and recurring problem for legal regulation.

4.   HOW SHOULD TIES BE BROKEN?

When rulemakers want to provide a procedure to break ties, several methods are available. For discussion of some of these, see Samaha, *Legal Tiebreakers*, at 1689–1700. As the case of weightlifting exemplifies, often more than one tiebreaker is provided, in hierarchical or lexical order. Consider whether the following menu of possibilities is complete. Consider too what are the relative advantages and disadvantages of each option and whether particular tiebreaking procedures with which you are familiar in sports or outside of sports should be changed.

(1)   *Continue standard play after regulation.* In sports that determine winners by count scoring, it is usually possible to break ties by continuing play past the regular termination of the contest. This can be done in at least two different ways. The first is to play for a standard pre-determined period of time; the second is to play only until a countable and fair difference is produced. Sometimes, both methods are used, the former as a first tiebreaker and the latter as a second tiebreaker.

The first method, overtime play for a predetermined period of time, is the rule in basketball; for example, 5-minute overtime periods are used in the NBA and in the NCAA. And there is no limit on the number of overtime periods, if the game remains tied after each. There have been three seven-overtime NCAA games: Black Hills over Yankton, 80–79, in 1956; Cincinnati over Bradley, 75–73, in 1981; and Skidmore over Southern Vermont, 128–123 in 2010.

The second method includes both true and equalized "sudden death" tiebreaking procedures. Under true sudden death (sometimes called "sudden victory"), the first team to score in an overtime period wins. The NFL used true sudden death prior to the 2011 postseason, at which time it introduced a slight modification (discussed below). From 1992 to 2004, FIFA also used true sudden death: the first goal scored during overtime was dubbed "the golden goal" and ended the match. That remains the tiebreaking device used in NCAA soccer.

In sports in which possession, or the realistic opportunity to score, is regimented rather than fluid, true sudden death is often considered unfair. Some of these sports deploy a modified version of sudden death in which the second team to gain possession, or otherwise have the better opportunity to score, is still awarded a chance to equalize or win even if the first team has scored. We can call this "equalized sudden death." Thus, the home team in baseball gets last licks even in extra innings, and in tennis a win the traditional way requires a two-game margin so that the first server does not have an advantage. Recall the celebrated match at Wimbledon in 2010 between John Isner and Nicolas Mahut, which Isner won 6–4, 3–6, 6–7(7–9), 7–6(7–3), 70–68. The final *set* itself lasted 8 hours 11 minutes, which was 90 minutes longer than the previous record for an entire *match*.

Starting with the 2011 playoffs, the NFL introduced a hybrid model between true and equalized sudden death. Under these new rules, the first team to score in overtime wins (true sudden death) except that if the team that receives the overtime kickoff scores a field goal on that initial possession, the other team is nonetheless entitled to one possession (equalized sudden death). The second team would then win if it scores a touchdown on its first overtime possession, and lose if it fails to score. If it too scores a field goal, then overtime progresses in true sudden-death fashion.

(2) *Play an altered form of competition.* The best known tiebreaking mechanism that employs an altered form of competition is soccer's. Many soccer matches are permitted to end in ties after 90 minutes of regulation play. In matches in which the breaking of a tie is more important (such as during the knockout stages of tournaments like the FIFA World Cup), the first tiebreaker is 30 minutes of overtime, played in two 15-minute periods without sudden death. If a tie remains after this overtime, the next tiebreaker is a shootout in which five players per team, on an alternating basis, take a shot on goal from the penalty mark. The team that registers more goals from the shootout wins. If they are still tied, then the shootout switches to a form of equalized sudden death, ending only after a round in which one team scores on the penalty kick and the other misses. Beginning with the 2005–06 season, the NHL has used a similar shootout after overtime, though with three initial shooters rather than five.

Similarly, in limited-over cricket and in tournaments, a "bowl-out" is sometimes used to resolve ties. In one form of bowl-out, five bowlers from each side deliver two balls each, but there is no batsman, so the wicket (three stumps with two bails on top) is unguarded. The winner is the team that puts down the greater number of wickets, knocking at least one of the bails completely off the top of the stumps (or, less likely, striking one of the stumps out of the ground). If the teams are tied after five bowlers, they continue the bowl-off and it is decided by (equalized) sudden death.

A less radically altered form of competition is to continue play under ordinary rules, but with fewer players, to increase the chance of scoring. Most prominently, in the NHL, since the 2015 season, each team must remove two skaters during overtime. An alternative would be to take just the goalies off. Players might also be taken off one by one after prescribed time periods if the game is still drawn. Commentators now and again propose that the shootout systems used in soccer and hockey be replaced with regular-play overtime periods in which players are removed sequentially until a tiebreaking goal is scored. The thought behind the proposal, of course, is that, within a relevant range, the lesser the density of players on the playing field, the easier it is to score.

NCAA football also uses a somewhat altered form of play in its overtime. As in baseball, teams take turns trying to score, and the game continues until one team is ahead at the end of a full round. But at the outset of overtime, each series begins with the ball 25 yards away from the goal line; also, beginning with the third round, if a team scores a touchdown it must go for a two-point conversion rather than kick for the safer one-point conversion. And, beginning with the 2019 season, from the fifth round on, teams alternate running two-point conversions from the three-yard line. Note also that the coin toss, to determine which team goes first, may affect the outcome, because the team that goes second has a distinct advantage in each round before the new conversion shoot-off. Arkansas and Mississippi played in a 7-overtime game (won 58–56 by Mississippi) in 2001. *Arkansas-Ole Miss football rivalry*, WIKIPEDIA, https://tinyurl.com/y689elvn.

(3) *Use some other measure of success, based on performance already completed.* In some sports, if neither side achieves its primary objective, then, instead of declaring a draw some other criterion for success is used. Recall that the old rule of boxing recognized only one basic way to win: by knocking out one's opponent. In modern boxing, what would have previously been a draw produced by the fact that neither boxer has knocked out his opponent at the conclusion of the bout will be broken in favor of the boxer who has scored more points, as determined by the judges. (How points are determined, and how the independent judgments of the several judges should be aggregated to reach a conclusion regarding which fighter has "more points," are separate questions addressed in Subchapters E1 and E2, below.) Similarly, in wrestling, if there is not a pin, the winner is determined by points. And there is a counterpart in some time-limited chess tournaments: If neither player achieves checkmate in the allotted time, a winner may be determined by adjudication of the final position.

In other settings, a tie is broken by using a secondary determinant of success that played a role in calculating the primary determinant, and so in some sense is being double-counted. For example, to determine season standings, a soccer league typically uses a formula such as three points for a win and one for a tie. When point totals are equal, one common tiebreaker is total goals scored (or total goals scored less total goals allowed). This is to double-count goals (or goal differential) because they are the components that determined the points total (i.e., the won-loss record) in the first place.

Fantasy football works just the same way. Most fantasy football leagues play their games head-to-head style: team A (consisting of players on different real teams) will be pitted against team B (also consisting of players on different real teams), with the winner being the team whose players totaled more fantasy points that week in the aggregate. Won-loss record is the first factor determining which fantasy teams go to the fantasy league playoffs. Total fantasy points scored is frequently the first tiebreaker.

(4) *Randomization.* As in the case of weightlifting, when sports use a random procedure to break a tie, such as the choice of lots or the flip of a coin, it tends to be the last in a series. Leagues often prescribe random choice as a final method to select teams with equal won-loss-tie records for postseason play. The NFL, for example, recognizes twelve (!) tiebreakers to determine a division champion when two or more teams tie for division lead based just on won-loss-tie record. These tiebreakers include: record in head-to-head competition (first tiebreak); record against divisional opponents (second tiebreak); strength of schedule (sixth tiebreak); and most net points in all games (tenth tiebreak). The final tiebreak is a coin toss. *NFL Tiebreaking Procedures*, NFL.com, https://tinyurl.com/y4tygajy.

Coin tosses are used outside of sports too. Occasionally, they have been used to break tied elections. *See, e.g.,* NEIL DUXBURY, RANDOM JUSTICE (2002); *Coin Toss Will Decide an Election in Illinois*, N.Y. TIMES, July 18, 1990, at A18.

(5) *Do-over.* At the 1928 Amsterdam Olympics, Argentina and Uruguay tied 1–1 in the goal medal match in soccer, necessitating a rematch three days later, which Uruguay won 2–1.

Recall the tie between Allyson Felix and Jeneba Tarmoh for the third and final spot on the U.S. Olympic team in the women's 100 meters. Incredibly, the governing body, USA Track and Field, did not have tiebreaking procedures already in place. After the tie was declared, however, it proposed that the two runners choose between a coin flip and a run-off to decide third place: if both women were to choose the same option, or if only one were to make any choice at all, that option would be used; if each selected a different option, a run-off would be held; and if both refused to choose, a coin flip would be used. Initially, the two agreed to a run-off, but the next morning, hours before it was to be held, Tarmoh—who had originally been awarded the spot and said that she still felt that she had earned it—withdrew, ceding the spot to Felix. (Tarmoh did participate in the Olympics, running a leg of the 4 × 100m relay in the qualifying round; she did not run in the finals, but was awarded a gold medal as a member of the team.)

COMMENTS AND QUESTIONS

1.   Generally. As the preceding review reveals, sports deploy a remarkable array of tiebreaking mechanisms, combining them in an even more impressive variety of ways. (And keep in mind that this is not a comprehensive list.) Do you think that most or all of the sporting authorities briefly canvassed have adopted tiebreaking schemes that are optimal for their particular circumstances, or do you think some have made bad choices? What considerations or desiderata do you think are most important when developing and assessing tiebreaking systems? For example, could you provide guidance regarding when it is better to use sudden-death or non-sudden-death overtime procedures? Is recourse to altered forms of competition, as in the soccer shootout, generally a bug or a feature?

2.   Field hockey. American collegiate field hockey uses a tiebreaking procedure similar to NHL regular season games: overtime consists of two sudden death periods with a reduced number of players on the field (from eleven to seven), and if the game remains tied after these periods have ended, each team selects five players to participate in a series of shootouts, with shootouts going to equalized sudden death if the teams remain tied after the five initial attempts. *See* Int'l Hockey Fed'n, Rules of Hockey 13 (Nov. 2020), https://tinyurl.com/yytcself; NCAA, 2020 NCAA Field Hockey Rules Modifications 8–11 (May 11, 2020), https://tinyurl.com/y5tzzc7v. Penalty shootouts in field hockey are akin to shootouts in ice hockey: a player takes on the goalie and has eight seconds to attempt to score, in any manner desired, in accordance with the normal scoring rules of the game. Some players prefer to shoot right away, while others will try to dribble around the goalkeeper.

Reducing the players on the pitch during the two overtime periods has largely forestalled recourse to penalty shootouts: during one recent season approximately 95% of collegiate field hockey games across all three NCAA divisions that ended regulation tied were resolved in the first or second overtime period. *E.g., 2019–20 Field Hockey D-I Overtimes Played,* NCAA Statistics, https://tinyurl.com/y5d74seh. Is this good news or bad? Given that a field hockey shootout involves more of the core excellences of the game, including dribbling, shooting, deception, reading the goalkeeper, and aggressive goalkeeping, than a simple penalty kick in soccer, which arguably involves little more than precision placement of the ball and good guessing by the goalkeeper, should we tolerate or even encourage the progression of more field hockey games to the shootout period to resolve the tie?

3.   Golf. Professional golf tournaments have experimented with a variety of tiebreakers. At one time, all of the men's major tournaments used 18-hole playoffs to determine a winner among any golfers tied after regulation. (Regulation is 72 holes over 4 days.) In 2018, the U.S. Open moved from an 18-hole playoff to a two-hole playoff. The Masters uses sudden death, while the British Open uses a 4-hole playoff, and the PGA Championship uses a 3-hole playoff. Which system is preferable? Tiger Woods, among other pros, prefers the full-round playoff on the grounds that it is a fairer and more accurate test of excellence than a couple holes. Many fans, in contrast, disfavor an 18-hole playoff because it requires an extra day. As one writer said after the 2018 change, "it's in everyone's best interest to crown a winner Sunday night." *Punch Shot: Bad call to end 18-hole U.S. Open playoffs?*, GOLF CHANNEL DIGITAL (Feb. 26, 2018). What would you recommend? If a tournament can be won and lost by a one-stroke differential after 72 holes, is there any reason why the same should not be true after 73 holes? And, if the first tiebreaker is anything other than sudden death, what should the *second* tiebreaker be? The U.S. Open now uses sudden death as its second tiebreaker (and so Woods won the 2008 U.S. Open over Rocco Mediate after 91 holes), but used to require yet another 18-hole round.

4.   *Marathon tennis.* Is the ordinary tiebreak—first to 7 points, win by 2—a good way to determine the winner of a set? Is there any justification for the rule used in the Olympics, Davis Cup, and, until 2019, all the Grand Slam tournaments other than the U.S. Open, that the tiebreak is used *except* in the last set, which must be won the old-fashioned way, by a margin of at least two games? (Note that in the 2010 Isner-Mahut marathon mentioned earlier, the third and fourth sets were resolved by tiebreaks.) The U.S. Open uses the ordinary tiebreak at 6–6 in a decisive set. Since 2019, Wimbledon has used an ordinary tiebreak if a decisive set reaches 12-all. The Australian Open instead now uses a 10-point tiebreak in a decisive set. The French Open now is the only one of the Grand Slam tournaments not to use a tiebreak in the decisive set; each of the four tournaments uses a different method of resolution when a decisive set reaches 6-all.

Should tennis instead resolve tied sets by using an alternative determinant based on performance already completed? The obvious solution would be to count total points in the set if the score in games reaches, say, 6–6. This approach would presumably eliminate marathon matches. It would also incentivize players to compete hard on every point, no matter what the score in the particular game. It would mean that a player could sometimes clinch a set by taking a 6–5 lead, or by scoring enough points in the following game. Would it be a good tiebreaking method overall? Why or why not?

5.   *Tiebreaking in baseball.* Baseball, we have noted, breaks ties that stand after the regulation nine innings by continuing standard play. But it could instead count some aspect of performance already completed. The game could go to the team that won the most innings, for example, or accumulated the most total bases, or had the most base runners, or got the most base runners safely to third base. How would a change along these lines affect the play of the game? If you prefer extra innings, do you think they should be the only tiebreaker, or would you favor recourse to another one—or a hierarchy of them—if the score remains tied after some specified number of extra innings (say, three, six, or nine)? Recall the fact, noted above, that the 2002 MLB All-Star Game was declared a tie after 11 innings. Should a secondary method of tiebreaking be used for all-star games even if not for other baseball games?

In the COVID-shortened 2020 MLB regular season, each half of an extra inning began with a runner on second base. The purpose of this rule change was to try to complete games faster to limit players' exposure to COVID-19 and avoid potential travel issues caused by the condensed season (teams played 60 games in only 63 days). The same rule has been used in the minor leagues to improve pace of play since 2018, and has caused a substantial increase in the percentage of extra-inning games to finish after 10 innings—from 45% (in the 2016 and 2017 seasons) to 73% after the rule change. *MLB Finalizes 2020 Rule Changes,* CBSSPORTS, https://tinyurl.com/y49rtdy5. However, MLB decided not to continue the rule for the 2020 playoffs and it is unclear if it will be used again in the future. What are the advantages and disadvantages of this approach? Should it be applied permanently? To the postseason?

6.   *A football auction.* The NFL and the NCAA use very different tiebreaking mechanisms. But consider instead an auction system: each team bids for the ball, it goes to the team that is willing to take it closest to the team's own goal line, and then the winner is determined by sudden death. At least three variations have been proposed. *See* Chris Quanbeck, *A New Overtime Format for the NFL—The Field Position Auction,* https://tinyurl.com/y2e9r2py. In one, the auction is open and starts from low yard lines, moving up one at a time; the coach who first throws a red flag gets the ball. In the second, the auction is also live, but it starts with high yard numbers, and the coaches take turns bidding lower numbers; the last bidder gets the ball. In the third, the bids are written, sealed in an envelope, and delivered to the referee. (To avoid the teams coming in with the same bid, one team might be told to use odd numbers and the other even, or one whole yard numbers and the other half-yard numbers.) In any version, the auction proposal has many virtues. Most significantly, it eliminates the influence of brute luck without introducing any new or wonky rules of play that differ from the rules that govern on-field play throughout the game. In addition, it creates a new and interesting tactical challenge for the coaches. Finally, it does without a kickoff, which is the most dangerous play in football. Would it be preferable to the system now being used? If so, do you prefer one of the three variants just mentioned, or another of your own devising?

If you favor the auction proposal, you might wonder why it hasn't gained more traction to date. Consider the possibility that a complete answer would involve the concept of **agency costs**. As a Wikipedia article explains,

Agency Costs

> "agency cost" is an economic concept concerning the cost to a "principal" (an organization, person or group of persons), when the principal chooses or hires an "agent" to act on its behalf. Because the two parties have different interests and the agent has more information, the principal cannot directly ensure that its agent is always acting in its (the principal's) best interests.

Common examples of this cost include that borne by shareholders (the principal), when corporate management (the agent) buys other companies to expand its power, or spends money on wasteful pet projects, instead of maximizing the value of the corporation's worth; or by the voters of a politician's district (the principal) when the politician (the agent) passes legislation helpful to large contributors to their campaign rather than the voters.

Agency cost, WIKIPEDIA, https://tinyurl.com/cu4sfp. Many legal doctrines and institutional practices are designed to minimize agency costs, to varying degrees of success. Plausibly, NFL coaches are agents, and NFL team owners are their principals. Can you think of any respects in which the interests of these principals and agents could diverge with respect to the resolution of ties, and with respect to the auction proposal in particular?

7.   *Avoiding the soccer shootout.* Here are some possible ways to resolve soccer ties, after 90 or 120 minutes. Consider whether they, or some other solution, are preferable to the current procedure, a shootout after 120 minutes. For all but the first, the rule could provide either for sudden death or for play to continue, in pairs of timed periods, until one team is ahead after completion of a pair of periods.

- Count some already-completed performance—perhaps corner kicks earned or shots on goal, or time of ball possession.

- Play on under ordinary rules, but provide that the goalie may not use hands on the ball.

- Remove one or more players from the field one every ten minutes so long as the game remains tied.

- Increase the size of the goal, perhaps progressively.

- Count corner kicks forced in overtime as the equivalent of a goal (if sudden death is used) or as a tiebreaker if the score is tied after a pair of overtimes.

Another proposal has been to revise shootouts so they more resemble those in ice hockey and field hockey; one possibility is to give an attacker the ball at midfield, and 30 seconds to score against one defender and the goalie. Tim Farrell, *ADG: Attacker Defender Goalkeeper*, (2008). http://www.theadg alternative.com.

8.   *Electoral nail-biters.* Consider the 1974 contest between Louis Wyman, the Republican candidate, and John Durkin, the Democrat, for a New Hampshire seat in the U.S. Senate being vacated by Norris Cotton. On Election Day, it appeared that Wyman had won by 355 votes, out of 223,363 cast. Durkin demanded a recount, which declared him the winner by ten votes. But then Wyman appealed to the State Ballot Commission, which reviewed disputed ballots and declared that Wyman had won by two votes. The New Hampshire governor rescinded the preliminary certification of election that had been awarded to Durkin and certified Wyman as the winner. (Cotton

resigned his seat three days early, and the governor appointed Wyman to complete the term.) Durkin then petitioned the Senate to review the case, but, after months of examination of disputed ballots by Rules Committee staff members, the Democratic majority was unable to overcome a Republican filibuster. Durkin ultimately agreed with Wyman to contest a new election, the seat was declared vacant in August 1975, and the governor appointed Cotton to fill his old seat pending the election. Durkin won the re-run comfortably, by nearly 28,000 votes out of 262,572 cast. *See Closest Election in Senate History*, SENATE HISTORICAL OFFICE, https://tinyurl.com/y9jv95ms.

Was a new election the right solution? Or should Wyman have been declared the winner after the second recount gave him a two-vote margin of victory? Or would you have favored a third alternative? For what it may be worth, you should know that Wyman's certified two-vote margin translated into an edge of just under .001%. (In a more recent contest, between Al Franken and Norm Coleman, for a Senate seat from Minnesota in 2008, a new election never seems to have been seriously considered. After an eight-month struggle, Franken was declared the victor, by a margin of about .01%.)

9. *Beyond the Electoral College.* We saw earlier that the U.S. presidential contest is determined by (weighted) unit scoring. Such a system is more likely than aggregate scoring to result in a tie. How should such a tie be broken were it to arise? The Twelfth Amendment to the Constitution (ratified in 1804) provides that the winner will be determined by vote among the incoming members of the House of Representatives, where each state delegation has one vote. (This method is used not only in cases of ties, but also in any multi-candidate presidential race in which no candidate has received a majority of the total electoral votes—that is, when the electoral vote is drawn as well as tied.) Is this a good tiebreaking method? Can you think up any better alternatives?

D. SHORTENED CONTESTS

Many tiebreakers require that play of some sort be extended beyond ordinary or "regulation" time. Sometimes, rules or circumstances provide for the opposite outcome: that play be suspended or terminated before the ordinary expiration of the contest. This occurs in at least two distinct (though occasionally overlapping) circumstances: to cut short a blowout, and when necessitated by intervening causes such as darkness or inclement weather.

1. MERCY RULES[e]

Mercy rules are common in youth sports. They are particularly common in baseball and softball, because if one team has trouble getting

---

[e]   The authors have drawn in this section on a student paper, "Mercy, Mercy Me," written by Kenneth Moreland of the Class of 2012 of the University of Texas Law School.

the other side to make three outs, the game, and even an inning, could last indefinitely. A typical rule provides that the game ends if one team is behind by 12 runs and has completed three innings at bat, or by 10 after four, or by eight after five. And in some competitions, there is a per-inning run limit—seven is typical, usually with the proviso that this limit does not apply in the last inning (for otherwise the game could be clinched earlier).

Other variations besides an abrupt end to the game are possible. Mercy rules in youth basketball and football are more likely to involve shortening the game by speeding up the clock. Even at the high school level, such rules are not unusual. For example, in Florida high school basketball, if a point spread of 35 points is reached in the second half, the clock runs continuously when a jump ball is called, on out-of-bounds, or during free-throw shooting for personal fouls. David Henry, *High School Basketball Mercy Rules Elsewhere*, Beaumont Enterprise (Feb. 13, 2011). Similarly, the National Federation of State High School Associations advocates a running clock in football whenever a team attains a 35-point lead. Greg Easterbrook, *TMQ Nation fires back*, ESPN.com (Sept. 19, 2007).

Mercy rules are less common in elite and professional sports, but they are not unheard of. In NCAA wrestling, if one wrestler has a 15-point advantage, the match is terminated and a technical fall is awarded. NCAA Wrestling Rule 2.14. Under the new rules of international wrestling, a wrestler who gains a seven-point advantage wins the match by technical superiority. *International Wrestling Rules* Article 19(j). Olympic baseball incorporated a 10-run, seven-inning mercy rule, and the NCAA allows conferences to set the same rule. *Baseball at the Summer Olympics*, WIKIPEDIA, https://tinyurl.com/yy96prnl; *NCAA Baseball 2019 & 2020 Rules Book*, Rule 2, § 79. The World Baseball Classic uses the same cutoff, and also a 15-run, five-inning one, in the early rounds of the tournament. *World Baseball Classic Qualifiers Rules and Regulations*, MLB.com, https://tinyurl.com/y5ordc2t. NCAA softball imposes an eight-run, five-inning rule—and allows it to be set aside only in games between the final two teams of the respective NCAA divisional championships. *NCAA Softball 2020 & 2021 Rules Book*, Rule 6.17.

What factors weigh in favor of mercy rules? One is certainly time. Especially in a tournament, in which playing space and time may be limited, there is a strong incentive to end a game in which the outcome appears clear. That is a stronger factor in baseball and softball—in which a blowout usually consumes more time than a close game—than in timed sports. Even in the latter, tournament organizers may be glad to take advantage of the opportunity to move the competition along and compensate for delays that might arise in other games. And even when there is no competing claim on the playing space, some of those involved—parents in youth sports, most notably!—may be happy to make other use of the time once the outcome appears clear. A college softball coach may be grateful for a mercy rule if it helps her team make a flight back home.

Another factor in youth sports is fear of psychological harm to those on the losing end. One commentator has written: "In youth sports, the sting of defeat can be particularly traumatic for kids at this age haven't yet developed the maturity and mental toughness to deal with a loss. They will feel ashamed and think of themselves as failures. And without the guidance and support of their coach and parent, they may feel so distressed that they may want to give up the game entirely." *Youth Sports: The Psychology of Winning and Losing*, LEAGUE NETWORK (May 17, 2017), https://tinyurl.com/y35ybgko. And in contact sports, there may be fear of physical injury as well.[f]

There are counterarguments, of course. In most competitions, a wide scoring margin does not suggest that the losing side is particularly vulnerable to injury if the contest continues to its natural end. As to the psychological angle, it is not necessarily clear that there is anything so terrible about being beaten badly in a sporting competition. There is no mercy rule in tennis, and no indication that young tennis players who get double-bageled—losing a match 6–0, 6–0—bear deep emotional scars for life; many of them will win other matches by the same score. Indeed, how to deal with and recover from a loss, even or especially a whopping loss or one that suggests the limits of one's talent, is one of the life lessons that sports can teach a youngster. (For a discussion of sport's value in teaching the virtue of resilience, see J.S. Russell, *Resilience,* 42 J. PHIL. SPORT 159 (2015). For a discussion not limited to sport, see ANGELA DUCKWORTH, GRIT: THE POWER OF PASSION AND PERSEVERANCE (2016).) Even if a contestant cannot win, he or she may derive considerable satisfaction from battling against, and even limiting, adversity. (One of the authors can report that a highlight of his non-illustrious wrestling career occurred when he spent nearly a full minute on his back—but not quite flat—and avoided a pin.) Moreover, it is hardly self-evident that it is more humiliating to lose by a large margin than for the game to be stopped abruptly and to know, "We got mercied."

Mercy rules prevent the possibility—improbable, but for that very reason especially fulfilling, exciting, and memorable when it does happen— of a dramatic comeback. And they may deprive bench-warmers on both sides of a valuable opportunity to play: Sometimes "garbage time" is when secondary players have their best chance to show what they can do. Even a speed-up rule alters the nature of the competition; for example, a running clock in football prevents execution of a "two-minute drill," which depends largely on managing the clock, especially by getting the ball out of bounds.

---

[f]   As Moreland has noted, "In a sport like football, fans calling for someone to 'stop the bleeding' might be using the phrase literally."

More broadly, and encompassing many of these considerations, is the argument that people play sports not just to win, but *to play*. There are many benefits of playing—exercise, development of skills, competing to achieve goals large and small—for both winners and losers, no matter the score. At least in timed sports, mercy rules short-circuit all that. In baseball and softball, a factor weighing in favor of mercy rules might sometimes be that *too much* play can be a bad thing—but one might ask whether a time limit rather than a mercy rule is the appropriate remedy.

COMMENTS AND QUESTIONS

1.   Amateur hour. Can you think of other considerations, besides those presented above, weighing for and against the use of mercy rules in youth and low-level amateur competitions? Do you believe that such rules are ever warranted? If so, in what circumstances, and what form should they take? How about per-inning run limitations in baseball: Can they be justified more easily than a mercy rule ending the game?

2.   Professionals. As noted above, mercy rules are used less frequently in elite-amateur and professional sports. The principal argument in favor of such rules at the youth level—some measure of protection for the competitors' supposedly fragile or vulnerable psyches—seems remarkably thin when applied to professionals. Moreover, several arguments against mercy rules seem particularly weighty at the professional level. To start, comebacks from very substantial deficits, although rare, constitute some of elite sports' most exciting and memorable events. Note, for example, the Buffalo Bills' comeback from a 32-point second-half deficit to beat the Houston Oilers in a 1993 NFL playoff game. *The Comeback (American football)*, WIKIPEDIA, https://tinyurl. com/nss4afx. The Bills won in overtime and reached that year's Super Bowl. Many participants and fans would not want to eliminate or substantially reduce the possibility of their occurrence. Additionally, broadcasters, especially of timed sports (like football and soccer, and unlike baseball), often count on scheduled events filling a predetermined time slot. Against this, cutting a blowout short can ease wear and tear on the athletes and reduce the danger of injury. (Of course, use of the scrubs in team sports mitigates this factor to some extent.) Are there other relevant considerations for and against mercy rules in professional and elite sports? In what circumstances, if any, do you think they might be appropriate?

3.   Alternatives. Can some of the supposed benefits of mercy rules be obtained through different mechanisms? Consider three:

a.   Continue the contest without shortening it but give the losing team a competitive advantage. For example, some indoor youth soccer competitions allow a team that is behind by five or more goals to put an extra player on the field, and another if the margin climbs to ten. What advantages and disadvantages does this approach have? Are there other sports in which it would be appropriate?

b.   Discourage running up a score. We will discuss later the question of when, and how, a team should avoid winning a contest by too much. For now, note that Connecticut high school football has a formal procedure, under which, if one team wins a game by more than 50 points, the two coaches and the referee must file reports, and a committee of the state interscholastic athletic conference determines whether the winning coach followed proper principles of "score management." If the conclusion is negative, the coach is suspended for the following game. Among the considerations are whether the coach made appropriate substitutions when the game was in hand, adopted a conservative game plan, let the clock run, had runners stay inbounds, and limited the passing game. CONNECTICUT INTERSCHOLASTIC ATHLETIC CONFERENCE, *38th Annual 2013 Football Playoffs*, https://tinyurl.com/yx8twj yn. Is this rule appropriate?

c.   Encourage retirement. In some contests, giving up is perfectly acceptable and unsurprising. Of course, this sometimes happens in individual sports when a contestant is unable to continue. Retirements are rather common in tennis, for example, and a boxer who has absorbed a great deal of punishment may decline to come out for a round, or the fighter's corner may (literally) throw in the towel. But in some settings, it also occurs simply because one side has virtually no hope of winning. In chess, a player with a hopeless position will routinely resign. In match-play golf, it is often even considered bad manners *not* to concede an easy putt, even if it will end the match. Of course, it is always possible for one side in any sport to give up, but in many sports that would be extraordinary, and it is frowned on. For example, though Roberto Duran had an illustrious boxing career, he is best remembered, and not favorably, for giving up in his second fight against Sugar Ray Leonard ("No más!") not because he was being hurt but because he was being beaten and frustrated. In some sports, if a team gives up, the game is reported as a forfeit, with the statistics wiped out, rather than as simply one that ended prematurely by concession. But note an incident reported by Kenneth Moreland, involving Don Mattingly as manager of a team in the Arizona Fall League, which offers off-season experience for developing baseball players. Behind by 15–1 after eight innings, and not wanting to risk injury to his pitchers, Mattingly gave up. The game was initially deemed a forfeit, but ultimately the league decided it had simply ended prematurely, to reduce the chance for injury. Aaron Gleeman, *Don Mattingly ran out of pitchers while managing in fall league*, NBC SPORTS.COM (Oct. 29, 2010). Should leagues encourage decisions of this sort when made to prevent injury? What if the principal motivation is simply not to wear out pitchers or other players, so that the team's chances of winning subsequent contests will not be impaired? If you believe a team should be able to concede a game, should the league set criteria on when, comparable to mercy rules—so many runs behind after so much time, for example? Do you agree with Moreland's suggestion that a team should be allowed to concede only with the agreement of the other side?

2. WEATHER AND OTHER INTERVENING CAUSES

Sometimes a game once started must be halted because of an intervening cause; most often it is weather, but it could include darkness, or a myriad of other problems such as a power outage. Depending on the circumstances and the governing rules, the game might, among other possibilities, be:

- resumed as soon as possible, presumably before the players have left the arena;

- suspended and continued from the same point at a later date;

- canceled—that is, completely wiped out (along with its statistics) as if it had never been scheduled;

- replayed from the beginning as if the first try had never happened (again, with the statistics wiped out); or

- terminated—that is, treated as if it were a complete game even though it was not.

Rules governing these situations differ widely, not only in the results they prescribe but in depth of detail and in the decisionmaker(s) to whom they leave the decision.

Thus, for example, NCAA rules, Sec. 3, Art. 3, provide four options if play of a football game must be halted and cannot be resumed: (1) resume the game at a later date; (2) terminate the game with a determined final score; (3) forfeiture; or (4) no contest. The rules provide:

> The option that takes effect shall be determined by conference policy if both institutions are members of the same conference. In non-conference competition, the directors of athletics at the participating institutions or their designees, in consultation with the coaches, must agree on one of the four options. This agreement will include the final score if the game is terminated (Rule 8–1–2).

But if play is halted during overtime and cannot be resumed, then the game is ruled a tie.

The NFL is considerably more reluctant to allow a game not to be played to its conclusion, and it gives the Commissioner a great deal of control over what to do. Rule 17, Sec. 1, Art. 4. The rules seek to ensure that the decisions whether to suspend or resume play are likely to be made by a representative of the Commissioner, by phone if none is present at the game. Art. 5. If play is interrupted and the game cannot be completed that day, the Commissioner ordinarily schedules it to be continued, from the same point, on another date, preferably no more than two days later. Arts. 8, 9. But, "[i]f, in the Commissioner's opinion, it is reasonable to project that the resumption of an interrupted game would not change its ultimate result or adversely affect any other inter-team competitive issue, he is empowered to terminate the game." Art. 4. Indeed, the Commissioner is empowered to terminate even a postseason game "if in his judgment, the continuation of the game would not be normally expected to alter the ultimate result." Art. 10.

Baseball has more detailed and prescriptive (and confusing and apparently self-contradictory) rules. Here is a summary of some of the more significant portions. If a game is called—that is, the umpire terminates play before it is concluded—it is still considered a regulation game if one team is ahead and the other has completed its fifth turn at bat. Rule 4.10. In older days, if a game had gone five or more innings and was tied, it would be considered complete as a tie. But baseball has now added the concept of a suspended game, which ordinarily must be resumed from the point of suspension at a later date, with the date and venue usually prescribed by the rules. A game becomes suspended if it is called at any time before completion for darkness or for light failure or other mechanical difficulty. The game also becomes a suspended one if it has become a regulation game and it is tied; or it is called for curfew or some applicable time limit (caused sometimes by a scheduled football game); or it is called for weather, the visiting team has taken the lead in the top of an inning that has not been completed, and the home team has not retaken the lead. Rule 4.12(c) provides:

> A suspended game shall be resumed at the exact point of suspension of the original game. The completion of a suspended game is a continuation of the original game. The lineup and batting order of both teams shall be exactly the same as the lineup and batting order at the moment of suspension, subject to the rules governing substitution. Any player may be replaced by a player who had not been in the game prior to the suspension. No player removed before the suspension may be returned to the lineup.

> A player who was not with the club when the game was suspended may be used as a substitute, even if he has taken the place of a player no longer with the club who would not have been eligible because he had been removed from the lineup before the game was suspended.

A game that has not become a regulation game ordinarily is replayed in its entirety, though the league has discretion to cancel it if it has not been played before the last regularly scheduled meeting of the teams and it appears unlikely to affect any team's status for the postseason.

The Philadelphia Phillies won three of the first four games of the 2008 World Series. With rain in the forecast for Game 5, the Commissioner told the teams that he would not allow the Series to be clinched in a rain-shortened game. After five wet innings, the Phillies, the home team, led the game 2–1. The visiting team, the Tampa Bay Rays, scored one run in the top of the sixth. At that point, play was stopped; Chase Utley, the Phillies' second baseman, said that "the infield was basically under water." Gene Wojciechowski, *Selig made correct call in suspending Game 5*, ESPN.com (Oct. 28, 2018). If the old rules had applied, the Phillies would have been declared the winner, because the score would have reverted to where it stood at the end of the fifth inning. Instead, the game was treated as a suspended one, and the Phillies completed their Series win two days later. In the offseason, MLB amended its rules to provide that all postseason games and games added to the schedule to determine postseason eligibility become suspended games, played to conclusion, no matter how many innings played or what the score.

COMMENTS AND QUESTIONS

1. In general. If a game is called, say for weather, what potential advantages and disadvantages are there in (a) replaying the game from the beginning; (b) considering the game to be complete when called; and (c) suspending the game, resuming it from the exact position at a later time? How gamewrights should reconcile the various considerations is obviously a very complex matter. Are each of the sets of rules summarized above optimal for the competitions they address, or could some improved?

2. Football. In an NCAA football game between teams not members of the same conference, what considerations do you think might determine whether the teams agree to terminate the game with a given score? *See* Paul Morgan, *Rain gives WMU the blues as Michigan collects win in washed-out football opener*, MLIVE.COM (Sept. 4, 2011) (football game ended, 34–10, with 1:27 left in the third quarter, after lightning strikes; losing coach doubts that going back onto the field after a lengthy delay "is the best thing for the student athletes," but acknowledges the calculus might have been affected by the score).

3. Baseball. In a regular-season baseball game, the home team is leading 2–1 after five complete innings. The visiting team scores seven runs in the top of the sixth. The home team makes two outs in the bottom of the inning, and then there is an electrical failure that makes resumption of the game impossible. What should happen? Does it matter if this is a major league game or a high school game between non-conference opponents?

4. Rowing. There is really only one university competition in Great Britain that generates anywhere near the attention that American collegiate sports do: the race between rowing eights from Oxford and Cambridge, often referred to simply as The Boat Race (though, in a sign that perhaps there will not always be an England after all, since 2013 it has been formally known as the BNY Mellon Boat Race). Since 1845, the race has been conducted on a course 4.2 miles (6.8 km.) on the River Thames. In 2012, when the race was about three-quarters complete, with Oxford holding a very slight lead but Cambridge having a very slightly better course before it, the race had to be halted because a swimmer (protesting elitism) was in the water near the boats. The disruption caused a delay of about a half hour, in part because of rough water; the race was resumed, with the boats even, a little further away from the finish.

Was this the proper resolution? In what circumstances, if you were the umpire, might you determine that the race should be rerun completely from the start? In what circumstances might you determine that the race should not be resumed or rerun, and the boat that had the advantage at the time of the disruption should be declared the winner?

The dénouement: Shortly after the restart of the 2012 race, the boats collided, and one of the Oxford men lost an oar. The collision was deemed Oxford's fault, and Cambridge won easily. At the finish, the Oxford bowman collapsed and was unconscious when he was lifted out of the boat, but he recovered fully. *Drama overshadows 2012 Boat Race*, WORLD ROWING.COM (Apr. 10, 2012).

E. JUDGMENTAL SCORING

Most sports employ objective scoring. Either a run is plated, a goal is scored, a point is won, or it is not. A runner either broke a plane first, or did not. An athlete either threw a discus furthest, or did not. True, it will sometimes be hard to discern whether these events occurred (see Chapter 11), but the rules of most sports contemplate that there is an objective fact of the matter. Sports that involve objective scoring are sometimes called "refereed sports."

Other sports, in contrast, involve at least some measure of subjective or evaluative scoring. In diving, gymnastics, figure skating, synchronized swimming, and dressage, for example, performances are scored in part on aesthetic criteria. Combat sports are frequently scored on criteria like "ring generalship" and "aggression." Sports with evaluative scoring are sometimes called "judged sports" or "performance sports."

Some years ago, the preeminent philosopher of sport, Bernard Suits, caused a modest stir in the philosophy-of-sport community by contending that judged sports, while genuine sports, are not games. *See* Bernard Suits, *Tricky Triad: Games, Play, and Sport*, 15 J. PHIL. SPORT 1 (1988). On his view, judged sports did not involve—as his theory of games (Chapter 1) required—a distinct goal, describable as a state of affairs, the realization of which it was the point and purpose of constitutive rules to make more difficult. Games, argued Suits, generate skills

by erecting barriers to be overcome, but performances do so by postulating ideals to be approximated. In games, *rules*, to repeat the point, are the crux of the matter. Just these rules generate just these skills. In performances, ideals are the crux of the matter. Just these ideals generate just these skills. That is why it is possible to speak of a perfect performance, at least in principle, without fear of contradiction, whereas a perfectly played game . . . seems to lead to a paradox.

Id. at 6; *see also* Bernard Suits, *The Trick of the Disappearing Goal*, 16 J. PHIL. SPORT 1 (1989).

It appears that few philosophers of sport were persuaded by Suits's new position that judged sports constitute a subcategory of sport that is not also a subcategory of games. For criticism, see Klaus V. Meier, *Triad Trickery: Playing With Sport and Games*, 15 J. PHIL. SPORT 11 (1988); Klaus V. Meier, *Performance Prestidigitation*, 16 J. PHIL. SPORT 13 (1989); R. Scott Kretchmar, *On Beautiful Games*, 16 J. PHIL. SPORT 34 (1989). (What do you think: are judged sports *games*, according to whatever definition or account of games you favor?)

We will address two basic issues here. Subsection 1 examines how the criteria for judging should be articulated. Subsection 2 asks how the assessments of the individual judges should be combined given that most judgmental sports use more than one judge.

1.   CRITERIA

Articulating the criteria by which judgmental scores should be awarded is a particularly vexing and important issue. If the criteria are too open-ended, there is too much room for incompetent judging that applies idiosyncratic standards, and corruption may become especially difficult to detect. On the other hand, an attempt to make the standards more particular may distort the competitors' incentives, rewarding the accumulation of achievements that seem not to be what the sport is principally about. We will focus on three sports: boxing, figure skating, and gymnastics.

Boxing.

Professional boxing, as noted previously, is scored on the basis of four criteria: clean hitting, effective aggressiveness, ring generalship, and defense. These are plainly evaluative or judgmental criteria. Olympic boxing also previously used such open-textured criteria. But some decisions struck observers as bizarre or worse. The most notorious was probably the one that gave the 1988 light middleweight title to Park Si-hun of South Korea, the host nation, over Roy Jones, Jr., of the United States; a quarter century later, *The Guardian* of Great Britain counted this the 14th most stunning moment in Olympic history. John Ashdown, *Roy Jones Jr cheated out of gold*, GUARDIAN (Feb. 15, 2012). In response to such embarrassments, Olympic boxing scoring has become almost entirely non-judgmental. Somewhat simplified, points are awarded for a blow landed with the marked part of the glove on the opponent's head or body (above the belt). Punches that are judged to have no force do not score points, nor do punches to an opponent's arms. Judges sitting in five-person panels press a button for a boxer when they believe that he has delivered a scoring hit. An electronic scoring system then registers a point whenever three or more judges press the button for one boxer within a second of each other. If fewer than three judges agree, no point is awarded.

The new system has not ended controversy concerning Olympic boxing. Before the 2012 Olympics, the CEO of the World Series of Boxing, an initiative of the International Boxing Association (AIBA, the A being a relic of the time when Amateur was part of the Association's title), which controls Olympic boxing, was accused of promising Azerbaijan two gold medals in exchange for a $10 million payment. ("First of all, no comment," the CEO, Ivan Khodabakhsh, replied, when questioned about the allegations. "Secondly, absolutely a lie.") At the Games themselves, among other incidents, Magomed Abdulhamidov of Azerbaijan was awarded a decision over Satoshi Shimizu of Japan, who had appeared to pummel him. AIBA overturned the result of the fight and expelled the Turkman referee, who had failed to give Abdulhamidov mandatory eight-counts on what appeared to be knockdowns. *See* Kelefa Sanneh, *Fixing the Olympics? Azerbaijan's Boxing Scandal*, THE NEW YORKER, Aug. 2, 2012.

Figure skating.

In the traditional system, each judge awarded each performer two grades, one on more technical criteria, the other on more artistic ones. As explained by the United States Figure Skating Association:

> The basic principle of the 6.0 system is a "majority" system. Each event is judged by an odd number of judges, and the winner of the event is the skater placed highest by a majority of these judges.
>
> For all singles and pairs events and the free dance, judges award two marks: one for technical merit and one for program presentation. The technical merit mark expresses a judge's evaluation of the quality of the required elements skated. The presentation mark reflects a judge's assessment of the program as a whole—its composition, originality, use of ice, skater's style and expression of the music.

The 6.0 System, U.S. FIGURE SKATING, https://tinyurl.com/y23zxe65.

The open-ended nature of these criteria led to frequent charges of favoritism and worse, including vote-trading. Matters came to a head after the 2002 Olympics in Salt Lake City, when an experienced French skating judge acknowledged that she had voted for a Russian pair, Yelena Berezhnaya and Anton Sikharulidze, over the Canadian pair of Jamie Sale and David Pelletier, because she was coerced by the head of the French skating federation; apparently, this was part of an explicit deal to enable France to win a gold medal in ice dancing.

Largely in response to this scandal, the International Skating Union (ISU) adopted a new system of scoring. Now a technical panel, supported by a video replay operator and a data operator, identifies each element of a program—for example, the type of spin—and its Base Value, a level of difficulty indicated in a chart published by the ISU. Meanwhile, each member of the judging panel gives the element a Grade of Execution (GOE) within a prescribed range, from −3 to +3 until 2018, and now −5 to +5. A "trimmed mean" of the GOEs given by each judge is determined—more on that later—and it is combined in a complex way with the Base Value to yield a total point score for that element; for example, in singles skating, the Base Values of all jump elements started in the second half of the program are multiplied by a factor of 1.1. And the scores for all the elements in the program, up to a prescribed limit on the number of elements, are added together to give the Total Element Score, also referred to as the Technical Score. Each judge also assigns a Program Component Score, on a 10-point scale, in .25-point increments, to express overall presentation and technical mastery. Judges in singles, pairs, and synchronized skating, for example, are supposed to assess Skating Skills, Transitions/Linking Footwork & Movement, Performance/Execution, Choreography/Composition, and Interpretation, each according to a prescribed set of criteria. A trimmed mean of the judges' scores on Program Components is multiplied by a factor that is meant to give it equal weight with the Total Element Score. The sum of those two, less any prescribed deductions (for example, one point for every fall in singles skating; two points for a fall by both skaters in pairs and ice dancing), then gives the Total Segment Score, and the Final Score is simply the sum of the two Total Segment Scores. Here, as an example, is one skater's score card from a free skate in the 2018 Winter Olympics; the x marks indicate jumps he performed in the second half of the program.

Rank	Name			NOC Code	Starting Number	Total Segment Score	Total Element Score		Total Program Component Score (factored)		Total Deductions
1	CHAN Patrick			CAN	4	179.75	87.67			93.08		−1.00

#	Executed Elements	Info	Base Value	GOE	J1	J2	J3	J4	J5	J6	J7	J8	J9	Ref.	Scores of Panel
1	4T+3T		14.60	2.14	2	3	2	2	2	3	2	2	2		16.74
2	4T		10.30	2.57	2	3	3	1	2	3	2	3	3		12.87
3	2A		3.30	−0.71	−1	−1	−2	−2	−1	−1	−2	−1	−2		2.59
4	ChSq1		2.00	1.90	3	3	3	3	3	2	2	3	2		3.90
5	3Lz+1Lo+3S		10.90	1.40	2	2	2	2	2	1	3	2	2		12.30
6	3A<	<	6.49 x	−3.00	−3	−3	−3	−3	−3	−3	−3	−3	−3		3.49
7	3Lo		5.61 x	−1.20	−2	−2	−1	−2	−1	−2	−2	−2	−1		4.41
8	CCSp4		3.20	1.14	2	2	2	3	2	2	2	3	3		4.34
9	3F+2T		7.26 x	0.40	1	1	0	1	1	0	1	0	0		7.66
10	2A		3.63 x	1.00	2	2	2	2	2	2	2	2	1		4.63
11	FSSp3		2.60	1.21	2	3	3	2	2	2	2	3	3		3.81
12	StSq4		3.90	2.10	3	3	3	3	3	3	3	3	2		6.00
13	CCoSp4		3.50	1.43	3	3	2	3	2	3	3	3	3		4.93
			77.29												87.67

Alex Abad-Santos, *Winter Olympics 2018: figure skating scoring explained for people who don't follow figure skating*, VOX (Feb. 14, 2018).

The new system has received decidedly mixed reviews. *See, e.g.*, Jim Caple, *New Scoring System Gets Mixed Reviews*, ESPN.com (Feb. 15, 2010). Critics have argued that, as the scorecard above suggests, it lacks simplicity—there is no longer any such thing as a perfect 6.0, and it can be hard to know just how good a total segment score of 158.08 is. More importantly, the system has significantly changed the incentives that shape how skaters structure their programs; for better or worse, "compete" has tended to replace "perform," as one journalist has put it. Gia Kourlas, *Amid Blunders on Ice, A Few Signs of Grace*, N.Y. TIMES, Feb. 19, 2014, at C1. Many skaters believe that, by encouraging them to amass points by cramming their time on ice with the same point-accumulating moves as each other, the system deprives their programs of individuality, personality, and artistic creativity. But others, including Evan Lysacek, former world and Olympic champion, believe that the system pushes skaters to be stronger, technically and even artistically. Caple, *New Scoring System*. And even critics of the system acknowledge that it is fairer to skaters. "You get credit for what you do well," former Olympian Johnny Weir (whom nobody could accuse of undervaluing individuality) has said. "It gives skaters from some countries that are not as strong politically an opportunity to do well. They don't get lowballed." *Id.* But it hardly seems that the system has eliminated all unfairness. An analysis by BuzzFeed News indicates that judges at the 2018 Winter Olympics demonstrated a strong preference in favor of skaters from their home country, and that this factor may have lifted Tessa Virtue and Scott Moir of Canada over their chief rivals, Gabriella Papadakis and Guillaume Cizeron of France, for the gold medal in ice dancing. John Templon & Rosalind Adams, *How Figure Skating Judges May Have Shaped the Olympic Podium*, BUZZFEED (Feb. 23, 2018).

Gymnastics.

Before 2006, the scoring system used in elite international gymnastics competitions began with a fixed start value—8.4 for men and 8.8 for women—and added bonuses for difficulty of moves, up to a maximum of 10. The athletes would then lose points for mistakes in execution. So a "perfect 10" meant a difficult routine that was performed without any significant error. Following controversy at the 2004 Olympics, FIG, the international gymnastics federation, adopted a new system that uses two separate scores. The Difficulty Score, determined by a two-member panel, measures difficulty and technical content, by adding points for each of the ten most difficult elements in the routine and, for some events, "connection value" by performing elements successfully in close succession. The Execution Score assesses execution, artistry, composition, and technique. It starts at 10 and works downward. In an attempt to limit subjectivity, the rules prescribe penalties for errors—for example, 0.8 points for a fall. Each of six panelists gives an independent score, and the middle four are averaged. The "D" and "E" scores are then added, and "neutral penalties"—such as for stepping out of bounds on the floor routine—are deducted to yield a final score. A total score over 15 will often earn a medal, but there have been scores over 17.

As Jordan Ellenberg, a mathematician, notes, "one thing opponents of the new system don't like" is that " '[a] perfect 16.9' lacks the ring of 'a perfect 10.' " But, Ellenberg argues, the new system should be easier to understand, because it disaggregates scores. While "the old unified score was an impenetrable combination of pluses and minuses," an E score of 10.0 really does mean "absolute perfection." Gymnasts rarely come close to that 10.0, though. More significantly, Ellenberg contends, the D score puts a premium, without a practical limit, on attempting difficult routines:

> Gymnasts can perform moves that no one's carried out before—that no one ever *thought* of carrying out before. Now, the sport has a scoring system that's built to reward that. In theory, yes, there's still an upper limit. There are only so many different possible elements in a routine and only so many possible connections between them, and each one, at least for now, is worth at most 0.7 points. But this new upper boundary is less like a perfect SAT score than a 1.000 batting average: a limit so far out of reach it might as well be no limit at all.

> . . . Before the new system, just about all elite competitors performed routines difficult enough to bring the start value up to a 10.0; sailing over that threshold earned you no more points than barely clearing it. With the new system, gymnasts have the incentive to keep making their routines tougher and more complex. In every other sport, the competitors in Beijing are superior to their predecessors and get better scores to prove it. Why should gymnastics be the only sport without world records?

> With the new system, gymnastics comes into compliance with the Olympic motto. That's "faster, higher, stronger," not "more graceful, more beautiful, closer to perfect." . . .

Jordan Ellenberg, *Down With the Perfect 10!*, SLATE (July 31, 2012).

COMMENTS AND QUESTIONS

1. Cheating. It is widely believed that judged sports are more susceptible to cheating by on-field officials than are refereed sports. Do you agree? In answering this question, note that most sports that involve objective *scoring* nonetheless have many standard-like regulatory rules that require officials to make subjective *judgments*. Football, for example, is a refereed "objective-scoring" sport, but the rules governing pass interference are sufficiently vague to give plenty of latitude to a corrupt field judge. Are judged sports more susceptible than refereed sports to simple incompetence?

2. *Remedies.* Recall the pairs figure skating at the 2002 Winter Olympics. If there were adequate grounds to award a gold medal to the Canadian pair of Sale and Pelletier, why wasn't it also appropriate to withdraw it from the Russian pair of Berezhnaya and Sikharulidze? Was this a principled or unprincipled compromise?

3. *World records.* Are world records meaningful in judged sports? Why or why not? If not, is that a mark against them?

4. *Weight of criteria.* It is sometimes said that professional boxing judges are supposed to weigh the four stated criteria equally. And in figure skating, as noted above, a multiplier is used in an attempt to give technical merit and more artistic aspects of the performance equal weight. What does it mean to speak of equal weight? To take an example that might be closer to your experience, suppose that a professor gives an exam in two one-hour parts, with 50 multiple-choice questions on Part 1 and four essays on Part 2. The professor says that she will give the two parts equal weight. What does that mean? Is it enough to say that the maximum score on the two parts is the same? Does even that matter? If the scores on the multiple-choice part are scrunched together, does that dictate that small differences in those scores should have a large impact on the final score? Or does it suggest that the multiple-choice part should not have a large impact on the final score? Or does it suggest something else, or have no significance at all?

5. *Counting all judges?* In addition to changing the way that scores are calculated, the new figure skating scoring system also changed for a time the way that scores issued by individual judges are selected and aggregated. Under the old rules, all scores from the nine judges used in major competitions were accepted and the highest and lowest dropped. For several years after the new system was adopted, 12 judges were named for each segment, but, by random selection, the scores of three of them were disregarded; for each skater, the highest and lowest were again dropped. Nobody, including the judges, would know which judges' marks were selected for consideration. What are the advantages and disadvantages of this system?

6. *Objectivity and subjectivity.* In the three sports presented above, the trend seems to be to move towards more objective systems of scoring. We'll focus on boxing (though you might want to consider comparable questions for the other sports). Which scoring system is better: an objective system that counts punches or a more avowedly evaluative system based on factors like aggressiveness, control of the ring, and power of blows landed? Is the distinction between *precision* and *accuracy* (see pp. 140–141) helpful here?

7. *Incentives?* In light of Ellenberg's contention that the new system gives gymnasts "the incentive to keep making their routines tougher and more complex," consider the controversy that arose over the difficulty value that the FIG's Women's Technical Committee awarded a new beam dismount that

Simon Biles—widely deemed the greatest gymnast in history—unveiled at the 2019 World Championships. The dismount, now called the "Biles," involves two flips and two twists; all agree that it is immensely difficult, probably achievable by nobody other than Biles herself. Yet the W.T.C. assigned it the same difficulty value as the maneuver would earn when performed during a floor routine, which all participants acknowledge is a far less demanding challenge. When criticized for undervaluing the move, FIG explained that "[i]n assigning values to the new elements, the W.T.C. takes into consideration many different aspects: the risk, the safety of the gymnasts and the technical direction of the discipline." Furthermore, "The W.T.C.'s task is to ensure the safety of all athletes around the world and decisions are not based purely on one gymnast." Biles was unpersuaded. "They keep asking us to do more difficulty and to give more artistry, give more harder skills. So we do, and then they don't credit it, and I don't think that's fair," she said. "Am I in a league of my own? Yes, but that doesn't mean you can't credit me for what I'm doing." Liriel Higa, *Don't Punish Simon Biles for Being the Best*, N.Y. TIMES, Oct. 9, 2019. Who's right?

8. *Radically subjective scoring.* Subjectively scored sports typically set forth standards by which judges are instructed to measure the athletes' performance. X Games Aspen 2020 implemented a more radically subjective system of scoring in which judges were instructed to rank skiers and snowboarders in the big air, slope style, and super pipe events by reference to nothing more than their own unguided assessment of the competitors' relative all-things-considered excellence. Proponents of the new system argued that wholly subjective scoring encourages greater creativity and allows competitors to try something spectacular with less fear that a single mistake would crush their medal hopes. Critics objected that radical judge discretion provides athletes with far too little guidance, not knowing to what extent judges will value huge ambitious tricks or clean, mistake-free runs. Do you think that judging a contest based solely on "overall impression" provides sufficient clarity to guide competitors, and to check judges' idiosyncrasies? Would other sports benefit from a purely subjective scoring system? Which ones? Do you think that the grading of law school exams is radically subjective? If so, is that a problem?

2. JUDGMENTAL SCORING AND SOME PROBLEMS OF VOTING

In a judged sport, gamewrights must make some crucial decisions, even apart from determining the criteria for judging. Among these are:

- *How many components, or segments, should be considered?* For example, figure skating competitions now usually include two segments, short and long competitions; boxing matches are divided into rounds, each scored separately.

- *How many judges should there be?* Judged sports usually use more than one judge. Not always, though. Dog shows use single judges for each breed and then a single judge to determine best of show. *See* THE WESTMINSTER KENNEL CLUB, *Dog Show 101*, https://tinyurl.com/y6ocmct7 (acknowledging "the sport's subjective basis: one judge, applying his or her interpretation of the standard, giving his or her opinion of the best dog on that particular day"). Bear in mind also that in Anglo-American trials there is usually only one judge, and many important decisions are left to the discretion of the trial judge. Is there good reason to have a single judge in litigation, which may involve disputes of great importance, but multiple judges in sports competitions? Use of multiple judges, we will see, poses a sometimes-difficult question of how their judgments should be aggregated.

- *Should ordinal or cardinal scoring be used?* Ordinal scoring, as we have seen, simply ranks competitors on any given component; cardinal scoring assigns a magnitude to the difference in performance between any two competitors. If there is only one judge in a competition and only one component used in scoring, then it does not matter whether the competition uses cardinal or ordinal scoring, no matter how many competitors there are: The winner will be the competitor that the judge believes performed best by that criterion, second place will be the one who performed next best, and so on.

If there are multiple scoring components, then at least at first glance it appears that cardinal scoring is preferable, for the same reason we have already seen (pp. 132–133) in the context of measured scoring: If, for example, two components are supposed to be weighted equally, then it seems a large margin, A over B, in one component should outweigh a small margin, B over A, in another component. But notice that even if there is only one judge (as when a single instructor grades a multi-section essay exam) complications may arise because if the spread of scores is different for two components, it may be unclear whether that reflects more a difference in how the judge graded rather than in how the competitors performed; note the discussion of grade scrunch above.

This type of complexity is intensified if there are multiple judges or multiple (here meaning more than two) competitors, and even more so if there are multiple judges *and* multiple competitors. If Judge 1 strongly prefers competitor Red over competitor Blue, and Judge 2 only mildly prefers Blue, then there is a good, though hardly incontrovertible, argument that Red should be declared the winner. (We address below the question of whether in multi-component, multi-judge events, the winner should be determined by aggregating the scores judge by judge or component by component.) But perhaps Judge 1 just used a more spread-out scale—perhaps on the understanding that by doing so her scores would have more of an impact on the ultimate outcome. So what should we do about that?

One partial solution, adopted in some figure skating competitions, is to take a "trimmed mean," calculated by deleting the highest and lowest scores and then taking the average of the remaining ones. (This approach also gives less importance to outliers, whose judgments differ significantly from most of the others.) Another, more complicated, solution would norm each judge's scores—that is, multiplying them by a scale factor so that the spread is about the same for each judge.

Arrow's impossibility theorem

How about using ordinal scoring instead, whereby each judge can only assign the ranks 1,2, 3, ... n, where n is the number of competitors? Ordinal rankings eliminate the problem of one judge having scores with a greater variance than another, and generally mitigate the impact of strategic, corrupt, or simply incompetent judging. Similarly, if there are multiple components, ordinal scoring eliminates the problem that one component will contribute more than it should to the ultimate result because its scores are more spread out. But ordinal scoring brings new problems of its own, partly owing to the intransitivity of group preferences.

Transitivity means that if a relationship R obtains between two elements, a and b, and also between the elements b and c, then it obtains as well between a and c. For example, the mathematical relations of equality and inequality are transitive. If $a > b$, and $b > c$, then $a > c$. It is generally thought to be a condition of rationality that an individual's preferences are transitive. If, on a given evening, Adam prefers going to the basketball game to watching a movie at home, and also prefers watching a movie at home to bowling, then he should also prefer going to the basketball game to bowling. He would be irrational were he to prefer bowling to attending the basketball game given the other preferences he holds.

But as the Marquis de Condorcet, an 18th century mathematician and philosopher, observed, transitivity does not apply to *group* preferences among three or more options. To illustrate, suppose that Adam, joined now by his friends Bakul and Claire, are deciding how to spend the evening together. Adam's preferences are as described above: he prefers basketball to a movie, and a movie to bowling. And because he is rational, he also prefers basketball to bowling. Bakul prefers bowling to basketball and a movie to bowling. Claire likewise prefers bowling to basketball, but prefers basketball to a movie. Their individual preferences are represented in the following table.

	Preference 1	Preference 2	Preference 3
Adam	Basketball	Movie	Bowling
Bakul	Movie	Bowling	Basketball
Claire	Bowling	Basketball	Movie

Given this set of individual preference rankings, what is the *group's* preference ranking? Put another way, were the options put up for a vote, what would be the result? Well, if the friends may cast a vote for *any* of the three options, there will be no winner: Adam votes for basketball, Bakul votes for a movie, and Claire votes for bowling. But what if the friends agree to vote in an "election" between only two options, not all three? If the choice is basketball or a movie, basketball wins by a vote of 2 (Adam and Claire) to 1 (Bakul). And if the choice is a movie or bowling, movie wins also by a vote of 2 (Adam and Bakul) to 1 (Claire). What, finally, if the choice is between bowling and basketball? Were group preferences transitive, then the winner would have to be basketball: if the group prefers basketball to movie, and movie to bowling, then, by transitivity, it must prefer basketball to bowling. But the group does *not* prefer basketball to bowling. By, once again, a vote of 2 (Bakul and Claire) to 1 (Adam), the group prefers bowling to basketball. This is the **Condorcet Paradox**, the most fundamental of the voting paradoxes: because *group preferences are not transitive,* a collective group ranking is not stable, but subject to **cycling**.

Cycling (etc.)

Now, you might think this is a modest result. Why should we care about transitivity? We should care because the failure of transitivity threatens the idea that there is any such thing as majority preference. We believe that many group decisions should be decided by majority vote, and that majority vote delivers what we might fairly term the collective will. But what this simple case appears to demonstrate is that there is often no stable majority will at all. Suppose that, once the friends see that they have divergent preferences, one proposes that they adopt a two-stage decision procedure: first vote in a two-way contest between two of the three options, and then vote in a second two-way contest between the winner of that first vote and the third option. However, the ultimate winner of this two-stage procedure will vary depending upon which pair-wise comparison they select to start. If they first vote between basketball and bowling, bowling will prevail, and then lose in a vote against a movie. If they first vote between bowling and a movie, the movie will prevail, only to lose in the second vote against basketball. And so on. The so-called will of the majority depends not upon what the voters "really" want, but upon an arbitrary choice among ways of structuring the vote. Obviously, this is just as true if Adam, Bakul, and Claire are not friends trying to decide upon a group activity, but rather judges ranking the performance of skaters (Red, Yellow, and Blue) in a competition.

	Skater 1	Skater 2	Skater 3
Adam	Red	Yellow	Blue
Bakul	Yellow	Blue	Red
Claire	Blue	Red	Yellow

Uncertainty regarding how best to aggregate the rank orderings of individual judges into a collective ranking provides the backdrop to another noteworthy figure skating incident from the 2002 Salt Lake City Winter Olympics, the same Games that featured corrupt vote trading in the pairs competition. The women's singles competition comprised two segments, the short program and the long program, with the latter counting twice as much as the former. In each program, each judge gave each skater two raw scores, one for technical merit and the other for artistic impression, which were added together. Although these scores were cardinal, they were converted into an ordinal ranking, 1 for the highest total score a given judge gave for any skater on that program, 2 for the second highest, and so forth. Those judge-particular scores were then combined by a complex system into a collective ordinal ranking for each skater, one for the highest ranked skater on the program, 2 for the second, etc.[g] At the end of the competition, a skater's collective ranking on the long program was added to half her collective ranking on the short program, the discounting of the short program ranking reflecting the fact that the long program counted double. That total determined the order of finish. Thus, if Skater A finished 3rd in the short program and 4th in the long program, she would have 5.5 points and finish behind Skater B, who was 6th in the short program and 2nd in the long and got 5 points. If two skaters had the same number of points, the one with the better score in the long program finished higher. (This was in a sense double counting, because the long program already counted for twice the short program.)

In the short program at Salt Lake, Michelle Kwan finished on top, followed, respectively, by Irina Slutskaya, Sasha Cohen, and Sarah Hughes: they received .5, 1, 1.5, and 2 points, respectively. The following evening, Slutskaya was the 23rd and final skater in the long program. Had she withdrawn, the top of the leaderboard would have been all-American:

---

[g] For a full explanation, see *Interpreting 6.0 Score Sheets*, SAN DIEGO FIGURE SKATING COMMUNICATIONS, https://tinyurl.com/y26m9bhd.

Place	Skater	Short	Long	Total
1	Kwan	1st/.5 pts	2nd/2 pts	2.5 pts
2	Hughes	4th/2 pts	1st/1 pt	3.0 pts
3	Cohen	3rd/1.5 pts	3rd/3 pts	4.5 pts

Slutskaya would have been far back, with 24 points (1 from the short program and 23 from the long.)

But Slutskaya didn't withdraw. She skated beautifully, giving her second place in the long program. And so this was the order of finish at the top:

Place	Skater	Short	Long	Total
1	Hughes	4th/2 pts	1st/1 pt	3.0 pts
2	Slutskaya	2nd/1 pt	2nd/2 pts	3.0 pts
3	Kwan	1st/.5 pts	3rd/3 pts	3.5 pts
4	Cohen	3rd/1.5 pts	4th/4 pts	5.5 pts

That Slutskaya's excellent routine knocked Cohen from third to fourth, and so off the podium, is not surprising. What might strike you as odd is that Slutskaya's performance could elevate Hughes over Kwan while both sat waiting in the locker room. How could one skater's performance affect the relative ranking of two others? (Hughes edged Slutskaya for the gold, although tied in total points, thanks to the tiebreaker.)

If you intuitively find this result perverse, it's worth putting a name to the principle or desideratum that it appears to violate. In the voting literature, it is called the *independence of irrelevant alternatives*, which means that the ranking of any pair of options should be independent of the presence or absence of a third option that does not bear on the choice between the two. In many prosaic contexts, the principle has substantial intuitive force. Suppose you are preparing to order at a restaurant, and have decided on the sirloin over the pasta. If, before you place your order, the server announces that the evening's special is tuna, it would be perfectly reasonable for you to choose tuna over the sirloin. But the tuna is an irrelevant alternative as far as the pairwise comparison of sirloin and pasta is concerned. It would be irrational—a violation of the principle of independence of irrelevant alternatives—for you to change your choice from sirloin to pasta just because tuna is now an option.

In this case Hughes's (figurative) leap over Kwan appears to violate the principle. Many people find it surprising. But it's built into this system of voting. (A similar instance occurred seven years earlier, at the 1995 World Championships in Berlin, when the final skater in the long program—14-year-old Michelle Kwan—turned in a 3rd place finish that catapulted France's Surya Bonaly over American Nicole Bobek for the silver.) If a scoring system uses ordinal rankings for multiple segments of a competition, then it reflects a premise that the gap between first and third place in one component is more significant in determining the ultimate order of finish than the gap between first and second on that component, so a third competitor, by widening the gap between the first two, might cause those two to reverse order. (Indeed, for this reason one of the authors believes that these cases do not involve a violation, real or apparent, of the principle, because a premise of the principle—that the third option does not bear on the choice between the other two—simply does not hold in the case of ordinal scoring.)

If you regard this result as a bug, you might want to devise a system of ordinal voting that respects, rather than violates, the independence of irrelevant alternatives. But in his 1951 Ph.D. dissertation, Kenneth Arrow

Arrow's Theorem

showed that no ordinal voting system can simultaneously satisfy that principle and three other basic desiderata: (1) *nondictatorship* (the group's ranking is never determined solely by the preferences of one of its members, but must account for preferences of all), (2) *unanimity* (if every individual in the group prefers option *a* to option *b,* then the group as a whole must as well), and (3) *unrestricted domain* (the system delivers a collective ranking whatever the individual rankings may be). This finding is now known as **Arrow's Theorem** or **Arrow's Impossibility Theorem**, a contribution to economic theory that helped win Arrow the 1972 Nobel Prize in Economics. Arrow's Theorem teaches us that oddities such as occurred in the women's figure skating competition at the 2002 Winter Olympics cannot be wholly eliminated. More fundamentally, there is *no* voting system that can reliably aggregate individual rank-order preferences into a coherent collective rank ordering.

COMMENTS AND QUESTIONS

1.   *Multiple judges, multiple criteria, ordinality, and cardinality.* What do you think? If you are troubled by departures from the principle of independence of irrelevant alternatives, would you prefer that figure skating aggregate raw cardinal scores rather than aggregating ordinal rankings derived from the raw scores? How would you do that in a way to curb the distorting influence of judges who, strategically or otherwise, employ unusually wide spreads between scores?

2.   *The independence of irrelevant alternatives and the presidency.* The Salt Lake City episode was (in the view of one author) a particularly conspicuous violation of the principle of independence of irrelevant alternatives only because tentative standings were broadcast before the competition was completed. For another probable, and more momentous,

example, consider the 2000 U.S. Presidential election. The outcome there came down to which candidate, the Republican George W. Bush or the Democrat Al Gore, won Florida, which was excruciatingly close. After all the shouting, and the litigation, was done, Bush had a 537-vote plurality, out of nearly 6 million votes cast. Ralph Nader, the Green Party Candidate, won 97,488 votes, a shade more than 1.6%; seven other candidates and write-ins collectively polled less than 0.7% of the vote. One careful study of has concluded that Nader voters preferred Gore to Bush by 3:2. *See* Michael C. Herron & Jeffrey B. Lewis, *Did Ralph Nader Spoil a Gore Presidency? A Ballot-Level Study of Green and Reform Party Voters in the 2000 Presidential Election* (Apr. 24, 2006). So, *if* Nader had not been on the ballot, and *if* the Nader voters nonetheless voted (an assumption that, admittedly, cannot be indulged blithely), and gone 3 to 2 for Gore, then (assuming no other changes) Gore likely would have won Florida by 20,000 votes. This suggests that the Florida result may have been the result of a violation of independence of irrelevant alternatives: remove the "irrelevant alternative" of Nader, and the order Bush-Gore order reverses.

This hypothetical result prevails only because in choosing its electors, Florida used the "plurality" or "winner-take-all" method that is dominant in United States elections: Each voter casts a single vote for the one candidate (or in this case, to be technically correct, for the one slate of electors pledged to the one pair of candidates for President and Vice President) that the candidate prefers. There are other plausible methods of voting under which Gore might have won even if Nader had been on the ballot.

Under one simple approach, each voter would rank her top three candidates, giving them three, two, and one points, respectively. It is plausible that most Nader voters would have given Gore two points, and more Gore voters than Bush voters would rank Nader second (because Gore was between Bush and Nader ideologically), enough to give Gore the victory. But notice that this simple ranked-order system is subject to manipulation: For example, a Bush voter who vastly prefers Gore to Nader or any of the other candidates might recognize that only Gore poses a threat to Bush and so refuse to give Gore any points at all.

Another, more commonly used, system, sometimes called instant-runoff voting (IRV), is more (but not completely) resistant to tactical voting. Each voter ranks her preferred candidates, as many as she wishes. If one candidate is preferred by a majority of voters, that candidate is the winner. If not, the candidate preferred by the fewest number of voters is eliminated, and the second choices of those voters are then treated as first choices. The process is repeated until one candidate is preferred by a majority of voters from among those remaining. IRV is now used for most statewide elections in Maine and Alaska, as well as in some municipal elections throughout the nation and in some important elections in other nations, most notably India and Australia. Had it been used to select Florida's electors in 2000, it is plausible, though hardly certain, that enough Nader voters would have ranked Gore above Bush that, when the race boiled down to the two leading candidates, Gore would have won a majority.

Ultimately, there is no single "correct" or "natural" way to aggregate the judgments or preferences of individuals in a group into a collective judgment or preference. There exist almost countless possible methods, of varying degrees of complexity, all involving different characteristic advantages and defects. This is as true in judgmental sports as it is in elections for office.

3. The countermajoritarian difficulty. The most commonly voiced arguments against judicial review as an institution, and against particular exercises of the judiciary's authority to declare acts of Congress unconstitutional and thus void, invoke what constitutional scholar Alexander Bickel famously dubbed "the countermajoritarian difficulty." *See* ALEXANDER BICKEL, THE LEAST DANGEROUS BRANCH: THE SUPREME COURT AT THE BAR OF POLITICS (1962). The claim, in a nutshell, is that when unelected judges invalidate actions of the elected branches, they act contrary to "majority will" as expressed by those representative institutions. How, if at all, do the Condorcet Paradox and Arrow's Impossibility Theorem bear on this argument?

The doctrinal paradox

For a very different voting paradox that arises both in sports and in other domains of life, we turn from figure skating to what some might think a near-polar opposite: boxing.

Boxing is competed in rounds. In pro boxing, there are three judges. The usual method of scoring is the "10-point must" system: Each judge must give one boxer 10 points for each round, and the other 10 or fewer. Usually, the second boxer will get 9 points; 10 points—a drawn round—is fairly common, 8 points—signaling a dominant round—is very infrequent, and scores under 8 are extremely rare. At the end of the fight, the scores on each judge's cards are added up. So each judge is counted as a single vote for one fighter or the other, or for a draw; if one fighter gets the votes of two or three judges, he wins the fight. Note that a one-point margin on a single card is as good as a 10-point margin. This aggregation method combines the votes at the judge level—looking at the bottom line on each judge's card and counting the judge's vote on the whole fight, without making anything depend on the round-by-round assessments that led to that vote.

Notice, however, that it is not inevitable that judges' judgments be aggregated in this way. Instead, the votes could be combined in the aggregate: add up all the points on all the judges' cards, and award the fight to whoever got more total points. Alternatively, the votes could be combined round by round, so that there is an overall winner for each round. There are several ways this could be done. For simplicity, let's consider a system in which the scores on a particular round that most favor fighter A and that most favor fighter B are discarded; only the score in the middle counts. *See* David J. Algranati & Daniel L. Cork, *Should Professional Boxing Change Its Scoring System? A Comparison of Current and Proposed Methods* (H. J. Heinz III School of Public Policy & Mgmt., Working Paper #2000–06, 2000). That might sound odd, but usually two judges or all three will score a given round the same, and if so the score they give is the one that counts. We'll call this the consensus system. To simplify matters further, let's take a schematic case in which each judge gives 10 points in each round to one fighter and 9 to the other, so effectively all that matters is whether a judge calls the round for fighter A or fighter B. This is a very common situation. Let us assume further that the judges score the fight as follows, with the right-most column showing how the round would be scored under the consensus system.

Round	Judge 1	Judge 2	Judge 3	Consensus
1	A	A	B	A
2	A	A	B	A
3	A	B	A	A
4	A	B	A	A
5	B	A	A	A
6	B	A	A	A
7	B	B	B	B
8	B	B	B	B
9	B	B	B	B
10	B	B	B	B
11	A	B	B	B
12	B	A	A	A
Total	B (115–113)	B (115–113)	B (115–113)	A (115–113)

If we apply the standard system, looking vertically first—down each judge's card—and then combine horizontally, B wins a unanimous decision, with a score of 115–113 on each card. But if we combine horizontally first—determining who won round 1, who won round 2, and so forth—and then add up those "consensus" round scores, then A wins, 115–113. Simply put, each judge individually thought that fighter B won 7 of the 12 rounds, but the judges taken as a group thought that fighter A won 7 of the 12 rounds!

Lest this schematic seem unrealistic, consider the scoring in the heavyweight championship bout between Evander Holyfield, the defending champion, and Lennox Lewis in New York City on March 13, 1999 (Holyfield-Lewis I). Many observers believed Lewis had won comfortably—but only one judge saw it that way. Another had Holyfield ahead, and the third scored it a draw. And so the bout was drawn. Because each judge scored each round either 10–9 or 10–10, we can simplify the presentation, indicating H for a vote for Holyfield, L for Lewis, and D for a drawn round. The table below shows the three judges' cards and, in the rightmost column, how the fight would have been scored under the consensus system.

Round	O'Connell	Christodolou	Williams	Consensus
1	L	L	L	L
2	L	L	L	L
3	H	H	H	H
4	L	L	H	L
5	L	L	H	L
6	H	L	L	L
7	D	L	L	L
8	H	H	H	H
9	H	H	H	H
10	D	H	H	H
11	H	D	H	H
12	L	L	L	L
Total (H–L)	115–115	113–116	115–113	113–115

Thus, if the consensus system had been used—determining an overall score for each round—Lewis would have won, effectively seven rounds to five.

Now consider the legal analogue: A multi-member court will sometimes be in a situation in which, if the judges vote on the case as a whole (analogous

Doctrinal Paradox

to looking at each boxing judge's whole card), one result will follow, but if they vote issue by issue (analogous to looking across the cards round by round) then the result will be the opposite. Lewis Kornhauser and Larry Sager, the legal scholars who first drew sustained attention to this phenomenon call it **the doctrinal paradox**, *see* Lewis A. Kornhauser & Lawrence G. Sager, *The One and the Many: Adjudication in Collegial Courts*, 81 CAL. L. REV. 1 (1993).

A classic illustration is *National Mutual Insurance Co. v. Tidewater Transfer Co.*, 337 U.S. 582 (1949). There the question was whether Congress could validly confer federal diversity jurisdiction on suits between a citizen of a state and a citizen of the District of Columbia. The relevant language of Article III of the Constitution provides that federal courts have jurisdiction over disputes between "citizens of different states," and for most purposes the District is not deemed to be a state. Nevertheless, there were two possible ways in which a justice might conclude that the conferral of jurisdiction was valid: He might conclude that (1) a grant of jurisdiction beyond the bounds of Article III was permissible in this context, or that (2) for this purpose "state" includes the District. Three justices (Black, Jackson, and Burton) accepted the first of these propositions, but the other six rejected it. Two justices (Murphy and Rutledge) accepted the second of these propositions—but the other seven rejected it. The other four justices (Vinson, Reed, Frankfurter, and Douglas) rejected both propositions. So solid majorities rejected both ways of concluding that the jurisdictional grant was valid—but the Court voted on the whole case rather than issue by issue, and the vote was 5–4 that the grant was valid. Professors Kornhauser and Sager report, "No Justice in *Tidewater* appears to have thought that issue-by-issue voting was the appropriate response to the embarrassment of the moment."

In other cases, however, Justices have acted on the basis that issue-by-issue voting is appropriate. For example, *Pennsylvania v. Union Gas Co.*, 491 U.S. 1 (1989), presented two principal issues: (1) Had Congress, in the statute involved in that case, expressed a clear intent to override the states' Eleventh Amendment immunity? (2) If so, had Congress acted constitutionally, given that it was legislating under the Commerce Clause (which predated the Amendment)? Justice White answered the first question in the negative. "However," he said, "a majority of the Court concludes otherwise, and therefore I reach the constitutional issue presented here." And on that issue, he joined a majority in concluding that override of the immunity was valid, and so allowing the suit to proceed—despite the fact that the result would have been the reverse if Justice White had been sitting on the case alone or if the Court had followed case-by-case voting.

Remarkably, Kornhauser and Sager point out that there is no common understanding of how a multi-member court should resolve the doctrinal paradox—that is, of when it should engage in one form of voting and when in the other. They do, however, offer some potential guideposts for resolving the problem. For example, they say that judges confronting the paradox "must decide whether the court, in the aggregate, is more durably committed to its judgment as to the pertinent rationales or its judgment as to the outcome," and that "where the salient issues are perceived to be independent of each other" there is good reason to vote issue by issue. But perhaps their most interesting suggestion is that in cases posing the paradox the court should conduct a "metavote," deciding whether to vote on the whole case or issue by issue.

COMMENTS AND QUESTIONS

1. *Skating and boxing.* Should judge-by-judge scoring on the competition as a whole, as is most common in boxing, be used in figure skating? Why or why not?

2. *Consensus scoring.* Do you believe that results like those that occurred in Holyfield-Lewis I are problematic? If so, do you believe that they would be eliminated or mitigated by switching from standard use of the 10-point must system to a "consensus" system that produces a single scorecard from three different scorecards? Why or why not? New Jersey boxing officials moved to a consensus system in light of Holyfield-Lewis I, only to return to the standard aggregation system when experience revealed that the consensus system, much like the standard system, could also produce outcomes that struck observers as mistaken. *See* Algranati & Cork, *Professional Boxing*.

3. A metavote? Deliberation? Holistic assessment? Algranati and Cork, in the working paper cited above, conclude that no change to the method of aggregating individual judges' judgments is likely to be superior to the present system and that the best way—and perhaps the only way—to improve boxing scoring is to improve "the education and training of boxing judges." It is worth exploring, however, whether the authors are too pessimistic regarding the prospects for positive reform of the method for aggregating the scores of individual judges.

To the extent that the contexts are analogous, the Kornhauser & Sager analysis suggests that no *categorical* rule in favor of either one of the two major approaches to aggregating judgments in boxing (a case-by-case protocol like the 10-point must system, or an issue-by-issue protocol like the New Jersey consensus system) is likely to be ideal. Do you think that the metavote they recommend is a good solution to the doctrinal paradox in law? Why or why not? If so (or even if not) could the metavote be adapted for boxing? How? Would it be an improvement to the choices presently on offer? (Recall the Zapata-Stephens fight discussed at p. 143. Would you say that the UFC used a "metavote" in the case of a majority draw? If so, couldn't it do the same in "paradoxical" fights?)

A less formal approach would be deliberation by the panel. Appellate judges confer before deciding a case—indeed, even if they confer orally only briefly, the case is not decided until the opinion is delivered, and the circulation of drafts gives the judges plenty of opportunity for exchange of views. Jurors, of course, do not simply vote; rather, they must confer first. Should boxing judges confer before filling out their cards? Should moot court judges do so? (It happens.) Should the winner of a boxing match simply be determined by a vote of the judges after deliberations, the scorecards being used essentially only as notes to assist in deliberations? What considerations bear on whether, when judgments of individual decision makers are aggregated, the decision makers should deliberate?

4. A novel proposal: the "conditional deferral." In advocating against categorical issue-by-issue or case-by-case resolution of doctrinally paradoxical cases in law, and in advocating in favor of a metavote, Kornhauser and Sager maintain that one factor that should prove relevant in any paradoxical case is each judge's subjective confidence level that he or she adjudged any given issue correctly. Could that insight be profitably leveraged to help resolve paradoxical cases in boxing? Consider the following proposal to supplement the 10-point must system with a "conditional deferral."

The idea in a nutshell is that scores given in accordance with the 10-point must system be aggregated at the whole-fight level and not at the individual-round level (that is, judge-by-judge, which is analogous to a judicial panel deciding on a case as a whole, and not round-by-round, which is comparable to issue-by-issue decision), but that a judge's score for a given round be adjusted if two conditions are satisfied: first, that the outcome of the fight would differ depending upon whether fight-level or round-level aggregation is used (that is, if the fight proves "paradoxical"); and second, that the judge, when scoring the round, noted at the time that it was not a score in which she had a high degree of confidence.

Here, in more detail, is how the proposal would work.

1. At the end of the fight, the judges' cards should be tallied both ways, judge-by-judge and round-by-round. If the two tallies agree on the outcome of the fight, then that outcome prevails, with the score adhering to the judge-by-judge protocol. If the tallies do not yield the same outcome, then the cards would be adjusted in line with conditional deferrals marked by the judges, as indicated below.

2. Each judge should score each round as under the 10-point must system, except that she has discretion to mark a "conditional deferral" for any given round. (This is to be done when the judge scores the round, not at the fight's end.) A conditional deferral is an affirmation that she is sufficiently uncertain about her score of that round such that, if both her colleagues award that round in the specified direction away from her score, and without doubts of their own, she would be willing to have her score changed to match the score that is closer to hers.

To illustrate:

- Suppose the three judges score a round as follows: 10–9, 9–10, 9–10. If the first judge marked a conditional deferral in favor of fighter B, her score would be liable to be adjusted to match those of her colleagues: 9–10.

- If the three scores were 10–9, 9–10, 9–10, and the third judge marked a conditional deferral in favor of fighter A, no adjustment would be made because it is not the case that judges 1 and 2 scored the round more favorably toward fighter A than the third judge did.

- If the scores were 10–9, 10–10, 9–10, and the first judge marked a conditional deferral toward fighter B, her score would be liable to be adjusted to a 10–10 draw. (It is a case like this that requires that the rule be stated in terms of permitting an adjustment whenever the scores of both other judges are in a specified direction away from the score awarded by the judge in question, and not in terms of permitting an adjustment to match the consensus score of her two colleagues.)

- If the scores were 10–9, 10–10, 10–10, and the first judge marked a conditional deferral in favor of fighter A—meaning that she was certain that A won the round, but thought it might be better scored as 10–8—then no adjustment would be made because judges 2 and 3 differed from judge 1 in the *opposite* direction of judge 1's doubt. (It is a case like this that requires that a deferral be marked as *directional*.)

- If the scores were 10–9, 9–10, 9–10, and judge 1 marked a conditional deferral in favor of fighter B, and judge 2 marked a conditional deferral in favor of fighter A, then no adjustments would be made.

3. After any adjustments are made on the judges' cards, the fight would be resolved according to the judge-by-judge protocol of the 10-point must system.

The principal motivation for this proposal is that it would sometimes result in dissolving the paradox by bringing the result under the judge-by-judge protocol in line with what it would have been under a round-by-round protocol. Consider Holyfield-Lewis I. (See the scorecards reproduced above.) Judge Williams, the third judge, acknowledged after the fight that she might have been wrong about round 5—one of the two rounds that she alone had scored for Holyfield. *See Boxing Judge has Change of Heart*, BBC NEWS, Mar. 19, 1999. Had Williams marked a conditional deferral in favor of Lewis on that round, then, because the bout was paradoxical, her score for that round would have been adjusted from 10–9 Holyfield to 10–9 Lewis. Suppose too that O'Connell had marked a conditional deferral also in favor of Lewis on round 7, a round he scored as a draw but that both other judges scored 10–9 for Lewis. As a consequence of these two adjustments, Williams's total score would be adjusted from 115–113 Holyfield to a 114–114 draw, and O'Connell's score would be adjusted from a 115–115 draw to 115–114 Lewis. If Christodolou's scorecard had remained the same, Lewis would have been awarded the victory—just as the consensus scoring systems would dictate.

Would this reform, if adopted, likely produce any other benefits? Would it produce any bad consequences? All in all, would you favor it? Could you improve upon it? What could be said for or against a system in which the scores on all the judges' cards are added up, the boxer who has the higher total winning the fight? (Under that system, Lewis would have won, 344–343.)

4. *The 10-point must system.* We have focused so far on possible methods for aggregating scores reached by individual judges. A much more commonly discussed problem with scoring in combat sports is that judges use too little of the scoring range that the 10-point must system creates. *See, e.g.*, T.P. Grant, *MMA: Four Steps To Fix Judging Under the 10-Point Must System*, BLEACHER REPORT (Dec. 6, 2010). In theory, the value of a ten-point range is that it allows judges to capture not only who won the round, but also how convincingly they won it. Take a five-round fight in the UFC in which Ferguson narrowly edges Santos for three rounds, but Santos beats Ferguson decisively in the other two. In theory, Santos's large margins of victory in the two rounds he won should outweigh the small margins of defeat he suffered in the three he lost, allowing him to outpoint Ferguson overall. In practice, though, that is unlikely to happen: well over 90% of rounds are scored 10–9, thus artificially limiting the impact of dominant rounds on the overall score. Why do judges employ such a narrow range of the available scoring spectrum? Might the notion of agency costs (introduced earlier in this Chapter) figure into the explanation? Can you

think of any reasons why interests of the principals (the UFC, the various boxing promotion authorities) and their agents (the judges) might diverge with respect to the effective spread used in the scoring of fights?

Do you agree that fight scoring would be improved if judges used more of the scoring range and awarded more 10–8 and even 10–7 scores? If so, what could be done to nudge judges to use more of the available spectrum? Would there be any substantial benefit to using a 20-point must system, in the hope that more scores more than one notch from the top would be given, or would that be like lengthening the basepaths in baseball to reduce the number of close calls at first base?

5.   *More judges?* Putting the doctrinal paradox aside, would the accuracy of boxing scoring be improved by increasing the number of ringside judges from three to five? The **Condorcet Jury Theorem** (yes, the same Condorcet, of course) provides that if a  group is going to reach a decision by majority vote, and if each member of the group, on average, has a greater than 50% chance of reaching the right outcome on their own, then the probability that the group will reach the right outcome increases as the number of group members (that is, voters) increases. Cost aside, is there any reason not to increase the number of judges?

6.   *Transparency.* In multi-stage competitions, like figure skating or gymnastics all-around championships, the scores of each stage are posted openly, as each competitor finishes each routine. Should the scores be posted only as each round is completed? (Note that in gymnastics all-around competition this would essentially mean that the scores would not be posted until the end, because the contestants rotate through the various stations.) Should boxing scores be posted openly each round? What advantages and disadvantages do you see in doing so? For a vigorous statement opposing open scoring, see Randy Gordon, *Why Boxing Must Not Employ an Open Scoring System*, https://tinyurl.com/y678u8ch. At the *end* of a competition, should the scorecards of the individual judges be announced? That is traditionally done in boxing. International skating preserves anonymity in voting; United States skating does not. INT'L SKATING UNION, *Frequently Asked Questions on the ISU New Judging System* (Sept. 8, 2003), https://tinyurl.com/y22nhkmq.

———

Exercise 5E

Starting in the 2014–15 season, college football has crowned a champion through a four-team postseason playoff. The four teams are seeded, with #1 playing #4, and #2 playing #3, and the winners later meeting in the championship game. How should the top four teams be selected?

Most sports that run a postseason after a regular season determine the competitors that meet in the postseason by a series of lexically ordered objective measures (e.g., won-loss record, head-to-head results, total points scored, etc.) that leave no room for subjective assessments by judges. But many informed observers believe that, in this context, exclusive reliance on objective selection criteria determined in advance would sacrifice too much accuracy for the sake of precision. As the official website of the College Football Playoff explains, "ranking football teams is an art, not a science," and the "selection process will inevitably need to select the four best teams from among several with legitimate claims to participate." COLLEGE FOOTBALL PLAYOFF, *Selection Committee Protocol*, https://tinyurl.com/y3qmadv7. Furthermore, objective criteria facilitate the ability of schools to "game" the system.[h] Accordingly, rankings of the top 25 teams, from which selections are ultimately made for the playoffs and for select bowl games, are determined at intervals beginning in the middle of the season by a 13-member selection committee whose members are instructed to base rankings on their "evaluation of the teams' performance on the field, using conference championships won, strength of schedule, head-to-head results, and comparison of results against common opponents to decide among teams that are comparable." The members' individual judgments are then aggregated into a collective ranking by means of a complex voting protocol, as described by the official directions:

1. Each committee member will create a list of the 30 teams he or she believes to be the best in the country, in no particular order. Teams listed by three or more members will remain under consideration. At the conclusion of any round, other teams can be added to the group of teams under consideration by a vote of three or more members.

2. Each member will list the six best teams, in no particular order. The six teams receiving the most votes will comprise the pool for the first ranking step. This is known as the "listing step."

3. In the first ranking step, each member will rank those six teams, one through six, with one being the best. The best team in each member's ranking will receive one point; second—best, two points, etc. The members' rankings will be added together and the three teams receiving the fewest points will become the top three seeds. The three teams that were not seeded will be held over for the next ranking step.

4. Each member will list the six best remaining teams, in no particular order. The three teams receiving the most votes will be added to the three teams held over to comprise the next ranking step.

5. Steps No. 3 and 4 will be repeated until 25 teams have been seeded. There will be seven rounds of voting; each round will consist of a "listing step" and a "ranking step."

COLLEGE FOOTBALL PLAYOFF, *CFP Selection Committee Voting Process*, https://tinyurl.com/yxd5k9yw. What are the strengths and weaknesses of this complex vote-aggregation protocol? Could you improve upon it?

CHAPTER 6

PENALTIES

■ ■ ■

Every sport prohibits some conduct because it frustrates or undermines (or threatens to frustrate or undermine) one or another of the sport's goals or values. For example, conduct might be prohibited because it causes or threatens physical injury, or makes sport-specific challenges too easy, or produces delay, and so on. In sports, as in the rest of life, prohibitions do not usually operate all by themselves: they are customarily backed by penalties. The principal functions of penalties are to deter violations and to remedy any competitive injury that the violation caused, though they may serve additional purposes as well. This chapter explores the many issues that attend the crafting of penalties.

First, we undertake some conceptual ground clearing. Things that rulemakers (and the rest of us) *call* "penalties" are not all of the same logical type. Accordingly, Subchapter 6A introduces a distinction, familiar from legal theory, between "prices" and "sanctions."

The remainder of this chapter concerns what Subchapter 6A terms "sanctions," and what might be deemed "true penalties." Subchapter 6B explores whether there are circumstances in which an infraction or violation should not draw forth a threatened penalty.[a] There are two common reasons, familiar (again) from ordinary life: because the infraction caused no harm ("no harm, no foul") or because the infraction was not intentional ("I didn't mean to!"). Subchapter 6C reviews types of penalties and Subchapter 6D discusses factors that bear on their appropriate magnitudes. Subchapter 6E presents a case study in optimal sanction design: NBA rules that mandate that players be ejected and disqualified for fighting.

A. INTRODUCTION: PRICES AND SANCTIONS

Let us start with some explicit and paradigmatic penalties in sport. In soccer, the referee may issue a "penalty card" (yellow or red) and a "penalty kick" for unsporting or serious foul play. In ice hockey, a player will be sent off the ice for two or five minutes as a "minor penalty" or "major penalty"

---

[a] It may be helpful to reserve the word "infraction" for non-compliance with a constitutive rule, and use "violation" for conduct that runs afoul of a regulative rule. As best we can tell, however, there is no standardly recognized distinction between "infraction" and "violation," except that some will view the former as less serious.

for any number of rules infractions. In basketball, a defender who fouls an opponent while in the act of shooting will be assessed a personal foul, and his opponent will be awarded free throws, as a penalty for the foul. In football, a team will lose five, ten, or fifteen yards as "distance penalties" for violations and fouls. In boxing, the referee can penalize a boxer for low blows by ordering a point reduction for the round.

All of the foregoing penalties—and countless others that could be cited—are, in a sense, the same sort of thing: they are *costs imposed on an individual or team in response to an infraction or violation.* Put another way, all these "penalties" are consequences imposed for the violation of a "duty-imposing" or "regulative" rule (see Chapter 4). When a rule provides "do not X; and if you X, then you will suffer the consequences Y," Y is the penalty for illegal Xing.

Or so it appears. But not all unwanted consequences that are *called* "penalties" assume this form.

Consider golf. Perhaps the most oft-quoted rule of golf, Rule 1.1, provides that, except as otherwise specified in the rules, a golfer must play her ball "as it lies." In general, the player must not improve the position or lie of his ball, or the area of his intended stance or swing. Rule 8.1. In stroke play, the "penalty . . . for a breach of most Rules" is two strokes. Rule 1.3(c)(2). Sure enough, this example conforms to our general definition: here, the "penalty" of a two-stroke addition to the score is a cost imposed for violating the rule that directs golfers to play their balls as they lie.

So far, so good. But what if a ball is lost in a water hazard? Rule 26–1 provides in part:

The player may under penalty of one stroke:

a.   Play a ball as nearly as possible at the spot from which the original ball was last played; or

b.   Drop a ball behind the water hazard, keeping the point at which the original ball last crossed the margin of the water hazard directly between the hole and the spot on which the ball is dropped, with no limit to how far behind the water hazard the ball may be dropped.

Suppose that, after losing your ball in a water hazard, you elect to drop and play a new ball as close as possible to the spot from which you played the ball that you lost. You will be assessed a one-stroke "penalty." For what, exactly? What rule did you violate? The following reading helps untangle this puzzle.

ROBERT L. SIMON, THE ETHICS OF STRATEGIC FOULING: A REPLY TO FRALEIGH

32 JOURNAL OF THE PHILOSOPHY OF SPORT 87 (2005)
© 2005 International Association for the Philosophy of Sport,
reprinted with permission of the publisher (Taylor & Francis Ltd.)

. . . The discussion over the ethics of strategic fouling is much more than a narrow debate over the use of a tactic in sport. Critics of strategic fouling admit that the practice is prevalent and tend to regard it as an example of how emphasis on winning has undermined the deeper and more fundamental values that make sport a morally attractive enterprise. In particular, critics fear that strategic fouling alters the kind of test that should be fundamental to a sports contest and so in effect gives priority to winning while undermining the kinds of skills that when exercised properly give winning its true significance. Undue emphasis is placed on results, and the external rewards such as fame and fortune that come with winning, and not enough on the integrity of the activity itself.

Philosophers of sport have discussed the ethics of strategic fouling from a variety of perspectives. Those who view the ethics of strategic fouling from perspectives influenced by formalism have stressed that such fouls are violations of the constitutive rules of the game. By this view, the rules are the basis of the (implied or explicit) contract between the competitors, or at least the basis of the public understanding that all competitors should be expected to follow. Hence, strategic fouls either violate the fundamental norm of conformity to the constitutive rules of the game or are perhaps not part of the game itself. According to the latter interpretation, strategic foulers are not really playing the game at all and so are unable to truly win, because the game is defined by the constitutive rules that determine what are and are not permissible moves within it.

Other writers who emphasize the social context of sport have argued that social conventions and practices, often referred to as the ethos of the game, legitimate strategic fouls in a way ignored by formalists, who focus too exclusively on formal elements of sport, particularly constitutive rules. Thus, there is alleged to be a common understanding among basketball players that losing teams will foul at the end of games to stop the clock. Because all teams do this and expect others to do so, as well, there is nothing illegitimate about such tactics.

A third group of theorists, including myself, has agreed with the conventionalists that formal rules are not necessarily all ethicists in sport have to take into account; they also have been wary of endorsing the conventionalist view that a practice is legitimate just because current practitioners of a sport accept it. These theorists have argued that in addition to rules, a broad interpretation of the best understanding of the game, including respect for its internal norms and values, can be fundamental to the ethical assessment of practices in sport. In my own case, I have tried to defend a theory of penalties that distinguishes punishments for prohibited behavior from prices for the exercise of strategic options and have argued that in some cases, such as fouling late in a basketball game to stop the clock and force the team in the lead to make foul shots, the penalties for strategic fouls are prices for allowable strategic choices rather than sanctions of moves not allowed in the game.

[Warren] Fraleigh's recent contribution takes the discussion farther by presenting new arguments, drawing in part on the work of Cesar Torres, against the acceptability of strategic fouling and by maintaining that the best overall theory of competitive sports supports the view that strategic fouls are unacceptable. Moreover, Fraleigh uses this line of argument to undermine the use of the price-sanction distinction to defend strategic fouling. . . .

[Fraleigh draws on Torres's distinction between constitutive and restorative skills. Constitutive skills, such as dribbling, passing, and shooting field goals in basketball, are required to meet the challenges posed by the sport's constitutive rules. Restorative skills are used to get the game back on track when something has gone wrong, such as a rules violation. Thus, shooting free throws in basketball is a restorative skill. Fraleigh argues that competitors undermine the central challenge of the sport if they transform it from one in which constitutive skills dominate to one in which restorative skills can determine the outcome. He also points out that rulemakers have made it clearer that certain penalties, such as those for intentional fouls in NCAA basketball, should be regarded as punishments rather than as prices.]

This critique of strategic fouling has considerable force, but before it is accepted we need to examine three distinctions more closely. The first is the distinction between constitutive and restorative skills, the second is between different kinds of strategic fouls, and the third is between a critique of indiscriminate strategic fouling and a critique of strategic fouling in specific situations in which it might add not only to the excitement and interest of the contest but also to the test it presents to competitors.

Constitutive and Restorative Skills

What exactly is the distinction between constitutive and restorative skills? In part, it is one of function. Restorative skills are those employed to get the game back on track after a constitutive rule has been violated. [Take foul shooting in basketball as an example of a restorative skill . . . .] Foul shooting is fixed and repetitive compared with the fluid motions of normal play in basketball. There is no opponent trying to defend against the shot. The shooter does not have to move to get open in the first place. Foul shooting, in other words, is less complex and therefore less interesting than shooting field goals. . . .

[But this is not always true of restorative skills.] Consider, for example, the art of killing penalties in ice hockey. The skills involved are hardly simple and repetitive. Penalty killing and the correlative power plays associated with it often are especially interesting and exciting parts of the game. Although a hockey game constantly disrupted by penalties can be regarded as defective to one degree or another and even spoiled in extreme cases, the skills employed by both sides during power play often are as intrinsically interesting or complex as those employed in the regular course of play. . . . Moreover, aspects of regular play might in themselves also lack complexity and exhibition of high levels of skill, such as a basketball player dribbling out the clock or a physically dominant player constantly scoring easy layup shots from under the basket against clearly mismatched opponents.

Finally, we need to distinguish between the complexity of an action during a game, such as shooting a foul shot, and the strategic complexities generated by the possibility of strategically fouling and sending an opponent to the foul line. The possibility of what I will later call the judicious strategic foul generates a whole set of complex options and choices that can make the overall game more interesting than otherwise for participants and spectators alike. . . . [For all these reasons,] sometimes a sports contest in which restorative skills are employed can be a better test of more varied abilities than one in which only constitutive skills are employed.

Types of Strategic Fouls

Although the distinction between constitutive and restorative skills might be complex, the main point of Torres's distinction is that constitutive skills are those the game is best construed as designed to test. Accordingly, intentional fouling changes the nature of that test and disrespects the central value of the game by eclipsing the role of constitutive skills and elevating restorative skills beyond their proper station. . . .

This argument is a strong one, and I believe it does establish strategic fouling as (at least presumptively) unethical in at least two kinds of cases. [The first occurs when a less skilled team fouls the other in an attempt to eliminate the other's skill advantage; Simon cites an example of an inferior ice hockey team resorting to roughhouse play to increase its chance of winning. The other, related kind of case is a foul committed to deprive an opponent of a particular advantage "already gained through superior use of constitutive skills," such as an intentional foul intended to prevent a score by a soccer player who has broken away ahead of the defense.] Not all strategic fouls, however, fall within these two categories.

First, and perhaps the less interesting kind of example for the issues involved here, are what might be called mixed or impure strategic fouls. Mixed strategic fouls occur when athletes play more aggressively at key points in the contest, knowingly taking on the increased risk of fouling because the price of fouling might be strategically worth paying. For example, basketball players on a team a few points behind in the last few minutes of a game might try to steal the ball from the offensive team but do so in a much more aggressive fashion than normal because, even if fouls are called, the offensive team might miss its foul shots. . . .

A kind of case that more directly challenges Fraleigh's argument is a strategic foul that does not deprive an opponent of an advantage already gained but that prevents play from being executed in the first place, that is, preventive strategic fouls. Thus, a basketball player might foul the recipient of a pass before the ball handler can pass, dribble, or make a move to shoot. Clearly, if a team repeatedly fouls in such a way, a basketball game can have no flow and the game is spoiled. A clearly inferior team that continually fouls in the hope of making the game so lacking in flow that the superior skills of the opponent are negated might be justly criticized. It does not follow, though, that this is the only kind of case in which a strategic foul of this kind might be employed. Let us consider the point further.

Judicious Strategic Fouls

[Simon posits the case of two teams of roughly even ability, having split their prior games, competing for a playoff spot; with 9 seconds left, Team A has possession and a 2-point lead.] Team B's coach realizes that his team's chances of stealing the ball with just 9 seconds to play are remote. Players on Team A might just hold the ball and not even attempt to advance it up the court. The coach also knows, however, that although both teams are roughly equal in constitutive abilities, Team A's players are not good foul shooters. He orders his team to foul to stop the clock, reasoning that if the opponents miss their foul shots, Team B will have a chance to tie or win the game.

Is this choice of strategy unethical? From the point of view of broad internalism (or interpretivism), we need to ask if basketball is a better game if judicious use of strategic fouling is regarded as appropriate. Although the answer certainly is debatable, it is not unreasonable to think that the game in question is a better one if it remains competitive until the end rather than ending anticlimactically by Team A simply holding the ball or not trying to advance it for the final 9 seconds.

What about the point that contests should, as far as possible, be determined by use of constitutive rather than restorative skills? This principle is presumptively correct, but in the previous example, it already has been established that the opponents are roughly equal in constitutive skills. Neither is better than the other in that regard. Although the suggestion that a tie might be the fairest resolution has merit, a tie is not feasible in this context because only one team can advance to the playoffs. . . . In such a case, if both teams are equal in terms of constitutive skills but one team is much better at exercising restorative skills, why isn't that team the better of the two? In other words, it is appropriate for differences in restorative skills to be tiebreakers. . . .

Of course, this example is an extreme case, but it does suggest a more general thesis. According to this thesis, strategic fouls are not ethically inappropriate when the following conditions are satisfied. First, it is reasonable to believe that the opponents are roughly matched in constitutive skills. Second, the team that strategically fouls has no alternative strategy based on the use of constitutive skills that gives it a reasonable chance to win. Third, the penalty for the foul must reasonably be regarded as the price of action rather than punishment for it; that is, the penalty must provide reasonable compensation for the offended team. Last, the strategic foul must not take away an advantage in play that the opponents have already earned through the exercise of constitutive skills. For example, this would rule out tripping from behind a hockey player who has broken away on an open goal. (We might also add that teams not employ a series of strategic fouls designed to prevent opponents from exhibiting constitutive skills by disrupting the flow of the game.)

One difficulty with this approach is that in my basketball example, it is not clear that the second condition is satisfied. Team B could try to double-team or trap players on Team A in an attempt to steal the ball. Such attempts sometimes are successful and involve the use of constitutive rather than restorative skills. But while this point has force, it is not clear that it applies fully to evenly matched teams with only a few seconds left in the game. A player on Team A might simply hold the ball and let the clock run out. . . .

Another difficulty, a critic might argue, is that the third condition is not satisfied. Penalties for many strategic fouls have been elevated to resemble punishments rather than prices. As we have seen, Fraleigh maintains that the evolution of the rules of basketball makes it clear that intentional strategic fouls are to be punished rather than purchased for a fair price. [Simon raises reasons to doubt this view. He notes that in most cases referees do not treat even clearly strategic fouls differently from others. This may be giving the team the benefit of the doubt, in light of the difficulties of distinguishing between pure and mixed strategic fouls. It may also reflect an understanding that the rules are not meant to eliminate strategic fouling. In support of this suggestion, he cites the rule that "allows a losing team to in effect trade two foul shots for the opportunity to attempt to make a 3-point basket," thus improving its chance of catching up, especially if its opponent is not strong from the line.] Is this a flaw in the rules, or does it provide the opportunity for strategic choices and excitement in the last few minutes of a contest that actually enhance the game? If, as I have suggested, the judicious use of strategic fouls in basketball games raises the competitive intensity of the game, making it a better test for the players, and if restorative skills can help determine which of two otherwise evenly matched opponents is superior, such fouls can have a defensible place in the game. . . .

COMMENTS AND QUESTIONS

1. Theoretical perspectives. Simon's article starts by distinguishing three groups of theorists: formalists, conventionalists, and internalists. But because his descriptions of these three approaches are fairly sketchy, a few additional words on the subject will prove useful. In particular, we should get clear on what these different theories are theories *about*, and on how they differ from each other.

As Simon uses the terms, **formalism, conventionalism**, and **internalism** are theories concerning ethics—the standards that govern what people ought, and ought not, to do. But these theories could alternatively be understood as concerning what the true norms of a practice are, or what gives a norm the contents that it has. Either way, formalism is, perhaps, the simplest or most intuitive of the positions. It maintains that the actual or valid rules of a practice are whatever the "formal" (written) rules say, or that judges should follow and enforce the meaning that is encoded in the formal provisions. Conventionalism, in contrast, maintains that the conventions or actual practices of a community can bear on what the true or valid rules are, or on what officials should do.

To understand the difference, consider jaywalking. Suppose a statute in some jurisdiction states that "it shall be an offense for a pedestrian to cross any street except at a designated crosswalk when the traffic signals authorize a crossing." Suppose too that pedestrians routinely flout this directive by crossing in the middle of streets and by crossing, in crosswalks, against the light. Moreover, when pedestrians do jaywalk, but do so safely, they are not criticized by other pedestrians or by drivers, and police officers who witness safe jaywalking do not issue citations. On these assumed facts, a formalist is apt to say that jaywalking is against the law ("that's simply what the formal rules say"), whereas a conventionalist is apt to say that jaywalking, when done safely, is not unlawful ("despite what the formal rules say, widespread and robust conventions permit it").

Internalism stakes out a middle ground of sorts. Internalists believe that there are (or at least can be) values and norms that are "internal" to a practice, such that they help make the practice what it is and help account for why people engage in it and what they get out of it. Internalism is therefore either another name for, or a close cousin to, the theory that the legal philosopher Ronald Dworkin dubbed "interpretivism." This theory holds that an interpretation of a practice must seek both to fit, tolerably well, certain facts about the practice (such as what the statutes say, and what participants in the practice, including officials, actually do and what they say about what they do), and to justify those facts or show them "in their best light." *See generally* RONALD DWORKIN, LAW'S EMPIRE ch. 2 (1986). Against formalism, internalism (or interpretivism) maintains that the norms are not necessarily fully determined by what formal authoritative texts say. Against conventionalism, internalism maintains that the norms are not necessarily fully determined by what actual practices happen to be. As applied to sport, internalists maintain that the norms are partially constituted or determined not only by what the formal texts say and by what participants do, but also by the values that undergird or inform sport in general or this sport in particular.

Do the differences among formalism, conventionalism, and internalism/ interpretivism make sense to you? Do you find yourself disposed in favor of any one of these approaches? Do you favor something else?

2. Strategy vs. tactics. Simon refers to strategic fouling. At least for the most part, he really should speak instead of "tactical" fouling. Strategy is the big picture, an overall plan to achieve a major objective. A tactic is a more narrowly focused method to achieve smaller objectives within the larger plan. Conquering the Nazis by attacking through Northern Europe was a strategy; building an artificial harbor in Normandy to help move men and materiel was a tactic. So fouling an opposing basketball player late in the game in the hopes of stopping the clock and increasing the chance of getting the ball back quickly is a tactic, not a strategy. If fouling an opposing player repeatedly in hopes of limiting his offense, knowing that he is a poor free-throw shooter, is a central part of the overall game plan—think Hack-a-Shaq—then it might be appropriate to call it strategic. But tactical fouling is far more common, and so that is the term we will use here except when referring specifically to Simon's definition.

3. Prices vs. sanctions. Simon's view about tactical fouling depends upon a "theory of penalties that distinguishes punishments for prohibited behavior from prices for the exercise of strategic options." Armed with this distinction, he has "argued that in some cases, such as fouling late in a basketball game to stop the clock and force the team in the lead to make foul shots, the penalties for strategic fouls are prices for allowable strategic choices rather than sanctions of moves not allowed in the game." Before evaluating his argument, we should clarify the terminology, for several terms are swirling around in just this single passage: "penalty," "punishment," "price," and "sanction." Although different writers use these terms in different ways, and it is not entirely clear that even Simon himself is wholly consistent in his usage, legal theorists widely believe that the key distinction lies between *prices* and *sanctions*.

As the legal scholar Robert Cooter explained in his classic treatment of the subject, "a sanction [is] a detriment imposed for doing what is forbidden, and a price [is] money extracted for doing what is permitted. Officials should create prices to compel decision makers to take into account the external costs

Prices
vs.
Sanctions

of their acts, whereas officials should impose sanctions to deter people from doing what is wrong." Robert Cooter, *Prices and Sanctions*, 84 COLUM. L. REV. 1523 (1984). On this account, criminal punishments are *sanctions* because they are imposed when somebody violates a prohibition; cigarette taxes are *prices* because buying and smoking cigarettes, even if not condoned let alone encouraged, is permitted. The *word* "penalty" might be used to refer to a *sanction*, or to a *price*, or to the class that is comprised of sanctions and prices jointly.

Based on your reading of Simon's article, as well as your background knowledge, is this how you would carve the relevant terrain? That is, although we use a variety of different *words* to refer to things in this general space— "penalty," "price," "punishment," "sanction," "exaction," etc.—do you agree that the phenomena really fall into two types: costs inflicted to punish or deter rule violations, and prices extracted for exercising an option?

4. A quibble. Given Simon's conclusion that the penalties for some tactical fouls are prices, what might be puzzling or mistaken about his initial definition of strategic fouls as occurring "when a competitor in an athletic contest deliberately and openly breaks a rule expecting to be penalized and with willingness to accept the penalty, in order to obtain a strategic advantage in the contest"?

5. Beyond prices and sanctions? The biathlon, a staple of the Winter Olympics, combines cross-country skiing and rifle shooting. A competition consists of a race in which participants ski around a cross-country trail system of varying distances, stopping at designated spots to shoot at five targets, alternating between standing and prone positions. If the competitor hits all five targets, she continues along the trail. For each target she misses, however, a "penalty" is imposed. The penalties assume different forms, depending upon the competition. One common penalty is the addition of 1 minute to the athlete's total time for each missed target. Another is the requirement that the competitor ski a 150-meter "penalty lap" for each miss, a lap taking approximately 30 seconds. As in most races, placement is determined by shortest total time.

How should we conceptualize the "penalty minute" or the "penalty lap"? They don't appear to be *sanctions* imposed for violating a rule (like the two-stroke "penalty" imposed by Rules of Golf 8.1 and 9.1 for improving one's lie). Even if the rules are rightly understood to require participants to *try* to hit the targets, it is implausible to suppose that they require competitors to *succeed*. But neither is it clear that these are *prices* that attach to the exercise of an option (like the one-stroke "penalty" imposed by Rule 17.1(d) if one chooses to drop behind a water hazard), for it seems inapt, or at least awkward, to describe a biathlete as facing a "choice" of either hitting the target or having a minute added to her time (or skiing a lap). What lesson should we learn? Are "penalties" in biathlon *sanctions* or *prices*, in your view? Or are they neither? Do they suggest that the reigning two-part distinction between *prices* and *sanctions* is too limited, and that the phenomena that we (sometimes) call a "penalty" should be divided into three categories, or even more? How would you carve the conceptual terrain?

6. Prices, sanctions, and basketball. In your view, are the foul shots awarded for tactical fouls committed by the losing team toward the end of a close basketball game better conceived of as *sanctions* or as *prices?* In answering this question, you might care to know that Rule 12 of the Official NBA Rulebook is captioned "Fouls and Penalties." It is divided into two parts: "A. Technical Foul" and "B. Personal Foul." Rule 12, Part B, is itself divided into ten sections, on such subjects as "Flagrant Foul," "Double Fouls," "Offensive Fouls," and "Loose Ball Fouls." The first section, denominated "Types," provides, in part, as follows:

> a.   A player shall not hold, push, charge into, impede the progress of an opponent by extending a hand, forearm, leg or knee or by bending the body into a position that is not normal. Contact that results in the re-routing of an opponent is a foul which must be called immediately.

> b.   Contact initiated by the defensive player guarding a player with the ball is not legal. This contact includes, but is not limited to, forearm, hands, or body check.

Does this language decisively resolve whether penalties for tactical fouls toward game's end are prices or sanctions? Is it probative even if not decisive? In thinking about this problem, do you find yourself moved more by formalism, conventionalism, or internalism?

If you believe that the penalties imposed for tactical fouls committed by the losing team toward the end of a close basketball game, to stop the clock, are prices, do you think the same is true of the other types of tactical fouls in basketball that Simon discusses, such as a foul to prevent the other team from scoring? Why or why not? Does the constitutive-restorative distinction have any force in this context? If the skill in free-throw shooting is less interesting than the range of skills necessary in other aspects of basketball, does that have any bearing on whether fouling is priced or prohibited?

Philosophical considerations aside, is basketball improved by tactical fouling? Is it improved by some types of tactical fouls and not others? If you think that tactical fouling is sometimes or always harmful to the game, do you have a fix?

7. Obamacare. In *National Federation of Independent Businesses v. Sebelius,* 567 U.S. 519 (2012), a divided Supreme Court upheld the critical "individual mandate" provision of the 2010 Patient Protection and Affordable Care Act (the act colloquially known as "Obamacare"). One 5–4 majority held that the individual mandate, which purported to require individuals to buy health insurance, was not a constitutional exercise of Congress's power to regulate interstate commerce. However, a separate 5–4 majority held that the mandate was a constitutionally permissible exercise of Congress's power to lay and collect taxes. Here is a snippet from Chief Justice John Roberts's pivotal opinion on this latter question:

> The most straightforward reading of the mandate is that it commands individuals to purchase insurance. After all, it states that individuals "shall" maintain health insurance. 26 U. S. C. § 5000A(a). Congress thought it could enact such a command under the Commerce Clause, and the Government primarily defended the law on that basis. But, for the reasons explained above, the Commerce Clause does not give Congress that power. Under our precedent, it is therefore necessary to ask whether the Government's alternative reading of the statute—that it only imposes a tax on those without insurance—is a reasonable one.
>
> Under the mandate, if an individual does not maintain health insurance, the only consequence is that he must make an additional payment to the IRS when he pays his taxes. See § 5000A(b). That, according to the Government, means the mandate can be regarded as establishing a condition—not owning health insurance—that triggers a tax—the required payment to the IRS. Under that theory, the mandate is not a legal command to buy insurance. Rather, it makes going without insurance just another thing the Government taxes, like buying gasoline or earning income. And if the mandate is in effect just a tax hike on certain taxpayers who do not have health insurance, it may be within Congress's constitutional power to tax.
>
> The question is not whether that is the most natural interpretation of the mandate, but only whether it is a "fairly possible" one. *Crowell* v. *Benson*, 285 U. S. 22, 62 (1932). . . . It is of course true that the Act describes the payment as a "penalty," not a "tax." But . . . that label . . . does not determine whether the payment may be viewed as an exercise of Congress's taxing power.

NFIB v. Sebelius, 567 U.S. at 562–564. What relevance, if any, does this discussion bear for your answer to the questions above in comment 6?

8.   *Daycare*. Consider also the results of a famous study of daycare centers in Haifa, Israel. Parents were supposed to pick their kids up by 4 pm. But before the study began, there was no fine or other formal penalty for coming late, and if a kid had not been collected by closing time one of the teachers would have to stay behind. When a modest fine was introduced in some of the centers for picking kids up late, lateness *increased*. Uri Gneezy & Aldo Rustichini, *A Fine is a Price*, 29 J. LEG. STUD. 1 (2000). Can you explain why?

9.   *Intentional fouls and violations in other sports*. How about tactical fouls in other sports—like intentional pass interference or intentional offensive holding in football, or the intentional tackle of an attacker in soccer? Are these actions priced or sanctioned?

NHL rules have long provided that a goalie commits an infraction by "[i]ntentionally dislodging the net from its moorings during the course of a breakaway." As a remedy, the opposing team is awarded a penalty shot. NHL Rules, Table 13, Rule 25(ii). Should this rule be understood as a priced option or a sanction-backed prohibition? In 2014, a goalie in the American Hockey League (the NHL's minor league), judging that he'd have a better chance defending the penalty shot than the breakaway, intentionally dislodged the net, and the tactic worked: he stopped the penalty shot. The league responded by toughening the sanctions. Now the goalie gets a game misconduct penalty and the backup goalie must come in to defend against the penalty shot. *See* Lindsay Kramer, *AHL's "Leggio Rule" stiffens penalty for goalies who intentionally dislodge the net*, SYRACUSE CRUNCH (Nov. 6, 2014). What lesson do you draw—that the tactic used to be priced but is now prohibited? That it was always prohibited? That it was, and remains, priced?

10. So what? Suppose that the rules of a sport impose "penalty" P for conduct C. What difference does it make (or might it make) whether P is rightly conceived as a *sanction* or as a *price*? One thing to say is that if P is a sanction of the sport then C is rightly conceived as prohibited by the sport, and if P is a price, then C is permitted. But what difference does it make whether the sport "prohibits C on pain of P" or "permits C on payment of P"?

Let us suppose that we all share a pretty clear sense of what it means for a sport to permit C on payment of P.[b] On that assumption, the question reduces to: What does it mean for a sport to prohibit C on pain of sanction P? This is an immensely difficult question on which normative theorists differ. Consider the following three possibilities:

(a)   if a sport prohibits C, then anyone who consents to participate in the sport assumes a moral obligation not to C;

(b)   if a sport prohibits C, then anyone who consents to participate in the sport is under a sport-specific obligation not to C (i.e., e.g., she assumes a "baseball obligation" or a "field hockey obligation" not to C), but it remains an open question whether she has a moral obligation not to C (and she often won't); or

(c)   the only type of obligation that exists is a "moral" or "all-things considered" obligation; and therefore there are no such things as sport-specific obligations, and any attempt by a sport to prohibit C can amount to nothing more than a statement of the consequences for Cing, in which case there is no difference between the two ways of characterizing a penalty in sport.

Does any one of these possibilities seem most probable to you? Can you think of any alternatives? We will revisit this question when we focus squarely on cheating, in Chapter 14.

---

[b]   But maybe we don't. Does this mean that a participant who Cs: (a) is obligated to pay or suffer P, or (b) makes herself liable to attempts by officials (or by opponents) to exact or impose P? If (a), then what sort of obligation is it—a moral obligation, or only a sport obligation?

11. Contracts as promises? The usual remedy for breach of contract is "expectation damages": the party that breaches must pay the promisee whatever sum would put her in the position she would have reasonably expected to be in had the first party performed. Suppose, for example, that Adam and Eve enter into a contract under which Eve promises to deliver one gross of apples to Adam on Friday and Adam agrees to pay Eve $50. If Eve fails to deliver the apples, and if the market price for a gross of apples has risen to $75 on Friday, then Adam's expectation damages are $25: by adding $25 to the $50 he had planned to pay Eve, Adam can purchase apples from another seller and be in exactly the position he expected to be in when he contracted with Eve. So what type of promise does one make by entering into a contract with another? Is it a promise to perform, with expectation damages serving as the sanction for breaking this promise (i.e., nonperforming)? Or is it a promise to perform-or-pay-expectation-damages—that is, a promise *either* to perform or pay expectation damages, as the promisor chooses? If it is cheaper for Adam to buy replacement apples than it is for Eve to deliver them, is it socially beneficial for Eve to breach and pay damages? For an entry into the substantial literature on this topic, see Matthew A. Seligman, *Moral Diversity and Efficient Breach*, 117 MICH. L. REV. 885 (2019).

Do you think the better answer to the previous questions are the same for all different types of contracts (both goods and services? all varieties of services?) and contracting parties (e.g., individuals, small businesses, multinational corporations)? Does it make any difference which way we conceptualize the contractual promise?

B. WHAT TO PROHIBIT? WHAT TO PENALIZE?

We focus now on penalties that are imposed in response to the violation of a rule—that is, on what the economic literature calls "sanctions." Such penalties depend upon a logically prior determination that this or that conduct should be prohibited. Even mixed martial arts, a sport that perhaps comes closest to open competition of any sport, prohibits a substantial array of conduct—including among others head-butting, eye-gouging, hair-pulling, and attacking the groin. Exactly what should be prohibited and penalized are highly sport-particular questions. If you want to figure out, say, whether baseball should no longer prohibit balks, whether basketball should allow goaltending, whether hockey should permit icing, or whether competitive eating should prohibit the practice of dunking food in water, you'll just have to predict how such changes in what is prohibited and permitted would affect how the sport is played and to evaluate, by reference to the kinds of considerations examined in Chapter 3, whether those changes in play improve the sport or not, on net. There is no shortcut.

Accordingly, this subchapter does not attempt to address particularistic questions about whether this or that sport should prohibit this or that conduct. Instead, we investigate two topics that the rulemakers of many sports will have occasion to address: (1) whether the existence of a violation, and the imposition of a sanction, should or should not depend upon whether normally proscribed conduct produced any bad results; and (2) whether the prohibition and sanction should or should not depend upon an actor's intent, or other mental state.

1. NO HARM, NO FOUL (OR PENALTY): THE (IR)RELEVANCE OF RESULT

Consider the following three rules:

1. "When a player or goalkeeper carries or holds any part of his stick above the shoulders of the opponent so that injury results, the Referee shall assess a double-minor penalty for all contact that causes an injury, whether accidental or careless, in the opinion of the referee." NHL Rule 60.3.

2. "Either batsman is out Obstructing the field if he wilfully obstructs or distracts the fielding side by word or action. Furthermore, it shall be regarded as obstruction if while the ball is in play either batsman wilfully, and without the consent of a fielder, strikes the ball with his bat or person, other than a hand not holding the bat, after the ball has been touched by a fielder. This shall apply whether or not there is any disadvantage to the fielding side." Laws of Cricket, Law 37.

3. "A player . . . is sent off if he . . . den[ies] the opposing team a goal or an obvious goal-scoring opportunity by deliberately handling the ball." FIFA Laws of the Game, Law 12.

Notice that of these three rules, only the second makes the existence of a violation, and the imposition of a penalty, insensitive to results. A soccer player (other than a goalkeeper) who intentionally handles the ball in an attempt to stop a shot on his goal will be shown a red card and sent off only if he succeeds. If the ball slips through his fingers and into the goal he has not committed an infraction because he has not "denied" the opposition a goal or goal-scoring opportunity. Likewise, a hockey player who carries his stick above the shoulders of an opposing player has not committed an infraction if his carelessness does not result in any injury. In contrast, a cricket player who deliberately interferes with the ball is out even if his interference causes no competitive impact—that is, "whether or not there is any disadvantage to the fielding side." Why these differences? What principles or considerations can explain and justify a decision to make regulative rules sensitive or insensitive to the downstream results of a competitor's actions?

Before tackling that question, one clarification is warranted. Some rules are insensitive to results by their very nature. This is true of many constitutive rules. Consider the rules governing traveling in basketball. The rules are surprisingly complex, but here's one component: "Upon ending his dribble or gaining control of the ball, a player may not touch the floor consecutively with the same foot (hop)." NBA Rule 10, Section XIII, h. A player who violated this rule but sought to escape the penalty for violation (loss of possession) on the grounds that his traveling didn't cause any bad results would be grievously misunderstanding the nature of the rule. Although written in terms that make it look like a regulatory rule backed by a penalty, this is probably better conceived as a fleshing out of a basic constitutive rule that requires players to advance the ball only by dribbling, passing, and shooting. (What reason do we have for this contention?) Traveling is simply not one of the permitted means of advancing the ball. It is prohibited because the constitutive rules rule it out—that is, because it tends to produce a game that the gamewrights regard as suboptimal (in this case, allowing the team with the ball to advance it too easily)—and not because it might produce some other disfavored state of affairs that can be identified independent of the conduct itself.

In contrast, much other conduct that is made the subject of a rule is regulated precisely because of its *tendency* to produce some disfavored consequence or result. The kinds of consequences or results that rulemakers disfavor are varied, but among the most important are these: injury, delay, and a change in the competitors' respective probabilities of victory. Grabbing an opponent's facemask in football, or executing a "horse collar" tackle, are prohibited, on pain of a 15-yard penalty, precisely because these actions tend to cause bodily injury. Calling a timeout in basketball when none remains is prohibited because it tends to cause delay or confusion. Physical interference with the batter, or with a receiver on a route, or with a soccer forward on a break, are prohibited because they impede those players' abilities to complete plays, reducing their chances of scoring, and thus winning.

At this point, it might prove useful to distinguish "between a general sort of thing and its particular concrete instances," where items of the

Type and Token

general sort are called **"types"** and the concrete particulars are termed **"tokens."** Linda Wetzel, *Types and Tokens,* STANFORD ENCYCLOPEDIA OF PHILOSOPHY (Edward N. Zalta ed., Fall 2018 ed.). Suppose that an acquaintance greets you with the declaration, "I own that very jacket!" They're thinking in terms of jacket *types* if remarking on your shared good taste, but jacket *tokens* if accusing you of theft. With this distinction in mind, the central question for the rulemakers is this: assuming the conduct type is regulated because of its tendency to produce results of a certain sort, when should the regulation or prohibition provide for a sanction only if the relevant token actually produced the result of the rulemakers' concern? Under what circumstances should the principle "no harm, no foul" (NHNF) apply? Does the appropriateness of imposing a sanction despite the non-realization of any harm or injury depend upon the functions that the sanction is designed to serve—functions like compensation, retribution, and deterrence?

COMMENTS AND QUESTIONS

1. Races. In the 1995 world track and field championships, Gwen Torrence ran a brilliant 200-meter final, finishing in 21.77 seconds. She finished far ahead of any competitor, but was disqualified for stepping on an inside lane, even though she did not interfere with any other runner. Should Torrence have been disqualified? Would a better rule have been to disqualify her only if she created some interference? To add some time to her time? Compare the rules governing Kentucky horse racing, which provide, in relevant part, as follows:

Section 12. Fouls.

(1) A leading horse if clear is entitled to any part of the track.

(2) If a leading horse or any other horse in a race swerves or is ridden to either side so as to interfere with, intimidate, or impede any other horse or jockey, or to cause the same result, this action shall be deemed a foul.

(3) If a jockey strikes another horse or jockey, it is a foul.

(4) If, in the opinion of the stewards, a foul alters the finish of a race, an offending horse may be disqualified by the stewards.

810 KY. ADMIN. REGS. 4:040. Are these good rules for horse racing? Should they be applied, or adapted, to foot racing? These rules came into play most notably, or notoriously, in the 2019 Kentucky Derby. Maximum Security crossed the finish line first, but 22 minutes later the stewards decided—unanimously, but to great controversy—that he should be disqualified for impeding other horses. Did the stewards make the right call? You can see the race at https://tiny url.com/y5wnzewl.

2. "And one . . ." In basketball, the victim of a shooting foul is awarded free throws even if his shot had gone in. This is an extreme case of "foul, regardless of no harm." Is it justified?

3. Golf. Golf is also notorious for rejecting NHNF. For example, a player is disqualified for signing a scorecard that reports a score for any hole lower than actually taken. Rule 3.3(b)(3). The rule applies even if officials discover the error soon afterwards; Rule 3.3(b)(2) allows no alterations after the card has been returned. Imagine the player who scores a 3 on hole 12 and a 4 on hole 13, but who accidentally switches the scores when recording them. The final recorded score is correct, but the player would be disqualified nonetheless. Is this a good rule?

Since 2016, there has been one limited exception: If the reason the reported score is lower than the actual one is that the player failed to take penalty strokes of which the player was unaware at the time, the player is not disqualified but subjected to an additional two-stroke penalty. This would have allowed Camilo Villegas to continue playing in the 2011 Hyundai Tournament of Champions; he was disqualified—on his birthday, no less—because after he returned his card officials determined, on the basis of a viewer's call, that he had violated Rule 23–1 (now Rule 11.3): while the ball was in motion he had moved a loose impediment that might affect the movement of the ball. Is this exception justified?

Another rule of golf (Rule 4.1(b)) limits the number of clubs a golfer can carry at any time to fourteen. In stroke play, the penalty for carrying more than 14 clubs is two strokes for each hole at which a breach occurred, with a maximum penalty per round of four strokes. Suppose it is discovered after a round that a player had 15 clubs in his bag. If, in fact, he only used 14 of them, would NHNF reasoning dictate that no penalty should be imposed? Why or why not? What if two of the 15 clubs were identical? What if the 15th club was in a separate zippered compartment, and neither he nor his caddy realized during the round that it was in the bag? What if the 15th club was a child's club? Arnold Palmer reports that Johnny Miller once played a full round at the U.S. Open before discovering one of his son's plastic clubs deep in his golf bag. "Miller asked the rules official if the club was actually considered a club. 'Let's see,' the official said, 'it has a head, a grip, and a shaft, so it's a golf club.' The penalty for Miller was four shots, the maximum allowed under the rule." ARNOLD PALMER, PLAYING BY THE RULES 37 (2002). Right result?

4. Football. Most infractions in football incur penalties regardless of whether the infraction affected the play. For example, when a long return of a punt or kickoff is called back because of an illegal block in the back by the receiving team, it is not uncommon for the announcer to observe, commiserating with the penalized team, that the infraction was particularly unfortunate because, given where it occurred, it could not possibly have had an impact on the play. (See Rule 12, Section 1, Art. 3, which seems to provide that this is the correct outcome.) The rule for pass interference is different: "Contact that would normally be considered pass interference [is not pass interference if] the pass is clearly uncatchable by the involved players." (Rule 8, section 2, article 5(c).) Encroachment is similar to pass interference: "It is a Neutral-Zone Infraction when a defender enters the neutral zone prior to the snap, causing the offensive player(s) in close proximity to react (move) immediately; officials are to blow their whistles immediately. If there is no immediate reaction by the offensive player(s) in close proximity, and the defensive player returns to a legal position prior to the snap without contacting an opponent there is no foul." Rule 7, section 2, article 3, note 2.

Should conduct be excluded from the definition of pass interference when it does not affect the outcome because the pass was uncatchable? If a defensive player moves into the neutral zone but returns before the snap, without touching an offensive player and without an offensive player moving, there is no infraction, presumably because the offense was not adversely affected. Is that the proper result? If so, then why shouldn't a player who blocks in the back while a teammate is running back a kick also be deemed not to have committed an infraction if that would-be infraction clearly did not affect the outcome of the play? Why shouldn't an offensive lineman who moves too soon but then resets before causing movement by the defense also be deemed not to have committed an infraction? Are these cases different *in principle* or is the only difference *epistemic*, which is to say that it's much easier in cases of pass interference or encroachment than in cases of other infractions for officials to be reasonably confident that the conduct at issue had no impact on the play?

5. *"No harm, no foul" vs. "no harm, no penalty."* The rules of football just mentioned that respect NHNF work this way: conduct that would be an infraction were it to adversely affect the opponent's play is not an infraction when it doesn't. The offside rule in soccer (Law 11) is similar: a player who is in an "offside position" does not commit an "offence" if he is not "involved in active play" by interfering with the play or with an opponent, or by "gaining an advantage by being in that position." So too is the anti-spinning rule in table soccer, better known as foosball: Rule 15 provides that "spinning of the rods is illegal," but Rule 15.2 clarifies that "spinning of a rod which does not advance and/or strike the ball does not constitute an illegal spin." Note that there is another way to achieve much the same result. The rules could provide that the conduct at issue (interfering with a receiver while the ball is in the air, being in an offside position, spinning the rod) *is* an infraction regardless of whether it affects play, while also directing that the officials *should not call the infraction or impose any penalty* if the infraction did not affect play. This approach is better described as "no harm, no penalty" (NHNP) rather than "no harm, no foul" (NHNF). In fact, the NFL does adopt NHNP instead of NHNF when it comes to offensive holding, providing that "When a defensive player is held by an offensive player . . . offensive holding will not be called . . . if the action occurs away from the point of attack and not within close line play." NFL Rule 12, Art. 3, Blocking Notes 1(e). How do the two approaches differ? Is one better than the other, in some or all circumstances, and why? Think about ordinary contexts, outside of sports, when somebody utters "no harm, no foul." In such contexts what is more often intended—that somebody's conduct should be deemed okay, or that, even though it wasn't, no adverse consequences should be imposed?

6. *Causation.* When a rule is result-sensitive—i.e., when it respects either NHNF or NHNP—it must have a way to link conduct to results. That is, it must incorporate some rules or tests for *causation*. In criminal law and the law of torts, the challenge of specifying fully satisfactory tests for causation has confounded courts and legal theorists alike. Sometimes we have an entirely adequate understanding of what causation consists of, but do not know whether, in a particular case, some conduct, C, did or did not cause some result, R.[c] Other times, however, uncertainty over whether some conduct caused some

---

[c] Prior to the 2008 season, NFL rules provided that if a receiver secured possession but failed to get both feet in bounds—ordinarily a requirement for a reception in the NFL—the officials should nonetheless award a reception if they adjudged that the receiver would have landed in bounds had he not been pushed out by a defender. This "force-out" rule was then eliminated: if a player doesn't land with both feet in bounds, the pass is incomplete (unless an opposing player

result isn't *empirical*, but rather *theoretical*. That is, we can sometimes agree about all the ordinary historical facts that are relevant, yet still be uncertain whether given those facts the specified action or course of conduct under consideration is rightly described as having caused the specified result.

To see how causation can raise theoretical difficulties, start with a simple case in which it doesn't. Suppose that, in a football game between Teams A and B, Team A has the ball and a 4-point lead with 3 seconds to play. Team A's quarterback need only kneel down after the snap to seal the victory. Instead, he fumbles the ball, and a defensive lineman from Team B scoops it up and runs it in for a touchdown as time expires, for six points and a two-point victory for Team B. It is intuitive to conclude that the fumble by Team A's quarterback *caused* the team to lose. In so concluding, we are relying, perhaps implicitly, on the principle that a given factor causes a consequence if but for the factor the consequence would not occur. This is what the law calls "but-for" causation. Here, Team A would have won but for the last-second fumble. Therefore, that fumble caused the loss. Or, more precisely, the QB's fumble was *a* cause of the loss, not *the* (sole) cause. Suppose that Team A's running back could have tackled Team B's defender after the latter recovered the fumble, but failed to do so. But for the RB's failure to make the tackle, Team A would have won notwithstanding its QB's fumble. So the running back's failure to make the tackle was a cause of the loss, just as the quarterback's fumble was. There can be many but-for causes of any event.

So far, so good. Yet there are at least two problems. The first is that we sometimes believe that a factor caused a result even when the but-for test is not satisfied. Alter the case we have just been imagining. Now suppose that the QB's last-second fumble occurred with Team A already down by 20 points. In this variation, it might seem that the fumble was *not* a cause of the loss because but for the fumble, the loss would still have occurred. And that might be right. But it seems that the same conclusion is likely to apply with respect to *every* bad play by members of Team A in that game: none is a cause of the loss because the loss would have occurred but for any one of them. And then the conclusion seems to follow that nobody or nothing caused the loss, which is disconcerting because if the loss occurred something must have caused it.

This is the puzzling problem of *causal overdetermination*. Consider the famous chestnut of the desert traveler, here as rendered by Leo Katz:

> Henri plans a trek through the desert. Alphonse, intending to kill Henri, puts poison into his canteen. Gaston also intends to kill Henri but has no idea what Alphonse has been up to. He punctures Henri's

---

actually carries the receiver or interceptor out of bounds). Tennessee Titans Coach Jeff Fisher, co-chairman of the NFL Competition Committee, explained the rule change as a blow for objectivity. "It's really the only part of the game where you're asking somebody that's trying to be objective throughout the game to make a subjective call on whether there was contact enough to get the receiver out of bounds," Fisher said. *The Fifth Down: Force-Out Rule May Get Flagged*, N.Y. TIMES, Dec. 5, 2007. Surely Fisher was mistaken. Subjective "judgment" calls abound under the NFL rules, and this one was hardly unique. The better explanation for the rule change is that officials often find it very difficult to determine whether a receiver's failure to get both feet in bounds was caused by an opponent's conduct or just his own momentum or lack of care.

canteen, and Henri dies of thirst. Who has caused Henri's death? Was it Alphonse? How could it be, since Henri never swallowed the poison. Was it Gaston? How could it be, since he only deprived Henri of some poisoned water that would have killed him more swiftly even than thirst. Was it neither then? But if neither had done anything, Henri would still be alive. So who killed Henri?

LEO KATZ, BAD ACTS AND GUILTY MINDS 210 (1987). What if, instead of poisoning Henri's water, Alphonse had filled Henri's canteen with quick-acting cement? Do you see why it could be thought to make a difference? Does it? Or suppose that a football defender interferes with a perfectly catchable pass— but the officials realize that the intended receiver had his head turned away from the pass and that he would not have caught the ball even absent the interference. Should a penalty be called?

In thinking about these problems, consider whether, as some scholars have contended, an act should be deemed to have caused a consequence if the act is a necessary element of a set of conditions that is jointly sufficient for the consequence to occur. This approach traces back to the work of J.S. Mill, and more recently has been developed by H.L.A. Hart and Tony Honoré and by Richard Wright, who labeled it NESS, for "necessary element of a sufficient set."[d] For example, defensive pass interference in the immediately preceding hypothetical was not *necessary* for the consequence, i.e., the incompletion: but for the interference, the pass would still have landed incomplete due to the receiver's inattention. But consider the set of circumstances that, by hypothesis, actually occurred, with just one change: the receiver was facing the ball. We can say that this (hypothetical) set of circumstances is sufficient for the incompletion, and that if we took the interference away the ball would have been caught (more likely than not). If so, the interference is a necessary element of a sufficient set to produce the result (incompletion). For a brief description of the NESS approach and of criticisms made of it, see Michael Moore, *Causation in the Law*, STANFORD ENCYCLOPEDIA OF PHILOSOPHY (Edward N. Zalta ed., Winter 2019 ed.); *see also* MICHAEL S. MOORE, CAUSATION AND RESPONSIBILITY: AN ESSAY IN LAW, MORALS, AND METAPHYSICS (2009).

The first problem with the but-for test of causation, we have said, is that sometimes it is intuitive that C caused R even though R would have occurred but for C. The second problem is the reverse: that sometimes we think that C did not cause R even though R would not have occurred but-for C. The well known facts of *Berry v. Borough of Sugar Notch*, 43 A. 240 (1899), illustrate: Berry, a street car engineer, was injured when a tree, negligently maintained by the borough, fell on him as the street car he was operating at an excessive rate of speed passed under the tree. Under the governing law, he could not recover damages from the admittedly negligent defendant if his negligence was

---

[d]   This approach is reflected in Restatement (Third) Torts § 27, which provides that "[i]f multiple acts occur, each of which . . . alone would have been a factual cause of the physical harm at the same time in the absence of the other act(s), each act is regarded as a factual cause of the harm." AM. LAW INST. 1998.

also a cause of his injury. It seems fairly plain that, but for his speeding, Berry would not have been injured by the falling tree because he would not have been in its path the moment it fell. Therefore, Berry's speeding was a cause of his injury and he should not be allowed to recover damages. Does that seem right to you? Could you articulate the reasons one might have for thinking not?

To return to sports, consider in conclusion this fanciful hypothetical. Suppose that Ivan, an ice hockey player, stabs at an opponent, Peter, with the point of his stick, trying to hit him. Ivan misses. Watching the episode and finding Ivan's ineptitude inexplicably hilarious, Peter's teammate, Nicholas, starts laughing uncontrollably. Losing his balance, Nicholas falls and breaks his wrist. NHL Rule 62, governing spearing, provides in part as follows:

> 62.1.   Spearing shall mean stabbing an opponent with the point of the stick blade, whether contact is made or not.
>
> 62.2.   A double-minor penalty will be imposed on a player or goalkeeper who spears an opponent and does not make contact.
>
> 62.4.   A match penalty shall be imposed on a player or goalkeeper who injures an opponent as a result of a spear.

What penalty or penalties should be imposed on Ivan? Did he injure Nicolas "as a result of a spear"? Should a different outcome obtain if 62.4 read instead ". . . who causes injury to an opponent by spearing"?

2.   INTERFERENCE: THE (IR)RELEVANCE OF INTENT

We have discussed intent earlier in this book, in Subchapter 3H. There our concern was with whether, when intent does matter in principle, rules should be crafted in intent-sensitive terms or, for reasons of greater administrability, should instead be written in intent-neutral terms that pick out a suitable *proxy* for the disfavored intention. Here we briefly examine whether intent *should* matter in principle.

Consider Official Rule of Baseball Rule 5.09(b)(3), which provides that a runner is out when "[h]e intentionally interferes with a thrown ball" or when he "hinders a fielder attempting to make a play on a batted ball." Insertion of the adverb "intentionally" to modify "interferes" but not to modify "hinders" was not an oversight. As a Comment to Rule 6.01(a)  emphasizes: "A runner who is adjudged to have hindered a fielder who is attempting to make a play on a batted ball is out whether it was intentional or not." Because the rulemakers evidently believed that umpires can determine when interference with a thrown ball is intentional, it is unlikely that they thought umps could not determine when interference with a batted ball, or a fielder trying to make a play on it, is also intentional. It's a reasonable inference, then, that MLB rulemakers believed that, practicalities of rule-enforcement aside, interference with a thrown ball should render a runner out only when that interference is intentional, but that interference with a fielder or a batted ball should make the runner out whether intentional or not. In the language of the law, the rulemakers believed that runner interference with a batted ball should be a "**strict liability**" offense—that is, an offense that is made out just by the actor's conduct—or their conduct plus the results thereof—and without regard to the actor's mental state.

What reason might MLB have for this pair of contrasting judgments? Often a choice between intent-based liability and strict liability is influenced by the behavioral incentives that each approach would create. In this context, if a runner were out for interfering with a thrown ball regardless of his intent, fielders would have an incentive to throw at runners. That would make for a different (and dangerous!) game. What if a runner were out for interfering with a fielder or a batted ball only when such interference is intentional? Possibly, that would give runners an incentive to intentionally impede fielders or redirect grounders while endeavoring to fool umpires into believing that the interference is accidental. But that's not obviously so; after all, we've already assumed that umpires can discern runner intent reasonably well (or, at least, that the MLB rulemakers so believe). One thing that is clear is that making runners strictly liable for interfering with fielders and batted balls incentivizes them to take care to avoid interference. And that would be a good outcome if the rulemakers determined that the game goes better when fielders have unimpeded opportunities to make plays, and when batted balls play true rather than caroming unpredictably off runners' bodies.

Of course, intent-based liability and strict liability do not exhaust the regulatory options. Criminal law is the department within Anglophone law that has done the most to systematically distinguish mental states, and partly due to the influence of the American Law Institute's Model Penal Code, criminal law scholars routinely distinguish five kinds of mental states (or quasi-mental states). A person acts: "purposefully" or "intentionally" with respect to some fact if it is their "conscious object" to bring that fact about; "knowingly" if they are aware that fact exists or will be bought even if it is not their object to bring it about; or "recklessly" if they act with conscious awareness of a substantial risk that the fact exists or will be brought about. In addition, if a person, unaware of facts that (in some sense) they should be aware of, acts in a fashion that deviates from the standard of care of an ordinary reasonable person, they act with ordinary (civil) "negligence"; if the person's action reflects a "gross deviation" from the ordinary standard of care, they commit "criminal negligence." *See generally* MODEL PENAL CODE § 2.02 (AM. LAW INST.).

These categories are available to sports leagues too. The laws of soccer provide that a direct free kick is awarded to the opposing team if a player commits any of several proscribed acts toward an opponent—kicking, striking, tripping, tackling, etc.—"in a manner considered by the referee to be careless, reckless or using excessive force." FIFA Law 12. " 'Careless' means that the player has shown a lack of attention or consideration when making a challenge or that he acted without precaution." " 'Reckless' means that the player has acted with complete disregard to the danger to, or consequences for, his opponent." Careless conduct is not disciplined; recklessness provokes a yellow card.

COMMENTS AND QUESTIONS

1.   Batter interference with catcher. Consider a famous incident from the 10th inning of Game 3 of the 1975 World Series: Ed Armbrister, a right-handed batter for the Cincinnati Reds, dropped a bunt right in front of home plate. Armbrister hesitated at first, thinking the ball was going foul, but as he broke for first base, he banged into Carlton Fisk, catcher for the Boston Red Sox, hindering Fisk's ability to field the ball and forcing him to rush his throw. Everyone was safe; no interference was called; the Reds went on to score and win the game; ultimately they won the Series, four games to three. For a full account of the play, see CJ Kelly, *The Bunt that Changed Baseball History*, HOW THEY PLAY.COM (June 10, 2020), https://tinyurl.com/yyt69zls; you can see the video at https://tinyurl.com/43muzu67.

Was the call correct? Despite Rule 5.09(b)(3) and the official Comment to Rule 6.01(a), a Comment to Rule 6.01(a)(10) provides: "When a catcher and batter-runner going to first base have contact when the catcher is fielding the ball, there is generally no violation and nothing should be called." And amateur umpires are instructed: "A catcher trying to field a batted ball that remains in the immediate vicinity of the plate cannot be protected because of the right of the batter-runner to begin his advance to first. Barring an intentional action on the part of either player, contact in this instance is incidental and is not interference or obstruction." CHRIS JAKSA & RICK RODER, THE RULES OF PROFESSIONAL BASEBALL: A COMPREHENSIVE REORGANIZATION AND CLARIFICATION (1997). Does this instruction make sense? Surely Armbrister engaged in an "intentional action": the intentional action describable as "running toward first base." So why wasn't he out, given that he engaged in an intentional action that hindered the fielder? Consider the suggestion that the rule governing interference by a batter-runner with a catcher attempting to make a play on a batted ball is the same as the rule governing interference with a thrown ball: the runner is out only if he intentionally interfered with the fielder (and not if he unintentionally interfered with the catcher by means of an intentional action). Do you agree that that's what's going on here? If so, do you think this is a sensible modification to the rules? If you don't agree, can you explain how to square Rule 6.01(a)(10) with Rule 5.09(b)(3)?

2.   Runner interference with thrown ball. Another famous non-interference call, this one on a thrown ball, occurred in Game 4 of the 1978 World Series. As described in a later account:

The Dodgers led 2 games to 1 and were leading Game 4 3–1 in the bottom of the sixth. With one out, the Yankees had Thurman Munson on second and Reggie Jackson on first with Lou Piniella up.

What happened: Piniella hit a low liner to shortstop Bill Russell. The runners had to hold to see if Russell caught the ball, but he dropped it, stepped on second to force Jackson and threw to first to complete the inning-ending double play. But Jackson remained in the baseline and appeared to move his hip slightly as the ball came toward him. The ball glanced off him, allowing Munson to score. Dodgers manager Tommy Lasorda argued interference with first-base ump Frank Pulli, saying Piniella should have been ruled out, but to no avail. The run stood.

David Schoenfield, *Five Worst Umpiring Calls in History,* ESPN.com (June 13, 2012). For a clip of the play see: https://tinyurl.com/yxt9vbr5. The Yankees tied the game up in the eighth inning, won it in the tenth, and won the next two games and the Series.

In response to Lasorda's repeated claim, "He's got to get out of the way!" Pulli said, "Where do you want the guy to go? . . . He didn't do it intentionally." Under the rule Pulli was correct in trying to determine Jackson's intention. *Should* that be the rule? Was Pulli right in determining that Jackson did *not* intentionally get in the way of the ball?

Suppose Pulli was uncertain whether Jackson intentionally interfered with the ball. How confident do you think he should have to be before calling intentional interference? (See Chapter 11.) If you conclude that it's not clear that Jackson intentionally moved *into* the ball, would you agree that he would have been able to get *out* of the ball's way had he wanted to? Should he be called out if he intentionally *refrained* from *not* interfering with the thrown ball? Rule 6.01(a)(10) provides that a batter or runner is out if "He fails to avoid a fielder who is attempting to field a batted ball, or intentionally interferes with a thrown ball." Is there a good reason why this rule doesn't provide more generally that a runner is out if he fails to avoid either a fielder who is attempting to field a batted ball or a thrown ball? Or, if there is a good reason why that rule would burden the runner unduly, is there also good reason the rules shouldn't provide that an offensive player who has been declared out (as Jackson was, due to the force) has an affirmative duty to avoid being hit by a thrown ball?

3.   *Beyond intention?* Rule 6.01(a)(6) provides that:

If, in the judgment of the umpire, a base runner willfully and deliberately interferes with a batted ball or a fielder in the act of fielding a batted ball with the obvious intent to break up a double play, the ball is dead. The umpire shall call the runner out for interference and also call out the batter-runner because of the action of his teammate.

What does "willfully and deliberately" add? One dictionary defines "deliberate" as "characterized by or resulting from slow careful thorough calculation and

Term of Art

consideration of effects and consequences," and emphasizes that the word "always indicates full awareness of what one is doing and, used precisely, implies careful and unharried consideration of procedures or consequences." WEBSTERS THIRD NEW INTERNATIONAL DICTIONARY 596 (1993). Do you think that MLB rulemakers intended that "deliberate" be given that meaning here? If not, might "willfully and deliberately" be a **"term of art"**—that is, a word or phrase that has a specialized meaning within a particular field or profession, and that might have different meaning in common usage? Do you think that "deliberate" does have a specialized meaning in baseball, either alone or when appearing in the longer phrase? Would the substance of the rule be different if the provision read: "If, in the judgment of the umpire, a base runner intentionally interferes with a batted ball or a fielder in the act of fielding a batted ball with the obvious purpose to break up a double play, the ball is dead, and the runner and batter-runner are both out"?

4.   More deliberation. Soccer rules provide that a player should be cautioned for "deliberately leaving the field of play without the referee's permission," and should be sent off for "denying the opposing team a goal or an obvious goalscoring opportunity by deliberately handling the ball (this does not apply to a goalkeeper within his own penalty area)." Law 12. Again, what does "deliberately" mean? Is there a good reason why a player (not a keeper) who intentionally leaves the field without the referee's permission or who intentionally handles a ball thereby denying the opposition "an obvious goalscoring opportunity" should not be carded unless his intentional action was characterized by "slow careful thorough calculation" that characterizes deliberation? Can you think of any conduct in soccer or any other sport that should constitute an infraction only when engaged in "deliberately"?

5.   Flagrant fouls in basketball. It is a personal foul in the NBA to "hold, push, charge into, [or] impede the progress of an opponent by extending a hand, arm, leg or knee or by bending the body into a position that is not normal." Rule 12B, section I. In addition, the referee shall assess a flagrant-1 foul "[i]f contact committed against a player . . . is interpreted to be unnecessary," and a flagrant-2 foul if the contact "is interpreted to be unnecessary and excessive." (Penalties for flagrant fouls include two shots and possession of the ball.) Rule 12B, section IV. What determines whether a personal foul is or is not "unnecessary" (or is or is not "excessive," for that matter)? Unnecessary toward what end? Would the rulemakers have better achieved their goal had they substituted "intentional" for "unnecessary"? Why or why not? If not, do you think "unnecessary" captures the idea they had in mind? Could you do better?

6.   Targeting in football. As part of its ongoing effort to reduce head injuries, NCAA rules provide that "No player shall target and make forcible contact against an opponent with the crown of his helmet." Rule 9, Art. 3. Similarly, the NFL directs that "[i]t is a foul if a player lowers his head to initiate and make contact with his helmet against an opponent." Rule 12, Art. 10. In both systems, violation of the rule calls forth a 15-yard penalty and the possibility of player ejection. The NCAA imposes an automatic ejection for confirmed targeting fouls,[e] while the NFL rule provides that a player "may be disqualified" for a violation but does not require disqualification or specify the considerations that should inform whether that sanction be imposed. Football is a fast-paced contact sport. All knowledgeable observers agree that even well-intentioned players are sometimes unable to avoid making forcible contact with an opponent with the crown of their helmets. Should intent matter? Neither set of rules specifies that contact with the crown of the head is a foul only when intentional, but both might imply that: intentionality might be baked into the very concept of "targeting," (NCAA) while purposiveness is implied by "lowers his head to initiate . . ." (NFL) Should the rules explicitly provide that the rule is violated only when contact is intentional? Or when reckless? Would you favor a two-tiered system, comparable to basketball's system for flagrant fouls, under which unintentional targeting ("Targeting I") results in a 15-yard penalty, but no ejection, and intentional targeting calls forth a yardage penalty and ejection ("Targeting II")? Is that better or worse than the NFL's discretionary rule? In early 2019, FBS coaches *unanimously* supported switching to such a system, but the NCAA Oversight Committee was not ready to make such a drastic change without additional study. According the committee's chairman, Shane Lyons, the committee doesn't "want to go back and look like we're doing something that's not in the well-being, health and safety of the student-athlete, so if you back off the penalty, is it sending the message that this is OK and this is not." Andrea Adelson, *NCAA Oversight Committee Open to Changes to Targeting Rule, Overtime*, ESPN.COM (Jan. 22, 2019).

C. TYPES OF SANCTIONS

Sports employ a wide array of sanction types. We discuss six: (1) addition or subtraction of points; (2) making it easier or harder to score; (3) removal of a player; (4) nullifying a play or a result of improper conduct; (5) disqualification or forfeiture; (6) fines and other out-of-competition penalties, such as reduction of draft choices.

(1) Addition or deduction of points. In numerous sports—boxing, tennis, golf, and ice skating are examples—addition or deduction of points is a routinely invoked penalty. Rugby also awards points when a foul prevents a score. In rugby union, a penalty try is awarded if in the view of the referee one "probably" would have been scored but for the foul. A rugby league referee "may award a penalty try if, in his opinion, a try would have been scored but for the unfair play of the defending team." RUGBY FOOTBALL LEAGUE, *Rules and Regulations*, https://tinyurl.com/y2sl8kna.

---

[e]   The NCAA automatically reviews every targeting foul. In 2019, the rules committee eliminated the option for referees to let a targeting call stand, requiring them to either confirm or overturn the call. (See Subchapter 13B(4)).

Point deduction may be an especially appealing remedy in multi-participant competitions. Various racing sports—in which time rather than points is the metric used to determine results—use an equivalent to deduction of points by adding increments of time as a penalty.

(2) Making it easier or harder for a side to score. Many sports penalize rule infractions by making it harder for the offending competitor or team to score, or by making it easier for the opponent. The standard penalty in football—yardage markoffs—is an example. Baseball also uses this sanction method: balks yield a free base, and some violations by a batter or runner cause an out. Free kicks and hits in soccer and field hockey are additional examples. In high-level soccer, including World Cup play, one-third or more of all goals come off set pieces: free kicks, corner kicks, and throw-ins.

The award of discrete point-scoring opportunities, such as free throws in basketball and penalty shots in soccer, ice hockey and field hockey, are strong forms of making it easier for the aggrieved team to score.

(3) Removing a player from play. One common subtype of penalty designed to alter the competitive balance—to make victory harder for an offender's team and easier for its opponent—is the removal of an offending player from play. Rulemakers who employ this form of penalty must confront two questions: first, whether the offender should be removed for a limited time or for the remainder of the game (or even longer); and second, whether the dismissed player may be substituted for or whether his team will be left to play shorthanded.

Because these are two separate design decisions, they interact to produce four obvious possibilities. Arrayed from least to most draconian, they are:

(a) player is removed for a limited time and substitution is allowed;

(b) player is removed for the remainder of the game and substitution is allowed;

(c) player is removed for a limited time and substitution is prohibited; and

(d) player is removed for the remainder of the game and substitution is prohibited.

Combination (c) is perhaps the most common. Many sports—among them, ice and field hockey, rugby league and union, indoor soccer, water polo, and lacrosse—all use a penalty box or "sin bin" for certain fouls. Combination (b) is used by basketball when players foul out. A red card in soccer exemplifies combination (d).

Although the four combinations just mentioned are the most obvious possibilities, they are not the only ones. Indeed, a red card in soccer might be viewed as a combination of choices (d) and (b) because the dismissed player must sit out his team's next game too, though a substitute is permitted for that game. A red card in team handball calls for the carded player to be sent off for the entire game but the team may insert a substitute after two minutes of shorthandedness.

(4) Nullifying the result. In various sports, points that would otherwise be scored are routinely not counted if an offensive player committed a foul. That certainly makes sense. Indeed, in football, one consequence of a penalty on an offensive team may in general be nullification of what would otherwise be a good play. Consider whether nullification is appropriate, or sufficient, in other settings.

In an NHL game between the New Jersey Devils and the Pittsburgh Penguins in October 2011, a double minor penalty was called on Patrik Eliáš, the Devils' star forward. Petr Sýkora, a teammate of Eliáš, decided that he didn't want Eliáš to go to the penalty box for four minutes, so he went instead. The Penguins protested but apparently the officials did not notice, until after Eliáš scored a short-handed goal. How should this situation be resolved? The closest NHL rule, Rule 70.4, provides that if a penalized player returns to the ice before his time has expired because of an error of the Penalty Timekeeper, he does not serve an additional penalty but must serve his unexpired time. Under International Ice Hockey Federation Rule 562, if a player illegally enters the game from the penalty bench by his own error or that of the Penalty Bench Attendant, any goal scored while he is on the ice is disallowed. Eliáš's goal was counted, but the Penguins won the game 4–1. *See* Petr Polák, *Penguins administer their own justice after Sýkora's trickery*, EUROHOCKEY.COM (Oct. 26, 2011).

(5) Disqualification and forfeiture. For significant violations, a competitor can be disqualified, both in individual and team sports, and a team can be charged with forfeiture. In combat sports, a fighter can be disqualified for repeated or flagrant fouls. In sumo, automatic disqualification applies for various fouls called *kinjite* (translated to "forbidden hand"), including the grabbing of an opponent's top knot. But in swimming and individual track events, competitors are routinely disqualified for what might appear a more modest infraction: a false start. As already noted (p. 58), Usain Bolt, the world's greatest sprinter, was disqualified in the finals of the 2011 100-meter race at the world track and field championship because he committed a false start.

Indeed, the IAAF (International Association of Athletic Federations, now known as World Athletics) has gotten progressively tougher on false starts. Until 2003, a runner was not disqualified unless they committed two false starts. Then the IAAF divided the rule for Combined Events (most notably the pentathlon and decathlon) and for other events, providing in its Rule 162.7:

> Any athlete making a false start shall be warned. Except in Combined Events, only one false start per race shall be allowed without the disqualification of the athlete(s) making the false start. Any athlete(s) making further false starts in the race shall be disqualified from the race.
>
> In Combined Events, if an athlete is responsible for two false starts, he shall be disqualified.
>
> *Note: In practice, when one or more athletes make a false start, others are inclined to follow and, strictly speaking, any athlete who does so has also made a false start. The Starter should warn or disqualify only such athlete or athletes who, in his opinion, were responsible for the false start. This may result in more than one athlete being warned or disqualified. If the false start is not due to any athlete, no warnings shall be given and a green card shall be shown to all the athletes.*

In 2009, by a contested vote, the IAAF amended the rule again. Rule 162.7 now provides:

> Except in Combined Events, any athlete responsible for a false start shall be disqualified.
>
> In Combined Events, any athlete responsible for a false start shall be warned. Only one false start per race shall be allowed without the disqualification of the athlete(s) responsible for the false start. Any athlete(s) responsible for further false starts in the race shall be disqualified.

See also Rule 200.8(c) (repeating the second and third sentences of the second paragraph of this Rule in the context of the track components of Combined Events).

What is the optimal rule to govern false starts in individual events? In combined events? Why should there be different rules for the two contexts? In either context, should a competitor be disqualified for her first false start? For her second? In either context, is it fair to have one collective "free" false start, with any subsequent ones being punished by disqualification?

(6) Out-of-contest sanctions. In some cases, authorities impose a sanction after a contest or outside the context of any particular contest. For example, players are sometimes suspended for egregious misconduct. NFL Commissioner Roger Goodell has docked teams draft picks for misbehavior that he concludes threatens the integrity of the game. Some such

sanctions—such as a fine imposed on a competitor or team—have little or no apparent competitive consequences.

Former safety Rodney Harrison—who was fined and suspended multiple times, and twice voted the dirtiest player in the NFL—has said that given players' salaries, even fines on the order of $15,000 for dangerous hits do not "get [their] attention." Rather: "You got my attention when I got suspended and I had to get away from my teammates and I disappointed my teammates from not being there." Josh Wright, *Optimal Sanctions for NFL Hits*, TRUTH ON THE MARKET (Oct. 19, 2010). Wright, a law-and-economics scholar (and later FTC Commissioner) notes that "a fine can be set so that the player loses the equivalent of one game's salary, two, three, and so on." With respect to the other point made by Harrison, that a suspension lets the team down, Wright suggests that "this reputational sanction can really only be harnessed by the league for the purposes of deterrence if it is suspending players for truly intentiona[l] and egregious hits that the player could have avoided"; extending the sanction to less flagrant conduct will diminish its impact.

COMMENTS AND QUESTIONS

1. *The list.* Do sports use additional sanctions that our list omits? Consider a sanction that the ATP imposed in 2016 on tennis player Nick Kyrgios for "Conduct Contrary to the Integrity of the Game": a $25,000 fine and suspension from the tour for eight tournament weeks. This is standard fare. However, the ATP simultaneously provided that the suspension would be reduced to three tournament weeks if Kyrgios "enters a plan of care under the direction of a Sports Psychologist, or an equivalent plan approved by ATP." *See* ATP TOUR, *ATP Sanctions Kyrgios* (Oct. 17, 2016). Could this penalty be redescribed as a three-week suspension plus a requirement that Kyrgios enter into an approved treatment plan, with a proviso that the penalty for failure to comply with the treatment requirement would be penalized by another five-week suspension? Does it matter which way we view it?

2. *Warnings.* Some playing rules are complicated and difficult for young athletes to grasp. Examples are the balk rules in baseball and the rules on obstruction in field hockey. With respect to such rules, it might sometimes make sense to issue warnings at first and impose a penalty only after subsequent violations. If we put aside the teaching function, is it ever appropriate to issue a warning rather than impose a penalty with immediate effect? In many sports, warnings are common even at the elite level. In tennis, for example, some tennis organizations impose a point penalty for the first code violation, but on the pro circuit a first code violation results only in a warning. CODE OF CONDUCT, ITF PRO CIRCUIT 109 (2012). And soccer and basketball referees appear to be warning players throughout a contest. (The yellow card in soccer is called a "caution," which is a near-synonym for "warning." Are soccer refs issuing warnings that they'll issue a warning?) Is the practice of warning players sensible? If conduct is wrong and sanctionable, can it be wrong

and sanctionable only if engaged in multiple times? Note that FIFA Law 5, which governs the referee's "powers and duties," specifically directs (in relevant part) that "The Referee: takes disciplinary action against players guilty of cautionable and sending-off offences. He is not obliged to take this action immediately but must do so when the ball next goes out of play."

3. Collective sanctions. Notice that the vast majority of sanctions in team sports penalize the team for the misdeeds of an individual. Outside of sports, in contrast, collective sanctions are presumptively disfavored. It is thought unjust to penalize innocent persons for the wrongs of another, even if the innocent actor and the wrongdoer are members of the same group or community. For an extensive discussion, see Daryl J. Levinson, *Collective Sanctions,* 56 STAN. L. REV. 345 (2003); *cf.* Richard Posner, *Collective Punishment,* THE BECKER-POSNER BLOG (July 23, 2006) (arguing that collective punishment is sometimes justified on the basis "that someone other than the actual perpetrator of a wrongful act may have more information [than the government has] that he could, if motivated, use to prevent the act"; citing liability of employers for acts of employees and liability of conspirators for acts of other members of the conspiracy as examples of collective punishment). Why the difference? Are we too accepting of collective penalties in sports, or too hostile to them outside of sports, or is everything just about right?

Instead of characterizing sanctions as either individual or collective, we may find a trichotomy more illuminating: some sanctions fall directly on the collective (e.g., yardage markoffs in football); some fall directly on the individual but impose substantial indirect costs on the group (e.g., ejection or suspension); and some fall directly on the individual and have slight impact, even indirectly, on the group (e.g., fines). If we look more closely, we may discover even more points along a spectrum. For example, ejection will have a greater indirect impact on the team if the team must play short-handed, as in soccer, than if it may replace the violator, as in baseball. Note also that, whatever costs are imposed on the individual by a formal sanction, the team may impose more, such as by benching a player who has collected gratuitous fouls. If we disfavor a collective sanction in a particular context, should we condone individual sanctions with indirect collective effects or should we work hard to identify and impose purely individual sanctions?

4. Incarceration as a collective sanction? It would be anathema to inflict criminal punishment directly on family members of persons convicted of crime. But our predominant mode of criminal punishment—incarceration—imposes enormous indirect costs on just those innocent family members, especially wives and dependent children. Does principled hostility to collective penal sanctions speak in favor of corporal punishment rather than incarceration as a method of criminal punishment? For an argument to this effect, see Jeffrey Brand-Ballard, *Innocents Lost: Proportional Sentencing and the Paradox of Collateral Damage,* 15 LEGAL THEORY 67 (2009).

5. *Lumping vs. splitting.* "It is sometimes said," one legal scholar observes,

> that the two most basic intellectual moves are "lumping" and "splitting"—that is, finding relevant common characteristics that allow us intelligently and usefully to group apparently distinct phenomena into a single category ("lumping"), and finding relevant distinguishing characteristics that allow us intelligently and usefully to separate otherwise similar phenomena into distinct classes ("splitting"). The best descriptive, interpretive, and analytical work, whether in law, medicine, biology, history, or any of a hundred other disciplines, does a good deal of both—lumping seemingly disparate phenomena into original categories that reveal unexpected patterns and lead to novel insights, while employing the chisel of penetrating distinction to sunder conventional, shopworn categories that may conceal more than they reveal.

Bradley C. Karkkainen, *Reply: "New Governance" in Legal Thought and in the World: Some Splitting as Antidote to Overzealous Lumping,* 89 MINN. L. REV. 471, 479 (2004). The design of penalties in sports and games often puts significant pressure on the decision to

Lumping vs. Splitting

lump or split. Basketball regulators must decide whether to treat "a foul as a foul" or to create a graduated scale of foul flagrancy. For most of its history, the NFL imposed a five-yard penalty for "incidentally grasping" an opponent's facemask, but fifteen yards for twisting, turning or pulling it. (In 2008, it repealed the penalty for merely incidental grasping.) Can you think of any penalty menus in sports that lump where they should split, or that split where they should lump?

6. *Goaltending.* In basketball, points are automatically added in only one context, defensive goaltending. Should basketball more aggressively award points for a foul but for which, in the officials' judgment, a basket would have been made? Should soccer adopt a similar rule—awarding a goal when a defender, not a goalie, uses his hand to block an obvious goal? The most memorable recent example, discussed below, p. 469, was the hand ball by Luis Suarez of Uruguay, denying a virtually certain decisive goal to Ghana in a quarter-final of the 2010 World Cup. *See* Isaac Fanin, *Ghana players 'cannot forgive' Suarez handball 10 years on,* BBC SPORT AFRICA (July 2, 2020). If you think a goaltending award is appropriate in basketball but not in soccer, is the difference that objective criteria are available in basketball but not in soccer? Is the difference that scoring is far more liquid in basketball than in soccer? Why should that make a difference? If a problem in calling goaltending in soccer is that the referee cannot be certain that the shot would have gone in, is an appropriate response to award fractional points or goals (or alternatively to inflate the value of a goal)?

7. *A comparative question: new possibilities for the penalty box?* Consider the variations already discussed in the section on "removing a player

from play." Is one approach or another generally preferable? If not, is there any good explanation for the wide variations we see in sports, other than that this is the way the respective sports have always done it? Can you think of any examples of sports that use combination (a) (the player is removed for a limited time and substitution is allowed)?

Would basketball be better if temporary removal were the primary means of punishment, as in ice hockey? How might such a system of penalties be structured?

8.   *Re-entry in basketball?* NBA Rule 3, Sec. I, provides: "No team may be reduced to less [that should be "fewer"!] than five players." If a player gets a sixth personal foul and there are no available substitutes on the bench, the player remains in the game but a technical foul is added to that personal foul and any subsequent ones on him. (This rule came into play in a game on February 5, 2014, allowing the injury-ridden Los Angeles Lakers to keep a fifth man on the floor in the closing minutes of a win over the Cleveland Cavaliers.) If a team is down to five eligible players and one becomes injured or is ejected, the last player disqualified by reason of receiving six personal fouls re-enters the game, but a technical foul is charged for the re-entry. In the NCAA, though, a team would have to continue with fewer than five players. In 1988, the United Tribes Technical College Thunderbirds beat another North Dakota junior college team, the North Dakota State University Lumberjacks, despite the fact that for the last five minutes of the game the underdog Thunderbirds played with only three men on the court. *See* Chuck Klosterman, *Three-Man Weave*, GRANTLAND (June 9, 2011). Which is the best approach—allowing a player who had fouled out to stay on or re-enter (perhaps with a technical foul added), requiring a team to play with fewer than five players, or providing that a team unable to complete the game with five eligible players has forfeited, or simply lost?

9.   *The scorecard in golf.* In the 1968 Masters tournament, Roberto de Vicenzo shot a birdie 3 on the 71st hole, but his playing partner, Tommy Aaron, entered a 4, and then a total of 66 rather than the 65 that de Vicenzo had actually shot. De Vicenzo signed the card. He was charged with the 4. But for this mistake, he would have tied for the lead and gone into a playoff with Bob Goalby; instead, he was the runner-up. "What a stupid I am!" de Vicenzo famously said. "I deeply regret Roberto's misfortune," Goalby said, shortly after donning a green jacket. Had the mistake been the other way around—that is, de Vicenzo signing for a *lower* score than he had shot—de Vicenzo would have been disqualified. If we have so much confidence in how many strokes he took, why care about the card?

Recall that a golfer is disqualified if she signs for a lower score than she obtained on any hole, even if she just transposed the scores for two holes and signed for the correct total for the round. Question 3, p. 205. Again, is disqualification appropriate in this case?

10.   *Relief.* In ice hockey, when one team is short-handed because of a penalty, icing cannot be called against it. What sense does that make? Is this

because the penalty would be too one-sided otherwise—but then why not just shorten the time of shorthandedness but continue to enforce icing? Or is it because it's more exciting to give the short-handed side a little countervailing edge?

Also, with respect to most minor penalties, if the team favored by the player advantage scores, the penalty ends. Why? But if both teams have players out for penalties and one team scores, the penalties continue. Does that make sense? Should soccer adopt a similar rule?

11. Penalty shots. What is the purpose of giving a penalty shot? To compensate for the opportunity the aggrieved side would have had absent the penalty, and yet require it to finish the job? To compensate with less than a full goal in a game in which scoring is not relatively liquid? In basketball, would it be better instead to put pressure instead on the fouling side—say, by giving the other team points unless the fouler made a difficult free throw? Are awards of free throws a sound approach because players are able to deter fouls against them by improving their free-throwing skills?[f] Is the varying ability of players to shoot free throws an argument against them, in that the value of the penalty is correlated with a skill that may have little to do with what happened on the court to lead to the penalty?

12. Football. Points are affirmatively awarded as a sanction for a violation only when the offense commits a violation in its own end zone, the result being a safety (two points) for the defense. NFL Rules, Rule 8, Section 6, Article 1(d). In a 1962 game between the Steelers and the Cowboys, Dallas had a 99-yard play nullified, and a safety called against them, because of holding in the end zone. *See* Ken Belson, *All That Work for Two Points,* N.Y. TIMES, Dec. 8, 2011; BOB ST. JOHN, LANDRY: THE LEGEND AND THE LEGACY (2001). Is this result justified on the ground that but for the violation the offense might have been stopped in the end zone?

Note by contrast that if a defender commits pass interference in his own end zone the result is not a touchdown. In the NFL, the ball is placed on the 1-yard line; in the NCAA, the maximum penalty is 15 yards. Should the two situations—offensive and defensive penalties in one's own end zone—be treated more similarly? For example, the rule could provide that if a team commits a foul behind its own goal line, the next play begins in its end zone, and if it chooses not to punt but fails to get the ball out of the end zone *then* a

---

[f]   David J. Hebert, *Who You Gonna Foul? How Players in the NBA Legally Deter Fouls* (May 10, 2011), https://tinyurl.com/y3pd3dzp.

> By committing fouls in basketball, one is essentially committing a crime. These criminals engage in rational economic decision making when choosing whether or not to foul an opponent. . . . Players who are better able to prevent a good outcome from fouls . . . are fouled less than players who are less able to do so. This research has broader implications into the world of crime, namely that individual people are able to deter criminal acts committed against them on their own by investing in capital, which reduces the payoff of committing a crime against them.

Is Hebert right that fouling basketball "is essentially committing a crime"? Would Robert Simon agree? See also the discussion of this paper in Sarah Lawsky, *Don't Do the Crime if the Other Guy Can Shoot from the Line?,* PRAWFSBLAWG (May 12, 2011).

safety is recorded. Or the dissimilarity could be eliminated from the other end, by awarding a touchdown when a defender commits pass interference in his own end zone. Insofar as it matters to you, NFL teams that face first and goal from the opponent's one-yard line have an 85% chance of scoring a touchdown and a 95% chance of scoring any points. *See* Andrew S. Rook, *Field Position and Scoring Probabilities: Half of the Red Zone is a Dead Zone (for Touchdowns)*, PHD FOOTBALL (June 24, 2013).

Consider the system of yardage penalties in football. The yardage awarded is generally insensitive to the position of the ball on the field, except that a penalty cannot bring the ball closer than half the distance to the goal line. Some defensive penalties, such as pass interference, carry with them an automatic first down, no matter the degree of the violation or the situation; note that this is a form of lumping. Is this a sound structure of penalties?

13. Intervention by the law. In a contact sport, when is it appropriate to treat contact that causes injury as tortious or criminal? Note the infamous case of Todd Bertuzzi's retributive attack on Steve Moore in an NHL game in 2004. *Todd Bertuzzi Sucker Punches Steve Moore—Full Incident*, YOUTUBE, https://tinyurl.com/yyyos6os. Bertuzzi pled guilty to a criminal assault charge, and a civil action by Moore proceeded for years until it was finally settled in August 2014. *Todd Bertuzzi*, WIKIPEDIA, https://tinyurl.com/y6rjy5xm. Given that fist-fighting is a common aspect of NHL hockey, what did Bertuzzi do that warranted such a stringent response? *See also, e.g., Roux v. Hattingh* (636/11) ZASCA 132 (S.A. S. Ct. App. 2012) (serious neck injuries in high school rugby game caused by "jack-knife" maneuver; liability upheld because maneuver contravened rules, spirit, and conventions of the game, was pre-planned and executed deliberately, and was "extremely dangerous . . . [,] likely to cause injury . . . and serious injury to boot").

D. HOW BIG SHOULD THE SANCTION BE?

Gamewrights must decide not only what types of sanctions to use, but also how big or onerous they should be. How should a sport system set the optimal level of sanctions? Consider again Josh Wright's discussion of how the NFL should punish dangerous hits. He asks: "Assuming that the league seeks to deter these types of hits back to the optimal level (surely the league doesn't think it is zero, right?), what is the optimal sanction?" On the one hand, if a sanction is too light, so that the costs to the player and his team are less than the benefits of his conduct, it may under-deter. Wright points to the example of James Harrison, a linebacker who was 2008 NFL Defensive Player of the Year for the Pittsburgh Steelers; Harrison was often fined but was nevertheless highly regarded by his teammates for his aggressive play. "He sets the tempo for everybody," said one. On the other hand, there are "error costs" in applying stiff sanctions: even as they reduce the undesirable conduct they target, they "threaten to chill beneficial conduct (in this case, aggressive play that consumers of the sport value and outweighs its costs but might expose the player to the sanction)." Wright, *Optimal Sanctions.*

COMMENTS AND QUESTIONS

1. Ouch! Do you agree with Josh Wright that the optimal level of hits to the head is not zero? Why or why not?

2. Sanction objectives. What goals are served by sanctions in sports? Insofar as we are discussing those "penalties" that are properly conceived as sanctions imposed for violations, one obvious point or function of the penalty is to deter future violations, whether by the violator herself or by others. Do or should sanctions serve any additional purposes? Which?

3. Optimal deterrence. It is tempting to think that the best way to deter some conduct, C, is to prohibit C on threat of very severe penalties. Now, very severe penalties might be undesirable for reasons having nothing to do with the efficacy of  deterrence. Consider life imprisonment as a penalty for littering. If the penalty did a near-perfect job of deterring the offense, we might nonetheless think it objectionable on the grounds that imposition of such a draconian penalty in just a small handful of cases is "unjust" or "unfair." But even putting aside values like justice and fairness, there are several deterrence-related reasons why severe penalties might be unwise. Here are three.

First, as suggested by the discussion of dangerous hits in football, severe penalties might make regulated actors overly timid, "chilling" them from engaging in permissible, even desirable, conduct adjacent to the conduct that rule makers want to deter. This is the problem of *overdeterrence.* Second, as the old English adage "as good as be hanged for a sheep as a lamb" reflects, very severe penalties for a given offense can leave rule makers with insufficient levers to deter yet more serious offenses. For example, if a criminal justice system punishes robbery with the death penalty, it might find that it lacks any means of deterring robbers from killing their victims. This is the need to preserve *marginal deterrence.* Third, if a threatened punishment far exceeds the community's sense of justice, regulated actors might predict that regulators will not impose it when push comes to shove. This prediction might embolden them to commit an offense that a less severe and thus more credible penalty could deter. (For this reason, bankers from more than 200 cities and towns petitioned Parliament in 1830 to end hanging as a penalty for forgery; juries were refusing to convict, and the bankers were convinced that the death penalty "ENDANGERS the property which it is intended to protect." The following year, more than 1100 "Merchants, Traders &c." joined in a petition arguing that "criminals who, under a more rational and considerable code of laws, would meet the punishment due to their crimes, escape with *complete* impunity," and so asking for the abolition of the death penalty for property crimes. THE PUNISHMENT OF DEATH: A SELECTION OF ARTICLES FROM THE MORNING HERALD 38–40, 166–67 (1836); CHARLES C. BURLEIGH, THOUGHTS ON

THE DEATH PENALTY 48 (2d ed. 1847).) We can call this third caution against severe penalties the *nullification* danger.

What sports penalties with which you are familiar are excessive because of one or more of these worries—that they *overdeter*, impede *marginal deterrence*, or invite *nullification*?[g]

4. Fines. Fines are the one commonly applied sanction that falls almost exclusively on the individual, assuming not only that they are formally imposed on the individual but also that the team does not reimburse him. Are fines used optimally? Is Rodney Harrison right that they are too low to have much impact? Should they be higher? Insofar as fines are intended to deter, shouldn't they be sensitive to offender wealth or income? Salary is a good (though imperfect) proxy for an athlete's income and one that is known to the league without intrusive investigation. Is there a good reason why the ordinary schedule of fines should be in dollar amounts (e.g., $5000, $25,000) instead of in percentages of player salary (e.g., 1%, 5%) or (what amounts to essentially the same thing, and is sometimes the metric) prescribed numbers of games' worth of salary? In Finland, fines for vehicular infractions and petty offenses are calculated in multiples of the offender's daily net income. Reima Kuisla, a Finnish millionaire, was fined €54,024 (about $58,000) for traveling 64 miles per hour in a 50 m.p.h. zone. Suzanne Daley, *Speeding in Finland Can Cost a Fortune, if You Already Have One*, N.Y. TIMES, Apr. 25, 2015.

Can fines or a counterpart be imposed on athletes in amateur sports?

5. Pass interference. Defensive pass interference is a spot penalty in the NFL (and also an automatic first down). In the NCAA, defensive pass interference is penalized at a maximum of 15 yards (plus an automatic first down) even if it occurs farther than 15 yards from the line of scrimmage. Which is the better rule and why? Does one system reflect too much lumping, or does the other reflect too much splitting? Or are the rules optimal, in both cases?

———

Exercise 6D

Recall the brief discussion, just pages ago, of lumping and splitting. Compared to most sports, soccer has a very limited menu of penalty types: yellow cards (caution), red cards (ejection of the offender, with no team right of substitution, for the remainder of the game, plus disqualification for the subsequent game), and indirect and direct free kicks, including a direct penalty kick when the offense occurs within the offender's own penalty area. Some soccer insiders believe that this menu is too limited, and that some greater splitting might be called for. More

---

[g] Another concern, unlikely to arise in a sports context, might be considered the *spoliation* danger. *See, e.g.,* the comments of William Ewart, 38 PARL. DEB. H.C. (3d ser. 1837) ("another reason why murder only should be punished with death was that by continuance of capital punishment in other cases an inducement was given to a criminal to put an end to the testimony against him by the absolute destruction of the person he had robbed").

particularly, some have wondered whether the sport could be improved if its penalty rules were modified to authorize referees to respond to some infractions by sending off the violator for some period of time, short of the remainder of the match. Craft a proposal for an expanded array of penalties for soccer. When doing so, you might find it useful to keep in mind how disparate the impact of a red card is depending only on when it is issued: In response to a red-card-worthy foul committed in the first minute of play, a team is ordered to play shorthanded for at least 89 minutes. If the very same foul is committed with a minute remaining, the penalty is that the team must play shorthanded for only one minute.[h]

E. A STUDY IN OPTIMAL SANCTIONS: PLAYER EJECTIONS IN THE NBA

NBA Rule 12A, Section VII.c, provides:

c.   During an altercation, all players not participating in the game must remain in the immediate vicinity of their bench. Violators will be suspended, without pay, for a minimum of one game and fined up to $50,000.

The suspensions will commence prior to the start of their next game.

A team must have a minimum of eight players dressed and ready to play in every game.

If five or more players leave the bench, the players will serve their suspensions alphabetically, according to the first letters of their last name.

If seven bench players are suspended (assuming no participants are included), four of them would be suspended for the first game following the altercation. The remaining three would be suspended for the second game following the altercation.

In addition to the fine, a player suspended for a game loses a *pro rata* portion, 1/82, of his annual salary.

The prohibition on leaving the bench area has been on the books for a long time, but at first it was enforced only by mild fines. The fine was raised from $100 to $150 in the 1977–78 season, and then to $500 in 1984–85 and $2500 in 1993, when a team fine of $5,000 for each violating player was added. A far tougher rule, with a much larger fine—then $20,000—and an automatic suspension, was adopted in 1994–95. The rule has remained

---

[h]   Does this immense disparity in impact suggest that referees should enforce penalties more strictly as the game progresses? See Chapter 12 on officials' discretion.

relatively stable since then, though the maximum fine has since been raised in stages to the current $50,000 level.

Looming over many discussions of the rule is a notorious incident of December 9, 1977, in which Rudy Tomjanovich of the Houston Rockets ran towards a fight, apparently in hopes of breaking it up; his arms were down. Kermit Washington of the Los Angeles Lakers turned and punched Tomjanovich, shattering his jaw and inflicting life-threatening injuries; spinal fluid leaked into his brain cavity. The incident may be viewed at https://tinyurl.com/y6jlpx27. A quarter century later, it became the subject of a book, JOHN FEINSTEIN, THE PUNCH: ONE NIGHT, TWO LIVES, AND THE FIGHT THAT CHANGED BASKETBALL FOREVER (2002).

The immediate impetus behind the automatic-suspension rule was two brawls in playoff games in the 1994 season. One was a wild melee in a game between the Miami Heat and the Atlanta Hawks. Three participants were fined $10,000 or more and suspended, but twelve additional players were fined the then-maximum $2500. Counting team fines, the total came to $135,000. Ira Winderman, *NBA Levies Suspensions, Fines in the Heat Brawl*, FORT LAUDERDALE SUN-SENTINEL, May 3, 1994. The second occurred less than two weeks later, in a conference semifinal game between the New York Knicks and the Chicago Bulls. A fight between Derek Harper of the Knicks and JoJo English became a full-teams brawl that spilled into the second row of the stands; Commissioner David Stern was sitting just behind, in the third row. Brian Chen, *Throwback Thursday: Bulls and Knicks Fight During 1994 Eastern Conference Semis*, BLEACHER REPORT (Dec. 18, 2014).

The new rule significantly affected a 1997 playoff series between the Heat and the Knicks. After Game 5 of the series, one player from each team was suspended for fighting (the Heat player for two games), and four Knicks were suspended for leaving the bench area. According to one report, none of the players who left the Knicks bench got involved in the fight: "[Patrick] Ewing merely stood at halfcourt watching the fray and at least one Knick, [Larry] Johnson, clearly tried to act as a peacemaker." Another Knick, Buck Williams, told Ewing, the team's biggest star, not to go out, but to no avail. Ernie Grunfeld, the Knicks' president and general manager, said:

> All of our players served as peacekeepers and the reason they came out was to protect one of their own. The reason they did it is the right reason. The action wasn't right because now unfortunately they're going to have to be suspended. But I'm proud that they stuck up for a teammate.

Charles Barkley of the Houston Rockets agreed. "That's a bad rule," he said. "They should clarify the rule and decide if a guy's going out as a peacemaker, or if he's going out to get involved. It's just a normal emotion when a fight breaks out, you go help your teammate." Mike Wise, *5 Knicks Barred for Melee; 3 to Miss Game 6*, N.Y. TIMES, May 16, 1997, at A1.

The NBA Players Association, contending that the new rule was a violation of the league's collective bargaining agreement, imposed on the players without their consent, threatened litigation, but it came to nothing. Because the rules then required a minimum of nine players, only three were suspended for Game 6—Charlie Ward, who was one of the fighters, and Ewing and Allan Houston, alphabetically the first two of the bench-leavers. *Id.* The Knicks, who held a 3–2 series lead, lost Game 6 at home. And they also lost Game 7, for which Johnson and John Starks were suspended.

The automatic-suspension rule also played a critical role in a 2007 playoff series, the Western Conference semifinals between the San Antonio Spurs and the Phoenix Suns. In the closing seconds of Game 4, Robert Horry of the Spurs threw a hockey-style hip-check on Steve Nash, the Suns' All-Star point guard, knocking him into the scorers' table. Gregg Popovich, coach of the Spurs, said shortly after the game that he did not think the foul was "such a big deal," and he may have been right; apparently, Nash admitted later that he gave the foul "a little bit of flair." Chris Barnewell, *Raja Bell admits that Steve Nash sold the Robert Horry hip check in 2007 playoffs*, CBS SPORTS.COM (Nov. 27, 2017). Raja Bell of the Suns received a technical foul for charging at Horry, and Horry, who hit Bell with his forearm, was ejected and suspended for Games 5 and 6. So far, Nash's flop, if it was one, seemed to have paid off, though Horry, nearing the end of a distinguished career, was then a role player, averaging under 5 points per game. But Amar'e Stoudemire, an all-NBA selection who was leading the Suns in the series with 23.5 points and 10.3 rebounds per game, left the bench in the direction of the incident, and so did Boris Diaw, his backup. Neither came close to making contact with anyone on the Spurs, but they were suspended for Game 5. Stu Jackson, executive vice president of the NBA, noted that the two had gone 20 to 25 feet from the bench, and he did not buy the contention that Stoudemire had a right to be at the table because he was about to check into the game. (You can see the play at https://tinyurl.com/37nejlw8.) The Suns complained that it was terribly unfair that they suffered more severe sanctions than the Spurs. It was "not a matter of fairness," said Jackson: "[T]his rule is clear. It's a bright line. Historically, if you break it you get suspended regardless of what the circumstances are." *Penalty 'punch in gut' for Suns*, TORONTO STAR, May 16, 2007. In any event, the Spurs beat the higher-seeded Suns, 88–85, in Phoenix in Game 5, and then clinched the series at home and went on to win the championship.

BILL SIMMONS, COMMON SENSE VS. THE NBA RULEBOOK

ESPN.com, May 16, 2007, updated May 30, 2007
© 2007 ESPN Internet Ventures, reprinted with permission

. . . You can't blame [NBA higher-ups] for the Stoudemire-Diaw suspensions because they correctly interpreted a stupid, idiotic, foolish, moronic, brainless, unintelligent, foolhardy, imprudent, thoughtless, obtuse and thickheaded rule. Can you blame them for having that rule in the first place? Yes. But you can't blame them for the actual interpretation—after all, Stoudemire and Diaw *did* leave their bench during an altercation, just like Tom Brady's right arm was still coming down as Charles Woodson popped him in the Tuck Rule Game.[i] Everyone knows about the leaving-the-bench rule. It's been around for more than a decade. It's the reason assistant coaches spin around during potential fights and hold their arms out like bouncers at a nightclub. It's the reason a really good Knicks team got bounced from the '97 playoffs (robbing everyone of a much-anticipated Bulls-Knicks Eastern Conference finals). It's also the reason why we haven't had a bench-clearing brawl since the rule was invented.

Here's the problem with that stupid, idiotic, foolish, moronic, brainless, unintelligent, foolhardy, imprudent, thoughtless, obtuse and thickheaded rule: It's currently designed as a black-or-white law that leaves no room for interpretation. As Barkley pointed out on TNT, Stoudemire and Diaw stopped after a few steps and never escalated the situation. In a way, it played out as poorly as the tuck rule did. In that playoff game against the Raiders, Brady pumped the football, brought it back down, got popped by Woodson and coughed up the ball. It should have been a fumble, but because of the stupid, idiotic, foolish, moronic, brainless, unwise unintelligent, foolhardy, imprudent, thoughtless, obtuse and thickheaded way that the tuck rule was designed, the play was interpreted correctly, the Patriots kept the ball and ended up winning in overtime.

The bothersome thing is that both rules should have been changed. After the Pats-Raiders game, the NFL should have softened that rule to leave some degree of interpretation depending on the game and the situation. Same with the NBA after the Knicks-Heat debacle in '97. Why didn't that happen? Because both leagues were so freaking stubborn and took so much heat for those two games, they obstinately kept the exact language of those rules in place. After all, a change of the rules would have been an admission that they failed. And as the old saying goes, those who forget the lessons of history are doomed to repeat them. . . .

But there's a larger issue that everyone seems to be missing, an issue that keeps popping up during these playoffs in various forms and might be fixable: Namely, that the NBA turned the competitive sport of basketball

---

[i]   See above, pp. 101–102.

into something else. It's still basketball, only it's a bastardized version of it. A certain amount of instinct and competitiveness has been compromised. Why? Because of the league's misguided attempt to create a fairy-tale universe in which world-class athletes can play basketball without ever raising their voices, trash-talking, bumping bodies, exulting after a great play or rubbing each other the wrong way. . . .

In an interview with Dan Patrick of ESPN, Commissioner Stern said:

> The entire intent as a rule, for the 10 years or so it's been in effect, was to make it clear that there's no way to know whether someone running out on the court is coming as friend or foe, and so when Rudy Tomjanovich came running out to see what was going on, to break up a fight, his face was forever changed. And it's a great concern that we have. So we made it as simple as possible.

Speaking of Stoudemire and Diaw, he said:

> They were 20 or 25 feet away from the bench. And they violated the rule. . . . Is it a red-letter rule? Absolutely.

> What changed the series is Amare and Boris ran out onto the court and they either forgot about it or they couldn't control themselves. I don't know which one. And there wasn't an assistant coach there, one of six, to restrain them. OK, so now either we have to have new rules, put up a fence, or hire more assistant coaches.

> And, by the way, we had a very easy rule to employ, it's been in for a decade, and not one Competition Committee, not one owner, not one Governors meeting has ever raised the subject for a change.

The Dan Patrick Show, *David Stern transcript: The commish answers questions about the suspensions*, ESPN.com (May 16, 2007).

Henry Abbott wrote in favor of the rule and its invocation:

> . . . There were some growing pains as everyone got used to the rule . . . . But eventually, just about everyone caught on.

> And, in part because of that rule, the NBA no longer has a chronic fighting problem. It worked. This rule helps many dozens time a year, when little sparks fly on the court and don't become big fires—because the few players on the court can't muster the energy to make that kind of trouble alone.

> . . . [T]he league, largely in response to fan criticism, has tried to make clear and enforceable rules where possible. The get-suspended-if-you-leave-the-bench-rule is one of the clearest and

most enforceable. You don't want to be suspended? You stay on the bench. Are there any players who don't know that?

Every rule has counterexamples that make it look bad. Speeding laws seem necessary, but does the government really not want police cars, ambulances, and the cars of women in labor to speed? And many of us like leash laws. But how about those frisbee dogs that perform at halftime sometimes—they're surely breaking the law almost everywhere they perform.

The Suns are the counterexample to the bench-clearing rule. It can suck to be a counterexample. . . .

True Hoop: Guess They Really Mean "Stay on the Bench", ESPN.com (May 15, 2007).

The automatic-suspension rule also drew attention in 2011, this time in the Finals, between the Heat (is there a theme here?) and the Dallas Mavericks, and this time for the League's decision *not* to penalize anyone. During a timeout in Game 6 a scuffle broke out near midcourt, and it was joined by several players who had not been checked in at the time but were on the court for the timeout. *2011 Game 6 NBA Finals Fight Between Mavs and Heat*, YOUTUBE, https://tinyurl.com/y443lr7e. Technical fouls were imposed, but no suspensions. Later in the game, the NBA issued a statement explaining, "A player will not automatically be suspended for leaving the bench if he has already left the bench because a timeout was called." This time, Henry Abbott objected to failure to enforce the rule:

Yes, the players were on the court because of a timeout. But, no, they were not *at midcourt in the scrum* because of the timeout.

And most importantly, the rulebook plainly does not make a commonsense exception for timeouts, despite the NBA's position.

What's more, on this particular rule, the league has scoffed at those who suggest the league interpret the situation beyond the letter of the law. . . .

The NBA has had dramatic success in reducing fighting and, more importantly, resulting severe injuries, and this ban on joining fights from afar is a lynch pin of the progress. . . .

Maybe that rule isn't quite as easy to employ as we thought. If there is, in practice, an allowance for players on the floor during timeouts, there ought to be that same leeway in the rulebook—especially in the case of this rule, whose stark clarity has underpinned the league's controversial positions in the past.

The rule is the rule is the rule is a reasonable position. The rule is the rule is the rule, except once in a while . . . that does not fly.

True Hoop: NBA Escapes a Scuffle, ESPN.com (June 14, 2011).

Another notable no-call of the rule occurred after Game 6 of the Indiana-Atlanta playoff series in 2014. Paul George, Indiana's star player, took at least one step away from the bench towards a scuffle, but an assistant coach stopped him from going further. After reviewing the video, which you can see here, https://tinyurl.com/y5gbcstb, the league decided not to suspend him. In the decisive Game 7, George led Indiana to a win with 30 points. Knicks and Suns fans, predictably, did not respond favorably to the non-suspension. But at least one journalist, Matt Moore of CBS, said that the decision indicated "a more level-headed approach from Adam Silver's league office vs. the literalist interpretations under David Stern," Matt Moore, *Paul George not suspended for Game 7 vs. Hawks*, CBS SPORTS.COM (May 2, 2014); Silver had become Commissioner just a month before. And in the 2018 Finals, Kevin Love was not suspended for leaving the bench to argue with an official—he had done so before an altercation between two players broke out. Colin Ward-Henninger & Kyle Boone, *NBA Finals: Tristan Thompson, Kevin Love avoid suspension for Game 1 altercation; Thompson fined $25K*, CBS SPORTS.COM (June 1, 2018).

The rule remains very much alive, however: Eight steps off the bench in a pre-season game was enough for C.J. McCollum of Portland to be suspended from the season opener in 2017. Dan Devine, *C.J. McCollum unhappy at suspension over 'eight expensive and costly steps'*, Yahoo! Sports (Oct. 6, 2017). The league invoked the rule to suspend Raymond Felton and Dennis Schröder of the Oklahoma City Thunder in December 2018, and Nikola Jokić of the Denver Nuggets the following month.

COMMENTS AND QUESTIONS

1.   Ejection? The relevant rule explicitly provides that players who leave "the immediate vicinity of their bench" during an altercation will be suspended for a minimum of one game. It does not say, however, that such players will be ejected for the remainder of the game in question. What kind of behavior warrants immediate ejection?

2.   Criticisms. As you can see, NBA Rule 12, Section VII.c, and the manner of its enforcement, have provoked many criticisms. Do you think the rule is optimal? (In evaluating this question, is it relevant to you that the two teams that many feel were treated unfairly in these episodes—the 1997 Knicks and the 2007 Suns—each lost the next two games, thus losing their series?) If it's not optimal, what's wrong with it? Identify all the plausible discrete objections to the rule and the manner of its enforcement. How, if at all, could the rule be improved?

3.   Fight . . . or flight. If, during an altercation, a player does not remain in the immediate vicinity of his bench, where he is likely to go? Well, toward the altercation, of course. But what if a player leaves the immediate vicinity of his bench to travel farther *away from* an altercation? Suppose, for example, that an altercation occurs close to Team A's bench and Player P, on Team A, moves away from the bench and the altercation precisely to avoid being drawn into the scuffle. Does the rule require that he be suspended?

4. *Inconsistency?* Were the NBA's responses to the 2007 Suns-Spurs and 2011 Mavericks-Heat incidents as inconsistent as Henry Abbott claims? What, if anything, could be said in defense of the league's 2011 ruling?

5. *How bright is the line?* Given that there is unavoidable ambiguity in determining when an altercation begins and where "the immediate vicinity" of the bench ends, does it follow that the rule is not really "bright-line" (or "red-letter," as David Stern, misspeaking, put it)? If so, is that troublesome?

6. *Accounting for the unexpected.* In 1997, Ronald Dworkin, the legal philosopher who championed "interpretivism" (and then a law professor at New York University), dismissed the NBA's "rules are rules" defense of its handling of the Knicks-Heat affair. Said Dworkin:

> You don't punish people for acts that not only don't cause harm, but aren't even of the kind to cause the harm that the statute was designed to prevent. Suppose Ewing saw somebody pulling a knife in the middle of a fray and he leapt off the bench and jumped on this person to try to prevent harm? It would be inconceivable in a case like that that you would interpret the law literally.

James Traub, *Asking Around: Did the Knicks get justice or did they just get the shaft? Bigdomes speak out.*, THE NEW YORKER, June 2, 1997, at 35. Do you agree? Does Dworkin's hypothetical prove that officials have more discretion than Commissioner Stern asserted? Was Stern committed to the conclusion that Ewing would have violated the rule in the case that Dworkin imagines, and therefore that the NBA would be obligated to suspend him, or could he distinguish the hypothetical case from the actual one?

Dworkin's hypothetical may appear far-fetched. But a problem is that we can never anticipate all the possibilities that might occur. Consider this analysis offered by Brian Simpson:

> Suppose we have a rule that the children are always to have a bath before going to bed, which seems a sensible enough rule. Obviously there need to be exceptions. For example, it would be silly to insist on a bath if one of the children was critically ill with pneumonia. We could try to think of all the exceptions in advance, but the task is hopeless, as becomes clear on the day when, through an accident to a travelling circus, we find a spitting cobra in the bath. Nobody would have ever thought of that possibility, and provided for it by the spitting cobra exception.

A.W.B. SIMPSON, INVITATION TO LAW 80 (1991). Does it follow that the NBA should just give up as futile its attempt to implement a bright-line suspension rule?

CHAPTER 7

WHO CAN PLAY?

■ ■ ■

Sports routinely restrict the eligibility of athletes to participate in particular competitions. Sometimes the rules are meant to place the athletes in appropriate competitive brackets. For example, age grouping is common in many sports—usually maximum ages for youth competitions and minimum ages for older athletes—and weight classes are used in most combat sports (not in sumo, however). Each of these criteria, though, is occasionally used to exclude participation entirely. For example, in order to participate in the Olympics in most sports an athlete must be at least 16, or turning 16 within the calendar year, and maximum overall weights are set for wrestling competitions. Individual horse racing competitions frequently establish maximum weights for jockeys, such as 126 pounds for the Kentucky Derby.

This chapter examines four types of eligibility rules common in sports: rules that limit participation to "amateurs" (somehow defined); rules based on residence or citizenship; rules concerning sex or gender; and (briefly) rules based on age.

A. AMATEURISM

The Olympic Games of ancient Greece began as amateur competitions, which meant that participation was largely limited to members of the aristocracy. But over time, Greek society and the game changed, and ultimately the city-states "subsidiz[ed] their leading athletes and shower[ed] them with rewards and privileges." Charles W. Thayer, *A Question of the Soul*, SPORTS ILLUSTRATED, August 15, 1960.

The modern Olympic Games, founded by Baron Pierre de Coubertin in 1896, have followed a similar arc. Although there was a long history of professional sports in the western world—there were professional boxers and cricket players as early as the second half of the 17th century—by the late 19th century, especially in Britain, an elevated sense of the "gentleman amateur" had taken hold. As Thayer puts it, "When the 'gentlemen' themselves decided to participate in sports, they were obliged to exclude the professional 'players,' because the strict social conventions of the day forbade gentlemen to associate with those who plied a trade considered by the upper classes to be demeaning." Coubertin was imbued, at least at first, with this sense of amateurism, and it was a principle underlying the first modern games, held in Athens in 1896. But the situation was not stable:

> [T]here was no way to enforce the policy and the next two Olympics, Paris in 1900 and St. Louis in 1904, both held over a five-month period in coalition with World's Fairs, witnessed professional athletes in sports such as fencing and cycling.
>
> Because many definitions of amateur existed, the IOC could not regulate amateurism globally. And despite honorable attempts initially on the part of British sport governing bodies and *Sporting Life* magazine, a lack of seriousness and agreement among the various sport federations provided no clear definition. Yet, the IOC chose to selectively punish athletes . . . .

Susan J. Rayl, *Olympic amateurism from de Coubertin to Samaranch: A story of professionalization and commercialization*, IDROTTSFORUM.ORG (Feb. 23, 2017) (reviewing MATTHEW P. LLEWELLYN & JOHN GLEAVES, THE RISE AND FALL OF OLYMPIC AMATEURISM (2016)).

The most prominent athletes tripped up by the amateurism rules were Jim Thorpe of the United States and Paavo Nurmi of Finland. Thorpe took gold in the decathlon and pentathlon at the Stockholm Olympics in 1912, leading King Gustav V to pronounce him—rightly, in the estimation of many experts—"the greatest athlete in the world." But the next year, after revelation of the fact that he had been paid to play in some low minor league baseball games in 1909 and 1910 (and had not exercised the precaution, as some college athletes did, of playing for pay under an assumed name), the IOC revoked his medals. Nurmi, the dominant middle- and long-distance runner of his time, won nine gold and three silver medals across three Olympics, but was prevented by the IAAF, the international track federation, from competing in a fourth, at Los Angeles in 1932, on suspicions he had taken money to race.

> Beginning in 1949, the Olympic Rules provided:
>
> An amateur is one who participates and always has participated in sport solely for pleasure and for the physical, mental or social benefits he derives therefrom, and to whom participation in sport is nothing more than recreation without material gain of any kind, direct or indirect. In addition he must comply with the rules of the International Federation concerned.

But that was more a credo than a definition. Avery Brundage, president of the IOC from 1952 to 1972, and a zealous defender of the principle of amateurism, said that it was "a thing of the spirit, and hence . . . very difficult to define." Thayer, *Question of the Soul.* A 1962 revision to the IOC's Eligibility Rules prescribed that "[a]n amateur is one who participates and always has participated in sport as an avocation without material gain of any kind," and that, in addition to complying with official interpretations of that rule, Article 26 and also with the rules of the pertinent federation, he must have "a basic occupation designed to insure his present and future livelihood" and must not receive or have received "a remuneration for participation in sport." Commitment to a requirement of amateurism meant that the IOC had to police many different boundaries. For example, it issued rules and decisions prohibiting athletes from: being given positions in the army or civil service, or as physical education teachers or coaches, to allow them to train; participating in training camps that operated for more than two weeks; profiting commercially in the media from their athletic fame; or receiving expense money beyond their actual outlay. But the constraints were widely violated—most flagrantly, but by no means exclusively, by the nations of the Soviet bloc—and even before the end of Brundage's reign they began to be chipped away.

The IOC eliminated the word "amateur" from Rule 26, as it was relabeled, in 1971 (though Rule 34 continued to require that participants in the Games be amateurs) and permitted athletes to receive "broken time payments"—replacement for lost earnings from foregone work time—shortly thereafter. It wasn't until 1986, however, that it authorized the international federations that govern individual sports to decide whether to open their sports to professional athletes, and some sports did so at the 1988 Olympics in Seoul. The most vivid marking of the new era came in Barcelona in 1992, when NBA players were eligible for the first time. The Dream Team, as the U.S. men's team quickly became known, crushed all its opponents—and in doing so generated tremendous new worldwide interest in the sport.

COMMENTS AND QUESTIONS

1.   *Amateurism in principle.* Has something been lost? Are there any good reasons to restrict the Olympics—or any other athletic competition—to "amateurs"? Are there any good reasons to exclude from the Olympics—or from any other athletic competitions—"professionals"? (Are these two questions equivalent?) Note that the United States Golf Association continues to maintain a series of amateur championships as well as its more renowned Open championships. There does not seem to be any disposition to change this state of affairs. Is this surprising, given the general renunciation of amateurism in the Olympics?

2.   *Definitions.* If the Olympics or some other sport or competition should be restricted to amateurs, how should that critical concept be defined? Is it enough to qualify as an amateur that one does not make a living competing in sport? Or that one does not make an *extravagant* living in sport? Or, more restrictively, should it be thought fatal to amateur status in a sport that one has been paid at all to compete in that sport—or even that one has been paid to compete in *any* sport?

While the Olympic movement has largely abandoned Pierre de Coubertin's commitment to amateurism, the ideology lives on at the NCAA. Is there any sound reason to require amateurism in college competition even though it is not required in the Olympics? The NCAA's initial 1906 Constitution declared that

> no student shall represent a college or university in any intercollegiate game or contest who has at any time received, either directly or indirectly, money, or any other consideration to play on any team, or for his athletic services as a college trainer, athletic or gymnasium instructor, or who has competed for a money prize or portion of gate money in any contest, or who has competed against a professional.

Perhaps echoing—or rather anticipating—Avery Brundage's view that amateurism "is a thing of the spirit," the NCAA added a definition of "amateur" to its bylaws a decade later: An amateur athlete is one whose participation in sports is "motivated primarily by education and by the physical, mental and social benefits to be derived." NCAA, 2020–2021 NCAA DIVISION I MANUAL, Bylaw 2.9 (2020). Does this mean that an athlete who participates in college sports in part because of the value of a scholarship, or in hopes of making it to the pros, is not an amateur? Is such an athlete ineligible for NCAA competition? Obviously not. How can you square that fact with the text?

The precise scope of the NCAA's insistence on amateur status has been debated throughout its history. For a summary, see Jason Kirk, *The endless argument at the center of college football*, BANNER SOCIETY (Oct. 4, 2019). At perhaps no time, however, has it faced such broad and repeated challenges to its insistence on amateurism and, even more, to the details of its rules designed to implement that commitment, as in recent years. In the fall of 2011, Pulitzer Prize-winning historian Taylor Branch published a long article in *The Atlantic* excoriating the NCAA for hypocrisy and calling for the payment of student-athletes. Taylor Branch, *The Shame of College Sports,* THE ATLANTIC, Oct. 2011. The article, subsequently expanded into an e-book, THE CARTEL: INSIDE THE RISE AND IMMINENT FALL OF THE NCAA (2011), gained substantial notice. For a ringing endorsement, see Joe Nocera, *Let's Start Paying College Athletes,* N.Y. TIMES, Dec. 30, 2011. For a biting criticism, see Seth Davis, *Should College Athletes be Paid? Why, They Already Are,* SPORTS ILLUSTRATED, Sept. 21, 2011.

3.   *Paying student athletes.* Let's focus first on the usual case, single-sport student-athletes. Traditionally, the NCAA has allowed athletic scholarships to cover tuition, room, board, books, and fees. A change of rules in 2015 allowed scholarships for some athletes to include so-called cost-of-attendance expenses, including transportation; at least some universities, rather than demanding a showing of receipts, implement the new policy by granting a flat stipend, which may be on the order of $3500. Is it reasonable

for the NCAA to insist that a student-athlete not be compensated more freely in a sport in which he or she competes intercollegiately? Should colleges and universities be permitted, or even required, to pay student-athletes stipends or salaries that have some relation to the income they produce for their universities? (For some athletes, of course, the scholarship gives the athlete more than market value; for some, much less.)

If a university should not be able to pay an athlete for playing *for it*, should a professional athlete nevertheless be allowed to play her sport in college so long as she does not receive compensation for her performances as a collegian? Consider, for example, the case of Jordyn Wieber, a world champion gymnast who was ineligible to compete for UCLA because she had turned pro before entering college.

4. Endorsement and media income. NCAA Bylaw 12.5.2.1 provides in general terms:

> **12.5.2.1 Advertisements and Promotions After Becoming a Student-Athlete.** After becoming a student-athlete, an individual shall not be eligible for participation in intercollegiate athletics if the individual:
>
> > (a)   Accepts any remuneration for or permits the use of his or her name or picture to advertise, recommend or promote directly the sale or use of a commercial product or service of any kind; or
> >
> > (b)   Receives remuneration for endorsing a commercial product or service through the individual's use of such product or service.

This rule, however, is made subject to Bylaw 12.5.1.3, which provides:

> **12.5.1.3 Continuation of Modeling and Other Nonathletically Related Promotional Activities after Enrollment.** If an individual accepts remuneration for or permits the use of his or her name or picture to advertise or promote the sale or use of a commercial product or service prior to enrollment in a member institution, continued remuneration for the use of the individual's name or picture (under the same or similar circumstances) after enrollment is permitted without jeopardizing his or her eligibility to participate in intercollegiate athletics only if all of the following conditions apply:
>
> > (a)   The individual's involvement in this type of activity was initiated prior to his or her enrollment in a member institution;
> >
> > (b)   The individual became involved in such activities for reasons independent of athletics ability;
> >
> > (c)   No reference is made in these activities to the individual's name or involvement in intercollegiate athletics;
> >
> > (d)   The individual does not endorse the commercial product; and
> >
> > (e)   The individual's remuneration under such circumstances is at a rate commensurate with the individual's skills and experience as a

model or performer and is not based in any way upon the individual's athletics ability or reputation.

Are these rules sensible? Should student-athletes be permitted to receive outside endorsement income? If this should be allowed in principle, is there a practical way to ensure that such income is not in effect payment by the university itself or boosters? Would it be worrisome if not? Given that Bylaw 12.5.1.3 allows a student athlete to earn income from certain endorsement activities, is section (a)—making the provision applicable only if "involvement in this type of activity was initiated prior to his or her enrollment in a member institution"—defensible?

Ed O'Bannon was a starter on UCLA's 1994–95 basketball team, which won the NCAA championship; O'Bannon was voted MVP of the tournament. Years later, the NCAA licensed EA Sports to represent classic teams in a video game, and a figure recognizable as O'Bannon was included. Should O'Bannon be entitled to a share of royalties? What if the use of his likeness had been made while he was still competing in college? *See O'Bannon v. National Collegiate Athletic Association*, 802 F.3d 1049 (9th Cir. 2015) (holding, murkily, that the NCAA's rules on student compensation were an illegal restraint of trade, but that schools are not required to compensate students unrelated to education), *cert. denied*, 137 S.Ct. 277 (2016).

    5.   *The multi-sport athlete.* Interestingly, NCAA Bylaw 12.1.3 provides: "A professional athlete in one sport may represent a member institution in a different sport and may receive institutional financial assistance in the second sport." So, for example, Jeremy Bloom, who competed in the Olympics and won the World Cup championship in freestyle moguls, was able to continue competing as a professional skier even while playing football for the University of Colorado. (He was good enough to be drafted by the Philadelphia Eagles, principally as a punt and kick returner.) Does that result violate the spirit of amateurism? What do you suppose Avery Brundage would say? What do you suppose Jim Thorpe would say?

    Bloom, however, had another problem. After achieving skiing success, he had numerous paid entertainment, endorsement, and modeling opportunities; for example, he contracted to model clothing for Tommy Hilfiger. Bloom wanted to continue these activities even after enrolling at Colorado and while playing football for it. He argued that, because he was allowed to be a professional skier and play college football, he should be allowed to earn whatever is customary for a professional skier—which comes primarily from endorsements and media opportunities. The NCAA disagreed, and so did the Colorado Court of Appeals. *Bloom v. National Collegiate Athletic Association*, 93 P.3d 621 (Col. App. 2004). They concluded that the Bylaws' restraints on endorsements and media activities were not sports-specific. It did not matter, the court said, "(1) when the opportunity for such activities originated; (2) whether the opportunity arose or exists for reasons unrelated to participation in an amateur sport; [or] (3) whether income derived from the opportunity is customary for any particular professional sport." So Bloom could earn prize money, or a salary if it were available, for his skiing, but not endorsement income. Is there any justification for that distinction? Bloom presented evidence supporting his contention that some of his acting opportunities "arose not as a result of his athletic ability but because of his good looks and on-camera presence." Should Bloom have been allowed, without jeopardizing his football eligibility, to continue to model Tommy Hilfiger clothes in ads if (a) he was unidentified in the ads (though of course some readers would recognize his face)? (b) he was identified as a freestyle ski champion? (c) he was identified as a freestyle ski champion and Colorado football player?

After playing football for Colorado for two years, Bloom decided he needed the endorsement income to continue to compete as a skier. As a result, he lost his NCAA eligibility.

6.   *The beginning of the end?* In September 2019, California passed a Fair Pay To Play Act, making it illegal, beginning January 1, 2023, for any postsecondary educational institution in the state to prevent a student-athlete "from earning compensation as a result of the use of the student's name, image, or likeness." (Five other states passed similar laws in 2020; Florida's will be the first to take effect, in July 2021.) California thus set up a potential showdown with the NCAA. But in October 2019, the NCAA Board of Governors voted unanimously to direct each of its three divisions to develop a plan that would allow student-athletes to profit from their name, image, and likeness. Among the criteria prescribed by the Board were the following:

- Assure student-athletes are treated similarly to non-athlete students unless a compelling reason exists to differentiate.

- Make clear the distinction between collegiate and professional opportunities.

- Make clear that compensation for athletics performance or participation is impermissible.

- Reaffirm that student-athletes are students first and not employees of the university.

Is this a salutary development? Will the distinctions envisioned by the NCAA be sustainable? Should the marketing divisions of college athletic departments be allowed to assist athletes in developing endorsement opportunities? Should such assistance be part of recruitment?

In January 2021, the NCAA Division I Council tabled a plan developed pursuant to this directive; among the reasons was an expression of concern from the Department of Justice that the proposal violated the antitrust laws. Meanwhile, the Supreme Court agreed to hear a case, *NCAA v. Alston*, that may decide the extent to which the NCAA can legally limit education-related benefits that its members can confer on student-athletes. It has become increasingly likely that Congress will step into this area.

———

Exercise 7A

Suppose that the NCAA directs each of its three divisions to develop plans to permit member schools to directly compensate student-athletes. Draft a statement of principles, along with implementing rules if possible, for Division I. (Division I comprises those schools with the largest student bodies and athletics budgets, including the Big 10, SEC, ACC, Big 12, and Pac-12 Conferences. But with nearly 350 colleges and universities, it also includes the Ivy League and such small private colleges as Davidson and Siena.)

B. RESIDENCE AND CITIZENSHIP

Residency requirements are common in youth sports, from little league baseball to high school athletics. In this subchapter, we examine the counterpart to residency requirements at the level of elite international competition: citizenship rules.

There are many elite international and supranational competitions, ranging from the Pan American and Commonwealth Games to the Rugby World Cup. The most prominent are surely the Olympic Games and the FIFA World Cup. We will focus on the Olympics.

Under Rule 42 of the Olympic Charter, a competitor must be a national of the country they are representing. (An athlete who holds more than one nationality can play for either.) But the IOC does not regulate the authority of competitor nations to grant citizenship on whatever terms they choose. Subject, then, to two qualifications, IOC policy facilitates a fairly free movement of athletes. The qualifications are these. First, when an athlete has represented one country in regional or world competition, she has to wait three years thereafter before switching to another, although that waiting period can be waived by the national Olympic committee of the first country. Second, although the IOC itself does not insist on more than nominal citizenship, it authorizes the international federations to establish more restrictive rules for the sports that they administer. Several do. For example, the International Swimming Federation requires athletes to have at least one year's residence in the country for which they are competing, the International Basketball Federation limits national teams to one player who acquired citizenship through naturalization, and FIFA (starting only in 2004) requires a player to demonstrate a "clear connection"—such as ancestry, birth, or residence—to the country he or she wishes to represent.

In recent decades, nations have been increasingly willing to fast-track citizenship for elite athletes from other nations. In some cases, there is an ethnic basis for the athlete to adopt a new nation. For example, Naim Suleimanov, a world champion weight-lifter known as the Pocket Hercules, was a member of Bulgaria's oppressed Turkish minority before defecting to Turkey and changing his surname to Süleymanoğlu. A substantial cash payment facilitated Bulgaria's willingness to drop its objections to Süleymanoğlu competing for Turkey, and he won three successive Olympic gold medals for that nation. And sometimes there is another basis for the change of citizenship. For example, the elite Jamaican sprinter Merlene Ottey had lived in Slovenia, the nation of her coach, for several years before changing her citizenship in the twilight of her career. But sometimes the connection has been tenuous at best. For example, Italy, host of the 2006 Torino Winter Olympics, put on the ice a men's hockey team with ten players from Canada. "They held only minimal ties to Italy; some of them had never visited the country." Ayelet Shachar, *Picking Winners: Olympic Citizenship and the Global Race for Talent*, 120 YALE L.J. 2088, 2093 (2011). Similarly, Azerbaijan included six South Koreans on its field hockey team at the 2008 European championships; all had been given Azerbaijani passports in time to play. *Id.* And sometimes the procedures for citizenship have been extremely expedited. On December 30, 2005, just weeks before those Torino Games, President George W. Bush signed an appropriations bill that included a rider providing for a virtually immediate grant of citizenship for aliens who had been in continuous residence for three years (rather than the usual five) so long as certain requirements were met— most significantly, that the expedited process was necessary to allow the applicant "to represent the United States at an international event." Amendment to Immigration and Nationality Act, Pub. L. 109–149, 119 Stat. 2882 § 518(a) (2005). And remarkably, the same legislation provided that this provision would be repealed effective two days later. *Id.* § 518(b). Maxim Zavozin, a Russian-born ice dancer, was granted citizenship on the day of enactment, and Tanith Belbin, an ice dancer born and raised in Canada, received it the next day, a Saturday; both had trained in the United States for several years. Belbin and her partner won a silver medal for the U.S. Afterwards, Zavozin took on a Hungarian partner—and Hungary granted him citizenship in time to compete for that nation in the 2010 Winter Olympics.

Shachar identifies three competing values that bear on an assessment of what she calls "Olympic citizenship": freedom, fairness, and community. On the one hand, it "without a doubt enhances the freedom of mobility across borders for those with exceptional talent." On the other hand, "[i]t hardly seems fair to train a person—be they a doctor or an athlete—only to have them 'poached' by another country once they reach success," and fast-tracking undermines "the expectation of a substantial attachment between the individual and the country that she represents." Shachar concludes that Olympic citizenship "is a collective action problem that calls for a collective response: it is in the interest of each competing nation to engage in passport swaps, but it is to the detriment of the whole system of fair play and sportsmanship to permit such unregulated and aggressive talent 'poaching.' "

COMMENTS AND QUESTIONS

1. Collective action problems. A **collective action problem** is a technical concept that falls under the more general rubric of **game theory**.

Collective Action Problem; Game Theory

Game theory is the study of decision problems among multiple agents in which the optimal move for one agent depends in part on the moves made by other agents. (Soccer penalty kicks present a commonly discussed example: the best decision for the shooter depends on what the keeper does, and vice versa.) Collective action problems are the subtype of game-theoretic problems in which two conditions are satisfied: each agent derives greater individual benefits if all players in the "game" cooperate than if each pursues individual self-interest; but, regardless of what other players do, each individual gains even greater benefits by not cooperating, i.e., by "defecting." In a true collective action problem, the pursuit of self-interest by group members is likely to result in outcomes that are, for each member, inferior to the outcomes that could be achieved through cooperation or coordination. For example, in the type of collective action problem known as a *prisoners' dilemma*, each of two players, A and B, has to choose separately whether to whether to defect (confess to the crime charged) or cooperate (remain silent). The four possibilities, from best to worst, for each player are (1) "I defect, you cooperate, (2) "We both cooperate," (3) "We both defect," and (4) "I cooperate, you defect." Note that each player would be better off defecting, whatever the other player does; hence, defecting is called a dominant choice for each player. But if each makes that choice, they each come out worse than if each had cooperated.

Is Shachar correct that rules and practices concerning the nationality of athletes in international competition present "a collective action problem that calls for a collective response"? If nations vary widely in the endowments they enjoy of athletes and money, then isn't it likely that their interests in a collective or coordinated policy on citizenship will be misaligned? Don't the examples presented above (and Shachar presents others) suggest that at least some countries will benefit from being able to award "form-over-substance, just-in-time citizenship grants" *even if* other countries are allowed to do so too? Put another way, if present practices present a problem for athlete-rich countries (like, in Shachar's example, South Korea), aren't they an opportunity for athlete-poor countries (like Azerbaijan)?

2. Fast-track. Whether or not citizenship rules implicate a collective action problem, how should nationality be defined for purposes of international athletic competition? Is there anything wrong with fast-track processes for what Shachar calls "Olympic citizenship"? Professor Ian Ayres argues that there is not. Nations, he says, "should be free to compete for the services of the world's best athletes." Such a competitive market in citizenship "would enhance meritocracy" and, by emancipating athletes, "reduce the sometimes arbitrary power of home-country Olympic committees." Moreover, he argues that on principle citizenship determinations should be a domestic affair, not the concern of international sports federations. And if this change reduced the importance of medal counts, that would be good, too, because under Rule 6.1 of the Olympic Charter the Games are supposed to be competitions among athletes, not among countries. Ian Ayres, *Room for Debate: The Olympics Should be a Competition Among the Best Athletes,* N.Y. TIMES, July 27, 2012. Do you agree? If Charter Rule 6.1 is to be taken seriously, should selection of athletes for the Games be made by the international federation for each sport, and based on past performance irrespective of nationality? Should athletes march into the opening and closing ceremonies together with their competitors, rather than with other athletes from their nation? Should they be required to compete in uniforms bearing no national identification? Should the raising of flags and the playing of national anthems at medal ceremonies be eliminated?

3.   *Eliminating citizenship requirements entirely.* If you think that fast-track processes for Olympic citizenship are perfectly okay, is that because you believe that there should be no nationality requirements for international competitions in the first place? Put another way, should Rule 42 and its equivalents in other international competitions be scrapped? Professor Peter Spiro finds the types of cases that Shachar discusses entirely untroubling. A professional baseball player need have no prior connection to the city for which he plays; Spiro believes the same should be true for Olympic athletes and their sponsoring countries. Such a change would eliminate what he regards as the unfairness of excluding from the London Games the table tennis player XuXin, who was the third best in China—and in the world—because each nation could only send two players to the singles event. And it would eliminate "draconian" rules such as the one limiting teams in international basketball competition to one naturalized player. Peter Spiro, *Room for Debate: Eliminate Nationality Rules,* N.Y. TIMES, July 27, 2012. Does Spiro go farther than Ayres? *Should Olympic competition be any different from domestic professional sports? Why or why not? Is there anything distinctive and valuable about the Olympic Games that Spiro disregards?*

4.   *The other extreme.* In *calcio storico,* a violent mix of rugby and bare-knuckle boxing played in Florence among teams drawn from the four districts that comprise the city, players are eligible to compete only for the district in which they were born. *See Home Game: Calcio Storico,* (Netflix release June 26, 2020). Is it ever appropriate to fix a person's eligibility to compete based on place of birth?

C. SEX AND GENDER

Some of the most controversial, and socially significant, issues of player eligibility relate to matters of sex and gender. This subchapter addresses first the most fundamental of these issues, on which the others depend—whether to sex-classify in athletic competitions at all, rather than to hold only competitions in which eligibility is unaffected by sex or gender. A closely related matter is whether, or the extent to which, competitions designed for one sex should nevertheless be opened to members of the other. We will then consider how sports that sex-classify should classify intersex and transgender competitors, and other persons who present non-standard sex or gender profiles, and finally whether sports that maintain separate male and female tracks or variants must equalize all rules across the two classes of competition.

1.　SEX-BASED CLASSIFICATION

JOHN COGGON, NATASHA HAMMOND & SOREN HOLM, TRANSSEXUALS IN SPORT—FAIRNESS AND FREEDOM, REGULATION AND LAW[a]

2 SPORT, ETHICS AND PHILOSOPHY 4 (2008)
Copyright 2008 Taylor & Francis, reprinted with permission

It is widely, though not universally . . . accepted that segregation of the sexes is a justified discrimination in sport. This acceptance can take a stronger and a weaker form: we might argue either that fairness requires sex discrimination or else that fairness is compatible with it. The former would make a mixed-sex sport impermissible even if consent was present. The latter would allow consent to govern the issue. But if we are to infer consent from mere participation, and the rules are set by persons other than the athletes themselves, attempting to recognise the distinction may ultimately be a fruitless task.

[Törbjorn] Tännsjö, in his work criticising sexual discrimination in sport, argues that there are four principal justifications in favour of maintaining the status quo:

1.　It is like having weight classes: it makes the result less predictable.

2.　If women beat men, it will cause violent responses from men.

3.　Giving up the sexual discrimination would mean that women nearly always lose, which will be discouraging for women generally and female athletes particularly.

4.　Female and male sports are different.

We would suggest a fifth justification, not discussed by Tännsjö, that in most societies females still suffer social discrimination which restricts

---

[a]　As an older term for persons whose gender identity does not match their biological sex or assigned gender, "transsexual" has largely been replaced by "transgender." When still used these days, "transsexual" most often refers to the subset of transgender people who have changed, or seek to change, their bodies through medical intervention. But given its long negative usage, many trans people find "transsexual" offensive.

the possibility of girls and women to fully actualise their potential in sports, for instance by not giving girls the same chances and encouragement to pursue athletic excellence in schools and so on. Sex discrimination in sports is thus justified in these societies, but the justification would disappear if social discrimination against women is ever overcome. In societies where social discrimination persists this can justify sex discrimination in sports, even if these are sports where men have no biological advantage (chess might be an example).

With regard to the first justification, it should be added here that weight classes may serve a broader purpose than that which Tännsjö suggests. They do not merely provide unpredictability; allowing weight classes permits a wider range of athletes to take part in a sport. In boxing, for example, were there no weight classes there would be many fewer professional or amateur boxers participating in competitive matches because, by and large, a person who is featherweight would lose to a heavyweight, even if the latter were of considerably lower talent. Furthermore, weight classes permit more subtle enjoyments.

There may be quite different skills used by bigger, stronger boxers than smaller, quicker boxers. Similarly, in single-sex sports a spectator enjoys the exercise of differing skills: for example, the markedly different style of men's and women's tennis.

Let us consider the five justifications. To start, we may dispense with numbers 2 and 4. The second reason—that sports that would be female-dominated would provoke violent reactions in men—does appear somewhat unconvincing as a policy argument. To dispose of it without comment, though, would deny us some valid insight. Think, for example, of the case of Zhang Shan; her great success at shooting directly preceded the event's return to being a single-sex sport.[b] Of course, this may not be described as a violent reaction, but it is a response that suggests some kind of intolerance of male subjugation. That intolerance, however, enjoys no obvious legitimacy and may therefore be disregarded.

The fourth reason—that male and female sports are different—is clearly somewhat question-begging, and may set us up for some circularity. But even if it is true that some sports appeal to inherently male or female characteristics, there are few sports that are denied to a whole sex. If we grant, for the sake of argument, that rugby is better suited to men than women and is therefore a 'male sport', we need not further advocate that women be prohibited from playing. Nor need we automatically decide that fairness demands joint participation. Fairness might permit it, but not merely by virtue of the sport's maleness or femaleness.

---

[b]   Zhang Shan, of China, won the gold medal in Skeet Shooting at the 1992 Olympics, when the event was open to men and women. She was unable to defend her title in 1996, because the event was open only to men. A women's event was added in 2000.

Justifications 1 and 3, however, do potentially provide good policy reasons for continuing segregation. If people are to identify themselves with a sex, draw role models from their particular sex and place themselves in a societal context with reference to their sex, it would indeed be regrettable if a whole sex—generally it is felt to be women—should lose sporting role models. This view is further supported by justification 5. While in an ideal world we might concede that sex should not affect our treatment or perception of athletes, we need to remember that we live in a world where social prejudice and sports systems create biases massively in favour of male dominance. Were we simply to have mixed events, we would effectively exclude women from the majority of Olympic sports (Schneider 2000). This position is born[e] out by the medical evidence, which suggests that generally men have a biological advantage over women both in terms of their aerobic capacity and their muscle strength (Cheuvront et al. 2005). Tännsjö argues that the fact that sex differences are general rather than particular is precisely why they should not be considered relevant: in this respect they are distinguishable from a weight class, which is specific (Tännsjö 2000, 103). The logic behind this argument makes sense, but it is surely better to have an imperfect system that fits more happily in a world that is also imperfect than a philosophically perfect system that disadvantages 50 per cent of the population in the present (imperfect) world.

It seems, then, that the principal justification for separating the sexes in sport lies in a combination of the first (with its additional justifications) and the third and fifth reasons enumerated above: it is justified similarly to weight classes, and it ensures that women are not excluded from taking part in the majority of sporting events at the highest level. Fairness in an unfair society recommends it, and the consent of the athletes legitimises it.

COMMENTS AND QUESTIONS

1. Fairness. The standard argument in favor of sex classification in athletics places heavy emphasis on "fairness." Due to no fault of their own, say many defenders of athletic sex classification, female athletes have no chance to beat men in elite competition. But because elite female athletes train just as hard as do their male counterparts, it is only fair that they be given a comparable chance to succeed. Sex classification is necessary to provide that chance. *See, e.g.,* Jessica L. Adair, *In a League of Their Own: The Case for Intersex Athletes,* 18 SPORTS LAWYERS J. 121, 130 (2011); Jill Pilgrim et al., *Far from the Finish Line: Transsexualism and Athletic Competition,* FORDHAM INTELL. PROP., MEDIA AND ENT. L. J. 495 (2003).

Do you agree that considerations of fairness demand that athletic competitions be segregated into separate male and female competitions? Most experts believe that the factual premise is almost certainly true. Due to much lower muscle mass, higher percentages of body fat, and lower levels of testosterone and androgen, the most talented and hardest working women athletes cannot compete successfully against top men in athletic competitions that depend significantly upon speed, strength, or explosiveness. For some evidence, consider that for all running and jumping events in which women and men both compete, the *women's world records* are slower or shorter than the American records for *high school boys*.[c]

So if the fairness-based argument for separate sex-based competitions bands is not compelling, it won't be because elite female athletes can compete successfully against elite male athletes in sports that reward male-typical attributes. Instead, the problem for the argument must be that this fact does not support the normative conclusion that failure to provide separate tracks or classes for women would be unfair. Why, precisely, is it unfair to the best women athletes to leave them effectively without a chance to win at the elite level? Is sex-segregation costless? If not, who loses?

2.   *"The Steve Rogers problem."* The fairness-based argument for sex classification starts from the premise that success in athletic competitions depends heavily upon one's basic biomechanical endowments. Those favored by the genetic lottery achieve greater success in sports, by and large, than do those who are less naturally gifted. All that is true. But it is as true within the sexes as across them. Do individual men who lack the genetic gifts enjoyed by elite male athletes have strong fairness-based claims that the organizers of athletic competitions should make special arrangements to ensure that *they* enjoy a real chance to win? (Think of Steve Rogers, of Marvel Comics fame, the scrawny young man who was too frail to join the army before he was transformed into Captain America.)

To make the question a little more concrete, imagine a male miler with basic biomechanical endowments comparable to those possessed by some particular elite female miler. Both have the same prospects for beating an elite male miler at that distance: close to none. Is it unfair to the sub-elite male runner to organize the competition as a single race pitting all comers against one another? If not, how can it be unfair to the elite female runner to organize the competition that way?

3.   *Race.* It is indisputable that persons of West African ancestry outperform all others in short foot races and (to a significant but less extreme degree) that persons of East African and North African ancestry dominate long distance races. Here's just a quick flavor of the extent of the dominance, as of 2012:

> The fact is, over the past fifty years, as the barriers to competition, at least for men, have gradually eroded, and equality of opportunity has steadily spread to vast sections of once poverty-stricken Asia and Africa, one might have expected that running results would have become more democratic. The medal podium should look like a

---

[c]   All data taken from TRACK & FIELD NEWS, *Records*, https://tinyurl.com/y6ansbk3.

rainbow of racial equality, a United Nations of sports. But just the opposite has happened.

The trends are eye opening: Athletes of African ancestry hold every major male running record, from the 100 meters to the marathon. (Although these same trends hold for female runners, the pattern is more dominant among male runners. This analysis focuses on men because the playing field for them is far more level, as social taboos remain that restrict female access to sports in many parts of the world.) Over the last seven Olympic men's 100-meter races, all 56 finalists have been of West African descent. Only two non-African runners, France's Christophe Lemaire, who is white, and Australia's Irish-aboriginal Patrick Johnson, have cracked the top 500 100-meter times. There are no elite Asian sprinters—or, intriguingly, any from East or North Africa.

Jon Entine, *The DNA Olympics—Jamaicans Win Sprinting 'Genetic Lottery'—and Why We Should All Care*, FORBES.COM (Aug. 12, 2012).

Many experts believe that these racially disparate performances are largely (though not entirely) the product of genetic differences across populations. *See generally* JON ENTINE, TABOO: WHY BLACK ATHLETES DOMINATE SPORTS AND WHY WE'RE AFRAID TO TALK ABOUT IT (2000). Some of the claimed biomechanical differences are these: East Africans have a higher percentage of slow-twitch fibers in their muscles, a slighter body, longer legs, and larger lung capacities, which help in endurance and long-distance running. Western African-descended runners dominate in anaerobic sports, including sprinting. People with ancestral roots in this region of Africa have bigger, more visible muscles along with a higher number of fast-twitch fibers in their muscles. They also have less natural body fat, narrower hips, and higher levels of testosterone. West Africans have higher centers of mass due to a relatively shorter torso than Caucasians: this favors them in running, and disadvantages them in swimming.

Other experts think this is false, and that demonstrated differences in athletic performance among racial groups are almost entirely the consequence of social factors. *See, e.g.,* JOHN HOBERMAN, DARWIN'S ATHLETES: HOW SPORT HAS DAMAGED BLACK AMERICA AND PRESERVED THE MYTH OF RACE (1996). But *if* we were to become persuaded that it is true, would it then be unfair to sprinters not of West African descent to require them to take their chances against the genetically superior (on this dimension) West Africans? If not, does it follow that it would be unfair to women to require them to take their chances against the genetically superior (ditto) men, or are the cases distinguishable?

    4.   *Modeling.* If you do not think that present practices are unfair to sub-elite male athletes or to European or Asian male sprinters, then you might conclude that failing to sex-classify in athletic competitions would not be unfair to elite female athletes. You might conclude, in other words, that sex classification in track is not justified by the supposed need to ensure fairness for the very best women runners. But that would not yet establish that there is not a powerful moral argument in favor of sex classification. It just means that if there is, it must have a different structure or logic. And a different argument for sex classification can be teased out of Tännsjö's suggestion (cited by Coggon, Hammond & Holm) that "[g]iving up the sexual discrimination would mean that women nearly always lose, which will be discouraging for women generally and female athletes particularly."

Start by imagining what the world would look like without sex classification in sport. Presumably, a massive percentage of elite female athletes—runners, swimmers, skiers, tennis players, and more—would be erased from our collective consciousness. That erasure would alter our collective picture of female potential. As Coggon, Hammond and Holm argue in the preceding article: "If people are to identify themselves with a sex, draw role models from their particular sex and place themselves in a societal context with reference to their sex, it would indeed be regrettable if a whole sex—generally it is felt to be women—should lose sporting role models." The philosopher Jane English has similarly observed, "When there are virtually no female athletic stars . . ., this is damaging to the self-respect of all women. Members of disadvantaged groups identify strongly with each other's successes and failures. If women do not attain roughly equal fame and fortune in sports, it leads both men and women to think of women as naturally inferior." Jane English, *Sex Equality in Sports*, 7 PHIL. & PUB. AFFAIRS 269, 273 (1978).[d] Finally, and in much the same vein, the sport philosopher Angela Schneider argues:

> Sports are complex social institutions that partially shape and define our images of who we are and what is possible for human beings. . . . [I]t would not help our view of either women or men only to see images of men in elite athletic competition. Seeing, and valuing, strong athletic women provides not only an example to younger women of the range of the possible for women, but it also changes our social views of what is appropriate and good for women to do.

Angela J. Schneider, *On the Definition of 'Woman' in the Sport Context, in* VALUES IN SPORT: ELITISM, NATIONALISM, GENDER EQUALITY AND THE SCIENTIFIC MANUFACTURE OF WINNERS 123, 137 (Torbjörn Tännsjö & Claudio Tamburrini eds., 2000).

On this view, sex classification is morally permissible—and possibly morally recommended or even obligatory—*not* out of regard for the fairness-based claims *of elite women athletes*, but out of concern that young women and girls (and men and boys too) should be presented with a broad and rich vision of life's possibilities—as broad and rich as young men and boys enjoy. We can conceive of this as fairness, not to the elite, but to the non-elite and pre-elite. Or maybe "fairness" provides the wrong vocabulary. Perhaps the moral claim is better couched in terms of a robust conception of equal opportunity for

---

[d]　The omitted language is: "or when women receive much less prize money than men do . . ." We address the case for equalizing prize money between the sexes below.

human flourishing. *See generally* JOSEPH FISHKIN, BOTTLENECKS: A NEW THEORY OF EQUAL OPPORTUNITY (2016). Are you persuaded?

5.   *Affirmative action in university admissions.* If you are attracted by the modeling argument for sex-based classification in sport, does it have any possible bearing on the propriety of race-based affirmative action in such contexts as admission to selective institutions of higher education? Supreme Court doctrine requires that all racial classifications made by a state must be subject to "strict scrutiny," which provides that a challenged distinction is unconstitutional unless "narrowly tailored" to achieve a "compelling state interest." The Court has held that a state interest's in securing the educational benefits of a more diverse student body is compelling. *Grutter v. Bollinger*, 539 U.S. 306 (2003). It has also held that a state's interest in combatting the current effects of entrenched societal discrimination is not. *Wygant v. Jackson Board of Education*, 476 U.S. 267, 274 (1986) (plurality). The combination of these holdings explains why public defenses of race-based affirmative action are always couched in terms of "student body diversity." Should the courts permit more race consciousness in university admissions by recognizing as "compelling" a broader array of state interests related to the promotion of racial justice? For example, should they deem "compelling" a state interest in ensuring that pathways to social advancement are visibly open to all Americans? Why (not)?

6.   *Sex-bias in the selection of sports.* If you are persuaded by neither the fairness-based argument for sex segregation nor the opportunity-based argument, consider the following suggestion. Sex segregation would not be morally recommended if sports in which women excelled relative to men— those involving such traits as balance, flexibility and perhaps endurance— enjoyed a more prominent place in our athletic universe. But the greater popularity of sports that favor male endowments relative to sports that favor female endowments is itself a cultural artifact. In effect, sports that would favor women have been artificially depressed by a patriarchal culture. *See* English, *Sex Equality in Sport,* at 275–76. Therefore, sex segregation is required as a corrective to this artificial depression of favorable sport opportunities for women.

Do you find this persuasive? How would you know whether or to what extent the present relative popularity of "male" and "female" sports is the product of cultural bias? If you believe that this is true, what could or should be done about it?

7.   *Alternatives to sex classification.* In lieu of classification based on sex, would it be possible and desirable to structure competitions in such a way as to give all persons a realistic chance to win so long as they maximize their basic biomechanical endowments? This is already done in combat sports, which arrange competition by weight classes. It's also done (though with only two divisions) in crew. And, though it draws very little attention, some American colleges have long competed in sprint football, previously known as lightweight

football, in which players must weigh no more than 183 pounds (or no more than 178 pounds if they have under 5% body fat). So, instead of a two-part classification drawn by sex, we could arrange competition groups by reference to specified measurable endowments, such as proportion of fast-twitch muscle fibers or levels of functional testosterone. For example, athletes in the top quintile of the endowment in question would compete against each other, persons who register in the next quintile would be grouped together, and so on. If the organizing endowment were sensibly chosen, almost all the competitors in the top group would be male. But "the division would be determined not by gender [or sex] but by actual physical advantages that gender supposedly, yet unreliably, supplies." Levy, *Either/Or,* at 55. Should American college athletics be organized in this way? And, whether or not this is done, should competition in more sports be separated on the basis of factors such as size? Should schools and colleges compete in height-limited basketball?

Alternatively, a sport could deploy a system of handicaps even at the highest level of competition. (See Subchapter 3A.) If, say, a golfer's handicap were subtracted from his nominal score, a middling tour professional who substantially outperforms what is usual for him could win the Masters even without shooting the lowest score. Runners could have seconds added to or subtracted from their times, as their personal performance baselines would warrant. In sum, then, we could structure competition to make things "fairer" to all persons, regardless of sex or race, who didn't win the genetic lottery. Would this be a better alternative to sex classification? How, precisely, would it work? Should it be adopted in addition to sex classification?

   8.   *From sex "classification" to sex "segregation."* Let us introduce some stipulated terms of art. "Sex classification" in athletics, let us say, has two features: (1) competitions are divided into male and female bands or tracks; and (2) males are barred from competing on the female track. On this definition of sex classification, females are *not* barred from competing on the male track if they so choose, so long as they meet whatever non-sex-based eligibility requirements the male competitors must satisfy. That is, the prohibitions in a system of sex classification are asymmetric: men are barred from participating in women's competitions, but not vice versa. Those prohibitions could, of course, be made symmetrical. Let us call it "sex segregation" rather than (mere) "sex classification" if the rules prohibit members of either sex from participating in the competitions designated for the other sex.

If we should sex-classify at all in athletics, should we move all the way to sex segregation? Golf and tennis have taken different positions. When Annika Sorenstam, widely considered the greatest woman golfer ever, was granted a sponsor's exemption to play the Bank of America Colonial Tournament, in Fort Worth, Texas, on the PGA Tour, several male golfers, including Vijay Singh, opposed the granting of the exemption. Phil Mickelson supported it, saying, "Guys who are having a tough time with this are thinking this is the men's tour. It's not. It's the best tour, for the best players in the world." Mickelson was right in the sense that the PGA's rules do not have a rule barring women.

But tennis bars women from competing in the men's draw just as it bars men from competing on the women's side.

What, if anything, justifies sex segregation in tennis? Is it merely a matter of carelessness—that the rules are written the way they are simply because the rulemakers, focusing on current reality, never considered the possibility of women competing in the men's draw? Is it demanded by a conception of fairness as evenhandedness—that is, if men are prohibited from playing in women's competitions, it's only fair that women are prohibited from playing in men's competitions? Or is it justified as a way to protect the women's game from the loss of popularity that it might suffer if the very best women left the women's tour and joined the men's tour, or if the best women players routinely lost to low-ranked men? Would it be fair for tennis to bar the few women, if there are any—Serena Williams is the most frequently mentioned example[e]—who might be able to successfully compete against professional male players from doing so in order to aid the many more women players who could not do so?

9.   *Mind sports.* The World Bridge Federation and the International Chess Federation both engage in sex classification but not sex segregation: they run tournaments in three categories: an "open" category for men and women of all ages, for women only, and for seniors only. Can you think of any reasons to sex-classify in bridge or chess? Do men possess a genetic advantage relative to women with respect to bridge- or chess-relevant skills? Or are the best bridge and chess players men only because more men than women (or more boys than girls) take up these games at an early age, thus producing a larger pool of serious players? For a study that reaches this conclusion, see Christopher F. Chabris & Mark E. Glickman, *Sex Differences in Intellectual Performance: Analysis of a Large Cohort of Competitive Chess Players*, 17 PSYCH. SCI. 1040 (2006). On this account, more top bridge and chess players are men than women for essentially the same reason that more men over 7′ tall are Chinese than Canadian.

10.   *Sex-based exclusions from participation.* The previous question asks whether it is appropriate to bar women from competing against men when a particular sport creates separate tracks for the two sexes. Is it ever appropriate for a sport to offer opportunities only for one sex? Consider the 50K walk. Since 1992, there has been a race walk for women at the Olympics as well as one for men at 20K, but the 50K walk has been only for men. The International Association of Athletics Federations (IAAF) said that interest among women in a 50K race is "pretty much nonexistent"; others have regarded this position as the last vestige of an attitude that for decades prevented women's competitions in distances from the half-mile to the marathon. Erin Taylor-Talcott, who had won three US women's titles in the 50K walk, had a best time

---

[e]   It is unclear how successfully Williams could compete against elite men. In 1998, when Serena was 16 and her sister Venus was 17, they claimed they could beat men ranked below 200. Karsten Braasch, then ranked 203 (though four years earlier he had reached no. 38) on the men's side, accepted the challenge and defeated the sisters in consecutive one-set exhibitions, 6–1 and 6–2.

easily good enough to win an invitation to the 2012 US Olympic trials. USA Track and Field allowed her to participate at the trials as a guest as long as she agreed not to try to participate in the men's race at the London Olympics themselves. Realizing that her chance of soon getting a time (4:09) good enough to qualify for the Olympics was remote, she agreed, and turned in a personal best of 4:33:23. Taylor-Talcott has said: "I'm a big proponent of 'if you build it they will come.' There's no way that if you create an international event for women that you won't get quality athletes who want to make the team. Since I've been fighting for a women's 50K I've had women from all over the world tell me that they want to do it." As a result of a lawsuit brought by Taylor-Talcott, USA Track and Field now offers equal prize money to men and women in the 50K national championships. *See* Jeré Longman, *Racewalking, but Not to London*, N.Y. TIMES, Nov. 17, 2011, at B14; Madeleine Pape, *Erin Taylor-Talcott and the question of "interest"*, HEAR SPORT ROAR.COM (June 23, 2014). In 2015, the IAAF changed its rules to recognize a women's world record in the 50K walk, and Taylor-Talcott was the inaugural holder of it. *Taylor-Talcott named to men's 50K World Race Walk Team Championships*, U.S.A. TRACK AND FIELD (Apr. 20, 2016). At the 2017 World Championships, a 50K women's walk was held. Seven women started, and four finished within the allowed time. Taylor-Talcott was disqualified early on, after the 5K mark, for repeated failure to comply with the definition of race walking. Inês Henriques of Portugal won in a world record time of 4:05:56. In March 2019, Liu Hong of China broke the 4-hour barrier, recording a time of 3:59:15. A women's 50K race was not scheduled for the Olympics that were originally to be held in 2020. *See* James Diamond, *US lawyer launches legal challenge to get women's 50km race walk into Tokyo 2020 Olympics*, INSIDE THE GAMES (Apr. 1, 2019).

Could there be any good reason why a woman should not be permitted to compete in the 50K racewalk at the Olympics if she made the qualifying time? Put another way, assume that in fact there is little indication of interest among women in a 50K racewalk; if, for no reason other than that, there is no *women's* 50K racewalk, can the creation or maintenance of a *men's* 50K racewalk be justified?

11. Youth sports. Issues related to sex classification arise with some regularity in high school and other youth sports. Little League baseball long barred girls from participation; its national director of public relations said that "all the medical and physiological evidence indicates baseball is a hazardous sport for girls to play on the same team with boys." He elaborated: "A girl's reaction time to a thrown ball is considerably less than a boy's. Girls are vulnerable to being hit. Their long bones in their arms and legs are more vulnerable than boys." But in June 1974, under pressure from litigation, Little League announced that it would open all competition to girls—though each girl who wanted to play would have to demonstrate "equal competency" with boys "in baseball skills, physical skills and other attributes used as the basis for team selection." Little League's Congressional charter was amended later that year to ensure that girls could play. *Jenny Fulle*, WIKIPEDIA, https://tinyurl. com/y6zvnwjf. Participation by girls is now rather routine—but the outstanding performance by Mo'ne Davis at the 2014 Little League World Series was sufficiently unusual to capture considerable national attention.

American high school athletic associations establish terms of competition for numerous sports. In some sports—such as soccer, basketball, track and field, cross-country, and tennis—competition is established both for boys and girls. But some sports, such as football and wrestling, are typically designated only for boys, and some, such as field hockey and competitive cheer, are typically designated only for girls. (Note that in many countries, field hockey—often termed simply "hockey"—is a significant sport for men as well as for women. Indeed, in large part because of its popularity in India and Pakistan, it is thought to be the third largest team field sport worldwide, in terms of number of participants, after soccer and cricket.) And sometimes, in middle school or high school, a young athlete wishes to play in a competition designated for the other sex. Consider these questions irrespective of legal constraints:

- An outstanding girl basketball player wishes to play on her school's boys' team, because the level of competition is better than on the girls' team and she will improve more. Should the athletic association allow her to play? Is the situation different if she wants to play on the boys' baseball team, and her school has a softball team, but not a baseball team, for girls?

- Now suppose a girl wants to wrestle on her school's boys' wrestling team; the school offers no sport for girls remotely similar to wrestling. Should she be allowed to wrestle? If she is allowed to wrestle and her prospective opponent in a championship tournament has a religious objection to wrestling against girls, what should the result be? *See* Dave Krider, *Boy forfeits to girl at Iowa state wrestling tournament*, MAXPREPS.COM (Feb. 17, 2011).

- A high school boy wants to swim, but his school has a swim team only for girls. Should he be allowed to compete for it? Does your answer change if he wants to play field hockey—he is from Belgium, where field hockey is popular among males—and his school has a field hockey team only for girls, but it has a lacrosse team for boys? In either of these situations, does it matter how old the boy is? Does it matter how good he is at the sport and whether he is likely to be dominant in the sport? Does it matter how many other boys, if any, also want to join the girls' team?[f]

---

[f] *See, e.g.*, Karen Crouse, *Boys Swimming on Girls Teams Find Success, Then Draw Jeers*, N.Y. TIMES, Nov. 19, 2011, at D1 (noting that two of four highest seeds in girls' state championship 50-meter freestyle event are boys); *Williams v. School Dist. of Bethlehem, Pa.*, 998 F.2d 168 (3d Cir. 1993) (reversing grant of summary judgment for a boy who wanted to play on a girls' high school field hockey team); *Boy field hockey star deemed 'too good' can play, committee rules*, FOX NEWS.COM (Nov. 30, 2015) (Long Island school district ruled that a 13-year-old boy could not play on an interscholastic girls' field hockey team, even though there was no boys' field hockey league,

- Should a high school athletic association make a rule that it will offer a sport either for both sexes or for neither?

12. Sex classification in the arts and sciences. Awards in the arts are routinely sex-segregated. Since its inaugural ceremony in 1929, the Academy of Motion Picture Arts and Sciences, has awarded separate Oscars for best actor and best actress, as do the Golden Globe Awards, the Screen Actors Guild, the Emmys, and so on. The Grammys has separate awards for male and female vocalists. Increasingly, critics object that the segregation is anachronistic and unjust. As one argued:

> [S]eparate is not equal. While it is certainly acceptable for sports competitions like the Olympics to have separate events for male and female athletes, the biological differences do not affect acting performances. The divided Oscar categories merely insult women, because they suggest that women would not be victorious if the categories were combined. In addition, this segregation helps perpetuate the stereotype that the differences between men and women are so great that the two sexes cannot be evaluated as equals in their professions.

Kim Elsesser, *And the Gender-Neutral Oscar Goes To . . .*, N.Y. TIMES, Mar. 4, 2010, at A35. Do you agree that male and female acting categories should be combined? What do you think the consequence would be?

The Nobel Prize in Physics was awarded to a woman, Maria Goeppert Mayer, in 1963, and not to another until Donna Strickland in 2018. (Nobels for women in Physiology or Medicine, by contrast, are relatively routine.) The Physics Prize was awarded every year in between, to 127 men. Should separate Nobel Prizes in Physics be awarded to men and women? If you think the answer is negative, but you also prefer to maintain separate acting awards for men and women, what reasons do you have, other than that this is the way these awards have always been given?

13. Sex classification in public safety: "The Steve Rogers Problem" revisited. Eligibility requirements for the military and for many public safety departments are sex-normed. Consider *Alspaugh v. Commission on Law Enforcement Standards*, 634 N.W.2d 161 (Mich. App. 2001). The Michigan State Police had a performance-skills test that candidates for the police academy, and ultimately for the police force itself, had to pass. It involved six events—a measure of handgrip strength, a 60-second pushup test, a timed half mile run, a timed obstacle course, a test of the time necessary to drag a 165-lb. dummy thirty feet, and a test of the time necessary to carry a 95-lb. duffel thirty feet and place it atop a 31" platform. The standards were "gender-normed," meaning that they were considerably more stringent for males than for females. The plaintiffs, male candidates who did not pass the test (but did

---

because he was "too good," then, after parents filed a complaint, reversed its decision, but only for the upcoming season).

satisfy the standards for females) sued, claiming sex discrimination. The trial court granted summary judgment for the defense, and the appellate court affirmed, accepting the defense's contention that the test was primarily intended to measure general physical fitness rather than establish minimum physical requirements necessary for law enforcement officers.[g] In your opinion, was the case rightly decided? Does *Alspaugh* teach us something of value about sex classification in sports? Do debates over sex classification in sports teach us something of value about issues like that involved in *Alspaugh*? Are the two contexts too different to be brought into productive conversation?

2.   ASSIGNMENT IN NON-STANDARD CASES

a.   Intersex Athletes

We have addressed the question of whether a sport should sex-classify (or sex-segregate) on the assumption that it is clear who is male and who is female, and that these are the only possibilities. But, as the bioethicist Alice Dreger notes, "Humans like their sex categories neat, but nature doesn't care. Nature doesn't actually have a line between the sexes. If we want a line, we have to draw it *on* nature." Alice Dreger, *Sex Typing for Sport,* 40 HASTINGS CENTER REP. 22, 23 (2010).

The case of Caster Semenya, a middle-distance runner from South Africa, vividly instantiates the issue. Having been raised in a poor Black village, Semenya was a virtual unknown when she burst on the international track scene in 2008 by winning a gold medal in the 800 meters at the Commonwealth Youth Games held in Pune, India. Her victory the following summer at the African Junior Athletic Championships qualified Semenya for her first senior event, the 2009 World Championships in Berlin. In Berlin, she struck gold again in the 800 meters with a personal best 1:55:45, more than two seconds faster than her nearest competitor and just two seconds off the women's world record set twenty-six years earlier by the Czech sensation, Jarmila Kratochvílová.

While Semenya was preparing to run in Berlin, however, the International Association of Athletics Federations (IAAF), track and field's worldwide governing body, was busily investigating charges that Semenya was in fact a man. Unquestionably, there were grounds for suspicion well beyond her remarkably fast times. *The New Yorker*'s Ariel Levy observed later that year, "Semenya is breathtakingly butch. Her torso is like the chest plate on a suit of armor. She has a strong jawline, and a build that slides straight from her ribs to her hips." Ariel Levy, *Either/Or: Sports, Sex, and the Case of Caster Semenya*, NEW YORKER, Nov. 30, 2009, at 48. Her voice is husky and her muscular running form is distinctly male in

---

[g]   The plaintiffs also claimed that if gender-norming was permitted, then the standards also ought to be age-normed, to control for decreases in muscular strength, endurance, and aerobic capacity attributable to the aging process. The appellate court rejected this contention as well, in part on the ground that the plaintiffs had failed to show their general physical fitness.

style; her 2009 performance in Berlin is viewable here: https://tinyurl.com/yx9bwmeo.

Over protests from the South African athletic federation, the IAAF subjected Semenya to sex testing by five medical experts—a gynecologist, an endocrinologist, an internist, a psychologist, and an expert on gender. Although the test results have never been released, Australia's *Daily Telegraph,* a tabloid owned by Rupert Murdoch's News Corporation, reported in the fall of 2009 that they revealed that Semenya had been raised as a girl and has external female genitalia but undescended testes in lieu of ovaries. According to this report, Semenya's body produces three times as much testosterone as the average female, with such consequent physical advantages as substantially greater muscle mass and blood oxygen capacity. It appears that Semenya has a condition referred to as 46XY DSD—the 46XY meaning that she has XY chromosomes and DSD standing for Differences of Sexual Development.

Citing confidentiality rules, the IAAF would neither confirm nor deny that report. In July 2010, without elaboration, it cleared Semenya to compete internationally. Still, the overwhelming consensus in track circles holds that Semenya is an intersex individual, a broad term for a range of distinct conditions—sometimes termed "disorders of sexual development" and formerly called hermaphroditism—involving the presence of intermediate or atypical combinations of physical features or hormonal characteristics usually relied upon to distinguish males from females. For example, an individual with Androgen Insensitivity Syndrome is genetically male but is insensitive to male hormones and so has some or all of the outer physical characteristics of a female. The most complete form of this syndrome is sometimes referred to as Testicular Feminization Syndrome. A set of biomechanical and hormonal features gives the average male greater strength and speed than the typical female—and to a lesser extent it grants such advantages to some intersex individuals.

In London, Semenya was originally awarded the silver medal in the women's 800 meters, finishing 1.04 seconds behind Russia's Mariya Savinova. Noting that the time was well short of her fastest and that she appeared relaxed at the race's end, several observers speculated that she might have tried not to win in order to avoid greater scrutiny. *See, e.g.,* June Thomas, *Did Caster Semenya Lose the Women's 800 Meters on Purpose?*, SLATE (Aug. 11, 2012). But ultimately Semenya won the gold, when Savinova was stripped of her title for doping. And at the Rio Olympics in 2016, Semenya won gold again. It is widely believed that those who joined her on the podium—Francine Niyonsaba of Burundi won the silver and Margaret Wambui of Kenya won the bronze—are also 46XY DSD athletes.

Assuming that a sport does sex-classify (or sex-segregate), how should it treat intersex individuals like Caster Semenya? Three possibilities are obvious: (1) allow people like Semenya to compete as and against women, (2) require them to compete (if at all) against men, or (3) develop a third classification specifically for intersex competitors.

The third option is entirely unrealistic: there just aren't enough intersex athletes—or enough athletes who are known, or even know themselves, to be intersex—to make a third classification viable.

Though the second option is realistic, what it amounts to in practice is not that elite intersex athletes will in fact compete against elite male athletes, but rather that they will stay home. As an illustration, consider Semenya's personal record in the 800 meters, 1:55:16. While blisteringly fast for elite women runners, it is over 14 seconds off the men's world record of 1:41:01. Indeed, in every single track event, the men's *qualifying times* for the 2012 Olympics were lower than the women's *world records*. Had Semenya been compelled to run against males, her best time would have left her off the medal stand in the top division at the 2012 Texas state high school championships. So the realistic options for intersex athletes in a world of athletic sex segregation would seem to reduce to just two: allow them to compete against women or leave them unable to compete at an elite level.

In response to criticism over its initial handling of the Semenya case, the IAAF pursued a fourth option that combines those two, allowing intersex athletes to compete as and against women if but only if they take specified steps to mitigate the athletic advantages their conditions confer. Regulations adopted in 2011 for handling cases of female hyperandrogenism (that is, an excess of androgens, or male hormones) would render an athlete eligible to participate in women's competitions at middle distances only if she had "androgen levels below the normal male range," defined to be total testosterone levels ≥ 10 nmol/L, or she was able to carry the burden of proving that she had "an androgen resistance such that she derives no competitive advantage from having androgen levels in the normal male range." *IAAF Regulations Governing Eligibility of Females with Hyperandrogenism to Compete in Women's Competition.*

The IAAF regulations were applied against Dutee Chand, an Indian sprinter who has been banned from women's competition for high testosterone levels. The IAAF told Chand that she might become eligible by taking hormone-suppressing drugs or undergoing surgery to inhibit her body's production of testosterone. Instead she brought a proceeding before the Court of Arbitration for Sport. In spring 2015, the CAS ruled in Chand's favor. *Chand v. IAAF & Athletics Federation of India*, CAS 2014/A/3759. The Court first opined that "[i]t is legitimate and necessary to divide athletes into male and female categories . . . because male athletes have such an advantage over female athletes that competition between the sexes is not fair." ¶ 230. It also ruled that "there should be an objective criterion or criteria to police this divide," and that "the level of endogenous testosterone and sensitivity to testosterone may provide an appropriate criterion to divide normal male and female populations." ¶ 510. But it concluded that, on the current state of the scientific evidence, the balance of probabilities did not establish

> that androgen-sensitive hyperandrogenic female athletes enjoy such a substantial performance advantage over non-hyperandrogenic female athletes that excluding them from competing in the female category, and thereby excluding them from competing at all unless they take medication or undergo treatment, is a necessary and proportionate means of preserving fairness in athletic competition and/or policing the binary male/female classification. In particular, while the evidence indicates that higher levels of naturally occurring testosterone may increase athletic performance, the Panel is not satisfied that the degree of that advantage is more significant than the advantage derived from the numerous other variables which the parties acknowledge also affect female athletic performance: for example, nutrition, access to specialist training facilities and coaching, and other genetic and biological variations.

¶ 532. In 2018, the IAAF adopted a new set of regulations of more modest scope, applying only to women competing in international competitions, or for recognition of world records, in events ranging from 400m to the mile. *IAAF Introduces New Eligibility Regulations for Female Classification*, WORLD ATHLETICS (Apr. 26, 2018), https://tinyurl.com/y4h7zcsq. These regulations cover any Relevant Athlete, a term defined to include an athlete who (1) has one of a prescribed set of DSDs, (2) "as a result . . . has circulating testosterone levels in blood of five (5) nmol/L or above," and (3) "has sufficient androgen sensitivity for those levels of testosterone to have a material androgenizing effect." First among the enumerated DSDs, and the one apparently applicable to Semenya, is 5a-reductive type 2 deficiency (5-ARD), in which a person with XY chromosomes is unable to convert testosterone into DHT, a powerful androgen that plays a vital role in the fetal development of the male sex organs (and has other effects such as causing male-pattern baldness). Under the regulations, a Restricted Athlete who wishes to compete in international competitions, or set a world record, in one of the prescribed events must, in addition to being recognized at law as female or intersex "or equivalent," reduce her blood testosterone level to below 5 nmol/L for a continuous period of six months, and then keep it below that level continuously so long as she wishes to maintain her eligibility.

Semenya and Athletics South Africa challenged these new regulations in the CAS. In 2019, a CAS panel upheld the regulations, though with some qualification. *Semenya v. IAAF*, CAS 2018/O/5794, 2018/O/5798 (2019). (Semenya and the IAAF each appointed one member of the panel, and the third, Annabelle Bennett, a former judge from Australia, was agreed on by the parties; not surprisingly, most of the panel's decisions on contentious issues were by majority vote.) The panel concluded that the regulations are "prima facie discriminatory"—they impose constraints on females and intersex persons, but not on males—but it said that this was "merely the starting point, and not the end" of analysis; the regulations would still be valid if they were "a necessary, reasonable and proportionate means of attaining a legitimate objective." ¶ 548. And the panel concluded that the regulations satisfied those tests. It accepted the IAAF's view that separate male and female categories in athletic competition are necessary "to protect one group of individuals against having to compete against individuals who possess certain insuperable performance advantages derived from biology rather than legal status," and so reference to biological factors rather than legal status alone may be appropriate. ¶ 560. After reviewing extensive scientific evidence from both sides, the panel concluded that the elevated levels of circulating testosterone possessed by 46XY 5-ARD athletes gives them "a significant sporting advantage" over 46XX athletes. ¶ 574. The panel emphasized "the notable statistical over-representation of female athletes with 5-ARD," ¶ 537, the population incidence of which is less than 1 in 100,000. ¶ 533. It was also satisfied that the decision to lower the testosterone threshold from 10 nmol/L to 5 was not arbitrary; there was evidence of significant physiological effects of increasing testosterone levels well below the 10 nmol/L level, and the 5 nmol/L level is well higher than the range for XX women, from 0.06 to 1.68 nmol/L, and enough to allow for higher levels for women with polycystic ovary syndrome (PCOS). ¶¶ 610, 611. But the panel expressed hesitation on this score. There are substantial side effects of medication to lower testosterone levels—Semenya testified to the difficulties lowering her levels below the prior threshold of 10nmol/L caused her—and there were risks of inadvertent fluctuation above the 5 nmol/L level. ¶ 615. Accordingly, the panel expressed "grave concerns" as to whether, as applied, the regulations would satisfy the proportionality standard. ¶ 620. In addition, it suggested that the IAAF defer application of the regulations to the 1500 m and 1 mile events until such time as more than "sparse" evidence of significant advantage for 46XY athletes becomes available. ¶ 623. Semenya promptly appealed the decision to the Swiss Federal Tribunal, which ultimately, in 2020, upheld the regulations.

COMMENTS AND QUESTIONS

1.   *The right approach?* What do you think is the best solution to this controversy? Consider the following argument:

The claims of unfairness lodged by women who find themselves competing against intersex athletes ring hollow. Lance Armstrong's heart is reportedly a third larger than that of an average man of comparable height and weight. Michael Phelps is widely believed to have Marfan Syndrome, a disorder of the connective tissue that could account for his uncommonly long arms and double-jointed feet. Usain Bolt has abnormally high calves and elongated Achilles tendons. Even Elisa Cusma, who lost to Semenya in Berlin, didn't reach the finals by dint of her hard work alone. She, like all elite athletes, is a lucky winner in the genetic lottery. It is little short of hypocritical for her to complain that others were luckier still.

Do you agree? Are the cases of Armstrong, Phelps, and Bolt analogous to those of intersex athletes such as Semenya? In what possible way are they disanalogous? If you are persuaded, what follows? Dreger, a fierce critic of the new IAAF regulations, has proposed that "the 'sex testing' policy should really just be a 'gender verification' policy: if you really were raised as a girl, you get to play as a woman." Dreger, *Sex Typing*, at 24. Would this be unfair to women without an intersex condition?

2.   *XY vs. $$*. Even if athletes such as Semenya (and Burundi's Francine Niyonsaba and Kenya's Margaret Wambui) hold biological advantages over their non-intersex rivals, they also face significant financial disadvantages relative to many. As one critic of the new regulations pointed out, "If the world of sport is going to look at factors that are strongly correlated with outstanding performance and medals, they should first look to personal and national income before anything else. Look at any medal table. It's lined up in favour of the richest countries and the richest families from those countries." Jamie Strashin, *What's the real problem with Caster Semenya?*, CBC SPORTS, May 18, 2018. What follows?

3.   *Scientific uncertainty*. The extent to which androgen levels alone confer performance advantages is disputed. For doubts see Katrina Karkazis, et al., *Out of Bounds? A Critique of the New Policies on Hyperandrogenism in Elite Female Athletes*, 12 AM. J. BIOETHICS 3 (2012) (arguing that "there are at least six markers of sex—including chromosomes, gonads, hormones, secondary sex characteristics, external genitalia, and internal genitalia—and none of these are binary"; that "any advantage that might be conferred by hyperandrogenism is so complex that testosterone levels alone are a nearly useless indicator of advantage, and certainly not an appropriate measure for determining eligibility"; and that, as a policy matter "all legally recognized females" should be allowed to compete); REBECCA M. JORDAN-YOUNG & KATRINA KARKAZIS, TESTOSTERONE: AN UNAUTHORIZED BIOGRAPHY (2019). If you believe the IAAF policy would be justified *if* its underlying empirical premises are sound, how confident must the IAAF (or a reviewing court) be that the premises *are* sound?

b. Transgender Athletes

The word *transgender* is used as an umbrella term to describe an individual whose gender identity does not match the person's assigned sex at birth. A male-to-female (MTF) transgender person is one who was born biologically male but who identifies as female, and a female-to-male (FTM) transgender person is one who was born biologically female but who identifies as male. Some but not all transgendered persons seek medical intervention to more closely align their bodies with their gender identities. *See, e.g., GLAAD Media Reference Guide—Transgender*, GLAAD.org, https://tinyurl.com/qvsdz84.

We will first consider general issues concerning the participation of transgendered persons by examining the NCAA's policy statement on the issue. And then we will consider a judicial opinion involving the tennis player Renee Richards, probably the most famous transgender athlete ever—not counting Caitlyn Jenner, who won the 1976 Olympic decathlon as Bruce Jenner, but who has not engaged in elite competitive athletics as a woman.

NCAA OFFICE OF INCLUSION, NCAA INCLUSION OF TRANSGENDER STUDENT-ATHLETES
http://www.ncaa.org/sites/default/files/Transgender_Handbook_2011_Final.pdf
August 2011
© 2011 NCAA Office of Inclusion, reprinted with permission

* * *

Should the Participation of Transgender Student-Athletes Raise Concerns About Competitive Equity?

Concern about creating an "unfair competitive advantage" on sex-separated teams is one of the most often cited reasons for resistance to the participation of transgender student-athletes. This concern is cited most often in discussions about transgender women competing on a women's team. Some advocates for gender equality in college sports are concerned that allowing transgender women—that is, male-to-female transgender athletes who were born male, but who identify as female—to compete on women's teams will take away opportunities for women, or that transgender women will have a competitive advantage over other women competitors.

These concerns are based on three assumptions: one, that transgender women are not "real" women and therefore not deserving of an equal competitive opportunity; two, that being born with a male body automatically gives a transgender woman an unfair advantage when competing against non-transgender women; and three, that men might be tempted to pretend to be transgender in order to compete in competition with women.

These assumptions are not well founded. First, the decision to transition from one gender to the other—to align one's external gender presentation with one's internal sense of gender identity—is a deeply significant and difficult choice that is made only after careful consideration and for the most compelling of reasons. Gender identity is a core aspect of a person's identity, and it is just as deep seated, authentic, and real for a transgender person as for others. Male-to-female transgender women fully identify and live their lives as women, and female-to-male transgender men fully identify and live their lives as men.

Second, some people fear that transgender women will have an unfair advantage over non-transgender women. It is important to place that fear in context.

Transgender girls who medically transition at an early age do not go through a male puberty, and therefore their participation in athletics as girls does not raise the same equity concerns that arise when transgender women transition after puberty.

Transgender women display a great deal of physical variation, just as there is a great deal of natural variation in physical size and ability among non-transgender women and men. Many people may have a stereotype that all transgender women are unusually tall and have large bones and muscles. But that is not true. A male-to-female transgender woman may be small and slight, even if she is not on hormone blockers or taking estrogen. It is important not to overgeneralize. The assumption that all male-bodied people are taller, stronger, and more highly skilled in a sport than all female-bodied people is not accurate.

It is also important to know that any strength and endurance advantages a transgender woman arguably may have as a result of her prior testosterone levels dissipate after about one year of estrogen or testosterone-suppression therapy. According to medical experts on this issue, the assumption that a transgender woman competing on a women's team would have a competitive advantage outside the range of performance and competitive advantage or disadvantage that already exists among female athletes is not supported by evidence.

Finally, fears that men will pretend to be female to compete on a women's team are unwarranted given that in the entire 40 year history of "sex verification" procedures in international sport competitions, no instances of such "fraud" have been revealed.

Instead, rather than identifying men who are trying to fraudulently compete as women, "sex verification" tests have been misused to humiliate and unfairly exclude women with intersex conditions.

The apparent failure of such tests to serve their stated purpose of deterring fraud—and the terrible damage they have caused to individual women athletes—should be taken into account when developing policies for the inclusion of transgender athletes.

Educators in collegiate athletics programs must develop thoughtful and informed practices that provide opportunities for all students, including transgender students, to participate in sports. These practices must be based on sound medical science, which shows that male-to-female transgender athletes do not have any automatic advantage over other women. These practices must also be based on the educational values of sport and the reasons why sport is included as a vital component of the educational environment: promoting the physical and psychological well-being of all students, and teaching students the values of equal opportunity, participation, inclusion, teamwork, discipline, and respect for diversity. * * *

NCAA Bylaws related to hormonal treatment and mixed teams.

Two areas of NCAA regulations can be impacted by transgender student-athlete participation: use of banned substances and mixed team status.

A mixed team is a varsity intercollegiate sports team on which at least one individual of each gender competes. . . .

- NCAA rules state that a male participating in competition on a female team makes the team a "mixed team." . . . Such a team is ineligible for a women's NCAA championship but is eligible for a men's NCAA championship.

- A female on a men's team does not impact sports sponsorship in the application of the rule—the team still counts toward the mixed/men's numbers. Such a team is eligible for a men's NCAA championship.

- Once a team is classified as a mixed team, it retains that status through the remainder of the academic year without exception.

NCAA Bylaw 31.2.3 identifies testosterone as a banned substance, and provides for a medical exception review for demonstrated need for use of a banned medication. It is the responsibility of the NCAA institution to submit the request for a medical exception . . . for testosterone treatment prior to the student-athlete competing while undergoing treatment. In the case of testosterone suppression, the institution must submit written documentation to the NCAA of the year of treatment and ongoing monitoring of testosterone suppression.

NCAA Policy on Transgender Student-Athlete Participation

The following policies clarify participation of transgender student-athletes undergoing hormonal treatment for gender transition:

1. A trans male (FTM) student-athlete who has received a medical exception for treatment with testosterone for diagnosed Gender Identity Disorder or gender dysphoria and/or Transsexualism, for purposes of NCAA competition may compete on a men's team, but is no longer eligible to compete on a women's team without changing that team status to a mixed team.

2. A trans female (MTF) student-athlete being treated with testosterone suppression medication for Gender Identity Disorder or gender dysphoria and/or Transsexualism, for the purposes of NCAA competition may continue to compete on a men's team but may not compete on a women's team without changing it to a mixed team status until completing one calendar year of testosterone suppression treatment.

Any transgender student-athlete who is not taking hormone treatment related to gender transition may participate in sex-separated sports activities in accordance with his or her assigned birth gender.

- A female-to-male (FTM) student-athlete who is not taking testosterone related to gender transition may participate on a men's or women's team.

- A male-to-female (MTF) student-athlete who is not taking hormone treatments related to gender transition may not compete on a women's team. . . .

COMMENTS AND QUESTIONS

1. The three assumptions. Regardless of whether you approve of the NCAA's ultimate policy, what do you think of its reasoning? Is it true that the concern that MTF athletes will have an unfair "competitive advantage over other women competitors" is based on the three assumptions that the report sets forth? Why or why not?

2. A fourth assumption. The report also points out that "[t]he assumption that all male-bodied people are taller, stronger, and more highly skilled in a sport than all female-bodied people is not accurate." That is, of course, correct. Were you guilty of making this assumption before reading the report? Do you know of *anybody* who assumes that *all* male-bodied people are taller, stronger, and more skilled than *all* female-bodied people? Regardless of your views on the bottom-line question of whether MTF athletes should be allowed to compete against ciswomen athletes, does the report gain or lose credibility by attributing this assumption to opponents of that policy?

("Cisgendered" individuals are persons whose gender identity matches their biological sex, or the gender they were assigned at birth.)

3. Beyond testosterone. The NCAA contends that "any strength and endurance advantages a transgender woman arguably may have as a result of her prior testosterone levels dissipate after about one year of estrogen or testosterone-suppression therapy." That is an extraordinarily important claim. If transwomen who have undergone hormonal therapy no longer enjoy biomechanical advantages over ciswomen then it is hard to see what good reason one could have for excluding them from women's competitions. (Note that we are not saying that transwomen athletes *should* be excluded if they *do* have biomechanical advantages accruing from their biological sex; we're saying only that they *shouldn't* be excluded if they *don't*.) But it is more controversial than the NCAA report appears to suggest.

The first and most important point is that the science on this topic is extremely underdeveloped. As one recent survey notes, "there have been very few studies on the performance of transwomen athletes at the elite level." Taryn Knox et al., *Transwomen in elite sport: scientific and ethical considerations,* 45 J. MED. ETHICS 395, 397 (2019). For this reason, contentions that male-typical performance advantages either do or do not survive hormone therapy are inescapably speculative. Nonetheless, the authors provide several reasons to be skeptical of the "advantages dissipate" claim. For one thing, "the phenomenon of muscle memory means muscle mass and strength can be rebuilt with previous strength exercise making it easier to regain muscle mass later in life even after long intervening periods of inactivity and mass loss." Perhaps more significantly, biological males have bigger and denser bone structure than biological females, along with greater lung capacity and larger heart size. And these

> indirect effects of testosterone will not be altered by hormone therapy. For example, hormone therapy will not alter bone structure, lung volume or heart size of the transwoman athlete, especially if she transitions postpuberty, so natural advantages including joint articulation, stroke volume and maximal oxygen uptake will be maintained.

Id. at 398. In sum, they conclude, the mere fact that a transwoman has undergone testosterone-suppression therapy "will not negate all the performance advantages accrued from having a male physiology prior to transition." *Id.* Do you think that sport governing bodies need greater grasp of the relevant scientific facts before settling on a policy for participation of transwomen, or is further investigation by experts in human biology beside the point?

4. Bottom lines. Does this policy statement draw the right balance with respect to MTF athletes by allowing them to compete on a woman's team, with it retaining its designation as a woman's team, but only after completing a year of testosterone-suppression treatment? Does it draw the right balance by allowing FTM athletes who have received medical exemptions for testosterone to compete on a men's team, but not on a women's team? Does it overlook or slight claims of trans athletes to a "human right" to participate in competitive athletics?

　　5.　A legislature weighs in. Compare the very different approach to the issue taken by the Idaho Fairness in Women's Sports Act, Idaho Code, Tit. 33, ch. 62 (2020), passed in March 2020, which provides that for purposes of determining eligibility to play on scholastic and collegiate teams in the state a student's sex, if disputed, may be established by a physician's statement that is based only on "the student's reproductive anatomy, genetic makeup, or normal endogenously produced testosterone levels." In August 2020, in *Hecox v. Little* (D. Idaho), a federal district judge enjoined enforcement of the Act, holding that it likely violates transgender students' constitutional rights under the Equal Protection Clause of the Fourteenth Amendment. At this writing, an appeal is pending before the Ninth Circuit.

RICHARDS V. UNITED STATES TENNIS ASSOCIATION
93 Misc. 713, 400 N.Y.S.2d 267 (1977)

ALFRED M. ASCIONE, JUSTICE.

　　Plaintiff, Dr. Renee Richards, née Richard H. Raskind, an ophthalmologist physician licensed to practice in the State of New York, underwent a sex reassignment operation about two years ago, at the age of 41, "at which time", Dr. Richards avers, "for all intents and purposes, I became a female, psychologically, socially and physically, as has been attested to by my doctors." Dr. Richards says that, "I underwent this operation after many years of being a transsexual, a woman trapped inside the body of a man."

　　As Dr. Richard H. Raskind, plaintiff was an accomplished male tennis player, and in 1974 ranked third in the East and thirteenth nationally in the men's [sic] 35-and-over tennis. Since the sex reassignment operation in 1975, plaintiff has entered nine women's tennis tournaments and has won two tournaments and finished as runner-up in three. Most recently, Dr. Richards, now 43 years of age, reached the finals of the Women's singles at the Mutual Benefit Life Open played on August 7, 1977 at the Orange Town Tennis Club in South Orange, New Jersey.

　　[Richards sued the United States Tennis Association (USTA) and other parties, seeking an injunction that would allow her to play in the U.S. Open as a woman. Until Richards sought to play as a woman, the USTA had not, in the nearly century-long history of its national championships, required a sex determination for competitors beyond a simple phenotype test (observation of primary and secondary sexual characteristics). But the USTA insisted that she take the Barr body test, which determines whether a person's cells have a second x chromosome. In the litigation, the USTA emphasized fairness concerns. It contended that there were as many as

10,000 transsexuals in the United States alone, and many more female impersonators or imposters, with the worldwide numbers unknown. It emphasized the financial and other rewards for success in the U.S. Open and "world-wide experiments, especially in the iron curtain countries, to produce athletic stars by means undreamed of a few years ago."]

The defendants have submitted the affidavit of Dr. Daniel Federman, professor and chairman of the Department of Medicine, Stanford University School of Medicine, in support of the applicability of the Barr body test for the determination of sexual identity. . . . It is Dr. Federman's opinion that the Barr body test reliably and inexpensively ($15.00) determines the presence of a second x chromosome in the "normal female". . . .

Dr. Federman says that the y chromosome is related to physical characteristics in the normal male that affect an individual's competitive athletic ability. The y chromosome controls the development of the testes, the source of the larger amounts of androgen (the male sex hormone) produced by the male relative to the female:

> "At puberty, the presence in the male of the y chromosome plus the much higher ratio of androgens to estrogens (the female sex hormone) results, on the average, in greater height, different body proportions, and a higher muscle mass than in the female. In the adult male beyond puberty, neither the removal of the testes by sex reassignment surgery, nor any subsequent treatment with estrogen can affect the individual's achieved height or skeletal structure. Removal of the testes plus ingestion of estrogens can reduce male strength, but any such effect is partial and depends upon continued ingestion of estrogen to be sustained."

It is Dr. Federman's view that sexual identity is a complex pattern of which some features are immutable (the nuclear and chromosomal); some can be effaced but not converted to their opposite (the gonadal and ductal structures); some are alterable by surgery or drugs (the external genitalia and hormonal balance); and some are largely subjective (the psychological and social sex). Under no circumstances can transsexual surgery produce the internal ductal organs or the gonadal identity of the opposite sex. . . .

Also submitted in opposition are affidavits of women's professional tennis players Françoise Durr, Janet Newberry and Kristien K. Shaw, each stating that based on her experience, "the taller a player is the greater advantage the player has . . . similarly, the stronger a player is, the greater advantage the player has, assuming like ability."

In another affidavit, Vicki Berner, Director of Women's Tennis for the USTA, formerly the number one ranked women's singles player from Canada, and then Tour Director in charge of players, asserts that she has been unable to find a record of any woman player over age 40 who has had such a successful competitive record as plaintiff, a record unparalleled in the history of women's professional tennis. . . .

What is a transsexual? A transsexual is an individual anatomically of one sex who firmly believes he belongs to the other sex. This belief is so strong that the transsexual is obsessed with the desire to have his body, appearance and social status altered to conform to that of his "rightful" gender. . . . Medical Science has not found any organic cause or cure (other than sex reassignment surgery and hormone therapy) for transsexualism, nor has psychotherapy been successful in altering the transsexual's identification with the other sex or his desire for surgical change.

Plaintiff's surgeon, Dr. Roberto Granato, who performed the sex reassignment operation on plaintiff, asserts that the male genitalia of Dr. Richards were removed and that as the result of the surgery the external genital appearance of Dr. Richards is that of female. Further:

> "With respect to Dr. Richard's internal sex, due to the operation I performed, one would say that Dr. Richards' internal sexual structure is anatomically similar to a biological woman who underwent a total hysterectomy and ovariectomy."

In addition, Dr. Granato states, that prior to and after the sex reassignment operation, Dr. Richards underwent endocrinological testing and administration of female hormones so as to change Dr. Richards' endocrinological hormonal balance to that of a woman. The removal of the testes, the main source of androgen (male hormones), decreases tremendously the male hormones in the blood and results in a decreased muscular mass, the structure of the muscle/fat ratio of the male is changed to a feminine type, together with the development of the breasts.

Dr. Granato sees no unfair advantage for Dr. Richards "when competing against other women. Her muscle development, weight, height and physique fit within the female norm." (Dr. Richards is 6'2 tall and weighs 147 lbs.) . . .

Dr. Donald Rubbell avers that he is Dr. Richards' gynecologist and that Dr. Richards examines as a woman and her perception of herself is entirely as a woman.

Dr. John Money, a psychologist presently serving as a professor and practitioner at Johns Hopkins Medical School in Baltimore, Maryland, and who has written and edited extensively on the subject . . ., has submitted an affidavit in support of plaintiff's application. . . .

Dr. Money . . . states that it is erroneous to assume that the [Barr] test will be accurate in determining the sex of all individuals since there are human beings who do not belong to the statistical average with respect to their chromosome pattern (e.g. Klinefelter and Turner's Syndromes, Androgen Insensitivity Syndrome and Testicular Feminization).[h]

As for Dr. Richards, Dr. Money says that the Barr test would work an injustice since by all other known indicators of sex, Dr. Richards is a female, i.e., external genital appearance is that of a female; her internal sex is that of a female who has been hysterectomized and ovariectomized; Dr. Richards is psychologically a woman; endocrinologically female; somatically (muscular tone, height, weight, breasts, physique) Dr. Richards is female and her muscular and fat composition has been transformed to that of a female; socially Dr. Richards is female; Dr. Richards' gonadal status is that of an ovariectomized female.

. . . Dr. Money also believes that Dr. Richards will have no unfair advantage when competing against other women. He says that her muscle development, weight, height and physique fit within the female norm. . . .

Finally, plaintiff submits the affidavit of women's tennis professional star Billie Jean King, holder of hundreds of titles including Wimbledon and the U.S. Open, and who defeated male tennis professional Bobby Riggs on national television, in support of plaintiff's application. Billie Jean King states that she and Dr. Richards were doubles teammates in one tournament and that she participated in two tournaments in which Dr. Richards played. It is Billie Jean King's judgment that, "she (plaintiff) does not enjoy physical superiority or strength so as to have an advantage over women competitors in the sport of tennis."

In this court's view, the requirement of defendants that this plaintiff pass the Barr body test in order to be eligible to participate in the women's singles of the U.S. Open is grossly unfair, discriminatory and inequitable, and violative of her rights under the Human Rights Law of this state (Executive Law, Article 15, Sections 290, et seq.). It seems clear that defendants knowingly instituted this test for the sole purpose of preventing plaintiff from participating in the tournament. The only justification for using a sex determination test in athletic competition is to prevent fraud, i.e., men masquerading as women, competing against women.

This court rejects any such suggestion as applied to plaintiff. This court is totally convinced that there are very few biological males, who are accomplished tennis players, who are also either preoperative or post-operative transsexuals.

When an individual such as plaintiff, a successful physician, a husband and father, finds it necessary for his own mental sanity to undergo a sex reassignment, the unfounded fears and misconceptions of defendants

---

[h]   Klinefelter Syndrome is the possession by a boy of at least one extra X chromosome, usually resulting in an XXY pattern. In the most common form of Turner's Syndrome, an entire X chromosome is missing.

must give way to the overwhelming medical evidence that this person is now female.

This court is not striking down the Barr body test, as it appears to be a recognized and acceptable tool for determining sex. However, it is not and should not be the sole criterion, where as here, the circumstances warrant consideration of other factors. . . .

[P]laintiff's application for a preliminary injunction is granted in all respects.

COMMENTS AND QUESTIONS

1.   Performance. In the 1977 U.S. Open, the tournament most immediately involved in this decision, Richards reached the finals, with Betty Ann Stuart, in women's doubles. Her highest rank as a women's singles player was No. 20, in February 1979. Later that year, she won the 35-and-over women's title at the Open.

2.   Motivation. Dr. Raskind, as he was known when he was married, and his wife divorced when he underwent sexual reassignment. In a later proceeding related to the divorce, the court said: "The husband had undergone transsexual plastic surgery in order to engage in professional athletics as a female, and the resultant publicity caused a decline in the practice which he (she) had sold." *Raskind v. Raskind*, 404 N.Y.S.2d 17 (N.Y. App. Div. 1978). Does that seem to be an accurate statement? Does it bear on whether Richards ought to have been allowed to compete in tennis as a woman? Would your view of the matter be changed if Raskind had changed sex at age 20 rather than when he was 41? Or suppose that Bruce Jenner underwent sex reassignment surgery in 1984, at age 35 and eight years after winning the Olympic decathlon, instead of in 2017; should Caitlyn Jenner then have been allowed to compete in track and field events as a woman?

3.   The norm. Drs. Granato and Money, experts for Dr. Richards, contended that physically she was "within the female norm." What exactly does this mean? A 6′2″ biological female would be in the 99.99th percentile for all women. U.S. CENSUS BUREAU, STATISTICAL ABSTRACT OF THE UNITED STATES (2011). Is their claim, then, that a MTF athlete would fall outside "the female norm," physically speaking, only if she were taller than every biological female ever? That wouldn't make the notion of a "female norm" very useful, would it? If that's not their claim, what is it?

4.   Sex-reassignment and the Olympics. In 2004, the Executive Board of the IOC adopted a policy laying out three conditions that a trans athlete must satisfy to compete in accord with their gender identity. The athlete must: (1) fully transition, which includes sex affirmation surgery (including removal of testes for transwomen) and two years of hormone therapy; (2) live in their experienced gender for at least two years; and (3) achieve legal recognition of the reassignment by the appropriate authorities. In 2015, the IOC amended its policy to no longer require surgical anatomical changes. The new policy allows transwomen to compete in the women's division so long as (1) they declared themselves to be women (for sporting purposes) for at least four years, and (2) their blood testosterone levels have, with hormonal treatment, stayed below 10 nmol/L (nanomoles per liter) for at least twelve consecutive months prior to competition. Michael Pavitt, *IOC confirms existing guidelines on transgender athlete eligibility to remain for Tokyo 2020*, INSIDE THE GAMES (Mar. 3, 2020). Was this a good change? Is the new policy too lenient? Too rigid? Just about right? In thinking about this, you might care to know that the 10 nmol/L cap was selected "because it is at the lower end of the testosterone level" for men under 40, and that "the normal healthy female testosterone range is 0–1.7 nmol/L." Knox et al., *Transwomen in elite sport*, at 396.

Exercise 7C

Given your success in crafting handicap rules for your school's intramural bowling league (see Exercise 3A), you've been asked by student body leaders to draft new rules for your school's fall intramural soccer league, and for your annual "fight night" held in the spring. For whatever its significance might be to you, the soccer league does not draw enough participants to form separate single-sex (or single-gender) teams, and some women have complained in the past that they spend too much time riding the bench in the co-ed league. Fight-night is a single-evening boxing tournament that pits law students against students from your business school. What rules of eligibility and participation do you propose?

3.   MUST SEPARATE BE THE SAME?

When men and women compete separately, they often compete under different rules, and for different purses. What differences, if any, are justifiable?

WOMEN'S SPORTS FOUNDATION, PURSE EQUITY IN PROFESSIONAL SPORTS

https://www.womenssportsfoundation.org/sitecore/content/home/
advocate/foundation-positions/athlete/purse_equity.aspx
© 2017 Women's Sports Foundation, reprinted with permission

It is the position of the Women's Sports Foundation that professional male and female athletes should receive equal purses when they are participating in the same competition (i.e., Wimbledon, X Games, a professional rodeo championship) that includes both male and female athletes participating in the same or comparable events. When men's and women's leagues are separate events in the commercial marketplace and operate solely on the dollars they earn, salaries of players may rightfully differ among leagues, whether male or female athletes are involved. But when men and women compete in the same sport venue for which a single ticket is offered and television advertising and rights fees are generated, any reason used to justify higher pay or purses for one sex over the other should be questioned.

How would the public react if there were higher purses for white athletes than athletes of color? Sex discrimination is no different than race discrimination.

- • MISCONCEPTION #1: Men should get larger purses than women because the women's events or competitions are not as exciting and/or the skills displayed by female athletes are not as high as the men (men jump higher, perform more risky tricks, hit a tennis ball harder).

Women athletes should be evaluated in their own right, not in comparison to men. Just as a heavyweight boxer and a lightweight boxer are not compared to each other when deciding prize money and the value of a boxer's skills and ability are not based on weight class and size, we cannot do this to classes of male and female athletes who are not competing against each other.

We also know that because of physiological differences between the sexes, men's events and women's events in the same sports may be different. Women generally have lower centers of gravity and superior balance but less upper body strength. Women compete in the balance beam in gymnastics and men do not; does that lessen the ability or perceptions about male gymnasts? Men compete in the rings in gymnastics and women do not; does that lessen the ability or perceptions about female gymnasts?

So, we should not be surprised if men and women don't perform the same types of tricks or stunts in competitions like the X Games. "Different" does not mean "better;" it just means "different."

It is also important to ask, in sports such as the X Games, whether differences in the size of the purses for male and female competitors affect the difficulty of tricks being attempted when difficult tricks create a significant risk of injury. Does a $100,000 pay differential make an athlete more or less willing to pull a risky stunt? How many more people would risk injury for a windfall than would do so for a pittance? As one female skateboarder said, "You pay me $5,000, I'll show you a trick that's good enough to win; you pay me $50,000, and I'll show you a trick that's on a whole new level."

- • MISCONCEPTION #2: Because female athletes do not bring in as much money in terms of sponsorship or television viewers as men, they shouldn't receive the same prize money.

Television ratings and promotion go hand in hand. We know that television ratings are a function of (1) how much the event is advertised and promoted, (2) whether the event is scheduled to be aired in prime time and (3) whether the event is aired in the same time slot and day (predictability, such as Monday Night Football). Thus, if a television network runs 100 ads promoting a televised game on Thursday night in prime time, it will yield a higher rating than a non-promoted event in that same time slot or a different time slot. Just as a non-promoted men's baseball game should not be compared with a promoted men's baseball game, men's and women's events shouldn't be compared if they are not promoted equally. In most cases, women's sports are not promoted and are not given prime time or predictable time slots. For example, if there is a competition where there are fewer women's events and the women's events are not equitably included in the telecast, it is misleading to argue that men's events receive higher ratings.

• MISCONCEPTION #3: Male athletes' competitions are longer than the women's competitions; their matches are longer, include more games and, therefore, the men should receive more money.

The length of the competition does not matter; it is the top celebrity athlete at the competition, male or female, who fascinates and draws the viewers and ticket buyers. For example, a celebrity musician, like Elton John, gets paid top dollar whether he performs a 45-minute set or a two-hour set. An athlete doesn't get paid less for defeating an opponent in straight sets in 50 minutes. Male volleyball players use a volleyball net that is higher than the women's volleyball net. Should they get paid more?

The nature, length and characteristics of the sporting event are appropriate to male and female athletes and their differences should not justify valuing one over the other.

The impact of unequal purses goes beyond the issue of money. Sport is too potent a force in society and our media culture to ignore. The implications of unequal pay extend beyond the playing field. When our sons and daughters watch a national network telecast and see the most celebrated female athletes valued less than their male counterparts, they are learning to believe that it is okay that females are less respected and less rewarded in our society. We are promulgating values for generations to come; we must be sure that the accepted values are acceptable ones.

COMMENTS AND QUESTIONS

1. *Not in dispute?* Notice what the Women's Sports Foundation (founded by tennis superstar and feminist icon Billie Jean King) does not challenge. First, it does not challenge pay discrepancies between male and female leagues. Those discrepancies can be vast. For example, the average player in the NBA earns an annual salary over $5 million; the average annual salary in the WNBA is just shy of $75,000. Nor does the Foundation challenge different purses in women's and men's tournaments that are conducted separately.

These too can be substantial. The total purse for the 2019 U.S. Open golf championship was $12.5 million; for the Women's Open it was $5.5 million. Should these disparities be tolerated? Why or why not?

2.   *The core of the debate.* What the Foundation does challenge is unequal purses in competitions that run separate male and female events within the same tournament. Tennis provides the most notable example. For years, men competed for larger purses in tennis tournaments than did women. Today, though, all major championships offer the same prize money to both men and women. The U.S. Open started the trend in 1973, followed by the Australian Open fully twenty-seven years later, and then Wimbledon and the French Open in 2007. In 2012, however, controversy over equal pay was reignited when Gilles Simon, the thirteenth seed in the men's bracket, argued that equal pay was not justified, in large part because the men play longer matches—best of five on the men's side, as opposed to best of three on the women's.

Who's right? Do you agree with the Women's Sports Foundation that "[s]ex discrimination [in prize money] is no different than race discrimination"? If it is different—and justifiable—why? Is failure to pay equal prize money when men and women compete in the same event sex discrimination?

If you are persuaded by the Foundation's position, would you apply it to a tournament that is run the way that the Western and Southern Open (a significant tournament in Cincinnati, now the last major warmup before the U.S. Open) was run for some years before 2014—with the men's and women's tournaments run one after the other, with barely any overlap? (Now this tournament runs men's and women's brackets simultaneously, but it still does not pay equal prize money, though the men's and women's singles winners did receive the same prizes in the unusual COVID-affected 2020 tournament.)

Would you apply the Foundation's position to prescribe equal pay for men and women in a tour of Olympic figure-skating medalists? In erotic films?

3.   *Popularity and promotion.* Consider in particular the second argument in favor of pay discrepancy that the Foundation identifies and aims to rebut. Could you flesh out this argument more fully than the Foundation does? Also, could you restate the Foundation's response? The core of that response appears to be that "television ratings and promotion go hand in hand." But what, exactly, does that mean? Is the claim that, if a tennis tournament promoted women's and men's matches equally, then viewership would be equal? If so, what reason do we have to believe that is true? If that is not the claim, what is it?

4.   *Does length matter?* Furthermore, even if the same number of viewers tuned in to men's and women's matches, the fact that best-of-five matches run longer, on average, than best-of-three matches would dictate that more commercials would be shown during the men's matches, producing greater advertising revenue. Would it be wrong to establish purses for each

competition in the tournament based on the revenue fairly allocated to that competition?

The Foundation position paper declares that "the length of the competition does not matter." Why not, exactly? Is it so clear that concert promoters would pay Elton John the *same* "top dollar" for a 45-minute concert as for a 2-hour one? Would you pay the same amount for a ticket to the two concerts?

And why are women's matches shorter than men's? Is there a good reason why women's Grand Slam tennis matches should not also be best-of-five affairs? Although the Foundation's position paper asserts that "[t]he nature, length and characteristics of the sporting event are appropriate to male and female athletes," it does not elaborate on *why* best-of-three is appropriate for female athletes while best-of-five is appropriate for male athletes. Do you think that this difference in appropriateness is biologically determined, socially determined, both, or neither? When "our sons and daughters watch a national network telecast" of a tennis tournament, which fact is likely to be more apparent to them: that the men are being paid more than the women or that the men play more sets? Does it matter? Is it unfair to men that they have to win three sets in a Grand Slam tournament to win a match, while the women only have to win two? Is it unfair to women that they get to play three sets at most, while the men may get to play five? *See* Juliet Macur, *Aching for Change in an Unequal Sport*, N.Y. TIMES, Aug. 28, 2014, at B9.

5.   *Double trouble.* Although the women's and men's winners at Wimbledon earn the same amount (£2,350,000 in 2019), both earn far more than do the winners of men's doubles and of women's doubles (£540,000 for each winning pair), and they earn more than do the winners of mixed doubles (£116,000 for the pair). What, if anything, justifies these discrepancies? Can these discrepancies be justified if the men's winners and women's singles winners are paid the same amounts? Given that not all brackets are paid at the same rate, what considerations do you suppose determine the respective prize amounts?

6.   *Beyond money.* That men must win more sets than must women to win a match at Grand Slam tennis tournaments is just one example of the fact that, putting prize money aside, the rules for men's and women's competitions can differ even when the sport is recognizably the same. (But *is* it "the same sport" for men and women when any of the rules differ? Recall the question, addressed in Chapter 3, of whether some rules of sports are more "essential" than others.) Consider the following examples:

- The height of the volleyball net is 7 ½″ greater in the men's game than in the women's.

- The three-point line in NCAA basketball is one foot further in the men's game than in the women's.

- In cross country championships administered by the NCAA and by the United States Track and Field Association (USATF), the men run a 10K race while the women run 6K.

- In gymnastics, women's floor routines must be 70 to 90 seconds and choreographed to music, whereas men's are 50 to 70 seconds and lack music.

- In lacrosse, the women's stick has a shallower pouch than the men's, designed to make maintaining possession of the ball more difficult but releasing it easier; men's sticks have a deeper pouch, requiring more force to remove the ball and more effort to release it.

- Body checking is allowed in men's ice hockey, but not in women's.

- In soccer, FIFA requires that men's World Cup matches be played on grass, but allows women's matches to be played on artificial turf. *See, e.g., Top Female Soccer Players Sue to Challenge Artificial Turf at World Cup*, WALL ST. J., Oct. 1, 2014,.

- Baseball is rarely played at elite levels by women. Instead, they play softball, with similar rules but on a smaller field, with a larger ball that does not travel as far and is pitched underhand, and for fewer innings.

Are any of these differences—or others of which you may be aware—problematic? Why or why not? Are there other rules that *are* the same for men and women that *should* be different? The height of the basket in basketball? The maximum weight of a bowling ball?

D. AGE

We conclude this chapter with brief discussion of a critical factor that pervasively affects athletic performance: age. In most settings, it is easy enough to see how age ought to affect eligibility. Up to a point, athletes tend to perform better with age. For that reason, it makes sense to have *maximum* ages for most youth competitions. Usually, there is no minimum age, and talented kids often "play up" in age, but sometimes safety considerations weigh against allowing this. Occasionally there are scandals as kids are placed in competitions for which they are no longer eligible; perhaps the most notorious is the case of Danny Almonte, who led a team from the Bronx to a third-place finish in the 2001 Little League World Series before it was discovered that he was two years over the age limit. But there is no particular conceptual difficulty here. Similarly, past some age in all sports performance tends to decline, and so many sports hold competitions for older athletes with *minimum* age brackets. Again, the idea is simple enough.

But now consider the curious case of women's gymnastics. Females tend to peak very early at some of the skills required for top performance in modern-day gymnastics. FIG, the international gymnastics federation, has long maintained, and has gradually raised, a minimum age for "senior"—i.e., the most elite—competitions, including the Olympics. The rules now prescribe that to be eligible a gymnast must turn 16 by the year of the competition. Given the abilities of some very young gymnasts, the minimum age threshold provides an obvious incentive for age falsification. Suspicion has arisen in many cases, and in a few FIG has concluded that the suspicion was justified and has taken punitive action; notably, in 2010, FIG stripped China of its bronze medal from the 2000 Olympics because Dong Fangxiao was underage. The stated reason for the age threshold is to protect young gymnasts from the physical and psychological risks of elite-level gymnastics. Assuming that such risks are substantial, is an age threshold for elite competition the appropriate response? In thinking about this question, make sure to take into account the intensity with which many youngsters prepare for and engage in top-level youth competitions.

CHAPTER 8

PERFORMANCE ENHANCEMENT

■ ■ ■

The Casey Martin case, presented in Chapter 2, served as a vehicle for introducing very basic questions about the relationship between sports (and games) and the rules that constitute them. The question in that case was whether and to what extent the PGA should make accommodations for a golfer's disabilities. We now examine a nearly opposite topic: the various forms of performance enhancement that a sport might decide to permit or forbid. Subchapter 8A is a quick introduction to issues raised by technological change, focusing on the use of high-tech suits in competitive swimming. Subchapter 8B examines whether a sport should accommodate a competitor's biomechanical enhancements made in response to physical disability. It focuses on the complex and controversial case of Oscar Pistorius, the former South African double-amputee middle-distance runner known as the Blade Runner. Subchapter 8C considers the use of performance-enhancing drugs.

A. TECHNOLOGICAL CHANGE

The role and importance of equipment vary greatly across sports. In most motor sports, manufacture and refinement of the equipment contribute at least as much to success as does the excellence of the athlete. At the other extreme, in some combat sports there is almost no equipment, and no competitively meaningful variation. For much of its existence, competitive swimming was also thought largely inhospitable to technological innovation (though the replacement of woolen suits by silk in the 1930s presumably had some effect). That changed a generation ago.

In the late 1990s, new materials that produced less hydrodynamic drag than even shaved skin led to a revolution in swimsuit design, including full-body suits. FINA, the international governing body for swimming competition, allowed these suits in time for the 2000 Olympics in Sydney, and a spate of world records fell. The next significant development came in 2008 with Speedo's introduction of the LZR Racer, which included polyurethane panels strategically placed to compress the body in key spots and help the swimmer stay higher in the water. At the Beijing Olympics that year, 23 world records were broken by swimmers wearing the LZR (including seven by Michael Phelps), and only two by swimmers who were not; 98% of all the medals were won by swimmers wearing the LZR. Soon, rival manufacturers introduced suits made fully out of polyurethane, such as the Arena X-Glide, which reduced drag even further, and rendered the LZR technologically obsolete by the time of the world championships in Rome in July 2009. Forty-three world records fell there, in what has been called "a ludicrous display of speed." Paul Newberry, *Will truce in swimsuit wars carry on past Rio Olympics?*, AP NEWS, Aug. 5, 2016. An academic analysis indicates that

> the introduction of new swimsuits increased performance in the majority of events between 2000 and 2010 in addition to the expected global improvement that would have taken place anyway. For example, performance in the men's 50 m freestyle was improved by the introduction of full body suits in 2000 by around 1%, then by an additional 3.5% with the introduction of polyurethane panels in 2008 or 5.5% with the use of polyurethane over the whole body in 2009. Similar, but smaller increases tended to be seen in almost all the other men's distances and in the women's events.

Leon Foster et al., *Influence of full body swimsuits on competitive performance*, 34 PROCEDIA ENGINEERING 712, 717 (2012).

Even before the Rome meet was over, FINA—responding to concerns that the new suits amounted to "doping on a hanger"—adopted regulations, effective January 2010, limiting how much of a swimmer's body could be covered and requiring that swimsuits be made of permeable materials. Swimwear must now be pre-approved by FINA. (Some variations of the LZR Racer are allowed.)

A day after FINA adopted the new regulations, the New York Times reported:

> The Briton Rebecca Adlington, who won gold medals in the 400 and 800 freestyles in Beijing, is sticking with the LZR Racer, but was critical of swimsuits that have recently been developed. "I would never in a million years take a drug to help me, so why would I wear a suit just to improve my performance?" she told The Daily Telegraph. "It's just not who I am." . . .

> Before this week, FINA did not have a bylaw expressly forbidding swimsuits that might aid speed, buoyancy and endurance. Some retired swimming greats were openly questioning the governing body's stewardship of the sport. Franziska Van Almsick, a former world-record holder in the 200 freestyle, recently told the German newspaper Der Tagesspiegel, "They can't allow the full-body condom where all you see is the swimmer's face." . . .

Not all the high-tech suits were created equal. But they enabled swimmers without an ideal physique or impeccable conditioning to be more competitive. Squeezed into the corset-like suit, a muscled and stocky body is as streamlined as a long and lean one; a soft abdomen as effective as six-pack abs. "The thing that's really hurt more than anything else is the whole suit situation has devalued athleticism," [University of Southern California swim coach Dave] Salo said. "A lot of kids who aren't in very good shape can put on one of these suits and be streamlined like seals."

Karen Crouse, *Swimming Bans High-Tech Suits, Ending an Era*, N.Y. TIMES, July 24, 2009.

More than a decade after the Rome meet, world records set there still stand in seven of the 20 men's long-course (50 m. pool) events—and none were set before 2008.

COMMENTS AND QUESTIONS

1. *High-buoyancy suits.* Do you agree that FINA was correct to ban high-buoyancy suits? If so, why? Is the problem that the suits allowed "swimmers without an ideal physique or impeccable conditioning to be more competitive" by making them more streamlined? If that is the concern, presumably the suits *increased* the relative importance of some other quality. If so, what was it—and why was the relative importance of factors that determine performance given the high-buoyancy suits less preferable than the relative importance without them? In considering this problem, do you draw a distinction between assistance given to those "without an ideal physique" and to those "without . . . impeccable conditioning"? Are corrective lenses improper in baseball because they allow players without excellent eyesight to be competitive? Swim caps also give swimmers an aerodynamic advantage. Should they be banned?

In evaluating the merits of the high-buoyancy swimsuits, is it a problem that they allow swimmers to swim faster than their predecessors, causing too many world records to fall and making transtemporal comparisons difficult? That the suits are expensive and therefore not easily available to all competitors? That they don't allow spectators to see enough of the swimmers' bodies?

Do different considerations apply to youth swimmers? In 2018, USA Swimming adopted a broad prohibition, effective in 2020, on "Technical Suits" in 12-and-under competitions. A technical suit is defined, with some qualifications, as one with "any bonded or taped seams regardless of its fabric or silhouette" or "woven fabric extending past the hips." USA Swimming News, *Tech Suit Restriction for 12-and-Under Swimmers*, Aug. 24, 2020, https://tinyurl.com/y2gksgas.

2. *A polyurethane asterisk?* Should world records set at the Rome meet be recognized? If so, should a separate set of records for performances not aided by the high-buoyancy suits of that brief era be recognized? (See Subchapter 17B.)

3. *Powerlifting.* Performance-enhancing equipment has essentially caused a divide in the sport of powerlifting (to be distinguished from the classic Olympic sport of weightlifting). Better performance can be achieved by wearing supportive equipment—snug garments that store elastic potential energy during the downward-motion portion of a lift and transfer it to kinetic energy during the upward portion. Some competitions and federations allow supportive equipment and some do not; the term RAW powerlifting is sometimes used for the latter type of competition. *See Powerlifting*, WIKIPEDIA, https://tinyurl.com/y29hnzoc. Do you think prohibiting supportive equipment makes powerlifting a more interesting sport? Is the issue of whether such equipment should be allowed different in any material way from the issue concerning high-buoyancy swimsuits? Is the result in powerlifting—essentially a bifurcation of the sport—a good one (more variety, appealing to different tastes and abilities) or a bad one (fragmenting interest and keeping competitors apart)? (See the schism in the competitive eating community, noted pp. 76–77.) Is it a useful model for how swimming could deal with high-buoyancy suits?

4. *Sportswear enhancements.* Another example of performance enhancing equipment is KYMIRA SPORT's infrared athletic clothing. See https://www.kymirasport.com. The infrared clothing generates "nitric oxide production, increased circulation, increased respiration efficiency [and] increased tissue oxygenation." KYMIRA's users include Olympians, professional rugby players, and cyclists. The fabric absorbs heat and infrared radiation from the athlete's body, and then transmits it back into the body, at a different infrared wavelength that penetrates 1.5 inches beneath the user's skin, without any electronics. Tom Taylor, *NASA-inspired infrared activewear from KYMIRA Sport says it can help with recovery*, SPORTS ILLUSTRATED, Mar. 14, 2017. These products are currently worn in training and recovery, but not competition. Should this technology be prohibited from in-game use? Is it more or less worrisome than buoyant swimsuits? Increasing circulation and breathing efficiency could improve stamina, thus improving cyclists' performance. Should cyclists be permitted to wear KYMIRA during the Tour de France?

And what about developments in running sneaker technology? The 2017 Nike Vaporfly shoes allegedly lower times by at least 4% because of the "carbon-fiber plate. . . which stores and releases energy with each stride. . . act[ing] as a . . . slingshot to propel runners forward." Kevin Quealy & Josh Katz, *Nike Says its $250 Running Shoes will make you run much faster*, N.Y. TIMES, July 18, 2018. As of 2019, the five fastest Men's marathoners wore Nike Vaporfly. Eben Novy-Williams, *Are Nike's Vaporfly Running Shoes Too Good?*, BLOOMBERG BUSINESSWEEK, Nov. 14, 2019. Buoyant swimsuits allegedly lowered times by about 2%. Jere Longman & Gina Kolata, *As Swimming*

Records Fall, Technology Muddies the Water, N.Y. TIMES, Aug. 11, 2008. Is there a specific percentage improvement in performance that should disqualify a new innovation?

    5. Tennis. Tennis rackets have seen radical change since the late 1970s. Up until 1978, the official rules specifically provided that the frame could be "of any material, weight, size, or shape." Nonetheless, for many years almost all rackets were made of wood and featured a hitting area of approximately 65 square inches. Metal rackets were introduced in the late 1960s, but soon other materials, most notably carbon-fiber composites, became dominant. These materials are stiffer than wood, giving the player more power, and also lighter and stronger, allowing for greater head size and giving the player greater control. In the 1970s, some manufacturers introduced oversize rackets with surface areas of more than 100 square inches. Continuing changes in racket size and composition have spurred the International Tennis Federation to amend its rules on the racket frame numerous times in recent decades; the rules put limits on the shape and size of the racket, prescribe the manner of stringing, and preclude it from including a power source, but do not limit the materials that may be used. INT'L TENNIS FEDERATION, 2020 RULES OF TENNIS, Appendix II (2020). Should rackets be unregulated? If regulated, what principles should shape the crafting of the regulations?

    6. Vaulting poles. When competitive pole vaulting began in the 1800s, rigid poles made of hardwood, typically hickory or ash, were used. After planting, the vaulter would climb the pole. Lighter and more flexible bamboo poles, which facilitated the new "swing-up" technique, were introduced in the early 1900s, and performances increased dramatically. In the second half of the twentieth century, the materials shifted again, to fiberglass and then to complex, layered poles of carbon-fiber composites, and again there was a sudden and sustained increase in performance level. Modern poles are the product of extensive scientific and engineering research. They are very efficient in absorbing and rapidly transferring kinetic energy; they are highly responsive, bending and quickly springing back to their original position, thus throwing the vaulter with great force. They are also lightweight, allowing the vaulter to sprint faster and to make the plant with greater ease. One commentator, writing from an engineering perspective, has said, "Despite advancements in the physical potential of athletes and in training techniques, the most important factor towards advancing the sport has been the development of better pole materials. Research into these new materials . . . inadvertently shifted the focus of the vault from the athlete to the pole." Matthew McCormick, *Soaring to New Heights: The Evolution of Pole Vaulting and Pole Materials,* 12 ILLUMIN, Issue 2 (2012), https://illumin.usc.edu/2702-2/.

    The composition of vaulting poles remains essentially unregulated as to size, weight, and composition. Craig Cooper, *Pole Vault: 2017 Complete Rules Comparison*, U.S.A. TRACK AND FIELD (2017). USATF does require that the basic material be smooth, but that is presumably to prevent the pole from doing damage, and not a performance-related constraint.

Should the composition of vaulting poles be regulated? If so, under what principles? Is there a better argument for leaving poles unregulated than for leaving swimsuits unregulated?

7. *From PEDs to PEEs.* Is Rebecca Adlington's analogy between performance-enhancing drugs and performing-enhancing equipment apt? In claiming that, just as she would not take a performance-enhancing drug, she would never wear a suit "just to improve [her] performance," is she implying that, were she a tennis player rather than a swimmer, she would never select a tennis racket for that purpose? Is it plausible that an athlete should reject some piece of equipment—a better racket, an improved golf club, the latest sneaker—if persuaded that it would help her perform better? If not, what exactly is left of Adlington's analogy?

B. BIOMECHANICAL ENHANCEMENT

PISTORIUS V/ IAAF

Arbitration CAS 2008/A/1480 (Court of Arbitration for Sport, award of 16 May 2008)
https://jurisprudence.tas-cas.org/Shared%20Documents/1480.pdf

Panel: Prof. Martin Hunter (United Kingdom), President; Mr David W. Rivkin (USA); Mr Jean-Philippe Rochat (Switzerland)

[Oscar Pistorius appealed from a decision by the International Association of Athletics Federations ("IAAF") that prostheses worn by Pistorius constituted a technical device that gave him an advantage over able-bodied athletes.],

Mr Oscar Pistorius is a South African citizen, born on 22 November 1986 without fibula bones in his legs. At the age of eleven months his legs were amputated below his knees. Since then Mr Pistorius has run, walked and undertaken many other physical activities using prosthetic lower limbs, and he will continue to do so for the rest of his life. Nevertheless, sport has dominated his life. During his time at school, Mr Pistorius competed in a number of different sports, including rugby, water polo, tennis and wrestling. During the hearing he stated that he had never thought of himself as being "disabled". He has no recollection of having his own natural legs. At the hearing, the IAAF's counsel described him as . . . *a great athlete, an inspiring athlete.*

. . .For participation in sporting activities Mr Pistorius uses a prosthesis known as the *Cheetah Flex-Foot,* supplied by a company headquartered in Iceland, Össur HF ("Össur"). The *Cheetah Flex-Foot* is designed for single and double transtibial (below-the-knee) and transfemoral (above-the-knee) amputees who intend to run at recreational and/or competitive levels. It has been used by many single and double amputees, almost unchanged, since 1997.

In 2004, only a few months after he started running competitively, Mr Pistorius competed in the Athens Paralympics, where he won the Gold Medal in the 200-metre event and the Bronze medal in the 100-metre event. At the time of this appeal process he is the paralympic world-record holder at 100, 200 and 400 metres. In 2004 Mr Pistorius also began to compete in IAAF-sanctioned events in South Africa alongside able-bodied athletes. He won a 100-metre open competition in Pretoria with a time of 11.51. In the following year he competed alongside able-bodied athletes in the South African Championship, in which he finished sixth in the 400 metre event. . . .

On 26 March 2007, the IAAF Council . . . decided to introduce an amendment to IAAF Rule 144.2 for the purpose of regulating the use of technical devices. The new rule prohibits: *(e) Use of any technical device that incorporates springs, wheels or any other element that provides the user with an advantage over another athlete not using such a device.*

. . . [In July 2007, in Rome, Pistorius] ran in a specially staged "B" race which the IAAF arranged to be videotaped by an Italian sports laboratory using several high-definition cameras from different angles. He finished in second place, and the video subsequently became an exhibit in this appeal.

For a non-scientific observer, the video appears to show that Mr Pistorius was slower than other runners off the starting blocks, during the acceleration phase (approximately the first 50 metres) and running around the first bend, but faster over the "back straight". The split times of the race provided by the IAAF confirmed this observation. The able-bodied sprinters ran their fastest 100 metre splits in the first and second 100 metres, but Mr Pistorius ran his fastest 100 metre splits in the second and third 100 metres. The initial scientific analysis of the videotapes by the Italian laboratory indicated that neither Mr Pistorius' stride-length, nor the length of time that his prosthesis was in contact with the ground, was significantly different from those of the other runners.

In order to take the evaluation further Dr [Elio] Locatelli [of the IAAF] asked Professor Peter Brüggemann at the Institute of Biomechanics and Orthopaedics at the German Sport University in Cologne if he could conduct a biomechanical study to demonstrate whether or not Mr Pistorius' prosthetic limbs gave him an advantage over other athletes. . . .

On 12 November 2007 Mr Pistorius and five "control" athletes of similar sprinting ability to him ran a sub-maximal 400-metre race on an outdoor track, followed by a series of maximal and sub-maximal sprints on a 100-metre track at the laboratory of the Institute. VO2 consumption measurements were taken and blood lactate levels were recorded. On 13 November 2007, anthropometric measures were conducted on all the participants using a 3D body scanner. The prostheses were measured using a materials testing machine. Two further tests were carried out, on an exercise bicycle, to measure the metabolic capacity of the athletes. Prof. Brüggemann and his colleagues Messrs Arampatzis and Emrich issued [a report referred to as "the Cologne Report"] on 15 December 2007.

The abstract of the Report contained the following conclusory passage: *The hypothesis that the transtibial amputee's metabolic capacity is higher than that of the healthy counterparts was rejected. The metabolic tests indicated a lower aerobic capacity of the amputee than of the controls. In the 400 m race the handicapped athlete's VO2 uptake was 25% lower than the oxygen consumption of the sound controls, which achieved about the same final time. The joint kinetics of the ankle joints of the sound legs and the "artificial ankle joint" of the prosthesis were found to be significantly different. Energy return was clearly higher in the prostheses than in the human ankle joints. The kinetics of knee and hip joints were also affected by the prostheses during stance. The swing phase did not demonstrate any advantages for the natural legs in relation with artificial limbs. In total the double transtibial amputee received significant biomechanical advantages by the prosthesis in comparison to sprinting with natural human legs. The hypothesis that the prostheses lead to biomechanical disadvantages was rejected. Finally it was shown that fast running with the dedicated Cheetah prosthesis is a different kind of locomotion than sprinting with natural human legs. The "bouncing" locomotion is related to lower metabolic cost.*

On 14 January 2008, the IAAF Council issued a Decision which included the following findings: *running with these prostheses requires a less-important vertical movement associated with a lesser mechanical effort to raise the body, and the energy loss resulting from the use of these prostheses is significantly lower than that resulting from a human ankle joint at a maximal sprint speed.* Based on these findings the IAAF ruled that the *Cheetah Flex-Foot* prosthetics used by Mr Pistorius were to be considered as a . . . *technical device that incorporates springs, wheels or any other element that provides the user with an advantage over valid athletes,* and therefore contravened Rule 144.2(e). Mr Pistorius was thus declared ineligible to compete in IAAF-sanctioned events with immediate effect. . . .

LAW . . .

The Panel's analysis . . .

Issue (ii) Was the process leading to the IAAF Council's Decision no. 2008/01 procedurally unsound?

[During the hearing, Pistorius abandoned the issue of whether the IAAF Council had exceeded its jurisdiction. On the question of whether the procedure leading to the Council's decision was procedurally unsound, the Panel concluded that the new Rule was likely introduced with Pistorius in mind, and that the process "began to go 'off the rails' " when the IAAF retained Prof. Brüggemann to carry out testing only when Pistorius "was running in a straight line after the acceleration phase"; IAAF officials must have known from the Rome observations that by excluding the start and the acceleration phase, in which Pistorius did relatively poorly, "the results would create a distorted view of Mr Pistorius' advantages and/or disadvantages."] . . .

Issue (iii) Was the IAAF Council's Decision unlawfully discriminatory?

24. Mr Pistorius claims that the IAAF Decision is in breach of its obligation of non-discrimination, because it did not search for an appropriate accommodation as required by law. He claims that, in finding Mr Pistorius ineligible in all IAAF-sanctioned events without attempting to seek any alternative solution, modification or adjustment that might permit him to participate in such events on an equal basis with all able-bodied athletes, the IAAF has denied Mr Pistorius his fundamental human rights, including equal access to Olympic principles and values. . . .

29. [D]isability laws only require that an athlete such as Mr Pistorius be permitted to compete on the same footing as others. [Sic!] This is precisely the issue to be decided by this Panel: that is, whether or not Mr Pistorius is competing on an equal basis with other athletes not using *Cheetah Flex-Foot* prostheses. As counsel for the IAAF rightly mentioned, if this Panel finds that Mr Pistorius' Cheetah Flex-Foot prostheses provide no advantage to Mr. Pistorius, he will be able to compete on an equal basis with other athletes. If the Panel concludes that Mr Pistorius does gain an advantage, the Convention [on the Rights of Persons with Disabilities, and its Optional Protocol] would not assist his case.

30. Mr Pistorius' submission based on unlawful discrimination is accordingly rejected.

Issue (iv) Was the IAAF Council's Decision wrong in determining that Mr Pistorius' use of the Cheetah Flex-Foot device contravenes Rule 144.2(e)?

31. The Panel's point of departure for this part of the analysis is Rule 144.2(e), adopted by the IAAF's Council [in] 2007. . . [It] reads as follows:

For the purposes of this Rule, the following shall be considered assistance, and are therefore not allowed:

[. . .]

(e) Use of any technical device that incorporates springs, wheels, or any other element that provides the user with an advantage over another athlete not using such a device.

32. Without implying any criticism of the draftsman, who faced an extraordinarily difficult task, the Panel considers that this provision is a masterpiece of ambiguity. What constitutes a *technical device*? For the purposes of the present enquiry, the Panel is prepared to assume that a passive prosthetic such as the *Cheetah Flex-Foot* is to be considered as a

"technical device", even though this proposition may not be wholly free from doubt.

33. What constitutes a device that *incorporates springs*? Technically, almost every non-brittle material object is a "spring" in the sense that it has elasticity. Certainly the *Cheetah Flex-Foot* is a "spring", but does it *incorporate* a "spring"? A natural human leg is itself a "spring".

34. Then there is the critical question of the meaning of an *advantage . . . over another athlete*. It was urged on the Panel by the IAAF's counsel that the ordinary and natural meaning of the word *advantage* is absolute, in the sense that if a *technical device* is used, and is determined (presumably by an appropriate and fair process) to provide an athlete with any *advantage*, however small, in any part of a competition, that device must render that athlete ineligible to compete regardless of any compensating disadvantages.

35. The Panel does not accept this proposition. Of course, athletes should not be forced to compete against persons who use powered aids such as motors, wheels, springs (as in "pogo sticks", for example), or other active propulsive devices. This is not in doubt, and interpreted in this way the new Rule 144.2(e) is a sensible and appropriate rule. But to propose that a passive device such as the *Cheetah Flex-Foot* as used by Mr Pistorius should be classified as contravening that Rule without convincing scientific proof that it provides him with *an overall net advantage* over other athletes flies in the face of both legal principle and commonsense. The rule specifically prohibits a technical device that . . . . *provides the user with an advantage over an athlete not using that device*. If the use of the device provides more disadvantages than advantages, then it cannot reasonably be said to provide an advantage over other athletes, because the user is actually at a competitive disadvantage. That is the only sensible reading of the terms of Rule 144.2(e).

36. The Panel notes that this interpretation of Rule 144.2(e) was effectively adopted by Dr Locatelli of the IAAF in his testimony at the hearing, when he said that the rule would not prohibit Mr Pistorius from running in 100-metre or 200-metre races. Dr Locatelli said that such distances did not allow Mr Pistorius to catch up from his slower start. Thus, Dr Locatelli focused on the overall effect of the prosthesis and not on whether Mr Pistorius had an advantage at only one point in the race.

37. Unfortunately, as Prof. Brüggemann made clear during the hearing, the IAAF did not ask him to determine whether or not Mr Pistorius' use of the *Cheetah Flex-Foot* prosthesis provided him with an overall net advantage or disadvantage. The Cologne Report therefore does not address the central question that the Panel is required to answer in this appeal.

[The IAAF acknowledged that it had the burden of proof, and the Panel agreed with it that the applicable standard was the "balance of probability."] . . .

The Panel's Assessment of the Evidence . . .

42. . . . [T]he finding of an advantage in using the *Cheetah Flex-Foot* prosthesis comes principally from two elements of the Cologne Report: First, Mr Pistorius, in using the device, does not have as much vertical force with each step; in other words, he runs in a flatter manner than able-bodied runners. All the experts agreed that these measurements were valid. Second, Mr Pistorius uses less metabolic energy in running, perhaps as a result of that flatter running. These test results were challenged.

43. The experts presented by Mr Pistorius conducted their own tests on him and on able-bodied athletes as controls at a laboratory in Houston in February 2008 (the "Houston Report"). Among other things, tests set out in the Houston Report found that Mr Pistorius used the same oxygen amounts as able-bodied runners at a sub-maximal running speed, and thus did not have a metabolic advantage. Other tests also showed that Mr. Pistorius fatigued normally. Again, the experts agreed that these test results were valid. The Houston Report also tested the amount of energy loss from the *Cheetah Flex-Foot* prosthesis against the intact human leg, which includes tendons and other elements that generate positive energy (and which, for obvious reasons, an amputated athlete would not have). It is common ground that the Cologne Report did not measure any of these elements.

44. In summary, the Panel determines that the IAAF has not met its "on the balance of probability" burden of proof that Rule 144.2(e) is contravened by Mr Pistorius' use of the *Cheetah Flex Foot* prosthesis for several reasons. First, as noted above, a violation would only occur if the user of the prosthesis gained an *overall net advantage* over other runners, and the IAAF did not ask Prof. Brüggemann and his colleagues to make that determination. The terms of reference put to Prof. Brüggemann and his team by the IAAF did not propose the appropriate question.

45. . . . The point was stated clearly by Dr Locatelli in one of his press interviews, when he said . . . . *we are looking for advantages, not for disadvantages.* The experts also agreed at the hearing that *neither the Cologne nor Houston studies have quantified all of the possible advantages or disadvantages of Mr Pistorius in a 400m race.*

46. Secondly, the Panel is not persuaded that there is sufficient evidence of any metabolic advantage in favour of a double amputee using the *Cheetah Flex-Foot*. Certainly, the evidence presented in the Cologne Report is not capable of satisfying the burden of proof that is acknowledged by the IAAF. The IAAF seemed to recognize this fact at the hearing as it focused on the biomechanical aspects of the Cologne Report, and it acknowledged

that most of the metabolic findings, including its blood lactate measurements, were not conclusive.

47. Similarly, the IAAF has not proven the other basis of the IAAF Decision: namely that the biomechanical effects of using the particular prosthetic device give Mr Pistorius an advantage over other athletes not using the device. In the last conferencing session among the experts and the Panel, the experts accepted that comparisons between the effective energy that can be used to increase the speed of sprinters using natural legs and prosthetic legs cannot be treated as providing definitive conclusions in the light of current scientific knowledge. They could not opine with certainty that the conflicting hypotheses they were advancing were indeed more than unprovable hypotheses. In particular, the scientists do not know if the fact that able-bodied runners create more vertical force than Mr. Pistorius is an advantage or disadvantage. There is at least some scientific evidence that sprinters, including 400m runners, train themselves to bounce more (ie, to use more vertical force) because it creates more speed. Thus, the Cologne Report's finding, on which the IAAF Decision relied, that Mr Pistorius uses less vertical force and runs in a flatter manner may be a *disadvantage* rather than *an advantage.*

48. In addition, while the Cologne Report found less energy loss in the *Cheetah Flex-Foot* prosthesis than in the human ankle, the scientific experts all agreed that the energy "lost" in the ankle could be transferred elsewhere in the body, through tendons, ligaments and muscles etc, because the human body does not like to lose energy. They agreed that such a transfer cannot be properly measured or currently understood. Thus, based on current scientific knowledge, it appears to be impracticable to assess definitively whether the *Cheetah Flex-Foot* prosthesis acts as more than, or less than, the human ankle and lower leg, in terms of "spring-like" quality.

49. Moreover, the scientific experts agreed that *a mechanical advantage provided by a prosthetic leg would be expected to lead to a metabolic advantage for a runner.* As noted above, neither the Cologne Report nor the Houston Report showed such a metabolic advantage.

50. In the light of the Panel's analysis of the facts, the scientific expert opinions and the legal principles involved, the Panel has no doubt in finding that the IAAF has failed to satisfy the burden of proof that it accepts. It follows that Mr Pistorius' appeal must be upheld.

51. The Panel is re-inforced in reaching this conclusion by the fact that the *Cheetah Flex-Foot* prosthesis has been in use for a decade, and yet no other runner using them—either a single amputee or a double amputee—has run times fast enough to compete effectively against able-bodied runners until Mr Pistorius has done so. In effect, these prior performances by other runners using the prosthesis act as a control for study of the benefits of the

prosthesis and demonstrate that even if the prosthesis provided an advantage, and as noted none has been proven, it may be quite limited.

52. The consequence of this ruling by the Panel is that the IAAF Council's Decision 2008/01 of 14 January 2008 is revoked with immediate effect, and Mr Pistorius is currently eligible to compete in IAAF-sanctioned events.

53. However, it is important to clarify what the result of this appeal does *not* decide.

54. First, the Panel's decision applies to Mr Pistorius while using the particular model of Cheetah Flex-Foot prosthesis that was the subject of the Cologne tests and shown to the Panel as exhibits during the hearing in Lausanne. It is not a general licence for Mr Pistorius to use any further developments of the *Cheetah Flex-Foot* that might be found to provide him with an overall net advantage.

55. Secondly, the Panel does not exclude the possibility that, with future advances in scientific knowledge, and a testing regime designed and carried out to the satisfaction of both Parties, the IAAF might in the future be in a position to prove that the existing *Cheetah Flex-Foot* model provides Mr Pistorius with an overall net advantage over other athletes.

56. Thirdly, the Panel's decision in this appeal has absolutely no application to any other athlete, or other type of prosthetic limb. Each case must be considered by the IAAF on its own merits. The ruling does not grant a blanket licence to other single or double amputees to compete in IAAF-sanctioned events using *Cheetah Flex-Foot* prosthetics, or indeed any other type of prosthesis. Each amputee athlete must collaborate with the IAAF to have his or her eligibility under Rule 144.2(e), as interpreted by this Panel, established on an individual basis. The Panel hopes that this will not impose a substantial new burden on the IAAF, because of the unique nature of Mr Pistorius' case. However, if it does create an additional burden, it must be viewed as just one of the challenges of 21st Century life. . . .

COMMENTS AND QUESTIONS

1. The CAS decision. The Court of Arbitration for Sport (CAS) issued at least four holdings in the Pistorius case: (1) that the appropriate question, for purposes of determining Pistorius's eligibility to compete against able-bodied runners, was whether his prosthetics provided him with an *overall net advantage*, not whether they provided him with any advantage at all; (2) that the federation proposing to exclude Pistorius shouldered the burden of proof; (3) that the standard of proof was the "balance of probability" or "more likely than not" standard; and (4) that the IAAF did not satisfy its burden.

With which of these holdings do you agree? Do you disagree with any or find them insufficiently defended? Why? Did the CAS issue other holdings of importance in this case?

With respect to the standard of proof problem, note this comment by Michael Johnson, a friend of Pistorius and then and for many years the world record holder in the 400-meter run: "My position is that because we don't know for sure whether he gets an advantage from the prosthetics that he wears, it is unfair to the able-bodied competitors. That is hard for a lot of people to take and to understand when you are talking about an athlete and an individual who has a disability." David Epstein, *Fair or foul? Experts split over whether Pistorius has advantage,* SPORTS ILLUSTRATED, Aug. 3, 2012.

2. *Net advantage.* What would it mean to say that the Cheetahs gave Pistorius a net advantage over able-bodied runners? They clearly made him better able to compete against able-bodied runners than he would have been able to do had he not worn them. Is the question whether actual-Pistorius-on-Cheetahs has an advantage over hypothetical-able-bodied-Pistorius, and if so, what specifications about hypothetical-able-bodied-Pistorius should we make? In trying to determine the issue of net advantage, what are all the factors that you would want to consider? Do you think a net determination is feasible? Does it depend on the length of the race?

Consider also the case of Blake Leeper, another runner who is missing his lower legs and whose use of prosthetics came before the CAS. In October 2020, the court ruled that the burden on the advantage issue should be on the governing body, not the disabled athlete. But the CAS concluded that Leeper's prosthetics "enable him to run at a height that is several inches taller than his maximum possible height if he had intact biological legs," and so "to run the 400m event in a time that is several seconds faster than the fastest time he would have been able to achieve with intact biological legs." *Leeper v. IAAF,* CAS 2020/A/6807 (2020), par. 390. Leeper's lawyer protested that the determination of Leeper's hypothesized height was "based solely on the body proportions of Caucasian and Asian athletes," and so unfair to Leeper, who is Black. See Press Release, *Court of Arbitration for Sport (CAS) Invalidates World Athletics Rule . . .,* Oct. 26, 2020, https://tinyurl.com/y2687ybl. World Athletics (as the IAAF has been renamed) rejected the characterization, saying, "The 15cm disparity found in Mr Leeper's case between his prosthetic leg length and his natural leg length is not due to racial differences in body dimensions." Press Release, *World Athletics' response to CAS announcement of decision in Leeper case,* Oct. 26, 2020, https://tinyurl.com/y48cfrnv.

3. *Hindsight.* Thanks to the CAS decision, and to his performance in Olympic qualifying, Pistorius was permitted to run against able-bodied runners at the 2012 London Olympics. He did not make the finals in the 400m individual race, and was part of a South African team that came in 8th in the final in the 4x400 relay. Do these results affect your judgment as to whether he should be allowed to compete against able-bodied runners? In what way?

4. *From Olympics to Paralympics.* Less than one month after the Olympics finished, Pistorius competed again at the Paralympics, where he was entered in 100m, 200m, and 400m, and the 4x100m relay. In the first of these four events, the 200m, Pistorius came in second to Brazil's Alan Oliveira and

created a minor controversy for complaining that it wasn't "a fair race" because Oliveira ran on longer blades, as approved for use in the Paralympics, than the ones that are approved for the Olympics. Owen Gibson, *Paralympics 2012: Oscar Pistorius erupts after Alan Oliveira wins gold*, GUARDIAN (Sept. 2, 2012). (He then came in fourth in the 100m and won gold in both the individual 400m and the relay.) Does Pistorius's complaint that the particular blades used by Oliveira gave him an unfair advantage over Pistorius himself have any bearing on the complaint, voiced by some able-bodied runners, that Pistorius's own blades give him an unfair advantage over them?

     5.   *Updating the evidence.* The CAS made clear that its decision on Pistorius's eligibility was based on the evidence then available to it and was revisable in light of new scientific findings. The Houston tests cited by the CAS for the proposition that Pistorius's proposition gave him no *metabolic* advantage were performed at a lab run by Peter Weyand, a physiologist at Rice University. Ironically, the year after the CAS issued its decision, Weyand published a paper concluding that the prostheses did give him a *mechanical* advantage. Peter Weyand, et al., *The fastest runner on artificial legs: different limbs, similar function?*, 107 J. APPLIED PHYS. 903 (2009) ("simultaneously similar to intact-limb runners physiologically but dissimilar mechanically").When you run, you apply enough force to the ground to lift your body in the air for a long enough time to reposition your legs before making contact with the ground again and repeating the process. That time for repositioning is called "swing time." Weyand had studied it extensively and concluded that virtually all humans—"[f]rom Grandma to Usain Bolt," as he later put it, David Epstein, *Fair or foul? Experts split over whether Pistorius has advantage*, SI.com, Aug. 3, 2012—have essentially the same swing time when they are running at top speed. The principal reason why one runner is faster than the other, apart from differences in leg length, is that the faster one applies greater force to the ground, therefore requiring less time before becoming airborne again. Peter G. Weyand, et al., *Faster top running speeds are achieved with greater ground forces not more rapid leg movements*, 89 J. APPLIED PHYS. 1991 (2000).

     Pistorius, Weyand and his colleagues found, did not fit the norm; his swing time, at 0.284 seconds, was 20% faster than the norm, which Weyand attributed to the fact that his limbs were so much lighter than those of able-bodied runners. Epstein's article reports a review of "more than 100 leg-swing times of professional sprinters taken with research-quality cameras, as well as peer-reviewed scientific journal reports on sprinters' swing times," with the fastest swing time reported, by a sprinter 8 inches shorter than Pistorius, being 0.30 seconds. The short swing time meant that Pistorius could run at high speeds even while applying less force to the ground, and keeping contact with it longer, than able-bodied runners. But the diminution of force was attributable at least in part to the softness of the prosthetic. Alena M. Grabowski, et al., *Running-specific prostheses limit ground-force during sprinting*, 6 BIOLOGY LETTERS 201 (2010). "It's like running on a mattress," is the way Hugh M. Kerr, one of the co-authors of the Grabowski study, put it.

Epstein, *Fair or foul, supra.*[a] And, as Epstein points out, the prostheses created another disadvantage: They had no ankles, meaning that Pistorius had to stand up straight in the blocks, which probably accounts at least in part for the fact that he was relatively slow at the start.

How do these advantages and disadvantages balance out? Matthew W. Bundle, a biomechanist at the University of Montana and second author of Weyand's 2009 study, contended that even factoring in the force reduction of the prostheses Pistorius was still seven seconds faster over 400 meters than he would be if his swing times were typical of able-bodied runners. *Id.* Epstein further reports:

> "Thousands of amputees have used these springs and haven't even come close to his times," Herr says of Pistorius. But, says Craig Spence, a spokesman for the International Paralympic Committee, "there aren't too many double-leg amputees who compete [in sprints]. There are two or three, so therefore they're combined with the single-leg amputees." Says Weyand, "single-leg amputees are limited by the speed of their biological limb. They can't swing both legs at drastically different speeds." . . . "It's innocent until proven guilty," Herr says.

6. But was he running? Should Pistorius have been excluded from able-bodied races on the ground that he was not engaged in the same competition—in particular, that he was not *running? See* S.D. Edwards, *Should Oscar Pistorius be Excluded from the 2008 Olympic Games?*, 2 SPORT, ETHICS & PHIL. 112 (2008). In answering this question, consider another technological innovation:

> USA Track & Field has worked with Nike to test carbon-sole shoe implants that harness energy normally lost when a runner's foot pushes off. Americans wore the shoes in the Sydney Olympics, meaning able-bodied sprinters have already used the type of carbon-infused prosthetics that got Pistorius banned. What's the difference between carbon shoes and carbon tibiae? Fashion? "It's a borderline case," says USOC sports technologist Peter Vint. "We're continuing to ask if that's legal or not."

Eric Adelson, *Let 'Em Play*, ESPN THE MAGAZINE, May 5, 2008, at 52.

7. Bionic athletes? Many experts in the fields of genetic and biomedical engineering believe that the carbon blades used by amputees like Oscar Pistorius represent a very early stage in the science of athletic performance enhancement. Thanks to advances in gene therapy and artificial organs and limbs, bionic athletes will be common in the near future. Already, for example, athletes, just like many of the rest of us, improve their vision through Lasik surgery. In the future, they may be able to receive bionic eyes with telescopic

---

[a] Herr, a rock-climber and MIT biophysicist, lost both legs below the knee at age 17 as a result of frostbite; he is renowned as a designer of prosthetics and is said to be "the first person with a major amputation to perform in a sport on par with elite-level, able-bodied persons." *Hugh Herr*, WIKIPEDIA, https://tinyurl.com/y5g2ls7y.

properties. Athletes receive artificial knees and hips. In the future, these artificial limbs will be stronger and more flexible than natural limbs and will be grafted directly to the skeleton, allowing for their direct control by the central nervous system. Artificial hearts will pump blood more efficiently than natural hearts. What principles should determine which enhancements and modifications are permissible and which are not? For a critical discussion, see MICHAEL J. SANDEL, THE CASE AGAINST PERFECTION: ETHICS IN THE AGE OF GENETIC ENGINEERING (2007).

8. *Preemptive surgery.* Consider that "[y]oung pitchers . . . have already started opting for preemptive Tommy John surgery because it makes tendons stronger." Adelson, *Let 'Em Play.* If such preemptive surgery gives a substantial competitive advantage, should players who have had it be barred from competing?

9. *Cybathlon.* Instead of trying to accommodate athletes who do and do not use prostheses or similar devices in a single competition, would it be better to expand competitions dedicated to the use of technological aids? Such a competition, called the Cybathlon, was held in Zurich in 2016. Competitors were encouraged to make use of "the most modern powered knee prostheses, wearable arm prostheses, powered exoskeletons, powered wheelchairs, electrically stimulated muscles and novel brain-computer interfaces." For each event, there were medals both for the device itself and for "the pilot, who is driving the device." Another Cybathlon was held in 2020, during the COVID-19 pandemic, with competitors participating from their home countries. *Cybathlon 2020*, ETH ZURICH, https://tinyurl.com/y66vy6n7.

10. *Digital dilemmas.* Baseball Hall of Famer Paul Waner once said that he would be a better hitter without the middle finger of one hand. Suppose that's true. Should baseball rules render ineligible someone who (a) was born with a finger missing? (b) had a finger removed to hit better? Consider also the case of Tom Dempsey, the first NFL kicker to make a 63-yard field goal:

> Dempsey was born without toes on his right foot and no fingers on his right hand. He wore a modified shoe with a flattened and enlarged toe surface. This generated controversy about whether such a shoe gave a player an unfair advantage. When reporters would ask him if he thought it was unfair, he said "Unfair eh? How 'bout you try kickin' a 63 yard field goal to win it with 2 seconds left an' yer wearin' a square shoe, oh, yeah and no toes either". Additionally, when an analysis of his kick was carried out by ESPN Sport Science, it was found that his modified shoe offered him no advantage—the smaller contact area could in fact have increased the margin of error. In 1977, the NFL added a rule, informally known as the "Tom Dempsey Rule," that "any shoe that is worn by a player with an artificial limb on his kicking leg must have a kicking surface that conforms to that of a normal kicking shoe."

Tom Dempsey, WIKIPEDIA, https://tinyurl.com/y2wrmr2w. Does this rule appear to be fair to kickers like Dempsey? Was the situation before the rule was adopted fair to other kickers?

C. PERFORMANCE-ENHANCING DRUGS

Most people, when they hear "performance-enhancing drugs" (PEDs), think first of steroids. Sure enough, anabolic steroids are paradigmatic PEDs. But the class of PEDs is huge, and includes countless substances that few people involved with competitive sports think seriously of regulating. Caffeine enhances performances by improving energy and focus. Ibuprofen enhances performance by relieving pain and reducing inflammation. Ambien does so by promoting restful sleep. The vast and disparate class of PEDs ensures that the interesting debates do not concern whether all use of PEDs should be banned in sports. Of course they shouldn't. Nobody thinks they should. The principal questions this subchapter addresses are what should be prohibited, why, and how.

The what and the why naturally go together. This subchapter's first task, accordingly, is to identify and evaluate the arguments given in favor of prohibiting this or that substance (or this or that *amount* of this or that substance) in this or that sport. Its second task is to explore how PED regulations can be implemented in a fashion that adequately deters and catches violations without unduly infringing the autonomy and dignitary interests of the regulated athletes. Bear in mind that neither of these questions concerns whether athletes who use PEDs *in violation of an applicable ban* are guilty of cheating. The issues here are whether the use of some particular PEDs (either in all sports or in some) should be banned in the first place and, if so, how a just and effective ban can be crafted and implemented. How to assess the acts of doping in violation of applicable rules is addressed below, in Chapter 14.

1. WHAT TO PROHIBIT

Before we discuss the arguments for banning PEDs, let's get a little clearer on the substances the arguments are about. The substances that PED critics have in their sights are of diverse sorts, but generally serve one or more of five basic functions: (1) *lean mass builders* (e.g., anabolic steroids, HGH) amplify muscle growth and speed recovery from injury; (2) *stimulants* (e.g., caffeine, cocaine, amphetamines) enhance energy, focus, and aggression; (3) *pain killers* (e.g., cortisone, toradol) reduce pain and inflammation; (4) *sedatives* and calming agents (e.g., beta-blockers, cannabis) reduce anxiety and slow heart rate; and (5) *blood boosters* (e.g., EPO) increase endurance by increasing oxygen-carrying capacity of blood.

Over the years, many reasons for prohibiting some usage of some substance have been offered. At one time, many critics of PEDs urged that they be banned because they were "unnatural" and threatened the very essence of athletic achievement. Those arguments are in some decline,[b] and today two sets of arguments predominate: that the substance is harmful to the user, and that the performance enhancement it offers degrades the athletic test. A full engagement with these debates would consume more pages than we can devote to it. This section summarizes these two lines of argument for prohibiting PEDs and the responses they've provoked. In all cases, the analyses must proceed substance by substance. But, by and large, health-driven arguments for prohibiting a given drug can be assessed from a sport-general perspective. (If EPO is harmful for bikers, it's probably harmful for swimmers, too.) Degradation-driven arguments, in contrast, largely proceed sport by sport. (An enhancement that degrades a challenge presented by baseball might not be degrading for the sport of soccer.)

a. Protect Against Harms to Health

Arguments to prohibit a substance on harm-minimization grounds come in two principal variants, not mutually incompatible. The essential premise common to both is that usage of the substance in question, in the amounts that some athletes would use if it were unregulated, risks serious adverse health consequences, acute or long-term. As the Australian Academy of Science summarizes:

- Anabolic steroids can cause high blood pressure, acne, abnormalities in liver function, alterations in the menstrual cycle in women, decline in sperm production and impotence in men, kidney failure and heart disease. . . .

- Amphetamines can cause damage to the liver, kidneys and cardiovascular system, and cause hallucinations and violent behaviour, while long term use can change the structures of the brain involved with memory and emotion. . . .

- After puberty, inflated levels of HGH can cause acromegaly, a disease characterised by excessive growth of the head, feet and hands. The lips, nose, tongue, jaw and forehead increase in size and the fingers and toes widen and become spade-like. The organs and digestive system may also increase in size, which may eventually cause heart failure. Acromegaly sufferers often die before the age of 40. Excessive use of HGH in adults may also lead to diabetes; muscle, joint and bone pain; osteoarthritis; cardiac limitations; hypertension; and

---

[b] For a discussion and attempted revitalization, see Sigmund Loland, *Performance-Enhancing Drugs, Sport, and the Ideal of Natural Athletic Performance*, 18 AM. J. BIOETHICS 8 (2018).

abnormal   heightened   symptoms   of   cardiovascular
disease. . . .

- If EPO levels are too high the body will produce too many red
  blood cells which can thicken the blood, leading to clotting,
  heart attack and stroke. In fact, EPO has been implicated in
  the deaths of numerous athletes, predominantly cyclists.
  Repeated doses of EPO can also stimulate the development of
  antibodies directed against EPO, which can result in
  anaemia.

Stephen Watt, *Drugs in Sport*, Australian Academy of Science, https://tiny
url.com/y7mpvh6h.

From the shared premise that abuse of many PEDs can significantly
harm the user's health, two lines of prohibitionist argument can be
distinguished, depending on whom the proposed regulations aim to
protect—the "willing user," or the "unwilling user," as we will call them.
Regulations justified as means to protect the health of willing users are
flatly paternalistic. They claim that it is appropriate for athletic governing
bodies to protect the health of those who want to use the substance to gain
the likely performance benefits, thus overriding the users' personal
preferences for their supposed own greater good. Regulations justified to
protect unwilling users are not paternalistic. Rather, they aim to protect
those who would prefer not to use the substance but believe that the
coercive logic of competition would compel them to do so, notwithstanding
the health risks, if their rivals chose to do so. "Clean athletes are harmed,
so the argument goes, because the dopers 'up the ante'. If some competitors
are using steroids, then all competitors who wish to compete at that level
will need to take steroids or other substances to keep up." Angela J.
Schneider & Robert B. Butcher, *A Philosophical Overview of the Arguments
on Banning Doping, in Sport, in* VALUES IN SPORT: ELITISM, NATIONALISM,
GENDER EQUALITY AND THE SCIENTIFIC MANUFACTURE OF WINNERS 185,
191 (Torbjörn Tännsjö & Claudio Tamburrini eds., 2000).

These arguments have provoked varied responses. Several responses
target the core premise that use of some of these substances is harmful to
the user. Critics advance at least three counterarguments: (a) that the
substances simply are not very harmful; (b) that, as harmful as they may
be, they're not more harmful than other practices that sports tolerate,
encourage, or even require; and (c) that a ban on PED use would be counterproductive.

The first counterargument challenges the health-based argument for
PED prohibition at its root, objecting that there is insufficient evidence
that the substances at issue impose significant health risks. As Dr. Norman
Fost, one of the most prominent skeptics, has argued:

Good ethics starts with good facts, and the claims on this point are, to understate the case, seriously overstated. Articles abound in the mass media on the life-threatening risks of anabolic steroids: cancer, heart disease, stroke, and so on. What is missing are peer-reviewed articles in scientific journals to support the claims. Quick: name an athlete who died, or was diagnosed, with steroid-related cancer, heart disease, or stroke. Cases are so hard to find that the prohibitionists have to make them up. So Lyle Alzado, the NFL all-star, is presented on the front page of the New York Times and the cover of Sports Illustrated because of an alleged steroid-related brain tumor. What is missing is a single article, or evidence, or even a quote from any authority on the topic to support any connection between steroids and Alzado's tumor.

Norman Fost, *Steroid Hysteria: Unpacking the Claims,* 7 AMA J. ETHICS 767 (2005).

The second counterargument maintains that, however harmful some PEDs may be, they're not more harmful than other practices that are allowed. As Angela Schneider and Richard Butcher argue:

There are many training practices, and indeed many sports, that carry a far greater likelihood of harm to the athlete than does the controlled use of steroids. If the reason for banning doping in sport really were a concern for the health and well-being of athletes, there would be many sports and many more practices that should be banned. So, at the very least, it seems inconsistent to argue in favour of the bans on doping and not the myriad other practices which are also harmful to the athletes.

Schneider & Butcher, *A Philosophical Overview,* at 189. Moreover, they add, even if the substances are harmful, a ban is as likely to exacerbate those harms as to reduce them because "athletes will continue to use them in clandestine, unsanitary and uncontrolled ways." *Id.* at 190.

While many critics of prohibition are skeptical of the health claims that regulators put forth, libertarians about PED use oppose prohibition even if the substances are proven to be more harmful than they believe they are. Most significantly, critics object that it is simply antithetical to basic liberal commitments to prohibit usage by competent adults for the user's own good. "Generally we foster and value independence and the right to make the important choices that affect one's own life," Schneider and Butcher argue. "We value autonomy. . . . [T]o ban steroids solely to protect their adult competent users is to treat those athletes as children unable to make the choices that most affect them." *Id.* at 188.

Bans designed to protect unwilling users from being "coerced" into taking substances they'd rather avoid are not paternalistic; they would promote, not restrict, the autonomy of the unwilling user. Nonetheless, persons more friendly to PED use criticize such regulations on grounds of consistency. Again, Schneider and Butcher put the counterargument well, emphasizing that

> elite-level sport is already highly coercive. If full-time training, or altitude training, or diet control, are shown to produce better results, then everyone is forced to adopt those measures to keep up. It is unclear why doping is any more coercive, and sufficiently so to warrant being banned than, say, full-time training. The feeling that somehow steroid use is worse than longer and ever more specialised training just raises the question of why it is worse. Some may argue that the question really is, Why can't an athlete accept two 'raises of the ante' but not accept a third, or an unlimited number? The answer to this question relies on a demand for consistency. There must be some reason why this, rather than that, practice is the one that is banned, and that reason cannot be merely that it was the third or the nth raise of the ante.

Id. at 191.

b.   **Protect Against Degradation of the Sport**

Degradation-based arguments for PED regulation are independent of harm-based ones. Their central thrust, very generally, is that use of the substance under discussion augments competitor performance in a way that unduly diminishes one or more challenges that the sport is designed and valued to test. An objectionable diminution in challenge can come about in many ways.

Perhaps most obviously, use of substances that increase muscle size and physical strength can threaten core challenges in sports that test strength, power, and explosiveness. In baseball, for example, the batter's twin challenges are to hit for average and to hit for power. As the rapid demise of longstanding home run records in MLB's "steroid era" (the 1990s and early 2000s) suggests (but does not firmly establish), use of steroids and similar drugs can increase strength and bat speed sufficiently to make that latter task significantly easier.[c] Similarly, golf becomes a considerably easier test if steroid-fueled golfers can reach the green in fewer strokes, and the game of tennis is made less complex if steroid use begets faster serves, which yield more aces. The balance of challenges served up by combat sports is likewise altered if fighters gain increased punching power.

---

[c]   For an analysis of the extent to which home run numbers during the era are likely attributable to doping or to other causes, such as slight changes in the composition of the ball, see Ben Lindbergh, *How Much of a Role Did Steroids Play in the Steroid Era?*, THE RINGER, Sept. 28, 2018.

Endurance sports require athletes to pace themselves—not only during competition, but also in training. "A good long distance runner is able to 'listen' to his or her body and balance on the right side of fatigue injuries." Loland, *Performance-Enhancing Drugs*, at 12. To the extent that bodily awareness and concomitant management of pain and soreness are viewed as features of a sport, substances that substantially speed recovery and enable more continuous hard training can diminish the sport's intended and valued challenges.

Many sports—including "shooting" sports such as archery, darts, and riflery, and "stroking" sports such as golf and billiards—require great calm and steadiness of hand. Biathletes learn to shoot between heartbeats. Calming agents, such as beta blockers, slow the heart rate, thereby lowering blood pressure and reducing muscle tremors. They make the task of steadying one's nerves much easier. If nerve-steadying is viewed not just as a de facto requirement of the sport but as among the sport's valued challenges, then it is a degradation of the challenge to achieve the goal by pharmaceutical means rather than by discipline and strength of will.

These are just illustrations. The extent to which a given PED threatens the integrity or value of a sport depends on the effects of the substance and the valued challenges inherent in the practice.

COMMENTS AND QUESTIONS

1. *How harmful is it?* As already noted, the harmfulness of PEDs cannot be assessed in general, but only substance by substance. About all that can be said at a general level is that almost every particular claim regarding the health risks associated with a given substance is uncertain and contested. That acknowledged, the scientific evidence that use of at least some of these substances carries significant health risks appears stronger today than when Fost wrote in 2005. A recent article in a peer-reviewed scientific journal identified varied and significant adverse health consequences from abuse of anabolic androgenic steroids, human growth hormone, and erythropoietin (EPO), including sexual dysfunction, anemia, aggression, suicidal ideation, and a host of cardiovascular complications extending to sudden cardiac death. *See* Vita Birzniece, *Doping in sport: effect, harms and misconceptions*, 45 INTERNAL MEDICINE J. 239 (2015). It also concluded that "data from research studies may in fact underestimate the side-effects of doping agents" because "[a]thletes often abuse substances in much higher doses than in the available placebo-controlled studies, and often combine several agents."

What degree of confidence of what degree (or character) of harm do you think should be required to justify restrictions on a PED, so long as the additional premises in the harm-prevention argument are satisfied?

2. *Internal and external harms.* After criticizing harm-based arguments for prohibition on the ground that many sports are intrinsically more dangerous to their participants than is PED use, Schneider and Butcher

anticipate the objection "that risks that are incurred by the nature of the sport, such as brain damage from having one's head pummeled in boxing, are different from risks that are incurred from practices that have nothing to do with competition in the sport *per* se—liver damage from steroid use, for example." Schneider & Butcher, *A Philosophical Overview,* at 189. Indeed, they grant that the significance of the difference might seem to draw support from Alasdair MacIntyre's distinction (in *After Virtue* (1981)) between the "internal" and "external" goods derivable from a practice, "where internal goods are gained from participation in the activity itself for intrinsic reasons (skill, strategy, etc.) and external goods are gained from societal recognition of success in the specific sport (fame, prestige, money, etc.)." But they conclude that "this distinction won't work if the justification for the ban is harm and harm operates on sport from the outside, because the athlete is harmed in either case; that is to say, both brain damage and liver damage are harmful." Schneider & Butcher, *A Philosophical Overview,* at 190.

What do you think? Is the distinction more promising than Schneider and Butcher allow? Is it incoherent or illogical for a participant to accept the internal risks that correspond to a practice's internal goods while refusing to accept the external risks that correspond to a practice's external goods? Can a plausible argument be made that we (the sporting public) or they (the players themselves) ought to tolerate the risk of brain damage that boxing, football, and hockey create, but not the risk of liver damage that steroid use creates? Think also about other risks. Suppose that the average player in the NFL confronts risk R of incurring game-related harms or injuries of magnitude H. Suppose too that Punter A, because of his position, faces a risk of only .5R of sustaining harms of magnitude H. Suppose finally that playing during the COVID-19 pandemic imposes an additional risk .5R of harms of magnitude H. (Obviously, the harms are different in type; we're asking you to assume that different types of injury can be roughly compared in magnitude.) Would Punter A lack grounds for objecting to playing during the pandemic given that football players generally incur those risks from ordinary participation in the game?

3.   *Counterproductive?* Do you agree that well-designed bans on the use of PEDs cannot protect athletes because they will still be tempted to use prohibited substances, albeit in clandestine and unsafe ways? Does the fact (if it is a fact) that very many competitors in very many sports claim to be "unwilling users" who support PED regulation for health reasons undermine that argument? If a ban would foreseeably increase dangerous use, why *would* competitors want it?

4.   *Paternalism and autonomy.* Do you agree that a paternalistic ban on PED use is an inappropriate intrusion into personal autonomy? Schneider and Butcher acknowledge that paternalistic interventions are sometimes permissible, citing mandatory "seat-belt and motorcycle helmet legislation" as examples. Do you think there is a sound distinction to be made between paternalistic laws such as those and paternalistic bans on substance abuse in sports? If not, how does that cut—for prohibition in both contexts, or against? (Recall our brief discussion of paternalism in Subchapter 3G.)

5.   *Paternalism and the Faustian bargain.* In their 1984 book, *Death in the Locker Room: Steroids and Sports,* Bob Goldman and Ronald Klatz reported survey results revealing that 50% of Olympic athletes would accept the Faustian bargain of a guaranteed gold medal for certain death in five years. If these results were to prove reliable, would they support or undermine the paternalistic argument for PED regulation? In fact, subsequent surveys conducted by other researchers cast significant doubt on the numbers Goldman and Klatz reported. A recent survey of 2888 athletes across fifty sports found that only (?!) 7–12% of respondents (depending on sport and level of competition) would accept that deal. *See* Juan Marcos Gonzalez et al., *Trading Health Risks for Glory: A Reformulation of the Goldman Dilemma,* 48 SPORTS MED. 1963 (2018). Do these new results strengthen or weaken the case for PED regulation to protect willing users? To protect unwilling users?

6.   *Coercion.* Schneider and Butcher are more sympathetic to prohibitionist arguments designed to protect clean athletes from competitive pressure to dope than to arguments based on paternalistic regard for the willing dopers. But they nonetheless reject the "ante-raising" argument. Why? Do you agree that proponents of that argument must maintain that "doping is . . . more coercive . . . than, say, full-time training"? Why couldn't they argue, instead, that doping and full-time training are comparably coercive, but that the former coerces (or pressures) competitors to engage in riskier behaviors? Note too that at least some sports do limit behaviors other than PED use (such as number of hours training) for the participants' own health. Should limitations on training time or methods be sufficient to permit the governing body of a sport also to prohibit some PED use on an anti-coercion rationale? Should they be necessary?

7.   *Coercion and collective action.* Suppose that all (or virtually) all competitors in a given sports community would prefer not to use (some class of) PEDs, but worry that they'd feel compelled by competitive pressures to do so if enough of their peers did. That is, all users in this community would be "unwilling users." On this assumption, the prohibition of PEDs would present a pure

Externality

collective action problem. (See p. 243.) A generally accepted solution to such a problem—at least where there are no negative externalities—is to empower a regulatory authority to impose and enforce the rule that the members would want to follow; the authority enforces the cooperative solution that the participants themselves would prefer. (An **externality** is a cost or benefit of a practice that affects third parties who did not engage in the practice and did not choose to incur that consequence. Externalities can be negative—such as increased health risks imposed by industrial pollution—or positive—such as a reduced risk of incurring illness if others vaccinate.) Would a ban on PED use in a community of unwilling users produce negative externalities? Would it be justifiable if not? Would it be justifiable if so?

8.   *Role models.* An additional argument for prohibition, perhaps in some decline, is that PED use by athletes encourages impressionable young people

also to use drugs, either the same PEDs (which might be significantly more harmful to developing brains and bodies) or illegal recreational drugs, from marijuana to heroin. Schneider and Butcher are unpersuaded, noting that "there are many things that we consider appropriate for adults but not for children. Alcohol and cigarettes are obvious examples, as indeed is sex, but, in North America at least, we don't ban these substances or activities for adults because they would be bad for children." Schneider & Butcher, *A Philosophical Overview*, at 192. Do you agree?

    9. *Treatment/enhancement*. For some time commentators pursued the notion that the prohibit/permit line should track the difference between treatments (or "therapy") and enhancement. "The idea here," Malcolm Gladwell explains,

> is that there is a big difference between the drug that "treats" some kind of illness or medical disorder and one, on the other hand, that "enhances" some preexisting trait. There is a huge amount of literature on treatment/enhancement among scholars, and with good reason. Your health insurance company relies on this distinction, for example, when it decides what to cover. Open heart surgery is treatment. A nose job, which you pay for yourself, is enhancement. This principle is also at the heart of most anti-doping policies. Treatment is OK. Enhancement is illegal. That's why Tommy John surgery is supposed to be OK. It's treatment: You blow out your ulnar collateral ligament so you get it fixed.

Exchange between Malcolm Gladwell and Bill Simmons, GRANTLAND, Dec. 20, 2013. But the utility of this distinction has come under considerable attack. As Gladwell proceeds to note, "[t]he tendons we import into a pitcher's elbow through Tommy John surgery are way stronger than the ligaments that were there originally. There's no way Tommy John pitches so well into his early forties without his bionic elbow. Isn't that enhancement?" Lasik eye surgery can deliver visual acuity well better than 20/20. Cases like these have fueled a growing consensus that the distinction can't do the work some had asked of it, either because too many substances could be plausibly classified both as treatment (or therapy) and as enhancement, or because some substances that seem pretty clearly to be enhancements should be allowed. Gladwell's own conclusion is that "[t]he treatment/enhancement principle sounds really clear and straightforward on paper. But in real life it gets confusing really fast. The only honest position, I think, is to admit that the doping issue is really hard and confusing and that the opinions most of us have on this need to be reevaluated."

    Bucking this trend, the philosopher of sport William Morgan has sought to defend a "treatment-enhancement distinction" that

> takes its point of departure from our historically changing collective views of what supplements, supports, and sustains certain widely shared standards of athletic achievement, and what exceeds those standards and in so doing implicates levels of performance never

previously observed because never previously achieved. What falls into the former category . . . belongs rightfully in the treatment domain, and what falls in the latter rightly belongs in the enhancement domain.

William J. Morgan, *Athletic Perfection, Performance-Enhancing Drugs, and the Treatment-Enhancement Distinction*, 36 J. PHIL. SPORT 162, 165 (2009).[d] As Morgan elaborates:

> In the 1970s and 1980s, . . . both the public and athletic bodies were one in their moral condemnation of doping, in their certainty that imbibing such substances thoroughly corrupted the standards of excellence that make sport the quintessential perfectionist practice that it is. . . .
>
> However, by the end of the 20th century, or so I want to claim, the public began to look at PEDs, or at least some of them taken in certain quantities, with a less morally jaundiced eye, while the mandarins of the sports world continued their strident moral campaign against them. For at least the larger public then, the moral and social distance that once separated sports from the rest of the world has been largely closed, and it has been closed less by a surge of recreational drug use, which, of course, is still trending upward, than a surge of performance-enhancing drug use in almost all walks of life. I am referring, among other things, to the astonishing increase of legal prescriptions for performance boosting drugs like Ritalin (up 1,700 per cent in the last fifteen years) and Adderall (up 3,000 per cent in the same time period), used to treat Attention Deficit Hyperactivity Disorder (ADHD), but increasingly used by high school and college students to boost their SAT scores and grades. Prescriptions for low doses of testosterone to improve the physical virility and well being of older males have similarly skyrocketed. This new permissive regard for PEDs no doubt further explains the candor with which leading intellectuals such as the world renowned physicist Freeman Dyson, whose PED of choice is over the counter No-Doz, and the prodigious mathematician Paul Erdos, whose PED of choice is amphetamines taken in massive doses, publicly talk about their use of these substances. And it also explains, I argue, the public's newfound tolerance for steroids and their kin in the athletic arena.
>
> What we are seeing here, therefore, is, I think, a sea change in the public's regard for performance-enhancing substances across the board, to include, of course, sport. [The philosopher Michael] Sandel nicely captures the mood behind this fundamental shift in the public's outlook on all things pharmacological. As he argues, "Unlike the drugs of the sixties and seventies, Ritalin and Adderall are not for

---

[d]   © International Association for the Philosophy of Sport, reprinted with permission of Taylor & Francis, publisher.

checking out but for buckling down, not for beholding the world and taking it in, but for molding the world. . . The steroids and stimulants that figure in [this embrace of] enhancement are not a source of recreation, but a . . . way of answering a competitive society's demand to improve our performance and perfect our nature." [MICHAEL J. SANDEL, THE CASE AGAINST PERFECTION: ETHICS IN THE AGE OF GENETIC ENGINEERING (2007), at 60–61.] What Sandel doesn't say here, however perceptive, that also should be said is that when drugs are enlisted in our effort to cope not just with the rigor and stress of everyday life, but further with the rigor and stress of performing music, or churning out new intellectual ideas and products, or pursuing athletic dreams, it suggests that what we are doing in all these cases is more so treatment than enhancement. In other words, part of the reason why substances like steroids are no longer considered morally toxic to everyday living, or music-making, or athletic pursuits, is that they now seem to be beneficial ways to sustain our performance in these disparate endeavors, that is, as treatments, rather than as ways to raise the level of the already impressively high standards that are regularly achieved in these endeavors, that is, as enhancements.

[Evidence for this claim] focuses directly on what I take to be not only the public's acceptance of the extraordinarily high levels of performance elite athletes routinely turn out today, but what can best be described as their public clamoring for such consistently extraordinary athletic achievements. For the arduous, even Herculean, training regimens necessary to support such levels of athletic accomplishment, not to mention the all-consuming commitment they require, could not be achieved at the rate they are nowadays were athletes not downing substances like steroids and amphetamines. Consider perhaps the most superhuman of all sports, the Tour de France. In the 2001 Tour, for example, medical doctors that tended to the riders were given official permission by the race directors to transport and administer up to 300 drugs just so they could complete the grueling feat of riding six hours a day at top-speed for 23 days. . . . So even athletic events like the Tour, which I think it is safe to say has attracted the most criticism of any major sport today for its doping problems, has not elicited from its still adoring public any hint that they want to walk back from the remarkable athletic accomplishments made possible by the use of PEDs. In their steadfast admiration and support for top performing cyclists, no matter how achieved, they are matched by their no less star-struck peers who flock to stadiums to watch, for example, their favorite intercollegiate or professional football teams, whose interior lineman now weigh in on average at a whooping three hundred plus pounds (think steroids here not simply hi-protein shakes and weight training), or their favorite professional baseball teams, whose long grinding season would be hard to endure at current levels of play without knocking back amphetamines or shooting up steroids. . . .

But the public's continued love affair with sports has not abated . . . . [T]he public for sports, unlike the sports industry itself, is now accepting of the idea that the use of specific PEDs in certain amounts is a morally permissible form of treatment to support present levels of athletic excellence rather than a morally impermissible way to enhance athletic performance to levels never before seen let alone envisaged . . . .

Id. at 169–74.

Put aside, for the moment, whether Morgan's observations persuade you that sports should permit steroid use by elite athletes. We'll address that contention shortly. Here we ask only whether you are persuaded that Morgan's argument (if successful) is a defense of a treatment/enhancement distinction. To say that a substance is being used for treatment purposes appears to be saying that it is meant to correct for some deficiency—say, in height or testosterone level—and that appears to require the choice of a baseline against which the asserted deficiency is measured. What baseline does Morgan assume?

Would Morgan's argument be any less persuasive if it proceeded as follows: (a) the use of steroids enhances athletic performance, and is *not* mere treatment or therapy, but (b) the mere fact that something is an enhancement does not alone resolve whether it should be banned, for (c) even enhancements should be banned only if they degrade the athletic test; and (d) use of steroids by elite athletes today does not degrade the test as judged by common widely accepted standards? Put another way, do you find Morgan's argument for permitting steroid use to be more persuasive when presented as an argument that such use should be permitted *because* it properly counts as *treatment*, or if recast as an argument that such use should be permitted *notwithstanding* that it properly counts as *enhancement*?

10. Morgan on steroids. Now we tackle the substance of Morgan's argument regardless of its packaging. Whether the use be deemed therapeutic or not, do you agree with his argument that because PEDs allow an athlete to train harder, thus attempting to achieve levels of achievement that enjoy wide public support, they should be deemed to cultivate rather than corrupt athletic excellence? Is he on firm ground in saying that "steroids and their kind don't make you a better athlete in the relevant sense of a more talented or a more skilled one, but a better prepared athlete in the sense of a more performance ready one"? Is he right that steroids merely "remove an irrelevant impediment to athletic success"? Is this a good description of the use of steroids, HGH, and EPO by professional cyclists? By professional baseball players? Similarly, are you persuaded that "the improved performance that comes with doping is irrelevant to [sport's] test of skill"—in contrast to the improved performance that comes with training—because doping "does not improve skill but merely provides a competitive advantage over those who do not dope"? Schneider &

Butcher, *A Philosophical Overview*, at 192 (summarizing but not endorsing this argument). Is Morgan right that if fandom shared sports administrators' hostile attitude towards PEDs they would have "massively defected" from sports in which it became apparent that use of PEDs was widespread?

11. Greatest comeback #33. In the summer of 2020, *The Athletic* ran a series of the 40 greatest comebacks in sports history. Number 33 on their list was New York Knicks' center Willis Reed's return from injury in Game 7 of the 1970 NBA Finals to lead New York to victory against the Los Angeles Lakers. Reed had suffered a torn thigh muscle in Game 5, and had sat out Game 6, before vowing to play in the finale. And he did, with an inspiring effect, thanks to two injections to his thigh he received before tip-off, one of Carbocaine, a numbing agent, and the other of cortisone. Mike Vorkunov, *The Comeback, No.33: 'Here comes Willis, and the crowd is going wild'*, THE ATHLETIC (Aug. 7, 2020).

There are two main classes of steroids: anabolic steroids, which bind to the body's androgen receptors, and corticosteroids, which bind to the glucocorticoid receptors. Both classes of steroid have similar primary effects in reducing pain and inflammation, and in facilitating recovery. But anabolic steroids contribute much more to muscle mass and strength, and have long-lasting effects, whereas corticosteroids, like cortisone, wear off quickly. Today, WADA prohibits use of anabolic steroids at all times—in competition, and out. It prohibits use of corticosteroids only in competition, subject to the grant of a therapeutic use exemption (TUE), which Reed presumably would have been granted. Should in-competition use of cortisone be prohibited entirely—that is, without exceptions for supposedly therapeutic uses? Should it be freely permitted—that is, without the need for an individualized TUE? Does your answer depend on the long-term health risks of significant repeated use?

12. Doping and bike racing. Morgan discusses the Tour de France, an event that most informed observers believe has seen rampant doping more or less continuously since its start in 1903. In 1924, for example, defending champion Henri Pélissier complained to an investigative journalist that "[y]ou have no idea what the Tour de France is like. It's a Calvary. But Christ had only 14 stations of the cross. We have 15. We suffer from start to finish." Then Henri and his brother Francis took out from their bags the cocaine, chloroform, and amphetamines without which the grueling race would not be possible. Patrick Mignon, *The Tour de France and the Doping Issue*, 20 INT'L J. HISTORY SPORT 227, 229 (2003). Forty years later the rider Tom Simpson died during a climb, and the subsequent autopsy revealed traces of amphetamines. *Id.* And consider an exchange with Italy's Fausto Coppi, Tour-winner in 1949 and 1952, when asked if he ever took amphetamines:

"Only when necessary," he said.

How often was that?

"Most of the time," Coppi replied.

Jacques Anquetil of France, a five-time winner, once said with sarcasm, "Do they expect us to ride the Tour on Perrier water?"

Jeré Longman, *Week in Review: The Deafening Roar of the Shrug*, N.Y. TIMES, July 29, 2007. Does this history have any bearing on the current propriety of PED use in cycling?

13. Beta-blockers. What about beta-blockers? Although he resists the treatment/ enhancement distinction, Gladwell also declares himself "pretty convince[ed]" by an argument from the bioethicist Carl Elliott (*In Defense of the Beta Blocker*, THE ATLANTIC, Aug. 2008) that beta-blockers should be deemed treatment and thus permitted. Paraphrasing Elliott, Gladwell reasons that

> they don't improve a performer's skills, but rather they prevent anxiety from "interfering" with their skills. A beta blocker won't turn a bad putter into a great putter. Rather, it will prevent nerves from getting in the way of a golfer performing according to his true ability. Elliott thinks of anxiety like asthma. And we wouldn't prevent a runner from taking asthma medicine, would we?

Gladwell and Simmons. Morgan disagrees, maintaining that

> people should be held hostage by their genetic endowments if they figure importantly in the aim and purpose of the human endeavors they participate in. So those of us, for example, who naturally lack poise under fire, that is, who have a hard time reining in our anxieties in tension filled situations, should refrain from using drugs like beta-blockers to ward off the debilitating effects of such anxiety in sport. That is because in sport it does matter very much how one responds to such pressure-packed situations, to whether one can think clearly, strategize appropriately, and perform skillfully in such nerve-racking conditions. In other words, unlike steroids, downing beta blockers doesn't remove an irrelevant impediment to athletic success but rather a crucial component of that athletic success, which is precisely why, again unlike steroids, drugs like beta blockers do make us better athletes. The point of this argument, therefore, is not that taking such substances alters the mental state of the participants, so does an effective pep talk, but that the tremors and other skill unfriendly tics that result from excess nervousness are things that we expect, by our present lights at any rate, athletes to be able to cope with sans chemicals. That doesn't mean that one is similarly disallowed from trying to deal with anxiety by simulating game conditions in practice, or by consulting a sport psychologist. For learning how to deal with anxiety producing situations is part of what we expect of athletes, whereas popping beta-blockers to chemically eliminate tremors and the like is not because, to reiterate, qualities like mental toughness and poise are, among other things, what athletic competitions are supposed to test. . . .

Morgan, *Athletic Perfection,* at 178. His conclusion, then, is that "substances like steroids and amphetamines, in the amounts presently ingested, belong in the treatment rather than the enhancement category" but "drugs like beta blockers that affect the psychological qualities valued by the athletic community and tested by the sports they admire and follow—things like mental toughness, poise, and more generally the ability to perform in pressure packed situations," count as enhancement and should be regulated. Who's right about beta-blockers? What more information would you need to have a confident judgment?

14. *Marijuana.* Are there any good reasons for a sport to regulate marijuana use? In the 1988 Winter Olympics, snowboarder Ross Rebagliati was stripped of his gold medal for testing positive for marijuana. On appeal, the medal was restored. Schneider & Butcher, *A Philosophical Overview,* at 199, approve that decision, arguing that "there is no evidence that marijuana enhances snowboarding performance, so testing for its presence is therefore an unjustifiable intrusion into an athlete's personal freedom." Do you agree?

For decades, marijuana use has been a contentious issue in the NFL, which has long suspended players for testing positive. In 2020, finally bowing to pressure from players who argued that cannabis is a safer and less addictive pain reliever than prescription medication, the league agreed to loosen its restrictions in several respects: by increasing fourfold the amount of THC (the principal psychoactive compound in marijuana) that would trigger a positive test; by limiting testing to training camp, instead of from April through August; and by penalizing positive tests with fines instead of suspensions. *See* Ken Belson, *N.F.L. Bows to Marijuana's New Status,* N.Y. TIMES, Apr. 13, 2020. Retired offensive lineman Eugene Monroe, who had been among the most vocal catalysts for change, was unimpressed. "Why are they still testing at all?" he wondered. "I don't understand. Just move on from this and do the right thing and let the players make the choice. There's no secret that players smoke marijuana." *Id.* Should the NFL get entirely out of the business of regulating and testing marijuana?

15. *Oxygen chambers.* Consider hyperbaric oxygen therapy (HBOT). As the Food and Drug Administration explains, "HBOT involves breathing oxygen in a pressurized chamber in which the atmospheric pressure is raised up to three times higher than normal. Under these conditions, your lungs can gather up to three times more oxygen than would be possible breathing oxygen at normal air pressure." Injured tissue may require increased oxygen levels to heal, and an increase in the amount of oxygen dissolved in the blood from HBOT can improve oxygen delivery. But, although HBOT has been approved for certain narrow uses, such as treatment of decompression sickness ("the bends"), the FDA has not approved it more broadly, and continues to warn about risks such as paralysis and air embolism. U.S. FOOD AND DRUG ADMINISTRATION, *Hyperbaric Oxygen Therapy: Don't Be Misled* (2013). Among the athletes who have slept in hyperbaric chambers are the tennis champion Novak Djokovic and several NFL players. Should this practice be allowed? If

you need more information to answer sensibly, what would it be, and what impact might it have?

16. Hypocrisy? Is there irony—or worse—in the fact that sports telecasts often feature ads for Viagra and similar products, which are, after all, performance enhancers?

2. FROM PRINCIPLE TO PRACTICE: REGULATORY CHALLENGES

When it comes to regulating PEDs, a decision that some conduct should be prohibited in principle is only half the job. For several reasons— including that the prohibited acts occur outside of play and involve ingestion into the athlete's body, and that the substances involved are often at the pharmacological cutting edge, exacerbating difficulties of definition and detection—the practicalities involved in crafting an administrable, effective, and tolerable regulatory regime are unusually challenging. Among the specific challenges a regulatory authority faces are: correctly identifying and clearly defining prohibited substances, combinations of substances, and methods of delivery; determining the considerations that would justify individual exceptions and creating systems for the granting of exceptions when warranted; crafting effective but minimally intrusive methods of enforcement, including testing protocols and standards of proof; and establishing a proper schedule of penalties.

Across the globe, different sports address these challenges in divergent ways. But the leading regulatory authority is the World Anti-Doping Agency (WADA). Founded at the initiative of the IOC in 1999, in the wake of the 1998 Tour de France EPO doping scandal, WADA's principal duties are to identify and list prohibited substances and methods; identify and promulgate best practices for education, investigation, and testing; and accredit testing laboratories worldwide. The World Anti-Doping Code, which WADA periodically updates, has been adopted by the IOC, and by hundreds of other international sports federations, and national sports leagues and anti-doping organizations. Key provisions of the WADA Code follow; capitalizations that might otherwise appear eccentric indicate terms defined elsewhere in the Code.

WORLD ANTI-DOPING AGENCY (WADA) WORLD ANTI-DOPING CODE (2021)

Copyright 2020 WADA, reprinted with permission

Fundamental Rationale for the World Anti-Doping Code

Anti-doping programs are founded on the intrinsic value of sport. This intrinsic value is often referred to as "the spirit of sport": the ethical pursuit of human excellence through the dedicated perfection of each Athlete's natural talents. . . .

The spirit of sport is the celebration of the human spirit, body and mind. It is the essence of Olympism and is reflected in the values we find in and through sport, including:

- Health
- Ethics, fair play and honesty
- Athletes' rights as set forth in the Code
- Excellence in performance
- Character and Education
- Fun and joy
- Teamwork
- Dedication and commitment
- Respect for rules and laws
- Respect for self and other Participants
- Courage
- Community and solidarity

The spirit of sport is expressed in how we play true.

. . . .

Article 2.   Anti-Doping Rule Violations

. . . .

2.1 Presence of a Prohibited Substance or its Metabolites or Markers in an Athlete's Sample

2.1.1   It is the Athletes' personal duty to ensure that no Prohibited Substance enters their bodies. Athletes are responsible for any Prohibited Substance or its Metabolites or Markers found to be present in their Samples. Accordingly, it is not necessary that intent, Fault, Negligence or knowing Use on the Athlete's part be demonstrated in order to establish an anti-doping rule violation under Article 2.1.

2.2 Use or Attempted Use by an Athlete of a Prohibited Substance or a Prohibited Method

2.2.1   It is the Athletes' personal duty to ensure that no Prohibited Substance enters their bodies and that no Prohibited Method is Used. Accordingly, it is not necessary that intent, Fault, Negligence or knowing Use on the Athlete's part be demonstrated in order to establish an anti-doping rule violation for Use of a Prohibited Substance or a Prohibited Method.

. . . .

Article 4.   The Prohibited List

. . . .

4.3 Criteria for Including Substances and Methods on the Prohibited List

WADA shall consider the following criteria in deciding whether to include a substance or method on the Prohibited List:

4.3.1   A substance or method shall be considered for inclusion on the Prohibited List if WADA, in its sole discretion, determines that the substance or method meets any two of the following three criteria:

4.3.1.1   Medical or other scientific evidence, pharmacological effect or experience that the substance or method, alone or in combination with other substances or methods, has the potential to enhance or enhances sport performance;[e]

4.3.1.2   Medical or other scientific evidence, pharmacological effect or experience that the use of the substance or method represents an actual or potential health risk to the athlete;

4.3.1.3   WADA's determination that the use of the substance or method violates the spirit of sport described in the introduction to the Code.

4.3.2   A substance or method shall also be included on the Prohibited list if WADA determines there is medical or other scientific evidence, pharmacological effect or experience that the substance or method has the potential to mask the use of other Prohibited Substances or Prohibited Methods. . . .

4.4 Therapeutic Use Exemptions ("TUEs")

4.4.1   The presence of a Prohibited Substance or its Metabolites or Markers, and/or the use or attempted use, Possession or administration or attempted administration of a Prohibited Substance or Prohibited Method shall not be considered an anti-doping rule violation if it is consistent with the provisions of a TUE granted in accordance with the international Standard for Therapeutic Use Exemptions.[f]

---

[e]   A comment to Article 4.3.1.1 adds that "there may be substances that, when used alone, are not prohibited but which will be prohibited if used in combination with certain other substances. A substance which is added to the Prohibited List because it has the potential to enhance performance only in combination with another substance shall be so noted . . . ."

[f]   The relevant standards provide that:

4.1   An Athlete may be granted a TUE if (and only if) he/she can show, on the balance of probabilities, that each of the following conditions is met:

Article 5.   Testing and Investigations

. . . .

5.2 Authority to Test

Any Athlete may be required to provide a [urine or blood] Sample at any time and at any place by any Anti-Doping Organization with Testing authority over him or her [except that, subject to further qualifications, only one organization shall have testing authority over an athlete during an event]. . . .

5.5 Athlete Whereabouts Information

[Covered Athletes] . . . shall provide whereabouts information in the manner specified in the International Standard for Testing and Investigations . . . .[g]

COMMENTS AND QUESTIONS

1. WADA's approach. Under Article 4.3.1 of the WADA Code, a substance is subject to prohibition if two of the following three conditions are satisfied: (1) it has the potential to enhance sport performance, (2) it presents a health risk to the user, or (3) it violates "the spirit of sport." Putting aside substances that might be prohibited as masking agents under section 4.3.2, do you think many substances would be prohibited that do not satisfy the first condition? If not, is it fair to say, as a practical matter, that a substance is subject to prohibition if (1) it has the potential to enhance sport performance and (2) it either (a) presents a health risk to the user or (b) violates the spirit of sport?

2. The spirit of sport. Insofar as the characterization of the WADA approach proposed in the preceding question is apt, how different is it from the suggestion, explored at the start of this subchapter, that a PED should (or may) be prohibited either if it is harmful to the user or if its use threatens to degrade challenges that the sport presents? The most obvious difference is that WADA defines or describes "the spirit of sport" by reference to a laundry list of values

---

a. The Prohibited Substance or Prohibited Method in question is needed to treat a diagnosed medical condition supported by relevant clinical evidence.

b. The Therapeutic Use of the Prohibited Substance or Prohibited Method will not, on the balance of probabilities, produce any additional enhancement of performance beyond what might be anticipated by a return to the Athlete's normal state of health following the treatment of the medical condition.

c. The Prohibited Substance or Prohibited Method is an indicated treatment for the medical condition, and there is no reasonable permitted Therapeutic alternative.

d. The necessity for the Use of the Prohibited Substance or Prohibited Method is not a consequence, wholly or in part, of the prior Use (without a TUE) of a substance or method which was prohibited at the time of such Use.

WADA, WORLD ANTI-DOPING CODE, INTERNATIONAL STANDARD: THERAPEUTIC USE EXEMPTIONS Art. 4.1 (2021).

g   The International Standard for Testing and Investigations is complicated. The basic idea is that athletes have an affirmative obligation to keep the applicable anti-doping organizations up to date on their whereabouts so that no-notice testing could be conducted at any time.

and ideals. How helpful is that list? Does it help you determine whether some substance that you feel uncertain or conflicted about (steroids? amphetamines? EPO? beta blockers?) should or should not be prohibited? Could you furnish better guidance?

3.   *Discretion?* If a substance meets two or three of the criteria, on what basis, if any, could WADA decide legitimately *not* to include it on the prohibited list? Given Article 4.3.1, should red meat be on the prohibited list?

4.   *Masking agents.* Article 4.3.2 specifically directs that potential masking agents be prohibited. Is that a sound decision? Should penalties vary depending on whether an athlete is shown to have ingested a substance prohibited under Article 4.3.1 or under Article 4.3.2?

5.   *Mistakes?* What if an athlete believes that a substance has been placed on the prohibited list erroneously? Article 4.3.3 provides that

> WADA's determination of the Prohibited Substances and Prohibited Methods that will be included on the Prohibited List, the classification of substances into categories on the Prohibited List, and the classification of a substance as prohibited at all times or In-Competition only, is final and shall not be subject to challenge by an athlete or other Person based on an argument that the substance or method was not a masking agent or did not have the potential to enhance performance, represent a health risk or violate the spirit of sport.

What considerations speak for and against this rule? If you think it's unnecessarily harsh, how would you improve it?

6.   *Strict liability.* Article 2 clearly imposes strict liability for ingestion of a prohibited substance. Generally, strict liability is strongly disfavored in the law. Is it justifiable in this context? Although neither WADA nor a governing sports body need establish fault on the part of an athlete whose urine or blood samples reveal a prohibited substance, penalties can be increased if the regulator establishes that violation was intentional or knowing, or reduced if the athlete establishes that they were faultless or merely negligent. See Article 10. Is this an appropriate compromise of sorts— liability attaches strictly, but the magnitude of penalty is sensitive to the user's mental state?

7.   *The burden and standard of proof.* WADA Article 3.1 provides that regulatory authorities charging an athlete with doping

> shall have the burden of establishing that an anti-doping rule violation has occurred . . . to the comfortable satisfaction of the hearing panel, bearing in mind the seriousness of the allegation which is made. This standard of proof in all cases is greater than a mere balance of probability but less than proof beyond a reasonable doubt.

Is "comfortable satisfaction" an adequately clear standard, either on its own terms or when supplemented with the note that it's more than a mere balance of probability but less than beyond a reasonable doubt? Could you do better?

8. *Enhancing treatment.* Suppose an athlete proposes to use a prohibited substance only to return her to her normal state of health after a significant impairment, but that doing so will in all probability enhance her athletic performance beyond its prior level. Is it appropriate to grant her a therapeutic use exemption?

9. *Testing, testing.* How often should covered athletes be required to provide blood or urine samples? Is some number of tests too many? Can anti-doping organizations assure athletes that testing won't be too onerous or intrusive without undermining their commitment to a no-notice testing policy?

10. *From enforcement back to prohibition.* Schneider and Butcher maintain that testing requirements constitute "an extreme intrusion into the private lives of athletes," and that they "can only be warranted by the need to protect others from serious harm." Does this brief encounter with the WADA rules and practices strengthen or weaken that claim? Does it matter whether participation in high-level sports is a "right" or a "privilege"? Do you agree with Schneider and Butcher that the permissibility of an intensive testing regime depends on a perception that sports are different from other activities?

11. *Therapy for Sharapova?* In 2015, WADA banned Meldonium, sometimes sold under the name Mildronate, effective January 1, 2016. Meldonium, which is prescribed in Eastern Europe but not approved in the United States or Western Europe, is used to treat ischemia, a lack of blood flow to parts of the body, especially to the heart. It increases exercise capacity in athletes, and WADA added it to the Prohibited List "because of evidence of its use by athletes with the intention of enhancing performance." The very first month of the ban, Maria Sharapova tested positive for Meldonium, which she had been taking regularly for more than a decade; a Russian doctor whom she consulted after suffering from frequent cold-related illnesses, tonsil-related problems, and upper abdominal pain, had prescribed it as part of a comprehensive regime. The doctor indicated she should take it on the day of competition and that she could, with consultation, up the dosage for matches "of special importance." Sharapova ended her consultation with that doctor in 2013, but continued taking Meldonium—including on the day of each of her five matches at the Australian Open, which inevitably led to her being caught; remarkably, she had been unaware of the change of rules. The violation led to a two-year suspension, later reduced to fifteen months. *See generally International Tennis Federation v. Sharapova,* CAS 2016/A/4643, https://tinyurl.com/y4bm63ld. Suppose Sharapova had been aware of the prospective ban and had applied for a TUE. Should it have been granted? Why or why not?

12. *Penalties.* It's impossible to say succinctly what the actual penalties for prohibited doping are. One thing that's clear is that "[a]n anti-doping rule violation in Individual Sports in connection with an In-Competition test

automatically leads to Disqualification of the result obtained in that Competition with all resulting Consequences, including forfeiture of any medals, points and prizes." Article 9. But the length of time for which an athlete will be suspended from competition can vary greatly, from a few months to permanent ineligibility. See generally Article 10. What factors should bear on the length of a suspension?

Consider the case of Chinese swimmer, and six-time Olympic medalist, Sun Yang. In 2014, Sun was suspended by Chinese authorities for three months after he tested positive for a banned substance, and suspicions of continued doping had followed him since. At the 2016 World Championships, fellow medalists refused to shake his hand or join him on the medals podium. Then, in September 2018, when antidoping officials tried to get samples from Sun at his home, he refused to supply a urine sample and his mother directed a member of his entourage to destroy a vial containing his blood with a hammer. In response, WADA imposed an eight-year ban, effectively ending Sun's career. The Court of Arbitration for Sport upheld the ban, *see* Victor Mather, Karen Crouse & Tariq Panja, *Sports Court Hands Chinese Olympic Swimmer an 8-year Doping Ban,* N.Y. TIMES, Feb. 29, 2020, at B8, but ten months later a Swiss court overturned the CAS's decision on the ground that one of the arbitrators who had upheld the ban had made racist comments about China on social media, thereby putting his neutrality into doubt. Tariq Panja, *Chinese Swimmer's Doping Ban Is Lifted After Accusation of Racism,* N.Y. Times, Dec. 23, 2020. The Swiss court held that the ban could be reinstated if upheld by a newly constituted arbitration panel. What should the CAS rule?

13. *Effectiveness.* A bottom-line verdict about whether a regime of PED regulation is justified probably depends, in part, on its effectiveness. What would make a regulatory regime effective? How effective do you think current schemes are, in sports with which you're familiar? Have you any idea how effectiveness could be measured?

Exercise 8C

Like their counterparts in many sports, two of the leading regulatory authorities that govern golf, the United States Golf Association (USGA) and the International Golf Federation (IGF) have, with minor modifications, adopted WADA rules and their associated international standards. *See* USGA, *Anti-Doping Policy for the United States Gold Association,* https://tinyurl.com/y69fsum2; IGF, *Medical & Anti-Doping Documentation/Regulations,* https://tinyurl.com/yxdlwvvg. Suppose, however, that these governing bodies were to consider going their own way. Write a set of principles or standards to govern the crafting of new rules. Among other topics, make sure to address: the considerations that determine whether a substance will be prohibited or permitted, the use of oxygen chambers, the schedule of penalties, and the role of athletes in the ongoing project of amending and implementing the rules.

CHAPTER 9

PROBLEMS OF LEAGUE AND TOURNAMENT PLAY

■ ■ ■

Thus far, we have focused primarily on the structure of competitions between two individuals or two teams. But much of organized competition is among more than two contestants. A tournament might be held over a weekend, for example, or numerous teams may compete for a championship over a season. How to structure such competitions raises numerous issues. This chapter focuses on two: First (Subchapter 9A), to what extent and in what ways, are and should leagues be structured to promote "parity" or a "level playing field" or "competitive balance"? Second (Subchapter 9B), how should tournaments and postseason play be structured?

A. LEAGUES AND PARITY

A central question that every sports league confronts concerns the extent to which league rules should either respect competitive advantages naturally accruing to particular clubs, by virtue, say, of their wealth or location, or try to counteract or dampen them to promote "parity." The principal levers that league can use in an attempt to promote (or retard) a trend towards parity are rules governing club finances and player assignment.

1. COMPETITIVE BALANCE

All teams in a professional sports league want to win on the field; winning provides a healthy return on the investment necessary to build a strong team, and nobody wants to waste money. Nevertheless, absent regulation, franchises in a given sports league often vary substantially in the amount of money they spend on players. This is for at least two reasons. First, some owners run their teams to maximize competitive success rather than to maximize profits. They will therefore be willing to use other resources to subsidize their teams, and wealthier owners have greater resources on which to draw. Second, teams can earn widely varying revenue based not only on factors largely within their control (like how efficiently they are managed) but also on factors that are significantly outside their control (like the population of the metropolitan areas in which they are located); the return on a given investment is likely to be greater in a big market than in a small one.

Leagues that want to reduce the impact of wealth disparities on competitive performance have used a variety of tools. Chief among the modern ones are salary caps and revenue sharing, both of which come in more modest or extreme versions. Salary caps are "hard" or "soft." A hard cap sets a firm upper limit to aggregate player salaries; a soft cap can be exceeded, but at the cost of incurring a "luxury tax," which is usually distributed to other clubs. Revenue sharing is more or less extreme depending upon the percentage of total revenues potentially available to each club that is shared. Clubs obtain revenue from national and local broadcasting agreements, gate receipts, concessions sold at games, joint-marketing agreements, and sales of licensed merchandise. Some or all of these sources of revenues can be subjected to sharing.

It is generally agreed that, of the four major American sports leagues, the NFL takes the most aggressive measures to reduce the competitive impact of disparities in club wealth, with a hard salary cap and significant (but not complete) revenue sharing. MLB takes the least aggressive measures, with modest revenue sharing and a very soft salary cap. In 2019, the Boston Red Sox, defending World Series champs, carried an aggregate player payroll of $226.3 million, compared to an MLB mean of $135.5 million and median of $126.7 million, and over three and a half times that of the tight-spending Tampa Bay Rays. The NBA and the NHL sit between these two poles. The English Premier League has salary disparities even greater than MLB: total spending by top clubs like Manchester United, Manchester City, Chelsea, and Arsenal can run as high as ten times that of bottom dwellers like Norwich City, Swansea City, and Southampton. *Premier League Guide*, SPORTING INTELLIGENCE.COM (Oct. 9, 2012), https://tinyurl.com/y5l9quto.

But are these measures really aimed at improving competitive balance? To the extent that is their aim, are they effective? And is competitive balance even a goal worth pursuing? Consider the following article.

AARON GORDON, THE MYTH OF COMPETITIVE BALANCE

sportsonearth.com, August 8, 2013
© 2013 MLB Advanced Media, L.P., reprinted with permission

. . . [There is a] commonly held belief that competitive balance is essential to the financial success of professional sports. . . . [A] long, unbroken chain of league commissioners . . . extol the virtues of parity and insist fans will not be interested in sports if these measures are not in place. . . .

The need for competitive balance is a myth: Fans will watch leagues without it, and even if they didn't, there's precious little evidence that leagues can do anything about it. There is one thing salary caps, revenue sharing, reverse-order drafts and luxury taxes do quite effectively: They transfer money from players to owners, increasing league profitability. . . .

[T]he concept of competitive balance is purposely vague. League commissioners and owners have rarely proposed their own clarifying definitions. The closest we have come was the Bud Selig-organized Blue Ribbon Panel On Baseball Economics to analyze the economic structure of Major League Baseball, which concluded: "Proper competitive balance should be understood to exist when there are no clubs chronically weak because of MLB's structural features. Proper competitive balance will not exist until every well-run club has a regularly recurring reasonable hope of reaching postseason play."

There are two separate but key concepts here to keep in the back of your head: That competitive balance is a function of the league's policies, and that if a club is well-run, it has a reasonable hope of basic success.

The former idea, that league policies affect the relative strength or weakness of clubs, has always been a part of sport history. [Gordon discusses the reserve clause, introduced into baseball in 1880 and followed by other major sports leagues, which bound the player to the owner for the player's entire player career. Owners argued in response to challenges that it was necessary to prevent the richest teams from acquiring a disproportionate share of player talent. But Gordon quotes Dean Chadwin, in *Those Damn Yankees: The Secret Life of America's Greatest Franchise*, that the reserve system "has enabled the best teams to squirrel away talented players in the minors where they can serve as insurance in case of injury, and more importantly be kept off the rosters of potential rivals."]

Even though the reserve system was largely a mechanism for the richest clubs to hoard talent and restrict labor costs—the very opposite of competitive balance—the argument had proven a worthy tool and received federal sanction.

. . . Today, the most discussed tools to promote competitive balance are concerned with keeping the top clubs from spending too much: salary caps, luxury taxes and revenue sharing. . . .

. . . [T]he preferred method of measuring competitive balance is looking at the distribution of wins over time. When sports economists do this, they almost invariably find that salary caps, luxury taxes and revenue sharing have no effect on competitive balance. John Vrooman found in his 1995 study that salary caps ironically promote competitive *imbalance* because [they] allow[ ] the league to behave as one entity, rather than each team acting as an individual firm. . . . Once MLB, for example, is a single entity, it's primarily concerned with the health of the entire league. So it institutes policies that may shuffle money around to make unprofitable teams profitable, but it doesn't mandate they become more competitive . . . .

[Sports economist Dave Berri] stated unequivocally in a 2011 blog post: "We found that none of these institutions [salary caps, luxury taxes, etc.] had any statistically significant impact on balance in any of these leagues [NBA, NHL, NFL, and MLB]." . . . [A] host of studies echo[es] the same conclusion: league policies don't affect competitive balance to any measurable degree. . . .

Even in the most unbalanced league, the best team almost always loses some games (thank you, 2007 New York Giants) and the worst teams almost always win some games (damn you, 2008 Detroit Lions). What the competitive balance debate really entails is probabilities of winning. Along those lines, as long as there's at least a slim probability of either team winning, fans remain interested.

To illustrate this point, Berri pointed out to me the amount of fan interest in the first two rounds of the NCAA tournament or regular season college football, two venues of runaway competitive imbalance, yet also two of the most popular American sporting spectacles. We watch sports for a multitude of reasons, one of which is to witness the improbable. (While on the subject, you rarely hear NCAA officials pining for greater competitive balance, perhaps because their labor costs are already zero.)

When I spoke to [sports economist J.C. Bradbury], he was unequivocal in his belief that the need for competitive balance is a myth. "If there was no uncertainty of outcome, yes that would be a problem for revenue. But we're nowhere near close to that point. So when owners say, 'look we don't have competitive balance, if we don't win more no one is going to come, therefore I need salary caps so that I can afford to pay players as much money,' that's really just a PR argument to try and hold down labor costs."
. . .

It's easy to imagine tormented fanbases caring deeply about competitive balance. Indeed, [a study by Martin Schmidt and Berri, *Competitive Balance and Attendance: The Case of Major League Baseball*, 2 J. SPORTS ECON. 145 (2001),] backs them up. It seems fans care about competitive balance to a statistically significant degree over three- and five-year stretches, implying fans don't mind waiting until next year to see their team win as long as every year doesn't become the proverbial "next year."

But remember the Blue Ribbon Panel's definition of competitive balance: ". . . when there are no clubs chronically weak *because of MLB's structural features*. Proper competitive balance will not exist until every *well-run club* has a regularly recurring reasonable hope of reaching postseason play" (emphasis mine). As the data has shown, clubs aren't weak *because* of a league's structural features; they're weak *independent of* what structural features leagues implement. In fact, the definition itself is circular. A well-run club can, by definition, field a competitive team by finding labor market inefficiencies to exploit. There have been far more small-market clubs able to do so than those that have lost money in any given year over the past three decades. "Moneyball" is the most obvious, culturally relevant and sexy example here, but it's hardly the most important.

Every year and in every sport, teams hire students straight from graduate school into their analytics departments . . . . Yes, the rich teams are hiring, too, but that's not all that important. The whole point of the statistical revolution is to properly value players based on what they contribute on the field, which is largely independent of market size or team revenue. Forget Hollywood's portrayal, the statistical revolution hasn't been about rich teams versus poor teams; it's about not overpaying, which is what salary caps and luxury taxes have been trying to prevent. In some ways, advanced statistics are accomplishing what lockouts, luxury taxes and salary caps have been attempting for decades. One of the reasons these league policies haven't affected competitive balance is because spending more money on players than they're worth isn't a good strategy for winning games.

To be fair, there is one measure leagues can implement that Berri acknowledges helps competitive balance . . .: the salary floor, or the mandatory minimum spending on players each team had to meet per year [under the 1993 NFL Collective Bargaining Agreement]. . . .

Similarly, reverse-order drafts are often—but not unanimously—believed to increase competitive balance, although to what degree is often contested. This is because—unlike revenue sharing which simply shuffles money around—drafts reallocate talent. But teams always have the choice of "selling" that talent for more prospects and picks as that talent demands higher salaries in future contracts. If the team is only interested in profits, this won't help it improve on the field.

However, salary floors don't come with that option. Teams simply must spend money on players, so they might as well try and do it on good ones. . . .

Salary caps and revenue sharing accomplish very calculated and important goals for league offices with massive payoffs, the same goal they've been fighting for since the inception of the reserve clause more than 130 years ago: to systematically lower player salaries. In 2003, Rodney Fort published a theoretical work showing that redistributing revenues from rich teams to poor teams will make winning less valuable for all teams, and therefore make labor less valuable as well. What he showed was that if the benefits of winning (money) are spread out more evenly, then everyone has less incentive to win and therefore will spend less money on players to try and win.

In a 2007 study [*Leveling the Playing Field or Just Lowering Salaries? The Effects of Redistribution in Baseball*, 73 SO. ECON. J. 947], John Solow and Anthony Krautmann . . . found that "[revenue] redistribution lowered [player] salaries by approximately 22 percent without affecting league balance." A 1998 study [Paul D. Staudohar, *Salary Caps in Professional Team Sports*, 3 COMPENSATION AND WORKING CONDITIONS 3, 10 (1998)] . . . examined the four major U.S. sports, and found, "Salary caps and payroll taxes may seem beneficial to owners, but their effects appear to be more symbolic and cosmetic than fundamental." . . .

However, to understand that salary caps restrict labor costs, one needs to look no further than the name itself: It is a cap on salaries.

If salary caps and revenue sharing don't affect competitive balance, what does? Berri had a simple answer: "Outcomes are determined by talent and luck." Since luck is, by definition, outside of human control, competitive balance is affected by the size of the talent pool the league is drawing from. The biggest changes to competitive balance happened during major supply shocks, such as integration in baseball, or widespread scouting in other countries.

In his seminal paper, [Berri et al., *The Short Supply of Tall People: Competitive Imbalance and the National Basketball Association*, 39 J. ECON. ISSUES 1029 (2005)], Berri articulates this argument right in the title in intuitive fashion as it pertains to the NBA. The NBA has been the least competitive league for some time because there are only so many athletic seven-footers, and there's nothing a salary cap or luxury tax can do about that. Those seven-footers (or the select few transcendent talents such as LeBron James or the unparalleled Andrea Bargnani) can be shuffled from team to team, but there will always be a few teams with them and many without.

But this made me wonder why we don't hear European soccer leagues talk more about competitive balance, even though they draw from a global talent pool. Berri's answer was the simplest one he could give: It would be illegal for them. You see, those darn socialists in the European Union make their sports leagues abide by all the same labor laws as every other industry: You can't own the rights to a worker before he signs a contract, you can't collude to determine how much money you will spend on employee salaries in order to artificially lower their value, and you can't penalize each other for spending too much money on employees.

(Some might counter this point by gesticulating feverishly at Financial Fair Play (FFP), which is basically an initiative to stop clubs from going into massive debt by signing players to heaping piles of money. FFP won't allow clubs to transfer money to each other, and it doesn't stop clubs backed by wealthy sponsors/oil billionaires/conglomerates/actual countries to simply even out the club's finances with their own pockets. On the contrary, it will likely widen the gap between small and large clubs, since smaller clubs, almost by definition, don't have wealthy backers to boost their bottom line, and they won't be permitted to take financial risks to climb the standings. Financial Fair Play is, in sum, very similar in spirit to what we have seen in the United States: a way for leagues to ensure clubs don't lose money, and not much else.)

The other wrinkle European soccer offers is the promotion and relegation system, combined with qualifying for lucrative tournaments based on the end-of-season standings, which keep fans interested in contests aside from the top of the standings. Beyond that, it creates a compelling incentive for most clubs to get results, lest they face the stiff financial penalty of relegation or not qualifying for an international tournament. This adds intrigue to contests that might be competitively imbalanced, in the American sense, because the bottom of the standings matter just as much (if not more) than the top.

COMMENTS AND QUESTIONS

1.   *What* is *parity?* For all the talk of parity and its importance, it is not entirely clear what parity means. The term is often used to encompass two distinct ideas: intra-seasonal competitiveness (roughly, the idea that, within a given season, the gap between the best teams and the worst teams shouldn't be very great), and inter-seasonal churn (the idea that, over the medium term, bad teams can become good and vice versa, or that no team is destined to long-term lack of success due to factors beyond its control). "Any given Sunday!" is an apt motto for proponents of intra-seasonal competitiveness, while "Wait 'til next year!" is a slogan for enthusiasts for churn. If you are disposed to think that parity is valuable in team sports, which notion—competitiveness or churn—do you think is more important?

2.   *How to measure it?* How can these different parity concepts be measured? Take churn. Is churn best reflected by the percentage of teams that make postseason play, or that win the league championship, over some X-year period? Or by something else? Gordon seems to suggest that churn is a function of "the distribution of wins over time." But how should *that* be measured? The percentage of teams with won-loss records between, say, 40% and 60%? Something else? The Schmidt & Berri study mentioned by Gordon uses the Gini Coefficient, which is often used to measure inequality in income or wealth. Imagine a graph with the horizontal axis running from 0 to 1 (or 100%), 0 representing the poorest person in the population and 1 representing the richest. The vertical axis represents cumulative percentage of total wealth held by the x poorest people. So the distribution is represented by a curve that starts at (0,0) and ends at (1,1) (because the entire population holds all the wealth). Perfect equality is represented by a 45° line (because the poorest 5% have 5% of the income, the poorest 10% have 10% of the income, etc.) The area between

the actual curve and this equality line, multiplied by 2, is the Gini Coefficient; it runs from zero (representing perfect equality), to 1 (representing perfect inequality, or all wealth held by one person). The Gini can easily be applied to the population of teams in a league and their wins in a season, or over a course of seasons.

3.   *Financial (un)fair play?* In 2009 the Union of European Football Associations (UEFA) introduced a new "break-even" financial requirement for clubs to be eligible to participate in the most prestigious and lucrative club tournament in the sport, the UEFA Champions League. The new Financial Fair Play (FFP) rules, discussed by Gordon, essentially limited the amount a club could spend on new player purchases and wages to no more than their incomed earned through sporting activities. The stated purpose of the regulations was to ensure long-term viability, a response to a relatively new trend of increased club debts resulting from wealthy investors purchasing small clubs looking to raise their global profile. Similar regulations were subsequently enacted for participation in Europe's five largest domestic soccer leagues.

The regulations have been controversial since implementation, with many questioning their legality under EU Sports Law. More important for our purposes however is the controversy stemming from an alleged decrease in parity and the creation of a "cartel of elite clubs" as a consequence of the regulations. Tom Serby, *The state of EU sports law: lessons from UEFA's 'Financial Fair Play' regulations*, 16 INTL. SPORTS L.J. 37 (2016). Financial Fair Play in effect created a salary cap that is proportional to a club's income. The obvious consequence of such a cap is vast disparity in funds available for player acquisitions. For context, in 2020 the revenue of top earner FC Barcelona (€840.8m) was over €300m higher than that of the ninth highest earner Chelsea (€513.1), with Europe's smaller clubs earning far less. DELOITTE FOOTBALL MONEY LEAGUE 23RD EDITION (2020). Many economists have pointed out that these restrictions function as a barrier to entry for clubs looking to challenge the historical elite, ensuring the current power hierarchies remain fixed. It has been alleged the rules were constructed in part to curb the rise of clubs like Manchester City and Paris Saint-Germain, whose record-breaking expenditures corresponded to on field successes threatening Europe's traditionally elite clubs.

Is the alleged lack of parity a reason to oppose these regulations? Is the fact that these regulations seem to benefit a select few clubs, impeding inter-seasonal churn, the fundamental issue? What about Leicester City, not a traditional European powerhouse, winning the 2016 English Premier League despite bookmakers giving them a 5000/1 chance before the season? What are the downsides of allowing wealthy owners to invest heavily in newly acquired clubs?

4.   *Whose benefit?* Are you persuaded by Gordon's argument that salary caps, luxury taxes, revenue sharing, and reserve clauses do not actually improve competitive balance (in the sense of churn), but only transfer wealth

from players to owners? Are you persuaded by his argument that competitive balance is not necessary to draw fan interest? Can you think of professional franchises that did well financially during prolonged periods in which they were not serious championship contenders?

5.   *Of finances and fairness.* Gordon's stated aim is to investigate the "commonly held belief that competitive balance is essential to the financial success of professional sports." His verdict is that that's not so. But what about the argument that churn is an element of the fairness of a sports league? Is that a plausible supposition, in your view? Does Gordon address it satisfactorily?

6.   *Higher-value users.* As Gordon notes, reserve clauses essentially gave the team that signed an athlete exclusive rights to his services for his entire career. In a celebrated article in 1956, Simon Rottenberg contended that

> [t]he position of organized baseball that a free market, given the unequal distribution of revenue, will result in the engrossment of the most competent players by the wealthy teams is open to some question. It seems, indeed, to be true that a market in which freedom is limited by a reserve rule such as that which now governs the baseball labor market distributes players among teams about as a free market would.

As Rottenberg explained, the reason for this similarity is the possibility of sale:

> Each team determines whether to use a player's services itself or to sell him, according to the relative returns on him in the two uses. If the return will be higher from sale, he will be sold, and vice versa. Now, if he can be sold to another team for a price higher than his worth to his present team, it is because he is worth more to the team that buys him than to the team that sells him. It follows that players will be distributed among teams so that they are put to their most "productive" use; each will play for the team that is able to get the highest return from his services. But this is exactly the result which would be yielded by a free market. The difference is only that in a market subject to the reserve rule part of the price for the player's services is paid to the team that sells his contract, and part of his value is kept by the team that holds his contract; in the free market the player gets his full value.

Simon Rottenberg, *The Baseball Players' Labor Market*, 64 J. POL. ECON. 242, 255–56 (1956). As Allen R. Sanderson and John J. Siegfried have pointed out, *Simon Rottenberg and Baseball, Then and Now: A Fiftieth Anniversary Retrospective*, 114 J. POL. ECON. 594 (2006), Rottenberg anticipated the ***Coase Theorem*** four years before it was presented in a seminal article by Ronald H. Coase, *The Problem of Social Cost*, 3 J. LAW & ECON. 1 (1960). (Not only was this article a principal basis for the award to Coase of the 1991 Nobel Prize in Economics, it

Coase Theorem

is also (at least as of 2012) the most cited law review article ever. Fred R. Shapiro & Michelle Pearse, *The Most Cited Law Review Articles of All Time*, 110 MICH. L. REV. 1483 (2012).) The thesis that Coase developed in that paper holds roughly (there is no canonical formulation of the theorem in that paper) that where property rights are clearly defined, and in the absence of obstacles to the sale of property rights among private parties (what law and economics calls "transaction costs"), property rights will end up in the hands of the highest valuer regardless of where they are initially assigned. So, for example, if Verizon is the highest valuer of some frequencies in the radio spectrum that the government is set to allocate, Verizon will end up with those frequencies whether they are initially assigned to Verizon, or to a competitor, or to your Great Aunt Ruth. Therefore—and again assuming, counterfactually, zero transaction costs—the initial assignment of property rights does not matter from the perspective of economic efficiency.

As Rottenberg indicates, this does not mean that there will be "an engrossment" (i.e., an absorption) of the better players by the wealthier teams—but it does mean that disproportionally the better players will likely go to larger markets, where their value will be maximized. Most observers probably regard that as unfortunate. Standen argues otherwise: "Indeed, why wouldn't MLB want to have strong teams in big markets like Boston and New York? Don't all the teams profit, if indirectly, from the Yankees' big profits, both from revenue sharing and from large gates when New York is in town? Baseball would be crazy to run its league any other way." Do you agree? Are there principled arguments for or against measures designed to mitigate wealth effects, or is the only consideration of relevance what structure will maximize total league revenue?

Standen also points out that notwithstanding the supposed interest in parity, no league precludes all possible ways in which large-market or wealthy teams can exploit their advantages. For example, MLB allows teams to sell local broadcast and telecast rights, "thus providing a huge revenue boost to teams in large, fan-crazy markets." Even in the NFL, the most parity-oriented of leagues, wealth matters: Valuable franchises like the Cowboys and Patriots cannot offer greater salaries or sell local telecast and broadcast rights, "but they can offer benefits that are uncapped, such as superior training facilities, stadium quality and comfort, and, most importantly, coaching acumen. Coaching salaries are uncapped, so teams can compete for players in that market."

7. *Limitations on sales.* As Standen notes, a 40-year-old rule in baseball severely restricts the ability of teams to sell their contractual rights in a player to another club, by limiting the amount of cash that can be included in such a transaction. Standen contends that this rule helps impoverish poor teams by forcing them "to take back most of their trade revenue in the form of risky minor league players," rather than in the most flexible possible asset, cash. Do you agree? In international soccer, in contrast, clubs routinely pay each other multi-million dollar "transfer fees" for players. Since 2013, when Spanish Football powerhouse Real Madrid was reported to have paid Tottenham

Hotspur of the English Premier League a record €100 million for the rights to 24-year-old Welsh winger Gareth Bale, there have been a total of ten transfers with over €100 million in fees. Mark Doyle, *The 100 Most Expensive Football Transfers of All Time*, GOAL (Oct. 6, 2020). The current record stands at €222 million for the transfer of Neymar from the Spanish Club Barcelona to the French Club Paris Saint-Germain (PSG). While most of the highest grossing transfers occur between some of the largest and wealthiest clubs in the world, the second highest transfer exemplifies a practice—the transfer of young talent from small, regional clubs to large, internationally recognized clubs—that is also quite common: the €180 transfer of Kylian Mbappe from AS Monaco to PSG. Like Monaco, many other less-wealthy teams survive, and even thrive through developing and selling talent. Other mid-sized teams will buy players from smaller clubs and resell them to even larger clubs after the players gain experience. Are there good reasons why baseball should disallow this practice?

8.   *Moneyball?* In his bestselling 2003 book *Moneyball: The Art of Winning an Unfair Game,* later made into a movie, financial journalist Michael Lewis explored how a small-market baseball club, the Oakland A's, could remain competitive in a sport that lacked structural mechanisms designed to promote churn. Lewis's answer was that the A's, led by its general manager Billy Beane, moved into evidence-based analytics earlier and more forcefully than did their rivals, allowing them to assign players more accurate values and thus exploit market inefficiencies. Over time, however, and partly as a result of Lewis's book, other teams, including those with the deepest pockets, followed the A's into the "sabermetric" revolution. Commenting on this development, Gordon argues that the fact that the rich teams are now doing what, at first, only some small teams did, is "not all that important" because "[t]he whole point of the statistical revolution is to properly value players based on what they contribute on the field, which is largely independent of market size or team revenue." Do you think that Michael Lewis would agree? Would Billy Beane?

9.   *Parity in international competitions.* If you believe that it is a bug, and not a feature, of domestic sports leagues that disparities in wealth should translate into disparities in on-field success, then do you think the same is true of supranational and international athletic competitions? Should the IOC implement some form of revenue sharing between wealthier and poorer national Olympic committees? Why (not)? How would an optimal scheme of subsidization work?

10.   *Parity in other contexts.* If you believe that it is a bug, and not a feature, of domestic sports leagues that disparities in wealth should translate into disparities in on-field success, then do you think the same is true of competitions outside the athletic realm—such as elections for public office, and civil litigation? For example, constitutional obstacles aside, should spending on elections for public office be capped to minimize the impact of wealth? If so, should the cap be hard or soft? If a well-financed candidate spends extravagant sums, should the government subsidize competing campaigns? Should wealthier litigants be

compelled to contribute some portion of the money they spend on attorneys or experts to subsidize the ability of their poorer adversaries to employ attorneys and experts of their own?

    11. Relegation. As Gordon notes, European soccer leagues use a system of promotion and relegation. In the twenty-team English Premier League, for example, the three lowest-place teams each season are sent down to a lower-tier league, the English Football League Championship, and are replaced by the two top teams from the Championship, along with the winner of a playoff series among the third through sixth placed clubs in the Championship. What ends does promotion and relegation serve? As you read the rest of this chapter, consider whether any North American leagues (perhaps the NBA?) would benefit, in principle, from adopting the system. If you think promotion and relegation would be desirable, can you figure out how it could be implemented?

2. PLAYER ASSIGNMENT

    As Gordon notes, many observers believe that competitive balance is improved by a reverse-order draft. In such a draft, which is used by most professional American sports leagues, teams select players each round in reverse order of their finish the previous season. Round by round, that is, the worst team the previous year picks first and the best team picks last.

    Structuring a draft requires a set of rules to determine the order in which teams make their picks. In the NFL, for example, any expansion teams get the first picks; if there are two or more, the order is chosen at random. Then come teams that did not make the playoffs, in reverse order of their regular-season records. Teams that did make the playoffs are ordered by the round of the playoffs in which they were eliminated. Thus, the team that lost the Super Bowl gets the next-to-last pick, and the Super Bowl winner gets the last pick. A system of tie-breakers is included. One frill is that if two or more teams within the same status group have the same record then they "cycle" picks from one round to the next. In the 2008 draft, for example, four teams had finished the season 8–8. In the first round their order of selection was Arizona, Minnesota, Houston, and Philadelphia; in subsequent rounds, the leader of that group of four went to the bottom of it.

    Other variations are possible. For example, while in the NFL the last team to pick is the Super Bowl champion (and comparably, in MLS, it is the winner of the MLS Cup), in MLB order is determined by regular-season won-loss record regardless of postseason accomplishments. (Naturally, tie-breaking rules must be used to order teams with identical won-loss records.) Additionally, some leagues add or subtract draft picks based on various competitive considerations. Starting in 2012, MLB has given small-market teams extra picks in special "competitive balance" rounds shoehorned between the first and second, and second and third, rounds of the standard draft. The NFL awards "compensatory picks" to teams that have lost more or better free agent players during the offseason than they gained.

The most notable variation on this common theme is the "draft lottery" used in one form or another by the NBA, the NHL, and the WNBA. In a lottery, the top pick does not necessarily go to the team that is rated dead last. Instead, the worst *teams* (generally identified as those that missed the postseason the previous year) are entered into a lottery that will assign draft position. The most discussed of these systems—the NBA's—has undergone many changes since it was introduced in 1985. Under current rules, all 14 non-playoff teams are entered into a lottery to determine the top four picks. The lottery is weighted so that the three teams with the worst record have the best chance to win the top pick (14%) and the three teams with the best record among the 14 have the worst chance (1%). After the first four picks, the remainder of the first-round draft order is determined just by won-loss record, thus ensuring that the team with the worst record can do no worse than pick fifth. In the NBA, the lottery does not affect the order of picks in the second (and final) round.

Although there are many ways to structure a lottery system, the root justification for it is straightforward: it is used to deter teams from intentionally losing—"tanking"—in order to guarantee themselves rights to a highly coveted player who will be entering the draft, especially "once in a generation" players such as Shaquille O'Neal, Sidney Crosby, or Andrew Luck. (We discuss the ethics of tanking for draft position later, in Chapter 15.) Still, most observers believe that, in the NBA at least, the lottery hasn't cured the problem. In recent years, for example, the Philadelphia 76ers management has acknowledged trading away talented players to enhance their lottery position, and many other teams, from the New York Knicks to the Sacramento Kings, are widely perceived to sit their best (if not very good) players when out of playoff contention. There is good financial reason to tank. Two MIT economics professors have estimated that winning the draft lottery increases attendance by five percent during the five-year period following the draft, and have also found strong evidence that teams do tank. Christopher Walters & Tyler Williams, *To Tank or Not to Tank? Evidence from the NBA*, MIT SLOAN SPORTS ANALYTICS CONFERENCE (2012).

COMMENTS AND QUESTIONS

1.   Why drafts? Why employ drafts at all? Law firms don't draft lawyers out of law schools, and they would violate the antitrust laws if they did: lawyers and law firms find each other by bilateral agreement in a competitive market. Major League Baseball did not institute a draft for first-year players until 1965. Even today, European soccer leagues do not employ player drafts: teams are free to sign players as they wish—usually by buying contracts from teams in inferior leagues. What are the advantages and disadvantages of draft-based versus market-based player assignment schemes? Are there alternatives to both?

2. Major League Baseball and the international market. While Major League Baseball maintains a draft for first-year American, Canadian, and Puerto Rican players, international talent is signed through a market-based system. League rules allow teams to sign any international player as young as sixteen, so long as their total spending stays under a specified cap for each year. Jesse Sanchez, *Here's where top int'l prospects are signing*, MLB (July 3, 2019), https://tinyurl.com/y3bc4svv. Small market teams are awarded competitive balance picks (see p. 332, above), and are given a higher spending limit. What do you think explains the continuance of this bifurcated system?

Competition has pushed scouts to track Latin American players as young as ten years old and agree orally with players as young as thirteen or fourteen. This has had detrimental effects on player health and has limited the effectiveness of international scouting. Ben Balder, *Trainers, MLB Teams Unhappy With Current International Signing System*, BASEBALL AMERICA (June 26, 2019), https://tinyurl.com/y62y2kts. MLB has begun conversations to implement a separate twenty-round international draft in the near future. Ben Balder, *MLB Targeting International Draft As Soon As 2020*, BASEBALL AMERICA (July 17, 2019), https://tinyurl.com/y2ft4rfs. Is this the right response? And if international players should be drafted, is there good reason to maintain a separate draft for them? Interestingly, the current proposal would rotate by division each year—for example, giving the first five picks one year to the teams in the American League East, and the next year to another division.

3. From reality to fantasy. Two different types of draft are widely used by fantasy leagues: "snake" drafts in which the order of selection is determined at random, and the order of selection in even-numbered rounds is the reverse of the order in odd-numbered rounds; and "auction" drafts in which each team gets a fixed budget and players are auctioned off. What considerations speak for and against each system?[a] Which makes more sense—a snake draft in which the team that gets the first pick in the first round gets the last pick in the next round (and so on), or the system generally used in pro leagues, in which the worst teams (or group of teams) pick first each round? Or does each system make better sense for the context in which it is deployed?

4. Different strokes for different folks. More generally, is one of the four methods outlined above—a snake draft as used in fantasy leagues, an auction draft, an NFL-style strict reverse-order draft, or an NBA-style lottery system— generally superior, or is each well adapted to the particularities of the competitive situation to which it is applied? Should the best teams be determined based only on regular season performance or on post-season performance? How should ties between teams with identical records be broken?

---

[a] A public service announcement from one of your authors: auctions are way more fun and interesting than snake drafts. If you play fantasy sports but haven't tried an auction, you should! You can thank us later.

5.   Earlier, or more? Assuming that it is desirable to give an edge in a draft to teams that did relatively poorly in the previous season, should that be limited to the order in which teams pick in each round? Alternatively or additionally, should leagues give low-ranked teams more picks in early rounds? What considerations bear on whether competitive balance is better promoted by giving low-performing teams higher picks or more picks?

6.   Missing seasons. Suppose a league misses most, or all, of an entire season—maybe, say, because of a global pandemic. How should the following year's player assignment system be run? Should the teams pick in the same order they picked in the previous draft? Should picking be randomized? Should teams bid, auction-style, for draft position, with the auction revenues divided between league and players? Should the league institute a snake draft for just this year, and assign draft positions randomly? Do you have a better idea?

7.   Fixing the NBA lottery. In tacit recognition that the NBA has a tanking problem, the league office proposed in late 2013 to scrap the lottery and replace it with a system in which a team's draft position would be entirely detached from its performance on the court. Under the proposed system— termed "the wheel"—each of the 30 teams would pick in a specific draft slot exactly once every 30 years. As Zach Lowe explains:

> Each team would simply cycle through the 30 draft slots, year by year, in a predetermined order designed so that teams pick in different areas of the draft each year. Teams would know with 100 percent certainty in which draft slots they would pick every year, up to 30 years out from the start of every 30-year cycle. . . .

The NBA's Possible Solution for Tanking: Good-bye to the Lottery, Hello to the Wheel, GRANTLAND (Dec. 23, 2013). The system is simpler to understand in pictorial form. Below is the wheel that outlines the order in which each team would cycle through the draft slots, showing that every team would be guaranteed one top-six pick every five seasons, and at least one top-12 pick in every four-year span:

27, 24, 13, 12, 1, 30, 19, 18, 7, 6, 25, 23, 14, 11, 2, 29, 20, 17, 8, 5, 26, 22, 15, 10, 3, 28, 21, 16, 9, 4,

Put another way: The team that gets the no. 1 pick in the very first year of this proposed system would draft in the following slots over the system's first six seasons: 1st, 30th, 19th, 18th, 7th, 6th. Just follow the wheel around clockwise to see the entire 30-year pick cycle of each team, depending on their starting spoke in Year 1.

In 2014, NBA owners rejected the wheel proposal, largely out of concern that weak teams could be stuck in rebuilding mode for over a decade. But the league has continued to tinker with the lottery.

In the spring of 2015, FiveThirtyEight.com asked readers to submit their own reform proposals and received nearly 7000 suggestions in response. Jody Avirgan, *How to Stop NBA Tanking: Tie Your Fate to Another Team's Record*, FIVETHIRTYEIGHT.COM (May 13, 2015). Here, in random order and in the proposers' own words, are the top four, as chosen by the website editors. (The first one presented was conceived by a student in the Jurisprudence of Sport course taught by one of the authors at the University of Pennsylvania Law School.)

1.   The Tombstone Date (submitted by Brett Schwab, Philadelphia)

Lottery balls would be determined by Elimination Wins. Elimination Wins are victories that occur *after* a team has been officially eliminated from playoff contention. *Tombstone Day is the day your team is eliminated from any possibility of making the playoffs. Whichever team gets the most wins AFTER their Tombstone Day gets the most lottery balls.*

A 2015 example:

- The Sixers were mathematically eliminated from playoff contention on March 19th. March 19th is their Tombstone Day. From March 19th on, the Sixers had 2 victories.

- The Magic were eliminated on March 25th. From their Tombstone Day on, the Magic had 3 victories.

- The Hornets were eliminated on April 10th. From their Tombstone Day on, the Hornets had 0 victories.

Under this system, the Magic would have the most lottery balls and thus higher odds of winning the draft.

2.   The Lottery Playoff (submitted by Chad, Champaign-Urbana)

At the end of the season, all playoff teams get a week off to rest and game plan. During that week, the 14 lottery teams play a single elimination bracket tournament for draft picks (the two teams with the best records get byes). *The winner of the tournament gets the first pick in the draft, second place gets the second pick. The rest of the teams are slotted according to record with the best teams getting higher picks.* So theoretically, every lottery team has a shot at the first pick, but if you lose a tournament game, it is in your best interest to have the most wins as possible, in order to be ranked higher than other teams.

Pros: Playoff teams have a chance to rest up before the big show. One and done games are magical. It's a playoff before the playoffs. Imagine two teams actually playing for the next MJ, instead of watching a dude grab balls out of a machine hoping for a chance to draft him.

Cons: None. You're welcome.

3.   The Tweaked Wheel (submitted by Adam Rosenthal, Seattle)

I propose a "draft number," which would be calculated by adding a number generated by a "wheel" approach to the number representing the team's reverse ranking in the standings. For example, a team with a wheel value of 17 that finished eighth-worst in the NBA standings would get a draft number of $17 + 8 = 25$. The lowest draft number would get the lowest pick, the second-lowest number would get the second-lowest pick, etc. Ties would be broken by the team with the lower wheel number.

4.   The NBA Futures (Samuel B. Feldblum & Cody Cutting, New York)

In a nutshell: Teams tank because they own their own picks. We could eliminate tanking by creating a world in which nobody owned their own pick, but instead owned stock market-style futures on other teams'. Teams get to pick other teams' finishing positions in the following year as their own. The worst team gets to pick the team whose draft position they would like to have next year (not their own), next the second worst team would pick whose draft position they want, etc.

Which method do you prefer—the existing system, the wheel, one of the four new proposals, or something else? Why?

B. ADVANCEMENT: BRACKET
PLAY AND POSTSEASONS

For many sports leagues, "the season" really comprises two seasons: the regular season and the postseason. A fundamental task for any league, accordingly, is to determine what the relationship between these two seasons should be. The central questions, perhaps, are: First, how hard or easy should it be to make the postseason? Second and relatedly, to what extent should the postseason be structured to advantage the teams that performed best during the regular season? This section explores the considerations and tradeoffs that properly bear on the answers to these questions. It also deals with closely related questions bearing on the organization of tournaments. Many tournaments, from the youth level all the way to the World Cup, are based on pool play and then bracket, or knockout, competition. A league's regular season can be thought of as an extended round of pool play, and the postseason is in essence the knockout phase of a tournament.

As an empirical matter, sports leagues vary considerably in how they structure their postseasons, although the trend in American sports is to increase the percentage of teams that qualify for postseason play.[b] For much of its history, for example, Major League Baseball's postseason consisted only of the championship series (oddly named the World Series) between the top teams in the American and National Leagues. For the last handful of years under this system, there were twenty major league teams, meaning that only 10% of teams made the postseason. MLB added rounds of postseason play in 1969 and then again in 1994. With the addition of a single-elimination wildcard game for each league in 2012, one third of MLB clubs (10 out of 30) make the postseason; in the COVID season of 2020, 16 teams made it. For comparison, about 40% of NFL teams now make the playoffs (14 out of 32), and 16, or about half of all teams, in the NBA and NHL do (30 teams in the NBA; 32 in the NHL beginning in 2021). In the top level of American college football (NCAA's Division I Football Bowl Subdivision) nearly 60 percent of all teams play in a postseason bowl game (70 out of 120).

Joe Posnanski, in *It's All About October* (Oct. 29, 2012), https://tinyurl. com/y6kqk5t6, explores the effects of the long-term trend by which Major

---

[b] The NHL is a striking counterexample to this trend. From 1943 through 1967, it consisted of only six teams (the Montreal Canadiens, Toronto Maple Leafs, Boston Bruins, Chicago Black Hawks, Detroit Red Wings, and New York Rangers), but sent four to the playoffs. If the teams were of roughly equal ability, you'd expect each to reach the postseason two of every three years. Those are good odds! In fact, though, three teams—the Canadiens, Maple Leafs, and Red Wings—averaged far better than that, while the other three fared much worse. (The Canadiens missed the playoffs just once in twenty-five years.) This disparity was due to a player assignment rule that gave each franchise exclusive negotiating rights to players located within 50 miles of its home ice. Because Canada developed so much more hockey talent than the States did, the Canadian teams enjoyed a massive built-in advantage against the U.S.-based teams, except for Detroit, which could draw from southwestern Ontario.

League Baseball has come to create an extensive tournament-like postseason. Until 1968, there were no preliminary playoff rounds—as just noted, there was only the World Series, between the champions of the two leagues. With the expansion of each league to twelve teams in 1969, and with the other major American team sports "chock full of playoff games," MLB divided each league in two and added the league championship series. At first these series were best-of-five, and later they were changed to best-of-seven. But a team still had to win its division or go home. That changed, though, beginning in 1994: the owners decided instead to divide each league into three divisions, creating an extra round of playoffs in which the division winners and one wild-card team from each league would compete. (As it turned out, there was no postseason in 1994 because of a labor stoppage.) And in 2012 they added a second wild-card team in each league; now the two play a single game for the right to compete against the division winners. And what has the effect been? As Posnanski says, "the natural progression of things" dictates that "[t]he more inclusive the playoffs, the less important the regular season." Some of his numbers are striking, though subsequent developments may make them somewhat less so:

- From 1903 through 1968, the team with the best record in baseball won the World Series a little more than 50% of the time.

- When four teams made the playoffs, from 1969 through 1993 (no postseason in 1994), the team with the best record in baseball won the World Series 28% of the time (7 out of 25).

- From 1995 through 2012, when he wrote, the team with the best record had won the World Series 17% of the time (3 out of 18) and one of those winners, the 2007 Red Sox, actually tied for the best record. (From 2013 through 2020, the team with the best record won the Series 4 times out of 8, with the 2013 Red Sox again tying for the best record. So the total from 1995 through 2020 is 7 out of 26, almost the same as in the 1969–93 period.)

And, he notes, of the 21 teams since 1995 that have won 100 or more games in a season, only two (the 1998 and 2009 Yankees) won the World Series and fourteen did not even reach it. (In the 2013–20 period, 11 teams won 100 or more games, 3 of them (the 2016 Cubs, 2017 Astros, and 2018 Red Sox) won the Series, and 2 others lost it; 4 of the 100+ teams that didn't make it to the Series played in the same league as a 100+ team that did. Also, the 2020 Dodgers, whose record in the COVID-shortened 2020 regular season corresponded to 116 wins for a full-length season, won that year's Series.)

Meanwhile, television viewership for the World Series has been in "free fall"—from an average of 37.6 million viewers in 1973–82 to an average of 17.2 million in 2003–12. And yet "baseball as a live spectator sport is in a golden era," with record-breaking ticket sales, a result that Posnanski says "is directly connected to the expanded playoffs with more teams having a shot at the postseason."

Given these changes in the game, Posnanski wonders whether teams have to change as well, to peak in the postseason. He points to the recent record of the San Francisco Giants. In 2010, the Giants had the fifth-best record in baseball, but won the World Series, largely on the strength of superb post-season pitching. In 2012, they were in a three-way tie for the fourth-best record in baseball, but again they won the Series, largely on the basis of heroics by pitchers who had been mediocre during much of the regular season. Posnanski wrote his piece in 2012, but his analysis of the Giants held true once again in 2014. The Giants finished the regular season with an 88–74 record—good, but hardly great. They had to win a wild-card game in Pittsburgh to advance further in the playoffs, and they did, 8–0. They then won three games (all by one run) out of four to eliminate Washington and four out of five (two of them shutouts) over St. Louis to reach the World Series. There, they faced the Kansas City Royals—itself a wild-card team, which had to come from behind in the bottom of the 12th inning against Oakland in the wild-card game to advance. The Giants won, four games to three, thanks in enormous part to the remarkable pitching of Madison Bumgarner. Bumgarner had had an excellent regular season—18 wins against 10 losses with a 2.98 ERA—but it did not foreshadow his amazing postseason. He shut out the Pirates in the wild-card game, threw 7 2/3 shutout innings in the first game of the LCS, and eight strong innings in the fifth and clinching game of that series. In the World Series, following up on a stellar performance in 2012, he pitched 21 innings, in three appearances, giving up exactly one run.

"It used to be," Posnanski says, "that you wanted to build the best team. Now, though, you want to build the best October team."

COMMENTS AND QUESTIONS

1.   October. Posnanski argues that Major League Baseball has made decisions over the past generation that "change the basic structure of a baseball season." Are you persuaded? Overall, are these changes for the better?

When baseball went to three divisions in each league, with one wild-card team in each league going into the playoffs, the wild-card team was essentially treated on an equal footing with the three division winners, but with the worst record among the four. Now that there are two wild-card teams in each league, advancement depends on the results of a single game, even if one team had a substantially better record than the other in the regular season. For example, in 2012, St. Louis won six fewer games than Atlanta during the regular season, but—with the help of that notorious call of an infield fly, *see* pp. 99–100—it won the wild-card game 6–3, and advanced. Is the new system fair? Is it an improvement?

2.   *Playing all competitors.* Before the baseball major leagues each expanded from eight teams to ten, each team played every other one in the league 22 times, half at each team's ballpark; expansion to ten teams brought the head-to-head number down to 18, but the schedule remained perfectly symmetrical. Now baseball more nearly resembles the other major American team sports: It features a divisional structure, with competition for wild-card spots as well as for divisional titles, and a limited amount of interleague play. As a result, a team may be competing for a position in post-season play against another team that has had a substantially different schedule. Moreover, those two teams may have played each other an odd number of times, meaning that one of the two has had a home-field advantage in their head-to-head competition. Are these asymmetries of concern?

The Big 12 Conference currently has ten schools. It used to have twelve— as the conference's name would suggest. The football season works differently with twelve schools from the way it does it does with ten. A twelve-team conference is divided into two six-team divisions. Each school plays all the others in its division and then plays some schools from the other division. The winners of each division play each other in a conference championship. With only ten teams, each team plays all of the others exactly once and, until 2018, there was no championship game. What are the competitive advantages and disadvantages of the two approaches?

3.   *Wins and losses.* In determining standings, the National Hockey League gives two points for a win and none for a regulation loss, but one for an overtime loss. Is that rule justified? Does it raise any potential problems? The CCHA gives three points for a win in regulation, two for a win in overtime, one for an overtime loss, and none for a loss in regulation. Is that system preferable?

4.   *Why post-season?* European domestic soccer leagues do not operate season-ending tournaments, though there are supranational tournaments among top finishers from the various domestic leagues. What factors might influence league organizers to eschew postseason tournaments and to crown the winner of the regular season the league champion?

5.   *Weather.* In competitions in which players do not all compete at the same time, changing weather conditions can affect performance. In golf, should all tournaments have a shotgun start—players starting at the same time but from different holes—to equalize weather conditions to the extent possible?

6.   *Home field.* Should championship series (or at least ultimate games, such as the seventh game of the World Series) in professional sports be played at neutral sites, as the Super Bowl ordinarily is, and as the NBA playoffs and the World Series were in the pandemic year of 2020? If the Super Bowl is scheduled for a site that happens to be the home field of one of the teams playing, as occurred in 2021, should it be moved?

7. *Match play and stroke play.* Most golf tournaments at the elite levels of the game use "stroke" or "medal" play—that is, players compete against the entire field (or however many are left after a cut partway through the tournament), and performance is assessed by the player's total score. But some tournaments—and some major team competitions, like the Ryder Cup—use match play, pitting one player (or pair) against another. In match play the virtually universal rule is to score by holes rather than by aggregate score. What are the relative advantages of each style of play?

8. *Match play in fantasy land.* In fantasy sports, a contestant's score depends entirely on the performance of the members of his team; he does not defend against other fantasy players. And yet many fantasy leagues are organized around match play. What, if anything, could be said for this structure?

9. *Seeding.* In a tournament organized around match play—including tournaments in all sports that are actually played head-to-head—the top competitors are generally seeded so that they do not meet each other early in the tournament. Is this fair—is a top seed an earned advantage? For whose protection is this done? The higher seeds? The lower seeds? The promoters and the observing public?

Assuming that the tournament is seeded, Nos. 1 and 2 will be on opposite sides of the draw, so that they don't meet before the final; seeds nos. 1–4 will each be in different quarters of the draw so that they don't meet before the semi-finals, and so on. That is as far as some tournaments go. In the U.S. Open tennis tournament, for example, the number 1 seed may play nos. 5, 6, 7, or 8 in the quarter-finals, the actual selection being done randomly. In the NCAA basketball tournament, by contrast, in the first full round the seedings of the two teams in each pair add to 17. That is, no. 1 in the region plays no.16; no. 2 plays no. 15; and so forth. Which system is preferable?

10. *Rearranging brackets.* When competitors are seeded, some systems rearrange brackets after each round, while others do not. Consider the NFL system. Seven teams make the playoffs from each conference: four division winners and three wildcards (non-division winners with the best records in the conference, subject to a complex system of tie-breakers). The top seed in each conference has a first-round bye, while the remaining division winners host wildcards: team 2 plays team 7, team 3 plays team 6, and team 4 plays team 5. In the next round, team 1 plays the lowest remaining seed, and the other two surviving teams play each other. In the NCAA basketball tournaments, by contrast, the brackets are fixed. In the first full round, the seeds (within the region) of the two teams in each game total 17 (#1 against #16, #2 against #15, etc.). If all games go according to seeds, then in the three subsequent rounds the seeds for each game total 9, 5, and 3, respectively, and in each round the #1 team (assuming it survives) would face the lowest seeded team remaining, #2 would face the second lowest, etc. But inevitably, there are upsets. If the #15 team beats the #2, as sometimes happens, then in the next round it faces the winner of the 7–10 game, rather than the #1 team.

Is one of these approaches generally preferable to the other? Rearranging brackets maximizes the probability that the top seed will reach the finals; one defending a fixed-bracket approach might argue that it maximizes the probability that the top two seeds meet in the finals. Do you think this is correct? Are there pragmatic reasons constraining some kinds of tournaments that might favor fixing the brackets even if rearrangement would be preferable in principle?

11. The playoff draft. To the extent seeding is designed to reward the competitors who have performed the best up to the tournament, should leagues institute "playoff drafts" in which teams, picking in order of their seed, get to select their next opponent until all the teams are paired up? In the NCAA basketball tournament, for example, the system would work like this. In the first round, the #1 seed in each bracket chooses its opponent from among the teams in the bottom-half of the draw; then the #2 seed chooses from the teams that remain, and so on, until all the teams are paired. Presumably, each team would most often choose to play against the lowest seeded of the teams remaining, but not always because injuries or matchups will sometimes make an opponent more or less attractive than its seeding suggests. Would this reform add more drama and strategy? Are there good reasons to oppose it? And if you do think it's a good idea, should it only be used in the first round, or in subsequent rounds as well?

12. Single elimination and beyond. The NCAA basketball tournaments are single elimination: lose and go home. The NCAA baseball and softball tournaments, by contrast, start with sixteen double-elimination regional tournaments of four teams each. The sixteen winners then pair up into eight best-of-three super-regional series. The eight winners then go to the College World Series, which essentially repeats the process: Each of two four-team brackets generates a finalist by double elimination, and a best-of-three series determines the champion. It is therefore possible for a team to lose four games—one at each stage—and yet win the championship. Are these differences justifiable?

13. Winners' bracket winner versus losers' bracket winner, even up. The Little League World Series also uses a double-elimination format to pick the international champion and the United States champion. But it is modified in a significant respect: In each case, the championship is determined by a single game between the respective winners of the winners' and losers' brackets— though by definition one of those teams has previously lost no games and one has lost one. The two champions then play a single game for the overall Little League World Series championship. Why do you suppose the tournament is set up this way? Is it justifiable?

14. The Swiss system. Some tournaments use a Swiss system: After the first round, contestants play against others with similar playing records. There are an immense number of variations on the system, but in most an attempt is made to prevent two contestants from playing against each other more than once. Scoring can be done simply, say, by counting one point for each victory, but usually there would have to be a tie-break to determine the order of finish (though if enough rounds are played there will be no ambiguity as to who the champion is). Under the Solkoff method, each player's tie-break score is the total of the scores of the player's opponents through the tournament. Another tie-break system is the cumulative method, which adds the player's scores at the end of each round, so a player who wins two, then loses two, and wins one would have a higher tie-break score (10 = 1+2+2+2+3) than a player who loses two and then wins three (6 = 0 + 0 + 1 + 2 + 3).

What advantages does the Swiss system have over single- or double-elimination tournaments? Over a round robin? What disadvantages? What tie-break method seems optimal?

15. *Multiple-round byes.* The 12U baseball tournaments at Cooperstown Dreams Park held each summer often feature more than 100 teams. The teams each play six scheduled games—the field is not divided into pools—and then all teams are seeded, the first criterion being fewest losses and the second criterion being runs allowed per game. All teams then enter a single-elimination tournament. In a typical week, the bottom-seeded third of the teams play first-round matches, against a team with a seed either one higher or one lower, beginning at 10 am on Wednesday. The teams with better seeds are given byes into the second, third, fourth, or fifth rounds of the tournament, which are all played that day; the better the seed, the more byes. At the end of the day, sixteen teams are left, and four rounds are played the next day to determine a champion. What advantages and disadvantages does this structure have?

———

Exercise 9B

You have organized a youth soccer tournament to run over a weekend. Sixteen teams have signed up. You have four fields, and can play from 8:00 am to 8:00 pm on Saturday, but need to end games earlier on Sunday to leave teams with enough time to return home. You have guaranteed each team that it will play at least three games, but have enough space and time that some, at least, can play more. The tournament should end with the selection of a champion and a runner-up, and perhaps other placements as well. How will you organize the tournament? If you decide to use pool play and then bracket play, bear in mind that you will need to set in advance a series of tie-breakers to determine seedings or advancement or both, and that, because of time limitations, individual games in the pool round may end in a tie. Bear in mind too that teams sometimes drop out at the last minute (usually because their funding falls through), too late to secure a replacement. How will your rules address that eventuality given your confidence that no team is going to be satisfied to learn that one of its three guaranteed games is a win by forfeit?

PART III

OFFICIATING

▪ ▪ ▪

We have, of course, been considering the decisions of officials throughout the entire book, because, if a sport has officials, it is they who implement the formal rules of the sport. But now we will focus on the officials' functions in detail. There are many different *types* of officials in sports, just as there are many different types in ordinary legal systems. For example, the commissioner of a sport along with various members of the league office might be termed "officials." In this Part, however, except when the context makes clear that a different meaning is intended, we are chiefly interested in those officials who enforce rules "on field" or "on court" in real time: "referees" in most sports, but "umpires" in several (e.g., baseball, cricket, and field hockey), and occasionally "judges" (as in "side judges" and "line judges"). One of us refers to these on-field officials generically as "officiators"; the other finds the term unnecessary and awkward.

On-field officials perform several tasks. The first is to interpret the written rules of a sport to determine what they provide, direct, or require. To the extent that sports are types of legal systems, this first task can be described as an effort to figure out what "the law" is. The second task is to find the facts that the rules, properly interpreted, make relevant. These two tasks are examined in Chapters 10 and 11. In addition, sometimes officials assume, or are delegated, discretion with respect to the enforcement of the rules. We examine various aspects of official discretion in Chapter 12. The fourth and final chapter in this Part, Chapter 13, explores how, if at all, official errors should be corrected.

CHAPTER 10

DETERMINING WHAT THE RULES PROVIDE

■ ■ ■

In the ordinary case, there is no significant doubt regarding what the rules of a sport provide or require. Usually, whatever the text "says" or "means" is the rule. In fancy terms, we might say that the rule (or "the law") is the semantic content or the ordinary meaning of the text.[a] For example, one formerly obscure provision in the NFL rulebook (Rule 2, Section 1) reads as follows: "The ball shall be made up of an inflated (12 1/2 to 13 1/2 pounds) urethane bladder enclosed in a pebble grained, leather case (natural tan color) without corrugations of any kind." The relevant rule, accordingly, is (among other things) that the ball must be inflated to a pressure of 12.5 to 13.5 psi, inclusive.

But sometimes we think that the semantic content or ordinary meaning of a stretch of text in the rulebook does not accurately capture what the rule really is, or what the rules truly require, or (to put the point differently) what the law of the sport is. There are at least two reasons why this might be so. First, there could be a disparity, or perceived disparity, between the meaning of the text and either what the rulemakers intended or what is sometimes termed the "purpose" or "spirit" of the rules. In such cases, we might conclude (though we might not) that the rule is what was intended or what comports with the purpose or spirit of the rules, and is not what the text says or means. This is the subject of Subchapter 10A. Second, what the text says might be inconsistent with how participants actually play the game and with how officials call it. When the meaning of the text (especially an old text) conflicts with consistent and longstanding practice, we might conclude (though, again, we might not) that the rule is what is practiced and not what is stated. This is the topic of Subchapter 10B. (Recall the discussion of formalism, conventionalism, and interpretivism/internalism at pp. 196–197).

---

[a]   Linguists and philosophers of language draw fine distinctions among such notions as "linguistic," "semantic," and "communicative" meaning or content. See, e.g., Mark Greenberg, *Legislation as Communication? Legal Interpretation and the Study of Linguistic Communication,* *in* PHILOSOPHICAL FOUNDATIONS OF LANGUAGE IN THE LAW 217 (Andrei Marmor & Scott Soames eds., 2011). We put those nuances aside.

A. TEXT, INTENTIONS, AND THE "SPIRIT OF THE RULES"

1. THE PINE TAR CASES

Baseball players smear substances such as pine tar on their bat handles to give them a better grip. Pine tar does not make a ball go farther or faster, but it can make balls dirty. And dirty balls have to be replaced; clean balls are easier to see, and discoloration of the ball was apparently a factor in the death of Ray Chapman from a thrown pitch in 1920. Accordingly, since 1955, the rules have limited the use of pine tar. Most notably, Rule 1.10(b) provided: "The bat handle, for not more than 18 inches from the end, may be covered or treated with any material (including pine tar) to improve the grip . . . ." Rule 2.00 defined an "illegally batted ball" to include "one hit with a bat which does not conform to rule 1.10." And Rule 6.06(a) directed that a batter "is out for illegal action" when among other violations, "he hits an illegally batted ball."[b]

So what happens if a batter uses a bat with excessive pine tar, and the violation is not noticed until after he gets a hit? There was a run of such cases in the major leagues (and more in the minors) within less than two months in the summer of 1975, with conflicting results. By that time, Rule 6.06(d) provided that, if a player uses or attempts to use a bat that "has been . . . tampered with in such a way to improve the distance factor or cause an unusual reaction on the baseball," then, "[i]n addition to being called out, the player shall be ejected from the game and may be subject to additional penalties as determined by his League President." And American League Regulation 4.23 provided: "Official playing rule 6.06d prohibits the use of 'doctored' bats. The use of pine tar in itself shall not be considered doctoring the bat. The 18 inch rule will not be cause for ejection or suspension." *See generally* Rachel Nall, *Why Do Baseball Players Use Pine Tar?*, SPORTSREC.COM (Oct. 31, 2018); Raymond Belliotti, *Billy Martin and Jurisprudence: Revisiting the Pine Tar Case*, 5 ALB. GOV'T L. REV. 210 (2012); Shane Tourtellotte, *The pine tar games,* THE HARDBALL TIMES, July 18, 2012.

On July 19, Thurman Munson of the New York Yankees, after having apparently gotten a two-out RBI single in the first inning of a game against the Minnesota Twins, was called out for excessive pine tar. The Yankees complained loudly but apparently did not protest formally. Tourtellotte, *The pine tar games.* The Twins won the game 2–1. Similarly, on August 18, Steve Stone, a pitcher for the Chicago Cubs, after hitting what appeared to be a single against the Los Angeles Dodgers, was also called out for excessive pine tar. The Cubs lost the game 3–1 but did not protest. But on

---

[b]   The rules have since been renumbered; Rule 1.10 is now Rule 3.02; the definitions in Rule 2.00 are now in an unnumbered definitions section; and Rule 6.06 has become Rule 6.03.

September 7, when John Mayberry of the Kansas City Royals got three hits, two of them homers driving in three runs, thus helping his team edge out the California Angels, 8–7, the umpires took no action against him despite the excessive pine tar on his bat. American League President Lee MacPhail denied a protest by the Angels. (The League Presidents were then responsible for ruling on protests; Commissioner Bud Selig eliminated these offices in 1999.) The key part of his ruling read as follows:

> The Playing Rules and the American League Regulations make it clear that pine tar is not to be considered in the same vein as a "doctored" or "filled" bat, under Rule 6.06(d). I would not consider that a ball hit with a bat with pine tar too far from the handle was necessarily an illegally batted ball under Rule 6.06(a), as one hit with a bat not conforming to Rule 1.10. Although Rule 1.10 limits a foreign substance to 18 inches from the handle, we are not talking about a material that improves the reaction or distance factor of the bat.

Rule 1.10(b) was amended after the 1975 season, to add that hitting a ball "treated with any material (including pine tar) which extends past the 18 inch limit . . . shall cause the bat to be removed from the game." And the American League office issued a supplemental directive to umpires saying in part:

> This penalty [of calling the batter out] was considered too severe to enforce for a bat that simply had pine tar more than 18 inches up the handle. The rules committee intended to keep the 18-inch limitation in effect, but the intended penalty was only that the bat be removed from the game.

In light of all these rules, regulations, rulings, and the directive, how should an umpire rule if, after a batter hits safely, the opposing team points out that the bat held too much pine tar? The opposing team's coach brandishes Rules 1.10(b), 2.00, and 6.06(a). How should the umpires respond? The question arose eight years later in what is far and away the most famous pine tar game of all. A video of the incident can be found here: https://tinyurl.com/y2aahlh3. Below is the text of the decision by League President MacPhail, on a protest filed by the Kansas City Royals.[c]

American League President's Decision on the Pine Tar Game

With two out in the ninth inning of the game of July 24th, Kansas City at New York, George Brett hit a home run with a man on to put the Royals ahead by a score of 5–4. Manager Martin objected, claiming that the pine tar on Brett's bat extended beyond the permissible 18 inches from the handle. Plate umpire Tim McClelland conferred with crew chief Joe Brinkman and with umpires Nick Bremigan and Drew Coble. The portion

---

[c]   *Text of League President's Ruling in Brett Bat Case*, N.Y. TIMES, July 29, 1983, at A16.

of the bat covered with pine tar was measured and found to be well over 18 inches. Brett was therefore called out ending the game and giving New York a 4–3 victory.

The umpires cite Official Playing Rule 6.06(a) which states "that a batter is out for illegal action when he hits an illegally batted ball." They state that Rule 1.10(b) provides that a ball hit with a bat "treated with any material (including pine tar) . . . which extends past the 18 inch limitation . . . shall cause the bat to be removed from the game;" and is therefore an illegally batted ball. They ruled that since the bat used by Brett was illegal under Rule 1.10(b) and since Rule 6.06(a) provides that a batter hitting an illegally batted ball is out, Brett must therefore be called out and the home run nullified.

Decision

It is the position of this office that the umpires' interpretation, while technically defensible, is not in accord with the intent or spirit of the rules and that the rules do not provide that a hitter be called out for excessive use of pine tar. The rules provide instead that the bat be removed from the game. The protest of the Kansas City club is therefore upheld and the home run by Brett is permitted to stand. The score of the game becomes 5–4 Kansas City with Kansas City at bat and two out in the top of the ninth inning. The game becomes a Suspended Game at that point and must be completed before the close of the season if practicable or at the close of the season if it should affect the first place position in either division.

The reasoning of this office in reaching the above decision is as follows:

(1)   Official Playing Rule 6.06(a) states that a batter is out for illegal action when "he hits an illegally batted ball." An "illegally batted ball" is defined in the rules as including one hit with a bat which does not conform to Official Playing Rule 1.10.

(2)   Rule 1.10 outlines several requirements affecting the legality of a bat. One of these is that "the bat handle, for not more than 18 inches from the end may be covered or treated with any material (including pine tar) to improve the grip. . .," but that no such material shall improve the reaction or distance factor of the bat. Rule 1.10 specifically provides that if the pine tar extends past the 18 inch limitation, the bat shall be removed from the game. If it was intended that this infraction should fall under the penalty of the batter's being declared out, it does not seem logical that the rule should specifically specify that the bat should be removed from the game. In fact, it is probable that a batter attempting to use a bat clearly outside other general requirements of Rule 1.10 (such as colored bats, etc.) would not be permitted by the umpires to do so. In fact, this is the manner in which batters attempting to hit with excessive pine tar have generally been restricted.

(3)   It is more logical to infer that the second part of the definition of an illegal batted ball, that pertaining to a bat which does not conform to Rule 1.10, is meant to refer to bats covered under Rule 6.06(d), which have been altered or tampered with in such a way to improve the distance factor or cause an unusual reaction on the baseball. This section specifically provides that "in addition to being called out, the player shall be ejected from the game and may be subject to additional penalties as determined by the League President." League regulations and bulletins specifically provide that pine tar violations do not fall under the provisions of this rule. American League Regulation 4.23 states that, "Official playing rule 6.06d prohibits the use of 'doctored' bats. The use of pine tar in itself shall not be considered doctoring the bat. The 18 inch rule will not be cause for ejection or suspension."

(4)   It is the conviction of the League President that the intent of the above rules is to declare a batter out and to inflict discipline upon him for use of an illegal bat, which has been "altered or tampered with to improve the distance factor or cause an unusual reaction on the baseball." (It has not been seriously contended that the pine tar on Brett's bat did either). It is not the intent of the rules to declare batters out or discipline them for improper use of pine tar. (The provision restricting the distance pine tar can extend up the barrel of the bat was primarily intended to keep from spoiling the ball and requiring new balls to be constantly brought into the game.) Conversations with several members of the Rules Committee reinforce this belief. The provision to prevent this is specifically spelled out in Rule 1.10 (i.e., remove the bat from the game).

(5)   As stated, it has not been the usual practice in the Major Leagues to call batters out for using a bat with excessive pine tar. The general procedure, when noticed by umpires or complained about by the opposing team, has been to require use of a new bat or require that the old bat be cleaned up. One exception to this occurred in July of 1975, when a hit by Thurman Munson of the Yankees was negated and Munson declared out in a game against the Minnesota Twins. Partly as a result of this, Rule 1.10(b) was amended and the following new language added, "material, including pine tar, which extends past the 18 inch limitation shall cause the bat to be removed from the game."

(6)   In September of 1975, the California Angels protested a loss to the Kansas City Royals on the grounds that player Mayberry of Kansas City had pine tar on his bat extending beyond the permitted 18 inch limit. The protest was denied by the American League office. The reasoning behind this denial as explained to the California Club was, in part, as follows: "The Playing Rules and the American League Regulations make it clear that pine tar is not to be considered in the same vein as a 'doctored' or 'filled' bat, under Rule 6.06(d). I would not consider that a ball hit with a bat with pine tar too far from the handle was necessarily an illegally batted ball

under Rule 6.06(a), as one hit with a bat not conforming to Rule 1.10. Although Rule 1.10 limits a foreign substance to 18 inches from the handle, we are not talking about a material that improves the reaction or distance factor of the bat."

Conclusions

A.   Protest is allowed based on the League's decision with respect to the proper interpretation of the rules involved. It is the League's position that that meaning and intent is to discipline and declare out batters using bats that have been tampered with to increase distance potential, but not to treat pine tar excesses in the same manner. Instead, the use of bats with pine tar extending beyond 18 inches should simply be prohibited. The opposing team has the right to call the infraction to the umpire's attention and ask that the bat be changed or cleaned up.

B.   Although Manager Martin and his staff should be commended for their alertness, it is the strong conviction of the League that games should be won and lost on the playing field—not though technicalities of the rules—and that every reasonable effort consistent with the spirit of the rules should be made to so provide.

C.   Although the umpires are being overruled, it is not in my opinion the fault of the umpires involved, but rather is the fault of the Official Playing Rules, which in some areas are unclear and imprecise. (The rules, which must cover many complicated situations, have been in effect for many years and have been amended repeatedly. At times, however, other rules affecting related situations have not been brought into conformity.) The responsibility for this, and the responsibility perhaps for the lack of clear, uniform instructions to the umpires on the interpretation of the rules must rest with those of us in administrative positions in baseball, including myself.

COMMENTS AND QUESTIONS

1.   A question of remedy. By allowing the protest, MacPhail caused the game to be continued from the moment of Brett's home run. The replay occurred on August 18. Brett, Manager Dick Howser, and Coach Rocky Colavito were ruled ejected because of their outbursts after the initial call; Gaylord Perry, closing out a long and successful pitching career that depended in significant part on the use of foreign substances, had also been ejected for trying to spirit the bat away in the clubhouse so it could not be sent to the league office. Neither team scored additional runs, resulting in a 5–4 victory for the Royals. Supposing for the moment that MacPhail interpreted the governing rules correctly, did he issue the appropriate remedy? What alternative remedies were possible?

2.   The merits. Now putting aside the question of appropriate remedy, what was the correct ruling on the merits? Should Brett have been called out, or should the runs have been allowed to stand? Consider the following possibilities:

(a)   The umpires ruled correctly and MacPhail incorrectly: the plain language of Rules 1.10 and 6.06(a) provided that Brett hit "an illegally batted ball" and that the penalty for such a violation was to be declared out. Rule-of-law and separation-of-powers principles dictate that the plain language of the official rules constitutes the law and must be enforced by the umpires and by members of the sport's "executive branch."

(b)   The umpires ruled correctly and MacPhail incorrectly not because the plain language of the rule must always be followed across all sports or across all legal systems but because one of the excellences that the sport of baseball particularly embodies is the wily manipulation and exploitation of the plain language of the formally promulgated rules for competitive advantage, and the Yankees were entitled to the fruits of their crafty gamesmanship. *See* Mitchell N. Berman, *On Interpretivism and Formalism in Sports Officiating: From General to Particular Jurisprudence,* 38 J. PHIL. SPORT 177, 186–88 (2011).

(c)   MacPhail ruled correctly and the umpires incorrectly: an interpretation of the rules must take into account all available legal materials, and in this case that included League regulation 4.23, MacPhail's own ruling in the Mayberry case of 1975, and the supplemental directive issued by the American League after the 1975 season.

(d)   MacPhail ruled correctly and the umpires incorrectly: when the intent of the rulemakers is clear, interpreters should follow that intent even in the face of conflicting statutory language, and the clear intent of the rulemakers in this case was that a batter should be declared out for doctoring a bat only if he did so in a way intended to gain a competitive advantage.

(e)   MacPhail ruled correctly and the umpires incorrectly not because of what the rulemakers might or might not have actually "intended" but because it is a general principle of adjudication in sport that "rules should be interpreted in such a manner that the excellences embodied in achieving the lusory goal of the game are not undermined but are maintained and fostered" and "the umpires' decision to discount Brett's homerun undermines the very aims and purposes that the game [of baseball] sets out to promote for no relevant reason." J.S. Russell, *Are Rules All an Umpire Has to Work With?,* 26 J. PHIL. SPORT 27, 35, 37 (1999). ("Lusory" means related to play. A lusory goal of a game is a good intrinsic to the practice, in contrast to extrinsic goods that the practice can deliver, such as wealth or fame.)

(f)   MacPhail ruled correctly and the umpires incorrectly assuming (as seems probable) that Yankee Manager Billy Martin was aware of the problem before Brett's at-bat in the ninth inning and therefore the Yankees should be deemed to have forfeited or waived their objection. *Compare* Fed. R. Civ. P. 32(d)(3)(B) (objection to form of question asked at deposition waived if not made timely at deposition).

(g)   MacPhail ruled correctly for one or more of the reasons presented in options (c), (d), and (e) above, but the umpires also ruled correctly because their task should be limited to enforcing the plain language of the rules, leaving more purposive or principled interpretation to supervisors. *See* Berman, *On Interpretivism and Formalism,* at 190–91. *Compare Rodriguez de Quijas v. Shearson/ American Express, Inc.,* 490 U.S. 477, 484 (1989) ("If a precedent of this Court has direct application in a case, yet appears to rest on reasons rejected in some other line of decisions, the Court of Appeals should follow the case which directly controls, leaving to this Court the prerogative of overruling its own decisions."). Interestingly, this seems to have been the opinion of at least one of the members of the umpiring crew. *See* Nick Bremigan, *Views of Sport: How Baseball Became Unstuck by a Rules Dispute,* N.Y. TIMES, Aug. 7, 1983.

Do you agree with one of the foregoing possibilities, or would you resolve the issue on other grounds? If you agree with option (c), was MacPhail's ruling in the Mayberry case correct? If you agree with option (f), how should umpires determine what Billy Martin knew when, and how confident must they be before concluding that the Yankees waived their objection? Would MacPhail have adequate grounds for determining that Martin waived his objection if the umpires had not made such a determination?

2.   THE BOBBY MARTIN CASE

Though born without legs, Bobby Martin of Dayton, Ohio, was a physically active teenager. Rick Reilly, in *Half the Size, Twice the Man,* SPORTS ILLUSTRATED, Oct. 3, 2005, reported: "He bowls, dances and does flips and cartwheels. He flies off staircases on his custom-made skateboard. He weaves down the hall between classes on it doing one-handed handstands." Very powerful in his chest and arms, he was able to move quickly on his hands—and he played football for his high school team. At halftime in one game, though, the officiating crew told his coach that Martin could not play, because he was not complying with a rule requiring that players wear shoes, knee pads, and thigh pads. The officials claimed not only that the rule was clear but that they were invoking it for his safety. Martin came out for the second half with a pair of cleats tied to his belt, but his school's athletic director told him this was "undignified" and he should take them off. "Though, by the refs' own black-and-white logic," Reilly contended, "it should've worked. Where is it written that the shoes have to be worn on the feet?" Before the team's next game, the Ohio High

School Athletic Association ruled that the officials were incorrect and that Martin could play; he finished the season with 48 tackles and won the next year's ESPY Award for Best Male Athlete with a Disability.

COMMENTS AND QUESTIONS

1. Pants without legs. Were the game officials in error, as the athletic association maintained? Why or why not? What, if anything, can be said in favor of the referee's enforcement of the rule against Martin? If (a) the referee had concerns about Martin's safety, but (b) the rules did not give the referee general discretionary power to exclude a player for safety concerns, would it be appropriate for the referee to invoke the shoe requirement as a ground for exclusion? If the opposing coach pointed out the apparent rules violation to the referee, what should the referee's response have been? (A video of Martin is available here: https://tinyurl.com/y5ebfxnc.)

2. Jewelry without jewels. High school sports delivered another challenging case of rule interpretation at a California track meet in May 2010. South Pasadena High School apparently completed an undefeated season, with a league championship, when Robin Laird cleared 7½ feet in the pole vault. But she had violated a California Interscholastic Federation (CIF) rule prohibiting athletes from wearing "jewelry," defined to include "anything that adorns the body," during competition: On her wrist was a little string bracelet that she had been wearing constantly since the previous November after buying it from a school club raising money for the World Wildlife Fund. The apparent violation was pointed out by a coach from Monrovia High School, which would win the championship if Laird was disqualified. And after coaches from both teams called the CIF, that was the result. One of Laird's teammates, Oliver Mittelstaedt, who had served as state youth governor in the California YMCA Youth & Government program, reported a conversation he had with a Monrovia coach: "I asked him if he felt like a winner. He said, 'No.' He said something along the lines of 'No one likes to win this way.' "

Mike Knowles, Monrovia's head coach, was quoted as saying, "I didn't want to do that. I've lost a CIF title because a girl had one diamond earring she forgot to take out in the 4-by-400 relay." Oliver Mittelstaedt's response to that was, "It's important not to take your own misfortune and pass it on to the next person." But Robin Laird said: "It would be unsportsmanlike for us to try to take [the championship] back. I think that in my experience with playing so many sports, I know that it's about more than just rules . . . but I'm accepting of the fact that rules are rules." Steve Lopez, *Young athlete transcends the rules*, L.A. TIMES, May 16, 2010.

Do you agree that Laird violated the rule? Is a little string bracelet "jewelry" in the ordinary meaning of that word? Are "Livestrong" bracelets "jewelry"? If not, should this bracelet be deemed to be jewelry as the rule book defined that term? Did it "adorn the body"? Look up the word "adorn" in a dictionary or two. If you were representing Robin Laird or South Pasadena High School what are the best arguments you could make against her disqualification? Should the question depend on when the Monrovia coach noticed the bracelet? And if Coach Knowles "didn't want to do" what he did, then why did he? Is there some reason he might have felt "compelled" to do it?

3. *Roller derby.* At one time, a uniform rule of flat track roller derby provided as follows: "Each Skater participating in a game must visibly display their roster number on each sleeve or arm. Roster numbers must be of high contrast and easily legible. . . . Roster numbers must be placed on the helmet in addition to the arm/sleeve. Numbers on helmets must match roster numbers." WOMEN'S FLAT TRACK DERBY ASSOCIATION, Rule 2.7.5.2. S1, a popular helmet manufacturer, puts the  logo "S1" on its helmets, as the photo shows. In some competitions, referees ruled that S1 helmets could not be used, invoking the final sentence of Rule 2.7.5.2. Right ruling? The rules have now been amended to provide that "if additional numbers are on the helmet (e.g., a brand name, model number, or tribute) they must be of a size, style, and position that is not confusing to officials." Presumably, that revision allows for S1 helmets. Should the formal amendment have been necessary?

4. *A rule with bite?* Reflect on the following anecdote related by golfing great Arnold Palmer, in ARNOLD PALMER, PLAYING BY THE RULES 18–19 (2002):

> It was 1988, and Tim Simpson and Raymond Floyd were playing together on Saturday [at the Bay Hill Invitation Tournament] when Tim hooked his ball near a water hazard on the third hole. As the two players walked over to where Tim's ball had stopped, they were alarmed to see a ten-foot alligator sunning on the bank. Inches from the alligator's mouth lay Tim's ball.
>
> Mark Russell, a PGA Tour rules official, was quickly dispatched to assess the situation, and after a couple of minutes of discussing the relative dangers of approaching an alligator of that size, Russell allowed Tim to put another ball in play in a safe spot not nearer the hole. The officials made that rule ruling because it was the only right and equitable thing to do.

Rule of Golf 13–1 then provided: "The ball must be played as it lies, except as otherwise provided in the Rules." (The same substance is now in Rule 1.1.) There was no rule that provides that the ball may be moved when near an alligator. However, Rule 1–4—colloquially termed the "rule of equity"—provided that "[i]f any point in dispute is not covered by the Rules, the decision should be made in accordance with equity." (Rule 20.3 now provides that the Committee governing the competition should "treat[ ] the situation in a way that is reasonable, fair and consistent with how similar situations are treated under the Rules.") In Palmer's judgment, Rule 1–4 licensed the official's decision to allow Tim Simpson to put another ball in play without incurring a penalty. Was he right?

     5.   More on the "rule of equity." Consider the following "Decisions on the Rules of Golf" issued jointly by the world's major governing bodies of golf, the R&A based in St. Andrews, Scotland, and the USGA. (The Rules referred to in these Decisions are from the pre-2019 version of the Rules of Golf.)

     Decision 1-4/10 addresses whether, under the rule of equity, a player whose "ball comes to rest in a situation dangerous to the player, e.g., near a live rattlesnake or a bees' nest," should be permitted to drop a ball elsewhere without penalty. The answer: "Yes. It is unreasonable to expect the player to play from such a dangerous situation and unfair to require the player to incur a penalty under Rule 26 (Water Hazards) or Rule 28 (Ball Unplayable)."

     Decision 1-4/11 asks: "If a player's ball comes to rest in or near an area of plants such as poison ivy, cacti or stinging nettles, should the provisions of Decision 1-4/10 apply?" The answer: No. "Decision 1-4/10 contemplates a situation which is unrelated to conditions normally encountered on the course. Unpleasant lies are a common occurrence which players must accept."

     Do you agree with the distinction drawn by these two decisions? What if the course is known by all to be home to several rattlesnakes (or alligators) but club officials and the golfers alike believe that groundskeepers have removed all poison ivy and are very surprised to discover that a ball has been hit into a large patch of it?

     If you believe that the Decisions resolve these two cases correctly, is that because whether the golfer in the first case can take a drop without penalty "is not covered by the Rules" whereas whether the golfer in the second case can take a drop without penalty *is* covered by the Rules? If so, how, exactly, do the Rules cover the second case but not the first? If not, is there a different distinction to be drawn between the cases of rattlesnakes, bees, and alligators on the one hand, and poison ivy, cacti, and stinging nettles on the other? Is the distinction simply fauna vs. flora?

     6.   Up a tree. What if a player's ball is lodged in a tall tree? At the Arnold Palmer Invitational in 2013, Sergio García hit a ball out of one, fifteen feet high, but injured his shoulder and withdrew from the tournament. *Sergio García climbs tree to play shot . . . but then injures himself,* GUARDIAN, Mar. 25, 2013. If García had requested permission to drop his ball near the tree without penalty, what result would have been appropriate given the text of Rule 1–4? Given the Decisions 1-4/10 and 1-4/11? Would it be "unreasonable to expect the player to play from such a dangerous situation"? If so, would it also be unfair to require him "to incur a penalty"?

     7.   When the rules are silent. According to former MLB player and manager Bobby Valentine, the checked swing is "the most argued call in baseball." David Waldstein, *Baseball Has a Rorschach Test: The Checked Swing,* N.Y. TIMES, Oct. 26, 2018. Whenever the call goes against their team, players, managers, and fans insist the umpire erroneously called a ball or strike, citing evidence such as whether "the batter's wrists broke," or "the bat broke the plane of the plate." These arguments are commonplace, but perhaps misguided. The official MLB rulebook defines a "strike," in part, as "a legal pitch when so called by the umpire, which—(a) Is struck at by batter and is missed." The rulebook provides no guidance regarding what it means to "strike at" a pitch, nor what the umpire's subjective judgment should be directed toward when considering if a batter "checked" his swing. More simply, there is no "checked swing" rule; it is a black box.

As an attempt to eliminate squabbles over the "checked swing," Valentine suggested that every attempt to check a swing should be a ball. The NCAA, on the other hand, provides the following:

Half Swing

SECTION 39. An attempt by the batter to stop the forward motion of the bat while swinging, which puts the batter in jeopardy of a strike being called. The half swing shall be called a strike if the barrel head of the bat passes the batter's front hip. This does not apply to a bunt attempt when the batter pulls the bat back.

Do you favor the NCAA's definition? Valentine's proposal? Or do you prefer the current MLB regime which constrains umpires only by unwritten traditional understanding in determining what constitutes a swing in general, and not only whether a given token event satisfies that definition? Whatever your answer, notice the asymmetrical appeals process for checked swings: if a checked swing is initially called a ball by the home-plate umpire, the catcher or pitcher can ask for an appeal to a base umpire (at first for a righty batter, at third for a lefty), who may call a swinging strike; if the home-plate umpire initially calls a strike, the batter cannot appeal the decision. Can you think of a justification for this asymmetry? Are checked swings a good candidate for temporal variance, makeup calls, or superstar treatment? (See Chapter 12.)

    8.   Textualism and non-textualism in the law. Disputes that pit **textualism** against **purposivism**, or that oppose "the letter" and "the spirit" of the text, are daily fare in courts of law. The topic is too big and the literature too vast to permit serious engagement here. But two brief clarificatory remarks are warranted. First, although noted commentators often describe

Textualism vs. Purposivism

textualism as the search for the meaning of the words that make up a text, sophisticated textualists recognize that the meaning of an utterance (a string of words, such as a sentence) is not entirely reducible to the meanings of the words that comprise it. This is due to the difference between semantics (the meaning that is conveyed, acontextually, by the words, given rules of syntax) and pragmatics (the meaning that is communicated by use of a string of words in a given context). Take an ordinance that provides that "children under eight may enter for free." This statement communicates, by negative implication, that children eight and older must pay. Textualists can agree that that's what the text, in context, means, even though dictionary definitions of the words used would not reveal that meaning. Second, the standard contrasting of textualism with purposivism can be misleading. It is true that purposivists, unlike textualists, will sometimes follow the legislature's (presumed) intentions or purposes rather than the meaning of the text it enacted. But there is an important asymmetry between the two approaches. Textualists do often limit themselves to the (pragmatically enriched) meaning encoded in the text. But almost nobody is a purposivist in a comparably single-minded way. Most thinkers identified as purposivists are really "pluralists." They believe that the interpretation of authoritative legal texts, such as statutes and constitutions, draws on many factors: original textual meaning, current meaning, legislative intentions and broader purposes, historical practice, avoiding absurd unforeseen results, and so forth. What distinguishes textualists from purposivists is that the latter are open to considering purposes *in addition* to the meanings encoded in a text, whereas the former generally are not.

Some much-discussed cases that implicate these distinct approaches to legal interpretation include *Smith v. United States*, 508 U.S. 223 (1993) (holding, over a dissent, that a federal statute that imposes enhanced penalties for "use" of a firearm during a drug-trafficking crime covers the exchange of a firearm for drugs); *Hans v. Louisiana*, 134 U.S. 1 (1890) (holding that the Eleventh Amendment to the Constitution, which provides that "the Judicial Power of the United States shall not be construed to extend to any suit . . . commenced . . . against one of the United States by Citizens of another State," also immunizes states from suit in federal court commenced by its own citizens); *Bolling v. Sharpe*, 347 U.S. 497 (1954) (holding that principles underlying the Equal Protection Clause, which provides that "No State shall . . . deny to any person within its jurisdiction the equal protection of the laws," also prevent the United States from maintaining segregated schools because it would be "unthinkable that the . . . Constitution would impose a lesser duty on the Federal Government"). For a celebrated examination of textualism and alternatives in the law, see Lon L. Fuller, *The Case of the Speluncean Explorers*, 62 HARV. L. REV. 616 (1949).

9. Textualism and alternatives in religion. The same sorts of interpretive debates that arise in law and sports also arise in religious practice, where they often travel under the labels "hermeneutics" or "exegesis." Speaking very generally, many scholars distinguish four schools or approaches to scriptural interpretation: literal, moral, allegorical, and anagogical (or mystical). For discussions, see KAREN ARMSTRONG, THE LOST ART OF SCRIPTURE: RESCUING THE SACRED TEXTS (2019); DAVID FERGUSSON, FAITH AND ITS CRITICS: A CONVERSATION ch. 6 (2009). How are sacred texts interpreted in any religious traditions that you're familiar with?

10. Judges and umpires. During his confirmation hearings for the Chief Justiceship of the United States, John Roberts sought to explain his jurisprudential philosophy by analogizing the role of a judge, and even of a Supreme Court Justice, to that of an umpire. "Judges are like umpires," he explained. "Umpires don't make the rules, they apply them. The role of an umpire and a judge is critical. They make sure everybody plays by the rules, but it is a limited role. Nobody ever went to a ball game to see the umpire."

Do you agree that judges are like umpires (and other sports officials)? In what ways yes, in what ways no? And what follows?

Consider the following suggestion. If we were to formalize Roberts's argument just a bit, it might take the following form: (1) the proper role of the umpire is limited to following and enforcing the preexisting law; (2) judges are like umpires; therefore, (3) the proper role of the judge is also limited to enforcing preexisting law. Many critics of the conclusion responded by rejecting the analogy: judges, they said, are *not* like umpires. Here's just one reason to think not. Because human foresight is limited, rules are likely to be under-determinate in proportion to the diversity and range of circumstances to which they might be applied. Law covers a vastly wider range of circumstances and possible fact patterns than do the rules of a sport or game. Therefore, law will be "gappier" than are the rules of sports, leaving judges with less guidance in resolving disputes and conferring upon them correspondingly greater discretion. This view grants premise (1) but denies the conclusion of the argument by rejecting premise (2). Judge Richard Posner, one of the most influential appellate judges of the last several decades, gave voice to this criticism when observing that "[n]either [Roberts] nor any other knowledgeable person actually believed or believes that the rules that judges in our system apply, particularly appellate judges and most particularly the Justices of the U.S. Supreme Court, are given to them the way the rules of baseball are given to umpires." RICHARD A. POSNER, HOW JUDGES THINK 78 (2008).

Of course, there's a second route toward rejecting the jurisprudential conclusion that Roberts would have his audience draw. One could accept premise (2) (at least arguendo) but deny premise (1). A proponent of this view would maintain that judges *are* like umpires, but *neither's* role is limited to just following the law laid down. Alternatively, of course, you could accept both Roberts's analogy and the conclusion he would draw. What do you think is right, wrong, or misleading about Chief Justice Roberts's analogy? How if at all do the incidents presented in this section, and others you are familiar with, affect your views?

B. THE RELEVANCE OF PRACTICE

Suppose that the ordinary meaning of a provision in the rule book captures the rulemakers' intentions and their more general purposes. But suppose that, over time, practice no longer conforms to that meaning: players and officials alike either simply ignore the rule, or act in accordance with a different norm that resides in the neighborhood of the norm that corresponds to the meaning of the text. What, then, is "the real rule" or "the real law"? Is it, as lawyers sometimes put it, "the law in the books" or "the law in action"? *See* Roscoe Pound, *Law in Books and Law in Action*, 44 AM. L. REV. 12, 35–36 (1910).

Conflicts between written law and practiced law pervade ordinary legal systems. We already noted, when introducing "conventionalism," the widespread disregard of jaywalking laws in some communities. Think too of speeding laws and criminal bans on fornication (sex between unmarried persons). It's not only that these laws are widely flouted in secret, but that they, and others like them, are disregarded so widely and openly as to raise doubts about whether the paper rules remain as norms of the legal system.

Sports serve up similar cases. Traveling in basketball, discussed below, is among the most commonly cited examples. In soccer, the Laws provide that a player taking a throw-in must "deliver[ ] the ball from the point where it left the field of the player," but players regularly deliver the ball five yards downfield from that point—or farther. And goalies routinely hold the ball, without penalty, for considerably more than the six seconds that Law 12 allots them. In baseball, longstanding and conspicuous departures from the law in the books include the location of the strike zone, the phantom double play, and the total disregard of the anti-fraternization rule.

In sports as in law, a pattern of substantial and consistent departure from the written rules raises several questions. The most important concerns the duties of on-field officials: when if ever is it improper to enforce a paper rule over a consistently practiced rule? A second concerns the options available to rule-making officials ("rulemakers" or "gamewrights"): how can they best restore the primacy of the written rule, when they have reason to do so?

COMMENTS AND QUESTIONS

1. Throw out the throw-in? The Laws of soccer direct how a throw-in must be executed:

At the moment of delivering the ball, the thrower:

- faces the field of play
- has part of each foot either on the touch line or on the ground outside the touch line
- holds the ball with both hands
- delivers the ball from behind and over his head
- delivers the ball from the point where it left the field of play

FIFA Law 15. That Law also provides that for certain infringements of this rule (not involving the placement of the throw), the opposing team will be awarded a direct or indirect free kick, and that, "[f]or any other infringement of this Law: the throw-in is taken by a player of the opposing team."

Suppose a thrower on Team Blue delivers the ball 3 meters from the point at which it crossed the touch line—not in compliance with the text of Law 15, but well within the parameters established by long practice. Would the referee act improperly in declaring the throw invalid and awarding a throw-in to Team Green? Would she act improperly in informing the Blue player that his throw was illegal and instructing him to re-throw?

2.   Fraternization. MLB Rule 4.06, captioned "No Fraternization," provides:

> Players in uniform shall not address or mingle with spectators, nor sit in the stands before, during, or after a game. No manager, coach or player shall address any spectator before or during a game. Players of opposing teams shall not fraternize at any time while in uniform.

The Rule was adopted after the 1919 Chicago Black Sox betting scandal, as part of an effort to convince the public that players were not manipulating game outcomes. Rob Neyer, *Why MLB (Officially) Frowns Upon Fraternizing*, SB NATION (May 13, 2011). It has not been complied with during the lifetimes of your (not young) authors, except during the pandemic year of 2020, and even then only very partially. In 2011, Joe Torre, newly appointed Executive Vice President for Baseball Operations, announced his intent to revive enforcement of the rule, opining that fraternization "sends the wrong message." George A. King III, *MLB wants to put end to frenemies on field,* N.Y. POST, Oct. 24, 2011. Commentators expressed doubt that Torre would succeed in the face of player resistance, *see* Buster Olney, *MLB feels players fraternizing too much,* ESPN.com (May 8, 2011), and within two years, the talk had shifted from restoring a seemingly defunct rule to scrapping it. As baseball analyst Buster Olney observed:

> [P]layers have effectively ignored the fraternization rule for years, given the constant on-field by-play between opposing players. Now, sources say, there is talk in some circles of eliminating the rule once and for all, rather than continuing to try to swim upstream against reality.

> Not that a rule change would necessarily change anything. Players have crossed over for handshakes and hugs and conversation with opponents during batting practice and when players do sprints on the field before the start of games . . . .

> Managers and coaches from rival teams talk constantly behind batting cages. There was no enforcement of the rule, and sources say that rather than keeping an empty regulation on the books, it's better to eliminate it altogether.

Buster Olney, *Factors that will create a wild winter,* ESPN.com (Nov. 4, 2013).

As of this writing, the formal anti-fraternization rule hasn't been scrapped, but neither (with the 2020 exception) has it been enforced. So how would you assess the situation? Do players on opposing teams who chat with each other before a game violate the MLB rules? Does a player or coach who addresses a spectator before a game violate baseball rules? Do the rules really prohibit players from signing autographs for spectators—or do they allow autograph-signing, while only prohibiting players from saying anything to a fan while signing? What should an umpire who sees such conduct do?

3.   *The strike zone.* Beginning in 1968, the upper limit of the strike zone, as defined in Major League Baseball's rules, was the batter's armpits. But umpires rarely called strikes above the batter's waist. In 1987, after years of unsuccessfully trying to cajole, threaten and importune the umps to call higher strikes, MLB settled on a surprising solution: it lowered the upper limit of the strike zone as defined in the books to "the midpoint between the top of the shoulders and the top of the uniform pants." Although this upper limit was still higher than what the umps had been calling, the rules committee reasoned that if the formal rule were closer to what the implementing officials, the umpires, were used to calling, it would more likely be enforced as, or close to the way, it was written. *See* Murray Chass, *Baseball Changes the Strike Zone*, N.Y. TIMES, Dec. 8, 1987, at D25. "We've actually made the strike zone larger," said Pat Gillick, general manager of the Toronto Blue Jays and a member of the committee. "What we did is establish a strike zone that we want to be enforced."

What lesson might rulemakers (in sports or elsewhere) draw from this episode? If gamewrights want to close a gap between the law in books and the law in action, what are their best ways to proceed?

4.   *All in the neighborhood.* Baseball's famous "neighborhood play" reflects yet another respect in which baseball practice has systematically departed from the rulebook. Also called the "phantom double play," the neighborhood play describes a practice according to which "a sliding baserunner is called out because the defensive player, with a clearly caught ball that is on target, is close enough to touch the base" but, in order to avoid being injured by the baserunner, does not actually touch the base while turning a double play. PAUL DICKSON, THE DICKSON BASEBALL DICTIONARY 577 (3rd ed. 2011). The neighborhood play is not recognized in the rulebook, and MLB's official position rejects it. Umpires deny calling it. "But," one commentator complained, expressing a common view, "we all know they're lying. The neighborhood play was an accepted part of baseball for decades, no different than a hit-batsman taking first despite no effort to get out of the way or a pitcher running his hand through his greased-up hair before every pitch." Larry Granillo, *Is the neighborhood play gone for good?*, SB NATION (June 27, 2013).

Interestingly, the neighborhood play did not describe a law-free zone. High school umpire David Emerling explains that

> when the "neighborhood play" *is* called, the pivot man should never be exempt from actually touching the base. He *must* still touch the base, however, he may not actually have the ball at the time he touches it. The umpire should not split hairs as to whether the pivot man was in contact with the base at the time he received the throw. But it has to be reasonably close and the play must be fluid.

The Official Forum: Phantom Double Play, OFFICIATING.COM (Aug. 8, 2005), https://tinyurl.com/y3srz59m. On this view, the neighborhood play rule has two rule-like aspects—the pivot man must possess the ball at some point and he must touch the base at some point—but also two standard-like aspects—those two events must occur in "reasonably close" time proximity and the connection must be fluid.

Of course, we don't want to take Emerling's view as gospel; there was undoubtedly some disparity in the way umpires called that play. But suppose that major league umpires consistently enforced the neighborhood play as Emerling describes the conflict with the plain language of the rulebook. Suppose that this consistent practice extended for several decades. Should an umpire under such circumstances continue to respect the informal practice or should he enforce the rules "as written"? Would the "law of baseball" include or not include the neighborhood play? Would a manager have a valid complaint if an umpire invoked the plain language of the MLB rule book to call a runner safe at second even if the pivot man did move his foot off the base immediately before he possessed the ball?

5.   *The neighborhood meets replay.* Notice that we have largely described the neighborhood play in the past tense. At least at the major league level, a pair of changes appears to have largely eliminated it. First, the play has been made reviewable, which allows for precise determination of whether the fielder had the ball in his possession while touching the bag. Second, a new Rule 601(j) requires runners sliding into second base to make a bona fide attempt to reach the bag "without changing his pathway for the purpose of initiating contact with a fielder." As one commentator noted, "Now that the fielder only needs to get a step or two clear of the bag to get out of range of the slide, it's fair enough to require him to actually touch the bag while he has the ball." Alex Hall, *There goes the neighborhood play*, SB NATION (Apr. 23, 2016). Do you doubt that, when calls are reviewed, umpires will demand full compliance with the rules as written? Is that a benefit or a cost of instant replay review?

6.   *Two steps, anywhere?* For decades, the NBA rulebook provided that a player was entitled to one step after completing his dribble.[d] But any fan of the game could tell you that players routinely take two steps or more without being penalized. Indeed, in 2009, the NBA Vice President of Referee Operations, Joe

---

[d]   Prior to amendment in 2009, Rule 10 provided:

A player who receives the ball while he is progressing or upon completion of a dribble, may use a two-count rhythm in coming to a stop, passing or shooting the ball. The first count occurs:

(1) As he receives the ball, if either foot is touching the floor at the time he receives it.

(2) As the foot touches the floor, or as both feet touch the floor simultaneously after he receives the ball, if both feet are off the floor when he receives it.

The second occurs:

(1) After the count of one when either foot touches the floor, or both feet touch the floor simultaneously.

This is not the most clearly crafted provision. But it appears to provide that a running player who catches a pass or picks up his dribble while a foot is touching the floor is entitled to just one more step before he must shoot or pass.

Borgia, admitted that referees "really don't reference the rulebook," but are instructed to allow players two steps. "Forever, as long as I can remember, a player has been allowed two steps," says Borgia, whose father was an NBA referee for the league's first two decades, and then a referee supervisor. "I've never heard anything other than that. . . . Everyone in the world knows you're allowed two steps." *NBA Traveling: "We Really Don't Reference the Rulebook,"* ESPN.com (Mar. 4, 2009). In 2009, the NBA amended its formal rule on traveling to bring the text into compliance with basketball practice. That turned out not to be so easy, however. The revised Rule 10 provided that "[a] player who receives the ball while he is progressing or upon completion of a dribble, may take two steps in coming to a stop, passing or shooting the ball." As one commentator persuasively explains, a rule that prohibits traveling in basketball needs "to account for momentum, because basketball would break down pretty quickly if players were required to come to an immediate stop in order to pick up their dribble while sprinting." Chris Thompson, *The NBA's Traveling Rule Tweak Doesn't Fix Its Real Traveling Problem,* DEADSPIN (Sept. 24, 2019). That need explains the two-step rule. At the same time, it makes no sense to

> grant a player who is dribbling while stationary two free steps in whatever direction they please, as part of the normal and not at all complex act of, you know, no longer dribbling. Those two steps for a player on the move are an acknowledgement that forward momentum is important to the basic flow of the sport, not some general, all-purpose allotment.

In 2019, the NBA revised its rules again in an effort to clarify that the two-steps-from-standstill gambit is not allowed. That revision incorporates into the traveling rules the concept of the gather, which is a term that basketball officials had used in implementing the rules and which "refers to a player picking up their dribble or taking control of the ball from a pass or loose ball, usually while on the move." In most circumstances, the gather occurs when a player "gains enough control of the ball to hold it, change hands, pass, shoot, or cradle it against his body." NBA Rule 4, Section III.b.3. (Does this remind you of the catch rules in baseball or football?) And, while "[a] player who receives the ball while standing still" may only pivot, a player who gathers the ball either while "progressing" or dribbling "may take two steps in coming to a stop, passing, or shooting the ball" (but a player who was not yet dribbling may take only one step prior to releasing the ball for the dribble). NBA Rule 10, Section XIII. When announcing these modifications, the NBA advised that "[t]he revision will not change the substance of the rule but will help eliminate the gap between the rule as written and how it has been applied in NBA games." NBA, *Official Release: NBA Board of Governors approves clarification of rule governing traveling violations,* Sept. 20, 2019. What does this clarification mean? Does it solve the problem to which it was addressed? Does it endorse the notion that the substance of a rule is determined by practice, not text?

CHAPTER 11

FINDING THE FACTS

■ ■ ■

We have begun our consideration of officiating by discussing rule interpretation, because the rules determine what facts are material: Whether a player touched an opponent here or there matters only if the rules provide that different consequences attach depending upon the location of the touch. That said, because there is usually little doubt about what the rules provide in a given context, as a practical matter fact-finding usually comprises a much larger part of the official's duties than does rule interpretation.

This chapter discusses three topics. Subchapter 11A introduces what is probably the single most important issue regarding fact finding, not only in sports but in many domains of life: how confident must a decision maker be that some particular fact obtains (that a ball is out of bounds, that a player committed a violation, that a team scored a point, and so on) in order to act on the premise that it is so. Subchapter 11B concerns the use of technological means for finding sport-relevant facts. Subchapter 11C examines a curious fact pattern that has arisen in cricket and that has analogues in ordinary legal disputes.

A. INTRODUCTION: UNCERTAINTY, DEGREES OF CONFIDENCE, AND ASYMMETRIC ERROR COSTS

In pretty much everything we do, we hope our behavior will accurately reflect the way the world is. We may be happy to eat a juicy apple in most circumstances—but not if it happens to be poisonous. We will be happy to find a defendant guilty if in fact he committed the crime charged—but if he did not, we would much prefer to find him innocent. And in sports as well, we hope that officials' calls will accurately reflect reality—that if a pitch was outside the strike zone, the umpire will call it a ball, and that if it went through the zone the umpire will call it a strike.

The difficulty is that uncertainty about the true state of the world is pervasive. Sometimes, we may say that we are certain about a given state of facts, but except perhaps in very limited circumstances that seems not to be absolutely true. The leading decision theorist Ward Edwards once put the point this way: If you are certain about a proposition, you must be willing to bet your life and everything you hold dear against a penny on the truth of that proposition—and believe that you got infinitely the better of the bargain. (Is this helpful, or does it suggest that perhaps "certainty" is something short of *certainty*? If so, what *does* "certainty" mean?)

As this analysis suggests, we do not view factual questions in binary terms—true or false—but in terms of probability, which is a matter of degree. We can think of the probability that an observer assigns to a proposition as the degree of confidence, from 0 to 100%, that the observer has in the truth of that proposition. We don't usually attempt to assign a number to a probability, but it can be done.[a]

As Edwards's statement also suggests, how we sensibly make decisions under uncertainty depends not only on our probability assessments but also on the stakes at issue. Let's suppose a simple situation in which there are only two possible states of the world and only two possible decisions to make—say, a player's conduct either was or was not a foul, and the official can either call it a foul or call it fair play. What is sometimes called Type I error, or a false positive, would occur if the official called a foul even though none was committed; the cost of Type I error is how much worse things are, given that no foul was committed, if the official (inaccurately) calls a foul than if the official (accurately) does not. And correspondingly, Type II error, or a false negative, would occur if the official called no foul even though one was committed; the cost of Type II error is how much worse things are, given that a foul was committed, if the official (inaccurately) fails to call one than if the official does (accurately) call the foul. It can be shown simply that, at least under an ideal set of rules, an official would call a foul only if the odds that it was committed are greater than or equal to the ratio of the cost of Type I error to the cost of Type II error.[b]

---

[a] Consider the following scenario. Three cards, one of them an Ace, are shown to a player face up and then scrambled face down. Alongside of them is placed face down a shuffled deck of 100 cards, 59 of them red. The player has a choice of two games to play; whichever she chooses, if she wins, she gets a prize of $100. Game 1 is Three-Card Monte; she must pick which of the three cards is the Ace. Game 2 is Pick-a-Red-Card; she picks one card at random, and if it is red she wins. Now suppose that before the player chooses, we have this conversation with her.

Q: Which game do you choose to play?
A: Game 1. I think the leftmost card is the Ace.
Q: Well, what if we changed the number of red cards to 61? Then what.
A: Well, that would put me over the edge. I'd play Game 2.
Q: OK. What if the number of red cards would be 6o?
A: Ooh. That's a really close call.

Then we can say the player assigns approximately a 60% probability to the proposition that the leftmost of the three cards is the Ace.

[b] Here is a quick mathematical demonstration. The expected value of calling a foul equals the probability that a foul was committed times the value of calling a foul given that one was committed plus the probability that a foul was not committed times the value of calling one given that it was not committed. In symbols, we can say

$$EV_F = (P_F \times V_{FF}) + (1 - P_F) \times V_{FN},$$

where V_{FF} equals the value of calling a foul when one was committed and V_{FN} equals the value of calling one when it was not committed. This equation uses the fact that the probability that a foul was not committed is equal to 1 minus the probability that a foul was committed. Similarly, the

You may be familiar with this type of analysis from considering the standard of persuasion in a criminal case. It is a premise of our system, and of many others as well, that an inaccurate conviction—a false positive on the proposition that the defendant is guilty—is far worse than an inaccurate acquittal.[c] In other words, the ratio of the cost of Type I error to the cost of Type II error is very high. Accordingly, a finding of guilt is justified only if the odds of guilt are extremely high, a principle that is usually expressed in the United States by saying that the jury should not find the defendant guilty unless it is persuaded of his guilt *beyond a reasonable doubt*. In most civil cases, by contrast, we say that an error in favor of the defendant is about as bad as an error in favor of the plaintiff. (One might question whether that is really so, and whether courts and juries act as if it is so, but that is the usual rhetoric.) This leads to the rule that the plaintiff should win if the facts are *more likely than not* in its favor—a rule rather well captured by the formula used in English courts, "balance of probabilities," and not so well by the formula usually used in American courts, "preponderance of the evidence." Sometimes also American courts use an intermediate standard, frequently expressed as "clear and convincing evidence"; for example, in some states a relative of a patient in a persistent vegetative state who wishes to terminate life support for the patient must satisfy the court to that standard that this would have been the patient's wish. And in some circumstances even a standard of less than 50% probability will suffice; thus, under *Terry v. Ohio*, 392 U.S. 1 (1968), a police officer may stop and briefly detain a person upon "reasonable suspicion" of involvement in a punishable crime.

Given the ubiquity of uncertainty and the frequent asymmetry of error costs, we might expect organized sports leagues to follow the law's lead by arming their officials with comprehensive and explicit standards of proof.

---

expected value of not calling a foul equals the probability that a foul was committed times the value of not calling a foul given that one was committed, plus the probability that a foul was not committed times the value of not calling one given that it was not committed, or

$$EV_N = (P_F \times V_{NF}) + (1 - P_F) \times V_{NN}.$$

Simple algebra leads to the conclusion that EV_F is greater than EV_N—which means it is better to call a foul than not to call one—if and only if

$$\frac{P_F}{(1 - P_F)} > \frac{V_{NN} - V_{FN}}{V_{FF} - V_{NF}}.$$

The left-side fraction represents the odds that a foul was committed. (The odds of a proposition are the probability that the proposition is true divided by the probability that the proposition is false. Thus, an 80% probability corresponds to odds of 4 to 1.) The numerator of the right-side fraction represents the cost of Type I error. And the denominator on the right side represents the cost of Type II error.

   [c] This perception is widespread, but not universal. Alexander Volokh, *n Guilty Men*, 146 U. PA. L. REV. 173 (1997), does a remarkable job of assembling expressions of this view made across many centuries and cultures. Volokh also cites some skeptics. German Chancellor Otto von Bismarck, for example, "is said to have remarked that 'it is better that ten innocent men suffer than one guilty man escape.' Feliks Dzerzhinsky, founder of the Soviet secret police, saw Bismarck's motto and raised him an execution: 'Better to execute ten innocent men than to leave one guilty man alive.'" *Id.* at 195 (footnotes omitted).

Yet most leagues treat factual uncertainty in surprisingly unsystematic fashion, sometimes specifying standards of proof, more often not, and sometimes using essentially meaningless formulas. As you read the following materials, consider whether this state of affairs could be improved.

COMMENTS AND QUESTIONS

1.   When in doubt, not out. Under Cricket Law 31.6, if one of the two umpires is doubtful about a matter that lies within his jurisdiction but believes that the other umpire may have been in a better position to see, he should consult with the other and then give his decision. The Law then provides: "If, after consultation, there is still doubt remaining the decision shall be Not out." In light of the discussion above, what do you take this provision to mean? Could it be improved?

2.   Default rules in baseball. Suppose you're a major league umpire. Rule 5.09(a)(1) provides that the batter is out if his batted ball is caught on the fly by a fielder. What call should you make if you're just not sure whether a fly ball is caught or trapped? In the absence of any explicit direction, should you assume that the more-likely-than-not standard should govern? Why or why not? Even if so, what should you rule if you are in perfect equipoise between the two possibilities, caught and trapped? Given that perfect equipoise represents a probability assessment of 50.000 . . . %, how often do you think it arises?

3.   And in football. As in baseball, football also makes concrete consequences turn on whether a ball is caught cleanly on the fly. (This is true of many ball sports, but not all: think basketball, lacrosse, or water polo.) But the NFL purports to give more guidance to its referees than MLB does to its umpires. "If there is any question by the covering official(s) as to whether a forward pass is complete, intercepted, or incomplete," says Rule 3, Sec. 2, Art. 7 of the NFL rulebook, "it always will be ruled incomplete." What if you're unsure whether a player engaged in unnecessary roughness? Here, doubt cuts in just the opposite direction: "if in doubt . . ., the covering official(s) should always call unnecessary roughness." Rule 12, Section 2, Article 8 (Note). Can you be more precise about what these rules really mean? Unfortunately, the NFL rules do not always direct which call to make in the face of uncertainty. For example, they provide no standard or burden of proof for holding or illegal use of hands to the face. What should a football official rule when uncertain?

4.   Varying confidence in basketball. At one time, the NBA embraced an unusual, perhaps unique, solution to the ineliminable fact of uncertainty. Instead of expressly varying the standard of proof for specific infractions (as the NFL does), the NBA rulebook contained this general instruction:

> The purpose of penalties is to compensate a player who has been placed at a disadvantage through an illegal act of an opponent and to restrain players from committing acts which, if ignored, might lead

to roughness even though they do not affect the immediate play. To implement this philosophy, there are times during a game where "degrees of certainty" are necessary to determine a foul during physical contact. This practice may be necessary throughout the game with a higher degree implemented during impact times when the intensity is risen, especially nearing the end of a game.

2006–07 OFFICIAL NBA RULES, *Comments on the Rules: I. Guides for Administration and Application of the Rules.* The second and third sentences of this comment are no longer in the rulebook. What do they mean—that, to call a foul in crunch time, a ref must be more confident than usual that the infraction occurred? Something else? Do they reflect a sensible solution to the problem of uncertainty in basketball? Should the NBA have deleted them? Should other sports leagues adopt something like this solution? We will examine the crunch-time problem below, in Subchapter 12C.

5.   *And beyond.* If a variable standard of proof does make sense in the NBA, would it work well in the ordinary legal system, too? As we have seen, the orthodox position in Anglophone criminal law regimes is that an erroneous conviction is far worse than an erroneous acquittal. How much worse is sometimes called "the Blackstone ratio." Is the Blackstone ratio constant (e.g., at 10:1), or might it vary based on such factors as the severity of punishment that the defendant will face if convicted; whether the defendant has any previous convictions for offenses of similar character or seriousness; the degree of likelihood that this particular defendant, if guilty and acquitted, will reoffend; and whether conviction and punishment of this offender are unusually likely or unlikely to purchase general deterrence? Should the criminal law standard of proof be responsive to factors like these or any others? Is it possible that the existing "beyond a reasonable doubt" standard does in fact encourage jurors to set a confidence level required for conviction in the particular case at whatever would be "reasonable" all things considered? If so, would that be a good thing or bad? *See generally* Erik Lillquist, *Recasting Reasonable Doubt: Decision Theory and the Virtues of Variability,* 36 U.C. DAVIS L. REV. 85 (2002).

6.   *Do-overs?* Suppose that, on a pivotal play, the officials are wholly uncertain what the correct call is. Would it ever be appropriate for the sport to authorize the officials to award a do-over instead of making a call that they believe is as likely to be wrong as right? Consider, for example, a high school football game in which officials simply cannot tell whether a receiver had control of the ball before falling out of the end zone as time expires on what would be, if complete, a game-winning catch. Is it preferable for the referee to make a call one way or the other rather than to order that time be put back on the clock and the play rerun? Why or why not?

7.   *Solomon on the court.* In a pickup basketball game, Oliver goes up for a layup, with Dwayne contesting. The ball ends up out of bounds, under the basket. Oliver contends that the ball was last touched by Dwayne, but Dwayne

says it was out off Oliver. Assuming that the other players are not sure what happened, what is a sensible outcome in a pickup game? What if the dispute is whether Dwayne fouled Oliver?

Should the outcomes be different if the situation arises in an officiated game, assuming that the referees, just like the players in the hypothetical unofficiated game, are unsure both about whether Dwayne fouled Oliver and about who last touched the ball? In an NBA game between the Cleveland Cavaliers and the Detroit Pistons on March 8, 2007, LeBron James of the Cavs was called for a charge and Jason Maxiell of the Pistons for a block on the same play, resulting in a jump ball at center court. Was this the right result if the officiating crew, taken as a whole, was in equipoise regarding which of the two players committed the infraction? Would it have been preferable that the officiating crew pretend to have a view one way or the other as to what happened? Should compromises of this sort be a more frequent occurrence in the NBA? Should the NCAA adopt a form of this compromise in a similar situation by giving the ball to the team with the possession arrow and switching the arrow to the other team? Should sports more generally adopt split-the-difference compromises of this sort?

8. Calling your own. In most amateur tennis matches, players themselves function as officials. Each player calls balls that land on their side of the net, and a player must abide by their opponent's calls. *See* USTA, *USTA Rules and Regulations, Part 3,* https://tinyurl.com/y69sp45b. The rules explicitly direct that "any doubt must be resolved in favor of an opponent." Why should that be? The USTA explains that "the game is much better played this way," but does not elaborate. Do you agree that the game is better this way? What would be the consequences of an alternative scheme in which players were instructed to issue the call they think more probable? The formal rules notwithstanding, many informed observers believe that often players do not give their opponents the benefit of the doubt. *See, e.g.,* Zoe Howard, *A first-hand experience with cheating and lost trust in junior tennis—and how to fix it,* SPORTS ILLUSTRATED (Mar. 20, 2017) (noting that in junior tennis, "cheating [by making knowingly incorrect calls] has unfortunately become accepted as 'part of the game.'"). Does a system of self-officiating inevitably produce self-serving calls? Could it have the opposite effect? Howard argues that the solution to the problem is a technological one: high-resolution cameras that record the match, and to which players can refer in resolving close calls. Is this a desirable solution? What would you propose?

9. Discounts in sports. What about discounting penalties by uncertainty? In an ordinary commercial market, prices for a good are sensitive to uncertainty about its quality or provenance. A used car with complete maintenance records that show it to be in great shape will cost more than a superficially identical car whose accident and maintenance history cannot be verified. A cow that has already borne healthy calves will cost more than a cow that may or may not be fertile. Roughly speaking, you would expect to pay half as much for a lottery ticket that offers a 1-in-a-million chance for a given jackpot as for a ticket that offers a 2-in-a-million chance for the same size pot.

Does it follow that the magnitude of penalties imposed for infractions in sports should be sensitive to the confidence that the official has that the infraction was committed? Should the same spot penalty be awarded for defensive pass interference if an official is .99 confident in their call as when they think it only barely "more likely than not" that the infraction was committed? Can you think of any rules of sport in which consequences should be adjusted to accord with an official's subjective confidence?

10. *Discounts in the law.* Should damage awards in tort or breach of contract be discounted by the factfinders' confidence regarding liability? That is, if a jury concludes that it is more likely than not—but only barely more likely than not—that the defendant was liable for plaintiff's injuries, should it award the plaintiff only half of her damages? Why (not)? All else equal, should a criminal defendant whose guilt is "certain" be punished more severely than one whose guilt is "beyond a reasonable doubt" but not without *any* doubt? For a provocative discussion of these issues, see LEO KATZ, WHY THE LAW IS SO PERVERSE ch. 3 (2011).

Exercise 11A

Write an exercise on standards of proof for the next edition of this textbook. Also, please explain why it's a good exercise—for example, how it can be satisfied by a variety of interesting answers, and why it's neither too easy nor too hard. If you prefer, you may instead craft an exercise for Subchapter 11B, which follows.

B. TECHNOLOGICAL AIDS

In some sports, electronic systems displace human officials entirely for some crucial determinations: In swimming, it is the timer attached to the touchpad, not a human official, that determines a swimmer's official time. In épée, it is the electronic scoring system that determines touches. In tennis, an electronic system such as Hawk-Eye is often used to call serves; if the Hawk-Eye system perceives the ball as long, it will blare, and the serve is deemed long without further ado.

For a technological system to be used to make, or assist in making, initial calls, it must, in most contexts, yield answers essentially immediately. (Note that here we are dealing only with the initial call; we will address replay review below, in Subchapter 13B.) Technological improvements make this more and more feasible in various settings. For example, determining whether a field goal attempt is good or not, if the ball sails higher than the uprights, is often a difficult call for human officials—

was the ball between the uprights when it crossed their plane?—but an easy one technologically:

> ... [A]ccording to engineers, precise, three-dimensional object tracking is done every day and it's easy to set up.
>
> A few high-speed cameras carefully positioned around the end zones and some ball-tracking software can get the job done for field goals, making it the easiest NFL scoring play for technology to handle. In fact, NFL broadcast graphics created by Sportvision already provide three-dimensional field goal tracking for television viewers.

Shira Springer, *New Technologies Ready to Assist NFL Referees*, BOSTON GLOBE, Nov. 4, 2012.

In soccer, some notorious official blunders generated increased interest in providing technological assistance to the referee; perhaps the biggest howler was the referee's failure, in England's 2010 World Cup match against Germany, to recognize that a shot by Englishman Frank Lampard that hit the underside of the crossbar landed a full two feet inside the goal. In 2010, the International Football Association Board (IFAB) approved in principle the idea of using goal-line technology (GLT) to detect whether a goal had been scored. IFAB laid down four basic requirements that a GLT system must fulfil:

i) The goal-line technology applies solely to the goal line and only to determine whether a goal has been scored or not;

ii) The GLT system must be accurate;

iii) The indication of whether a goal has been scored must be immediate and automatically confirmed within one second; and

iv) The indication of whether a goal has been scored will be communicated only to the match officials (via the referee's watch, by vibration and visual signal).

FIFA now maintains a detailed set of specifications that systems must satisfy. FIFA QUALITY PROGRAMME FOR GOAL-LINE TECHNOLOGY: TESTING MANUAL (2014). FIFA approved two systems, Hawk-Eye and GoalRef, in 2012, and use in some matches began. Another system, GoalControl, was implemented at the 2014 World Cup in Brazil and successfully used in all 64 matches, providing crucial assistance in calling several goals. *Goal Line Technology at Brazil 2014*, FIFA.com (July 29, 2014). FIFA used GoalControl again at the 2018 World Cup, but at the 2015 and 2019 Women's World Cups it used Hawk-Eye. (At the 2018 World Cup, FIFA also began to use a Video Assistant Referee (VAR) system, a form of replay review; that is discussed below, p. 436.)

COMMENTS AND QUESTIONS

1.   Decision-aid technology in general. If some use of decision-aid technology would improve the accuracy of calls and would not incur delay, are there any considerations other than expense that might reasonably weigh against deployment of that technology? For example, recall the suggestion made earlier (Subchapter 3F) that considerations of standardization or uniformity might dictate that decision-aid technology should not be used in some venues if it cannot be used in all, or should not be used at one level of competition if it cannot be used at lower levels. Is this persuasive to you? What other factors should be considered?

2.   Room for interpretation? Consider an observation by Dr. Andy Harland, director of the Sports Technology Institute at Loughborough University in Great Britain, that "[i]f the game becomes too mechanistic, if there's no room for interpretation, then suddenly there's no room for supporters"? What "room for interpretation" is proper or desirable with respect to calls such as whether a football team achieved a first down, or whether a soccer player scored a goal, or whether a pitch is a ball or a strike? What would make determinations of questions like these "too mechanistic"? *See* Chris Jaffe, *10th Anniversary: Curt Schilling vs QuesTec camera*, HARDBALL TIMES (May 24, 2013) (relating incident in which major league pitcher Curt Schilling expressed his displeasure with the impact of the QuesTec system by destroying a camera).

3.   The mission of GLT. FIFA has said that the objective of using GLT "is not to replace the role of the officials, but rather to support them in their decision-making." FIFA, TESTING MANUAL, at 6. But why? Is this a sound decision? In particular, is the requirement that the system communicate the indication of a goal only to the official an appropriate one?

4.   Balls and strikes. Beginning in 2001, MLB used an Umpire Information System (UIS), supplied by QuesTec, in some ballparks to rate the performance of umpires and to allow them to review their own calls. UIS is widely believed to have made the calling of balls and strikes more consistent. Now, PITCHf/x is installed in every park. This technology is accurate to within one centimeter. What would be gained and what would be lost if ball and strike calls were made automatically by the system instead of by the human umpire behind the plate?

In answering this question, consider whether the following data are relevant. Two researchers who determined that plate umpires are 85% accurate in calling balls and strikes also determined that umpires are considerably less accurate on pitches that are delivered with either 3 balls or 2 strikes (but not when the count is 3 balls *and* 2 strikes). Putting full counts aside, when the pitch is in the strike zone and the batter already has 2 strikes, umpires erroneously call the pitch a ball 39% of the time; and when the batter is sitting on 3 balls and the pitch is outside the strike zone, umpires erroneously call strikes 20% of the time. That is, umpires increase their error rates to avoid issuing walks and strikeouts—so much so that the strike zone actually enforced is 188 square inches larger on 3–0 pitches than on 0–2 counts. TOBIAS MOSKOWITZ & L. JON WERTHEIM, SCORECASTING: THE HIDDEN INFLUENCES BEHIND HOW SPORTS ARE PLAYED AND GAMES ARE WON 18 (2011). *Should* the strike zone get larger or smaller as the count changes? (Note that if so, this would be a form of contextual variance, a topic addressed at length in Subchapter 12C.) If so, is that a consideration against the use of decision-aid technology? Why or why not?

5. *Better than the naked eye?* The Hawk-Eye system used in tennis is not a true videographic representation of the ball. It is, instead, a "Reconstructed Track Device" (RTD), which applies a statistical algorithm to information drawn from visible-light cameras and reconstructs the flight and impact point of the ball. Hawk-Eye reconstructs the ball's most likely path using images from cameras; thus, as used in tennis, it does not faithfully reproduce what *actually happened*, but rather what statistically is *most likely* to have happened. While the company behind Hawk-Eye does not publish the math behind its system in detail, its margin of error on average is 2.2 millimeters (0.087 inches) and some new research suggests that it can be off by as much as 10 millimeters (0.394 inches). *See* Harry Collins & Robert Evans, *Sport-decision aids and the "CSI-effect,"* 21 PUB. UNDERSTANDING SCI. 904 (2012). ATP data suggests that roughly 94% of all challenges occur within 100 millimeters, so this margin of error is not negligible. *See* George Mather, *Perceptual uncertainty and line-call challenges in professional tennis,* 275 PROC. R. SOC. B. 1645 (2008).

Because of the need to reduce congestion on the courts, numerous tennis tournaments during the COVID-19 pandemic—including the 2020 U.S. Open and the 2021 Australian Open—replaced line judges with Hawk-Eye Live, a souped-up system that makes instantaneous calls (and features a pre-recorded voice announcing "Out"). Should they continue to do so even absent a pandemic? (Novak Djokovic thinks so.) *See, e.g.,* Shahid Judge, *Explained: How Hawk-Eye Live is replacing line-officials and decongesting tennis courts in COVID times,* INDIAN EXPRESS, Feb. 3, 2021.

Consider whether a clear understanding of how RTDs work complicates the cost/benefit analysis that properly attends their use. As sociologist of science Harry Collins points out, there is ambiguity if part of the ball, looked at from above, overlaps the line, but the part of the ball touching the court is fully outside the line. In that case, he says, the human eye—including that of "an optimally skilled and perceptive" official—would perceive the ball as 'in,' and that would be the traditional call, but "an optimally accurate machine working with impact footprint would indicate 'out.'" Harry Collins, *The Philosophy of Umpiring and the Introduction of Decision-Aid Technology,* 37 J. PHIL. SPORT 135, 142 (2010). And so Collins wonders whether an 'out' call by machine in such a case is appropriate. *Id.* at 142. What do you think is more important in cases like this—"[c]oherence with tradition and the way the nontechnically assisted game is played" or accurate and consistent implementation of a roughly similar but not identical standard? Or something else? In addressing this question, note that cricket, which also uses Hawk-Eye (usually to determine whether a ball would have hit the stumps if the batsman's leg had not blocked it), is transparent about when Hawk-Eye is uncertain. When it is uncertain, umpires are instructed to use their own judgment. Which approach do you find preferable—that of tennis or of cricket? Or do the different approaches appropriately reflect differences between the sports?

    6.   And again. Are Collins's concerns even weightier in soccer? Consider this commentary, by law professor David Pozen, on the Video Assistant Referees (VAR) recently deployed in soccer:

> VAR-induced delays at this summer's Copa América and Women's World Cup have unsettled the rhythm of both competitions. A sport with no timeouts or commercial breaks now finds itself repeatedly interrupted by VAR reviews. . . . Worse still, the outcomes of multiple matches have been swung by VAR determinations that a goalkeeper left her line early during a penalty kick, allowing the shooter a second chance after an initial miss. Scotland is heading home from the World Cup after such a call was made last night.

> VAR's supporters insist that "rules are rules," and these goalkeepers violated the rules. The official laws of soccer currently state (on p. 121) that when a penalty kick is taken, the goalkeeper "must have at least part of one foot touching, or in line with, the goal line." VAR seemed to show that the Scottish goalkeeper Lee Alexander had both feet off the line when the Argentinian midfielder Florencia Bonsegundo struck the ball. Alexander was therefore in breach. Case closed.

> Legal realism, however, suggests an alternative perspective. In Karl Llewellyn's classic formulation, there are "paper rules" and "real rules." The paper rules are written down in authoritative law books. The real rules, as Frederick Schauer puts it, "are the ones actually applied by real officials in real institutional settings." While we may have cause to worry about especially large or arbitrary gaps between the paper rules and real rules, the two pervasively come apart to some degree.

> Schauer gives the example of a highway speed limit. In many jurisdictions, the official speed limit—the paper rule—is 65 miles per hour. All the signs and statutes indicate as much. But the real rule is often 74. Everyone knows that they won't receive a speeding ticket for going 66 miles per hour, even if they might be given a ticket for going 75. Drivers adjust their behavior accordingly.

> Soccer's penalty-kick rules for goalkeepers are similar—or at least, they used to be. Every goalkeeper knew that she couldn't take a giant step off the goal line well before the ball was booted. But stealing a few inches of ground a fraction of a second early? That was commonplace. Indeed, it was part of the art of good goalkeeping.

Perhaps in implicit recognition of the draconian nature of the penalty-kick sanction, the real rules permitted more flexibility than the paper rules. Alexander's subtle shimmy against Argentina was consistent with the former though not the latter.

Yet now, under VAR, the cops are doling out tickets to drivers going 66. And with multiple cameras trained on every blade of grass, they don't miss a single infraction. No wonder England's goalkeeper Karen Bardsley describes the new enforcement regime as a "cruel and pedantic" crackdown that is forcing players to unlearn deeply ingrained habits.

. . . [T]he president of FIFA Gianni Infantino likes to say that "VAR is not changing football, it is cleaning football." Llewelyn's distinction helps show why Infantino's slogan is misleading. VAR *has* changed the rules of soccer, the real rules, not to mention the flow and feel of the game.

Is the added "cleanliness" worth it when goalkeepers try to inch off the line? At least when it comes to putting speed cameras on the streets, there may be benefits to public safety and public coffers. Yet most people nevertheless hate speed cameras, for good reasons, and the use of VAR to close the gap between the paper rules and real rules of penalty kicks strikes me as even harder to justify. Simply asserting that "rules are rules" obscures much and resolves little.

What Are the Rules of Soccer?, BALKINIZATION (June 20, 2019).

C. A LARK: "THE UMPIRE'S DILEMMA"

In cricket, there are various ways in which a batsman can be "given out." He is "out Caught" if "a ball delivered by the bowler . . . touches his bat without having previously been in contact with any fielder, and is subsequently held by a fielder as a fair catch . . . before it touches the ground." Laws of Cricket 32–1. In general, he is "out Bowled if his wicket is put down by a ball delivered by the bowler . . . even if it first touches his bat or person." Law 30–1. (The wicket consists of two small bails on top of three stumps; it is put down "if a bail is completely removed from the top of the stumps, or a stump is struck out of the ground." Law 28–1(a).) And he cannot prevent himself from being bowled by getting between the ball and the wicket. Accordingly, he is "out LBW" (or Leg Before Wicket) if, in addition to other conditions, "the ball not having previously touched his bat, the striker [batsman] intercepts the ball . . . with any part of his person, . . . and but for the interception, the ball would have hit the wicket." Law 36–1. (There are other ways as well that the batsman may be given out, but this is all we need to know for now.)

In 1985, the philosopher Colin Radford posited a case in which the bowler delivers a ball which strikes the batsman on his pads and then carries through to the wicket-keeper, who catches it. . . . The difficulty for the umpire is that he is not sure whether the ball made contact with the batsman's bat before striking his pads. If it did, the batsman is out caught; if it did not, he is in this case out lbw.

Colin Radford, *The Umpire's Dilemma,* 45 ANALYSIS 109, 110 (1985). This is a problem because, at least under one view of the Laws, the umpire cannot decide that the batsman is out "caught or lbw"; rather, to dismiss a batsman, he must determine one particular reason.[d]

Indeed, an incident very much like Radford's hypothetical occurred during the final Test match of the Ashes—the traditional series between England and Australia—in 2009. With Ricky Ponting of Australia batting, a ball deflected off something and was caught by the wicket-keeper. If the ball had hit Ponting's bat, he was out caught; if not, it must have hit him or his pads, and he was out lbw. And yet, after long consideration, the umpire, Asad Rauf, decided that he could not give Ponting out one way or the other, and Ponting continued to bat. Ian Rumfitt, *Ricky Ponting and the judges,* 70 ANALYSIS 205 (2010). This, says Rumfitt, is "an instance of the general point that a thinker might know (or have strong evidence for the truth of) a disjunction without knowing (or having strong evidence for) either disjunct." "The pressing question," he adds, is "whether it ought to be possible to give a batsman out on disjunctive grounds." The question, in other words, is whether the Laws of cricket *should* allow the umpire to say something like, "out, either caught or lbw."

Assuming that the Laws of cricket do not allow for such a result, what do you think of the suggestion by the legal philosopher Joseph Raz, in a personal communication to Rumfitt, "that Rauf should have plumped for one of the grounds and given Ponting out on that ground"? Rumfitt says:

> [Raz] points out that, in criminal appeals, the appellant loses even if the decision is shown to be faulty, so long as the fault did not cause any injustice. Justice is rarely pristine, and a no-nonsense judge might well cut through the problem in the way Raz suggests. But those of a more delicate sensibility may still admire

---

[d]   Previous editions of the Open Learning Manual published by the Marylebone Cricket Club, keeper of the Laws of Cricket, said, "To be dismissed, he [the batsman] must be out under some Law." According to Ian Rumfitt, the widely understood meaning of this passage was that the batsman must be out under a particular Law that the umpire was able to specify.

The quoted passage from the Manual appears to have been a mistaken exposition of Law 27.2(b), and it has since been changed. That Law provides that a batsman is dismissed if "he is out under any of the Laws and leaves his wicket"; it governs only the situation in which the batsman leaves the wicket.

The Open Learning Manual now appears to conform to the Law. It provides: "To be dismissed [the batsman's] innings must be terminated either by an umpire giving him out (on appeal), or by leaving his wicket of his own freewill and being out under some Law."

Rauf's scrupulousness in resisting the temptation to do the right thing for the wrong reason.

Ricky Ponting, at 209 n.4.

COMMENTS AND QUESTIONS

1.   *Disjunction or disjuncts?* What is your answer to Rumfitt's "pressing question"? Should the laws of cricket allow an umpire to rule the batter out "either caught or lbw"? Whichever way you conclude, what are the best arguments for a contrary judgment?

2.   *The umpire's duty.* Suppose that the applicable cricket rules do not allow for a disjunctive ruling. In that case, should an umpire in Rauf's situation be "scrupulous" and rule the batter not out, or should he declare the batter out, naming one or the other grounds, to better promote "justice"?

3.   *Criminal-law analogues.* Analogous cases sometimes arise in criminal law; some of these cases raise the question of what facts the jury must agree upon. Consider the following:

- *Jack's Destruction of Evidence.* The jurors are confident that Jack willfully destroyed evidence, but they are divided as to whether he burned it or flushed it down the toilet. *See* Peter Westen & Eric Ow, *Reaching Agreement on When Jurors Must Agree,* 10 NEW CRIM. L. REV. 153, 158–59 (2007). Should the jurors be allowed to find him guilty of destroying evidence?

- *Two-City Robbery.* Aaron is charged with robbing two banks at 12 noon on the same day, one in Anchorage and the other in Fairbanks, 350 miles away. Some jurors believe beyond a reasonable doubt that he robbed the Anchorage bank, and some believe beyond a reasonable doubt that he robbed the one in Fairbanks. *Id.* at 159–60. Should the jury be able to convict him of bank robbery? Suppose that the reason for the jurors' indecision is that video and DNA evidence provide ample proof that each robbery was committed either by Aaron or by his identical twin. Does this make a difference? Should the jurors be allowed to find Aaron guilty of bank robbery? Would it matter if, instead of bank robbery, the charges were intentional homicide? Car theft? What if one were intentional homicide and the other car theft? *See generally* Alon Harel & Ariel Porat, *Aggregating Probabilities Across Cases: Criminal Responsibility for Unspecified Offenses,* 94 MINN. L. REV. 261 (2009).[e]

- *Schad v. Arizona,* 501 U.S. 624 (1991). The trial judge instructed the jurors that they could find the accused guilty of first-degree

---

[e] For a real-life case from Germany in which charges had to be dismissed because prosecutors could not determine which of two identical twins was implicated by the evidence, see Claudia Himmelreich, *Despite DNA Evidence, Twins Charged in Heist Go Free,* TIME, Mar. 23, 2009.

murder if they found *either* that he had killed the victim intentionally *or* that he had unintentionally caused the death, directly or indirectly, while committing the felony of robbery. The United States Supreme Court, by a 5–4 vote, with no majority opinion, upheld the conviction. Does this seem to be the right result?

- *Richardson v. United States*, 526 U.S. 813 (1999). Richardson was charged with being a so-called kingpin in a continuing criminal enterprise. As the governing statute, 21 U.S.C. § 848, was understood, conviction required that, through the agency of five or more persons that he managed, he committed three violations of any of a long list of federal statutes. The trial judge instructed the jury that to find Richardson guilty it had to agree unanimously that he had committed three or more such violations—but the instructions did *not* say that it had to agree unanimously on which three he committed. By a 6–3 vote, the Supreme Court reversed. Should it have allowed the conviction to stand?

- *R. v. Giannetto* (1997: 1 Cr. App. Rep. 1). The defendant was convicted of murdering his wife. He argued that the jury should have been instructed that to find him guilty it must agree either that he had killed her or that someone else had done so on his behalf. The Court of Appeal held that the jurors "were entitled to convict if they were all satisfied [beyond reasonable doubt] that if the defendant was not the killer he at least encouraged the killing." Do you agree?

Westen & Ow present this formula as a solution to cases of this sort:

In all cases in which a defendant is alleged to have committed an offense by one or another, or all, of multiple means, judges must decide if there is sufficient evidence by which individual jurors can find beyond a reasonable doubt that, if the defendant did not commit the alleged offense by one of the alleged means, he must have committed it by another of the alleged means. If such evidence is lacking, judges must instruct jurors that they cannot convict without agreeing on which means the defendant used. If such evidence is present, jurors may convict if, as among the various alleged means, one particular means exists that each juror believes beyond a reasonable doubt is either the very means the defendant used or the means (or among the means) he must have used if he did not use any of the other alleged means.

Reaching Agreement, at 154. Is that persuasive? Suppose the jurors are convinced that the accused either murdered his wife himself or that he aided and abetted someone else to kill her, but they are unable to decide between those two. What implications would this have for the accused's punishment? *Cf. R. v. Thatcher*, [1987] S.C.R. 652 (Can.) ("Where there is evidence before a jury that points to an accused either committing a crime personally or, alternatively, aiding and abetting another to commit the offence, provided the jury is satisfied beyond a reasonable doubt that the accused did one or the other, it is a matter of indifference which alternative actually occurred.") Does the Westen & Ow analysis help resolve the case of Ricky Ponting?

CHAPTER 12

THE OFFICIAL'S DISCRETION

■ ■ ■

As the legal philosopher Ronald Dworkin helpfully explained, there are different forms of discretion:

> The first thing to notice is that the concept is out of place in all but very special contexts. For example, you would not say that I either do or do not have discretion to choose a house for my family. It is not that I have 'no discretion' in making that choice, and yet it would be almost equally misleading to say that I do have discretion. The concept of discretion is at home in only one sort of context: when someone is in general charged with making decisions subject to standards set by a particular authority. It makes sense to speak of the discretion of a sergeant who is subject to orders of superiors, or the discretion of a sports official or contest judge who is governed by a rule book or the terms of the contest. Discretion, like the hole in a doughnut, does not exist except as an area left open by a surrounding belt of restriction. . . .

> Sometimes we use 'discretion' in a weak sense, simply to say that for some reason the standards an official must apply cannot be applied mechanically but demand the use of judgment. We use this weak sense when the context does not already make that clear, when the background our audience assumes does not contain that piece of information. Thus we might say, 'The sergeant's orders left him a great deal of discretion', to those who do not know what the sergeant's orders were or who do not know something that those orders vague or hard to carry out. It would make perfect sense to add, by way of amplification, that the lieutenant had ordered the sergeant to take his five most experienced men on patrol but that it was hard to determine which were the most experienced.

> Sometimes we use the term in a different weak sense, to say only that some official has final authority to make a decision and cannot be reviewed and reversed by any other official. We speak this way when the official is part of a hierarchy of officials structured so that some have higher authority but in which the patterns of authority are different for different classes of decision. Thus we might say that in baseball certain decisions, like the

decision whether the ball or the runner reached second base first, are left to the discretion of the second base umpire, if we mean that on this issue the head umpire has no power to substitute his own judgment if he disagrees.

I call both of these senses weak to distinguish them from a stronger sense. We use 'discretion' sometimes not merely to say that an official must use judgment in applying the standards set him by authority, or that no one will review that exercise of judgment, but to say that on some issue he is simply not bound by standards set by the authority in question. In this sense we say that a sergeant has discretion who has been told to pick any five men for patrol he chooses or that a judge in a dog show has discretion to judge airedales before boxers if the rules do not stipulate an order of events. We use this sense not to comment on the vagueness or difficulty of the standards, or on who has the final word in applying them, but on their range and the decisions they purport to control. If the sergeant is told to take the five most experienced men, he does not have discretion in this strong sense because that order purports to govern his decision. The boxing referee who must decide which fighter has been the more aggressive does not have discretion, in the strong sense, for the same reason. . . .

We must avoid one tempting confusion. The strong sense of discretion is not tantamount to license, and does not exclude criticism. Almost any situation in which a person acts (including those in which there is no question of decision under special authority, and so no question of discretion) makes relevant certain standards of rationality, fairness, and effectiveness. We criticize each other's acts in terms of these standards, and there is no reason not to do so when the acts are within the center rather than beyond the perimeter of the doughnut of special authority. So we can say that the sergeant who was given discretion (in the strong sense) to pick a patrol did so stupidly or maliciously or carelessly . . . . An official's discretion means not that he is free to decide without recourse to standards of sense and fairness, but only that his decision is not controlled by a standard furnished by the particular authority we have in mind when we raise the question of discretion.

RONALD DWORKIN, TAKING RIGHTS SERIOUSLY 31–33 (1977).[a]

The first weak sense of **discretion** that Dworkin identifies implicates our discussion of rules and standards (in Subchapter 3H). The second

---

implicates the discussion, in the next chapter (Chapter 13), of the situations in which, and the standards by which, decisions made by on-field sports officials should be subject to review by hierarchically superior officials. This chapter explores the circumstances in which officials do or should assume, or are or should be granted, discretion in what Dworkin terms the "strong" sense.

A. CONTEXTUALLY VARIABLE ENFORCEMENT: AN INTRODUCTION

BRUCE WEBER, AS THEY SEE 'EM: A FAN'S TRAVELS IN THE LAND OF UMPIRES

pp. 113–14 (2009)
© 2009 by Bruce Weber.
Reprinted with the permission of Scribner, a division of Simon & Schuster, Inc.

It's fair to say my umpiring beginnings were modest. My first game was a Little League contest; I was on the bases. And my first call of any consequence I got wrong on purpose. The team at bat had scored a dozen or so runs in the third inning, largely because the first baseman had dropped three perfectly good throws, and with the score something like 20–1, the poor kid finally held on to one. The runner, however, had beaten the throw by a stride and a half. I did my job. "He's out!" I bellowed.

The reactions were interesting. The center fielder, sprinting by on his way to the dugout, said, "Thank you, thank you, thank you, Mr. Umpire," with the plaintive gratitude of a squirming boy who'd been excused early from an overlong church sermon. One of the parents on the sideline growled at me, "You're kidding, right, Blue?"

"I'd had enough, hadn't you?" I said.

"That's bullshit."

My partner, one of the league's regular umpires, stared daggers of disgust in my direction and didn't talk to me for the rest of the game, which thankfully ended, owing to a local slaughter rule, after the fourth inning.

Afterward, the coach of the winning team came over and shook my hand and winked at me. "Nice job on that call," he said.

I didn't think a lot about it at the time; it became just a small, funny story I enjoyed telling. But in retrospect it was a good introductory lesson in the distinctions among an umpire's authority, his power, and his job. Is an umpire only supposed to get it right, with nothing to come between him and the pure call? Or does he more appropriately consider context? Things such as sportsmanship, the personality of the players, just deserts, the way the game "ought" to be played? And if it is okay to consider context, is it always okay? And if it's not always okay, when isn't it? What sorts of calls should or shouldn't be affected?

COMMENTS AND QUESTIONS

1. Weber's ruling. Was Weber right to purposely call out a runner he knew to be (according to the sport's formal rules) safe? If not, is that because you believe that all rules of all sports should be strictly enforced or because, although baseball umpires should properly enforce some rules more or less strictly depending upon context, in this particular situation Weber exercised poorly the discretion that rightly belongs to umpires? One way of viewing Weber's decision is that he created an on-the-spot mercy rule for this particular inning. Was it appropriate for him to do so? If you think it was not, would it have been appropriate for him to call the coaches in and say, "First time the first baseman catches a ball, I'm going to call an out, OK?" If you think that even that was not appropriate, was there *any* remedy that could properly be implemented in this situation?

2. Invariant enforcement in general. Is it plausible that all sports rules should be enforced invariantly even in youth leagues? If not, is there good reason to believe that fully invariant or acontextual enforcement is required at higher levels of competition? If so, does this follow from the nature of rule-governed activity or for some other reason? Is invariant enforcement of the rules the practice in the sports with which you are most familiar?

3. Invariant enforcement in life. Is rule-enforcement discretion more or less palatable or desirable in sports than outside of sports? Consider the police. Is it ever appropriate for police officers to exercise discretion not to enforce laws? What are the costs or dangers inherent in according the police such discretion? What are the costs or dangers of not doing so? Is it ever appropriate for a cop not to stop—or to let off with only a warning—a motorist who committed a traffic infraction? Or to not arrest somebody the officer knows to possess a small amount of illegal drugs? What factors should properly govern the exercise of police discretion? How should the exercise of police discretion be policed?

4. Types of context-variance. Weber rightly observes that, if the exercise of some measure of enforcement discretion by sports officials should be tolerated, or even applauded, it becomes critical to identify the factors that properly bear on the exercise of official discretion. The remainder of this chapter focuses on three factors that knowledgeable observers believe often influence the discretionary enforcement or non-enforcement of sport rules: (1) whether the officials have made previous officiating errors in the same contest that could and should be "evened up"; (2) whether the contest is at a critical juncture, particularly what is sometimes called "crunch time"; and (3) whether one or more of the participants in the play is a "star" and thus should be accorded special treatment. What other contextual factors do you think might properly influence the exercise of enforcement discretion by sports officials?

More generally, what answers might you supply to the questions that Weber raises at the end of the passage quoted above?

B. THE MAKEUP CALL

MARK HAMILTON, THE MORAL AMBIGUITY OF THE MAKEUP CALL

38 JOURNAL OF THE PHILOSOPHY OF SPORT 212 (2011)
© 2011 by International Association for the Philosophy of Sport, reprinted
with permission of the publisher (Taylor & Francis Ltd.)

. . . So accepted is the existence of makeup calls that Subway ran a national television advertisement during the 2008 Super Bowl season in which an official in what appears to be a real game turns to the crowd with fan noise reverberating, looks toward the audience as he switches on the microphone and announces, "I totally blew the call. In fact, it wasn't even close. But don't worry. I will penalize the other team. For no good reason. In the second half. To even things up." Every sports fan watching this commercial knew exactly what the commercial was satirizing, the makeup call. . . .

Once an official becomes aware that an incorrect call has been made there is a psychological impact on the arbiter. The awareness that she has missed a call presents the official a dilemma about how to carry on. Rather than correct it without delay herself by reversing a call and consequently appearing clumsy or incompetent by publicly admitting this error, the official sticks it in the back of her mind that a mistake has been made and then, consciously or more likely subconsciously, reciprocates or gives back what was taken away when she has an opportunity to make a call in favor of the team that had been short-changed by the first call. This ideally restores balance and creates a type of reconciliation such as when one person "makes up" with another. . . .

A type of self-talk may occur in the mind of the official, "I gave the other team the 'benefit of the doubt' in the last call so this time I will give the benefit of the doubt to the other team." The reasoning that may go through the head of the official is that "Person or Team A" should never have received this advantage, so it is an unfair advantage because of "my error." With this in mind the official assumes personal blame and responsibility though it may only manifest itself as a quasi-ill feeling lasting only a moment. Based on this combination of a twinge of guilt and need to right a perceived wrong the official then provides a call that creates an advantage giving the "benefit of the doubt" to the second competitor "Person or Team B" in an attempt to restore justice or fairness to the game. It is an easy rationale. The first call was motivated by a desire to be just and to apply the rules fairly but did not successfully achieve this aim, so the second is provoked by a desire to keep the game even and to not permit either team to have the game tilted in their direction and thus it is motivated by a desire to maintain the game's equilibrium. . . .

The Argument Against Makeup Calls

. . . Makeup calls may be intentional and conscious or unintentional and subconscious; by intentional is meant that it is purposefully done and by conscious is meant that the official making the call is aware of what she is doing. Intentional conscious makeup calls are most troublesome. I will provide four reasons these should be considered immoral and not permitted.

First, it is dishonest. Officials are expected to make calls within the constitutive and regulative rules of the game and an intentional makeup call opposes this by breaking these rules. No one believes that umpires have the discretion to make novel calls outside of the constitutive and regulative understandings of sports. To do so is ignoring what one "sees" and subverts integrity. Second, it creates partiality. It is logically contradictory to think that a referee should knowingly make a bad call. Officials with a personal itinerary can no longer call the game through unbiased lenses. . . . Third, a Formalist would consider makeup calls to be logically inconsistent and equivalent to not playing the game.

Finally, it is an act of injustice to perpetuate injustice through further injustice. Philosophically one might phrase it this way: two wrongs do not make a right. . . .

. . . Graham McFee asserts, "Any referee caught making a makeup call should be banned for life from officiating—he has abandoned the duty to judge the event impartially." These should be eliminated from discussion as they are obviously illegal and immoral.

The more common type of makeup call is one where the official is not aware she is doing so and lacks intent to miss a call but wants to remain objective and evenly divide borderline calls; this is motivated by a desire for justice and impartiality. The official is not cognizant of her action or subconscious motive for the call. This second type of makeup call is deficient of malicious intent and is more likely to occur in fast-paced sports such as basketball or soccer or sports like baseball where decisions must be immediate without opportunity for deliberation.

But even this type of unintentional subconscious decision by an official to perform a makeup call presents varied problems. One problem is proportionality, the assumption that the makeup call is equivalent to the originally missed call. The initial justification for the makeup call is that it is based on desert. It assumes that a ball called a strike can be compensated for later by a strike called a ball, or that a charging call now and one called later in a game are equivalent, but this is not so in sports. No two calls are likely equal in value. A foul called now and one called soon after even if it is a similar type of play will more than likely not be identical in value. Game contexts change, games progress and the consequences of one call may be wholly different from the context of a previous call even when it is the same or similar call. It is quite an assumption of an official to believe she can make the game "fair" by making bad calls. . . .

Officials who make themselves more important than the rules of the game create suspicion. It could be argued that an official who initiates a makeup call even subconsciously is no longer calling the game since he is bypassing the rules. By declaring a makeup penalty or foul the official is purposely rejecting the game and its foundations. It has been well argued in the philosophy of sport that cheaters are no longer playing the game.[b] Analogous to this cheating athlete who is no longer playing the game, the biased official who formulates a makeup call is no longer "calling" the game but creating some new game according to his own rules. . . . He is taking justice into his own hands and practicing vigilante justice. . . . [Hamilton also raises the possibility that the original call was correct, in which case, he says, the so-called makeup call "has not succeeded in bringing justice but has actually compounded the error."]

Finally an argument can be made that makeup calls violate Kant's second formulation of the Categorical Imperative. Kant states, "Act in such a way that you treat humanity, whether in your own person or in the person of another, always at the same time as an end and never simply as a means." . . . Yet the makeup call does just that; it uses another rational person or team of persons as a means to an end to correct the official's error. [Hamilton posits a case in which an umpire compensates for a bad call of ball four on a full count in favor of Batter "X" with an inaccurate full-count call of strike three against the next batter, "Y".] Batter "Y" is not being respected for his own individual humanity but has become a pawn for the umpire to use to ease his own conscience. These criticisms place the burden of proof upon those who would support the moral justification of makeup calls.

Seeking Moral Justification for Makeup Calls

[Hamilton canvasses various theories of justice in search of a justification for makeup calls.]

. . . Corrective justice is grounded in the second Aristotelian theory of justice and encompasses aspects of retributive and restorative justice. It offers the best hope at finding a useable theory to justify makeup calls. Like retributive justice it tries to provide a remedy for a wrong that has occurred. And though two wrongs do not make a right, there is a

---

[b]   This proposition is called the Logical Impossibility Thesis. We examine it in Chapter 14. Recall also Robert Simon's discussion, at p. 191, in Subchapter 6A.

responsibility to correct a wrong and this theory takes this responsibility seriously. . . .

The makeup call attempts to make the game as fair as possible and to remove the official from being a determining factor in the outcome of the game. The official who subconsciously makes a makeup call is not motivated by a desire to change the course of a game. She simply wants to keep the game in harmony and to not personally be a causal determining factor to the outcome of the game. This is a good motive and is the only real compensation available to the official. A bad call is unfair and one side will suffer. The makeup call attempts to restore rightly to a team or player as much as possible what has been unfairly taken from them even at the unfortunate expense of another. All forms of corrective justice limit restitutionary damages insofar as they correspond to the injustice that the accused party has done to the injured party. The good official understands this and is restricted by a fair sense of proportionality knowing that no call is precisely equivalent in value to a previous call but it could be relatively of the same value. The position arguing for corrective justice says sporting games are not a series of consecutive unrelated plays but are part of a whole contest of interconnected and interdependent plays and actions. Games have an obvious gestalt to them and calls are interconnected affecting how a game should be officiated. This holistic approach to contests could allow discretionary use of makeup calls by officials, but not every type of makeup call in every sport.

Each sport develops its own higher sense of internal justice as part of its evolving ethos . . . . One sport may believe makeup calls are quite immoral and should not be an accepted part of its competition; it is outside the justice system of that sport. Other sports may find them quite acceptable. Officials and participants must be cognizant of the way their sport is to be played (regulative rules) and officiated and what the acceptable parameters of the ethos of the sport are. It can be argued that in some sports the unstated contract of play assumes the makeup call as part of the unspoken regulative rules of the game. This is justified by arguing that makeup calls can be a lawful way of restoring harmony to the competitive contest as most basketball, baseball, and soccer enthusiasts know. . . .

. . . Makeup calls seem to be an almost necessary part of the basketball or baseball ethos possibly to the degree that not making a makeup call violates the spirit of the game. Thus a game may build within it a form of corrective justice which permits officials to keep a game "fair" and in harmony with opportunities for each team or competitor having equal or relatively equal opportunity for success by having discretion to make makeup calls. But this should be limited to not distorting the nature of the game, not merely using another team or player as a means to an end to satisfy or soothe the official's conscience due to an errant or inept call, and it should be limited to calls which really are close enough to have been debatably called either way.

Conclusion

. . . There still seems something offensive about makeup calls. I believe they are self-evidently immoral and compromise the integrity and impartiality of officials. The imperative of our officials remains to get each call correct. Because of this the burden of proof continues to rest upon those who would morally justify makeup calls.

Games are not perfect and neither are our officials though we expect them to be. We can improve our games, however, and one way to do so is to reduce or even eliminate the need and desire for makeup calls. There are several specific ways I would suggest. [First, Hamilton suggests altering the ethos of sport, through education, to generating greater acceptance of bad calls as part of the game, as bad bounces are. Second, he suggests that improving the accuracy of the call of the first play—both through better training of officials and expanded use of replay review—would decrease the need for makeup calls.]

We should fine-tune our discussions about what the primary duties and responsibilities of an official really are. Why should character matter in our officials? Which should be the higher priority: to get each individual particular call independently correct or see the contest as a whole and calls as interrelated? This last philosophical underpinning seems to be foundational to this whole discussion on makeup calls and directly relates to justice in sports. A clearly articulated philosophy of officiating needs to be understood by participants, audiences, and officials and whether this or that action is worthy of being a penalty, about the role of dissent, and acceptance or rejection of the regulative and constitutive rules of the game and officiating within them. . . .

COMMENTS AND QUESTIONS

1. The Subway ad. You can see the Subway ad mentioned by Hamilton at https://tinyurl.com/y4h9efqr. Why is the ad funny? Because makeup calls seem so inappropriate? Because it's unlikely a ref would candidly admit what they're doing?

2. Makeup calls and morality. Hamilton maintains that makeup calls are "self-evidently immoral." Do you agree? Should a conscientious official ever intentionally issue a "makeup call"? If so, under what circumstances? Are you persuaded by Hamilton's argument that the official cannot know whether he is helping or hindering fairness? And what does fairness represent in this context?

3. Makeup calls and the standard of proof. Hamilton distinguishes between conscious and subconscious makeup calls. Consider whether it might also be helpful to distinguish two different types of conscious makeup calls. Let us say that a "strong" form of makeup call exists when an official makes what they "know" (or confidently believe) to be the wrong call in order to compensate for what they confidently believe was an earlier wrong call that went against the side they now advantage. In contrast, a "weak" form of the intentional makeup call involves the purposeful adjustment of the standard of proof such that the official makes a call that they do not "know" or confidently believe to be mistaken but that is the opposite of the call that they would make were they not putting a figurative thumb on the epistemic scales. An official makes a weak makeup call when they believe that it is more likely than not that Team A did not commit some infraction but make the call against Team A because they have already made several similarly close calls in Team A's favor. Is there any meaningful difference between strong and weak intentional makeup calls? Can you think of any reasons why weak intentional makeup calls might be permissible even if strong intentional makeup calls are not? Or vice versa?

In evaluating the merits of weak intentional makeup calls, does it matter whether the hesitation on the part of the official is attributable to (a) uncertainty as to what happened, or (b) indecision as to how to characterize it? Compare the two functions to those performed by a jury in assessing, say, a medical malpractice claim: The jury must determine both what happened and whether to characterize it as malpractice.

4. *Makeup calls and the constitutive/regulative distinction.* Is the distinction between constitutive and regulative rules of any relevance here? The weak makeup call introduced in Question 3 involved the possible commission of an infraction, which we take to be a violation of a regulative rule. Is the case for weak makeup calls—or even strong makeup calls—any more or less persuasive when the call in question would concern whether a competitor's action conforms or does not conform to a constitutive rule, such as whether a team has completed, or failed to complete, a reception in football, or an out in baseball, or which team last touched a basketball before it sailed out of bounds?

5. *Official errors.* Do you agree with Hamilton that we ought to recondition our mindset towards officials to be more tolerant of errors? How could this be accomplished? Even if it could be accomplished, would it be worthwhile? Would it have benefits beyond the context of sports?

6. *Makeup calls in hockey.* In 2013, Kerry Fraser, a former NHL referee, created a stir by admitting to behavior that looks like a makeup call. As he wrote:

> I can tell you there were many times I felt my stomach in knots after being fooled on a play or calling a marginal infraction. A two minute power play seemed like an eternity when the other team pressed hard and there was absolutely nothing I could do to make it right. That means that I would not compromise the game further by "inventing" a penalty against the team on the tainted power play. If, on the other hand, a "gift horse" presented itself in the form of some infraction that could be deemed an illegal advantage gained by the team on the

power play I was quick to grab it; perhaps a pick, interference or anything of the sort. If a team killed the penalty I would breathe a sigh of relief—if a power play goal was scored I gulped as the air escaped my lungs hoping my error would not affect the final outcome of the game. That is all part of being human.

Greg Wyshynski, *Kerry Fraser admits refs use 'makeup calls' after questionable penalties; also, water is wet*, YAHOO! SPORTS (Apr. 9, 2013). The suggestion is that Fraser would make calls that were "technically" correct but that he would not ordinarily make when doing so would correct an error he had previously made. Is this acceptable? For a study by economists that concludes that hockey referees exhibit a "striking . . . tendency to not call a penalty on the same team 'too many' times in a row," see Jason Abrevaya & Robert McCulloch, *Reversal of Fortune: A statistical analysis of penalty calls in the National Hockey League*, 10 J. QUANT. ANALYSIS SPORTS 207, 220 (2014).

WILLIAM T. PIZZI, "MAKEUP CALLS" IN SPORTS AND COURTS

11 GREEN BAG 2d 333 (2008)
© William T. Pizzi, reprinted with permission

"Makeup Calls" in Sports

* * * [W]hat can be done in an imperfect world where referees make mistakes, there is a lot at stake, and there is no challenge procedure that might permit errors to be corrected? There is no alternative for coaches and managers but to do what they have always done in these situations. NFL coaches must continue to slam their headsets on the ground, the better to run onto the field to confront the nearest referee to protest the unfairness of a call or non-call. In the NBA, coaches must continue to sprint along the sideline next to the offending referee to give voice to the injustice of what just transpired. And, finally, baseball managers must run as best they can onto the field and go chest to chest with an umpire—without quite touching him—to protest the call. When this yields no change in the ruling, the manager must do something quite beautiful and extraordinary. He must kick a small amount of dirt onto the pants of the offending umpire. For an older and portly manager who never played soccer as a child, the symbolic kicking of dirt can be difficult if the ground is damp or hard. But it must be done to say to the umpire, "I do not respect your decision and, therefore, I must increase your dry cleaning bill."

What is the point of vehemently protesting rulings that the protesters know well cannot and will not be reversed? Obviously, they plead their case in the hope that the referee will see the injustice of what he has done and give the offended team the benefit of the doubt on the next close ruling. (Notice that the berating of lines-persons—"What?! Are you blind?"—such a common occurrence in the John McEnroe era, has largely disappeared from tennis matches when the new technology is employed.)

But do referees pay attention to these protests? Of course they do. While it is easy to philosophize that referees should turn a deaf ear since mistakes will balance out in the long run, we don't have the long run at hand. Instead, we have a specific contest and no referee wants to be in the position of having decided a hard fought contest by denying a team a touchdown or by giving possession of the ball to the wrong team as the result of a refereeing error. . . .

It is perhaps not surprising that the term "makeup call" had its origins in the period when jumbotron screens in sporting venues became ubiquitous. These screens replay immediately what has just taken place so that everyone, including the offending referee, can see why a ruling clearly was wrong. . . .

The term "makeup call" is most closely and controversially linked to basketball, a sport where often a refereeing error in the waning seconds can directly determine the outcome. Commentators contend that sometimes when, for example, a referee has erroneously given possession of the ball to team A, the referee will quickly whistle a "makeup call," such as traveling or an improper zone defense on team A in order to restore possession to team B. This is a controversial assertion as it insists that referees sometimes assess fictional penalties in order to right a previous wrong. League officials deny that this happens, yet players and coaches insist that it does. . . .

Part of the reason [the] fictitious ruling [in the 2008 Subway ad] strikes us as comical is the fact that referees cannot speak with candor "on the record" on these matters. Thus, refereeing supervisors are required to deny the existence of makeup calls. But everyone familiar with professional sports not only sees makeup calls, but accepts them as a part of sports.

Makeup Calls in the Legal System

Judges are in a position analogous to sports referees in that they must make decisions quickly, the rules are complicated, interlocutory review is not possible for most rulings, and many decisions involve judgment calls. The difference between the two realms of refereeing is, of course, that the legal system cannot tolerate a game the outcome of which was distorted by a ruling that was wrong. For this reason, we have an appellate system to review what happened at trial.

Usually, appellate courts are good at seeing individual rulings in broader contexts so that a denial of a certain discovery request may have been balanced out by more liberal rulings on other requests. Or perhaps a very generous evidentiary ruling for one side at trial was balanced by a similar showing of latitude to the opposing side on a request to admit certain evidence. Appellate courts understand that even the most conscientious trial judges are not perfect; they make mistakes. But mistakes often balance out.

There are times, however, when appellate courts ignore the way the "game" is played at trial and refuse to see individual rulings in a broader context. Instead, they place a single ruling in isolation under their microscope and see the ruling as serious error, when, in context, the error may have been balanced out by other rulings.

To illustrate my point, let me turn to *Shane v. Commonwealth*, [243 S.W.2d 336 (Ky. 2007),] . . . reversing a conviction because a judge made a jury selection error in not removing a particular juror for cause. Because the defense had to use a peremptory challenge to remove this particular juror, the impact of the error, the court concluded, was to leave the defense one challenge short of the nine to which it was entitled and this was automatic reversible error.

Not all jurisdictions view the loss of a peremptory as automatic reversible error, but many jurisdictions do, including Vermont, Colorado, Virginia, and California. *Shane* is thus typical of many appellate cases that focus all their attention on a single ruling at the jury selection stage with no appreciation that rulings on challenges are often interrelated.

The issue in *Shane* is not complicated. The defendant, Timothy Shane, was in a Colorado Best prison in 2003 when DNA evidence extracted from cigarette butts left at the crime scene linked him to a 1993 Kentucky burglary/sexual assault. He was charged, brought to Kentucky and convicted of burglary as well as of being an habitual offender ("Persistent Felony Offender" under Kentucky law). The issue on appeal concerned the failure of the trial judge to remove for cause Juror 138.

Juror 138 was a police officer who had not been a police officer at the time of the crime, but who had worked in the same district as two of the officers who had been involved in the investigation (one of whom testified at trial). He said his past association with police officers would not affect his ability to be an impartial juror, but he also said that he was "absolutely" pro-police and he did not believe police would lie under oath because they took the oath more seriously. The defense asked the judge to remove Juror 138 for cause and, when the judge refused, the defense used a peremptory on Juror 138.

Let's assume the court is wrong on Juror 138: he gave some "good" answers and some "bad" answers, but, on balance, he should have been struck for cause. So what? Maybe this was a makeup call. Perhaps the judge was thinking to himself, "I have given the defense three very favorable rulings on challenges for cause. One of them, in particular, I think was definitely not necessary. This is another close one, but I think this is a conscientious person who can be fair so I will make the defense use a peremptory." So maybe the defense never lost a peremptory in the end because the calls on challenges for cause balanced out.

I realize that the "official" position of any spokesperson for the judiciary, just like the official position of Major League Baseball, the National Football League, and the National Basketball League, has to be to insist that makeup calls are a myth and could never happen in an American court. Judges, the spokesperson would assure us, are made of sterner stuff than the rest of us so that, even subconsciously, they would never balance equities in this way.

But I think we can be fully confident that makeup calls happen in court just like they happen on the court. The reason is that makeup calls are a part of parenting, of social sports, and of life. We all try to balance the equities, and if we have been harsh on one occasion, we try to be more generous on the next. Thus, we have to understand the error with Juror 138 as part of a series of rulings to appreciate its impact.

Another way in which this ruling may have been a makeup call relates to the way the judge was ruling on the prosecution's challenges for cause. For example, maybe the judge thought to himself, "I have been very tough on prosecution challenges for cause. There were two jurors whom I probably would have dismissed for cause, but I trust people when they say they can be impartial. I made the prosecution use two peremptories on those two jurors. So I am going to be equally tough on the defense."

When a referee has to make rulings that are somewhat subjective, athletes understand that one referee may rule differently from another on the same issue. Baseball players know that some umpires have smaller strike zones than others and basketball players understand that some referees call games "more closely" than others. But what is important is that they call the game the same way for both sides.

The same logic applies to jury selection errors. To understand this error, we need to understand how the judge rules more generally on challenges for cause. Sure, the defense was entitled to nine peremptories under Kentucky law and this error meant the defense only had eight. But maybe the defense lost a peremptory but the prosecution lost two or three?

. . .

Conclusion

In the end, we know some things about Juror 138, but nothing about the rest of the game. We don't know how the judge ruled on other defense challenges or on the prosecution's challenges. I don't think this is fair to the judge. Judges, like referees, have to rule quickly and sometimes they make mistakes. But sometimes a mistake is not as serious in context as it might appear and sometimes it may even be balanced out completely by other rulings that went in favor of the wronged party. At least we ought to look.

COMMENTS AND QUESTIONS

1. Transparency. Is Pizzi right that the official position of courts and major sports leagues "has to be to insist that makeup calls are a myth"? Is that true even if makeup calls do in fact occur? Is it plausible to argue both that makeup calls *should* occur and that leagues should deny that they do? Note that the Official Rules of Major League Baseball include this General Instruction to Umpires: "You no doubt are going to make mistakes, but never attempt to 'even up' after having made one. Make all decisions as you see them and forget which is the home and visiting club." Suppose you concluded that umpires sometimes *should* "even up" after having made a wrong call. Would it follow that this general instruction should be repealed? Would it follow that the rules should instruct umpires regarding the circumstances in which makeup calls are permitted or even required?

2. Makeup calls and defamation. An NBA referee sued the Associated Press and one of its reporters for defamation for suggesting that the ref had made a make-up call. The reporter, Jon Krawczynski, had tweeted that "Ref Bill Spooner told [Timberwolves' coach Kurt] Rambis he'd 'get it back' after a bad call. Then he made an even worse call on Rockets. That's NBA officiating folks." *Bill Spooner sues AP writer over tweet,* ESPN.com (Mar. 15, 2011). Spooner eventually settled with the AP, agreeing to drop the suit in exchange for removal of the tweet from Jon Krawczynski's Twitter account and a payment of $20,000 for his litigation costs. In your opinion, is the suggestion that an official has made a makeup call defamatory? Is it significant that Spooner (apparently) *thought* the suggestion was defamatory?

3. The analogy. Are you persuaded by Pizzi's analogy between makeup calls in sports and in courts? Is there any basis for concluding that the trial judge's ruling on Juror 138 was a makeup call? If it was or might have been one, should that affect the appellate court's treatment of the situation? Is Pizzi right in contending "that the legal system cannot tolerate a game the outcome of which was distorted by a ruling that was wrong"? (By the way, Pizzi suggests that Shane may not have needed all his peremptories; he used them all, but that may have been so that he could complain on appeal that he was prejudiced by the denial of a for-cause challenge to Juror 138.)

4. Exam grading. Another analogy, which may hit closer to home, is to exam grading. Suppose a teacher is grading a set of essay exams. There are two essays on the exam, and she grades in full points. Suppose that on Question 1 she gives a student a 9, but thinks that the question is almost good enough to give a 10 instead. And her evaluation of the second question is about the same; if she graded on a continuous point scale, she would give each essay a 9.4, for a total of 18.8. What score should she give the second essay?

5. From the classroom to the octagon. Suppose that the teacher in the preceding question moonlights as a UFC judge on weekends. In one fight she believes that Fighter A won the first round, but just barely, and has scored it 10–9 for A. She believes that Fighter A also won the second round, and by an equally narrow margin. The fight is three rounds, and 10–8 rounds are very rare. How should she score round two? Is your answer the same whether our protagonist is grading exams or judging fights?

C. WHISTLE-SWALLOWING IN CRUNCH TIME

MITCHELL N. BERMAN, "LET 'EM PLAY": A STUDY IN THE JURISPRUDENCE OF SPORT
99 GEO. L.J. 1325 (2011)
© 2011 Mitchell N. Berman

Introduction: One Step Over the Line

Kim Clijsters was the feel-good story of the 2009 U.S. Open. A former world #1, the 26-year-old Belgian had been retired for 2 years, during which time she had married and borne a child, when she surprised the tennis world by announcing her return in the summer of 2009. Entering the tournament as an unranked wildcard, Clijsters defeated Denmark's Caroline Wozniacki in straight sets to become the first unseeded player ever to win the U.S. Open and the first mother to win a grand slam event in 30 years.

The match that made the headlines, however, was not the final. It was Clijsters's semifinal contest against the #2 seed, Serena Williams. Straight off her victory at Wimbledon, Williams had powered through the women's draw at the Open without losing a set; with the third-round defeat of #1 seed Dinara Safina, she was the odds-on favorite to win her third grand slam tournament of the year. Instead, Williams lost the first set 4–6 and found herself serving to Clijsters at 5–6 in the second. Down 15–30, Williams's first serve to the ad court was wide. On her second serve, the line judge called Williams for a foot fault, putting her down double-match point. At this, Williams exploded, walking over to the judge several times, gesticulating with her racket in an ominous manner, shouting, and threatening to do things with the ball that the lineswoman was bound to find unwelcome. Because Williams had already committed a code violation earlier in the match for racket abuse, this second code violation called forth a mandatory one-point penalty. That single point gave the match to Clijsters.ᶜ

Williams has few defenders. Her outburst was further penalized with a $10,000 fine that, after many commentators bemoaned its inadequacy, was raised to $82,500 and supplemented with a two-year probation. But without condoning or excusing Williams's response to the foot fault call, I'm interested in a different question: whether the call should have been made at all. CBS color commentator and former tennis great John McEnroe thought not. As he remarked at the time: "you can't call that there." His

---

ᶜ   You can view the incident at https://www.youtube.com/watch?v=gNwc7o_0Sgg.

point was not that the call was factually mistaken,[6] but rather that, even assuming arguendo that it was factually supportable, it was an inappropriate call to make at that point in the match: the lineswoman should have cut Williams a little slack. Many observers agreed. As another former tour professional put it, a foot fault "is something you just don't call—not at that juncture of the match."[7]

The McEnrovian position—that at least some rules of some sports should be enforced less strictly toward the end of close matches—is an endorsement of what might be termed "temporal variance." It is highly controversial. Indeed, some people find it simply incredible that a call conceded to be correct at one time could be thought improper at another. As one letter writer to the *New York Times* objected: "To suggest that an official not call a penalty just because it happens during a critical point in a contest would be considered absurd in any sport. Tennis should be no exception."[8] On this view, which possibly resonates with a common understanding of what it means to follow "the rule of law," rules of sports should be enforced with resolute temporal invariance.

Now, perhaps McEnroe was wrong about the Williams foot fault. But the premise of the letter propounding the competing view—that participants and fans of any other sport would reject temporal variance decisively—is demonstrably false. Indeed, one letter appearing in *Sports Illustrated* objected to the disparity of attention focused on Williams as compared to U.S. Open officials, precisely on the grounds that "[r]eferees for the NFL, NHL and NBA have generally agreed that in the final moments, games should be won or lost by the players and not the officials."[9] I am unsure just how general this supposed agreement is. But I'd warrant that most fans of professional basketball would affirm that contact that would constitute a foul through most of the game is frequently not called during the critical last few possessions of a close contest. Moreover, most fans I have spoken with believe this is not only how it is, but how it ought to be.[10] In any event, precious few of those who disagree would contend that

---

[6]   The rule governing foot faults provides that, "During the service motion, the server shall not . . . [t]ouch the baseline or the court with either foot." International Tennis Federation, Rule of Tennis 18.c (2010). *See also* USTA Comment 18.3 (2007) ("A player commits a foot fault if after the player's feet are at rest but before the player strikes the ball, either foot touches . . . the court, including the baseline.").

[7]   Michael Wilbon, *A Call and a Response That Can't Be Defended*, WASH. POST, Sept. 14, 2009, at D03, *available at* http://www.washingtonpost.com/wp-dyn/content/article/2009/09/13/AR 2009091302533.html.

[8]   Vince Bray, Letter to the Editor, N.Y. TIMES, Sept. 20, 2009 (Sports Sunday), at 5.

[9]   J. Everett Prewitt, Letter to the Editor, SPORTS ILLUSTRATED, Oct. 12, 2009.

[10]   An anonymous reader of this paper expressed puzzlement that I should appeal to intuitions widely held by sports fans, opining that "the point of introducing the analytical apparatus" should instead be "to provide a structure within which those intuitions could be corrected." Well yes, of course, the analytical apparatus will allow us to correct intuitions when they should be corrected. But that we should not hold ourselves hostage to pre-reflective intuitions does not mean that we should disregard them entirely. Reflective equilibrium—the method that I employ—insists that our general principles and "analytical apparat[i]" do not enjoy categorical

the status quo is absurd. So an insistence on rigid temporal invariance requires argument not just assertion.

However, advocates of temporal variance ought not to be too smug either. For while the negative import of temporal variance is clear—namely, the *denial* of categorical temporal *in*variance—its positive import is anything but. Surely those who believe that the foot fault ought not to have been called against Serena Williams in her match against Kim Clijsters mean implicitly to invoke a principle broader than "don't call foot faults in the twelfth game of the second set of semi-final matches in grand slam tournaments." But how much broader? Is the governing principle that *all* rules of *all* sports should be enforced less rigorously toward the end of contests? Presumably not. Few proponents of temporal variance, I'd wager, would contend that pitchers should be awarded an extra inch or so around the plate in the ninth inning, or that a last-second touchdown pass should be called good if the receiver was only a little bit out of bounds. So even if categorical temporal invariance is too rigid, the contours and bases of optimal temporal variance remain to be argued for.

That, indeed, is the topic for this subchapter: are there any good reasons to enforce some rules of some sports less strictly toward the end of close contests, and, if so, how do those reasons apply to particular rules of particular sports? Much of our discussion will focus on basketball, the major sport with respect to which it is probably most obvious to knowledgeable observers that some measure of temporal variance is respected in actual practice. *See, e.g.,* KYLE GARLETT & PATRICK O'NEAL, THE WORST CALL EVER! 43 (2007) (nominating, as one of the worst officiating calls in NBA history, a shooting foul whistled against the Chicago Bulls' Scottie Pippen in the closing seconds of Game 5 of the 1994 Eastern Conference semifinals, with the Bulls leading the Knicks 86–85; conceding that Pippen did bump Knicks's guard Hubert Davis after the shot but decrying that the call broke "the long-standing NBA philosophy of not calling ticky-tack fouls in the closing seconds of playoff games"; you can see the play at https://tinyurl.com/y3rbaow5; note that commentator Hubie Brown says that the foul comes after the shot but that Pippen "definitely fouls" Davis).

We will consider two accounts of temporal variance in sports. The first, offered by economist Tobias Moskowitz and sports journalist and lawyer Jon Wertheim, seeks to explain (but not to justify) the practice as a manifestation of the cognitive bias that psychologists call "omission bias." The second, developed by one of the authors of this book, seeks to justify

---

priority over our case-specific judgments. Rather, it counsels that we try to bring into coherence our considered judgments about principles at various levels of generality and case-specific outcomes.

(but not necessarily to explain) the practice as a way to promote the desideratum that the outcome of athletic contests should reflect the competitors' relative excellence in executing the particular athletic virtues that the sport is centrally designed to showcase and reward. The latter argument depends upon the claim that the absolute magnitude of the difference or "gap" between the competitive cost of an infraction and the competitive cost of the sanction imposed for the infraction can change during a game and can become unacceptably large near the end of close contests.

TOBIAS J. MOSKOWITZ & L. JON WERTHEIM, SCORECASTING: THE HIDDEN INFLUENCES BEHIND HOW SPORTS ARE PLAYED AND GAMES ARE WON

pp. 11–14 (2011)
© Tobias J. Moskowitz and L. Jon Wertheim, reprinted with permission

People view acts of *omission*—the absence of an act—as far less intrusive or harmful than acts of *commission*—the committing of an act—even if the outcomes are the same or worse. Psychologists call this *omission bias*, and it expresses itself in a broad range of contexts.

In a well-known psychological experiment, the subjects were posed the following question: Imagine there have been several epidemics of a certain kind of flu that everyone contracts and that can be fatal to children under three years of age. About 10 out of every 10,000 children with this flu will die from it. A vaccine for the flu, which eliminates the chance of getting it, causes death in 5 out of every 10,000 children. Would you vaccinate your child?

On its face, it seems an easy call, right? You'd choose to do it because not vaccinating has twice the mortality rate as the vaccination. However, most parents in the survey opted *not* to vaccinate their children. Why? Because it *caused* 5 deaths per 10,000; never mind that without the vaccine, their children faced twice the risk of death from the flu. Those who would not permit vaccinations indicated that they would "feel responsible if anything happened because of [the] vaccine." The same parents tended to dismiss the notion that they would "feel responsible if anything had happened because I failed to vaccinate." In other words, many parents felt more responsible for a bad outcome if it followed their own actions than if it simply resulted from lack of action.

In other studies, subjects consistently view various actions *taken* as less moral than actions not taken—even when the results are the same or worse. Subjects, for instance, were asked to assess the following situation: John, a tennis player, has to face a tough opponent tomorrow in a decisive match. John knows his opponent is allergic to a particular food. In the first scenario, John recommends the food containing the allergen to hurt his unknowing opponent's performance. In the second, the opponent mistakenly orders the allergenic food, and John, knowing his opponent might get sick, says nothing. A majority of people judged that John's *action* of recommending the allergenic food was far more immoral than John's *inaction* of not informing the opponent of the allergenic substance. But are they really different?

Think about how we act in our daily lives. Most of us probably would contend that telling a direct lie is worse than withholding the truth. Missing the opportunity to pick the right spouse is bad but not nearly as bad as actively choosing the wrong one. Declining to eat healthy food may be a poor choice; eating junk food is worse. You might feel a small stab of regret over not raising your hand in class to give the correct answer, but raise your hand and provide the wrong answer and you feel much worse.

Psychologists have found that people view inaction as less causal, less blameworthy, and less harmful than action even when the outcomes are the same or worse. Doctors subscribe to this philosophy. The first principle imparted to all medical students is "Do no harm." It's not, pointedly, "Do some good." Our legal system draws a similar distinction, seldom assigning an affirmative *duty* to rescue. Submerge someone in water and you're in trouble. Stand idly by while someone flails in the pool before drowning and—unless you're the lifeguard or a doctor—you won't be charged with failing to rescue that person. . . .

This same thinking extends to sports officials. When referees are trained and evaluated in the NBA, they are told that there are four basic kinds of calls: correct calls, incorrect calls, correct non-calls, and incorrect non-calls. The goal, of course, is to be correct on every call and non-call. But if you make a call, you'd better be right. "It's late in the game and, let's say, there's goaltending and you miss it. That's an incorrect non-call and that's bad," says Gary Benson, an NBA ref for 17 years. "But let's say it's late in the game and you call goaltending on a play and the replay shows it was an incorrect call. That's when you're in a *really* deep mess."

Especially during crucial intervals, officials often take pains not to insinuate themselves into the game. In the NBA, there's an unwritten directive: "When the game steps up, you step down." "As much as possible, you gotta let the players determine who wins and loses," says Ted Bernhardt, another longtime NBA ref.

It's a noble objective, but it expresses an unmistakable *bias*, and one could argue that it is worse than the normal, random mistakes officials make during a game. Random referee errors, though annoying, can't be predicted and tend to balance out over time, not favoring one team over the other. With random errors, the system can't be gamed. A systematic *bias* is different, conferring a clear advantage (or disadvantage) on one type of player or team over another and enabling us—to say nothing of savvy teams, players, coaches, executives, and, yes, gamblers—to predict who will benefit from the officiating in which circumstances. As fans, sure, we want games to be officiated accurately, but what we should *really* want is for games to be officiated without bias. Yet that's not the case.

MITCHELL BERMAN, "LET 'EM PLAY"

Blog postings to the Volokh Conspiracy, July 19, 2011
© 2011 Mitchell N. Berman

One rationale for temporal variance invokes essentially aesthetic considerations: the referee's whistle disrupts play, thereby reducing spectators' enjoyment of the action. And while disruption of play almost always incurs an aesthetic cost, disruption during crunch time is especially costly from an aesthetic perspective inasmuch as dramatic tension is especially high.

There is something to this justification for temporal variance. It would seem to apply, though, only when play would continue uninterrupted but for the calling of a foul. However in some sports that arguably respect temporal variance play stops either way.

For example, it appears to me—and not only to me[d]—that football officials are often more reluctant to call defensive pass interference during crunch time even though an incompletion stops play just as surely as does a penalty flag. Because an aesthetic or dramatic preference that play not be disrupted would seem not to explain or justify temporal variance in the calling of fouls and the enforcement of penalties across the board, it might not provide the whole story even in basketball. So without denying that appreciation for dramatic excitement can help explain why officials should give the competitors somewhat greater slack during moments of high drama, it behooves us to explore the possibility of an alternative account too.

The alternative account that I favor can be parsed as follows:

(1) In the main, a sanction imposed for an infraction has a greater expected impact on contest outcome (against the rule-violator) than does the infraction itself (in the violator's favor). This must be so if the sanction

---

[d] Here is *Sports Illustrated*'s lead NFL columnist, Peter King, explaining his naming Browns cornerback Hank Poteat "goat of the week":

> With Cleveland holding a 37–31 lead and no time left on the clock in the fourth quarter, Detroit quarterback Stafford let fly with a rainbow to the end zone and Poteat tackled Calvin Johnson with the ball in the air. *If Poteat had jostled Johnson, there's little chance a flag would have been thrown.* But a full-scale body slam to the ground . . . That has to be called. Pass interference. With the extra play, Detroit threw a touchdown pass to win it. On the goat scale, Poteat's play ranks about as high as you can go.

Peter King, *Monday Morning QB: Matthew Stafford's gutsy comeback in Detroit was one for the ages*, SPORTS ILLUSTRATED, Nov. 23, 2009 (emphasis added).

is to serve not only a restitutionary function, but a deterrent function as well.

(2)   The expected impact of all outcome-affecting contest events—e.g., scores, base hits, yardage gains, infractions that confer a competitive benefit on the rule-breaker, penalties imposed for infractions, etc.—are not constant, but context-variant. For one thing, the impacts vary in inverse proportion to the closeness of the contest. The variance that matters for my purposes, however, is temporal: when the contest is close (and holding the closeness of the contest constant), the expected impact of outcome-affecting events varies in inverse proportion to the distance remaining to the contest's completion. For example, a touchdown or a basket, a 15-yard penalty markoff or a free throw opportunity, all have greater impact on the expected outcome when they occur 2 minutes before the end of a then-tied game than when they occur 2 minutes from the start of a then-tied game.

(3)   From (1) and (2) it follows that the absolute magnitude of the gap between the competitive impact of the infraction (say, a non-shooting foul) and the competitive impact of the penalty imposed for the infraction (say, the award of free throws) is significantly greater in crunch time during close games than earlier in the same contest.

(4)   It is a general desideratum of sport that athletic contests go better insofar as the outcome of the contest reflects the competitors' relative excellence in executing the particular athletic virtues that the sport is centrally designed to showcase and reward. This general principle might well benefit from further refinement, but it's a good first cut. This is why we prefer to reduce the impact of luck on outcomes (e.g., we generally want playing surfaces to be regular thus reducing unpredictable bounces). It is also why almost everybody agreed, in Casey Martin's lawsuit against the PGA, that *if* (as the Supreme Court majority essentially concluded, but as the dissent denied) the central athletic challenge the PGA Tour presented was the ability to hole a ball by means of striking it with a club, in the fewest number of strokes, while battling fatigue, then golf is less good—it exemplifies a core value of sport less well—if it requires competitive golfers to walk the course even when it is extraordinarily difficult for them to do so and when they are greatly fatigued without walking.

(5)   From (3) and (4) we have a reason (not a conclusive reason) to enforce restrictions on minor or incidental contact less strictly toward the end of close contests if—as is contestable but surely plausible—the ability to refrain from minor bodily contact with opponents is a peripheral athletic virtue in basketball as we know it. If this is so, then a penalty of nominally constant magnitude that it is optimal to impose early in a contest may become suboptimal to impose later in that same contest. To be clear: I do not claim that this excellence is something that, in the nature of things, no sport could wish most to valorize. My argument for temporal variance in

basketball is explicitly contingent on its being the case that this particular excellence does not rank so highly among the excellences that basketball wishes to feature and encourage. Whether this is so is an interpretive question.

That's my proposed pro tanto argument for temporal variance in the enforcement of non-shooting fouls in basketball. The argument can be easily extended to similar fouls in sports like football and hockey. At bottom, it's based on the same aversion that we often see in the law (from the harmless error doctrine to contract law's material breach doctrine) to the awarding of windfall remedies disproportionate to the harm suffered.

COMMENTS AND QUESTIONS

1.   Omission bias. Do you agree with our characterization of the Moskowitz & Wertheim account as an explanation but not a justification, and of the Berman account as a justification that is not necessarily an explanation? Is it helpful to recall the concept of cognitive biases that tend to bound rational thinking, see p. 74, and to note that omission bias is one of these?

2.   Evaluation. Do you find Berman's pro tanto justification of temporal variance in basketball plausible? (A pro tanto justification for a practice is an argument or consideration that provides *some* justificatory force, or reason, for it, without maintaining that the justificatory force is sufficient to render the practice right or optimal all things considered.) Do you find Berman's pro tanto justification persuasive? Which parts of his account are most vulnerable? If you believe that Berman's account does not justify the temporally variant enforcement of the rules governing fouls in basketball, do you conclude that the practice is not justifiable, or can you think of a better justification?

3.   From court to rink. What about hockey? It is generally agreed that the NHL observed a practice of temporal variance for much of its history. Ron Hoggarth, a retired referee who worked more than 1,000 N.H.L. games from the 1970s through the 1990s, later recalled, "We put our whistles in our pockets during overtime and in the playoffs. A player had to interrupt an unbelievable scoring opportunity for us to call a penalty." Dave Seminara, *Power Plays Rising as Referees Show Less Tolerance, Even Late in Games*, N.Y. TIMES, Sat., Feb. 9, 2013, at D6. Knowledgeable observers, however, believe "that the league ha[s] gradually moved away from situational refereeing to a more consistent application of the rules." *Id.* Is that a positive development? Should the refs give players a little more leeway in overtime than in regular time? In the postseason relative to regular season? For purposes of temporal variance, are basketball and hockey properly distinguishable from each other on the ground that free throws in basketball, much like yardage markoffs in football, are a necessary evil, whereas power plays in hockey are a positive good?

———————

The "omission bias" explanation for temporal variance in basketball would seem to apply just as well to tennis. If officials are asymmetrically averse to *making* a call that has a large competitive impact and to *refraining* from making a call that has the same impact, then we should expect to see temporal variance in the enforcement of foot-fault rules. That is precisely what Moskowitz and Wertheim do expect, which is why they agree that the call on Serena Williams, made by line judge Shino Tsurubuchi, was so unusual. And yet, consistent with our characterization of the omission bias account as a mere explanation without justificatory force, they appear to conclude that Tsurubuchi did the right thing:

> Her call—her resistance to the omission bias to which we've become accustomed in sports and in life—may have earned her widespread ridicule and disapproval, but she also won fans that night, including [NFL Referee] Mike Carey: "Making the hard call or the unpopular call, that's where guts are tested, that's the mark of a true official," he says. "You might have a longer career as an official if you back off. But you won't have a more accurate career."

MOSKOWITZ & WERTHEIM, SCORECASTING, at 29–30.

Does Berman's analysis offer any more support than does the Moskowitz & Wertheim account for the view, apparently widespread in tennis circles,[e] that Tsurubuchi should have held her tongue? In his blog postings, Berman recognizes that his argument justifying temporal variance in basketball might not justify it in other contexts. For example, he says, calling of balls and strikes in baseball is not a proper candidate for temporal variance on the analysis presented above, which depends upon the widening of a gap between the competitive cost of an infraction and the competitive cost of the penalty it incurs. In terms used earlier in this book, the rules governing balls and strikes may be considered constitutive (they are part of what makes up the game) rather than regulative ("Don't do this, or else . . . ."). If a pitch is a ball, it is not an infraction of the rules, and so it makes no sense to speak in this context of a gap between the cost of an infraction and the cost of a penalty for it. So hardly anybody would say that at a crucial time in a game an umpire ought to call balls and strikes more or less generously to the pitcher, or be more or less generous to the runner in calling force plays at bases. Nor would many people think that tennis officials ought to be more or less generous in crunch time in calling "zone faults"—that is, failure to serve the ball into the service box. Should foot faults be considered differently?

One possible argument would be that the rule on foot faults, unlike that on zone faults, is a regulative rule, in which case the argument for

---

[e] We already noted that John McEnroe and another anonymous player thought the call inappropriate at that juncture. For citations to other expert commentators who expressed the same view, see MOSKOWITZ & WERTHEIM, at 29.

temporal variance might be much the same as in basketball. But Berman puts that possibility aside to make a different type of argument.

Seeking to identify the "competitive desideratum" underlying the rules, Berman suggests that the service rules are meant to formulate a test of the ability to serve the ball into a precisely defined target space—the type of challenge common to many sports—but from a generally defined launching site; "precision in the placement of the served ball might be of far greater concern to the sport than is precision in the placement of the server's body." He argues not that the foot-fault rule should become a loose standard, but merely that the underlying norm the rule is meant to reflect is a standard. He refers to is as a "rulified standard." This stands in contrast to the rule on zone faults, which is a "true rule" because it reflects an "underlying athletic challenge that is *itself* sharp-edged and rule-like: get the ball *in* the pre-defined space." It does not follow that line judges should routinely call foot faults only when the player goes unreasonably over the line, for a rulified standard is still a rule. Berman continues:

> That said, that we must not *routinely* pierce a rulified standard does not mean that we must *never* pierce it. Whether and under what circumstances to disregard the rule's form in favor of its underlying considerations is always at least askable with regard to rulified standards. Indeed, that is the most obvious upshot of the distinction between rulified standards and true rules. Plausibly, two additional requirements should be satisfied in order to go beneath the surface of a rulified standard: (1) that enforcing the rule as a rule would produce unusually high costs; and (2) that disregarding the rule's form on this occasion would incur low costs on the dimensions, such as predictability and the like, that justified its rulification in the first place.

> These two additional conditions, it seems to me, are probably satisfied by foot faults in crunch time. The high cost of enforcing the rule as a rule are plain: doing so allows the foot fault to have an undue impact on the match outcome—that is, it thwarts what we have called the "competitive desideratum." At the same time, the costs of piercing the rule are very low precisely because the fact of the supposed nonconformity with the rule is hidden from public view. And it's hidden from public view because the Hawk-Eye electronic system that determines whether a ball lands within the lines is not used to judge foot faults. From the perspective of optimal game design, that might be a good thing. In general, rule makers who want to preserve the rule-enforcers' option to sometimes apply the standard that animates a rulified standard should arrange things so that non-compliance with the rule isn't apparent. Transparency is not always a virtue.

Of course, even if an ideal system would have (non-expressly) authorized line judges to adjudicate crunch-time foot faults against the underlying standard of reasonableness and not in terms of the nominal rule, that does not determine whether Serena Williams's step on the line should have been called. It could be that it was unreasonable or unfair all things considered— if, for example, her transgression was substantial or repeated. My sense is that it was neither, but I make no strong claims about it. I claim more strongly that Williams's step on the line did not apparently put Clijsters at a competitive disadvantage: the ball landed squarely in the service court and was easily returnable. In sum, if I'm right that the foot fault rule is a rulified standard not a true rule, that would be a promising (though not conclusive) basis for supporting the McEnrovian intuition: the line judge should have cut Williams some slack.

"Let 'em Play"—Day 4: Of Rules and Standards, VOLOKH CONSPIRACY (July 21, 2011).

COMMENTS AND QUESTIONS

1.   Other considerations. As Berman emphasizes, his analysis does not take into account all the possible costs of temporal variance. What are the other costs, and are they significant? Loss of confidence in the integrity of the game? Alteration of behavior in crunch time, in anticipation of temporal variance? If the variance is not acknowledged, does that diminish the probability that players will in fact alter their behavior?

Should some penalty calls be considered investments, impairing the immediate quality of the current game in hopes of improving long-term qualities of the sport, such as safe behavior? If so, does that argue in favor of temporal variance, on the ground that the cost of the investment is greater in crucial situations but the benefits are unlikely to vary much? Does this support the idea that players should not be readily ejected from important games for offensive behavior that might cause them to be heaved in more mundane games?

2.   20/20 hindsight? Does the fact that Williams's serve "landed squarely in the service court and was easily returnable" have the significance that Berman attributes to it? Is this *ex post* analysis appropriate? Is it plausible that the foot-fault violation *helped* Williams make a better serve? If a player feels confident that a foot fault will not be called in a given situation, will that give her an advantage?

3.   Constitutive and regulative rules revisited. Should the rule on foot faults be considered a regulative rule rather than a constitutive or power-conferring one? If the answer is yes, what bearing does this have on the question of whether Williams should have been given slack?

4. Fairness. Suppose that you were the line judge in the Williams-Clijsters match, that you declined to call the foot fault, and that Williams went on to win the match. And suppose that early in the match, when Clijsters had engaged in essentially identical conduct, you had called a foot fault. After the match, you are asked, "How could that be fair?" Would you have a persuasive answer? Would the persuasiveness of your answer be any different if you declined to call a foul late in a close basketball game, but early in the game you called a foul on the other team for essentially identical conduct?

5. Expectations. Berman says that penalties "have greater impact on the expected outcome when they occur 2 minutes before the end of a then-tied game than when they occur 2 minutes from the start of a then-tied game." That is certainly true, assuming that by "impact on the expected outcome" we mean the impact as judged at that moment. Is there a different way to understand "expected outcome"? Should we care about "expected outcome" at all? After all, in basketball, a point is a point, and each point counts the same toward the final score regardless of when it occurred. From whose perspectives, and for what purposes, is it useful to care about how events in the game change the expected outcomes, as viewed from that moment?

6. Comparing foot faults and zone faults. If you are not persuaded by Berman's analysis, do you nonetheless think that the case for temporally variant enforcement of foot-fault rules is somewhat stronger (or at least somewhat less weak) than is the case for temporally variant enforcement of zone-fault rules? If so, how would you explain that sense? Should foot faults be called lets rather than faults, given that they represent a failure at the start of action?

7. Foot faults in other sports. If you accept Berman's view, would you also say that (1) on a long jumper's last jump the officials ought to be relatively lenient in determining whether or not the jumper stepped over the foul line? (2) a baseball umpire should be willing in a crucial situation—say, tie game, bottom of the ninth, two outs, runner on third—to overlook the fact that the pitcher's foot was a little off the rubber at the time of the pitch (which, calling the game by the book, would balk the winning run home)? If your answers to these questions are negative, why?

8. Different rules for different times? Assuming that Ron Hoggarth is right that, in the past, NHL referees would all but put the whistle away during overtime and the playoffs, how would you expect players to respond? Does it make sense to have a rule that applies during regulation time of the regular season but not otherwise? Does your answer vary from rule to rule?

9. All things considered. Taking all relevant considerations into account, do you believe that Tsurubuchi should have called a foot fault on Serena Williams at that point of her match against Kim Clijsters, assuming that doing so was consistent with the standards she had used through the match? (And should a code violation have been called on Williams for her comments to Tsurubuchi, given that the impact was to end the match?) Is the question distinguishable from that of another famous foot-fault call made against Williams, at the 2019 Australian Open, when she had a match point at 5-1 in the third set against Karolina Pliskova? (She then twisted her ankle and lost the next six games and the match.)

Note that Berman says that Hawk-Eye does not call foot faults. That is changing. Hawk-Eye Live, the system used to replace line judges during the COVID-19 pandemic, does call foot faults, though official intervention is still necessary. But if the system advances so that no human intervention is necessary on foot faults, as on ordinary calls, presumably its operation would not vary with the context. Would that be a beneficial development? Or should temporal variance somehow be programmed into the system?

10. Balls and strikes. Berman assumes that temporal variance would not be appropriate with respect to called balls and strikes; hence, he observes that his defense of temporal variance in basketball would not directly apply to foot faults in tennis if the rules governing foot faults are constitutive or power-conferring rules rather than regulative or duty-imposing rules. And he predicts that "hardly anybody" would think that umpires should cut pitchers a little more slack toward the end of a close game. But "hardly anybody" is not "nobody." Consider this account of Don Larsen's perfect game in the 1956 World Series by the famed Harvard zoologist-cum-Yankees fan Stephen Jay Gould. It was penned on the death of the home plate umpire for that game, Babe Pinelli:

> Babe Pinelli was the umpire in baseball's unique episode of perfection when it mattered most. October 8, 1956. A perfect game in the World Series—and, coincidentally, Pinelli's last official game as arbiter. What a consummate swan song. Twenty-seven Dodgers up; twenty-seven Bums down. . . . [T]he agent was a competent, but otherwise undistinguished pitcher, Don Larsen.
>
> The dramatic end was all Pinelli's, and controversial ever since. Dale Mitchell, pinch hitting for Sal Maglio, was the twenty-seventh batter. With a count of 1 and 2, Larsen delivered one high and outside—close, but surely not, by its technical definition, a strike. Mitchell let the pitch go by, but Pinelli didn't hesitate. Up went the right arm for called strike three. Out went Yogi Berra from behind the plate, nearly tackling Larsen in a frontal jump of joy. "Outside by a foot," groused Mitchell later. He exaggerated—for it was outside by only a few inches—but he was right. Babe Pinelli, however, was more right. A batter may not take a close pitch with so much on the line. Context matters. Truth is a circumstance, not a spot. . . .
>
> Truth is inflexible. Truth is inviolable. By long and recognized custom, by any concept of justice, Dale Mitchell had to swing at anything close. It was a strike—a strike high and outside. Babe Pinelli, umpiring his last game, ended with his finest, his most perceptive, his most truthful moment. Babe Pinelli, arbiter of history, walked into the locker room and cried.

Stephen Jay Gould, *The Strike That was Low and Outside*, N.Y. TIMES, Nov. 10, 1984, at 23. (Note that Gould's piece was mistitled. Video of the play makes clear, as the body of the essay suggests, that if the pitch wasn't the right height, it was too high, not too low. Gould also took poetic license in another way; the perfect game, Game 5 of the Series, was Pinelli's last game behind the plate, but he worked Game 6 at third base and Game 7 at second.)

Is Gould right that Pinelli should have called that non-strike a strike? Is this an appropriate case for temporal variance? Why or why not?

11. Stricter in the crunch? Is there an argument that officials should be *more* rigorous in sanctioning violations when the stakes are high? Consider the decision by college mock trial officials to strip Yale of its 2019 national title for improper invention of facts. An unsuccessful appeal of the decision contended that Yale's conduct was no more egregious than a violation in a preliminary round the prior year that had been lightly punished; the appeal argued that it was unjust to impose greater punishment on the Yale team because the incident was "far more high profile and . . . sparked more public outcry": "Trial conduct should be treated the same, regardless of whether it happens in the National Final or in the first round of Regionals." What do you think?

D. SUPERSTAR TREATMENT

Across sports—from the NBA and the NHL to England's Premier League—fans, journalists, and even players frequently complain that superstars get the calls. It is said that officials give them more latitude to commit infractions and give the defensive players guarding them less latitude. *See, e.g.,* Greg Swartz, *10 NBA Superstars Who Get Most Preferential Treatment from Referees*, BLEACHER REPORT (June 26, 2012).

We are unaware of any sports whose rules formally provide for superstar treatment. Therefore, if superstars do get the calls, the officials are responsible: either their pro-superstar bias is entirely subconscious or, to at least some extent, officials are exercising discretion to enforce rules more leniently against the stars. If the latter is the case, can the exercise of such discretion be defended? The principal objection to such a practice is straightforward, and is likely to sound in norms of fairness and "equal treatment." (See Subchapter 3A.) The objection in a nutshell is that superstar treatment is unfair to the ordinary players who don't get the calls. This is an intuitively powerful objection. What can be said against it?

Consider three responses:

(a) Equal opportunity, not equal treatment. Superstars are treated better than regular players in many respects. Most conspicuously, they are paid more. In addition, management often treats the stars more solicitously in other ways, including by giving them more days off and by consulting them on trades, draft picks, and even coaching changes. Moreover, disparity of treatment exists not only within a sport but between sports

and between professional sports as a class and other domains of life: NBA players earn more than MLS players, all of whom earn more than public school teachers. The lesson is that fairness does not require that everyone—by which we mean, in this context, superstars and average players alike—be treated the same, but that no structural barriers are imposed to prevent people from becoming superstars and thus eligible for preferential treatment. What fairness requires is only equality of opportunity. Insofar as league rules and practices do not place obstacles in the way of any player becoming a superstar, fairness is satisfied. Put another way, it's fair to treat superstars better than average players for the same reason it's fair to treat players in the NBA better than those toiling in the D-League: they've *earned* the favorable treatment.

(b) Fairness is phony. Fairness is not a genuine value; all that matters is aggregate welfare. As two Harvard law professors argued:

> Satisfying notions of fairness can make individuals worse off, that is, reduce social welfare. Furthermore, individuals will be made worse off overall whenever considerations of fairness leads to the choice of a regime different from that which would be adopted under welfare economics because, by definition, the two approaches conflict when a regime with greater overall well-being is rejected on grounds of fairness . . .

> We find that little explicit justification for notions of fairness—even those developed by prominent writers over the years—has in fact been offered. Relatedly, many theorists seem to rely heavily on conclusory metaphors . . . .

> Also, fairness proponents often appeal to intuitions or instincts. Yet . . . this source of insight is an unreliable grounding . . . and reliance on these sources is self-defeating because an important purpose of explicit normative analysis of legal policy is to identify when our intuitions or instincts may lead us astray.

Louis Kaplow & Steven Shavell, *Fairness Versus Welfare*, 114 HARV. L. REV. 961 (2001).

If, as Kaplow and Shavell argue, rulemakers should care only about aggregate welfare, then superstar treatment may well be justified. The practice of treating superstars more favorably than other players plausibly maximizes *aggregate* welfare by increasing the welfare of the superstars themselves and most fans more than it decreases the welfare of non-superstars.

(c) Everyone wins. The previous argument for superstar treatment does not deny that superstar treatment is disadvantageous to all players who aren't superstars. Rather, it makes two claims: first, that arguments against the practice that invoke notions of "fairness" (or equality) should

be rejected and that the practice should be evaluated *only* in terms of whether it improves *total* welfare; and second, that superstar treatment improves the welfare of superstars and fans more than it reduces the welfare of other competitors. A stronger variant on this argument would deny that superstar treatment leaves non-superstars worse off.

Although this claim might be counterintuitive, the success of many sports leagues and enterprises depends heavily on the presence and success of superstars. In the NBA, for example, as the superstars go, so goes the league. And during the period of Tiger Woods's dominance, TV ratings for golf were much higher at tournaments when he was in contention. The superstar effect on public attention, as reflected most notably in TV ratings, is sometimes so great that average players actually *benefit* financially from superstar bias: Even if it narrows their slice of the pie, they are better off because the pie is so much greater. Because journeymen benefit long-term from a pro-superstar bias, there is, according to this argument, no good objection to the practice.

Arguments (b) and (c) correspond to two notions of economic efficiency. On the first notion, termed "**Kaldor-Hicks efficiency**," a change is efficient so long as the winners' gains exceed the losers' losses, so that the winners *could* (in theory)  pay enough to induce the losers to agree to the change, even if they don't (in fact) pay the losers anything. On the second notion, "**Pareto efficiency**," a change is efficient so long as there are some winners and *no losers*; a "Pareto optimal" state is one in which it is impossible to improve somebody's lot without making at least one other person worse off. Both notions of efficiency are centrally important to welfare economics and to the economic analysis of the law.

COMMENTS AND QUESTIONS

1. The bottom line. All things considered, is superstar treatment justifiable? If it does not exist, should it? Are you persuaded by any of the responses, alone or in combination? Can you think of additional arguments in favor of superstar treatment? Can you think of additional arguments against it?

2. Other earned advantages. Even if you are not persuaded that superstars have earned different substantive rules—on fouls, bigger strike zone, etc.—might they have earned some advantages? For example, have they earned special treatment with respect to standards of personal behavior? Should a baseball umpire be willing to take more guff from a superstar than from a rookie before throwing him out of the game?

Have superstars earned "epistemic deference"? That is, should an official take a player's past performance into account as *evidence* when trying to determine some particular fact on a given occasion, such as whether a football receiver known for great hands secured possession of the ball or whether a close pitch was just within, or just outside, the strike zone? It is sometimes said that Ted Williams, the great baseball hitter, was allowed to call his own game. In one often-told story, possibly apocryphal, a catcher questioned the home plate umpire about his calls after Williams walked on four straight pitches, provoking the ump to respond, "Mr. Williams will let you know when it is a strike." Is this objectionable or epistemically defensible?

3. *Superstar mistreatment?* What about treating superstars worse, not better, than other players? Would this be justified on the same grounds that support the use of handicaps in other sports, as in club golf? In the 2013 Masters, after hitting a ball into the water, Woods took a drop, but he did not place the ball immediately behind his divot, as he should have. The violation was called to the attention of officials by a TV viewer, of whom he has many more than the average golfer, and he was assessed a two-stroke penalty. Was this unfair to Woods? (Many observers felt he should have been disqualified for signing a scorecard that did not reflect the penalty.)

4. *Rule changes.* If you don't think that sport rules should be enforced *more* strictly against superstars, is it okay to change rules with the specific goal of nullifying or mitigating an advantage enjoyed by one or another superstar? For example, in 1964 the NBA widened the lane from 12' to 16' specifically to curb Wilt Chamberlain's dominance. The next year the league changed the rules to prohibit offensive goaltending. Of course, these rules formally applied to everybody, not just Wilt. But the rule change was directed at Wilt and he's about the only player who suffered from the change. Is this problematic?

5. *Superstar teams?* Earlier we discussed frequent fan complaints that the NBA is biased in favor of big-market teams. (See Subchapter 3H.) Suppose for the purpose of argument that officials, or the league itself, do tend to favor certain teams, such as the New York Knicks and Los Angeles Lakers. Could there be any justification for such a practice?

CHAPTER 13

CORRECTING OFFICIATING ERRORS

■ ■ ■

Officials in professional sports tend to be very accurate. For example, the NFL grades its officials on every call in every game and has determined that over 97% of the plays are called correctly. *See* Judy Battista, *In NFL, Wrong Calls and Wrong Assumption,* N.Y. TIMES, Nov. 1, 2008. Major League Baseball employs a system of cameras, PITCHf/x, installed in every ballpark to track the speed, location, and movement of every pitch. A review of over 4.3 million called pitches between 2008 and 2013 concluded that plate umpires make the correct call 86.8% of the time on balls inside the strike zone and 85% on balls outside—and presumably most of the errors are on very close pitches. *See* Scott Lindholm, *How well do umpires call balls and strikes?,* SB NATION (Jan. 27, 2014).

But to say that officials in professional sports are very accurate is also to say that they make mistakes. Indeed, officiating errors are an inevitable part of most sports. ESPN researchers used broadcast footage to review every call, other than balls and strikes, in each of the 184 major league baseball games played during two weeks in the 2010 season. They found that on average 1.3 calls per game were so close that replay review was necessary to determine whether the umpire's call had been correct. The umps had indeed gotten it right in 65.7% of those cases, and wrong in 20.4%; the remaining 13.9% remained too close to call even after replay review. T.J. Quinn & William Weinbaum, *Study shows 1 in 5 close calls wrong,* ESPN.com (Aug. 13, 2010).

So, suppose it appears that an official made a mistake. Should anything be done to correct the situation—and if so, what? That is this chapter's topic.

As you will suspect, and as we will see, the answer plausibly depends on a range of factors. We start with what is arguably the easiest case: an official realizes she has just made an erroneous call and knows that, if she corrects it promptly, her error will produce no competitive injury. For a simple example of such a case, imagine a basketball or soccer referee who first calls that an out-of-bounds ball was last touched by a player on Team A and then realizes, before the throw-in, that it deflected off a player on Team B.

One could, of course, maintain that even in a situation such as this, the mistake should not be corrected, that all officiating decisions should be treated as sacrosanct, or for some other reason unchangeable. That will strike many observers as an indefensibly dogmatic view. In most areas of life, we care about truth and getting things right. And truth often goes hand in hand with another value we care a lot about: justice.

> We want the contest to proceed on the path that the players' own efforts and accomplishments warrant. If you catch the ball cleanly for a ten-yard gain, your team deserves to move ten yards down field. If you kick the ball off the crossbar and over the goal line, your team deserves to be credited with a goal. If the ball beats the batter-runner to first base, the fielding team deserves to record an out. Every mistaken call—the failure to register as a reception a ball cleanly caught, the imposition of a yardage penalty for a phantom infraction, and so on—is something to be avoided and regretted precisely because it upsets this scheme of institutional desert, of how the contest ought to proceed. . . . [B]ecause justice is, plausibly, the virtue of allocating goods in accordance with desert, any steps taken to reduce mistaken final calls promote justice.

Mitchell N. Berman, *Replay*, 99 CAL. L. REV. 1683, 1712–13 (2011).

Accordingly, the practice in most sports is to allow, or even to require, officials to correct mistakes when the mistake can be corrected promptly, and when the prompt correction allows the competition to be placed in exactly the condition it would have been had the initial error not been made. In football, for example, it is not uncommon for referees to "pick up" an errant flag, and announce that "there is no foul on the play." In tennis, before the use of RTDs (see Subchapter 11B), players could call on the chair umpire to reverse a line judge's call. Immediate reversal is rarer in baseball, and in some settings it virtually never happens. (When is the last time you heard an umpire call "Steerike! . . . Actually, that was a little outside. Ball"?) But the Official Rules of Baseball do direct that an umpire should be prepared to change "*a manifestly wrong* decision when convinced that he has made an error." (How confident should the decisionmaker be before reversing herself, or before overturning a call made by an inferior or subordinate official? That is, how weighty should be the thumb that the mere fact of an initial decision places on the decisional scale?)

As our description of this situation suggests, the case for reversing a mistaken call is strongest when two conditions are satisfied: (1) officials need not be persuaded by the participants that their initial call was erroneous and can reverse themselves quickly; and (2) simply by issuing the correct call, officials can put the competition back on the track that it would have been on had the correct call been made initially. Very plausibly, the case for reviewing calls that are claimed to be mistaken, and for reversing those that are deemed to be mistaken, will be weaker if review is time-consuming or if reversal will not automatically cure the effects of the mistake. This observation structures the material that follows.

But before proceeding further, think about this question: *Even assuming* that these two conditions are both satisfied, what arguments are there that the officials should not reverse the mistaken call? In doing so, it might help to consider this famous story told about Hall of Fame umpire Billy Evans:

> He once called a ball foul before it stopped rolling. When the ball struck a pebble and bounced back into fair territory, the manager of the team at bat rushed onto the field, cursing Evans and demanding that he reverse his ruling. Billy responded, "Well, it would have been a fair ball yesterday and it will be fair tomorrow and for all years to come. But right now, unfortunately, it's foul because that's the way I called it."

David W. Anderson, *Billy Evans*, SOCIETY FOR AM. BASEBALL RESEARCH (2017). Suppose that Evans knew immediately on the ball touching the chalk that he had blown the call, and suppose that it was abundantly clear that absent the bad call the batter would have reached first before the fielding team could make a play. Was Evans nevertheless justified in refusing to correct his call?

Subchapter 13A examines cases in which the first condition is satisfied but the second isn't: correction of the error, even when prompt, does not leave things as they would have been. Subchapter 13B concerns the use of instant replay to review calls during the contest, a process that generally produces delay and therefore raises special questions of institutional design. Subchapter 13C addresses whether, and under what circumstances, calls should be reviewed and potentially reversed after play has continued.

A. ERRORS THAT AFFECT PLAY

Official errors are unfortunate. But in many cases they do not create a particularly pressing problem if quickly corrected: prompt correction can return the contest to its proper path. In some fluid situations, though, an official error may affect the course of play. Such cases present difficult questions of remedy.

1. INADVERTENT WHISTLES

Inadvertent and otherwise premature whistles occur with some frequency in some sports. Premature whistles create an obvious problem. In some cases they do not appear to affect play but we cannot easily act on the assumption that they do not, given that players are instructed to "play the whistle." Is any remedy possible? This is in fact an area of surprising complexity. See, for example, the memo of the National Federation of State High School Associations (NFHS), *The 'Dreaded' Inadvertent Whistle: NFHS Rule 4.2.3*. Here is the summary overview from that memo:

The ball becomes dead, the clock shall be stopped, and the down is ended.

Therefore, penalties AFTER an inadvertent whistle must be DEAD BALL fouls.

If there are NO penalties, or if the penalty for a foul during the down is DECLINED. . .

The down is always replayed if the whistle occurs while a legal forward pass or snap is in flight during a legal kick.

If the ball is loose following a backward pass, fumble, illegal forward pass or illegal kick. . .

the team last in possession has a choice

Replay the down.

Count the down, put the ball in play where possession was lost.

If the ball is in player possession. . .

that team has a choice

Replay the down.

Count the down, accept the results of the play at the spot of the inadvertent whistle.

If the penalty for a foul during the down is ACCEPTED. . .

The penalty takes precedence and the inadvertent whistle is IGNORED.

The clock starts with the ready-for-play (except following a free kick), following an inadvertent whistle.

The period MUST be extended by an untimed down if inadvertent whistle sounds during the last timed down.

———

Here are three plays and the prescribed rulings on them as described in this memo:

4. 2. 3A.   **Play:** With fourth and 2 from K's 38-yard line, a scrimmage kick by K1 is muffed beyond the neutral zone by R1 following his signal for a fair catch. While the ball is loose following the muff, an official sounds his whistle inadvertently.

Ruling: Because the whistle was inadvertently sounded during a kick, the down will be replayed even though R1 was first to touch the scrimmage kick beyond the neutral zone. The clock will start on the ready-for-play signal. (3–4–2c)

4. 2. 3Ba.   **Play:** While a legal forward pass is in flight B1 interferes with eligible A1 and then there is an inadvertent whistle.

Ruling: If the captain accepts the penalty for a foul which occurred prior to the inadvertent whistle, the whistle is disregarded. It will be a new series for A, 15 yards in advance of the previous spot. (7–5–10a; 9–4–2b)

4. 2. 3Bb.   **Play:** While a legal forward pass is in flight a whistle is inadvertently sounded after which B2 contacts A2 while the ball is still in flight.

Ruling: The contact by B2 occurred during a dead ball period and unless it is a personal foul, will be ignored. Because the whistle was inadvertently sounded while a legal forward pass was in flight, the down shall be replayed.

In the NBA an inadvertent whistle is ordinarily treated as a suspension of play, after which "[p]lay shall be resumed at the point of interruption." Rule 4.XIII. Rule 7.II.j provides:

> If an official inadvertently blows his whistle and the 24-second clock buzzer sounds while the ball is in the air, play shall be suspended and play resumed by a jump ball between any two opponents at the center circle, if the shot hits the rim and is unsuccessful. If the shot does not hit the rim, a 24-second violation has occurred. If the shot is successful, the goal shall count and the ball inbounded as after any successful field goal. It should be noted that even though the official blows his whistle, all provisions of the above rule apply.

COMMENTS AND QUESTIONS

1. To speculate or not to speculate? Should a play be ruled dead on an inadvertent whistle no matter how confident officials are that they can determine what would have happened had the mistaken whistle not be blown? *Cf.* Ben Austro, *Despite inadvertent whistle, Panthers TD is allowed to stand, incorrectly,* Football Zebras (Nov. 5, 2012). If no, how would you craft an ideal rule for inadvertent whistles in football? In other sports that you know?

2. Advertent mistaken whistles. The cases we have considered so far involve inadvertent mistaken whistles. They are relatively rare. Entirely common are *advertent* mistaken whistles—that is, whistles that are blown intentionally but based on a mistaken view of the facts or a mistaken understanding of the rules. They occur whenever an official's call stops play under circumstances in which the correct call would have allowed play to continue. Take a forward pass in football that a back judge whistles incomplete. If the line judge has a better angle on the play and determines that the ball was caught, the back judge's call could be reversed, but unless the receiver was promptly tackled or pushed out of bounds it may be impossible to know what the final outcome of the play would have been had the correct call been made initially. What result? What difference, if any, should it make whether a whistle that stops play was *accidental* or *mistaken*?

A well-known example of a mistaken whistle occurred in the final minute of a September 2008 NFL game between the San Diego Chargers and the Denver Broncos. With the Chargers leading 38–31, Denver faced second and goal at the San Diego one-yard line. Jay Cutler, the Broncos' quarterback, dropped back to pass and the ball squirted out of his hand for what should have been ruled a fumble. But referee Ed Hochuli (one of the league's top-rated officials, moonlighting from his position as a prominent member of the Arizona civil defense bar) blew the play dead, ruling that it was an incomplete pass. Hochuli realized his error immediately and replays confirmed that it was a fumble, allowing the officials to change the call from incomplete to fumble. But, by NFL rules, possession remained with Denver (because the ball was dead on the whistle) even though a Chargers linebacker had scooped up the loose ball. As Dallas Cowboys owner Jerry Jones later explained: "Nothing can be done. I understand that after that whistle blows, you can't speculate, 'Well, did everybody get the best shot at recovering the ball if some of them heard the whistle and some of them didn't?' " *NFL to give Hochuli lower grades after call in Chargers-Broncos game*, ESPN.com (Sept. 15, 2008). Retaining the ball at the San Diego ten (where the ball had landed), Denver proceeded to score a touchdown and convert a two-point conversion for a 39–38 win.

If this play were to occur now, the outcome might be different. NFL Rule 15, Section 2, governing replay review, now provides in part:

> If an on-field ruling of a dead ball (down by contact, out of bounds, or incomplete forward pass) is changed, the ball belongs to the recovering player at the spot of the recovery, and any advance is nullified. The recovery must occur in the continuing action following the loss of possession.

In other words, because the replay determined that the call of a dead ball (accompanied by a whistle) was improper, a fumble recovery after the improperly blown whistle is recognized—but only if it is part of "continuing action" after the fumble, and without any possibility of advancing the ball. So in a situation like that of Hochuli's blown call, this rule gives the recovering team part of what it probably would have earned had the call not been made. *See Hochuli 'devastated' following blown call*, NFL.com (Sept. 18, 2008) (Mike Pereira, then the NFL's supervisor of officials, suggesting such a change for this reason). But it also gives players an incentive to play after a whistle, and assumes that the whistle did not have any effect. Is it a good rule?

3. When the remedy is clear. Consider the converse case: an incorrect call allows the play to continue when it should have been blown dead. This is usually not a problem. If the back judge calls a forward pass complete and the receiver runs it in for a touchdown, but that call was mistaken, the officials can simply change the call to incomplete and (assuming the clock is set back a few seconds) the teams are in the position they would have been had the correct call been made initially. But is it ever appropriate to allow the mistaken call to stand even though the problem could be corrected—that is, reversal of the call would produce the situation that would have obtained had the call been correct initially? And when can we be sure that this will be the result? Consider the following case.

Michigan State was playing Duke in the Round of Sixteen in the men's NCAA basketball tournament on March 25, 2005. With the game tied at 32–32 and the half almost over, a Michigan State player stole the ball and scored on a layup with 0.2 seconds left. But the officials disallowed the points after determining that the timekeeper had not started the clock immediately after Duke's in-bounds pass was touched, before the steal. *See Recap: Spartans bottle up Redick; Izzo notches first win over Coach K*, ESPN.com (Mar. 25, 2005).

Note that in this case the problem is not that the officials let play go on too long; then it is relatively simple to say that anything that happened after play should have been stopped doesn't count. Here, rather, the problem is that the officials waited too long before letting time begin to run. So did their ruling reach the proper result? It says, in effect, "You scored with X seconds left showing on the clock, but the clock was started Y seconds late, and Y is greater than X, so if the clock was started when it should have, you wouldn't have scored." Is that fair? Given that Y is greater than X, does it matter how large each one is? Should Duke be foreclosed from objecting after the score if it did not object beforehand?

2. JEOPARDY

Inadvertent whistles raise this question: what should officials do when they stopped play short, so we may not know what would have happened had the error not occurred? But not all calls end plays. Sometimes officials make calls during the course of play, and the play unfolds differently from the way it would have had the mistaken call not been made.

A memorable incident occurred in Game 4 of the 1980 National League Championship Series, between the Philadelphia Phillies and the Houston Astros. This is widely considered one of the great post-season series ever. Game 4 was an elimination game for the Phillies, because they were down two games to one, and in those days the LCS was best-of-five.

Bake McBride and Manny Trillo of the Phillies led off the top of the fourth inning with singles, so there were runners on first and second with no outs. Gary Maddox then hit a soft line drive that Vern Ruhle, the

Houston pitcher, caught near his left foot. But did he catch it on the fly or trap it?

Doug Harvey, the home plate umpire (and future Hall of Famer), put his palms down, indicating the ball had hit the ground. But Ruhle was sure he had caught the ball in the air. He threw over to first (rather than to second or third, where he might have gotten a force out if he had caught the ball on the ground). Ed Vargo, the umpire at first, put his hand up to indicate an out. Dallas Green, manager of the Phillies, and other members of the team ran out to protest; apparently they understood correctly that Vargo was indicating that Ruhle had caught the ball in the air and so Trillo was doubled off first. Meanwhile, Art Howe, the Astros' first baseman, ran to tag second base. Jerry Crawford, the second-base umpire, indicated that McBride, who was standing on third, was out. After consulting with Vargo, Harvey ruled that the Astros had made a triple play. And then, as reports of the game indicated, bedlam broke out.

The Phillies argued that there should be runners at second and third with one out, Maddox, the batter, having been thrown out at first on a ground ball. The Astros, of course, claimed that they had made a triple play—the batter out on a fly ball and the two runners caught off base after having failed to tag up.

After a long conference among themselves and with League President Chub Feeney, the umpires came up with an intermediate ruling: Ruhle had caught the ball on the fly, Trillo was doubled off first, and McBride was safe at second.

Both teams protested: The Phillies eventually withdrew their protest because they went on to win the game, 5–3 in 10 innings. (They also won the series, and then the World Series, for the team's first major league championship ever.) Feeney disallowed the Astros' protest on the ground that, given that the Phillies did not score in the fourth, the play did not affect the outcome of the game.

Harvey explained that his view had been blocked by the batter, and so he deferred to Vargo and Bob Engel, the third base umpire, both of whom thought Ruhle had made the catch. He said further:

> I felt that my no-catch call put the runner at second base in jeopardy. He went to third base on my call. I felt the runner on first broke immediately and never could have gotten back no matter what my call was.

> The jeopardy rule has been in the rule books for a long time. It gives the umpires the right to correct a mistake if he feels his call has put a runner in bad position. That's exactly what happened.

The rule that Harvey presumably had in mind is now codified as Rule 8.02(c). It provides:

If the umpires consult after a play and change a call that had been made, then they have the authority to take all steps that they may deem necessary, in their discretion, to eliminate the results and consequences of the earlier call that they are reversing, including placing runners where they think those runners would have been after the play, had the ultimate call been made as the initial call, . . . all in the discretion of the umpires.

The rule itself does not use the word "jeopardy." One of the comments to it does, but ironically the implication is the opposite of the one that Harvey suggested. Addressing appeals by the plate umpire to the base umpires on half swings, the comment warns: "Base runners must be alert to the possibility that the base umpire on appeal from the plate umpire may reverse the call of a [fourth] ball to the call of a strike, in which event the runner is in jeopardy of being out by the catcher's throw." In other words, runner beware; the initial ruling may be wrong. Does that seem to be the right solution in the situation the comment addresses? Is that situation materially distinguishable from that of the Ruhle play?

For a video recounting of the Phillies-Astros series, with particular coverage of the Ruhle play, see https://tinyurl.com/y4rwk3z8.

COMMENTS AND QUESTIONS

1.   *The proper outcome.* What should the outcome have been? (a) Stick with Harvey's initial call—a call that we are assuming was mistaken—leaving runners on second and third with one out? (b) Triple play? (c) Double play with runner on second? Are there any other plausible possibilities? Which do you think is best all things considered?

2.   *Time out?* One other question was whether the result could not be a triple play because time had been called after Vargo called Trillo out at first, before Howe tagged second. *Could* time be called then? Assuming that time was not formally called then, should the umpires nevertheless have ruled that time was out, on the ground that the dispute began immediately after Vargo called Trillo out and Green ran onto the field? (Note that this would at least explain how the umpires came up with the resolution that two outs were recorded on the play, a result that otherwise seems to have the sole merit, apart from Harvey's "McBride relied; Trillo didn't" explanation, that two is exactly halfway between one and three.)

3.   *"The replay shows our guy was out, so we score a run."* Compare the Vern Ruhle incident with this incident from a game in July 2014 between the Toronto Blue Jays and the Oakland A's. The Blue Jays had the bases loaded with one out in the second inning of a scoreless game, when Anthony Gose grounded to Nate Freiman at first base. Freiman swiped a tag at runner Munenori Kawasaki, who was on his way to second, but first base umpire Vic Carapazza said there was no tag. Freiman threw to home plate immediately after the tag, apparently getting Edwin Encarnacion on a force play.

Blue Jays manager John Gibbons challenged the play, arguing that his own player Kawasaki had been tagged and was therefore out. Upon instant replay, the umpires agreed, so Kawasaki was ruled out. But that removed the force play at the plate, and because catcher Stephen Vogt didn't tag Encarnacion—even though Vogt had more than enough time to do so (he just didn't think he had to)—the Blue Jays were awarded a run, and a 1–0 lead.

Oakland protested on the grounds that they were entitled to rely on the initial call by Carapazza. Indeed, had Carapazza called the tag on Kawasaki correctly in the first place, the obvious play would not have been to make a risky throw home for a tag but rather to go to first base for a far easier inning-ending out. Oakland's protest was denied.

Was this the right result? Can this case be reconciled with Doug Harvey's ultimate ruling in 1980? If not, which is right?

4. Fifth down. On October 6, 1990, in the Colorado-Missouri football game, which turned out to have significance for the national title, Colorado was down 31–27 with time running out and no time-outs left. A backup Colorado quarterback, Charles Johnson, completed a first-down pass a few yards short of the goal line, giving the Buffaloes first and goal with about 40 seconds left. On first down, Johnson spiked the ball to stop the clock. On the next play, a Colorado runner, Eric Bieniemy, was stopped just short of the goal line. The officiating crew failed to flip the down marker, so it continued to show second down. Johnson handed off to Bieniemy again, who was again stopped short. Johnson then spiked the ball with two seconds left. On the following play—Colorado's fifth in the series, but only 4th down according to the marker—Johnson kept the ball himself, and the officials ruled that he had crossed the plane of the goal line. Only then did officials—and apparently television commentators as well—realize the mistake. The officiating crew conferred for 20 minutes, and ruled that the touchdown would stand. Colorado had to run a conversion play, but, with the lead and no time showing on the clock, they simply downed the ball, rather than risk a fumble recovery and runback.

One factor in assessing what should be done about this error is that the time of the game expired with the touchdown-play-that-never-should-have-been. But for now let's put this factor aside; we will consider it later. Let's assume that the controversial series occurred at the end of the first half. Would it be proper for the touchdown to stand?

First, suppose that Johnson looked over to the down marker and, before spiking the ball on what should have been 4th down, concluded in reliance on the marker that it was in fact 3rd down. (The fact that he spiked then suggests that, in reliance or not, he believed it was not 4th down.) Would that reliance be proper? Should we instead say that Johnson—and the whole Colorado team—was responsible for keeping the down count straight? What if the referee, orally or by holding up fingers, indicated the proper down?

Now assume that it's clear that Johnson never looked over to the down marker; forgetting his first spike, he independently believed that it was still 3rd down, so that it made sense to spike. What then? Should the rule be that even though he did not in fact rely on the error, we should act as if he did, because the difficulty of determining whether there was reliance might be too great?

And if in any of these scenarios you are inclined to think that Colorado should not get the benefit of the touchdown, what significance do you give to the fact that for three plays the down marker indicated that Colorado had a play more than it should have, but Missouri did not object?

Absent any suggestion that the officials gave Colorado an extra down intentionally, should Missouri suffer the consequences of its failure to flag the officials' mistake before Colorado ran additional plays? If you believe so, what result if Missouri noticed that the official down marker was wrong after the *second* handoff to Bieniemy?

Note that while Colorado might argue that the touchdown should stand, Missouri might argue that it should get the ball back near its goal line with two seconds left in the half, because that's where the ball was after Colorado's first four plays. Would an appropriate solution be rather to give Colorado the ball back, fourth and goal at the two, because that is the last situation it would have faced if there had not been any confusion about the downs?

Now compare the Colorado-Missouri game with an incident that occurred almost exactly half a century before, on November 16, 1940, when Cornell, defending national champions riding an 18-game winning streak, visited Dartmouth. With less than a minute remaining, Cornell, down 3–0, got the ball on the Dartmouth 6-yard line. Three running plays brought the ball very close to the goal line. Cornell was then penalized for delay of game, and the referee moved the ball back outside the 5. With 9 seconds left, Cornell threw an incomplete pass. The linesman indicated that Cornell still had the ball, and the referee agreed. As time expired, Cornell threw a touchdown pass, and— though it didn't matter—it kicked the extra point. So the game appeared to be a 7–3 Cornell victory. But when Cornell realized the error later, it offered to forfeit the game, and Dartmouth accepted.

After the 1990 game, Colorado made no comparable offer to forfeit. Is there any material difference between these two incidents—was one error more appropriately subject to correction than the other?

5.   *Long counts.* In a heavyweight championship boxing match in 1990, Buster Douglas, the challenger, was outboxing the heavily favored champion, Mike Tyson. But near the end of the eighth round, Tyson caught Douglas with an uppercut and knocked him down. The referee was slow starting the count. As a result, Douglas had about 12 seconds to get up; he rose as the count reached 9 and the bell rang to end the round. Fully recovered before the next round, he continued to dominate Tyson and knocked him out in the 10th. (The

enduring image is of Tyson, down for the first time in his career, groping around for his mouth guard while he was being counted out.)

Suppose that before the next round began, Tyson contended that he should be ruled the winner by knockout. What should the result be? Does it matter what condition Douglas was in when the count should have reached 10 or whether he was relying on the referee's count? According to sports journalist Jeremy Schaap:

> When Douglas got knocked down at the end of the eighth round, he appeared to be clearheadedly following the referee's count. The count was about two seconds behind the timekeeper's, but that's not very unusual, and Tyson was late retreating to a neutral corner. The fighter's sole responsibility is to beat the referee's count—which Douglas did with ease, deliberately.

Jeremy Schaap, *Busting the myths of Tyson-Douglas*, ESPN.com (Feb. 10, 2010). That seems clearly correct as a matter of principle; if Douglas was gearing himself to the referee's count, it would be unacceptable to say to him, "But in fact you took more than 10 seconds to get up. So you're out by a knockout." But suppose the facts were not as Schaap reports. Suppose that the ref had clearly started the count five seconds late, that Douglas had risen just after the ref counted to nine, and that ringside observers agreed that Douglas was *not* "clearheadedly following the referee's count"? Then would it be appropriate to declare Tyson the winner? As in the Colorado-Missouri game and the Vern-Ruhle incident, a key question is whether the result should depend on a fact-based inquiry into reliance on the official error.

6.   *"I would have returned it."* Suppose a pro tennis player hits a hard serve that lands on or near the sideline. The line judge immediately yells, "Out!" The receiver does not return the ball. The server challenges the call, and the chair umpire rules that the serve was good. But now what? Should the server be awarded the point on the ground that she hit a good serve that her opponent did not return? Or should a let—a replay—be called, on the ground that the call might have dissuaded or impaired the opponent from hitting a good return? Should the rule be a *per se* one, one way or the other? If not, what should the standard be for making the determination?

7.   *Reliance in the law.* Mistake and ignorance of law are among the most controversial issues in criminal law. You have probably heard the saying "mistake of law is no defense." That is generally true, but there are exceptions. One exception arises when a defendant has relied on a legal ruling by a legal official that is afterwards determined to be mistaken. Anglophone criminal law tends to grant defenses in such cases very grudgingly. For example, claims of reliance on erroneous advice from a lawyer or police officer are usually rejected categorically. Jurisdictions grant more readily a defense for reasonable reliance on a mistaken ruling by a judge. For example, the influential Model Penal Code provides in part: "A belief that conduct does not legally constitute an offense is a defense to a prosecution for that offense based upon such

conduct when . . . he acts in reasonable reliance upon an official statement of the law, afterward determined to be invalid or erroneous, contained in a judicial decision, opinion or judgment." MPC § 2.04(3)(b)(ii). Yet even in this context the defense is very narrowly circumscribed. In particular, many courts have held that an actor who acts in reliance on a trial court ruling that her conduct is lawful is not entitled to the defense if the trial judge's ruling is subsequently overturned on appeal. The rationale is that the actor's reliance on the lower court was not reasonable as a matter of law because the actor knew or should have known that it could be reversed on appeal.

In a representative case, one Ostrosky fished without a required state permit and argued unsuccessfully at trial that the permit requirement was unconstitutional. Ostrosky appealed his conviction to the intermediate state appellate court, which agreed that the permit law was unconstitutional and vacated his conviction. While the state appealed that ruling, Ostrosky again fished without a permit and was again arrested. After his second arrest, the state supreme court reversed the intermediate court, holding the permit requirement constitutional and restoring Ostrosky's conviction. At trial for the second incident of fishing without a permit, Ostrosky argued that he was entitled to rely on the earlier appellate court decision that had invalidated the permit law. The U.S. Court of Appeals rejected that argument, reasoning that, when Ostrosky relied on the earlier decision in his favor, he assumed the risk that it would be reversed on further appeal, as it was. *Ostrosky v. State of Alaska*, 913 F.2d 590 (9th Cir. 1990). Was *Ostrosky* rightly decided? If so, does it follow that Bake McBride's reliance on Doug Harvey's initial not-caught call was unreasonable (because he knew or should have known that it could have been reversed), leaving the Phillies without any good argument against a triple play? Or are the cases distinguishable? And how should such considerations have played out in the 2020 election? For example, Wisconsin election officials allowed ballots to be collected at two "Democracy in the Park" events. If the state supreme court later determined that this was not proper, should those ballots be disallowed? *See Trump v. Biden*, 951 N.W.2d 568 (Wis. 2020) (applying the equitable doctrine of laches, by a 4–3 vote, to reject challenge).

B. INSTANT REPLAY

In most of the cases we have been considering thus far, the officials determine on their own that they have erred—either because the initial action was an accident, rather than a mistake (hence not truly a "call" at all), or because there was an intra-crew disagreement that the crew (or crew chief, as the case may be) resolved against the initial decision. Many times, though, a competitor believes there has been a mistake that the officials do not acknowledge. Should there be a system that allows competitors to get review of the initial call, in something close to real time, not after the contest?

To be sure, many sports offer limited forms of appeal without special technology. Baseball allows the pitching team to appeal to the first or third base umpire when the batter attempts to check a swing and the home plate umpire does not call a strike. And tennis players were long permitted to appeal line calls to the chair umpire. But the most common and frequently discussed method of in-contest review of calls is review by use of instant replay technology. Because the in-contest use of instant replay to review calls is expanding rapidly across the world of sports, and because its use raises many difficult and interesting questions of system design, it warrants separate discussion. *See generally* Berman, *Replay.*

The basic rationale for use of instant replay is straightforward: for interrelated reasons of truth and justice, we want to get things right; and given current technology that permits high-definition videography from multiple angles, many or most sports can improve accuracy by using instant replay to review at least some on-field calls in close to real time. Putting expense aside, perhaps the chief (though, as we will see, not sole) objection or countervailing consideration is that "close to real time" isn't real time, and that gamewrights should resist any rule changes that introduce greater delay to the conduct of competition. The challenge for any gamewright designing a system of review is to balance these interests, and others as well.

The issues that a designer of instant replay must address are startlingly complex, as evidenced by the fact that MLB regulations governing the use of instant replay run over 8500 words—or longer than the U.S. Constitution with its twenty-seven amendments (and nearly twice as long as the original Constitution of 1787). Here we examine three principal issues: what calls should be reviewable; what the procedures for initiating review should be; and what standard of review should apply. These questions are interrelated.

1. REVIEWABLE CALLS

Most contests would break down if every call were reviewed. Some selection must be made. Indeed, as far as we can tell, every sport that provides for instant replay review specifies which calls are, or are not, reviewable.

In the NFL, for example, reviewable calls include: all those related to whether a player or ball did or did not cross a goal line or side line; whether a pass was completed or intercepted; whether a pass was touched by an ineligible receiver or by a defender, and whether it was thrown beyond the line of scrimmage; whether a ball carrier was down by contact before losing control of the ball; whether a kick attempt was good, when not higher than the top of the uprights as it crossed the goal post; whether there were too many players on the field; the spotting of the ball when a correct spot might determine whether the offense is awarded a first down; and calls regarding "the game clock, in situations in which time is deemed to have expired during or after the last play of the first or second half, or of an overtime period in the preseason or regular season, or of an overtime half in the postseason." NFL Rule 15, § 2, Article 4.

The list of unreviewable calls is longer. Some of the more common and consequential include: offside, holding, unsportsmanlike conduct, status of the play clock, forward progress not relating to touchdowns or first downs, and recovery of a loose ball in the field of play. As for pass interference, well, we'll get there very soon.

Section V of the MLB regulations governing replay review provides an exhaustive list of "the only calls eligible for Replay Review." It lists eleven categories of reviewable calls, with many elaborations and qualifications. This section itself runs nearly 2,000 words. MLB, *Rules: Replay Review*, https://tinyurl.com/yxwld6cs. Some of the choices made by these regulations may be obvious. For example, a call as to whether a batted ball was a home run or rather struck the top of the fence or a railing and stayed within the field of play is reviewable. Others may be more mysterious. Here are two sample paragraphs from the regulations:

C. **Specified Fair/Foul Ball Calls.** Calls involving a decision regarding whether a batted ball was "A FOUL BALL," within the meaning of the Official Baseball Rule's Definition of Terms (formerly Rule 2.00) but only with respect to balls that first land at or beyond the set positions of the first or third base Umpire. (In the case of a three-man crew, the home plate Umpire has the discretion to determine where the first or third base Umpire would have been set for the purpose of determining whether a fair/foul ball call is reviewable.) Line drives fielded by a defensive player in the infield and balls that first land in front of the set positions of the first or third base Umpire shall not be subject to review. The Umpire shall determine whether a purported foul ball landed in front of his position and thus is not subject to review. Such a determination by the Umpire is not reviewable. . . .

E. **Catch Plays In The Outfield.** An Umpire's decision whether a fielder caught a fly ball or line drive in flight in the outfield before it hit the ground (or an object other than the fielder.) See Official Baseball Rule Definition of Terms (formerly Rule 2.00) of "A CATCH"; and "IN FLIGHT".) Fly balls or line drives fielded by a defensive player in the infield shall not be eligible for review. Any outfielder who stations himself in the infield on the play shall be considered an infielder for the purpose of this Regulation. A fly ball (but not a line drive) touched by an infielder (other than the pitcher or catcher) in an area behind the original positioning of the nearest infielder (other than the pitcher or catcher) shall be considered a fly ball or line drive in the outfield subject to review. The Umpire shall determine whether a call is reviewable under this provision. Such a determination by the Umpire is not reviewable.

COMMENTS AND QUESTIONS

1.   Everyone saw it but the ones who mattered. One particularly notorious incident may loom over your consideration of the issues on reviewability—a no-call of pass interference (PI) in the 2018 NFC Conference Championship game (played on January 20, 2019), between the New Orleans Saints and the Los Angeles Rams. The game was tied 20–20 with 1:49 remaining in regulation. New Orleans had the ball on the Los Angeles 13-yard line, third and 10. Los Angeles had only one timeout remaining. Drew Brees, the Saints quarterback, threw to Tommylee Lewis at around the 6, near the right sideline. Before Lewis could catch the ball, he was knocked down by Nickell Robey-Coleman of the Rams. You can see the play at https://tinyurl.com/y75yxb45. Both Lewis and Robey-Coleman (not to mention 73,000 fans at the game, millions of TV viewers, and the head of NFL officiating) appeared to expect a flag; after watching the sequence in a post-game interview, Robey-Coleman said, "Ah, hell yeah, that was PI." It was also a helmet-to-helmet hit. If the penalty had been called, New Orleans would have had a first down, which would have allowed it to run down almost all of the clock and kick a short field goal, leaving L.A. hardly any time to score. Instead, it faced fourth down and so had to kick the field goal immediately. This gave L.A. the ball with 1:41 in the game. Sure enough, L.A. tied the game in regulation and won in overtime, earning a spot in the Super Bowl.

The furor was predictable and sustained. In response, the NFL decided to make calls and non-calls of pass interference reviewable on an experimental basis for the 2019 season. But, the Competition Committee said, because interference "involves a greater degree of subjectivity than other reviewable plays," stricter criteria are necessary before booth review can be made. "Accordingly," the Committee prescribed, "the Replay Official will stop the game when there is clear and obvious visual evidence that a pass interference foul may or may not have occurred, based on viewing the play live or any initial available line feed views." A decision on the field should only be reversed if, applying the usual standard for reversal (from Rule 15, Sec. 2, Art. 3), review yields "clear and obvious visual evidence" that the call on the field was in fact incorrect. *Competition Committee Finalizes Replay Rule for 2019 Season*, NFL OPS (June 20, 2019).

By common consensus, the experiment was an abject failure. The chief criticism was that Senior Vice President of Officiating, Al Riveron, who was given authority to make the final call on every challenge from the league's New York command center, imposed an impossibly high standard of review in practice, routinely failing to reverse calls or non-calls that almost all observers thought obviously mistaken. Indeed, out of 33 pass interference challenges made from Week 4 through Week 10, Riveron's team reversed exactly one call. One columnist reported after the season that he had "spoken to two knowledgeable officiating sources who independently identified about 50 pass interference calls that Riveron judged incorrectly on any reasonable scale of review," Kevin Seifert, *Goodbye, pass interference replay review: Lessons learned from the NFL's failed officiating experiment,* ESPN.com (May 28, 2020), a contention that nobody who followed the season would find hard to credit. But application of an overly demanding review standard was only part of the problem. The other part was that when, after Week 10, replay officials did start overturning calls and non-calls at a brisker clip, they were just as likely to reverse calls that most observers thought should have been sustained. *See, e.g.,* Danny Heifetz, *The NFL's New Pass Interference Rule Fixed Nothing and Broke Everything,* THE RINGER (Nov. 20, 2019); Adam Stites, *The NFL's pass interference challenge is looking worse every week,* SB NATION (Nov. 19, 2019). All told, the experiment fared so poorly that the league decided without any debate not to renew it for the 2020 season. "We failed, and we failed miserably," admitted NFL Executive Vice President of Football Operations, Troy Vincent. *NFL executive vice president Troy Vincent pans launch of pass interference replay,* ESPN.com (May 25, 2020).

What do you think? Was the league right to shelve the experiment after a single season, or should it have given Riveron and his crew more time to get better? If the 2019 replay rule was not good, could it have been improved, or is pass interference effectively unreviewable, perhaps because on-field officials apply such varied standards for what constitutes pass interference in the first place? *See* Heifetz, *The NFL's New Pass Interference Rule* (quoting former referee Terry McAulay's judgment that pass interference is the "most highly subjective call in football"). Most calls and non-calls of fouls are not reviewable. *If* we assume that most should not be, is there any good reason to make PI calls and non-calls reviewable, apart from the fact that a missed call in an extraordinarily visible and critical moment happened to involve PI? *See* John Breech, *Ex-NFL VP of officiating explains why the new pass interference rule might not be such a great idea,* CBS SPORTS.COM (June 21, 2019). Does it make sense to apply the "clear and obvious visual evidence" ("COVE") standard at the threshold, in deciding whether to stop play, as well as in deciding whether to reverse the call on the field?

2.   *Underlying principles?* Notice that neither the NFL nor MLB provides a general rule or principle, or set of rules or principles, to explain which calls are or are not reviewable. Instead, both leagues simply provide a list of reviewable calls (supplemented in each case by an explicitly nonexhaustive list of nonreviewable calls). Of course, the reviewable calls are not selected randomly or (recall Chapter 2) "arbitrarily." Can you distill any principles that explain which calls are, or are not, reviewable?

A common suggestion is that replay review is not appropriate for what are sometimes called "judgment calls." The argument for that principle ordinarily runs like this: Even if we should try harder to get calls right when there is a true fact of the matter to discover (like whether the ball hit the ground or crossed the plane of the end zone), there just aren't simple truths about matters of evaluative judgment (like whether some amount of contact was excessive), so subjecting such calls to replay review would amount to substituting one official's judgment for that of another. *See, e.g.,* Chad M. Oldfather & Matthew M. Fernholz, *Comparative Procedure on a Sunday Afternoon: Instant Replay in the NFL as a Process of Appellate Review,* 43 IND. L. REV. 45, 51–52 (2009). Do you agree that a distinction between judgment and non-judgment calls *does in fact* explain which calls are, and are not, reviewable in either the NFL or MLB? If this distinction does not *fully* explain what's reviewable and what isn't, does it partially explain the reviewability decisions? For example, is it fair to say that no judgment calls are reviewable and that some non-judgment calls are?

Do you agree that a distinction between judgment and non-judgment calls *should* explain which calls are, and are not, reviewable? Consider that, though some decisions in litigation are committed to the discretion of the trial court, appellate courts can, and sometimes do, conclude that the trial court exceeded the permissible bounds of its discretion. Should review of judgment calls in sports be conducted in a similar manner—that is, the fact that the call required judgment should not preclude replay review, but the reviewing official should give wide latitude to the judgment of the official who made the call?

3. *Judgment calls in baseball.* As we noted in the previous section, MLB allowed managers to appeal some umpire decisions long before it introduced review by instant replay. Those appeals are still permitted. Rule 8.02(a) provides that "[a]ny umpire's decision which involves judgment, such as, but not limited to, whether a batted ball is fair or foul, whether a pitch is a strike or a ball, or whether a runner is safe or out, is final. No player, manager, coach or substitute shall object to any such judgment decisions." In what sense are decisions regarding whether a batted ball is fair or foul, and whether a runner has been tagged out, "judgment calls"? If those are judgment calls, what types of calls are *not* judgment calls? In any event, is Rule 8.02(a) consistent with the fact that many fair-or-foul calls, and virtually all calls regarding whether a runner is safe or out, are reviewable by instant replay?

4. *Neighborhood play revisited.* We just said that "virtually all" safe-or-out calls are reviewable. Until 2016, the MLB regulations expressly provided that, although most force/tag calls are reviewable, a few such calls would "not be subject to review"—including in particular:

> The Umpire's judgment that a runner is clearly out on a force play at second base under circumstances in which the defensive player may or may not have touched second base in his attempt to complete a double play and avoid a collision with the runner. All other elements of the call shall be subject to review, including whether the fielder caught the ball, had control of the ball, was drawn off the bag, or tagged the runner. In this regard, a determination as to whether the fielder made a catch before dropping the ball while in the act of making a throw following the catch shall be reviewable.

Why was this call not reviewable? Does this have any bearing on our earlier discussion (see Subchapter 10A) regarding what the rules truly provide with respect to "phantom double plays"? In 2016, the rules were amended to delete this language. Was this change a sound one?

5. *Mixed calls of fact and of judgment.* Does the distinction between "factual" and "judgment" calls overlook the possibility that many unreviewable "judgment" calls involve elements that are purely factual and that some reviewable "factual" calls involve elements that are evaluative or judgmental? For an example of the former possibility, consider pass interference once again. How much contact is necessary to constitute forbidden interference might well be a matter of judgment and therefore, let us suppose, not properly reviewed in the NCAA. But what if replay shows that there was no contact at all, that the receiver tripped over his own feet? Is there any good reason why a defensive pass interference call should not be reviewable when the coach of the defending team contends that the defender made no contact with the receiver?

As for the possibility that reviewable calls can contain unnoticed elements of judgment, consider a potentially game-altering play in the Giants' 45–38 loss to the Eagles in Week 14 of the 2009 season. After scrambling for a 15-yard gain to escape a sack, Giants QB Eli Manning fell to the ground and lost the football. The Eagles recovered and were awarded possession. Calls of fumble and change of possession are reviewable to determine whether the ball carrier was down by contact before losing control of the ball, and the Giants challenged. Replay showed indisputably that Manning's knee was down before he lost the ball. So ordinarily the call would be reversed. But while it was clear that Manning was down, it wasn't as clear that he was down *by contact:* Eagles' defensive tackle Brodrick Bunkley had grabbed a piece of Manning's jersey as he escaped the pocket, but Manning took a few steps before hitting the turf, making it unclear whether the defensive contact had caused Manning's contact with the ground. If it had, there was no fumble; if it hadn't, there was. Should the question of whether Manning was down by contact have been deemed a judgment call, hence not reviewable?

6. *Review more?* Are there calls in either baseball or football that are not reviewable but should be? For example, NFL rules allow review of kick attempts only when the ball was "not higher than the top of the uprights as it crossed the goal post." Is there a good reason to disallow review of extra point and field goal attempts when the ball was higher than the uprights? If it's likely to be very hard for a replay official to determine the success of a kick when the ball is so high, is that a reason to make such calls unreviewable, or simply to expect that such calls will be very rarely overturned? In baseball, is there good reason why the question of whether a fly ball in the infield was caught before it hit the ground—the very question involved in the Vern Ruhle play—should not be reviewable? How about this "simple" solution offered by journalist John Breech: "Let every potential call be reviewable. Every. Single. One." Breech relies on limits on the number of challenges a team can make to keep replay from swallowing up the game. John Breech, *Rams-Saints ends*

with ugly pass interference no-call, here's the simple fix for the NFL going forward, CBS SPORTS.COM (Jan. 21, 2019).

7. *Beyond baseball and football.* Think about the use of instant replay in a sport that you know well. Does that sport make a good choice regarding which calls are reviewable by instant replay?

For example, for years the NHL made review available only to determine whether the game clock shows the correct time, or whether a goal was scored— that is, whether the puck crossed the goal line entirely and before time expired, whether the puck entered the net before the goal frame was dislodged, and whether a puck that entered the net was directed by a hand or foot or deflected by a high stick or an official. Is this too limited? Consider the suggestion, from sports journalist Joe DeLessio, that "[i]f an event that immediately precedes a goal should negate it, the referees should be allowed to ask for a review, even if it doesn't fit one of the criteria already on the books." Joe DeLessio, *Quest for Perfection*, SPORTS ON EARTH (Jan. 21, 2014). DeLessio offers an example from the 2012–13 season in which the Avalanche's Matt Duchene scored against the Predators after receiving the puck when he was egregiously offside:

> The play couldn't be reviewed, but the call could have easily been overturned if it was. (The NHL later admitted the linesman blew the call.) Offsides calls wouldn't be universally reviewable, and ultimately a decision would need to be made on what would happen if a goal was scored 10 or 20 or 30 seconds after a missed offsides call. Still, officials should be given the leeway to review, and disallow, a goal like Duchene's.

Do you agree with DeLessio? The NHL did, amending its rules starting in 2017 to allow a coach to challenge a goal on the ground "that the play should have been stopped by reason of an 'Off-side' infraction by the attacking team." NHL Rule 78.7. The rules further provide that "[i]f a review is not conclusive and/or there is any doubt whatsoever as to whether the call on the ice was correct, the original call will be confirmed," and the challenging team will be assessed a two-minute minor penalty "for delaying the game." Is this a good solution?

2. PROCEDURES FOR INITIATING AND UNDERTAKING REVIEW

A sport could decide that any call that falls within the set of calls deemed reviewable will be reviewed as a matter of course. And one can find pockets of that approach; the NFL now automatically reviews every scoring play and every turnover. But for the most part, just because a play *could* be reviewed does not mean that it *will* be reviewed. And so a sport needs some procedure to decide which ones will actually be reviewed. And, however the decision to review may be made, the sport needs a procedure to determine how review shall be conducted. Among the procedural questions that need to be resolved are the following: (1) Who will have power to initiate review—the competitors themselves (by which we mean, in this context, to include coaches or managers), the officials (on or off the field), or both? (2) Insofar as competitors initiate review, should the number of available challenges be limited and, if so, how? (3) Insofar as officials call for instant replay review on their own initiative, how if at all should their calls for review be limited or regulated? (4) Who undertakes review when initiated? Sports that use instant replay review resolve these design choices in strikingly diverse ways.

The NFL was the first major sports league to use instant replay and has, on many issues, provided a model for other leagues to follow. Through most of the game, power to initiate review is vested with the coaches, not the officials, and is limited to only two per game, except that, if a coach makes two challenges and both are successful, the team receives a third. The cost of an unsuccessful challenge is loss of a timeout, which means as well that a coach is not allowed to challenge a call unless the team still has a timeout to lose. During the last two minutes of each half, coaches are disabled from challenging calls, and authority to seek review is assigned to the same specialized replay officials who undertake review when called for. Thanks to rule changes in 2011 and 2012, all scoring plays and called turnovers are reviewed automatically, without a coach having to spend a challenge.

NCAA football flips principal authority to challenge calls from the coaches to the officials. Officials have general power throughout the game, and may review as many calls as they wish, but they may call for review only if "there is reasonable evidence to believe" that a reviewable call was erroneous, and only if "the outcome of a review would have a direct, competitive impact on the game." NCAA Football Rule 12, Section 5, Art. I. Coaches are allowed one challenge through the game, and a second if the first is successful. Unsuccessful challenges are not penalized.

In professional tennis, a player is allowed three unsuccessful challenges per set, and an extra one in a tie-break; a successful challenge does not count against the limit. There is no cost of challenging, other than the **opportunity cost** of using up one of a very limited supply of challenges. (The economic concept of "opportunity cost" refers to the value of the next-highest-valued alternative that an agent forgoes when selecting their highest-valued  alternative. It is the loss of benefit that an agent could have enjoyed had they not made the choice they did.) Similarly, coaches in MLB are allowed one unsuccessful challenge per regular season game, and two unsuccessful challenges in the postseason, in tiebreaker games to qualify for the postseason, and in the All-Star game; successful challenges do not count against these limits. The crew chief is authorized to call for review of home run calls at any time, and of other reviewable calls after the seventh inning.

Opportunity Cost

As of the 2019–20 season when the English Premier League (EPL) adopted the system, soccer's Video Assistant Referee (VAR) system is now in use by all the major soccer international competitions, domestic club leagues, and many domestic cups. The system varies slightly in implementation among competitions—for example, the 2018 FIFA World Cup used four VAR officials, each focusing on a different aspect of the game, while the EPL uses three officials—but the procedures and standards remain the same across competitions. VAR officials constantly monitor the match, but may step in to correct "clear and obvious errors" or "serious missed incidents" in only four "match-changing situations": (1) goals and offenses leading up to a goal, (2) penalty decisions and offense leading up to a penalty, (3) direct red card incidents (but not second yellow cards), and (4) mistaken identity. The EPL contends that it has a "high bar for VAR intervention on subjective decisions to maintain the pace and intensity of the matches." However, "[f]actual decisions, such as offside or if a foul was committed inside or outside the penalty area, will not be subject to the 'clear and obvious error' test." English Premier League, *VAR* (June 1, 2020), https://www.premierleague.com/VAR. Whether the call is subjective or objective, and whether initiated by the VAR or by the on-field referee, the final decision whether to overturn a call is always held by the on-field referee. FIFA, *VAR at the 2018 FIFA World Cup*, https://football-technology.fifa.com/en/innovations/var-at-the-world-cup/.

COMMENTS AND QUESTIONS

1. Automatic review? Under what circumstances, if any, should review be undertaken as a matter of course, as is done in the NFL for scoring plays and turnovers? When a call is a matter that can be discerned by a mechanical system, such as line calls in tennis, should the system itself be allowed to announce its findings? Note that this is done in tennis with respect to calls on the serve, but not others. Why not others?

2. Competitive impact. Should replay officials be required, as in the NCAA, to assess whether reversal of a call would have a "direct, competitive impact on the game"? Will it always be apparent to an official what the competitive impact of a reversal will be? For example, suppose a team with third down and five to go on its opponents' thirty throws a pass that is ruled incomplete—but the pass is short enough that even if the call is overturned the team will still face fourth down. Does the ruling have competitive significance? Does your answer depend on just how much of a gain the play would be deemed to make if the pass is ruled complete? Doesn't each inch of gain marginally improve the team's chance for a field goal, or for a first down? Does this sort of case cause trouble for the NCAA rule? If not, why not? If so, how could the rule be improved?

3. Caps on challenges. Sports that allow competitors to challenge calls cap the number of challenges that any side may make. In one possible model, a competitor is allowed a fixed number of challenges, whether they are successful or not. In another model (used in baseball and tennis), competitors are allowed a fixed number of *unsuccessful* challenges; challenges that prove successful are unlimited. Football uses a hybrid model: a team is allowed two challenges but if both are successful, it is allowed one more. Is this a principled or unprincipled compromise between the two forms of hard cap? Consider a football game in which one coach makes two challenges and both are upheld, giving him a third. If he makes that third challenge and it too is upheld, he won't get another. Why not? Why should the team run out of challenges just because its three successful challenges show that it has suffered numerous bad calls? Is one of these approaches best in general, or are different approaches better for different sports? If the latter, what factors or considerations bear on which approach is best for a given sport?

Should challenges be bankable? Consider, as an illustration, a revision to the NFL rules that would permit a team to transfer one unused challenge to its next game. What would the effects of this rule change be?

4.   *Unlimited challenges.* Is it clear that the formal rules should limit at all the number of challenges a competitor is allowed? If the formal rules allowed unlimited challenges, how great is the risk that teams would abuse the privilege? Is this something that can be policed effectively by informal norms, given that the participants are repeat players? After all, if the coach of Team A challenges calls excessively, we might expect that the coach of Team B will respond in kind, and that the threat of such retaliation would suffice to prevent excessive challenges. If you think that informal norms would not suffice here, why not? (In the law, each side is given a limited number of peremptory challenges to use during jury selection but an unlimited number of challenges for cause. There are no limits on issues a party can raise on appeal or on objections counsel can raise during trial.)

5.   *Charge for failure.* In the NFL, not only are there caps on challenges, but an unsuccessful challenge costs a timeout. Is this appropriate or unduly punitive? Why isn't the fact that challenges are limited in number enough to deter frivolous challenges or to incentivize care? Or does some other factor justify the timeout charge?

6.   *Power to initiate review.* In the last two minutes of a half, power to initiate review in the NFL shifts from coaches to officials. Why? The most commonly voiced rationales suggest the rule is protective of coaches. First, the rule relieves coaches from having to worry about challenges when they must also focus on clock management; second, it immunizes coaches from criticism for using up their timeouts and therefore disabling themselves from issuing a two-minute challenge. Are these compelling rationales? Are there other good reasons to give review power in the final two minutes to officials? Are there other good reasons to withdraw that power from coaches? Note that officials could be empowered to initiate review in the final two minutes without coaches also being disabled from doing so. How would you allocate power to initiate review in football?

7. *The reviewer.* Who should undertake review and make the final decision when a call is subject to instant replay review: the chief on-field official (as in the NFL and in the World Cup), the on-field officials as a crew (as in the NBA), a special replay official at the game (as in NCAA football), specialized replay officials housed in an off-site command center (as in the NHL and MLB)? Somebody else? A combination? What are the various considerations?

3. THE STANDARD OF REVIEW

Replay rules usually state highly restrictive standards for reversal of an on-field call. For example, before 2016 the NFL maintained a standard requiring "indisputable visual evidence" (IVE) for reversal; the NCAA uses the nearly identical "indisputable video evidence" standard. If we take this standard literally, it is more restrictive even than the "beyond a reasonable doubt" standard necessary to convict a criminal defendant. This may explain the NFL's decision to use a somewhat softer "clear and obvious visual evidence" (COVE) standard for reversal since the 2016 season.

MLB rules provide:

> To change a reviewable call, the Replay Official must determine that there is clear and convincing evidence to change the original call that was made on the field of play. In other words, the original decision of the Umpire shall stand unchanged unless the evidence obtained by the Replay Official leads him to definitively conclude that the call on the field was incorrect.

MLB REPLAY REVIEW REGULATIONS, Section III ("Standard for Changing a Call") (2014). (Are those two sentences consistent? That is, does the second accurately reflect what the "clear and convincing evidence" standard requires in Anglophone law?) Similarly, the NBA provides that "[t]he call made by the game officials during play will be reversed only when the replay provides the officials with 'clear and conclusive' visual evidence to do so." NBA Rule 13.III.a, d.

Are such highly deferential standards of review desirable? Consider the following discussion, which focuses on the IVE standard previously employed in the NFL.

MITCHELL N. BERMAN, REPLAY
99 CAL. L. REV. 1683, 1691–97 (2011)
© 2011 Mitchell N. Berman

The goal of instant replay is to correct officiating errors—or at least those errors that are both correctible at reasonable cost, and consequential. Because form should follow function, the instant replay system should be designed to minimize (consequential) officiating errors. More precisely, the various features of the system—including the standard of review—should be chosen to maximize error correction up to the point at which the marginal cost exceeds the marginal benefits. Call this the Pinchbeck Principle, in honor of the NFL VP [Val Pinchbeck] who . . . explained that instant replay was instituted to ensure that no team missed the Super Bowl because of a correctible officiating error. Stripped to its essentials, the argument against IVE is that it does not satisfy this desideratum, and that a more relaxed standard of review—something like the law's *de novo* standard of review—would.

A. The Heart of the Argument

"Indisputable visual evidence" is an extraordinarily stringent standard—on its face, more demanding than the "beyond a reasonable doubt" standard of proof that governs criminal trials. The intended consequence is to drastically minimize the number of times a correct initial call is reversed. A second consequence—not intended, but surely foreseeable—is to ensure that a large number of mistaken initial calls are permitted to stand uncorrected. Put another way, if the standard is complied with, correct on-field calls will be overturned very rarely. That's good. But incorrect on-field calls will be allowed to stand very frequently. That's bad. From an error-minimization standpoint, the only question is which effect is greater relative to a more neutral or less deferential standard of review: the reduction in erroneous reversals or the increase in erroneous affirmances?

Surely, however, this is not a difficult question. On the assumption that reviewing officials' beliefs track reality tolerably well—or, more precisely, that they are not systematically biased in one direction or the other[25]—the league would minimize the combination of erroneous final calls by instructing each official to announce the ruling that he believes is more likely than not correct. Error minimization, after all, is precisely the rationale behind the law's preponderance of the evidence—or "more likely than not"—standard of proof. Much as unbiased jurors will, in the aggregate, minimize the sum of false negatives and false positives by announcing verdicts in accordance with the facts they believe more likely

---

[25] This is a critical assumption that, although generally reasonable, isn't always. Consider three-card monte. What makes this con successful is that the mark's beliefs are poor guides to truth. If you're looking for, say, the red ace, you might do better not picking the card in which you have most confidence. The possibility of similar and systematic mismatch between facts and beliefs is something a legal system should take into account. For example, controlled experiments repeatedly demonstrate that people place vastly too much credence in eyewitness testimony—a proposition that the large number of cases of DNA exoneration vividly bolster. So when only one party to a lawsuit introduces such testimony, factfinders are likely to be more confident in that party's case than is warranted. Or suppose that jurors systematically overweight the testimony of police officers. If so, then use of the preponderance standard in criminal trials might produce more false positives than would an epistemically unbiased factfinder. A standard of proof greater than preponderance could help counter this bias, and actually increase total accuracy. Unsystematic biases—biases that sometimes favor one party, sometimes the other—might wash out in the long run. But when a legal system is infected by recurring and nonrandom biases, then the more-likely-than-not standard of proof might not minimize total errors relative to a heightened (or lowered) standard designed to offset the bias.

than not correct, so too would replay officials minimize the sum of erroneous affirmances and erroneous reversals by announcing the rulings in which they have the greater confidence. If, as would appear, replay officials have good access to the facts, strongly deferential review all but ensures more errors than necessary.

C. Summary

Epistemic standards that provide that an initial call cannot be corrected after instant replay review unless the reviewing official deems the evidence of error "indisputable" or "conclusive" strongly entrench initial calls against reversal. The argument against strong entrenchment—and, equivalently, the argument in favor of something like de novo review—can be parsed as follows:

1. The NFL should employ that standard of review that would maximize the correction of consequential errors except insofar as correcting the marginal error is outweighed by marginal costs of the system. (The Pinchbeck Principle)

2. *De novo* review corrects more (consequential) errors than does IVE. (The error-minimization premise)

3. *De novo* review does not incur more costs than IVE—or not enough to outweigh the increased benefits in the coin of error correction. (The not-prohibitively-costly premise)

4. Therefore, *de novo* review is preferable to IVE.

COMMENTS AND QUESTIONS

1. Validity of the argument for de novo *review.* In logic, an argument is **valid** if the conclusion follows from the premises. That is, a valid argument would produce true conclusions if the premises are true, which they might not be. (The following argument is valid, even though none of the premises is true: 1. All alligators can fly; 2. Roger Goodell is an alligator; 3. Therefore, Roger Goodell can fly.) Is the four-step argument summarized above valid? If not, why not?

 Validity and Soundness

2. Soundness of the argument. An argument or premise is **sound** if true. If the argument summarized above is valid but not sound then one or more of the premises must be false. Which of the premises do you think are most vulnerable? What objections can you think of before you continue reading?

3. Error minimization. In Anglo-American law, rulings of law made by a trial court are reviewed *de novo* by the appellate court. (Recall that, in the Pistorius case, the Court of Arbitration for Sport emphasized that it reviews *de novo* rulings made by any sport federation.) One consideration sometimes offered in support of this principle is that the appellate judges are more expert in the law than are trial judges—or at least are not less expert. A more persuasive rationale is that if the appellate court deferred to the trial court with respect to legal questions, the law would be unstable, because different trial courts within the same appellate jurisdiction might generate conflicting legal rulings. By contrast, findings of the facts that bear on the particular case are generally reviewed on appeal under a deferential standard—in particular, a finding of fact made by a trial judge must be upheld unless the appellate judges are persuaded that it was "clearly erroneous." One rationale for this deferential standard is that the trial judge "sees more and senses more" than "his loftier brothers" because he has direct access to witnesses, whereas the appellate judges are limited to the written record. Maurice Rosenberg, *Judicial Discretion of the Trial Court, Viewed from Above,* 22 SYRACUSE L. REV. 635, 663 (1971). For much the same reason, one argument favoring a deferential standard of review of on-field calls is that the on-field official is more likely to get the call right than is the reviewing official, so the *de novo* standard of review will actually produce more total final errors than does a deferential standard like IVE. This is an objection to the second premise presented by Berman. Is it persuasive? Is it generally true that the initial call made by an official on the field is more likely to be accurate than a call made by a referee or booth official after reviewing, in slow motion, the video shot by multiple cameras? *See* Berman, *Replay,* at 1700–02. Do your answers depend on the nature of the call and the quality of the replay? What other rationales can you think of for why a deferential standard of review is applied to fact-finding both in litigation and in sports officiating?

4. *Beyond error minimization.* Even assuming that a system of instant replay review should be structured to minimize total officiating mistakes and that a lower standard of appellate review like *de novo* would yield fewer total errors than would a highly deferential standard like IVE, would the lower standard be too costly for reasons apart from error-correction? That is, are there good reasons to dispute the third premise from the argument above?

One common defense of the existing standard is that a lower standard would produce more total replay-associated delay. Is this true? What is the chain of reasoning that yields that conclusion? (Recall that, under the existing NFL system, each coach is entitled to only two challenges for the entire game, except that he is allowed a third if his first two are both successful. If a coach issues a challenge that is unsuccessful, his team loses a timeout.) *See* Berman, *Replay, supra* at 1703–06.

5. *Two types of error.* Perhaps the most interesting arguments for IVE, COVE and similar standards challenge the premise—reflected in what Berman calls "the Pinchbeck Principle"—that the goal of replay review should be to minimize total final errors. This challenge can proceed along two very different lines. The first is that the goal of review should not be to correct mere mistakes (not even mere mistakes that significantly affect the contest's outcome) but rather to correct only really bad mistakes—the mistakes that seasoned officials really should be expected to avoid. Even assuming arguendo that *de novo* review will catch and correct more "mere mistakes" than will IVE, this line of reasoning goes, IVE is preferable because it is better designed to

limit overturns to "whoppers." Are you persuaded? Why should the goal of review be to correct only big errors and not those errors that, while more understandable or excusable, nonetheless have a big impact on the game? Furthermore, is IVE well-tailored to catch all and only (or nearly all and only) the whoppers? Why (not)? *See* Berman, *Replay,* at 1721–24.

6.   *Asymmetrical error costs.* The second avenue for challenging the Pinchbeck Principle maintains that the goal should be to minimize, not total errors, but total weighted errors, and that a highly deferential standard is necessary to achieve that end. The distinction between error-minimization and weighted-error-minimization is best illustrated by the criminal law. A criminal verdict can be erroneous in two different ways: an innocent defendant can be convicted, or a guilty defendant can be acquitted. Because we believe that these two types of errors are not equally bad, we set the standard of proof at a level calculated to produce very few errors of the first type (Type I errors, or "false positives") (see Chapter 11), even though such a standard foreseeably produces many more errors of the second type (Type II errors, or "false negatives"), and more errors of the two types combined. Because the two types of error do not have equal negative value, our goal is not to minimize the sum of all errors (the number of false positives plus the number of false negatives) but the weighted sum of all errors, which means that we accept more total errors if we can have fewer of the worse type.

Notice now that instant replay review also produces four possible outcomes—two different types of correct final calls (affirming a correct initial call and reversing an incorrect initial call), and two different types of incorrect final calls (erroneous reversals and erroneous affirmances). These possibilities are displayed in the matrix below. If the two different types of error are not equally bad, then the goal for instant replay review should be to minimize weighted errors and not total errors—just as it is in criminal trials. And if erroneous reversals are significantly worse than erroneous affirmances, then a highly deferential standard of review will minimize total weighted review error even if it produces more total errors than would a nondeferential standard.

		Result of Review	
		Affirm	Reverse
Initial Call	Correct	Correct Final Call	Mistake (Erroneous Reversal)
	Incorrect	Mistake (Erroneous Affirmance)	Correct Final Call

The last sentence is put conditionally: deferential review would produce less weighted error *if* erroneous reversals are significantly worse than erroneous affirmances. But this is far from obviously true, for both types of error seem equally bad in this straightforward way: both make it the case, and make it the case equally, that the game proceeds down a path that is different from the path that the two teams' own play has earned them. So what reason have we to conclude that the two different routes to a final error are not equally bad, all things considered?

Here are two possibilities. *See* Berman, *Replay,* at 1714–21. The first idea is that there is always something harmful about a public reversal of an on-field call even when that reversal sets things right. The harm is that the public reversal tends to undermine the officials' authority or promotes disrespect for them. (See the discussion on pp. 543–544 regarding what Gottfried von Cramm told Don Budge about showing up an official.) Therefore, a final mistake produced by erroneous reversal *is* worse than a final mistake produced by erroneous affirmance because the former has two elements of disvalue, not just one: the element of mistake and the element of reversal. (By the same token, a final correct call produced by reversal of an incorrect initial call has less positive value than a final correct call produced by affirmance of a correct initial call.) Is this a persuasive argument for IVE? In a world in which millions of viewers at home, and increasing number of spectators at the game, have access to video replays from multiple cameras in high definition and super slo-mo, which fact is more likely to undermine respect for the officials: the fact that an initial call is reversed or the fact that the initial call, whether reversed or not, appears to have been mistaken?

Loss Aversion; Endowment Effect

The second argument that it is worse to make an incorrect reversal than to let an incorrect call stand depends upon a psychological bias known as loss aversion.

Roughly, spectators of any sporting event can be divided into two groups: those who care who wins that particular contest (call them "partisans") and those who don't ("enthusiasts"). Every call is experienced as a benefit by some of the partisans and as a detriment by others; some gain utility from the call, others lose it. So too with every reversal of a call already made: to adopt a hedonic idiom, each reversal confers pleasure on partisans of the team that benefits while inflicting pain on partisans of the team that loses. . . .

Th[is] observation plausibly becomes relevant to debates over standards of review . . . if **loss aversion** and the **endowment effect** are true psychological phenomena. Briefly, the endowment effect is the experimental finding that people value goods they already own more highly than an identical good they do not own. Loss aversion is the preferred explanation: people prefer avoiding losses to realizing gains. If these cognitive biases exist and apply in this context, then partisans want not to lose a call already made that had been to their benefit more than they want to gain the benefit of the reversal of a call already made that had been to their detriment, even when the magnitudes of the loss and the gain, in terms of probable impact on contest outcome, are the same. Similarly, if the call is reversed, it is experienced as a more profound welfare setback by partisans who lose what had been theirs than it is experienced as a welfare gain by partisans who did not "own" the call to begin with. If this is true, then holding all else constant (like the size of each team's fan base), each reversal is utility-reducing on net. Therefore, each reversal is a cost and, as before, the total cost of an erroneous reversal is greater than the total cost of an erroneous affirmance.

Berman, *Replay,* at 1720. Do you agree that the NFL should set its standard of review at whatever level would foreseeably maximize partisans' welfare? Why or why not? If so, should the league also favor teams with many fans over those with few?

7. *The appearance of justice.* It is often said in ordinary legal contexts that the *appearance* of justice is as important as the *fact* of justice. Consider in that light the suggestion that those with a stake in a contest—players, coaches, partisan fans—are likely to *believe* that a reversal is mistaken and therefore unjust unless they are confident that the initial call was wrong. Does this consideration support a highly deferential review standard such as the NFL's IVE or MLB's "clear and convincing evidence"? How does this rationale differ from the loss aversion rationale discussed in the previous question?

8. *Selection effects.* If calls were selected randomly for review, one might argue that *de novo* review could hardly be worth the effort: it might create nearly as many errors as it would correct, because most of the selected calls would in fact be correct, and with respect to those review could only create an error, not correct one. But calls are not randomly selected for review. *For the most part,* the selected calls are close and there is some reason to doubt their accuracy. Does this fact weigh in favor of *de novo* review?

9. *All things considered.* Can you think of any good arguments for or against the IVE or COVE standards of review in addition to those already canvassed? What do you think the standard of review should be?

10. *Another way to reduce reversals.* If you conclude that erroneous reversals are in some fashion worse than erroneous affirmances, and therefore that a sport should be more concerned to minimize the former type of error than to minimize the sum of both types of error, is the use of a highly deferential standard of review the best way to achieve that goal? Possibly another way to achieve that same end is to mandate a *de novo* standard of review but to increase the number of reviewers and provide that a challenged call is reversed only if some specified supermajority of reviewers agrees. For example, a sport could send all replay challenges to a centralized location where three (five? twenty?) specially trained replay officials will review the call and are authorized to reverse only if all agree that the on-field call was mistaken. What considerations favor one method or the other of "entrenching" the initial call—using one replay official who deploys a highly deferential standard, or using several replay officials who deploy a nondeferential

standard but can reverse only by supermajority (or unanimous) agreement? If you prefer the latter solution, should the reviewers consult or not?

———

Exercise 13B

Recall our discussion (pp. 430–431) of the NFL's failed experiment with instant replay to review pass interference calls and non-calls. Although the league scrapped the experiment after only one season, stakeholders were not happy to return to the status quo ante that had brought us the egregiously mistaken, yet unreviewable, non-call in the 2018 NFC Championship Game. Could the league do better? In trying to design a better approach, consider what the root difficulties are. Are the problems with the standard of review or with the review procedures? Is the problem simply that the replay officials needed more training and experience? Is it possible that part (or more) of the difficulty lies in the substantive content of the interference rules themselves, or in the penalties that interference brings forth? All things considered, what reforms would you propose?

4.　THE "STANDS"/"CONFIRMED" DISTINCTION AND THE CRIMINAL LAW

Notice that the discussion thus far asked a question about sports—how should sports use instant replay?—and drew on practices in law, and frameworks development by legal scholars, to help answer that question. The direction of illumination in this subchapter has been from law to sports. Now it is time for sports to return the favor.

In collegiate and professional football, officials are instructed to use different language to report two different reasons they may have for denying a replay challenge. As the NCAA rules explain, the referee should make one of these announcements:

> 1.　If the video evidence confirms the on-field ruling: "After further review, the ruling on the field is confirmed."

> 2.　If there is no indisputable (conclusive) evidence to reverse the on-field ruling: "After further view, the ruling on the field stands."

Similarly, MLB directs that "[t]he Replay Official will . . . inform the Crew Chief of his decision either to change the call on the field, confirm the call on the field or let stand the call on the field due to the lack of clear and convincing evidence to change it."

We might say, in short, that these leagues employ a system of three verdicts for reporting results of replay review ("reversed," "stands," and "confirmed") rather than a simpler and more straightforward two-verdict system ("reversed" and "not reversed").

Why do the rules make this distinction? Why do they insist on three verdicts where two would seem to do? The answer seems plain. Although the first verdict—that the ruling "is confirmed"—and the second—that it (merely) "stands"—have the same *tangible* effects, they plainly differ in *expressive* or *communicative* significance. They say or express different meanings. When replay officials stop play and initiate formal replay review, they highlight and broadcast a suspicion that the on-field official got it wrong, and thus in a sense failed. A ruling of "confirmed" expunges that suspicion. It announces to the public: "He got it right." A ruling of "stands" says only, "Well, we can't say that he got it wrong." The first verdict offers a vindication—of both the official and the call—that the second withholds.

If we know that a challenged call will not be reversed, should we care as well whether it was in fact correct? Maybe not. Maybe all we should care about is whether there is sufficient basis for overturning it. But the very fact that several sports leagues that adopt a heightened standard of review instruct their officials to clearly distinguish those challenged calls that replay confirms to be correct from other calls that must also be allowed to stand suggests that we *do* care, because the existence of the "stands"/"confirmed" distinction is hard to explain otherwise. And if there is any reason to care about this difference in the context of sports officiating, it seems the reason should weigh much more forcefully in other areas of life where it should matter to us what really happened and not only what the formal institutional response to a dispute should be.

Indeed, a three-verdict system is at least an option anytime a decision procedure employs a standard of proof (or of review) more demanding than the default more-likely-than-not standard. That is, the institution could announce, "The facts justify taking action X," "The facts do not justify taking action X," or "We are not sufficiently confident that the facts justify taking action X."

The longest standing, most widespread, and most familiar decision procedure using an elevated standard of proof is the criminal law. In our system, an accused may be found guilty only if the trier of fact concludes that guilt has been proven "beyond a reasonable doubt." And if an American jury decides that it cannot reach that conclusion, it pronounces a verdict of "not guilty." But that is clearly a misnomer. It does not mean, "We believe that the defendant is not guilty," but rather, "We believe that the state has failed to prove the defendant's guilt beyond a reasonable doubt." A state could, however, authorize, or require, a jury that is not voting for conviction to select between two different forms of acquittal: "innocent" when it is persuaded that the defendant is not, in fact, guilty;

and "not proven guilty" when it believes that the defendant is guilty more likely than not, but it is left with too much doubt to convict.

That's how they do it in Scotland, which, although part of the United Kingdom (as of this writing), has its own, unique, legal system. Among the more distinctive features of Scottish criminal law is the availability of three verdicts. As in American criminal law, Scottish judges and juries are required to convict a defendant if persuaded of his guilt "beyond a reasonable doubt." In that case, the verdict is "guilty." But if not so persuaded, the factfinder may return either one of two verdicts: "not guilty," which is regarded as "a positive declaration of innocence," or "not proven," which "is thought to imply solely that the accused's guilt has not been conclusively demonstrated." Peter Duff, *The Scottish Criminal Jury: A Very Peculiar Institution*, 62 LAW & CONTEMP. PROBS. 173, 193 (1999).[a] The Scottish criminal verdict system, in other words, is directly analogous to the instant replay system in American football.[b]

COMMENTS AND QUESTIONS

1.   Consequences in criminal law. Who would win and who would lose if we imported a third verdict of "innocent" into our criminal law? Presumably virtually all defendants who would be acquitted in a two-verdict system would also be acquitted in a three-verdict system. Those declared "innocent" under the three-verdict system would be better off for the switch. Obviously, if you were to be prosecuted for a crime, you'd want to be acquitted, but you'd especially want the jurors to announce that they find you innocent of the charges and not merely that they are unable to find you guilty. That degree of vindication is unavailable in our current two-verdict system. On the other hand, some defendants who would be acquitted under the two-verdict system would move in the other direction: They would also be acquitted in a three-verdict system, but by reason of "not proven guilty." The expressive significance of an acquittal on those terms is more stigmatizing when a separate verdict of "innocent" is an available option (in a three-verdict system) than when it isn't (in a two-verdict system).

How about the effects on defendants who would be found guilty under a two-verdict system? One might think that adding a new form of acquittal verdict shouldn't alter the percentage of all defendants who are acquitted rather than convicted. After all, the line that separates acquittal from conviction remains in exactly the same place in two-verdict and three-verdict systems: it is defined by the beyond-a-reasonable-doubt standard.

---

[a]   The Scottish system also allows verdicts by majority vote of the fifteen jurors.

[b]   We should recognize that in some cases an American jury also has more than two options. In some cases, for example, it may acquit the defendant on the principal charge but convict on a lesser one—or it might find the defendant not guilty by reason of insanity.

Although intuitive, this prediction is likely to be mistaken. There is good reason to anticipate that more people will be acquitted under the three-verdict system than in a two-verdict system.

The reason derives from a psychological bias called "extremeness aversion" or "the compromise effect," the tendency of people to evaluate a given option more favorably when it appears as intermediate in a choice set rather than as an extreme. In one suggestive set of experiments, a summary of facts concerning a homicide was presented to two groups of subjects. *See* Mark Kelman et al., *Context-Dependence in Legal Decision Making*, 25 J. LEGAL STUD. 287 (1996). Subjects in the first group were asked to decide whether the defendant's actions satisfied the legal definition of manslaughter (punishable by eight years imprisonment) or of murder (punishable up to life imprisonment with the possibility of parole). Subjects in the second group were offered, in addition, a third possibility of aggravated murder (punishable by death or life imprisonment without possibility of parole).

Forty-seven percent of the subjects in the first group (the two-option group) chose manslaughter, while 53% chose murder. We should therefore expect that the percentage of subjects choosing manslaughter in the second group (the three-option group) would remain about the same: as a logical matter, if the defendant should be found guilty only of manslaughter when the alternative is murder, he should still be convictable only of manslaughter when an additional more extreme form of murder is put on the table. But only 19% of the subjects in the second group chose manslaughter, the remaining 81% dividing about equally between murder and aggravated murder. One plausible explanation invokes the compromise effect: once murder became outflanked, it appeared more attractive to some who otherwise would favor manslaughter. The apparent implication for a three-verdict system is that some juries that would have convicted a defendant when given a choice between two "extremes" will acquit on the grounds of "not proven" when that is the intermediate option.

That appears to be a principal ground of resistance on the part of some Scottish defense lawyers to the possibility of eliminating the "not proven" verdict: In some cases, if the only way to avoid letting the accused get off without a stain is to find him guilty, the jury may do just that, even though it would find the charges "not proven"—and so not convict the accused—if that were a possibility.

How does this speculation affect your judgment about whether our criminal law regime would be better with three verdicts than with two? What other factors do you think are relevant when choosing between these two systems? Given that a criminal defendant is acquitted, *should* the judicial system indicate that it considered, and rejected, the option of declaring him innocent? For extensive analyses of the tradeoffs and procedural details, see Samuel Bray, Comment, *Not Proven: Introducing a Third Verdict*, 72 U. CHI. L. REV. 1299 (2005); Andrew D. Leipold, *The Problem of the Innocent, Acquitted Defendant*, 94 NW. U. L. REV. 1297 (2000). For an empirical study, see Michael Smithson, et al., *Guilty, Not Guilty, or . . .? Multiple Options in Jury Verdict*

Choices, 20 J. BEHAV. DECISION MAKING 481 (2007) (asserting that the study contradicts the view that the Not Proven option attracts jurors away from returning a conviction and that the option more often supplants outright acquittals—but presenting evidence suggesting that diminution of convictions is in fact substantial). Note that the system is controversial even in Scotland. *See, e.g.,* Duff, *Scottish Criminal Jury.* at 173 ("even many Scots regard [the three-verdict choice] as illogical and unprincipled").

2. *"Stands" and "confirmed" in football.* Putting aside the criminal law, do you think sports that use instant replay and adopt a heightened standard of review *should* distinguish calls that are confirmed from those that merely stand, even if no tangible consequences follow? For that matter, *should* any tangible consequences follow? For example, we observed earlier that, in the NFL, a team loses a timeout for an unsuccessful challenge. Should coaches who challenge a call unsuccessfully lose a timeout only when the call is confirmed, and not when it is merely allowed to stand?

C. THE TIMING OF REVIEW

1. DELAYED REVIEW IN GENERAL

Ideally, error correction will occur immediately, before any further play occurs. And the rules tend to enforce that principle. For example, in the NFL, a coach who wants a play reviewed must throw the red flag "before the next legal snap or kick." Rule 15, Sec. 2, Art. 1. And review called for by the replay official must be initiated "before the ball is next legally put in play." Rule 15, Sec. 2, Art. 2, Note 2. Similarly, MLB's Replay Review Rules, Sec. II.D, in general require that a team challenge a play, or the Crew Chief initiate review, "before the commencement of the next play or pitch," and they provide a definition of when the next play is deemed to commence. (Additional constraints apply when a pitching change is made, when the play appears to end the inning, and when it appears to end the game; in the last case, the challenge must be made "immediately upon the conclusion of the play.")

But there are cases in which review is permitted notwithstanding the fact that play has proceeded.

COMMENTS AND QUESTIONS

1. *Sorry—that three was a two.* Suppose an NBA player sinks a long shot—but there is doubt whether it was for two points or three. If the play occurs before the third full timeout in the fourth period, then review is delayed until the next timeout or period break. After the third full timeout in the fourth period, and throughout overtime, review takes place at the next clock stoppage. In the last two minutes of regulation and of overtime, the clock stops after a successful field goal attempt, so review occurs immediately. But before then,

play may continue without anyone knowing the score—or put another way, whether the score already achieved will soon be readjusted.

Is this a sound rule in that (a) until the closing segment of regulation, it allows play to continue for what may be a considerable stretch before the doubtful shot is reviewed? (b) even late in the game, or in overtime, but while there are more than two minutes on the clock, the play remains unreviewed until the clock stops? Why do basketball rulemakers allow postponed review of some plays, even though that appears to be anathema in most sports?

Note, on the other hand, that if a player is fouled while shooting and there is doubt whether he is entitled to two free throws or three, review is conducted immediately, "so referees know how many shots to award." NBA, *Instant Replay Situations & Procedures, 2019–2020 Season*, https://tinyurl.com/y2kkagln. Given that review is postponed in some cases if the shot is made, and that the review may result in points being taken off the board, would it make sense for the referee to award three shots in doubtful cases, the first one to be considered provisional, not to count if later review shows that the proper call was only two shots?

2.   *Finish your round and then we'll rule on the fifth hole.* Multi-member competitions provide particularly interesting problems concerning postponed review. A notable example occurred at the 2016 U.S. Open Golf Championship. As Dustin Johnson, who was in contention for the title, stood over a six-foot putt on the fifth hole of the final round, and shortly after he had taken practice strokes, his ball moved slightly. Rule 18–2 of the Rules of Golf as they then stood provided that he incurred a one-stroke penalty if he caused the ball to move but not, under a very new amendment to the Rule, if something else caused the movement. (Under the 2019 codification, these provisions are in Rule 9.4.) Decision 18-2/0.5 provides that "[a]ll relevant information must be evaluated," and that the penalty applies "[i]f the weight of the evidence indicates that it is more likely than not that the player caused the ball to move, even though that conclusion is not free from doubt." Johnson stepped back and called over Mike Newell, one of the officials who was following Johnson and his playing partner, Lee Westwood. Newell, who as it happens was chair of the USGA's Rules of Golf Committee, conferred with Johnson and Westwood and ruled that there had been no violation. But other USGA officials reviewed video of the incident, and met Johnson at the 12th tee to discuss the situation; the time for the review and the difficulty of reaching Johnson on a crowded course apparently accounted for the delay. The officials alerted Johnson to the prospect that a penalty might be imposed after all and to ask him whether he had any other explanation, other than his practice strokes, for why the ball moved. The officials concluded that they were not yet ready to make a definitive decision, but they did alert other golfers to the situation. After Johnson completed his round—but before he signed his scorecard!—the officials told him that he had indeed incurred the penalty.[c] As it happens, the

---

[c]   Under Rule 18–2, if the player causes the ball to move before taking his shot, not only does he suffer a one-stroke penalty but he must restore the ball to its original position. The USGA determined before the tournament that, because of green conditions, there might be doubtful cases

penalty did not matter—Johnson won the tournament by three strokes—but it generated a firestorm of discussion, much of it highly critical. Some of the criticism concerned the substance of the decision that Johnson had more likely than not caused the ball to move. But much of it concerned the delay in imposing the penalty.[d] The next day the USGA issued a statement that said in part:

> Upon reflection, we regret the distraction caused by our decision to wait until the end of the round to decide on the ruling. It is normal for rulings based on video evidence to await the end of a round, when the matter can be discussed with the player before the score card is returned. While our focus on getting the ruling correct was appropriate, we created uncertainty about where players stood on the leader board after we informed Dustin on the 12th tee that his actions on the fifth green might lead to a penalty. This created unnecessary ambiguity for Dustin and the other players, as well as spectators on-site, and those watching and listening on television and digital channels. . . .

> In keeping with our commitment to excellence in all aspects of our work on behalf of the game of golf, we pledge to closely examine our procedures in this matter. We will assess our procedures for handling video review, the timing of such, and our communication with players to make sure that when confronted with such a situation again, we will have a better process.

Statement Regarding Dustin Johnson Ruling, USGA (June 20, 2016).

What *should* the USGA do in such a situation? The ideal would be to issue a definitive ruling before any other play occurred, but with golfers playing all over the course that would raise severe practicality problems. One could say that the ruling of the official on site should be final, but then that would deprive the USGA of the video evidence, which is particularly valuable in deciding what caused a very slight ball movement. One could say that the USGA should rule definitively and promptly on the basis of the video evidence, but that would probably deprive it of the opportunity to hear from Johnson before making its decision. One could say that after reviewing video evidence and consulting with Johnson at the 12th tee, the USGA should have been prepared to rule definitively, because it already had all the information it needed, but that would still mean that a penalty was imposed on Johnson six holes after the incident.

---

as to whether a player caused the ball to move, and if an initial ruling that he had not done so was later overruled he should not be penalized for failing to restore the ball to its original position. Probably few observers would doubt that this was a sensible decision.

[d] Sources for this incident include: Alex Micelli, *USGA ruling on Dustin Johnson at U.S. Open muddies water for future*, USA TODAY GOLFWEEK (June 20, 2016); Jaime Diaz, *What Really Happened: Dustin Johnson, the USGA and the U.S. Open Fiasco*, GOLF DIGEST, Sept. 2016; and *FAQs Regarding Dustin Johnson Ruling*, USGA, https://tinyurl.com/yyzwd295.

The USGA expressed regret that it had expressed "uncertainty" and "unnecessary ambiguity" by delaying its ruling. What is wrong with such uncertainty? When you take an exam, presumably you do not expect to get a score on each question before moving on to the next. Boxers do not know what is on the judges' cards until the fight is over; a boxer who thinks that in the final round he only needs to avoid being knocked out may be sorely disappointed if the judges see the fight differently. A figure skater deciding whether to do a planned triple jump near the end of her routine or settle for a safer double might like to know how her routine has been assessed up to that point, but she doesn't. Should golfers, or other athletes, be told in effect, "Just play. Your job is to do the best you can. If you think there is a chance that the score will later be adjusted, and that uncertainty affects your choice of tactics, well, that's part of the game. Use your best judgment"?

2. POST-COMPETITION REVIEW

Note that by the time the USGA imposed the penalty on Dustin Johnson, the competition was over. Post-competition review poses special issues. On the one hand, after the results have been declared, there is a strong value in finality. Depending on the circumstances, it might be particularly difficult to restore the competitive situation, or even to resume competition at all. But in some cases countervailing considerations weigh in favor of allowing review even after the contest is over. And post-competition review might be particularly tempting if the official error in question occurred at the very end of the contest.

a. The Importance of Finality: Yang, Hamm, and the False Start Value

Consider a notorious incident from the finals of the men's all-around individual gymnastics competition at the 2004 Olympics. The top six contenders were on the parallel bars, the fifth of six events, with only the high bar remaining. Yang Tae Young of South Korea, last of the six on the parallel bars, performed a routine that he had done twice earlier in the Olympics. Both times it had been assigned the highest possible Start Value, 10.0. The Start Value is really a measure of degree of difficulty, and despite the name judges determine it during the routine, not before it begins, based on the maneuvers the gymnast actually attempts. This time, Yang's routine was assigned a Start Value of 9.9, but it should have been 10.0; the judges responsible for setting the Start Value had misidentified one element, a Belle, labeling it instead as a less difficult Morisue. Although the Start Value was posted on a three-sided electronic scoreboard near the apparatus, Yang's coach was not positioned where he could see it, and he was not immediately aware of the disparity. That tenth of a point turned out to make a large difference: After the final rotation, Yang was in third place, 0.049 points behind the winner, Paul Hamm of the United States, with Yang's countryman Kim Dae-Eun in second, 0.012 points behind Hamm; if the crucial one-tenth of a point were added back in, Yang would be in first place, .051 ahead of Hamm. According to the South Korean team, it made an oral protest shortly after the conclusion of the competition, around the time of the medal ceremony. The next day, it followed up with a written protest.

FIG, the international gymnastics federation, suspended the three judges responsible for the scoring error, but it rejected the protest, saying, "The rules do not allow a protest against the judges' marks. The judges' marks have to be accepted as a final decision and cannot be changed." (That, as explained below, was incorrect.) The Korean Olympic Committee (KOC) then proposed that two gold medals be awarded, and at first the U.S. Olympic Committee was willing to go along, but Jacques Rogge, chair of the IOC, said nothing doing: FIG could change the recipient of the gold, but there would be only one gold. FIG then sent a letter to Hamm asserting that because of the error the "true winner" of the event was Yang and suggesting that Hamm should return his gold medal, "as the ultimate demonstration of fair play." (In August 2001, the Russian trampolinist Irina Karavayeva returned a gold medal that she had been awarded the previous month at the Trampoline World Championships after a judging mistake; she said, "I consider that it is necessary to correct this mistake and I decided to give the Gold Medal to my friend Ana Dogonadze from Germany in the spirit of friendship and fair-play.") The USOC declined even to convey the letter to Hamm.

Yang and the KOC then brought a proceeding before the Court of Arbitration for Sport (CAS). The court noted that in fact FIG rules provided a mechanism for reversing judging errors. The Chair of the Apparatus Jury had the power, with the approval of the Chair of the Competition Jury, to change "an extremely incorrect score," and the Superior Jury was authorized to take such action as it deemed necessary in case of "a grave error of judgement" by the judges—an authorization that, according to the CAS, was "large enough to embrace reversing marks as well as disciplining judges." *See Yang Tae-Young v. FIG*, CAS 2004/A/704, ¶ 3.6. But the rules did not say clearly *when* review must be sought, or when it must be made. Previously, the rules had required submission of a written complaint (in French or German) within 15 minutes of the incident, but for some reason that provision had been repealed more than a decade before. *Id.* at ¶¶ 3.10, 3.11.[e]

Nevertheless, drawing on what hints it could glean from the rules and also recognizing its limited authority to intervene, the court concluded that "any appeal must be dealt with *during, not after* a competition." "This interpretation," the court said,

---

[e] It was reported soon after the incident that "[t]he rules say a team can file a protest, called an inquiry, but only within one event after the one in question." Alan Abrahamson & Diane Pucin, *U.S. Gymnast May Share Gold Won in Scoring Error*, L.A. TIMES, Aug. 22, 2004. If in fact there was a rule to that effect, whether formal or informal, it escaped the notice of the court.

conforms with the natural expectation of both participants, spectators and the public at large that at the close of a competition in any sport, gymnastics included, the identity of the winner should be known, and not subject to alteration thereafter save where exceptionally, for example, the purported winner is proved to have failed a drug test and so been disqualified.

Id. at ¶ 3.7.

COMMENTS AND QUESTIONS

1. It's over when it's over—but when is it over? The result of the Hamm-Yang case reflects the dominant approach to post-contest review across the world of sports: governing bodies generally refuse to correct mistaken officiating decisions after the competition has ended. The CAS decision emphasizes the value in finality, or closure. As Sandy Hamm, Paul's father put it: "when a game is over, it's over." Abrahamson & Pucin, *U.S. Gymnast May Share Gold.* But just what does this mean? *Assuming that a given judging decision is ordinarily subject to review,* it would be bizarre to say that it could not be reviewed because the competition ended with that call. So far as we are aware, no sport adopts such an approach. Indeed, given that play is not expected to continue, there may be good reason to be *more* lenient as to the time during which review must be sought. Thus, for example, under MLB rules, a protest based on alleged misapplication of the rules requires that the umpires be notified at the time of the controverted call "and before the next pitch, play or attempted play"—but "[a] protest arising on a game-ending play may be filed until 12 noon the following day . . . ." Comment to Rule 7.04.

Note in this light some confusion, or at least ambiguity, in the CAS decision. As noted above, the court said that an appeal "must be dealt with" during competition. But later, the court concluded that "any protest to be effective within the ambit of the FIG rules had to be *made* before the end of competition." *Yang,* ¶ 4.3(i) (emphasis added). So which is it? If the Korean team had made a timely complaint, would it effectively expire if FIG had not reached a definitive resolution by the time the competition ended? Consider again the MLB protest rules. Not only must the protest be timely, but it must be based on an alleged violation or misapplication of the rules, not a judgment decision, and one that is deemed to have "adversely affected the protesting team's chances of winning the game." Rule 7.04. Accordingly, protests are rarely upheld. For example, the Astros' protest after the Vern Ruhle incident was not upheld because the Phillies did not score in that inning, *see* p. 421, though a creative advocate could articulate ways in which failure to call an extra out *might* have adversely affected the Astros' chance of winning the game. But it is possible for a protest made timely to be upheld, and if so it will almost certainly be after the competition is over. The most notable protest that was upheld within recent memory was that in the George Brett pine tar game. *See* pp. 350–355. Do the MLB rules suggest that the strongest factor counseling against post-contest review is not so much the need for closure as the need for the sport's governing structure to respect judgments made by those who are actually officiating the competition?

2.   *Why then?* Even assuming that the CAS meant to emphasize the time at which a complaint is made, rather than when it is resolved, why should "the end of competition" be vested with special significance? Should it matter whether the Korean team complained a few minutes before the competition ended or a few minutes after? Was FIG's previous 15-minute rule—which meant that a complaint might be made shortly after the close of competition if the challenged call occurred shortly beforehand—more sensible?

b.   Reconstructing the Competitive Situation

The comments above raise the question of whether the principal problem in a case like Yang-Hamm isn't that the competition was completed by the time that the complaint was made or resolved but that it is impossible to reconstruct the competitive situation that would have existed had the proper call been made in the first place. This is a problem that we have seen may arise whenever play continues before a call is reversed. The obvious remedy in Yang-Hamm was to add to Yang's final score the 0.10 points that the judges improperly deducted from his Start Value. But, as Olympic insiders pointed out at the time, "it can never be known how Yang or Hamm would have performed" in the remainder of the competition had the correct Start Value been assessed initially. Abrahamson & Pucin, *U.S. Gymnast May Share Gold.* Focusing on Yang, the CAS elaborated:

> We have no means of knowing how Yang would have reacted had he concluded the competition in [the parallel bars] as the points leader rather than in third position. He might have risen to the occasion; he might have frozen (his marks on the high bar were in fact below expectation[)] and speculation is inappropriate. So it needs to be clearly stated that while the error may have cost Yang a gold medal, it did not necessarily do so.

Yang, ¶ 4.8.

COMMENTS AND QUESTIONS

1.   *The proper burden?* Granting that one cannot know with certainty what would have happened had the judges gotten it straight from the start, is that the proper standard? Should the matter depend instead on an assessment of what *most likely* would have happened had the proper ruling been made initially? And in this case, is there any better basis for assessing what would have happened than what did happen? Note that it does not appear in this case that Hamm could plausibly contend that, had the error not been made, either he or Yang would have made a different tactical decision on the high bar, the last event. The argument that performances could have come out differently therefore appears to depend entirely on psychological factors of the type

identified by the CAS. If Hamm wanted to avoid review, should he have had the burden of demonstrating that more likely than not performances would have been different had the proper call been made from the beginning?

Put another way, suppose that the Koreans had complained immediately after the judges posted Yang's Start Value, but that (as in Dustin Johnson's case) it took some time to resolve the matter by reviewing video evidence, while the competition continued. Would it then have been proper to deny Yang the Start Value to which he was entitled because of difficulty in reconstructing what would have happened had the proper assessment been made from the start?

2. *Timely appeal.* The comments above suggest that perhaps Yang's real problem was delay in complaining—not so much that the complaint was made after the competition was over but that it created a *gratuitously* long interval of competition before the problem could be corrected. (Recall that Yang's coach was not in position to notice the improper Start Value when it was posted.) So what is the optimal rule on timeliness? As noted above, the CAS indicated that FIG's rules were unduly vague on this question. FIG rules now permit a gymnast (or, more precisely, his or her federation) to protest the Start Value for his or her routine (i.e., the difficulty score) at the competition by filing what it calls an "inquiry." The inquiry must be made "verbally"—that really should be "orally"—"immediately after the publication of the score or at the very latest before the score of the following gymnast or group is shown. For the last gymnast or group of a rotation, this limit is one minute after the score is shown on the scoreboard."

Moreover, "[t]he inquiry must be confirmed as soon as possible in writing, but within 4 minutes at the latest after the verbal inquiry," and it must be accompanied by an agreement to pay a prescribed sum—$300 for the first complaint, more for subsequent ones—if the complaint is not upheld. FIG Technical Regulation 8.4. Note that this rule still allows a gap, during which competition continues, between the time of the incident and the time the inquiry is filed.

When must the matter be resolved? The Technical Regulation says that the Superior Jury must make a final, non-appealable decision

at the very latest:

- at the end of the rotation (or group) for the qualifying competitions, the all-around competitions and the team competition (final)

- before the score of the following gymnast or group is shown for the finals. . . .

Perhaps this provision strikes you as ambiguous and as hopelessly incompatible with the time limit for making the inquiry; if an inquiry is made at the last permissible minute, and confirmed in writing a few minutes later, just when is it that the Superior Jury is supposed to rule? Has FIG learned what it should have from the 2004 fiasco?

Suppose that Technical Regulation 8.4 had been in force, the Korean Federation had filed an immediate inquiry, and by the time it was resolved Hamm had already performed on the high bar, but his score had not yet been published. What would have been an appropriate remedy in that case?

3. *Standing to challenge.* Although a gymnast's federation is permitted to file an inquiry if it believes that the Start Value assigned the gymnast is too *low*, no federation representing any of a gymnast's opponents is permitted to file an inquiry on the ground that the start value assigned that gymnast is too *high*. *See* Technical Regulation 8.4 ("A [national federation] is not allowed to complain against a gymnast from another federation."). Can this asymmetry be justified? Suppose that a candidate for elective office is permitted to appeal a ruling against her on some disputed matter such as, for example, whether absentee ballots cast for her satisfy certain procedural requirements. Shouldn't it also follow that the candidate's opponents must be permitted to appeal a ruling on the disputed ballots that went in the candidate's favor? Why (not)? If so, then are there any good reasons to treat the gymnastics case differently from the elections case?

4. *The bottom line.* Did FIG act properly in this case? How about the CAS? The IOC? What do you think would have been the optimal outcome in this dispute? Should Hamm have given up his gold? What more, if anything, would you want to know about the Karavayeva-Dogonadze incident to assess whether Karavayeva should have held onto her gold?

c. Other Considerations

As noted above, the CAS, despite its paean to the importance of finality, identified disqualification for drug use as a situation that might justify post-contest reversal of an outcome. There have been some notable examples, such as Ben Johnson, who was stripped of an Olympic title and a world record in the 100 meter dash, and Lance Armstrong, who lost seven Tour de France titles. Other forms of competitor misconduct have also led to retrospective disqualification. For example, Jim Thorpe was stripped of the gold medals for the pentathlon and decathlon that he had won at the 1912 Olympics, because he had played professional baseball and so ended his amateur status. *See* Subchapter 7A. The University of Michigan forfeited 113 men's basketball victories because of improper financial support given to players by a booster in the 1990s. And as a result of the Jerry Sandusky scandal, 112 football wins were taken away from Penn State—but later restored. See Subchapter 17B. On the other hand, team victories are not ordinarily stripped because players used PEDs. And nobody would likely advocate post-contest reversal of the result of a football game because, say, video evidence showed incontrovertibly that a linesman on the winning team got away with a flagrant hold on a crucial play. Nor, for that matter, did MLB seriously consider vacating the Houston Astros' 2017 World Series title because of their sign-stealing violation. (See p. 477.)

Can you state a set of criteria for when competitor misconduct should and should not lead to post-contest reversal?

With respect to officiating error, the CAS indicated that, despite its general stance of non-intervention, it would review decisions if the rules governing the competition "have been applied in bad faith, e.g., as a consequence of corruption." *Yang*, ¶ 3.15, *quoting Segura v. IAAF*, CAS O.G. 00/013 (2000), ¶ 17. Why should that matter?

Are there other situations in which mistakes should be corrected even after the competition has concluded? Consider the following cases.

On December 19, 2007, with the host Atlanta Hawks ahead of the Miami Heat 112–111 and 51.9 seconds left in overtime, a foul was called on Shaquille O'Neal of the Heat. "[T]he Hawks' Official Scorer," in the terms later used by the League, informed the referee that this was O'Neal's sixth personal foul, so that he had fouled out of the game. O'Neal departed, without any complaint being made by the Heat. Al Horford of the Hawks sank two free throws, and the Hawks held on for a 117–111 win, *see Hawks outlast Heat*, GAINESVILLE TIMES, Dec. 31, 2007—or so it appeared. Charts kept on the Miami bench showed only five fouls on O'Neal, and sheets distributed immediately after the game showed the same, but minutes later Hawks personnel changed those—supposedly as a correction—to indicate that he had six. Shea Serrano, *Weird NBA: Ten Years Ago, the Hawks Won a Game Without Scoring a Point*, THE RINGER (Mar. 7, 2018). Under NBA rules, a protest may not be made during a game and must be made within 48 hours after the game concludes. Comment II.F. The Heat filed a timely protest. A review of the game indicated that, as stated by a press release issued by the NBA the following month, "the Hawks' Official Scorer mistakenly attributed to O'Neal a foul at 3:24 remaining in the fourth period that was actually called against the Heat's Udonis Haslem." It appears that a factor contributing to the error was that—pursuant to a league policy aimed at getting more fans close to the action—the part of the crew that ran the official scoring computer was located 26 rows behind the floor, where the official scorer's book was kept.

Commissioner David Stern ruled that when the Heat returned to Atlanta in March, the last 51.9 seconds would be replayed, with the Hawks leading 114–111. According to the press release, Stern

> found that the Hawks were grossly negligent in committing this scoring error, since they failed to follow league-mandated scoring procedures and failed to respond effectively when the members of the statisticians' crew noticed the mistake. Because of this conduct by Atlanta's personnel, Miami suffered a clear competitive disadvantage, as O'Neal—the Heat's second leading scorer and rebounder that night—was removed from a one-point game with only 51.9 seconds remaining. Under this

unprecedented set of circumstances, the Commissioner granted the Heat's protest, and fined the Hawks $50,000 for their violation of league rules.

Nobody scored during the replay, so the game finally went down as a 114–111 win for the Hawks. *See, e.g., Heat file protest, content Shaq only committed five fouls vs. Hawks*, ESPN.com (Dec. 21, 2007); *Heat appeal is upheld, rare NBA replay set*, L.A. DAILY NEWS, Jan. 12, 2008.

COMMENTS AND QUESTIONS

1.   Gross negligence. When deciding to correct the official scorer's mistake, even after the game had ended, David Stern was careful to explain that it wasn't a case of ordinary error or carelessness, but of "gross" negligence. Do you think that cases of gross negligence should generally be treated more like cases of ordinary carelessness or mistake (post-contest review highly unlikely) or more like cases of corruption (post-contest review more readily available)? Or do you think that situations are too varied to permit helpful generalizations one way or the other? In any event, was Stern right to correct the error and vacate the result of the game?

2.   Variations. What if the Heat and Hawks were not scheduled to play again in the regular season? What if they were scheduled to play again, but only in Miami? Should the Hawks have had to take the free throws again? What should the result have been if the game were played in Miami and the error was made by the Heat's stat crew? What if it were Haslem, or a lesser player, rather than O'Neal, who was mistakenly ruled to have fouled out?

Because of roster changes in the interim, the league had to issue complex rules on who was eligible in the replay. *Guidelines set for Heat-Hawks reply*, UNITED PRESS INTERNATIONAL, Mar. 3, 2008. As it happened, between the time of Stern's ruling and of the replay, O'Neal was traded to Phoenix. After O'Neal was traded, should Stern have said, "Never mind"? What if he had been traded *to the Hawks*?

Should it have mattered that the Heat did not claim that O'Neal had not fouled out until after the (initial playing of) the game, or more precisely the overtime period, was over? True, the *protest* was timely. But note also NBA Rule 2.VI.D, which provides (and did at the time):

> A record keeping error by the official scorer which involves the score, number of personal fouls, team fouls and/or timeouts may be corrected by the officials at any time prior to the end of the fourth period. Any such error which occurs in overtime must be corrected prior to the end of that period.

Is this rule sound? Too generous? Too lenient? Does it, or should it, limit the ability of the Commissioner to correct an official error, if the aggrieved team did not complain during the specified time? Pat Riley, coach of the Heat, said: "It's basically on them. It's on the scorer's table. We're coaching games and training players and making sure everything else is going on. I don't think we should be doing their job. But we try to." *Heat considering filing a protest over contested foul on Shaquille O'Neal*, USA TODAY, Dec. 20, 2007. Is that persuasive? Granting that it is the job of the scorer's table to get the situation right in the first instance, should it be the job of the bench to count fouls and raise objections in a timely manner, preferably before play resumes or at least before the end of the period?

3.   *Pine tar revisited.* In ruling on the George Brett pine tar game (pp. 350–355), American League President Lee MacPhail did not follow Sandy Hamm's maxim that "when a game is over, it's over." But notice that, far from suggesting that the umpires were guilty of gross negligence, let alone corruption, MacPhail absolved them of any fault. "Although the umpires are being overruled," he said, "it is not in my opinion the fault of the umpires involved." Why, then, even recognizing that the Royals made a timely protest and that the umpires did not adhere to the rules as MacPhail later interpreted them, should this protest have been granted? After all, even if you believe that he was right to hold that a batter should not be ruled out for using a bat with too much pine tar, MacPhail could have made that ruling prospective only, allowing the outcome of the disputed game to stand. Should he have followed Hamm's maxim? Why or why not?

4.   *Mistakes of law and mistakes of fact.* Whether or not MacPhail was correct to make the ruling retrospective, the Royals' protest was viable only because it concerned an officiating error of law (what the authorized remedy is when a batter uses excessive pine tar) rather than one about an ordinary matter of fact (how far up the bat handle pine tar was smeared); recall that a protest must be based on an alleged violation or misapplication of the rules, not a judgment decision. Are there good reasons for governing bodies to be more liberal in correcting legal errors after the contest than factual errors?

Consider the following cases:

(a)   In 2005, Uzbekistan and Bahrain had a two-leg playoff for advancement towards the World Cup finals. The first leg was played in Uzebekistan, which took an early 1–0 lead. In the 38th minute, an Uzbek player was awarded a penalty shot and made it. But one of his teammates had entered the penalty box too early. The referee disallowed the goal and awarded Bahrain a free kick. The game ended in a 1–0 victory for Uzbekistan. But because advancement depended on the cumulative score across the two games, Uzbekistan protested, on the ground that under the rules the referee should have ordered the penalty shot retaken. FIFA upheld the protest. But instead of awarding Uzbekistan a second goal it declared the match invalid.

(b)   In a playoff game between high school football teams in Oklahoma, the Douglass High School Trojans scored on a 58-yard touchdown pass with 1:04 remaining, to take a 25–20 lead over the Locust Grove Pirates. During the play, however, a Douglass High coach, running along the sideline, bumped one of the officials, provoking a flag. Under the governing rules, this was a 5-yard penalty that should be assessed on the extra-point attempt or the ensuing kickoff. But, misunderstanding or misremembering the rules, the referee annulled the touchdown, over the protests of the Douglass High coaches. The Trojans failed to score and lost, 20–19. After the game, the Oklahoma Secondary School Activities Association apologized to Douglass High, calling the referee's error "inexcusable," but insisting that the result would stand.

Were these two protests decided correctly? Is there a good reason why (putting aside the nature of the remedy) Uzbekistan won its protest but Douglass High lost, or are the cases not meaningfully distinguishable? If the two cases should have been resolved the same way, what would have been the right outcome: both protests granted, or both denied?

5.   *A question of remedy.* In all the cases discussed in this section, if the governing body decides to correct an officiating error after the competition has ended, it must also decide on a remedy. League commissioners prescribed the same remedy in both the Hawks-Heat game and the Brett pine tar game: reverse the mistaken officiating decision and order the game replayed from that point forward. But there is at least one other obvious possibility: declare the contest a nullity and order it replayed from the beginning. Under what circumstances, if any, is that the preferable remedy?

Take the Brett pine tar game in particular. Once MacPhail determined that he would reopen a game that had already been completed, should he have given the Yankees the option of replaying the game from the start instead of having to resume the game down by one run with two out in the top of the ninth inning? Would a compromise of this sort have been principled or unprincipled?

In the Uzbekistan-Bahrain game, FIFA took the opposite tack from that taken by MacPhail: it ordered the entire match replayed, from the first minute. A representative of the Uzbek football federation said, "The referee stole our second goal and now FIFA is stealing our first goal." *FIFA set precedent and anger Uzbeks*, IRISH EXAMINER, Sept. 6, 2005. In the event, the replay ended in a 1–1 draw. The second leg, in Bahrain, was a 0–0 draw. Bahrain advanced because of an unusual tiebreaking rule: it had more goals away. *Bahrain national football team*, WIKIPEDIA, https://tinyurl.com/y5f4p9tp. So it appears that Uzbekistan failed to advance because of its protest. What lesson should we draw: that FIFA should have ordered the game replayed from the 38th minute, with the score 1–0 and Uzbekistan up for a second attempt at a penalty shot? That FIFA should have denied Uzbekistan's protest entirely? That FIFA ruled correctly on both matters, and that Uzbekistan just shouldn't have protested? Or something else?

———

We have thus far considered situations in which there are arguably compelling reasons for a sport's governing body to correct errors after the contest notwithstanding that substituting the correct call for the mistaken one does not by itself put the competitors back in the position they would have been in had the correct call been made initially. But just as, sometimes, correcting errors *during* the competition does *not* put the competitors just where they would and should have been (see Subchapter A), sometimes correcting errors *after* the competition *can*. For example, suppose that a mistaken call is made on the last play of a contest, as time expires, and that the call results in mistakenly denying (or allowing) a score. If adding (or subtracting) the score would change the contest outcome without any uncertainty, is there a good reason not to fix things after the fact?

COMMENTS AND QUESTIONS

1.   *Fifth down.* Consider again the 1990 Colorado-Missouri football game, discussed above (pp. 424–425). Recall that Colorado scored a decisive touchdown as time expired, but only after it was given an extra down; the officiating crew had failed to flip the down marker after a spike earlier in the series. What was the right result in this game? Big 8 Commissioner Carl James agreed with Missouri that the seven game officials had erred in counting the downs and suspended all of them. However, he also allowed the final score to stand, ruling that "the allowance of the fifth down is not a correctable error." See GARLETT & O'NEAL, WORST CALL EVER, at 132–34. Should it have been? The prior analysis suggests that it might be unfair to Colorado to wipe out the touchdown—even if the game were not over—because its quarterback, Charles Johnson, may have relied on the official error when he spiked the ball on what should have been fourth down with two seconds remaining. But let's put that aside. Assume either that Johnson did not rely on the error or that you conclude that he had no right to rely on it, and that if the entire sequence had occurred at the same point in the first half the proper result would have been to nullify the touchdown play, which should not have occurred, and give Missouri the ball near its own goal line with two seconds left in the half. On that assumption, should the officials, once they recognized their error, have adopted that solution, given that in fact the sequence occurred as time in the *second* half expired? On the same assumption, but given that the game officials let the touchdown stand, should the Big 8 have nullified it and declared Missouri the winner?

Compare the Colorado-Missouri game once again with the 1940 Cornell-Dartmouth game. Cornell, like Colorado, scored a decisive touchdown as time expired when it was improperly given a fifth down, but only after it had run four plays that failed to get the ball into the end one; it never spiked the ball. When Cornell later realized the error, it offered to forfeit the game, and Dartmouth accepted; Colorado never made a comparable offer. Is there any material difference between these two incidents—was forfeiture more justified in one case than in the other? Does the fact that Cornell forfeited and Colorado did not reflect a difference in the eras? A difference in the competitive settings?

If you think that voluntary forfeiture or official reversal was appropriate in either of these games, is it critical that in each case the score came as time expired? Would your judgment differ if five seconds remained on the clock after the score? One second—which would still require a play to be run? Or is the relevant time how much was on the clock *before* the fifth-down touchdown, on the ground that if the game officials had given the defense the ball at that point, it would have had to run a play?

2.   *Saved by the bell—and the slow count?* By rule, a boxing match ends, even if a boxer is down, with the final bell; if the count has not reached ten, then the winner is determined by decision on the basis of the judges' cards. So alter the facts of the Douglas-Tyson fight (pp. 425–426) this way: Douglas was well ahead on all cards, but as the final round neared a close, Tyson knocked him out stone cold; he was on the canvas when the bell rang and did not get up for two minutes afterward. The count should have started 11 seconds before the bell, in which case Tyson would have been declared the winner by knockout. But in fact it started only 8 seconds before, and, dazed though Douglas is, he has his hand raised as the winner by decision. Tyson protests. What result?

3.   *Wrong even on the replay.* With 2:07 remaining in the Toledo-Syracuse football game of September 24, 2011, Syracuse scored a touchdown to take the lead 29–27. The officials on the field ruled that the kick for the extra point was good, and the replay official confirmed the ruling. Toledo then drove far enough to score a game-tying field goal as time expired, but Syracuse won the game in overtime. Later that day, the Big East coordinator of football officiating issued a statement saying that the replay official erred in failing to reverse the ruling on Syracuse's crucial extra point; one of the replay videos showed conclusively that the ball passed outside one of the uprights. *See Big East: Replay official made the wrong call on Syracuse PAT*, SYRACUSE POST-STANDARD, Sept. 25, 2011. Should the result of the game be reversed? Would it make any difference if the incorrectly called extra point tied the game at the end of regulation?

4.   *Galarraga's imperfect game.* In the summer of 2010, Detroit Tigers pitcher Armando Galarraga was one out from a perfect game when first base umpire Jim Joyce called a batter safe at first on a grounder. Replays revealed that Joyce's call was clearly mistaken. Because Joyce's error came with two outs in the ninth inning, if he had correctly called the batter out, the game would have been over at that instant. Should MLB Commissioner Bud Selig have reversed that call after the fact, thereby awarding Galarraga the perfecto that he had, in a sense, earned?

If you think that Selig should have reversed the call after the game, do you think that would have been the correct outcome if Joyce's error had come with *one* out in the ninth? If so, how, if at all, would the case differ from the Yang/Hamm controversy? If you think Selig should have reversed the call in the actual case, do you think that he should also have done so if "only" an ordinary no-hitter (much more common than a perfect game but still perhaps a career highpoint for the pitcher) were at stake? A shutout? The win?

5.   *Missed pins.* Suppose Jones and Smith are engaged in an amateur wrestling match and that Jones pins Smith early in the first period, but the referee mistakenly rules that Jones had not secured the pin. The match continues for two more action-packed periods and Smith is eventually ruled the winner on points. If the relevant wrestling federation conclusively determines after the match that Jones had pinned Smith in the first period, and that Jones should therefore have been declared the winner right then, should it then overturn the result? If not, why not? Does your answer change depending upon whether the referee had made a factual mistake (e.g., he just didn't see, as other ringside observers had, that Smith's shoulders were in fact touching the mat) or a legal mistake (e.g., he believed that, to count as a pin, a wrestler's shoulders must be down for two seconds, when the rules for this level of competition require that the pin must be held for only one second)? If so, why?

6.   *From the field to the court.* In the Oklahoma state high school football game discussed on p. 460, Douglass High promptly filed suit in the district court in Oklahoma City after the Oklahoma Secondary School Activities Association denied its protest. It asked either that the Trojans be awarded the touchdown and the game be replayed from that point, or that a new game be ordered. See Jeré Longman, *After Referees Blunder, Next Call Is a Judge's*, N.Y. TIMES, Dec. 9, 2014, at B12. What should the court do? More generally, should officiating errors ever be challengeable in ordinary courts of law? If so, under what circumstances?

PART IV

PLAYING THE GAME

■ ■ ■

Parts II and III concerned rules, rulemaking, and officiating, for participants need to know what the rules are, and how they are enforced. But they need to know more. They need to know *how to play the game.* In saying that, we don't mean that they must learn skills and tactics. That is of course true, but not our concern in this book. We mean that competitors need to grasp and learn to navigate the largely informal norms that help make games and sports the rich normative systems that they are.

Members of a sporting community—officials and spectators, in addition to players and competitors—care greatly about how competition is undertaken. We condemn cheating, denounce bad sportsmanship, and celebrate good sportsmanship. But as important as these notions are to us, we don't have a very clear grasp of what these concepts are and what they involve. We don't know just what distinguishes cheating from intentional fouls that are just "part of the game." We aren't sure what defines the borders of good sportsmanship and bad sportsmanship, or what territory lies between. We accept that deception, stalling, and other forms of gamesmanship are often allowed, occasionally acclaimed, and sometimes abjured, but we may puzzle over what principles, if any, drive these judgments. We sometimes demand that participants "respect the game" (or their opponents) but we disagree strongly about what the requisite respect involves. In short, most of us are convinced that sports and games do demand of their participants much more (and also, perhaps, less) than what the rules provide, yet we are deeply uncertain about what that more (or less) encompasses. This Part investigates such matters. Loosely speaking, Chapter 14 concerns cheating and other forms of disreputable sporting behavior. Chapter 15 examines the scope of the duty to compete and its implications for the supposed virtue of sportsmanship.

465

CHAPTER 14

MISCONDUCT

■ ■ ■

Here's a straightforward two-part idea: players are required to compete within the rules, and that's it. Although there is at least a kernel of truth in this view, it is certainly too simple—in both directions. First, as the ubiquity of tactical fouls suggests, sometimes it seems permissible to intentionally break the rules. Second, if intentional *noncompliance* with rules is sometimes *okay*, the fact that we sometimes condemn "loopholing" suggests that strict *compliance* with the rules is sometimes *not* okay. Subchapter 14A begins a general examination of when rule-breaking is okay, when it's cheating, and when it may be neither. Subchapter 14B examines the puzzle of loopholing. Subchapters 14C and 14D explore deception and stalling, respectively. Subchapter 14E discusses a cluster of behaviors—taunting, trash-talking, and excessive celebration—that are sometimes disparaged, and occasionally prohibited, as unsporting or disrespectful.

In places, we will be asking what attitude the formal rules should take toward some type of conduct—whether, for example, this or that sport should prohibit this or that form of deception. The focus of this Chapter, though, is not on what the rules should be, but on how players should conduct themselves in light of the rules. This emphasis is important because in complex sports, as in complex rule-governed activities more generally, rules are unlikely to cover everything. A central theme of this chapter is that sports and games will invariably present occasions on which it is appropriate to wonder whether thus-and-such conduct is either (a) permissible notwithstanding that the rules prohibit it, or (b) improper notwithstanding that the rules allow it.

A. INTENTIONAL RULE-BREAKING

Let's start with this simple and common thought: it's not okay to cheat. And to cheat, let us suppose, is to intentionally violate a rule in order to gain an advantage over others. Therefore, it's not okay for players of a game or sport to intentionally break a rule in order to gain an advantage over an opponent. To play a game is, in some fashion, to be required or obligated to comply with its rules.

That's a natural enough idea, but it encounters obvious counterexamples. It is routine in many sports for a competitor to intentionally break a rule based on the instrumental calculation that the competitive benefit thereby secured exceeds the competitive cost of the expected sanction discounted by the expected probability of its imposition (which could be close to 1, representing certainty, but need not be). Common examples include intentional fouls in basketball, holding of a defender by an offensive lineman in football, grabbing of a wide receiver in football by a defensive back, and lots more grabbing, holding, and pulling in soccer, hockey, and countless other sports. Few if any observers would call *all* conduct of this sort "cheating." Just as importantly, few would deem all such conduct wrongful or improper. So the flat contention that participants are "required" to comply with all game rules, or that a sport or game "demands" full compliance with its rules seems, at the least, to require qualification.

We will soon investigate qualifications. Before we do so, let's first consider a possible *clarification*. The supposed counter-examples we are considering arise in the following context: provisions in a rulebook say "Do not commit foul F. If you commit F, then you are liable to penalty P"; a player intentionally Fs, in apparent violation of the rule. Yet as our previous discussion of the price/sanction distinction taught (see Subchapter 6A), it might be open to argue that, notwithstanding the language of the text, the "real rule" actually provides "You may F, but the cost of Fing is to be liable to extraction of price P." In other words, it could be that some particular rules that purport to *prohibit* various forms of physical contact in sports such as basketball, football, and soccer, on pain of *sanction*, are more accurately or more properly characterized as *permitting* the conduct for a *price*. If this is so, then seemingly rule-breaking conduct that we think permissible might not be examples of permissible rule-breaking; it could be that they don't amount to rule-breaking at all.

This is possible. But is it convincing? Do you agree that in all cases in which it is permissible (or not "cheating"?) for a competitor to intentionally break a rule of her sport, that is because the rule at issue does not "really" prohibit her conduct in the first place? Consider that question as you read the materials that follow. If you conclude that it is sometimes acceptable within the context of sporting competition to break a rule for advantage— that is, if it's sometimes acceptable to engage in conduct that the sport really does *prohibit*, and not *price*—then what determines when it is and when it isn't?

COMMENTS AND QUESTIONS

1. Prices, prices, everywhere? What do we mean by asking whether a competitor is "required" or "obligated" to comply with the rules, whether she "ought" to do so, or whether the sport "demands" compliance? Is this terminology confused or misplaced? Is it more accurate to say that *all* sanction-backed prohibitions in sports are nothing other than a complicated schedule of prices? For example, while it might *seem* that golf *prohibits* golfers from intentionally moving a ball before hitting it (or, equivalently, that golf *requires* that golfers *not* move the ball before hitting it), is the more sophisticated and more accurate way for a golfer to understand things simply that if she does move the ball, she is likely to face certain consequences?

If you believe that there are no duties, obligations, requirements, and prohibitions in sport, but only prices, can you defend and not merely assert this view? Can you explain what about the common view is mistaken? Do you believe that the same is true of duties, obligations, prohibitions and the like in *law?* For example, should we understand the criminal law not as imposing obligations not to rape, rob, or murder, but as announcing the prices that might be exacted for engaging in such conduct? *Cf.* Oliver Wendell Holmes, Jr., *The Path of the Law,* 10 HARV. L. REV. 457, 459 (1897) ("If you want to know the law and nothing else, you must look at it as a bad man, who cares only for the material consequences which such knowledge enables him to predict . . ."). Do you believe that the same is true of *morality*?

2. Intentional fouls across sports. There are many types of tactical fouls in a wide variety of sports. Perhaps the most common type occurs when a defender intentionally fouls an offensive player to prevent a scoring opportunity. In Quidditch, such fouls have been considered cheating by reputable authorities. *See* J.K. ROWLING, HARRY POTTER AND THE SORCERER'S STONE 188 (1997) (commentary by Quidditch announcer Lee Jordan). What about in such sports as basketball, football, soccer, and hockey? Must it be cheating in all sports or in none, or could the same or essentially similar behavior constitute cheating in some sports but not all? If the latter is true, what would determine whether some type or token of tactical fouling is cheating or not?

3. If covert, then not okay? The first-pass definition of cheating that we offered above is not the one most favored in the literature. It is more common to define cheating as the *covert* or *surreptitious* violation of a rule in order to gain an advantage. *See, e.g.,* Warren P. Fraleigh, *Intentional Rule Violations— One More Time,* 30 J. PHIL. SPORT 166, 168 (2003); Nicholas Dixon, *On Winning and Athletic Superiority,* 26 J. PHIL. SPORT 10, 13 (1999); Michael Sean Quinn, *Practice-Defining Rules,* 86 ETHICS 76, 78 (1975). This definition can explain why many intentional (or "tactical") violations aren't cheating, and may be entirely permissible: they're committed out in the open. Intentional fouls in basketball to stop the clock are a good example: the defensive team could not achieve its aim if such fouls were committed surreptitiously. But many intentional fouls *are* committed covertly. Although an offensive lineman in football might hold or even tackle a defender brazenly when necessary to protect his quarterback, offensive linemen generally prefer not to be caught and penalized when they hold. Do you agree that an offensive lineman who holds openly does not cheat, whereas an offensive lineman who tries to conceal his holding does cheat? Putting aside the concept of *cheating,* do you believe that intentional fouls and other intentional rule violations are permissible or acceptable if and only if they are done entirely openly?

4.   If not covert, then okay? The case of the surreptitious hold in football might suggest that covert rule-breaking can sometimes be acceptable. Even if that's so, it could still be true that open rule-breaking is always acceptable, or that it can never be cheating to break a rule openly. In other words, even if non-covertness (i.e., "openness") is not a necessary condition for rule-breaking to be permissible, it could be a sufficient condition. Is it? Consider a much-discussed incident from the Uruguay-Ghana quarter-final in the 2010 FIFA World Cup. Luis Suarez, the Uruguayan striker, used his hand to prevent a virtually certain last-minute tie-breaking goal by his Ghanaian counterpart, Dominic Adiyiah. Suarez was red-carded and Ghana was awarded a penalty kick, which failed when the ball hit the crossbar. Within minutes the game went to a shootout, which Uruguay won, advancing to the semi-finals. But Suarez could not play in that match; the red card not only caused him to be ejected from the match against Ghana but disqualified him from playing in the team's following match.

Opinions on Suarez's conduct were decidedly mixed. Very possibly, the dominant opinion among soccer cognoscenti was that what Suarez did was not permitted but neither, exactly, was it cheating. For example, Uruguay's coach, Óscar Tabárez, contended that "[s]aying we cheated against Ghana is too harsh a word to use. . . Yes, he stuck his hand out, but it's not cheating. What else do you want?" *List of 2010 FIFA World Cup controversies*, WIKIPEDIA, https://tiny url.com/yylbv2nn. Tabárez was far from an impartial observer, of course, yet his judgment reflected a widely shared (but far from unanimous) sentiment that, although Suarez's conduct was not wholly kosher, "cheating" is "too harsh" a verdict. Indeed, of those who did accuse Suarez of cheating, many qualified or elaborated upon their judgments in a fashion that left a much more nuanced or ambivalent impression. Asomoah Gyan, Adiyiah's teammate who took and missed the ensuing penalty kick, exemplified this more subtle view when opining that "it was cheating" but that, "in the end, he [Suarez] was right. . . . I'm a footballer and I know if I had been in his place, I would have done the same." Ian Holyman, *Gyan Forgives Suarez Handball*, ESPN.com (June 18, 2014).

What do you think? If you think that Suarez cheated, and that he ought not to have done as he did, what do you suppose his teammates and countrymen would have said if he told them that he could have prevented the ball from going through but didn't think it would be the right thing to do? Does that matter? If you think that he did not cheat, is that because handling the ball in soccer is not prohibited, but permitted for a price? If you think that he did not cheat, should he be applauded for quick-thinking? Should he be neither condemned nor applauded? If you think that he did not cheat, what limits on permissible behavior to prevent a goal would you discern? For example, if Suarez could have prevented the goal only by tackling Adiyiah from behind, would you still regard that as permissible? Praiseworthy?

5.   Lefty on the run. Phil Mickelson, one of the world's great golfers, has won five major championships and finished in or tied for second six times at the U.S. Open, but has never won the title to complete a career Grand Slam.

Coming to the par-4 13th hole in the third round of the 2018 U.S. Open at Shinnecock Hills, Mickelson had pretty well played himself out of contention, bogeying four of the last five holes. And then he completed the job. His approach shot ran over the back of the green. His chip went past the hole again and over the front edge. He chipped back, and the ball stayed on the green—but 18 feet past the hole. Then it got bad; you can see the sequence at https://tinyurl.com/y35rjojf. His putt sent the ball on a fourth trip past the hole, and it appeared very likely to roll down a steep slope past the green again. But Mickelson didn't let it. He trotted past the ball, and while it was still moving putted it back up the slope—and past the hole for a fifth time. His next putt lipped out—passing the hole once more—and then he tapped in, on his eighth stroke. But that was before a penalty for striking a moving ball. Rule 14–5 of the Rules of Golf as they then stood provided: "A player must not make a *stroke* at his ball while it is moving." (Rule 10.1(d) of the 2019 version of the Rules speaks in the second person, providing with exceptions not relevant here, "You must not make a *stroke* at a moving ball.") The penalty, in stroke play, is two strokes. So under this Rule, Mickelson got a 10 on the hole. Immediately after the round, he was unrepentant, saying:

> I didn't feel like continuing my display, and I gladly take the 2-shot penalty and move on. I don't mean it [to be] disrespectful. If you're taking it that way, that's not on me. I'm sorry you're taking it that way. It's certainly not meant that way. Sometimes in these situations it's just easier to take the 2 shots and move on.

Ian O'Connor, *Why Phil Mickelson should apologize, then withdraw from the U.S. Open*, ESPN.com (June 16, 2018). Four days later, though, perhaps because he recognized that many fans were outraged, he issued a very different statement: "I know this should've come sooner, but it's taken me a few days to calm down. My anger and frustration got the best of me last weekend. I'm embarrassed and disappointed by my actions. It was clearly not my finest moment and I'm sorry." *Mickelson apologizes 4 days after violating golf rules*, FOX Sports.com (June 20, 2018).

Did Mickelson have anything to apologize for? If he believed that, even taking the two-stroke penalty into account, he was better off hitting the moving ball, did he make an acceptable decision? Is there in fact something appealing about seeing a world-class golfer make a quick pro-and-con calculation and move (relatively) quickly to implement his decision?

Many observers believed that Mickelson should have been disqualified under Rule 1–2(i), which provided that a player must not "take an action with the intent to influence the movement of a *ball in play*." This Rule also prescribed a two-stroke penalty—but it provided in addition that "in the case of a serious breach" of the Rule, the Committee governing the competition could disqualify the player. Note 1 to the Rule provided that a breach that allowed the player "to gain a significant advantage" should be considered significant. The USGA (a frequent target of pungent criticism by Mickelson) took the view that this Rule did not apply, because Rule 14–5 more specifically addressed

Mickelson's conduct. (Was that the correct decision? Does it make sense that actually trying to redirect a moving ball towards the hole could only incur a two-stroke penalty, but stopping it from moving further away could lead to disqualification? The 2019 Rules do not authorize disqualification for purposely stopping or deflecting the ball. Rule 11.2(c) provides, in addition to the 2-stroke penalty, that if the shot was taken from off the green, the player must take the next shot from a spot near where the ball would have come to rest; if the shot was from the green, the stroke does not count but the player has to putt again from the same spot.) Assuming for the sake of argument that Rule 1–2(i) *did* apply, would this have been an appropriate case for disqualification? What arguments might Mickelson make against?

6. *Ravensgate.* Consider this ending to a 2016 football game between the Baltimore Ravens and Cincinnati Bengals:

> The Ravens led 19–12 with 11 seconds remaining and were lined up in punt formation. Rather than risking a punt that might be blocked or returned, and rather than giving the Cincinnati offense enough time for a Hail Mary pass or two, the Ravens snapped the football and then had all of their blockers grab, hold, bear-hug and tackle the Bengals' rushers. Punter Sam Koch backpedaled, moved back and forth and stood with the ball in his hands while penalty flags flew and the time ticked off the clock, finally stepping out of the back of the end zone for a safety.

> Game over.

> Ravens win, 19–14.

Mark Maske, *The Ravens' penalty-on-purpose tactic against the Bengals was legal. It shouldn't be.*, WASH. POST, Nov. 28, 2016. Video of the incident is available here: https://tinyurl.com/y4sntp9q.

NFL Rule 4, Sec. 8, Art. 2(a), provides that if the defense commits an infraction on the final play of a period, the offense has the option of playing a single untimed additional down. But the rules don't ordinarily allow the defense to extend a period after an *offensive* infraction. *Id.*, Art. 2(b). It's that asymmetry that allowed the Ravens' gambit to work. An announcer calling the game, former NFL quarterback Dan Fouts, lauded the play as "brilliant." Do you agree? Do you think that NFL rules should tolerate it by allowing it to have its desired effect? Insofar as they do, should the Ravens be applauded or denounced for engaging in the gambit? Given that it had been done once, the next coach who did it probably could not be credited with brilliance. What should we think of that next occurrence?

Art. 2(b) does have some exceptions, allowing extension of a period after an offensive foul in certain circumstances. One of those, now as in 2016, is for "a palpably unfair act." Art. 2(b)(3). But nowhere do the Rules define this term. Maske reported that "in the league's view, a palpably unfair act is defined as successive or repeated fouls." Perhaps, but nothing in the Rules provides much support for that interpretation. (Rule 12, Sec. 3, Art. 2 does provide that "[t]he defense shall not commit successive or repeated fouls to prevent a score," and that a score shall be awarded if the violation is repeated after a warning, but that is a different matter.) So should the officials have required the Ravens to run another (clean) play? If not, because they did not act unfairly, or for some other reason? Should the officials have deemed the Ravens to be on defense, and awarded the Bengals one more play?

In any event, the Ravens' ploy now clearly would be disallowed. Another one of the exceptions in Rule 4, Sec. 8, Art. 2(b) allowed an extra play if the offensive penalty was for "a personal foul or unsportsmanlike conduct foul committed prior to an interception of a forward pass, the recovery of a backward pass or fumble, or [the] offensive team failing to reach the line to gain on fourth down." Art. 2(b)(4). In a 2017 amendment, the league added "a safety" after "prior to" in this provision. (Subsequently, the provision was further amended, for clarity, by adding "during a down" before "prior to.") And at the same time, the league added a new Article 3 to Rule 12, Section 3:

> **ARTICLE 3. INTENTIONAL FOULS TO MANIPULATE GAME CLOCK.** A team may not commit multiple fouls during the same down in an attempt to manipulate the game clock.
>
> Penalty: For multiple fouls to run off time from the game clock: Loss of 15 yards, and the game clock will be reset to where it was at the snap. After the penalty is enforced, the game clock will start on the next snap.

7.　*(Not) making weight.* Combat sports that are competed in weight classes (almost all of them) impose diverse penalties for not making weight. In amateur boxing, for example, a fighter who misses weight is disqualified. In the UFC, overweight fighters are allowed one-pound overage (except in title fights), but must, if they exceed that margin, surrender 20–30% of their purse to their opponent (the percentage depends on how much they're over the limit); occasionally, a bout is canceled if the overage is too great, such as for Rafael Alves's 11.5-lb. miss in 2021. Also, in championship fights, overweight fighters are ineligible to claim the title if they win. For many fighters, cutting weight is as challenging and painful as the fight itself. Consider a fighter who consciously decides not to even try to cut the final five pounds for a particular fight, reasoning that it's worth paying the 30% penalty to avoid the pain of the cut and to give himself a better chance in the bout. Cheating?

8.　*Covertness in conclusion.* Whatever you may think about the Suarez, Mickelson, and Ravens incidents, do you agree that there cannot be cheating without covertness or deception? Consider two proposed counterexamples in addition to the case of intentionally missing weight: (1) the driver who "drives on the soft shoulder of the freeway in order to avoid sitting in a line of traffic waiting to get around an accident or other obstruction," STUART P. GREEN, LYING, CHEATING, AND STEALING: A MORAL THEORY OF WHITE-COLLAR CRIME 57 (2006); and (2) the corporate president who improves his lie at the company golf tournament, in plain view of others but knowing that they won't challenge him. BERNARD GERT, MORALITY: ITS NATURE AND JUSTIFICATION 192 (1998).

Are these instances of cheating? Do they establish that neither deception nor covertness is a necessary criterion of cheating?

9. *The ethos of the game.* Consider the suggestion that cheating is the intentional violation of a rule to gain advantage, except where the "ethos of the game" or "conventions of the sport" allow such violations. *See, e.g.,* ROBERT L. SIMON, FAIR PLAY: THE ETHICS OF SPORT 55–57 (3rd ed. 2010); Fred D'Agostino, *The Ethos of Games,* 8 J. PHIL. SPORT 7 (1981). NFL Rules prohibit wide receivers from coating their hands with stick 'um. Golf rules prohibit players from carrying more than 14 clubs in their bag. If football players who do use stick 'um do not thereby cheat, but golfers who carry too many clubs do cheat, the explanation is simply that the ethos or conventions of football allow it, and the ethos or conventions of golf don't. Does this strike you as correct? Adequate? If this is true, is this *all* we can say? Can we explain what makes it the case that the football ethos is what it is and the golf ethos is what it is? If an ethos-based or convention-based account of cheating is correct, does it follow that, in all disagreements over whether some given conduct is cheating, the majority is necessarily right? For example, if a majority of members of the soccer community conclude that Suarez did not cheat, then can there be no more room for argument? Does it follow that any novel instance of rule-breaking is inevitably cheating because no convention has yet arisen to allow it? Or is a novel instance necessarily *not* cheating because no convention has arisen to prohibit it?

10. *Deflategate.* Consider the long-running soap opera known as Deflategate. After their 2015 AFC Championship Game against the Indianapolis Colts, the New England Patriots were found to be using footballs that were underinflated relative to NFL requirements. NFL Rule 2 provides that balls shall be inflated to between 12 ½ and 13 ½ psi. The eleven Patriots' balls were tested at halftime of that game and were measured to range from 10.50 to 12.30 psi. All were below the requisite minimum inflation. Underinflated balls are easier to grip and throw, especially in cold and wet conditions, as prevailed during the game. Supplemental league regulations, termed Guidelines and incorporated into the League's Policy Manual for Member Clubs, provide further:

> Once the balls have left the locker room, no one, including players, equipment managers and coaches are allowed to alter the footballs in any way. If any individual alters the footballs, or if a non-approved ball is used in the game, the person responsible and, if appropriate, the head coach or other club personnel will be subject to discipline, including but not limited to, a fine of $25,000.

After a months-long investigation, attorney Ted Wells of the Paul, Weiss law firm issued a report that stated this conclusion:

> It is more probable than not that [Jim McNally and John Jastremski, two members of the Patriots equipment staff] participated in a deliberate effort to release air from Patriots game balls after the balls were examined by the referee. . . . [And] it is more probable than not

that Tom Brady (the quarterback for the Patriots) was at least generally aware of the inappropriate activities of McNally and Jastremski involving the release of air from Patriots game balls.

Theodore V. Wells, Jr., *Investigative Report Concerning Footballs Used During the AFC Championship Game on January 18, 2015*, 2, https://tinyurl.com/nfqby2w. As a result, the League, through Executive VP Troy Vincent, imposed penalties on both the Patriots and Brady himself. The Patriots were fined $1 million and were deprived of a first- and a fourth-round draft pick. Brady was suspended without pay for the first four games of the 2015 season (though as a result of litigation the suspension was postponed to 2016). In a letter to the Patriots, Vincent explained:

> As you know, we regard violations of competitive rules as significant and deserving of a strong sanction, both to punish the actual violation and to deter misconduct in the future. In this case, the footballs were intentionally deflated in an effort to provide a competitive advantage to Tom Brady after having been certified by the game officials as being in compliance with the playing rules.

NFL releases statement on Patriots' violations, NFL.com (May 11, 2015).

NFL Commissioner Roger Goodell upheld the penalties on appeal, prompting Brady to challenge his suspension in federal court. On September 3, 2015, U.S. District Judge Richard Berman ruled in Brady's favor and vacated his suspension.

Before Judge Berman issued his ruling, an ESPN poll of players revealed that 72% believe that the Patriots deflated footballs. But only 42% concluded that the Patriots cheated. Kevin Seifert, *Player survey: Majority think Patriots deflated footballs but aren't 'cheaters,'* ESPN.com (Aug. 12, 2015). It thus appears that a substantial percentage of NFL players believe that intentionally and surreptitiously underinflating rules in violation of the rules is not cheating. Is that because they think that intentional under-inflation is permitted for a price? Is that a plausible understanding of the rules, under a formalist, conventionalist, or internalist understanding? (See Subchapter 6B.) If not, what can explain the judgment of many players that *even if* the Patriots broke the rules, this wouldn't be a case of cheating? Put another way, if this isn't a case of cheating, what would be?

11. Trifles. If you think that intentionally and surreptitiously deflating footballs, in violation of league rules, is not cheating (regardless of whether you think that Brady or anybody associated with the Patriots did in fact deflate balls), is that because you think that the conduct could only have brought about a minor advantage, and that cheating requires that one pursue or obtain a major advantage? Is that plausible? Golf rules provide that a player may carry a maximum of 14 clubs. If a golfer intentionally carries a fifteenth, does the question of whether she is cheating depend upon the likelihood that she'll use that extra club? Is it not cheating to mark only a single card in a deck?

12. *Spygate.* Compare Deflategate with another imbroglio involving the Patriots from nine years earlier.

Article 9.1(C)(14) of the NFL's Constitution and Bylaws provides:

(C) No member [club], nor any stockholder, director, officer, partner, or employee thereof, or person holding an interest therein, nor any officer or employee of the League shall: * * *

> (14) Use at any time, from the start to the finish of any game in which a club is a participant, any communications or information-gathering equipment, other than Polaroid-type cameras or field telephones, including without limitation videotape machines, telephone tapping or bugging devices, or any other form of electronic devices that might aid a team during the playing of a game.

In September 2006, Ray Anderson, the N.F.L's senior vice president for football operations, sent a memo to all NFL teams, purporting to interpret this rule. The memo said: "Video taping of any type, including but not limited to taping of an opponent's offensive or defensive signals, is prohibited on the sidelines, in the coaches' booth, in the locker room, or at any other locations accessible to club staff members during the game." It was apparently motivated by reports that the New England Patriots had been videotaping opponents from the sidelines.

And indeed, in September 2007, in the season opener, a Patriots employee on the team's sideline was discovered videotaping signals by coaches of the New York Jets. The NFL imposed stiff penalties on the Patriots—$250,000 plus the loss of one or more high-round draft choices. In imposing the penalty, Commissioner Roger Goodell wrote the Patriots, "This episode represents a calculated and deliberate attempt to avoid longstanding rules designed to encourage fair play and promote honest competition on the playing field." Bill Belichick, coach of the Patriots, apologized for his "mistake." *See, e.g.,* Judy Battista, *Sideline Spying: N.F.L. Punishes Patriots' Taping*, N.Y. TIMES, Sept. 14, 2007.

In May 2008, Belichick gave an interview about the episode with Armen Keteyian of CBS. It is available at https://tinyurl.com/y2ej7zso. Belichick elaborated on his "mistake":

> . . . [T]here was a memo that Ray Anderson sent out at the beginning of the 2006 season, and that was an error on my part. I take full accountability for that. At that point, I feel like I should have gone to the league. I made a mistake. I should have gone to the league and said 'Look, are we OK doing this, even though we're not using it within the game?' I didn't do that. We continued to do what we had done previously, at times. It wasn't every game, but it was a significant number . . . .

But Belichick also offered a multi-part (and quite lawyerly) defense in mitigation of his conduct. He made the following points, among others:

- The Constitution and Bylaws allowed what the Patriots did, because the tape was not used during the game; instead, it was intended to assist preparation for future games.

- The Patriots gained no real advantage because opposing teams change their signals regularly.

- The Patriots gained no real advantage because they could have accomplished the same objective by having someone watch the signals and take notes, later examining what the play was.

- Stealing signs is part of the game.

- A participant can take reasonable precautions to defend against stealing of signs.[a]

- The Patriots conducted the taping in the open.

How do you assess this incident: cheating or not? Are Deflategate and Spygate distinguishable, or if one case is cheating, must the other be as well?

13. Sign-stealing in baseball. Many players acknowledge that stealing signals from the field—usually from second base, but also from the coaching boxes or the dugouts—is a legitimate part of the game. "Hey," said one player, "if you're dumb enough to let me see your signs, why shouldn't I take advantage of it?" But a common view is that one must not "be too obvious," and that "[i]f you get caught you have to stop" (for how long?) and must "be prepared to get drilled." JASON TURBOW WITH MICHAEL DUCA, THE BASEBALL CODES 157–61 (2010). Does this combination of rules—if such we may call them—make sense?

Furthermore, most baseball people regard sign-stealing from closer in as more problematic. It is generally considered disreputable for a batters to peek at the catcher's signs, or even to see where the catcher is setting up. *Id.* at 168–71 ("If on-field stealing is generally considered a gentleman's challenge, peeking is its evil twin."). Does this distinction have any merit?

And sign-stealing from further out—typically from beyond the outfield fence—is generally condemned. But there is a long history of it, going back at least to 1900. *See* TURBOW, THE BASEBALL CODES, at 172–81; PAUL DICKSON, THE HIDDEN LANGUAGE OF BASEBALL: HOW SIGNS AND SIGN-STEALING HAVE INFLUENCED THE COURSE OF OUR NATIONAL PASTIME (2d ed. 2019). According to Joshua Prager, when Bobby Thomson hit "the shot heard 'round the world"—the famous walk-off home run (as it would now be described) that gave the Giants the 1951 pennant by winning the decisive game of a playoff series against the Brooklyn Dodgers—he was tipped off to the pitch; Prager says that Thomson received signals relayed from a coach who was armed with a telescope in the Giants' clubhouse, which was in centerfield of their home ballpark, the Polo Grounds. JOSHUA PRAGER, THE ECHOING GREEN: THE UNTOLD STORY OF BOBBY THOMSON, RALPH BRANCA AND THE SHOT HEARD ROUND THE WORLD (2006). Thomson denied receiving any information about

---

[a] *See* Patrick Hruby, *Can Oregon's placard code be broken?*, ESPN.com (Jan. 7, 2011) (placard system used by Oregon football team as a precaution).

the fateful pitch. But suppose he was tipped off. Was that cheating? If so, why? *See* NPR, *The Shot Heard Round the World*, https://tinyurl.com/y5hayh6x.

- Is it because the spying came from off the field of play? Does it matter whether the spy is in the scoreboard or in the bullpen?

- Is it because the spying was technologically aided, in this case by binoculars? What if a spy from beyond the outfield wall is able to pick up signs with the naked eye? (TURBOW, THE BASEBALL CODES, at 171, reports that Don Lee, a reliever with the Los Angeles Angels in the early 1960s, could do this.) What if he could do so wearing glasses?

- Is it because (let us assume) the spy was dedicated to this one assignment—that is, he had no function during the game other than spying?

- Is it because this type of spying seems less commonplace than stealing signs from second base?

- Is it because the batting team is better able to protect itself from spying from the field than from spying from anywhere, by any means?

MLB directives now explicitly prohibit electronically aided sign-stealing. And yet some teams have continued to engage in the practice. The 2017 Red Sox apparently relayed signs picked up from viewers in the Fenway Park video room to a trainer in the dugout through his Apple watch. DICKSON, HIDDEN LANGUAGE OF BASEBALL, at 115. The Houston Astros of that same season, en route to the World Series title, also picked up signs electronically, and relayed them to the batter by the refreshingly low-tech method of banging on a trash can. Commissioner Rob Manfred imposed stringent punishment on both teams, and on the executives he deemed most involved, but let the players off without sanction, eliciting substantial criticism from fans and many players of opposing teams. For an overview, see *Everything you need to know about MLB's sign-stealing scandal,* ESPN.com, Feb. 13, 2020.

14. Spitballs and corked bats. The two essential pieces of equipment in baseball are the ball and the bat. The official rules of Major League Baseball expressly prohibit various forms of doctoring either. Rule 6.06(d) provides that "A batter is out for illegal action when . . . [h]e uses or attempts to use a bat that, in the umpire's judgment, has been altered or tampered with in such a way to improve the distance factor or cause an unusual reaction on the baseball. This includes bats that are filled, flat surfaced, nailed, hollowed, grooved or covered with a substance such as paraffin, wax, etc." Rule 8.02(a)(2) provides that "[t]he pitcher shall not . . . [a]pply a foreign substance of any kind to the ball." And yet, from the inception of baseball to the present day, players have done all those prohibited things. Batters sometimes hollow out their bats and fill them with cork or another light material to permit them to swing their bats faster. Pitchers put all types of substances on the ball to increase movement on their pitches.

Virtually everybody agrees that it is cheating to doctor the bat. Many casual fans believe the same is true of doctoring the ball. But many sophisticated observers do not. *See, e.g.,* J.S. Russell, *Is There a Normatively Distinctive Concept of Cheating in Sport (or anywhere else)?*, 41 J. PHIL. SPORT 303, 312 (2014); Randolph M. Feezell, *On the Wrongness of Cheating and Why Cheaters Can't Play the Game*, 15 J. PHIL. SPORT 57, 65 (1988). Gaylord Perry, a notorious spitballer, was elected to baseball's Hall of Fame in 1991 with few critics complaining that it was inappropriate to bestow such an honor on a cheater. Similarly, when Yankees pitcher Michael Pineda was suspended for ten days early in the 2014 season for applying pine tar to the ball, the dominant criticism was not that he violated the rules but that he was so darn brazen about it. On this view, it's not cheating to use a foreign substance for the purpose of affecting the ball's flight, but the umpires can't be expected to condone it when such usage is obvious to all. So here's the puzzle: Bat doctoring and ball doctoring are equally against the rules, yet they are not viewed equally as cheating. It would be too strong to assert flatly that the former is viewed as cheating and the latter isn't. But, almost certainly, ball doctoring is widely adjudged to be a more doubtful or borderline case. A spitballing pitcher might be labeled a cheater too, but is as likely to be adjudged a scamp as a scoundrel.

Do you think bat corking is cheating? Do you think spitballing is cheating? Whatever your personal views about these cases, can you make any sense of the fact (if it is a fact) that at least some observers view the two types of rule-breaking differently? Can appeal to covertness, ethos, or conventions help here?

15. PEDs revisited. We examined earlier (Subchapter 8C) how sports should regulate the use of performance-enhancing drugs. Suppose now that a particular sport does ban some particular drug. Do you agree that, ordinarily, it would be cheating to use such a drug in the face of the ban? If so, does this conclusion change if many or most other competitors are doing it too? That others are doing it is not a good defense to most charges in law or morals. But might it nonetheless be a valid defense to a charge of cheating? Consider the suggestion that a competitor cheats, or otherwise acts improperly, only in breaking a rule to gain an *unfair* advantage over others, and there is no unfairness in trying to gain an advantage that others are already obtaining. Is this a promising line of argument? Can it help us make sense of other cases of acceptable rule-breaking?

16. Cheating oneself? If cheating is a form of proscribed advantage-seeking behavior, must a cheater be trying to gain an advantage over another competitor? Is it possible to cheat at solitaire?

17. What's in the name? Throughout this discussion, we have used the term "cheating" with great frequency. But is there any significance to whether given conduct is considered to be cheating or not cheating? Should we instead be asking whether the conduct should be considered morally blameworthy and, separately, whether there should be any sanction for it?

B. LOOPHOLING: CHEATING WITHIN THE RULES?

What are loopholes? Although it might prove difficult to craft a very precise definition, most of us probably share at least a rough and ready sense of what they are. The legal theorist Leo Katz describes them as "seeming glitches in the formulation of a law . . . that allow clever lawyers to help their clients do things that appear to subvert its purpose." KATZ, WHY THE LAW IS SO PERVERSE, at 73. The criminal law scholar Sam Buell defines them as "spaces that actors reveal through new behaviors that render law underinclusive in ways lawmakers did not foresee and may have been unable to foresee." Samuel W. Buell, *Good Faith and Law Evasion,* 58 UCLA L. Rev. 611, 616 n.14 (2011) (emphases omitted). If something along these lines is right, then loopholing is the intentional exploitation of a glitch or overlooked space to secure the law's benefits in a manner that is inconsistent—and *understood by the actor herself to be inconsistent*—with the law's animating "purpose" or "spirit." Many people believe that loopholing is, at least sometimes, wrong or dodgy in some way—cheatingish, if not fully cheating. What do you think? Is loopholing ever normatively comparable to paradigmatic cheating? Under what circumstances? Consider the following cases.

COMMENTS AND QUESTIONS

1. Victory Victoria. Tennis rules provide that "[a] request for a Medical Time-Out may be made by a player to the Referee, Chair Umpire, or other official at any time during the match or warm-up." They then direct the officials not to grant the timeout if the player does not have a qualifying medical condition. But they do not by their terms provide that a player may not request the timeout without a bona fide belief that she has a qualifying condition. And because the regulations specifically authorize up to 12 minutes for evaluation and 3 minutes for treatment, a player can secure a lengthy delay even when it is determined that she does not present a condition that permits treatment. That is (by hypothesis) what Victoria Azarenka did in her semifinal match against Sloane Stephens at the 2013 Australian Open: call for a medical timeout without a medical need, wait for trainers to determine that she needed no treatment, and cheerfully return to the court, refreshed and refocused, after a ten-minute delay.[b]

Stephens's coach described Azarenka's conduct as "very unfair—cheating within the rules." Do you agree? Consider the view that a competitor can never warrant criticism for strictly *complying* with the rules, and that if exploitation

---

[b]   We assume here that Azarenka knew at the time she called for the medical timeout that she lacked a medical need. That is what she said or implied in response to an on-court question immediately after the match. Her tune changed a little at the post-match news conference. *See Was Azarenka 'Cheating' Within the Rules?,* USA TODAY, Jan. 24, 2013. So we can treat the animating assumption as a stipulation for purposes of analysis.

of an apparent loophole leads to results that members of the practice community do not like, the only upshot is that those who draft the formal rules should revise them. See KATZ, WHY THE LAW IS SO PERVERSE at 86; Leo KATZ, ILL-GOTTEN GAINS: EVASION, BLACKMAIL FRAUD, AND KINDRED PUZZLES 12 (1996). What, if anything, can be said against this view?

2. *Ready Reddy.* In an 1887 American Association baseball game, a base runner for the Louisville Colonels, Reddy Mack, safely crossed home plate and then turned to tackle the Brooklyn Grays' catcher to prevent him from making a play on the two runners behind him. At the time, league rules stated that no runner may interfere with a fielder. But Mack, having already scored, was no longer a runner. See Russell, *Are Rules All an Umpire Has to Work With?,* at 28. Did Mack cheat?

3. *Underarm bowling.* One of the most notorious episodes in international cricket occurred at the end of a 1981 one-day match between Australia and New Zealand. With one ball of the final over remaining, New Zealand needed a six (analogous to a home run in baseball) to tie the match. To prevent that from happening, the Australian captain, Greg Chappell, instructed his bowler (and younger brother), Trevor Chappell, to deliver the last ball underarm, along the ground. At the time, no rule of cricket specifically barred underarm bowling, but it was universally viewed as not within the spirit of the game. As the ball was being bowled, an Australian commentator on the match—Ian Chappell, Trevor and Greg's older brother—exclaimed: "No, Greg, you can't do that." Another Australian commentator, the former Australian captain Richie Benaud, denounced the act as "disgraceful" and "one of the worst things I have ever seen done on a cricket field." *See, e.g., The Infamous Underarm bowling incident,* THE NATION (Sri Lanka), Aug. 22, 2010. Shortly after the match, the official cricket rules were amended to specifically outlaw underarm bowling.

Virtually everybody—including Greg and Trevor Chappell—agrees that the tactic was unsporting at best. But why? Why was it not comparable to a quarterback taking a knee in the last seconds of a football game? At the other pole, was it worse than unsporting? Was it cheating? If it wasn't cheating, is it any less objectionable? Why (not)?

4. *Loopholing and PEDs.* Suppose that a formal rule of a sport prohibits the use of specific substances, and defines the banned substances by their chemical composition. Would it be cheating to ingest or otherwise avail oneself of a newly synthesized substance, not yet recognized by the rules, that is functionally identical to the banned substances?

5. *Loopholing the game clock.* An NFL game is governed by two clocks: the game clock, which counts down from 15 minutes to zero each quarter, and the play clock, which counts down from 40 seconds to zero each play. If the offense doesn't snap the ball before the play clock expires, it is subject to a 5-yard penalty for delay of game. Sometimes the offense will think this a good deal—if it wants to back up to give its punter a few more yards of field in which to land a punt, or if it has a large lead with not much time remaining and places

a higher value on running time off the game clock than on maximizing field position. In a 2019 game against the Jets, the Patriots were up 33–0 and facing fourth down at New York's 33-yard line with 11 minutes remaining in the fourth quarter. New England coach Bill Belichick intentionally allowed the play clock to expire to give his punter more room. As is common in this situation, Jets' coach Adam Gase declined the penalty, figuring that a punt from that distance would likely reach the end zone, thereby giving the Jets a touchback and possession on its own 20. Had New York accepted the penalty, the game clock would have remained stopped until the Patriots snapped the ball. But because New York declined, the game clock restarted.

As a purely tactical matter, should Belichick have let the play clock expire again? One might suppose that, by doing so, New England could force the Jets to accept the penalty so as to stop the game clock, lest, by tolerating successive delays of game, they watch the game clock expire in 40-second increments. But the NFL had anticipated this gambit: NFL rules provide that two consecutive delay-of-game infractions incur an unsportsmanlike conduct penalty and an automatic stoppage of the game clock. So Belichick did not commit a second intentional delay of game infraction. Instead, he instructed one of his offensive linemen to commit a false start just as the play clock was about to expire. Again, the Jets declined the penalty, and the game clock continued. This time, before the play clock expired, the Patriots punted. So New England was able to milk another 40 seconds off the game clock all because the NFL rulemakers had failed to anticipate that a wily coach might follow up an intentional delay-of-game infraction with an intentional infraction of a different rule. "It was just the way the rules are set up," Belichick explained after the game. "We were able to run quite a bit of time off the clock without really having to do anything. It's a loophole that probably will be closed, and probably should be closed, but right now it's open." Was this permissible loopholing or cheatingish? Was it distinguishable from Ravensgate? Should this really be considered an example of tactical fouling instead of (or in addition to) loopholing? *See* Subchapter 6A, pp. 191–201. Note that the tables were turned two months later when the Tennessee Titans, coached by former Patriot linebacker Mike Vrabel, employed the same maneuver against New England to seal a playoff victory. The NFL closed the Belichick loophole (if that's what it was) during the subsequent offseason.

      6.   *Cheating in fantasy.* As fantasy football players may know, on many hosting sites, players dropped from a team are placed on waivers and cannot be picked up by any other team until some specified period has elapsed, say 72 hours. You learn Friday evening that your lone QB broke his hand in practice and is ruled out for Sunday's game. When you go online to pick up a replacement you discover that your opponent for that week has already picked up and then dropped, seriatim, every starting QB not already on the roster of any of your league's teams. The only QBs who remain available for you to claim are backups who aren't even expected to play. If your league had not thought to enact a rule to prevent this gambit, should your fellow owner be

congratulated for clever gamesmanship or condemned as a cheater? Or neither?

7. *Edge sorting*. We assume that it is cheating to play poker with marked cards or to deal off the bottom of the deck. But some cases in which casino players try to gain an advantage against the house are more ambiguous. We have already addressed the issue of card-counting in blackjack (Subchapter 3A). Now consider the practice of edge sorting. In 2012, Phil Ivey, one of the world's greatest poker players, used the practice with an associate, Cheng Yin Sun, to take the Borgata Hotel Casino in Atlantic City for $9.6 million by playing baccarat, or Punto Banco, as the North American version of the game is known in other parts of the world. And then they used similar tactics to win an even greater sum, about £7.7 million, at Crockfords, a London casino. But then they wound up in litigation on both sides of the Atlantic.

Baccarat, which uses ordinary playing cards, is like roulette in that you can decide what outcome to place your bet on and how much to bet, but you have no control over the outcome. Because it is a game of pure chance, casinos are willing to indulge all sorts of superstitions that players may have, especially if they are heavy bettors like Phil Ivey. But what the casino thought was a pile of superstitions on Ivey's part was actually a methodical effort to gain an informational advantage.

Bets are placed before the cards are dealt, so the bettor can only see the back of the first card of the deal. If a baccarat player has any information indicating what that first card will be, that may be enough to overcome the house edge, which is very narrow. Edge sorting is possible because the backs of some playing cards are not absolutely symmetrical. For example, if the back features a pattern of small diamonds, it may be that there are complete diamonds running down one edge of a given card but not down the other. So Ivey asked the Borgata for the use of a particular style of Gemaco cards, the asymmetries of which Sun could spot regularly, in an 8-deck shoe, which was to be used all day. He also asked that the cards be shuffled by machine, that he have a private pit, and that the dealer speak Mandarin Chinese. The casino went along with all these demands, which Ivey explained as rooted in superstition. Then he and Sun sat patiently at the baccarat table, and after a card was turned over Sun sometimes asked the dealer in Mandarin that it be rotated 180°—supposedly again for superstition. (In London, she spoke in Cantonese; Ivey said he had better luck with Asian dealers.) The dealer complied, and the cards were put in the shuffling machine without turning them back around. As a result, little by little the shoe was sorted so that by looking at the edges on the back Ivey had useful information as to whether the first card about to be dealt was a 7, 8, or 9, which would greatly increase the probability that a bet on the so-called player's hand would pay off. Ultimately, this advantage paid off enormously.

But when the casinos figured out what had happened, they took action. Borgata accused Ivey and Sun of cheating and sued to recover the money. Crockfords returned their stake of £1 million, and Ivey and Sun sued to get their winnings. Crockfords won its case at every level. Mr. Justice Mitting, the trial judge, concluded that the deception by Ivey and Sun did not mean that they were not indeed playing Punto Banco, and he even asserted that "[i]t was by itself on the right side of the line separating cheating from legitimate gamesmanship. By itself it was no different in principle from a shrewd and numerate poker or Blackjack player pretending to be a fool, a legitimate technique in playing games in which the perception of one player of another may influence his play." But then he noted that cheating at cards "does not necessarily involve deception"; it might include, for example, looking at an opponent's cards.[c] And, he said, "as far as the civil law is concerned, there is no general agreement as to what one might term the industry standard of cheating or not cheating." Ultimately, he concluded that for purposes of the civil law Ivey and Sun had cheated because (1) Ivey "gave himself an advantage," (2) "[h]e did so by using the croupier as his innocent agent or tool," and (3) "he was doing so in circumstances in which he knew that she and her superiors did not realise the consequence of what he had done at his instigation." The Court of Appeal affirmed the judgment, by a 2–1 vote, and so did the Supreme Court of the United Kingdom, by the decision of a unanimous five-justice panel. *Ivey v. Genting Casinos (UK) Ltd t/s Crockfords*, [2017] UKSC 67. Lord Hughes, for the Court, wrote that the conclusion that Ivey's actions were cheating was "unassailable":

> It is an essential element of Punto Banco that the game is one of pure chance, with cards delivered entirely at random and unknowable by the punters or the house. What Mr Ivey did was to stage a carefully planned and executed sting. . . . It may be that it would not be cheating if a player spotted that some cards had a detectably different back from others, and took advantage of that observation, but Mr Ivey did much more than observe; he took positive steps to fix the deck. That, in a game which depends on random delivery of unknown cards, is inevitably cheating. That it was clever and skilful, and must have involved remarkably sharp eyes, cannot alter that truth.

Are you persuaded that Ivey and Sun cheated, even though no rule specifically prohibited edge sorting? Was the trial court's decision internally consistent? Are you persuaded by the distinction drawn by the Supreme Court?

Should it matter that the casinos could have protected themselves by simple expedients, such as rotating some of the cards before putting them in the shuffling machine or covering the shoe before the bets are made? Mr. Justice Mitting found this possibility immaterial: "The casino can protect itself by simple measures against cheating or legitimate advantage play. The fact that it can do so does not determine which it is." Are you persuaded? (Mr.

---

[c] One might ask whether looking at an opponent's cards could be effective cheating absent some form of deception—that is, acting in a way that raises no suspicion that one is actually looking. A form of gambling cheating that involved no deception appears in the musical *Guys and Dolls*: Big Julie insists on playing craps with his own dice, which have no spots; he had them removed for luck. But, he says, "I remember where the spots formerly were." Nobody is fooled, but Big Julie has a gun.

Justice Mitting's judgment is available at https://tinyurl.com/y5zvessk; the UK Supreme Court's judgment is available at https://tinyurl.com/y4259t9m.)

On the American side, Borgata sued not only Ivey and Sun but also Gemaco. Ivey and Sun counterclaimed, charging spoliation of evidence. Separately, Ivey complained that Borgata was guilty of unfair competitive methods by "plying him with free alcohol served by only the most curvaceous and voluptuous females in the industry." Wayne Parry, *Poker Pro: Borgata uses booze, sexy servers to distract gamblers,* NBC NEW YORK.COM (Aug. 27, 2015). "It distracts you from your playing," Ivey said. "I mean, anything they can do to give themselves an advantage. Everyone knows that alcohol impairs your judgment, and they offer that, and they have the pretty cocktail waitresses and they're all very flirty. They're talking to you, you know. I got quite a few numbers." *Id.* If proven, should that conduct be deemed illegitimate?

Judge Noel Hillman of the U.S. District Court for the District of New Jersey held that Ivey and Sun had not committed fraud against the casino or violated federal and state RICO statutes by misrepresenting their true motives for their game requests—but that they had breached their contract with the casino to play baccarat in compliance with New Jersey gambling laws; they violated N.J.S.A. 5:12–115(a)(2) and (b), which prohibit the use of marked cards in gambling, "when they knowingly engaged in a scheme to create a set of marked cards and then used those marked cards to place bets based on the markings." *Marina District Development Co., LLC v. Ivey*, 216 F. Supp. 3d 426, 433 (D.N.J. 2016). Thus, he ordered Ivey and Sun to return all their winnings (including more money that Ivey won at craps with his Baccarat winnings, *Marina District Development Co., LLC v. Ivey*, 223 F. Supp. 3d 216, 220–21 (D.N.J. 2016)). He also threw out the counterclaims, because no examination of the actual cards used was necessary, so Ivey and Sun were not injured by the alleged spoliation. 216 F. Supp. 3d at 429 n.2. In 2018, he held that Borgata had no viable tort claim against Gemaco for providing defective playing cards; he declined to resolve whether it had a breach-of-warranty claim, for which its recovery would be limited to $26.88. *Marina District Development Co., LLC v. Ivey*, 2018 WL 1469013 (D.N.J. 2018). After an appeal was argued, the parties participated in a court-annexed mediation program and settled.

Other sources on this incident include *Edge Sorting—The Complete Guide*, YOUTUBE, https://tinyurl.com/y2rswarz; Chad Holloway, *Details Emerge in Borgata's Lawsuit Against Phil Ivey*, POKER NEWS.COM (Apr. 16, 2014); Maurice VerStandig, *Sorting out the Law Behind Phil Ivey's Edge Sorting Debacle at Borgata*, POKER NEWS.COM (Apr. 18, 2014).

8.   *Disney disability.* Disney World has made special entrances to its attractions available to disabled guests. These entrances, and their vastly shorter wait times, can be used by disabled persons in wheelchairs or motorized scooters and up to six members of their parties. Plainly, an able-bodied guest who feigned a disability to use these special entrances would be cheating. Some wealthy able-bodied visitors have hit upon a different way to avail themselves of the special entrances: they hire disabled "guides" at about

$1000 for the day. Dr. Wednesday Martin, a social anthropologist who uncovered the scheme, quoted one proud mother as crowing, "My daughter waited one minute to get on 'It's a Small World'—the other kids had to wait 2 ½ hours." Tara Palmeri, *Rich Manhattan moms hire handicapped tour guides so kids can cut lines at Disney World,* N.Y. POST, May 14, 2013.

9. *Contrived defenses.* The law governing the use of deadly force in self-defense varies across jurisdictions. Generally speaking (and putting aside both the castle doctrine and stand-your-ground laws), it is permissible to use deadly force against an aggressor to protect oneself from the aggressor's anticipated use of force only when "necessary"; the use of such force is not deemed necessary if safe retreat is possible. Suppose that Hatfield, anticipating that McCoy will launch an attack on Tuesday, takes pains on Monday to ensure that he, Hatfield, will have no avenue of safe retreat when the attack comes. He blocks an easy escape route, say, or ties his own shoelaces together. He then awaits his nemesis, gun at the ready. When the armed McCoy arrives for Hatfield on Tuesday, Hatfield's use of deadly force in self-defense is necessary, for he has rendered safe retreat impossible. Hatfield shoots McCoy dead and pleads self-defense. Should the criminal law close this loophole? How could it do so?

10. *Allow vs. permit.* It is commonly thought that if some system of rules, S, does not prohibit some conduct, C, then it follows logically that S permits C. Some commentators, however, distinguish between "strong" and "weak" permissions. *See, e.g.,* Eugenio Bulygin, *Permissory Norms and Normative Systems, in* ESSAYS IN LEGAL PHILOSOPHY 324 (Eugenio Bulygin et al., eds., 2015). According to this way of carving things, not to prohibit is tantamount to weakly permitting, but not to strongly permitting. Using a slightly different vocabulary, we might say that if S doesn't prohibit C, then it follows logically that S *allows* C; but it does not necessarily follow that S *permits* C. That is, a permission (but not an allowance) is more than the mere absence of a prohibition. Do you anticipate that some form of an allowance/permission distinction will feature in a satisfactory explanation of when loopholing is permissible? If so, how might you distinguish allowance from permission?

C. DECEPTION

Charles W. Eliot, president of Harvard from 1869 to 1909, once explained why he wanted to drop baseball as a college sport: "Well, this year I'm told the [Harvard] team did well because one pitcher had a fine curve ball. I understand that a curve ball is thrown with a deliberate attempt to deceive. Surely that is not an ability we should want to foster at Harvard." PAUL DICKSON, BASEBALL'S GREATEST QUOTATIONS 127 (1991); *see* 2 HENRY JAMES, CHARLES W. ELIOT: PRESIDENT OF HARVARD UNIVERSITY, 1869–1909 69 (1930) ("To pitch a curved ball seemed to him to be a resort to a 'low form of cunning.' "). Today, the view that all deception is cheating, or should be prohibited, will strike most people as someplace between quaint and crackpot. Games are replete with deception that athletes, leagues, and sports fan consider entirely permissible—from decoys to fake handoffs to blind passes, and countless more. Indeed, many routine moments and many memorable ones in sports involve deception of opponents. For example, a football team may line up on fourth down in punting formation and then run a pass play. And in a famous play in 1994 against the New York Jets, with time running down, Dan Marino of the Miami Dolphins acted as if he were about to spike the ball—slamming the ball to the ground, wasting a down but stopping the clock—but instead he threw an easy touchdown pass.[d] The Dolphins were on the other end when Aaron Rodgers of the Green Bay Packers used a similar play to gain critical yardage against them in a game on October 12, 2014. As Bruce Weber notes in an article presented below, "deception is inherent to competition and it is fundamental to games of all types, including hide and seek and chess." *Cf.* SUN TZU, THE ART OF WAR (Lionel Giles trans., 1910) ("All warfare is based on deception."). But what deception is permissible, and what not? We will divide the topic into two basic parts: deception of opponents and of officials.

1. DECEPTION OF OPPONENTS

JOHN BRANCH, RODRIGUEZ KEEPS STRADDLING BASEBALL'S FOUL LINE

New York Times, June 1, 2007
© 2007 The New York Times Company, reprinted with permission

It was clever or childish, cunning gamesmanship or borderline cheating, or maybe something in between. But when Alex Rodriguez of the Yankees shouted something to a Toronto Blue Jays infielder Wednesday night, helping cause a pop-up to drop and leading to three runs, the debate began.

The only certainty is that the play further blurred the line between what is fair or foul in the unwritten code of baseball—and solidified Rodriguez's reputation as a player willing to test boundaries. Players, coaches and baseball observers interviewed yesterday routinely struggled to articulate what was permissible and what was not, and why.

"If I could explain it clearly, there would be no fine line," said the Fox baseball broadcaster Tim McCarver, a former major league catcher. "You just have to be there. That's how fine the line is."

---

[d] *See Dan Marino ICONIC Fake Spike (11/27/1994)*, YOUTUBE, https://tinyurl.com/ y3sbwoug. The play has become rather legendary. *See Clock Play*, WIKIPEDIA, https://tinyurl. com/y3k2tbfx; *2008 Miami Dolphins Dan Marino fake spike play ad*, YOUTUBE, https://tinyurl. com/y2925k37.

Deception in baseball has long been alternately applauded and cursed. Games are filled with attempts to trick the opponent, like children in the outfield imploring the batter-batter-batter to swing and fielders applying a tag without a ball or trying to steal signs.

Baseball lore is filled with memorable examples of bamboozlement, from a minor league catcher carving a potato to look like a baseball to infielders serving as decoys to help win the World Series.

On Wednesday, with the Yankees leading, 7–5, in the top of the ninth inning, Jorge Posada hit a two-out high pop that third baseman Howie Clark settled under. But as Rodriguez casually ran behind him toward third, he shouted something—"Ha!" according to Rodriguez; "Mine!" according to Clark.

Clark scooted away. The ball dropped.

It was ruled a hit for Posada, not an error on Clark. Hideki Matsui scored and Rodriguez was safe at third. Jason Giambi singled to drive in Rodriguez and Posada, and the Yankees went on to win, 10–5.

The play infuriated the Blue Jays. As Clark watched sheepishly, shortstop John McDonald had to be restrained from going after Rodriguez. Toronto Manager John Gibbons argued with the umpires. He later called the play "bush league."

Their complaints had little to do with the rules and everything to do with an unwritten code of sportsmanship. According to Rule 7.08(b), a base runner is out if he "hinders a fielder attempting to make a play on a batted ball." But the rule equates interference with contact. That leaves a void, open to interpretation. Can players shout anything? What if Rodriguez had moved closer, or shouted it louder?

"That's what makes baseball so great," McDonald said yesterday before the Blue Jays played the Chicago White Sox. "There's the rule book, and there are other things that are passed down from older players when I was first starting my career. So it's something I may take offense to, but other people may not."

Apparently, the code permits some words or noises but not others. It may also depend on where the play occurs. It is telling that there is some discrepancy over what Rodriguez said. He denied saying "mine," though Clark repeated that accusation yesterday.

"Maybe that's a little bit out of line," Rodriguez said.

Others agreed.

"It's not like he said, 'I got it,' " Yankees Manager Joe Torre said after the game, suggesting that such a claim would be inappropriate. "He just made a noise."

Players and coaches differed widely on how common the practice was. San Francisco Giants shortstop Omar Vizquel, in his 19th season, said that he had never had an opponent try to distract him from catching a pop-up, and was not sure it was legal. But White Sox Manager Ozzie Guillén, a former shortstop, said that it happened all the time. "It's the first time it worked at the big-league level," he said.

"Why not do it?" he said. "We all do everything to win games."

Torre, Rodriguez and others said that such attempts to break the concentration of fielders, if not fool them completely, were common, at least in foul territory.

"When a catcher comes over to the opposing dugout, everybody yells, 'I got it. I got it,'" Torre said. . . .

In the eighth inning of a scoreless Game 7 of the 1991 World Series, Lonnie Smith of the Atlanta Braves was on first base, and he ran toward second as the pitch was thrown. He saw Minnesota Twins second baseman Chuck Knoblauch crouch to field the batted ball and fake a throw. He did not immediately see that Terry Pendleton had hit the ball toward the wall between two outfielders. Smith should have scored on the hit, but he stopped at second momentarily before scurrying to third.

Smith was stranded there, and the Twins won, 1–0, in 10 innings. Smith was widely criticized, and Knoblauch's play was complimented. McCarver worked the game as a broadcaster, and he still considers it a great play by Knoblauch.

Why? "Because that's a decoy," he said, explaining that it was Smith's fault for losing track of the ball's flight and having to rely on the fielders for an indication of where it went.

Jerry Manuel, a coach for the Mets, differentiated between a decoy and other attempts at deception, although the difference is difficult to delineate. "Decoy is part of the game," he said. "When you scream or yell, that is not a decoy."

A true decoy was used by a minor league catcher named Dave Bresnahan. In 1987, with the Williamsport (Pa.) Bills, he carved a potato to look like a baseball. With a runner on third base, Bresnahan threw the potato into the outfield in an apparent pickoff attempt. The runner raced home, and Bresnahan tagged him out with the real ball.

After some confusion, the runner was declared safe, and Bresnahan— whose number was later retired by the minor league team—was cut the next day by the Cleveland Indians organization. . . .

COMMENTS AND QUESTIONS

1.   *A-Rod's shout.* What do you think—was A-Rod's shout "cunning gamesmanship or borderline cheating, or maybe something in between"? Do you think the answer depends on whether he yelled, "Ha" or "Mine" or "I got it"? Is there a useful distinction in this context between distraction and deception?

Is there a safety consideration at play? What should Clark, the third baseman, have done when he heard a sound coming from behind him?

Rodriguez himself defended his conduct: "In a situation like that, that play happens to me three or four times a week, except it's not at third base—[it's] over by the dugout, foul territory. Sometimes it works, sometimes it doesn't. . . . I get screamed at all the time on the field." Brian Hoch, *A-Rod defends controversial shout*, MLB.com (May 31, 2007). Are you persuaded? Are the situations comparable? If not, why not?

If you believe that A-Rod's shout—under whatever hypothesis you choose as to what he said—was *not* proper competitive conduct, do you think the Official Rules of Baseball should formally prohibit and sanction it?

2.   *Balks.* In baseball, there is a set of complicated rules prescribing how a pitcher must act when there is a runner on base. According to an official comment, "the purpose of the balk rule is to prevent the pitcher from deliberately deceiving the base runner." Comment to Rule 8.05. Thus, for example, Rules 805(b) and (c) provide:

(b)   The pitcher, while touching his plate, feints a throw to first or third base and fails to complete the throw;

(c)   The pitcher, while touching his plate, fails to step directly toward a base before throwing to that base . . . .

(Note that a feint to second base is allowed.) Violation of these rules results in a balk, which advances each runner one base. Why *should* the balk rules attempt to prevent the pitcher from deliberately deceiving the runner?

3.   *Hesitation versus change-of-pace.* In the hesitation pitch, formerly used by Satchel Paige among others, the pitcher hesitates for a moment in his delivery to throw off the timing of the batter. This pitch is now illegal. What possible purpose could the prohibition serve? A change of pace, which also attempts to accomplish the same objective, is perfectly legal. Does this make sense? *See* Craig Burley, *The Hesitation Pitch*, BATTER'S BOX (Aug. 23, 2004).

4.   *Decoys: fake throws, fake handoffs, thrown potatoes, hidden balls, and the wrong guy in the on-deck circle.* Let's assume for simplicity that A-Rod shouted, "Mine!" That is an overtly communicative act, like the motion a quarterback makes when rushing to the line to signal to his teammates an intent to spike the ball, and unlike, say, a fake handoff or throwing a potato into the field. Note that McCarver and Manuel distinguish between a communicative act like A-Rod's and a decoy like Knoblauch's. Is the distinction sound? If it is, what makes a move a decoy?

And if decoys are OK, what, if anything, was wrong with the potato move, which as Branch notes used a "true decoy"? If your response is that it makes a joke out of the game, what exactly is wrong about adding a funny play to the game? And is the joke on the runner who fell for the move? Or is the problem merely one of time and information (and conservation): If the ploy is allowed, would the field be littered with potatoes? Would runners be put at too much of a disadvantage, not knowing whether a thrown sphere was the game ball or a carved tuber?

What then about a hidden-ball play? A fake handoff is one, and is obviously permissible; of course it requires considerable athletic ability to sell the move. The same is often true in lacrosse, in which hidden-ball plays are rather common, *see Rahme: Weather Woes Stir Up Debate, Syracuse's Hidden-Ball Trick and Miles' New Look*, INSIDE LACROSSE (Feb. 19, 2014), though sometimes the skill necessary to bring the play off seems more like acting. *Hidden Ball Trick*, YOUTUBE, https://tinyurl.com/y3e6l8ry. And that is usually true in baseball, in which the play is more static; it results more from distracting the runner's attention than from making a skillfully deceptive handoff while play is in active motion: If the runner thinks that the pitcher rather than a fielder near him has the ball, then he may step off the base and be surprised by a rapid tag. Although the Official Rules of Baseball allow the play, they constrain how it may be made.[e] Should it instead be barred, on the ground that it has nothing to do with the excellences that baseball is meant to test?

Also characterized as a decoy was a fake script supposedly listing Oklahoma's opening plays that a Texas student assistant found during warmups before the teams' 1999 football showdown. Texas believed it had gotten a big break, until it fell behind 17–0. Jake Trotter, *The untold story of Mike Leach's 'lost' OU play script that fooled Texas*, ESPN.com, Oct. 3, 2018.

As a final example of a decoy, consider this incident from a game between the Colorado Rockies and the Pittsburgh Pirates, on April 8, 2011. With the score tied in the bottom of the 14th inning, the Pirates had two outs with a man on first. José Tábata, a good hitter, was up for the Pirates, who had the pitcher's spot up next as a result of an earlier double switch, and then Andrew McCutchen, a dangerous hitter. (The double switch is a move National League managers sometimes make late in a game if they pull a pitcher from the mound in the middle of an inning when his spot in the batting order is coming up soon: They also replace another player who has just batted and put the new pitcher in what was the position player's spot in the batting order and the replacement

---

[e] It cannot be made immediately after a suspension of play, because under MLB Rule 5.11 play cannot resume until "the pitcher takes his place on his plate with the ball in his possession." Furthermore, the play cannot be made if the pitcher is standing "on or astride" the rubber, because it is a balk if he does so with men on base and without the ball. Rule 805(i). *Hidden ball trick*, WIKIPEDIA, https://tinyurl.com/y56jo34j. Are these sensible limitations? *See* BILL DEANE, FINDING THE HIDDEN BALL TRICK: THE COLORFUL HISTORY OF BASEBALL'S OLDEST RUSE 164 (2005) (Mike Lowell, playing third base, holds onto ball after play; pitcher catches on and roams around mound, until runner takes a lead: "I just walked around and tried to stall. I was running out of things to do. I was going to touch my toes.").

position player in what was the pitcher's spot. The result is often that the pitcher's spot is moved to the heart of the batting order, rather than at the weak end.) The Pirates had no hitters on the bench. It therefore made sense to walk Tábata, even though it would move the winning run to second base, because the pitcher would have to hit and would probably make an out to end the inning. But the Pirates' manager, Clint Hurdle, put McCutchen in the on-deck circle. The Rockies' manager was apparently fooled into thinking McCutchen would bat next, and they pitched to Tábata, who hit a game-winning double.[f]

Hurdle was asked after the game whether he put McCutchen in the on-deck circle to fool the Rockies.

> "Oh, come on," he said, his voice dripping with sarcasm. "Why would we do that? No, we put him up there in case of a play at the plate, Andrew was the more experienced guy there in case of a slide. I didn't want to have to have Garrett go through that."

Recap: Jose Tabata's RBI double lifts Pirates in 14th, ESPN.com (Apr. 9, 2011). In other words, if there were a close play at the plate, it would be better to have McCutchen, rather than a pitcher who did not bat often, in the on-deck circle; it is the on-deck batter's responsibility to advise a runner coming home whether to slide. Do you believe Hurdle's explanation? If you think that in fact he did it to fool the Rockies, and succeeded, was this proper conduct—and why do you think he denied engaging in it?

5.   *From deception to distraction.* Some deceptions, like the hidden-ball play, depend on distraction. Athletes may distract their opponents in many ways without attempting to deceive them. In women's tennis, one method of choice is grunting. Speaking of the Portuguese player, Michelle Larcher de Brito, "a precocious 16-year-old possessed of sharply angled ground strokes and an extended battle cry that sounds like something an anthropologist might travel across the world to study," Hall of Famer Martina Navratilova protested: "The grunting has reached an unacceptable level. It is cheating, pure and simple. It is time for something to be done about it." Christopher Clarey, *A Player's Reputation Precedes Her, Loudly*, N.Y. TIMES, June 21, 2009. If de Brito's grunts were intentional—which we can take to mean that they were louder or more extended than would be optimal for the quality of her play—was she cheating? Now suppose they were indeed at a level that enabled her to play her best. Should they nevertheless have been constrained?

2.   DECEPTION OF OFFICIALS

Ideally, officials make accurate decisions, and accuracy in decision-making depends to a large extent on accuracy of information. So should conduct by a competitor designed to transmit inaccurate information to an official, in hopes of gaining a competitive advantage, be deemed improper

---

[f]   Eric Seidman, *Clint Hurdle's Excellent Decision*, FANGRAPHS (Apr. 11, 2011) (noting that no rule of baseball suggests that Hurdle acted improperly).

conduct? On considering the following materials, you may well conclude that the question is not a binary one, to be answered either yes or no. But then the issue becomes when such deception is appropriate and when not.

BRUCE WEBER, A BOY SCOUT PULLS A FAST ONE

The New York Times, Sept. 18, 2010
© 2010 The New York Times Company, reprinted with permission

OMG! Derek Jeter cheated?

For those who missed baseball's latest instance of purported turpitude, on Wednesday night in a game against the Tampa Bay Rays, Jeter, the Yankee shortstop and generally perceived-to-be Boy Scout, feigned being hit by a pitch. He pretended that the ball had ricocheted off his hand, though as stop-action replay made evident (and as he readily acknowledged after the game), it actually hit the knob of his bat. Nonetheless, his charade fooled the umpire; he was awarded first base, and even though the Yankees ultimately lost, it was a seemingly significant ploy. The following batter, Curtis Granderson, homered, putting the Yankees in front.

The next time Jeter got to the on-deck circle, Rays fans chanted the convenient rhyme "Jeter, Cheater," and the following day, sports blogs and talk radio were congested with persnickety rectitude and upright indignation. Do truth-telling and accountability have no place in sport? This is the example professional athletes are setting for our children?

Yikes! First of all, can we please just call a halt to the professional-sport-as-a-metaphor-for-life thing? Morality is complicated and context-based, isn't it? The difference between right and wrong is not automatically transferable from one arena (so to speak) to another, from the context in which an actual score is kept and the idea is to win, to the larger context, in which duping other people has actual, potentially harmful consequences or undermines the purpose of effort. It doesn't seem an especially difficult concept for a child to grasp or an adult to explain that it is, in fact, O.K. for a ballplayer to pretend to be safe when he knows he was out, but it isn't O.K. to shortchange the unwitting waitress or plagiarize a homework assignment.

Now, about the morality of sport generally and baseball particularly. To begin with, deception is inherent to competition and it is fundamental to games of all types, including hide and seek and chess. (One thing that has gotten buried in the seriousness of the Jeter hoopla is that fooling people can be fun.)

Second, that one player or one team might be interested in putting one over on an opponent is one reason, a big reason, that organized sports have officials—who have no expectation, by the way, that the players are guided by the honor system.

Indeed, I'd argue that a prime function of officials is to relieve players of the burden of honor. After all, on a bang-bang play at first base, when the runner is called safe but knows in his heart he was out, he does not feel compelled to correct the umpire's misimpression.

Officials, not athletes, are the ones who make sure that the game is fair. One thing that means is that opponents have equal opportunity to influence them. This is why it is not only acceptable but entirely accepted that soccer players will careen to the ground after a slight jostle, hoping to induce a yellow card; that offensive and defensive linemen will point at each other after a whistle on the line of scrimmage, each accusing the other of moving first; that catchers habitually tug an outside pitch toward the plate in an effort to convince the ump that a ball is a strike, the baseball version of "Who are you going to believe? Me or your own lying eyes?"

Baseball, especially, has a long history of such behavior. In the early days, when only a single umpire presided over each contest, it wasn't unusual for players to take advantage of his back being turned; a base runner might take a shortcut across the diamond from first to third or a fielder might delay a runner by grabbing hold of his belt. Jeter's alleged transgression is hardly worth mentioning in comparison.

There is, of course, such a thing as cheating in sports, and it deserves opprobrium, but it is qualitatively different from the sort of gamesmanship that makes games more interesting. I would describe the dividing line this way: If a player's ruse is spontaneous, if it occurs in response to the action on the field, then it's legit.

Deviousness plotted in advance or off the field, however, is a problem, the sporting equivalent of malice aforethought. That's why a base runner's decoding an opposing catcher's signs and flashing them to the batter is good baseball, but hiding a sign-stealing coach inside the center-field scoreboard with a pair of binoculars is not. It's why an outfielder who short-hops a line drive ought always to hold the ball aloft in case the umpire didn't see it bounce, but why a hitter who corks his bat, a pitcher who secrets Vaseline under the bill of his cap to be able to smear it on the ball, or anyone who uses steroids should be suspended.

As for Jeter, there is something puritanical and prudish to the charge that he cheated. As someone must have said sometime, baseball ain't church. That Jeter recognized the situation of the ball hitting his bat as an opportunity, then deployed his histrionics to persuasive effect, all in a split second, is testimony to a first-rate athletic instinct. I'm with Joe Maddon, the manager of the Rays, who was ejected from the game for arguing over the Jeter call.

"If our guys did it, I would have applauded that, too," Maddon said. "It's a great performance on his part."

CESAR TORRES, ON DIVING: SOCCER'S INTEGRITY IS AT STAKE

The New York Times Soccer Blog, Sept. 17, 2009
© 2009 Cesar Torres, reprinted with permission

Like all other games, soccer is created and regulated by rules. These rules establish the goal of the game and the means allowed to accomplish it. Notice that the rules prohibit the use of more efficient physical skills (for example, handling the ball, hacking opponents, or diving) to accomplish the stipulated goal. In this sense, soccer is designed primarily to test proficiency in a distinctive set of complex kicking skills. Soccer focuses on the multiple ways in which the feet can control the ball. This is exemplified by the Uruguayan writer Eduardo Galeano's description of soccer as a "show performed by twenty-two men in shorts who chase a ball and kick her to prove their love."

Diving clearly falls outside the means allowed to accomplish the goal of soccer and consequently undermines what the game is meant to test. Soccer does not seem to be about simulating infractions to deceive referees, winning undeserved penalty or free kicks and influencing referees to unjustly punish opponents. Divers deny the centrality of soccer and its distinctive set of complex kicking skills. That is, divers fail to honor the game's excellence that they are supposed to cultivate and celebrate.

It is logically contradictory to simultaneously accept the rules of soccer and to circumvent them when opportunities arise. Strictly speaking, this is the case with of all forms of cheating: intentionally breaking the rules surreptitiously to gain an advantage that would not probably be obtained otherwise. Divers, then, excuse themselves from following the rules and treat opponents simply as means to their own ends while avoiding the game's core objective. . . .

The argument . . . that diving is a complex skill that adds difficulty, interest, and drama to soccer does not go too far either. It goes without saying that successful diving requires cunning and talent. Clumsy or blatantly obvious diving is not only ineffective but also not amusing. Not all skillful behavior, however, falls within the confines of the game.

In an article entitled "What Counts As Part of a Game?: A Look at Skills" . . ., [27 J. PHIL. SPORT 84 (2000)], I have argued that there are two kinds of skills in sport.

One is known as constitutive skills; they are required to negotiate soccer's problem and are implemented during open play. In soccer, they include different forms of kicking the ball, dribbling and heading it, marking and opening up spaces to score, to mention a few. The other kind is known as restorative skills; they are employed when the game is stopped and there is a need to put it back on track. In soccer, they include, for example, penalty, free, and corner kicks as well as throw-ins. Both constitutive and restorative skills legitimately belong to soccer, although the former are more central than the latter.

While diving is a physical skill in its own right, it is neither a constitutive nor a restorative skill. Divers implement a skill that is not meant to be tested or needed to resume play. It is what I have called an extra-lusory skill, one that should not be considered part of soccer and has no place in it. In this sense, diving is no different than sneakily elbowing an opponent or pulling his/her shirt to obtain a competitive advantage. This is why a player lacking in diving ability is not perceived as a lesser player, whereas one lacking in passing or dribbling skills is perceived as such. Using the same rationale, it is possible to affirm that whatever degree of difficulty, interest, and drama is added to soccer by diving, it comes from a spurious source. It is, then, not a coincidence that the rules of soccer explicitly penalize this extra-lusory skill, for it downgrades the set of skills by which players are to distinguish themselves qualitatively on the pitch.

Soccer does not flourish when diving occurs. On the contrary, when diving is tolerated, accepted and celebrated, soccer's integrity as a sport comes into question. Diving should be condemned by those on the pitch as well as by those who are devotees of the game, irrespective of whether the diver is clad in one's favorite team's jersey or not. Likewise, all diving should be equally discouraged, not just the cases involving high-profile players. Perhaps, the more diving is condemned, the less players will be inclined to use it.

COMMENTS AND QUESTIONS

1. *Cheating revisited—Weber's definition.* According to Bruce Weber, what, precisely, *is* the "qualitative difference" between cheating and gamesmanship? Is "deviousness" okay—i.e., gamesmanship, not cheating—if it is *either* spontaneous *or* "in response to the action on the field," or is it okay only if *both* criteria are satisfied? Or is Weber's claim something else entirely? Do you read him to be maintaining that old-time baseball players did nothing wrong by cutting across the infield from first to third behind the back of an umpire? Do you agree?

2. *Spontaneity.* Why is spontaneity relevant at all to the existence of cheating? Weber contends that it is "good baseball"—and not cheating—for a base runner on second to try to steal the catcher's signs and relay them to the hitter. This appears to be a nearly universal judgment. *See, e.g.*, TURBOW, THE BASEBALL CODES. Would it be cheating if the base runner had planned in advance to try to steal signs in the event that he were to reach second? If it is not plausible that action which would not be cheating when spontaneous necessarily becomes cheating when planned in advance, is it any more

plausible that spontaneity necessarily prevents a ruse from counting as cheating? Consider the A-Rod incident. Even he seems to acknowledge that he might have crossed some important line had he shouted "Mine!" instead of "Ha!" Do you agree? If so, would it matter whether the shout was premeditated? Does a student who copies answers from a fellow student's exam not cheat if she hadn't planned to do it before the opportunity presented itself?

3.   *Sport as metaphor.* To ask that last question is to invite a consideration of Weber's plea that we all "just call a halt to the professional-sport-as-a-metaphor-for-life thing." What exactly do you think he is calling for? Do most people who employ the metaphor in one form or another generally claim or believe that moral or evaluative judgments that are proper in one domain are "automatically transferable" to the other, or does the metaphor serve somewhat more modest ends? If you agree that it is not difficult for an adult to explain *that* it is okay for a ballplayer to pretend to be safe when he knows he was out, but not okay for a student to plagiarize, is it comparably easy to explain *why* that is? Put another way, if an adult is unable to provide her child with a full and comprehensive catalogue of permissible and impermissible types of deception, and wishes instead to supply the child with a general principle or test that he can use to sort out for himself future cases that might arise, what should she say?

4.   *The logical incompatibility thesis.* Note Torres's claim that it is "logically contradictory to simultaneously accept the rules of soccer and to circumvent them when opportunities arise." He is here invoking what sports philosophers call "the logical incompatibility thesis" (briefly flagged in Mark Hamilton's argument against make-up calls, p. 389): it is *logically* impossible to win games by willfully breaking rules because, insofar as games (including sports) just are collections of rules, one who willfully breaks the rules is not in fact playing the game. And you can't win a game that you aren't playing. *See* WARREN FRALEIGH, RIGHT ACTIONS IN SPORTS: ETHICS FOR CONTESTANTS (1984). Is this correct? If not, why not? If you think it's mistaken, would you agree that it is impossible to win a game by intentionally violating the game's *constitutive* rules?

5.   *Jeter cheater?* After the game, in admitting that the ball hit his bat, Derek Jeter said: "He told me to go to first base. I'm not going to tell him I'm not going to first, you know. It's part of the game. My job is to get on base." That's a convenient way to spin things, but his critics did not contend that Jeter should have declined when the umpire directed him to first; they did not maintain that he had an affirmative duty to correct the umpire's misimpression. (We explore this possibility below, pp. 541–548.) Rather, they objected to his engaging in theatrics designed to deceive the umpire into believing that he had been hit—a dance of pain, followed by a visit from the Yankees trainer.[g] Was this cheating? If not, why do you think that, after the fact, Jeter was less than forthright when describing the nature of his conduct?

---

[g]   *See, e.g.,* Dan Welin, *MLB Replay Debate Resurfaces: Is Derek Jeter a Cheater?*, Bleacher Report (Sept. 16, 2010); Four Corners, *Was it OK for Jeter to fake getting hit by pitch?*, CHICAGO

6. Flopping. In some sports, notably soccer and basketball, flopping (also known as diving and simulation) is a recurrent issue: A player purposely falls or otherwise reacts in a way suggesting that he has been fouled by an opponent. Flopping raises several interesting issues, explored below.

a. Social contingency? Weber asserts that "it is not only acceptable but entirely accepted that soccer players will careen to the ground after a slight jostle, hoping to induce a yellow card." As the article by Cesar Torres proves, Weber's claim is surely wrong as a purely descriptive matter: although views regarding the propriety of flopping vary widely across soccer subcommunities, many observers think the practice is not remotely acceptable. For example, in a 2000 survey administered by the English Premier League, a whopping 89% of fans identified players "pretend[ing] to be fouled" as the single aspect of the sport that most angered them. *See also, e.g.,* Natalie Alvarez, *Foul Play: Soccer's "Infamous Thespians" and the Cultural Politics of Diving,* DRAMA REVIEW 10 (2016) ("In the xenophobic imagination, diving has become a means of delineating the dividing lines between those who do ('them') and those who don't ('us'), suggesting that the world FIFA imagines in its official slogan—'Football means hope and brings the peoples of the world together'—is perhaps less united than it is willing to admit.")

Is flopping by soccer players cheating? Does the answer vary across soccer subcommunities? How about flopping by basketball players? Is there a critical difference between exaggerating minor contact and feigning contact that did not occur at all?

b. Flopping and the formal rules. In 2008, FIFA amended its rules to provide specifically: "Any simulating action anywhere on the field, which is intended to deceive the referee, must be sanctioned as unsporting behaviour. This act of misconduct is punishable by yellow card." FIFA Law 12, Decision 5. Does an in-game penalty for flopping imposed by an on-field official make sense? Doesn't it amount to punishment for the official's perception of bad acting—with the risk that in fact the penalized player *wasn't* acting and the wrong side is penalized? If the official is persuaded that the player on the ground is flopping, why isn't it a satisfactory response to say, "Play on!," knowing that the player has put his team at a competitive disadvantage by taking himself out of the play to no advantage?

In the United States, Major League Soccer has been more aggressive. In June 2011, it fined D.C. United forward Charlie Davies $1,000 for putting the game into disrepute for a dive in a match against Real Salt Lake. The League's Disciplinary Committee ruled that Davis "intentionally deceived the officials and gained an unfair advantage which directly impacted the match," the League's Executive Vice President, Nelson Rodriguez, said. "This type of behavior tarnishes the image of the League, is detrimental to the game and will not be tolerated." *MLS Disciplinary Committee fines Davies for dive vs. RSL,* MLS SOCCER.COM (June 24, 2011) (noting that players and coaches had

TRIBUNE, Sept. 16, 2010; Larry Brown, *Derek Jeter Made the Right Baseball Move,* LARRY BROWN SPORTS (Sept. 16, 2010).

expressed a wish to see a decrease diving, embellishment, and other simulation intended to deceive the officials). And the following month, the Disciplinary Committee suspended as well as fined a player for diving. Mr. Rodriguez said, "We will continue to impose sanctions, and even increase their level, if necessary, in an attempt to eliminate this type of behavior." *RSL's Saborío fined, suspended for dive vs. Quakes,* MLS SOCCER.COM (July 29, 2011).

Is this approach correct? Does it have any advantage over IFAB's Decision 5? What problem(s), if any, does it leave unsolved?

c.   *But is it a flop?* If flopping is to be penalized one way or another, then officials must determine, either on the spot or afterwards, that the conduct really was a flop. That is not always so easy. Consider, for example, the crucial call of a dive made on the Italian star Fernando Totti in a 2002 World Cup match against South Korea. Watch the play: https://tinyurl.com/y5fvppml.

What was the proper call here? No foul by the defender, and a penalty on Totti? (That was the actual call; Totti's yellow card, his second, removed him from the game.) "Play on"—no foul either way? A foul by the defender? If so, with a card?

Four years later, the shoe was on the other foot: In a World Cup match against Australia, the referee ruled that Totti's teammate, Fabio Grosso, was fouled by Lucas Neill. Italy eventually won the Cup. But did Grosso dive? Watch the play: https://tinyurl.com/y4a45xz7.

Grosso later said: "[M]aybe I accentuated it a little bit. . . . I felt the contact so I went down." Matthew Hall, *Grosso owns up,* THE WORLD GAME (Nov. 13, 2012). For other possible dives in soccer, see a clip of Christiano Ronaldo in Euro 2008, *Ronaldo is a cheater,* YOUTUBE, https://tinyurl.com/y4cqq48x, and a collection, *The Worst Football Dives Ever—Ham Actors,* YOUTUBE, https://tinyurl.com/nqjuvu7.

d.   *Flopping for competitive balance.* Assuming Cesar Torres is right that soccer was originally "meant to test" a set of skills that does not include flopping, does the prevalence of flopping alter the situation so that refusal to flop is essentially a counterpart to unilateral disarmament? *See* Sam Borden, *Where Dishonesty Is Best Policy, U.S. Soccer Falls Short,* N.Y. TIMES, June 16, 2014, at A1. After noting American players' disinclination to flop, Borden quotes one American player as saying, "[I]f you're the U.S., at what point do you say, If you can't beat 'em, join 'em?" And he quotes Tim Howard, the veteran American goalkeeper, as saying that he had "no problem" with a seemingly obvious flop by a Brazilian player and, "I would encourage my own players, if they felt contact, to go down."

e.   *The skill of flopping.* Does Torres beg the question in referring to "what the game was meant to test"? Given the complexity of a game such as soccer or basketball, is this even a sensible question to ask—or is there any sensible answer other than that the game was meant to test the complex combination of skills that maximizes the chance of winning?

If you doubt that flopping requires skill, consider the remarkable article by Frank Ramsey, then of the Boston Celtics and a future Hall of Famer, with Frank Deford, *Smart Moves by a Master of Deception*, SPORTS ILLUSTRATED, Dec. 9, 1963, at 57. Complete with illustrations, the article gives detailed instructions on how to draw an undeserved foul. For example, under the heading, *Why I Fall*, Ramsey writes, "Drawing fouls chiefly requires the ability to provide good, heartwarming drama and to direct it to the right audience." Discussing a situation in which his opponent has a clear lane to the basket, Ramsey says:

> I shift my weight to get as much of my body as I can in front of him without moving my feet. If the official is anywhere behind me, it will appear as if I am in front of my man.

> Then, at the first contact, I fall down—as if my man had charged right into me. With any luck, the foul I deserve will be called on the other guy.

Is Ramsey advising proper conduct?

Should the outcome of a trial depend on the dramatic flair of the lawyers? Does it? Should lawyers decline to be dramatic? In determining whether diving ought to be regarded with contempt, should it matter whether skill is required to perform it well?

7. *Framing, disguised traps, and other optimistic presentations.* Weber endorses a baseball catcher's "framing" of pitches—drawing them towards the strike zone as he catches them. Do you agree? *See generally, e.g.*, Ben Lindbergh, *The Art of Pitch Framing*, GRANTLAND (May 16, 2013).[h] Is framing materially different from any of these practices?

- A batter has three balls, looks at the next pitch, and starts breaking to first base, without really knowing that the pitch was a ball; perhaps she is unsure, or perhaps she thinks she was fooled by a pitch on the corner.

- In basketball, players from both teams handle the ball just before it goes out of bounds—and as soon as it does, they each head towards their own basket, as if they are sure (though obviously they can't both be correct) that the ball was last touched by the opponent.

- A gymnast is very dissatisfied with her performance on the uneven bars. But as she does her final dismount she makes sure to smile and thrust her arms up in apparent triumph.

---

[h] *Compare* Dave Weaver, *Don't Ever Let Your Catchers Frame a Pitch!*, HITTING WORLD.COM (2005):

> I do not want to see my catchers catching a pitch that clearly is a ball and pulling, pushing, or somehow moving the glove to try and reposition the pitch at a spot they feel will get them a strike call. I don't want them trying to "Make a ball look like a strike." The best way to keep a strike looking like a strike is to never do anything that would make it look like a ball.

- One successful trial lawyer made a practice of smiling broadly and noticeably after every sidebar in a jury trial, no matter what the outcome had been. (One opposing lawyer was so rankled that he asked the court to prevent this practice.)

If a baseball fielder or a football receiver holds aloft a ball that he has caught near the ground—perhaps trapping it on a very short hop—is there any plausible way to understand the conduct other than as an attempt to deceive the officials into thinking he caught it? Assuming that it is an attempt at deception, do you think it is proper? If so, is it also permissible for a cricket fielder to do the same? Ed Smith, former professional cricketer and author, contends that it isn't. In cricket, he says, it's cheating for a fielder to try to deceive the umpire into believing (mistakenly) that he caught the ball on a fly, but it is not cheating for a batsman to try to deceive the umpire into believing (mistakenly) that he did not nick a ball subsequently caught by the wicket keeper. ED SMITH, WHAT SPORT TELLS US ABOUT LIFE: BRADMAN'S AVERAGE, ZIDANE'S KISS AND OTHER SPORTING LESSONS 123 (2008). Can these views be reconciled? Do they lend support to the idea that what is permissible and what isn't in sport depend solely on what the customs of that sport just happen to be, and that nothing more can be said?

8. *The hand of God.* Luis Suarez has denied that his intentional handball against Ghana, see p. 469, constituted cheating or was otherwise improper. To the contrary, he proudly proclaimed that "The 'Hand of God' now belongs to me. Mine is the real 'Hand of God.' " *World Cup 2010: Uruguay Striker Luis Suarez says it was 'Hand of God' against Ghana*, TELEGRAPH, July 3, 2010. He was referring to the infamous handball goal scored by Argentina's Diego Maradona against England in the quarter finals of the 1986 FIFA World Cup. Wikipedia has identified that goal as "[o]ne of the most famous instances of cheating" in sports history. *Cheating*, WIKIPEDIA, https://tinyurl.com/p2yg3 nb.

Was it cheating, or was Maradona fully entitled to try to deceive the referee? Note that players who score off a handball do not always stay mum. In a game in Italy's top soccer league, Serie A, Lazio forward Miroslav Klose was credited for a fourth-minute goal against rival Napoli before he informed the referee that he had accidentally handled the ball. The goal was disallowed, Lazio went on to lose 3–0, and Klose won praise from his teammates and from FIFA President Sepp Blatter, for his honesty. See Miles Chambers, *Klose handball confession draws praise from FIFA president Sepp Blatter*, GOAL.COM (Sept. 27, 2012).

9. *Any limits?* Most attempts by an athlete to deceive officials are not verbal. But occasionally, an athlete has an opportunity to lie to an official. For example, in one youth baseball game, the umpires could not tell, because the sun was in their eyes, whether a batted ball had gone over the fence on the fly. They asked the center fielder, who had a better view (and who knew the ball had indeed gone over on the fly). What should he have said or done? If you think it would have been inappropriate for him to lie to the umps, how do you

distinguish this case from any of the ones discussed above in which you thought the deception was permissible conduct?

D. STALLING

A basketball shot clock reflects a bright-line rule: If a team fails to shoot within the time allowed, it loses possession, no matter how aggressively it was trying to score, and if within the allowed time it gets off a shot that hits the rim it can, if it gets the rebound, retain possession, no matter how much it was attempting to kill time before shooting. Compare sports such as wrestling and judo, which penalize stalling, by open-textured rules that may be more accurately characterized as standards. Here is the definition of stalling in wrestling from the Rule Book of the National Federation of High Schools (NFHS):

> Each wrestler is required to make an honest attempt to stay within the 10 foot circle and wrestle aggressively, regardless of position or the time or score of the match. Action is to be maintained throughout the match by the contestants wrestling aggressively whether in the top, bottom or neutral position and both contestants are equally responsible for initiating action. It is the responsibility of contestants, coaches and referees to avoid the use of stalling tactics or allowing the use thereof. This shall be demonstrated by those responsible with strict enforcement by referees.

Rule 5–25–1 & Rule 7–6–1. In an article presented by the NFHS, an experienced wrestling referee explains:

> For as long as interscholastic wrestling has been contested, the question of stalling has been of [paramount] concern to both coaches and officials. Every year, questions arises as to how stalling is to be called or how can I coach a wrestler to stall without being penalized. All must realize that stalling is an art, it is coached, and it is a violation and it must be penalized. Coaching stalling as a tactic, in either the offensive, defensive or neutral position, is well documented. Coaches and athletes must accept the fact that if they do stall, they will be penalized for stalling. Rules 5–25 & 7–6 requires each wrestler to make an honest attempt to wrestle aggressively. Coaches need to coach this and officials need to penalize when aggressive wrestling does not take place. . . .

Dick Loewenstine, *NFHS Wrestling "Stalling,"* https://tinyurl.com/y4b7 wuza.

What, if anything, is wrong with stalling? Is it comparable to a basketball team with a big lead slowing the ball down, or a football team with a lead running the clock out, perhaps by taking a knee near the end of the game? (We consider a famous incident of a team that did *not* take a knee below, p. 523.)

COMMENTS AND QUESTIONS

1. *A slow trip to the mound.* Baseball and softball are ordinarily played without time limits, and so they take a relatively lenient stance to mid-inning timeouts. But as a matter of necessity games in youth tournaments are time-limited. Consider this incident from a girls' 14U softball tournament, in Kalamazoo, Michigan, July 22, 2007: The team designated as the home team was losing a game narrowly in the bottom of the sixth inning with two outs and nobody on, one strike on the batter, and seconds to go before time expired. If the inning finished before time ran out, the game would continue another inning, and the home team would have the top of its order coming up in its half of the inning, with a far better chance to score. But the visiting coach came out to talk to the pitcher—for what reason was not readily apparent—and time ran out.

Was the coach's conduct appropriate? If not, should the formal rules governing a tournament, or umpires' practices, be amended to prevent such conduct or take away the incentive for engaging in it? If so, how should this be accomplished? Assuming no such change, what criteria should guide an ethical coach in determining whether to come out to talk to the pitcher when time is close to expiring and her team is ahead? Consider comparable questions for the other cases—should formal rules or official practice be changed, and if not what ethical principles should constrain the actors?

2. *Why stall?* Consider these three distinct reasons why a competitor might be moved to intentionally slow the contest. First, in timed sports, stalling allows a side that's ahead to reduce its opponent's opportunities to overcome a scoring deficit or otherwise improve an outcome (as by getting a pin in wrestling). This might explain the slow trip to the mound and kneel-downs in football. Second, a side might stall if unable to compete effectively at an opponent's preferred faster pace of play. Third, stalling can serve to check an opponent's momentum. This is a common function of stalling in tennis. Can you identify other common purposes behind stalling? Do you think that any are more or less discreditable than others?

E.   TRASH TALKING, TAUNTING, AND CELEBRATION

The 2006 World Cup championship match between Italy and France may have turned on a remarkable incident that occurred deep into overtime. After Marco Materazzi of Italy and Zinedine Zidane of France exchanged words, Zidane head-butted Materazzi. The referee apparently did not see the incident, but another official called his attention to it. Thus, after a short delay, Zidane—the great star of the France side, playing in his last game—was given the red card, and France had to play a man down the rest of the way. Ultimately, Italy won 5–3 in a shootout. (Italy shot first; only one French player missed his shot.) A short clip including the head butt itself is at https://tinyurl.com/yyjagq8w.

Two months after the match, Materazzi said: "I did not provoke him, I responded verbally to a provocation. We both spoke and I wasn't the first. I held his shirt but don't you think it is a provocation to say that 'if you want my shirt I will give it you afterwards'?" *Materazzi reveals insult to Zidane*, CNN.com (Sept. 5, 2006). In a 2014 interview, Materazzi gave a fuller account:

> . . . I was close enough to Zidane to stop him jumping. I put my arm around him and gave him a little tug, with my body on him. Pretty standard stuff: it happens 100s of times a game.
>
> I quickly apologised, but he kept saying, over and over again, that if I wanted his shirt so badly, I could have it after the game. He wouldn't stop. So I said that, instead of his shirt, I'd rather have his sister. That was it. That's all it was.
>
> Maybe it was the adrenaline; maybe it was the fatigue; maybe it was the occasion. But the next thing that happened was so difficult to understand. He walked towards me and, out of the blue, headbutted me in the chest.
>
> It was the last thing I expected. Had I anticipated it and raised my hands, odds are we would both have been sent off. I have no idea what went through his mind. . . . What I said wasn't very nice perhaps, but it was no different from the trash talking that takes place at any level of football, from the schoolyard to, as we saw, the World Cup final. I'm sure he heard far worse many, many times.

World Cup Memories: 'I have no idea what went through his mind,' ESPN.com (May 22, 2014).

Materazzi's "That was it" assertion appears not to square perfectly with his report, in yet another interview, a year after the episode, that his exact words were, "I prefer the whore that is your sister." *And Materazzi's exact words to Zidane were. . .*, GUARDIAN, Aug. 18, 2007. But Materazzi took great umbrage at reports in three British tabloids that he had called Zidane "the son of a terrorist whore"; he sued the three and secured substantial settlements from all three and apologies from two. *Materazzi wins British libel damages over Sun's claims about Zidane head-butt,* GUARDIAN, Feb. 6, 2009. Part of his objection to this rendition was its racial overtones; Zidane's parents came from a Berber-speaking region of Algeria. But Materazzi was principally offended by the accusation that he had referred to Zidane's mother. "I may have said nasty things over my career,"

Materazzi said in the 2014 interview, "but I have never referred to anyone's mother. I lost my own when I was 15-years-old and it's something I have always avoided." As for Zidane's sister, Materazzi acknowledged in the 2006 interview that if he owed an apology to anybody it was to her, but he insisted, "I swear, before all this mess I didn't even know Zidane had a sister."

The Zidane-Materazzi incident appears to exemplify a point made by Jeffri Chadiha, writing in the context of the NFL:

> What most players understand is that trash-talking isn't really about humiliating an opponent. It's about controlling minds, by any means necessary. It's a big mental victory when a guard becomes more concerned with beating up an opposing defensive lineman instead of executing his block. It's exhilarating for a receiver to know a defensive back is more concerned with laying him out than maintaining his coverage responsibilities. And we haven't even mentioned the thrill of coaxing opponents into penalties. The players who talk trash savor all those rewards and they don't waste time getting started. . . .

Jeffri Chadiha, *Trash talk: All about finding an edge*, ESPN.com (Jan. 29, 2014).

Chadiha describes a remarkable 1998 incident involving two ultimate Hall of Famers: Shannon Sharpe, a tight end for the Denver Broncos, learned the phone number of the girlfriend of Derrick Thomas, a linebacker for the Kansas City Chiefs, and recited it one digit at a time during the Bronco's final drive of a 30–7 victory. Thomas committed three personal fouls—one involving Sharpe's face-mask—and was suspended for a game by his own team. *See* Leonard Shapiro, *Chiefs Suspend Thomas After Defense Meltdown*, WASH. POST, Nov. 18, 1998. "It was my finest moment," Sharpe later reflected.

Chadiha notes the "one unwritten rule of trash-talking: You had better have serious game if you're going to do it." A corollary, he says, is that one of two ways to silence a trash-talker is to win. And the other

> is to not engage him. [Former defensive end, and noted trash talker Chuck Smith] spent years trying to aggravate Hall of Fame offensive tackle Willie Roaf—they faced off twice a year for seven seasons when Roaf was playing in New Orleans—and that never worked out. Smith would talk smack after plays. He'd nudge Roaf when he was walking back to the huddle. Every time the stoic Roaf would shrug it off and line up to go right back at his nemesis. . . .

As for potential official responses to trash talk, consider Kurt Helin's take on a 2010 incident in which Kevin Garnett, then of the Boston Celtics, allegedly called Charlie Villanueva of the Detroit Pistons a "cancer patient"; Villanueva in fact has alopecia universalis, which causes total hair loss. After noting that the league had the technical power to fine or suspend Garnett, Helin wrote:

> But what Garnett is a vocal practitioner of is common in the NBA. Guys get on each other. Hard. Mountains of trash talk fly around an on an NBA court. It is vicious and nothing is sacred— questioning manhood, family and everything else goes on. Nightly. And has for generations—Michael Jordan was ruthless with his mouth just like his game. Same with Larry Bird. And so on and so on. . .
>
> If you fine or suspend Garnett for this comment, you are on a slippery slope. A derogatory term for homosexuals gets used during games often, is that worthy of a fine every time? Curse words? Only when a referee hears it?
>
> . . . Trash talk takes place on playground courts, high school gyms and the YMCA. Guys grew up doing it. Then they get to the NBA and have to be saints?
>
> There was a time when this could be enforced on the court. When Villanueva or a team's designated enforcer could inflict some physical pain on Garnett for these antics, and said enforcer would get tossed for the game for it. And that was all. So teams had enforcers. Now the fines and suspensions make that kind of retribution impossible.
>
> Trash talk is part of the game. You don't have to like it. But you can't fine and suspend for it, not even over-the-line comments about cancer.

Kurt Helin, *Kevin Garnett talks trash. The league should do nothing about it.*, NBC Sports.com (Nov. 3, 2010).

COMMENTS AND QUESTIONS

1. Of sticks and stones. Should trash talk be prohibited and penalized by rule? If so, what should the standard be for determining just what trash talk is to be punished? Racial or other ethnic insults? References to a player's anatomy or medical condition? To a player's manhood? To a player's femininity? Hairstyle? Girlfriend? Ability in the sport? Chances of winning? Anything at all (on the theory that in most sports a player ordinarily has no need whatsoever to address remarks to an opponent)?

If trash talk should be prohibited, should a professional league make efforts to detect it (such as by miking players or amplifying the sound track of a tape of the game)? Assuming that a league makes no such efforts, is it troublesome that trash talk will be punished only if noticed by an official, and that usually it will not be noticed?

If trash talk should be penalized, should the penalty be an in-game sanction (for example, a technical foul or yardage, or ejection), or one imposed afterwards? And if the latter, what should the nature of it be? A fine? Suspension? A requirement that the player prepare a video emphasizing the need for civility? Something else?

Does "who started it" matter? Is Materazzi's conduct excused or mitigated by any of these facts (assuming they are so): That Zidane had provoked him? That comments like Materazzi's are common in elite soccer? That the comment referred to Zidane's sister rather than to his mother? That the comment appears, or should have appeared to be, a generic insult, not one based on actual familiarity with the life of Zidane's sister? Is Materazzi's comment materially different from a common generic two-word insult purporting to refer to intimate relations between the target and his mother?

NFL Rule 12, Section 3, Article 1, provides:

> There shall be no unsportsmanlike conduct. This applies to any act which is contrary to the generally understood principles of sportsmanship. Such acts specifically include, among others: . . .
>
> (b) The use of abusive, threatening, or insulting language or gestures to opponents, teammates, officials, or representatives of the League.
>
> (c) Using baiting or taunting acts or words that engender ill will between teams.

Is this a well-formulated rule?

2. *Walking the talk.* How disapproving of "insulting language" and "baiting or taunting acts" do you believe the NFL actually is? *See Picking the best trash-talker for all 32 NFL teams,* ESPN.com (Jan. 31, 2016).

3. *Out of bounds?* Should leagues specially prohibit taunts based on what American law often calls "protected classes," such as people of a given race, religion, or sexual orientation? Note that in 2014 the NFL's Competition Committee considered but decided not to adopt a rule specifically targeting racial slurs and references to sexual orientation—but it noted at the same time that the current rules empower officials to punish them, and it said this would be "a very significant point of emphasis." Chris Burke, *NFL Competition Committee passes on n-word rule, considers extra point changes,* SPORTS ILLUSTRATED, Mar. 19, 2014.

In 2011, the NBA fined Kobe Bryant $100,000 and Joakim Noah $50,000 for antigay slurs directed at a referee and a taunting fan, respectively. Were these appropriate? If so, would they have been appropriate if the slurs had been directed at players? In answering the last question, would it matter what the sexual orientation of the targeted player was understood to be? What if Bryant or Noah had responded to taunts from a significantly overweight fan with slurs about his weight? In answering this question, consider these comments from British singer Sam Smith, who is gay and at times has been overweight:

> "If someone called me fat, that affects me way more than someone calling me a f-----," said the crooner. "I think just because I've accepted that, if someone calls me a f-----, it's like, I am gay and I'm proud to be gay so there's no issues there."

> Smith said the "fat" comments resonate more because "that's something [he] can change."

Lindsay Kimble, *Sam Smith Says Being Called Fat Hurts Him More Than Anti-Gay Slurs*, PEOPLE, Apr. 19, 2015.

    4.   *Butt out?* In the closing seconds of the 2014 NFC championship game, Richard Sherman, cornerback for the Seattle Seahawks, swatted away a pass intended in the end zone for Michael Crabtree, a receiver for the San Francisco 49ers; the pass was then intercepted by Sherman's teammate Malcolm Smith, effectively locking up a win that sent the Seahawks to the Super Bowl. Sherman patted Crabtree on the butt and offered a handshake. Such a nice friendly gesture—and Sherman was rewarded with a shove to the face mask by Crabtree, an unsportsmanlike-conduct penalty, and later a $7,875 fine. (He did also make a choke sign towards the San Francisco bench and belittle Crabtree in a televised postgame interview.) Kevin Patra, *Richard Sherman: 'I'm the best corner in the game'*, NFL.com (Jan. 19, 2014); *Richard Sherman vs. Michael Crabtree*, YouTube, https://tinyurl.com/yydvrkso. Just what, if anything, was wrong with Sherman's conduct immediately after the play?

    5.   *Celebration.* Until 2017, the NFL's Rule 12, Section 3, Article 1, prohibited the following, along with insulting and taunting language and conduct:

> (d) Individual players involved in prolonged or excessive celebrations. Players are prohibited from engaging in any celebrations while on the ground. A celebration shall be deemed excessive or prolonged if a player continues to celebrate after a warning from an official.

> (e) Two-or-more players engage in prolonged, excessive, premeditated, or choreographed celebrations.

> (f) Possession or use of foreign or extraneous object(s) that are not part of the uniform during the game on the field or the sideline, or using the ball as a prop.

Despite this rule, NFL.com has long presented a celebratory video of the Top 10 touchdown celebrations of all time. Several of them appear to have violated this rule, especially the prohibition on choreographed celebrations; LaDainian Tomlinson, the Ickey Shuffle, Deion Sanders' high step, and Billy "White Shoes" Johnson's Funky Chicken were choreographed *and* used the ball as a prop.

What is wrong with choreographed celebrations? If after a touchdown two players did the Parent-Trap handshake, *see The Parent Trap Handshake*, CAMP CRESTRIDGE FOR GIRLS, https://tinyurl.com/yxlyfgxr (though they might choose not to identify it that way), should that be prohibited? If so, how much of it could they do before crossing the line?

6. Grounded. What is wrong with celebrations on the ground? In September 2014, safety Husain Abdullah of the Kansas City Chiefs returned an interception against the New England Patriots for a touchdown. Several yards after crossing the goal line, he slid to his knees and in a continuous motion took a prayerful position near the back of the end zone. Chris Chase, *NFL refs defend penalty on Husain Abdullah (but not because of the prayer)*, USA TODAY, Oct. 2, 2014. He was charged with unsportsmanlike conduct, but the next morning an NFL spokesman said that the call was incorrect: "[A] player who goes to the ground as part of religious expression should not be penalized. While he did slide immediately before beginning his prayer, this was not a correct call and the play should not have resulted in a penalty." Monique N. Jones, *NFL referee association says league graded Husain Abdullah call as correct*, USA Today, Oct. 2, 2014. Two days later, though, the NFL Referees Association issued a statement asserting that the penalty was correct as graded by the league. Scott Green, a former president of the Association, said:

> Both the officials and the player involved in the unsportsmanlike conduct penalty were not confused as to why a flag was thrown. The player was flagged, correctly, for the slide on his knees in the end zone, not for going to the ground in a prayerful gesture. . . . On field officials are aware of the prayer provision and respect the right of players of all faiths to express themselves.

The "prayer provision" did not appear to exist in the Official Rules. But assuming that such a provision is read into the Rules, was penalizing Abdullah a sensible application of the Rule as it stood? Did the Rule make any sense?

In any event, the NFL has now taken a much less aggressive stance towards celebrations. Clauses (d), (e), and (f) of Rule 12, Section 3, Article 1 now prohibit only:

> (d) Any violent gesture, or an act that is sexually suggestive or offensive.
>
> (e) Prolonged or excessive celebrations or demonstrations by an individual player or multiple players.
>
> (f) Using any object as a prop, or possessing any foreign or extraneous object(s) that are not part of the uniform on the field or the sideline during the game, other than the football after a scoring play or change of possession.

Does this set of provisions give adequate guidance on what is and is not allowed?

7.   *Spikes*. In 2013, Jimmy Graham, a receiver for the New Orleans Saints, knocked the goalpost crooked while dunking the ball over the crossbar after catching a touchdown pass against the Atlanta Falcons; the game was delayed while workers set the post aright. *Jimmy Graham TD/breaks goal post*, YOUTUBE, https://tinyurl.com/y4z48ko2. Before the 2014 season, the league announced that it would interpret the "ball as a prop" restriction to prohibit dunks like Graham's. In a preseason game against the Tennessee Titans in 2014, Graham dunked twice—costing him $30,000 and his team a total of 30 yards, which led him to promise he would not do it any more. Was the prohibition sensible? If so, because the ball was used as a prop—which is no longer prohibited—or for some other reason? Was this a sound way of implementation?

The elimination of the prohibition on using the ball as a prop after a scoring play was a bow to reality. After all, spiking the ball appears to have been using it as a prop even without the ball going over the goalpost. What *could* a player do with the ball after scoring? Barry Sanders always simply handed it to the officials—was that a subtle use of the ball as a celebratory prop?

8.   *Race*. Are the NFL rules on celebration attempts to curb a largely Black style of play in deference to white tastes? Is that a problem if so, or simply a financially defensible response to the market?

9.   *Fans*. The NCAA is stricter than the NFL in at least one respect; players are not allowed to interact with fans or go into the crowd. What is wrong with gesturing to the fans? *See SEC: Penalty on Green a bad call*, ESPN.com (Oct. 5, 2009) (conference declares that crucial call in Georgia-LSU game was incorrect; on-field official had incorrectly thought that player gestured to crowd after scoring touchdown). Thus, Number 5 on the NFL.com video, the Lambeau Leap, by which Green Bay Packers players vault into the home crowd at Lambeau Field after a touchdown, would be illegal in college ball; should it be legal in the NFL? Is the Lambeau Leap preferable to some forms of team celebration because it is off the field? *Because* it involves the fans? If a baseball crowd calls for a "curtain call" after a routine home run, is it proper for the player who hit the homer to come out and take a bow?

10.   *Hanging on*. NBA Rule 12.A provides in part:

Section IV—Basket Ring, Backboard, or Support

a.   An offensive player who deliberately hangs on his basket ring, net, backboard or support during the game shall be assessed a non-unsportsmanlike technical foul and a $500 fine.

b.   A defensive player who deliberately gains or maintains height or hangs on his opponent's basket ring, net, backboard or support shall be assessed a non-unsportsmanlike technical foul. If he touches the ball during a field goal attempt, points shall be awarded consistent with the type of shot.

EXCEPTION: An offensive or defensive player may hang on the basket ring, backboard or support to prevent an injury to himself or another player, with no technical foul assessed.

c.   Should a defensive player deliberately hang on the basket ring, net, backboard or support to successfully touch a ball which is in possession of an opponent, an unsportsmanlike technical foul shall be assessed.

High school and college basketball have similar rules. But the widespread perception is that enforcement becomes looser at the more elite levels of the game. "[I]n reality," says one observer, "this 'rule' does not exist; kind of like 'travelling.' Which is OK, but then the league should just admit that it doesn't exist. Guys do it all the time. The great king LeBron himself swears by it." Mark Vandeusen, *Did the NBA secretly eliminate the "hanging on the rim" technical foul?*, NEXT IMPULSE SPORTS (Apr. 25, 2013). Doing chin-ups while on the rim, however, appears to be inviting a technical foul. *See, e.g., Nate Robinson alley-oop dunk*, YOUTUBE, https://tinyurl.com/y29kepkm.

Just what is wrong with hanging on the rim? Should it be treated as misconduct only if it is deemed to be taunting? If so, how should an official determine whether it is taunting?

Is hanging on the rim comparable to an athlete roaring and thumping his chest after a big point? Novak Djokovic, the tennis champion, does that routinely. Though some players and fans don't like it, it isn't penalized.

11.   At contest's end. After winning the Australian Open in 2012, Djokovic not only bellowed and beat his chest but also ripped off his shirt. Is there, or should there be, any greater tolerance for celebration, even if choreographed, after a contest is over? In September 2009, Prince Fielder of the Milwaukee Brewers hit a walk-off home run in the 12th inning of a game against the San Francisco Giants. His teammates gathered about the plate. The game ended when Fielder jumped on the plate and held his arms aloft—and as he did, the Brew Crew collapsed around him, as if they were bowling pins struck by a very large ball. https://tinyurl.com/yxs2uztp. Longtime outfielder Torii Hunter said, "Baseball is not like the NFL, where you can celebrate in the end zone. You've got to keep your cool, play the game. You can't do that." During the off-season, the Brewers' manager apologized to the Giants' manager, but the books were not closed on the incident until March, in the first inning of a preseason game, when Barry Zito of the Giants plunked Fielder on the back; this was understood to be retaliation for the September incident. Jerry Crasnick, *Zito hits Fielder, without further incident*, ESPN.com (Mar. 4, 2010). (On pitcher retaliation and informal norms, see generally pp. 114–118.)

12.   Informal norms. As the previous question evidences, many sports police taunting and celebration, not through formal rules crafted and enforced by league officials, but by means of informal norms enforced by the players themselves. What are the advantages and disadvantages of allowing the players to police themselves?

13. The home run trot. Are informal norms regarding taunting and excessive celebration in fact very sensible? Consider, for example, that a baseball pitcher who gives up a home run is likely to take great umbrage if the batter stands too long at home plate watching the ball or if he takes too long circling the bases. *See, e.g.,* TURBOW, BASEBALL CODES, at 62 ("At or near the top of any pitcher's peeves is the home run pimp, a hitter who lingers in the batter's box as the ball soars over the wall.") But such conduct is likely to be more a product of the batter's wanting to savor the moment than trying to show up the pitcher. Bernie Augustine, *David Ortiz sets record for slowest home run trot after hitting game-winning homer for Red Sox against Rangers*, N.Y. DAILY NEWS, Apr. 10, 2014. Should a pitcher tolerate it?

14. Formal rules and informal norms. Even if you conclude that informal norms should play a significant role—perhaps even a leading or exclusive role—in establishing and enforcing proper norms regarding taunting and celebration, that does not mean that formal rules should play no part. As Larry Lessig's analysis of indirect methods of regulation taught (see p. 114), leagues can use formal rules to try to shape informal rules. Should leagues attempt to alter the norms that produce trash talking and similar behaviors? How might they proceed?

———

Exercise 14E

The NBA undertakes an annual rulebook review, aiming to head off problems before they arise. This year (let us suppose), the taunting rules were on the agenda.

NBA Rule 12.A, Section V provides in relevant part as follows:

(a) An official may assess a technical foul, without prior warning, at any time. A technical foul(s) may be assessed to any player on the court or anyone seated on the bench for conduct which, in the opinion of an official, is detrimental to the game. . . .

(d) A technical foul shall be assessed for unsportsmanlike tactics such as:

1. Disrespectfully addressing an official

2. Physically contacting an official

3. Overt actions indicating resentment to a call or no-call

4. Use of profanity

5. A coach entering onto the court without permission of an official

6.   A deliberately-thrown elbow or any unnatural physical act towards an opponent with no contact involved

7.   Taunting

Taunting is not defined. Comment P of the Official Comment on the Rules adds:

> If a player blatantly taunts an opponent, a technical foul shall be assessed. The opponent WILL NOT, automatically, be assessed a technical foul. His behavior will be the determining factor.
>
> Simultaneous taunting is a verbal altercation. Verbal altercations and unsportsmanlike conduct will be administered as a double technical foul and no free throws will be attempted.
>
> Technical fouls assessed to opposing teams during the same dead ball and prior to the administering of any free throw attempt for the first technical foul, shall be interpreted as a double technical foul.
>
> A PLAYER(S) GUILTY OF TAUNTING MUST BE SINGLED OUT AND PENALIZED.
>
> If a previous unsportsmanlike act has been committed and if this situation is BLATANT, a technical foul must be assessed and the guilty player(s) must be ejected.

As with other non-simultaneous technical fouls, taunting is penalized by awarding the victimized team a free throw followed by possession. In addition, the Commissioner is empowered to suspend the offending player and/or impose a fine not to exceed $50,000. Rule 12 Section VII.

You are a staffer in the Commissioner's office. If you think the rules governing taunting could be improved, provide a draft of the changes that you would propose. If you think that the rules are optimal as they are, provide a brief memo explaining why.

CHAPTER 15

SPORTSMANSHIP, GOOD AND BAD

■ ■ ■

What is sportsmanship? It is probably a type of virtue, like courage or generosity. But what does it consist of? Is it definable? Do we know it when we see it? What is the relationship between good sportsmanship and bad sportsmanship? It seems that somebody is to be praised for exhibiting good sportsmanship and criticized or blamed for exhibiting bad sportsmanship. Is bad sportsmanship merely the failure to exhibit good sportsmanship when the opportunity presents itself, or is it something more than that? If blamable bad sportsmanship is more than merely the absence of good sportsmanship, what more is required?

Many questions of sportsmanship arise out of the question of whether in a given setting a competitor should decline to maximize her chance of winning by taking full advantage of the situation. We address questions of that type in Subchapter 15B. But first, in Subchapter 15A, we address what is in some ways the opposite type of question—whether in a given circumstance a competitor has an obligation to try to win the particular contest, and to put forth her best efforts in doing so.

A. DUTIES TO TRY

A chief goal for participants in competitive sports is to win. One might suppose, therefore, that Competitor A could have no objection if her opponent, B, puts in little effort: the less hard B tries, the greater A's probability of victory. In fact, though, competitors frequently do complain when their opponents "don't even try." And the complaint is often seen to have force. Here we explore the scope, and implications, of competitors' duties to try. We first examine the scope of supposed duties to try to win. We then consider whether competitors have broader obligations to put forth "best efforts."

1. TRYING TO WIN

At the 2012 London Olympics, four pairs of badminton players were expelled for purposely losing matches. The badminton competition began with pool play and then continued into knockout rounds. Some doubles teams qualified for the knockout rounds before playing their last pool match, and then found that, for one reason or another, they would be in a more advantageous position if they lost that match. The problem began when the Danish team, in a shocking upset, won its final pool match over one of the Chinese pairs. This meant that the only way that the two Chinese teams could avoid meeting before the final—and so the only way they could preserve the possibility of winning both gold and silver—was for the second Chinese team to lose its final pool match, against a South Korean team. But the South Koreans also determined that, in light of the Danish victory, they would have a better matchup later on if *they* lost the pool match. So both sides tried, rather comically, to lose, in part by repeatedly making bad serves. It appears that the match was competitive in the sense that both teams were doing their best to lose without being obvious about it. The Chinese managed to lose the match.

But that wasn't the end of the difficulty. The second Chinese team's loss in the pool match distorted the incentives in a pool match between a second South Korean team and one from Indonesia. Both teams tried to lose that match as well, in an attempt to set up better matchups in the next round. The Badminton World Federation then conducted an investigation and expelled all four tanking teams for unsportsmanlike conduct in violation of Section 4.17 of its Players' Code of Conduct, which prohibits "conducting oneself in a manner that is clearly abusive or detrimental to the sport." *See, e.g.,* Justin Peters, *Shuttlecock and Bull*, SLATE (Aug. 1, 2012).

Was this the right decision?

SAM BORDEN, THE GOAL IS WINNING GOLD, NOT WINNING EVERY MATCH

The New York Times, August 2, 2012
© 2012 The New York Times Company, reprinted with permission

LONDON—Abby Wambach, the veteran forward on the United States women's soccer team, said the other day that "no one gives you anything for finishing at the top of your group." And the goal of every Olympic athlete, from Wambach to Usain Bolt to Ann Romney's horse Rafalca, is to win a medal. The rest is just a journey.

So why the uproar over the tactics used by the four women's badminton teams that were disqualified for trying to lose their final preliminary-round matches? Where exactly did the badminton players veer off into corruption?

They did not organize the tournament. They did not arrange the draw.

They simply looked at the information that was presented to them, looked at their ultimate goal and went in the direction that seemed to have the best chance of leading them there. A loss in those matches, they decided, would give them a better path to winning a medal. How is this different from, say, a swimmer who coasts to the wall in a preliminary heat or a runner who jogs past the finish line in a semifinal to conserve energy for the final? Is it even that much different from a baseball player bunting?

Derek Jeter is a career .313 hitter. And yet in certain situations, sometimes even important situations in important games, Jeter goes up to the plate with the intention of not getting a hit. If he is successful—that is, if he succeeds at failing—he will be congratulated by his teammates when he returns to the dugout. The rules of baseball and other sports create situations in which a type of failure can be good strategy.

In the badminton case, the teams' ultimate goal was clear: win a gold medal. And what is one way to help do that? Avoid the best teams for as long as possible. This was not a sacrifice bunt because there was no sacrifice. The teams, after evaluating the tournament setup that was presented to them, saw an opportunity to give up nothing in the hope of gaining something significant. One could argue it would have been silly for them not to seize that opportunity.

It is worth noting, too, that the notion of "always give it your all" or whatever other hoary chestnut you can imagine a hyperactive Little League coach spewing in a pregame huddle is largely Western. As the British have been so quick to remind us over the past two weeks, fair play and sportsmanship were invented here. But what does that truly mean? Play to win in a meaningless match, only to be rewarded with a more difficult path later on?

To some, that defies sporting sensibility; to others, it defies logic.

One can only imagine, too, how the local reaction to this situation might have differed four years ago in Beijing. After all, Sun Tzu taught a more sophisticated approach to combat in "The Art of War," imploring a big-picture savvy that put a premium on positioning and strategy and an unflinching attachment to remembering the desired end result.

That is what the badminton teams did, and the theory is put to use to varying degrees in every sport. Sometimes it is a football team purposely taking a 5-yard penalty so its punter can have more room to try to land his kick near the end zone. Sometimes it is a cyclist slowing down to help his teammate kick to the finish. Sometimes it is a basketball team playing less talented players to help its chances of receiving a higher draft pick.

On Tuesday in Cardiff, Wales, the Japanese women's soccer team purposely played for a draw in its final group game, hanging back in the second half and never pushing forward to try to score. This strategy was ordered by the team's coach, and his reasoning was simple: a draw meant his team would stay put and play its quarterfinal in the same city a few days later. A win meant the Japanese would have to travel to Scotland to play the knockout game.

To that coach, Norio Sasaki, less travel meant a better chance at winning the tournament. To those badminton players, a loss in the final group game meant the same. Fans who complained about having bought tickets to see something like that are not seeing the athletes' big picture. The competitors' main obligation is to do what sets them up best to win a medal. They trained to play well, yes, but more important, they trained to win a medal. And Tuesday, losing gave them the best chance to do that. If fans are still angry, they should be angry at the organizers who made the situation possible, not the athletes themselves.

Was it pretty? No, it was not. And no one says fans have to celebrate losing to win. But we should also not be so foolish as to act as if it isn't sometimes just another part of the game.

COMMENTS AND QUESTIONS

1. *A simpler case.* One way to understand the divergent views surrounding the Olympic badminton scandal is as a debate over whether athletes in competitive sports have a duty to try to win and, if so, what the precise nature and contours of that duty are. To start with a possibly easier case, suppose that the two Chinese teams met in the gold medal match and one of the two intentionally lost, perhaps out of deference to the more senior team or because they (the tankers) had won gold the previous Olympiad. Would this violate any important principle of sport ethics? Does Sam Borden provide any reason to believe that it would be acceptable? What if, as has also been charged, one Chinese competitor lost a pool match intentionally because doing so was thought to increase the chances that a teammate would win the championship?

2. *Winning at* what? If Borden would agree that it would not have been permissible for badminton players to try to lose the championship match, then why, precisely, was it permissible for them to try to lose an earlier match? Consider the suggestion that it is largely uncontroversial that participants in competitive sports must try to win, and that the badminton case simply highlights that we reasonably disagree about the *level* or *unit* of competition to which the duty to try to win attaches. A batter takes the first pitch to see "what the pitcher's got." A poker player intentionally misplays a hand to set up her opponent for a change in tendencies later in the tournament. Nobody would object that the former violated his duty to try to win the pitch or the latter violated her duty to try to win the hand. Similarly, the reason why it's okay for swimmers to coast to the wall in a preliminary heat is because their obligation is to try to win the medal race, and not the preliminaries. If this is right, then does it follow that the badminton players' obligation was also to try to win as high a place as possible on the podium and they had no duty even to try to win other matches except insofar as doing so would increase their chances of winning or placing well in the whole enchilada?

3. *A better way?* If you agree with Borden that a team ought to be allowed to try to lose a preliminary match in order to improve its chances in an overall competition, should it have to go through the charade of trying to lose?

Would it be better to allow it simply to take a forfeit? But then what happens if both teams forfeit? A flip of the coin? The loss goes to the first team to forfeit, on the basis that once it does so the other team is declared the winner and has no chance to forfeit? Both teams are "credited" with a loss?

Alternatively, could the structure of the competition be altered to avoid the problem altogether? If so, how? Would a solution lie in giving the top-seeded teams, in order, a choice of opponents for the next round? What if the leaders of different groups have the same record? Or is the sport better off under the current rules, in which the teams might compete in trying to lose, but to do so subtly enough not to be discovered?

4. *The Macolin Convention.* In 2014, the Council of Europe adopted the Macolin Convention in order to fight the global phenomenon of "match-fixing." The Convention imposes an obligation on States parties to criminalize under their domestic laws "manipulation of sports competitions," defined as "an intentional arrangement, act or omission aimed at an improper alteration of the result or the course of a sports competition in order to remove all or part of the unpredictable nature of the aforementioned sports competition with a view to obtaining an undue advantage for oneself or for others." It specifies that an "undue advantage" does not have to be a financial profit, but rather can take the form of "intangible advantage, such as advancing to a higher level in the competition, or simply the 'glory' of winning." EXPLANATORY REPORT TO THE MACOLIN CONVENTION, Art. 55 (2014), https://tinyurl.com/y6pfpn3f. Since its adoption, Portugal, Norway, and Ukraine have ratified the convention. Given that a minimum of five ratifications is required for the convention to enter into force, it has not yet come into effect.

5. *The right unit in soccer?* Many soccer tournaments, including the FIFA World Cup, have a two-part structure similar to that used in Olympic badminton: teams compete in round-robin format to pass through a "group stage" in order to reach a single-elimination "knockout stage." If, as Borden maintains, the badminton players did not act improperly, does it follow that a soccer team that is already assured of making it through the group stage also acts properly in throwing its last group game in order to position itself for a more favorable matchup in the knockout stage?

Consider the 1982 FIFA World Cup soccer match played between West Germany and Austria in Gijón, Spain. Wikipedia explains:

> The match was the last game of the first-round Group 2, with Algeria and Chile having played the day before. With the outcome of that match already decided, a win by one or two goals for West Germany would result in both them and Austria qualifying at the expense of Algeria, who had beaten West Germany in the first game. West Germany took the lead after 10 minutes, thereafter the remaining 80 minutes was characterized by few serious attempts by either side to score. Both sides were accused of match-fixing although FIFA ruled that neither team broke any rules.

Disgrace of Gijón, WIKIPEDIA, https://tinyurl.com/jnu7qt5. Was this acceptable? If so, why is the match known in German as *Schande von Gijón* ("Disgrace of Gijón")? If it was not acceptable, does it follow that the badminton players' conduct wasn't either? Did the Japanese women's team mentioned by Borden act properly in aiming only for a draw in Wales?

6.   *The right unit in tennis?* The ATP Code of Conduct provides that "[a] player shall use his best efforts during the match when competing in a tournament." Section 8.04(M)(4)(h). Consider a player who withholds her best efforts during several points or even games in order to conserve energy for a final decisive set. Should this be understood to violate the Code? Does the answer depend upon what prevailing practices are? *See* Douglas Robson, *Men's Tennis Wants to Crack Down on Tanking, but What, Exactly, is Tanking?*, N.Y. TIMES, Nov. 20, 2016, at SP10.

7.   *Advancing by losing in baseball?* In 1981, a mid-season strike divided the Major League Baseball season in two. In that era, the leagues were divided into two divisions; ordinarily, the winners of each division played in the League Championship Series (LCS). But the owners decided that year to hold an extra round of playoffs, with the winner of the first half of the season in each division playing against the winner of the second half, and a wild card getting a chance if one team won both halves. Originally, the wild card team was supposed to be the second-place team with the best overall record. But some observers noticed that if Team A had won the first half and was in contention with Team B to win the second half, and team C would likely have the second best overall record but was not in contention for the second half title, C would have an incentive to lose its games to A—thus increasing the chance that A would win the second half as well as the first, and therefore that C would make it to the playoffs as a wild card. The system was then changed, so that the wild card would be the team with the second-best record in the second half.[a] If the system had not been changed, would it have been improper for a team in the position of C to lose its games intentionally to A, or to forfeit them? (Did the change eliminate the possibility of a perverse incentive? Assuming it did so, was it a proper solution? Would it have been better to give a two-half winner a bye into the LCS?)

8.   *The victim?* If a competitor purposely loses a contest, just who or what is hurt? To what extent is concern for fans who had paid for tickets appropriate? Does that concern vary depending on whether the contest is a pool-play match? On whether the ticket covers other contests besides the one in which the tanking occurs? If you are not worried about the fans who bought Olympic badminton tickets, how about those who (like one of the authors) paid good money in 1980 to see the second bout between Sugar Ray Leonard and Roberto Duran—who suddenly quit out of frustration in the middle of the eighth round, telling the ref, "No más" ("No more")?

---

[a]   In the end, the teams with the best overall records in each of the National League divisions failed to make the playoffs.

9.   Basketball. On November 29, 2012, the San Antonio Spurs played a game in Miami against the Heat. These were two of the top teams in the NBA: The Heat were the defending champions, and the two teams would meet each other in the finals of both that season and the next one. But the Spurs were at the end of a grueling road trip, and Gregg Popovich, their coach, decided not to bring four of the team's starters—Tim Duncan, Tony Parker, Manu Ginobili, and Danny Green—to Miami. The team Popovich put on the court hardly embarrassed itself—it was leading by five with 2:14 to go, before the Heat went on a 12–2 run to win 105–100. Nevertheless, the League responded sternly (apologies): Commissioner David Stern (a lawyer) imposed a $250,000 fine on the team. He made a statement laying out the basis for his decision that the Spurs' conduct violated a decision of the league's Board of Governors in April 2010 that a team should not rest players "contrary to the best interests of the NBA":

> The result here is dictated by the totality of the facts in this case. The Spurs decided to make four of their top players unavailable for an early season game that was the team's only regular-season visit to Miami. The team also did this without informing the Heat, the media, or the league office in a timely way. Under these circumstances, I have concluded that the Spurs did a disservice to the league and our fans.

Spurs fined $250,000 for 'disservice,' ESPN.com (Nov. 30, 2012).

Did Stern make the right call? How did each of the factors he cited play into his decision? Was the Spurs' conduct bad sportsmanship, or non-competitive behavior—or just bad commerce? If you agree with Stern, but also think that it's okay for tennis players to take it easy on discrete points or games, what's the difference? Is it that spectators buy tickets for basketball *games* and tennis *matches*? Would it matter if most basketball tickets were sold as season tickets, not as individual game tickets?

10.   When the playoffs are locked up. Suppose, as sometimes happens, that near the end of the NFL season one team has locked up its playoff position, so that in that sense the game is meaningless for it, but it is playing against a team that is in competition with one or more other teams for a spot. To what extent, if any, is the playoff-bound team obligated to play its starters? Is the situation any different in other team sports?

Before playing Stanford in football on November 24, 2012, UCLA had locked up the southern division of the Pac-12, and therefore a spot in the conference championship game, the winner of which would go to the Rose Bowl. Stanford was contending for the northern division lead with Oregon. Though many observers regarded Oregon as the stronger team, Stanford would advance unless it lost to UCLA *and* Oregon won its game that week. Was UCLA under an obligation to do its best to win the November 24 game? Is this different in any material respect from the badminton situation? (Stanford beat UCLA 35–17 on November 24, and then again in the championship game, but only by a 27–24 margin.)

11. Suck for Luck. If it is permissible for teams that have already locked up a spot in the playoffs to rest players during the regular season, even when they expect to lose as a result, may teams do the same when they are already *eliminated* from the postseason? Borden refers to this possibility in the context of basketball, but perhaps the best-known recent example comes from football. In the final stretch of the 2011 NFL season, teams that had already been mathematically eliminated from the playoffs knew that whichever of them ended with the worst record would have the first pick of the following draft and with it the opportunity to select Stanford quarterback Andrew Luck, widely recognized as the most promising quarterback to enter the draft in a generation. Accordingly, fans of some of those clubs urged their teams to "Suck for Luck." Clever gamesmanship or something else? Should draft procedures be altered to minimize the incentive to engage in this kind of behavior? (See Subchapter 9A2.) Note that when Doug Pederson, coach of the Philadelphia Eagles, benched his starting quarterback in the final quarter of a tight final game in January 2021—when the Eagles were eliminated from playoff contention and the difference between a loss and a win was three draft slots—players on his own team, and many fans, responded with fury, and Pederson was fired barely a week later, less than three years after winning the Super Bowl.

2.   DUTIES OF BEST EFFORTS

If players are under some form of obligation to try to win a given contest, are they also under a duty to try to put forth the best performance of which they are capable?

Consider the January 2011 game between the girls' teams from two Utah high schools, Christian Heritage High and West Ridge Academy. The final score was 108–3 in favor of Christian Heritage—but it didn't feel that close. Christian Heritage scored 28 points in each of the first three quarters, and West Ridge didn't score until the final quarter. Rob McGill, the Christian Heritage coach, said he had little choice, because he had only nine players available for both varsity and junior varsity games, and he felt it would be disrespectful to West Ridge if he told his players to pass the ball around the perimeter rather than using their ordinary offense. "I have been on the other side of this equation," he said:

> It was very insulting when teams slowed the ball down and just passed it around. That's why I'd rather have a team play me straight up, and that's why I played them straight up. Because I didn't want to taunt them, I didn't want to embarrass them, I didn't want them to think we could do whatever we want.

He didn't speak about defense; Christian Heritage reportedly never used a full-court press.[b]

---

[b]   *See, e.g.,* Cameron Smith, *108–3 girls basketball rout raises questions,* YAHOO! SPORTS (Jan. 2011); *cf.* Cameron Smith, *100–2 middle school blowout may have repercussions,* YAHOO!

The Christian Heritage head of school apologized to West Ridge, and the schools agreed to hold a meeting before the teams' next game two weeks later to avoid a recurrence. The final score in that game, held at West Ridge, was 62–7 in favor of Christian Heritage. West Ridge may, of course, have benefited from the home court advantage. (The next night, by the way, the West Ridge boys won at Christian Heritage, 66–29; in the rematch at West Ridge two weeks later, they won 62–27.[c])

The 108–3 game generated considerable nationwide attention and discussion. One commentator, Joe Carter, wrote that "it is shameful and dishonorable to treat a sports opponent as if they are not worthy of your full effort. When you step onto the playing field you want your competitor to play fairly and to the utmost of their skills and talent." Noting the apology by Christian Heritage and the head of school's promise that "we're going to do things differently next time," Carter wrote:

> What terrible lessons to be teaching these children. On one side they are told that if they work hard at honing their skills and teamwork, that they'll be expected to hold back—give less than 110%—so that they don't hurt anyone's feelings. On the other side they are being told that adults believe they are so fragile that the only recourse is to ask the other team to condescend to them and treat them as inferior.
>
> The fact is that sometimes you win, sometimes you lose, and sometimes you get thrashed like Walter Mondale in '84. That's life. If we don't have the courage to tell that to our children, then let's adjust our expectations—and coaching clichés—accordingly.

Joe Carter, *Why You Should Always Run Up the Score*, FIRST THINGS (Jan. 26, 2011).

COMMENTS AND QUESTIONS

1. Keeping the pedal to the metal. Do you agree with Joe Carter that Coach McGill and Christian Heritage were ethically obligated to play "to the utmost of their skills and talents?" Is this conclusion compelled by the judgment that the badminton federation reached in London? Do you believe that they were obligated to maximize their score?

2. Going easy. If you disagree with Carter, do you believe that Christian Heritage had a contrary obligation *not* to run up the score? What, precisely, should Coach McGill and his players have done? Should he have pulled his starters? What if the Christian Heritage substitutes were themselves far better than the West Ridge starters? Should he have instructed his players to

---

SPORTS (Nov. 28, 2011) (up 25–0 after less than two minutes, coach pulls starters; up 70–0 at the half, he tells his team to stop playing defense).

　　[c]　*Game Details—Basketball (Boys)*, DESERET NEWS, Feb. 4, 2011; *Game Details—Basketball (Boys)*, DESERET NEWS, Feb. 22, 2011.

go easy on defense, or to intentionally miss shots? Was the school right in apologizing? Or is there no obligation either way? Should the second game have been played?[d] For an introduction to the philosophical literature on blowouts, see, e.g., Randolph M. Feezell, *Sportsmanship and Blowouts: Baseball and Beyond,* 26 J. PHIL. SPORT 68 (1999).

3. *The lose-for-pay problem.* Recently, another problem has arisen in Grand Slam tennis. The number of first-round retirements has grown alarmingly large. Some players who were not fit were playing nonetheless because even first-round losers get a good payday for appearance. Tournament officials responded with a carrot—half the appearance money for players who withdraw before the tournament begins—and with a stick, the following section, III.G, added in 2018 to the Official Grand Slam Rulebook:

G. FIRST ROUND PERFORMANCE.

All players are expected to perform to a professional standard in every Grand Slam match.

With respect to First Round Performance, if in the opinion of the Referee the player did not perform to the required professional standard, the Referee may determine that the player be subject to a fine of up to first round prize money.

Factors that may be considered by the Referee in making such a determination include, but are not limited to, the following:

(i) the player did not complete the match;

(ii) the player did not compete in the 2–3 week period preceding each Grand Slam;

(iii) the player retired from the last tournament he/she played before the Grand Slam Main Draw;

(iv) the player was using a Protected or Special Ranking for entry;

(v) the player received a Code Violation for failure to use Best Efforts.

This rule has been invoked several times, both against players who were deemed not to have put forth best efforts (*e.g.,* Bernard Tomic, after losing 6–2, 6–1, 6–4 to Jo-Wilfried Tsonga at Wimbledon in 2019) and players who were deemed unfit to play (*e.g.,* Anna Tatishvili, who because of an ankle injury that required surgery had not played a tournament in more than a year and a half, after losing 6–0, 6–1 to Maria Sakkari at the 2019 French Open). Is the new rule an appropriate response to a problem that needs fixing?

---

d *See also 108–1 girls basketball rout in Ohio another in long line of prep blowouts,* USA TODAY HIGH SCHOOL SPORTS, Feb. 18, 2016 (losing school in 108–1 game congratulates winner "on their victory and pursuit of a championship"); Nate Scott, *Girls high school basketball coach suspended after team's 161–2 win,* USA TODAY, Jan. 15, 2015 (two-game suspension for winning coach, who ran full-court press for first half, ending in 104–1 score; coach said he was eager to have team get a good half of play in as preparation for next game, and that opposing coach had agreed).

4. Best efforts in motorsports. In NASCAR, a rule adopted in 2013 requires drivers

> to race "at 100% of their ability with the goal of achieving their best possible finishing position in an event." That means no more deal-making, giving up a position for a teammate or "artificially altering" the finish of a race. Any driver or team engaging in such behavior, which could include intentional cautions or pulling off the track to give an advantage to another competitor, is subject to penalty.

Jeff Gluck, *New NASCAR rules aim to end teamwork on track*, USA TODAY, Sept. 14, 2013. Is this the right rule for NASCAR? If so, does it follow that teams in all or most sports should always try to maximize their point totals?

5. "The fumble." Any fan of the New York Giants, of a certain age, remembers, with agony, the muffed handoff between quarterback Joe Pisarcik and fullback Larry Csonka that lost the 1978 Giants a game to the rival Philadelphia Eagles.

> The Giants were 5–6 when they blew a 17–12 lead with 30 seconds left in a game that would have put them back in the playoff picture. Instead, it hurtled the Eagles toward their first postseason in 18 years when The Fumble, on third-and-2 with 31 seconds left, was returned by [Eagles' cornerback, Herm] Edwards for a 26-yard touchdown, to give the Eagles a 19–17 victory. . . .

> It was before today's "victory formation," in which quarterbacks simply take a knee to kill the clock. They had to be touched down. The story goes that with the Eagles blitzing, [offensive coordinator Bob] Gibson didn't want to get his quarterback injured. He called a handoff from his seat in the press box. . . .

> "Three quarterback falldowns and we would have been out of there," said Pisarcik, noting that he just fell on the ball on first down without a play call. "The play should not have been called. But it wasn't just his fault. Everybody deserves a little bit of fault."

Hank Gola, *30 years later, Giant disappointment of 'The Fumble' still lingers*, N.Y. DAILY NEWS, Nov. 18, 2008.

> What most Giants fans don't know is that the call wasn't the product of a simple brain freeze, but arose from a sense of sporting honor.

> Everyone watching expected quarterback Joe Pisarcik to take one more snap and kneel with the ball, thus running out the clock and preserving a 17–12 Giants upset.

> Nowadays, teams in this situation let the play clock run down to the last possible second and have the quarterback take a knee. . . .

> Gibson did not want to expose his quarterback to further risk of injury (he had already taken some hits earlier in the season). Nor did he want to risk his players being fined for violating the league's rules

against fighting. Most importantly, the last thing he wanted was for his team to get a penalty, which could stop the clock and require getting another first down to secure the win. He also personally despised the kneeling play, considering it unsporting and somewhat dishonorable (a view popular among a lot of coaches of the period). . . .

[Eagles coach Dick] Vermeil refused to question McVay's judgment but allowed that he, too, disliked sitting on the ball to preserve a victory.

The Miracle at the Meadowlands, WIKIPEDIA, https://tinyurl.com/y5pkzle9. Was Gibson's sense of honor misplaced? Is it sporting or ethical for a football team to run the clock down by "taking a knee" (often multiple times)? Should the formal rules prohibit it?

    6.   *Changing times.* If the kneel-down was viewed with suspicion in 1978, that is no longer the case. Indeed, it is now so broadly accepted that some football people regard it as bad form for a defensive team to try to get to the quarterback in a kneel-down situation before the ball is declared dead. During the 2012 NFL season, a contretemps arose when defensive linemen on the Greg Schiano-coached Tampa Bay Buccaneers charged the line and knocked over Giants quarterback Eli Manning on a kneel-down in the concluding seconds of a Giants victory. New York coach Tom Coughlin scolded Schiano for violating an informal rule that defenses take it easy on such plays, but Schiano refused to apologize and insisted that the play was simply smart and hard-nosed football. *See, e.g.,* Toni Monkovic, Fifth Down, *Schiano, Coughlin, and the Unwritten Rules*, N.Y. TIMES, Sept. 17, 2012. Who was right? What more would you need to know to answer that question?

    7.   *Lying down on the job.* Consider the final minutes of Super Bowl XLVI, in 2012. With 1:03 left to play and holding one final timeout, the New England Patriots were leading the New York Giants 17–15, but the Giants faced second down and goal on the Patriots' six-yard line. In this situation, the smart play for New York would arguably be to run two plays short of the goal line, thus forcing New England to use its last time out, and putting the G-Men in position to attempt a field goal—nearly automatic at that distance—that, if successful, would give them a one-point lead and leave New England only about 20 seconds to score again. To prevent the Giants from executing this strategy, the Patriots' defense, acting on instructions from Coach Bill Belichick, did not tackle the Giants' ball carrier, Ahmad Bradshaw, thereby allowing him to score and giving New England more time to retake the lead (though a touchdown was then required). As it happened, New England did not score, and the Giants won. But most commentators praised Belichick for his quick thinking. Were they right to do so? Are there any grounds for criticizing his decision, on ethical if not tactical grounds? Would Bradshaw have acted properly had he fallen to the ground intentionally to avoid scoring the touchdown that the Patriots were offering him?

    8.   *A sacrifice goal.* Note also the remarkable Barbados-Grenada soccer match in pool play in the 1994 Caribbean Cup. Barbados needed to win by at

least two goals to advance; goal differential rather than head-to-head play was the tie-breaker, and Grenada had the edge. Two unusual rules generated an anomaly: All pool games had to have a winner, so if drawn at the end of regulation they would go into sudden-death overtime. And the sudden-death goal counted double. In the last few minutes of regulation, with Barbados leading 2–1, it realized it would have a better chance in sudden death than in regulation of scoring the further goal it needed. So it scored an own goal. That put Grenada in the position of advancing, without a need for overtime, if *either* team scored a goal in regulation—which meant that Barbados had to defend both goals for the remaining few minutes. Barbados did so successfully, scored in sudden death, and advanced. *See Barbados 4–2 Grenada (1994 Caribbean Cup qualification),* WIKIPEDIA, https://tinyurl.com/ntc4jy9. Did the teams act properly? Should such an unusual form of competition be welcomed?

   9.   The ethics of record-breaking. Soviet pole-vaulting champion Sergey Bubka was one of the most dominant athletes of the late twentieth century. Starting in the mid-1980s, Bubka broke the men's world-record for pole vaulting, indoor and outdoor, on thirty-five separate occasions over the course of a decade. However, as one commentator explains, Bubka's feats were

> not always met with unfettered enthusiasm. When Bubka became the first athlete to clear six meters in 1985 (having missed a chance at the 1984 Games, due to the Soviet boycott) or twenty feet (6.096 meters), that was something. Nearly every record-breaking event after, though, was a minor height increase from the prior record. The problem with Bubka's performance is that he was so dominant, the competitions became boring, and it became evident that Bubka was deliberately not vaulting for the maximum he could perform. Record-breaking is a lucrative side of federation sport, and Bubka was cashing in every time he broke a record. In other words, even though he was breaking records, he was not actually doing the best that he could. Bubka was violating a major ethos of elite competition inherent in the value of record-breaking.

Shayna M. Sigman, *Are We All Dopes? A Behavioral Law and Economics Approach to Legal Regulation of Doping in Sports,* 19 MARQ. SPORTS L. REV. 125, 188–89 (2008). Do you share Sigman's assessment?

   10.   Personal records in team sports. If you do agree with Sigman, compare the situation in which a team helps an individual player achieve dramatic personal numbers. A striking example is the November 2012 NCAA Division III basketball game between Grinnell and Faith Baptist Bible. Grinnell won, 179–104. Ho hum. What was truly remarkable about the game was the performance of Grinnell guard Jack Taylor. Taylor scored 58 points in the first half, taking Grinnell to an 85–46 lead. In the second half, he heated up, finishing with 138 points, which smashed the NCAA's prior single-game individual scoring record of 113.

   Taylor was 27 for 71 on 3-pointers, 25 for 37 on two-pointers, and 7 for 10 on free throws. He played 36 of 40 minutes; none of his teammates played more than 15. He had a grand total of 0 assists. Virtually overlooked was the performance of David Larson of Faith Baptist Bible, who played all 40 minutes and scored 70 points—34 of 44 on 2-pointers, 0 for 2 on 3-pointers, and 2 for 4 on free throws, with 1 assist. (Taylor, by the way, made no personal fouls, and Larson made 2.)[e] Did Grinnell act properly by facilitating Taylor's record-breaking performance?

11. The basketball gods. After recording a triple-double in a game after his team, the Lakers, had already been eliminated from the playoffs, LeBron James explained why he still put forth his best efforts as follows:

> I would never cheat myself. . . know we're out the playoff race, but if I'm on the court, I'm going to play how I play, and I play to win. So, I will never cheat the game. . . There's such a thing called 'game gods.' And they're watching no matter what you're doing, and it's our obligation to go out and be a professional, and that's what I'm about. . . When I'm on the floor, I've got to play the game no matter what our circumstances is, no matter how many minutes I'm out on the floor, through the basketball gods, I've always respected the basketball gods. . . ."

Dave McMenamin, *Lebron on triple-double: I won't 'cheat the game,'* ESPN.com (Mar. 25, 2019). Do you think that James believes in basketball gods? Is his view intelligible and attractive without invoking the supernatural?

B. SPORTSMANSHIP AND RELINQUISHING ADVANTAGE

Perhaps competitors are under an obligation to try to win. If so, that obligation stands in tension with the widespread sense that ideals of sportsmanship sometime permit, and might possibly even require, competitors to relinquish advantages to their opponents. We now focus on that type of issue, breaking the broad question into three smaller topics: (1) whether participants are required not to fully exploit competitive advantages that accrue by virtue of an opponent's accident, mistake, or mishap; (2) whether participants should or may go further and render affirmative assistance to an opponent, even at competitive cost to oneself; and (3) whether a competitor should or may correct an official's error in her favor.

1. FORGOING ADVANTAGE

Ordinarily, we expect competitors to take advantage of opponents' errors or weaknesses. If a shortstop overthrows first base, the batter will happily run to second. If an interior defensive lineman is also an inferior one, we may expect the offense to run at him repeatedly. But not always.

---

[e] The box score is available at https://tinyurl.com/y4rsod88. *See also, e.g.,* Myron Medcalf, *Grinnell Guard Erupts for 138,* ESPN.com (Nov. 20, 2012).

In some cases, competitors do *not* take full advantage of a situation. In this section we will focus on the questions of when such behavior is laudatory, and when it should be expected.

Edward Wyatt, BackTalk; Stopping for Armstrong's Spill Draws the Second-Guessers to Ullrich

The New York Times, August 10, 2003
© 2003 The New York Times Company, reprinted with permission

None of the other runners waited when Mary Decker fell after colliding with Zola Budd in the final of the 3,000-meter race at the 1984 Olympics. Nor did rival jockeys slow the pace after War Emblem stumbled out of the gate at the 2002 Belmont Stakes, ruining his chance to win the Triple Crown.

But when Lance Armstrong caught his handlebars on a fan's tote bag and crashed to the pavement last month during the 15th stage of the Tour de France—a crucial climb to the Pyrenees ski village of Luz-Ardiden—Armstrong's rivals slowed down and waited for him to recover, forsaking the chance to leave him behind.

At the time, race fans heard much about cycling's first unwritten rule: Thou shalt not ride away from the race leader when he is on the ground, stopping to relieve himself, or at other unsporting moments. Commentators agreed after the race that all of Armstrong's closest rivals appeared to heed the rule, including Jan Ullrich, who at the time trailed Armstrong in the overall standing by a mere 15 seconds.

But by doing so, Ullrich and the others not only allowed Armstrong to catch up. They also gave him a chance to win the stage—and arguably the Tour itself, both of which he did. Ullrich finished second, for the fifth time over all and the third time to Armstrong.

The incident has sparked a still-growing debate among cycling fans about whether Ullrich and the others should have, or did, wait for Armstrong. At the time, Armstrong graciously acknowledged Ullrich's gesture, noting that two years ago, he had waited when Ullrich crashed on the descent of the Col de Peyresourde, another storied Pyrenees peak.

But after the race, Armstrong released a bombshell, one that so far has received little notice.

"I watched the footage, and I'm not so convinced that Jan Ullrich was waiting," Armstrong said in a post-Tour interview with Outdoor Life Network, the cable television network that showed the Tour. "I think everybody said that and that was the feel-good story, but I'm not so sure he was waiting."

In the OLN interview, . . . Armstrong maintained that it was only after Tyler Hamilton rode to the front of the group and told the other riders to slow down that they waited. Hamilton, Armstrong's former teammate on the United States Postal Service squad, is the leader of the rival CSC team.

"If you look at the minute before that, or the half minute, I saw Ullrich on the front—in his normal position, with his normal face, going," Armstrong said. "That's what I saw," he added, shrugging.[f]

Ullrich has been largely mum since the incident, but shortly after, he told The Los Angeles Times: "Of course I would wait. If I would have won this race by taking advantage of someone's bad luck, then the race was not worth winning."

Some former racers, however, believe Ullrich would have been well within his rights to ride away and try to take the yellow jersey off Armstrong's back, particularly on the Tour's last mountaintop finish and with no more than a handful of seconds separating the two.

"I believe he gave away the Tour de France right there," said John Eustice, a former United States pro cycling champion who works as a television commentator and whose company, Sparta Cycling, organizes professional races.

Eustice said that Ullrich, by waiting for Armstrong, lost his rhythm, a fatal error for a rider who is far more dependent on maintaining an even pace than is Armstrong, who prefers zippy accelerations and who can quickly recover.

"It was a great, chivalrous move on Ullrich's part, but I think it was over the top," he said. "He was within his right to continue racing. If I were his race director, I would have killed him."

Eustice's opinion is not universally shared. David M. Chauner, a former Olympic cyclist and president of Threshold Sports, the organizer of the New York City Cycling Championship and other races, said opinion would probably be split among racers on what Ullrich should have done.

"In a certain sense, it would be a hollow victory if you win because another guy has an accident," Chauner said. "But it's a sentiment not necessarily shared by everyone in the race." Frequently, he said, when a competitor gets up from a crash, he is so pumped that he is stronger than he was before the accident, something that rivals must factor in.

Armstrong said after the stage that his post-crash attack was fueled by adrenaline. It caught Ullrich off guard and allowed Armstrong to open a 40-second gap. Once Ullrich recovered his rhythm, he was able to match Armstrong's pace, but not to close the gap.

Paul Sherwen, the former racer who provides commentary for OLN's race broadcasts, said he wondered how Ullrich was feeling at the time.

---

[f]   Armstrong gave a similar assessment in his book *Every Second Counts* (2003).

Immediately before the crash, Armstrong was attacking. "Ullrich might have been thinking about getting a breather," Sherwen said, who added that he believes Ullrich did wait and had a responsibility to do so.

Phil Liggett, also an OLN race commentator who along with Sherwen conducted the post-Tour interview with Armstrong, disagreed, saying he believes that Ullrich did not wait, at least until Hamilton rode to the front and slowed the group. Asked what he would have said to Ullrich had he been the Bianchi team's race director, Liggett said, "My reflex action would have been to say to race."

It is a tough decision, one that has to be made within seconds and depends on a multitude of variables. In the 1998 Tour de France, Ullrich was leading the race when he suffered a flat tire shortly before the final climb of the 11th stage. Marco Pantani waited for Ullrich to rejoin the group before he attacked, winning the stage. Pantani went on to win the Tour.

This year, a few days before Armstrong's crash, Joseba Beloki, who finished second to Armstrong in last year's Tour, fell during a descent of the Cote de la Rochette. The fall happened directly in front of Armstrong, who had to ride off the road and across a field to avoid going down himself. No one waited—for good reason, as it turned out. Beloki broke his femur and was out of the race.

"It's something you can't have rules for," Sherwen said. "I think it's a gut feeling, and a decision that has to be made on the ground."

And one that will be debated for years to come.

COMMENTS AND QUESTIONS

1. Beyond rules. Do you agree with Paul Sherwen that proper etiquette regarding what competitors should do when the leader is temporarily down to a fall, mechanical failure, or a call of nature is "something you can't have rules for"? If you agree with him, is it because a rule is unlikely to take into account adequately the "multitude of variables," as Wyatt puts it, that should determine competitors' conduct in situations of this sort? Why can't a more standard-like rule consider all those factors?

If you agree with Sherwen, does that suggest that the issue should be left to policing by informal norms—or that even informal norms that sometimes require competitors to wait do not work and that instead the governing norm should give riders free rein to exploit the misfortunes of other competitors, including the leader? Bottom line, do you believe that Ullrich had, or should have had, a responsibility to wait for Armstrong? And if so, why is the situation different from those of Decker's fall in the 3000-meter race at the 1984 Olympics or War Emblem's stumble in the 2002 Belmont Stakes?

2. The chain reaction. An incident somewhat similar to the Armstrong-Ullrich episode of 2003 occurred in Stage 15 of the 2010 Tour. When the stage began, Andy Schleck of Luxembourg, the second-place winner the prior year, held the yellow jersey as the overall leader of the Tour, with a 31-second lead over Alberto Contador of Spain, the defending champion. As Schleck mounted an attack on the final climb of the day, his chain came off. While Schleck was stopped, Contador sped by, gaining 39 seconds and capturing the yellow jersey. Schleck reacted with fury, saying, "I can tell you, my stomach is full of anger and I want to take my revenge." The manger of his team, Bjarne Riis, a former Tour racer (with a win in the 1996 Tour of complicated official status, because he later admitted to doping), was much more measured, saying that Contador "had to go with [Lulu] Sánchez and [Denis] Menchov," because those other riders were high in the overall standards.

At first, Contador defended his conduct, saying,

> I planned to attack anyway, and when I knew what had happened to him, I was already ahead and racing. Of course, I know it's a delicate situation and could lead to debate, but I don't believe that to lose or win 30 seconds at this point will make you win or lose the Tour de France.

But he quickly had second thoughts, and that night posted on YouTube a video in Spanish with English subtitles, apologizing for his move. "The race was totally launched," he said, "and maybe I did a mistake. I'm sorry." He did jab at Schleck, though, saying that in Stage 2 he had waited after Scheck crashed, but that Schleck "took advantage" of him in the next stage when Contador was caught behind a crash on cobblestones. Juliet Macur, *Etiquette Debate Follows Tour De France Lead Change*, N.Y. TIMES, July 20, 2010, at B11; *see also, e.g., Opportunist Contador learns that winning isn't everything*, CNN.com (July 20, 2010). For a partial transcript of Contador's apology video, see *Contador makes YouTube apology to Schleck*, CYCLING NEWS (July 20, 2010). In the end, Contador won the Tour by . . . 39 seconds.

Did Contador act improperly in this incident? Are his comparisons to earlier incidents apt? Would this incident have appeared different if it had occurred earlier in the race? If Schleck were not leading overall? If Contador were not second? If Schleck had not been attacking when his chain flew off? Does it matter whether Schleck's losing his chain is, as some riders thought, attributable at least in part to his own fault? Should Contador have just stopped altogether? Should the determination of what was proper for Contador to do depend on what other racers were doing in response to the situation?

What would have happened in a comparable incident if this were auto rather than bicycle racing? Is one resolution generally preferable to the other, or does each reflect the circumstances of its own sport?

3. A soccer norm for injuries. A soccer player is injured but the whistle has not blown. A player on the opposing team kicks the ball out of bounds to stop play, with the expectation that the injured player's team will return the ball when play resumes. Is kicking the ball out of bounds in that situation proper? Required? What should happen if a teammate of the injured player intentionally kicks the ball out of bounds to stop play?

Here is a description of a famous 1999 soccer match between Sheffield United and Arsenal, in the 5th round of the FA Cup:

> With the score 1–1 and ten minutes to go, the United goalkeeper, Alan Kelly, kicked the ball out of touch so that treatment could be given to an injured [United] player. When the ball was thrown back into play by [Arsenal player] Ray Parlour, although it was intended for Kelly, [Arsenal player Nwankwo] Kanu was unaware of the circumstances. Thinking it to be an attacking move, he chased the throw-in down the right wing unchallenged, and centred the ball for Marc Overmars, who promptly scored to make the match 2–1. Immediately after the match Arsenal manager Arsène Wenger offered to right the error and replay the match; in the end, Arsenal won that match 2–1 as well.

Nwankwo Kanu, WIKIPEDIA, https://tinyurl.com/y49uwrs2. The offer to replay the match is said to have been "a first in the 127-year history of the F.A. Cup." DONN RISOLO, SOCCER STORIES: ANECDOTES, ODDITIES, LORE, AND AMAZING FEATS 280 (2010). Should Arsenal instead have scored an own-goal immediately after the goal scored by Overmars? In 2019, in roughly comparable circumstances, Leeds United allowed Aston Villa to score an unopposed goal to compensate for a goal its coach believed it should not have scored; the match, with ramifications for promotion to the Premier League, ended in a 1–1 draw.

4.   *Exploiting short-handedness.* Consider this situation, from a game in a 13U baseball tournament, June 12, 2011: Through a series of unfortunate events, the Michigan Blue Jays are short-handed, playing against the Milan Reds with only eight players. As a result, every time the ninth spot comes up in their order, an out is automatically recorded. (Parenthetically: Does this rule make sense? Why not let the team bat with eight? Should it suffer a penalty on offense as well as on defense?) So at least say the official rules. Should the Reds be allowed to decline the automatic out, and if so should they decline it, as a matter of good sportsmanship?

Now assume that the Reds are indeed taking the automatic out every time the Blue Jays' ninth spot comes up. The Blue Jays' number five and six batters lead off one inning by making outs. The number seven batter reaches base. Is it proper for the Reds to walk the number eight hitter intentionally? In answering this question, does it matter what base the number seven batter reached?

Now suppose it is the last inning and the Reds have a one-run lead. The number four and five hitters make outs. Is it proper for the Reds to walk the next three hitters intentionally?

5.   *Exploiting an apology.* On September 17, 2011, in the fourth round of a WBC welterweight title bout, Victor Ortiz head-butted Floyd Mayweather. The referee properly took a point away from Ortiz and reprimanded him. The boxers touched gloves and Ortiz offered Mayweather a hug and even a kiss on the cheek in apology. While Ortiz was defenseless, Mayweather hit him with a left hook. Ortiz looked towards the referee—who had his head turned, apparently to speak with the timekeeper—and Mayweather knocked Ortiz out with a right hand to the face. You can see the critical sequence at https://tiny url.com/y5ucptfs. The whole fight is at https://tinyurl.com/yynjy2ek, with that sequence beginning after 32 minutes.

Mayweather was unapologetic after the fight. "In the ring," he said, "you have to protect yourself at all times. After it happened, we touched gloves and we were back to fighting and then I threw the left hook and right hand after the break. You just gotta protect yourself at all times."

The referee, Joe Cortez, said, "Time was in. The fighter needed to keep his guard up. Mayweather did nothing illegal." Dan Rafael, *Mayweather scores controversial KO*, ESPN.com (Sept. 17, 2011). Ortiz denied having heard Cortez call time in. *Victor Ortiz at the post fight press conference after his fight with Floyd Mayweather*, YOUTUBE, https://tinyurl.com/y3sa254s.

Among the commentary on this incident is this video comment by Jeremy Jahns: https://tinyurl.com/y2mz2ulh.

Did Mayweather act improperly? At what point was time in?

2.   RENDERING ASSISTANCE

WHEN SPORT BECAME MORE THAN JUST A GAME

The Independent (U.K.), July 30, 2009
© 2009 James Corrigan/The Independent, reprinted with permission

JACK NICKLAUS AND TONY JACKLIN

American concedes most famous 'gimme' in history, writes James Corrigan

"Tony, I don't think for a second you're going to miss that putt. But I'm not going to give you the chance." Golf is proud of being a game of sportsmanship, but nowhere in what it likes to think of as its gentlemanly history has a gesture so encapsulated this cherished spirit than the above quote. The scene was the 18th at Royal Birkdale, it was 1969 and Great Britain and Ireland had lost every Ryder Cup but one in 13 stagings. Tony Jacklin and Jack Nicklaus were the last singles out on the course on the final day and with the scores level the significance of Jacklin's short but eminently missable two-footer for a half was as obvious as it was ominous. Make it and for the first time in the match's then 42-year history, the Ryder Cup would be tied. It was then that Jack Nicklaus stooped down, picked up Jacklin's marker and uttered the famous words to the young Open champion. What made it so much more remarkable was the backdrop to the "gimme". Twenty minutes before on the final green the Welshman Brian Huggett had cried after winning his singles in the belief he had just landed the cup. Huggett had heard a huge cheer from the 17th, which he took as Jacklin beating Nicklaus. In fact, Jacklin's 50-footer for eagle had merely levelled his encounter. As they walked to the 18th tee, the pair realised it all rested on them. Recalled Jacklin: "Jack asked me, 'You nervous?' 'Petrified,' I replied. 'If it's any consolation, I feel exactly the same way,' said Jack." Both found the par-four green; Jacklin 30 feet away, Nicklaus 20 feet. Jacklin went first, his centre cup effort just dying short. Nicklaus had the putt to win and typically gave it every chance. It shot past almost five feet. "I would've loved to have offered a half, but he hit it so far by, it was impossible," said Jacklin. Nicklaus confidently rammed it home. And so followed what his opponent called "the greatest single sporting gesture in golf".

COMMENTS AND QUESTIONS

1.   Saint Nick? In conceding a putt to Jacklin, Nicklaus did not merely refuse to fully exploit an advantage; he affirmatively relieved his opponent of the need to successfully perform a challenge of the sport. We might therefore think that what he did goes beyond what cycling demanded of Ulrich and what some boxing observers demanded of Mayweather. Precisely because Nicklaus went beyond what could reasonably have been demanded or even expected of him, his concession to Jacklin has been highly praised. But his Ryder Cup teammates were not impressed at the time. As the preceding article continues:

> The American captain, Sam Snead, was furious; and so, apparently, was the rest of his team. "All the boys thought it was ridiculous to give him that putt," snarled Snead. "We went over there to win, not to be good ol' boys." Nicklaus, however, remained unrepentant. "I believed good sportsmanship should be as much a part of the Ryder Cup as great competition," was the way he saw it.

Who's right? Was Nicklaus's concession required by the norms of the sport or otherwise? Did it show proper respect to his opponent? To the competition? To his teammates? Is there an agency problem here? Nicklaus is the agent and the team is the principal; perhaps they have different agendas, with the team aiming only to win within the rules and Nicklaus also eager to make himself look like a good guy. Would your assessment of the concession be different, and in what way, if

(a)   it had given the British-Irish team a win, rather than a draw, in the Ryder Cup?

(b)   it had been made in a dual match between rival college teams?

(c)   the match had been in the United States, or at a neutral site, rather than in England?

For other discussions of this incident, see, e.g., Matt Hardisty, *The Concession—September 20, 1969*, Ryder Cup (Sept. 21, 2018) (calling the concession "one of the greatest examples of sportsmanship ever seen in golf or anywhere else"); Jim Munro, *18 Memorable Ryder Cup Moments*, SUNDAY TIMES (commentary of Nicklaus: "I didn't think it was in the spirit of the game to make Jacklin have a chance to miss a two-footer to lose the match in front of his fans.").

2.   *Softball and soft hearts?* Compare the 1969 Ryder Cup with this remarkable incident from a 2008 softball game between Western Oregon and Central Washington, two Division II schools. It was Senior Day, the last home game of the regular season for Central Washington, and a critical game for both teams, each of which had hopes of reaching the NCAA tournament for the first time. With two runners on base and the game scoreless in the top of the second inning, Sara Tucholsky, a light-hitting Western Oregon senior who had never hit a home run, knocked a ball over the centerfield fence. Naturally excited, she missed first base on her home run trot, and as she turned back to touch the bag her right knee gave way. She fell in agony, with an apparent ligament tear. It soon became clear that she could not make it around the bases unaided. If she had been helped by a member of her team, including coaches or trainers, she would have been called out. The umpires therefore ruled that Western Oregon's only option was to put in a substitute for Tucholsky at first base, which would result in her hit being a single rather than a home run. (It appears that she was able to crawl back to first under her own power.) In fact, as the NCAA later explained, this was wrong: NCAA Softball Rule 8.5.3.2 provides, "If an injury to a batter-runner or runner prevents her from proceeding to an awarded base, the ball is dead and the substitution can be made. The substitute must legally touch all awarded or missed bases not previously touched." But the ruling on the field is what controlled. The Western Oregon coach was about to make a substitution when Mallory Holtman, the Central Washington first baseman—also a senior and her team's outstanding offensive player, the league's all-time leader in home runs and RBIs—asked, "Excuse me, would it be OK if we carried her around and she touched each bag?" There being no rule in the books against an *opponent* aiding a runner, the umpires decided it would be all right. So Holtman and Liz Wallace, the Central Washington shortstop, carried Tucholsky around, gently dipping her so that she could touch each base with her left foot. Holtman later said:

> Honestly, it's one of those things that I hope anyone would do it for me. She hit the ball over her fence. She's a senior; it's her last year. . . . I don't know, it's just one of those things I guess that maybe because compared to everyone on the field at the time, I had been playing longer and knew we could touch her, it was my idea first. But I think anyone who knew that we could touch her would have offered to do it, just because it's the right thing to do. She was obviously in agony.

The three received a standing ovation as they reached home plate, and then Holtman and Wallace returned to their positions and the game resumed. Western Oregon held on for a 4–2 win.

Pam Knox, the Western Oregon coach, said the incident "came from character," and that Holtman and Wallace were "playing for a coach [Gary Frederick] who instills it." Refusing to say that the incident demonstrated a difference between men's and women's sports, she said, "As coaches, we are so competitive, we forget this stuff. By God, I would hope I would have done the same thing":

> It kept everything in perspective and the fact that we're never bigger than the game. It was such a lesson that we learned—that it's not all about winning. And we forget that, because as coaches, we're always trying to get to the top. We forget that. But I will never, ever forget this moment. It's changed me, and I'm sure it's changed my players.

Graham Hays, *Central Washington offers the ultimate act of sportsmanship*, ESPN.com (Apr. 28, 2008); George Vecsey, *A Sporting Gesture Touches 'Em All*, N.Y. TIMES, Apr. 30, 2008.

Do you agree that this incident was a display of commendable good sportsmanship by Central Washington? It's hard to doubt it. The incident won the 2008 Best Moment ESPY award and has been praised far and wide. But ordinarily a competitor does not help an opponent, and in particular if an opponent suffers an injury or mishap a competitor ordinarily does not help the opponent overcome the consequences. Suppose that a ball carrier in football gets past the last line of the opposing team's defense for what appears to be a sure touchdown before pulling up short with a hamstring injury. Would it be appropriate for defenders who had been beaten on the play to allow the now-injured player to hobble across the goal line unmolested? If not, what can explain a different verdict in the case of Holtman and Wallace? Is there any relation between this incident and the Casey Martin case?

Is there a meaningful difference between what Holtman and Wallace did, and what Nicklaus did nearly forty years earlier? Is it possibly significant that Tucholsky was injured and Jacklin wasn't?

3.   The stronger claim. If Holtman and Wallace deserve our praise or admiration for their gesture, does that suggest that they would have been neither praiseworthy nor blameworthy had they refrained? If so, is that conclusion correct? Or can we make a stronger claim that they *should* have carried Tucholsky? Consider carefully Holtman's statement that "I think anyone who knew that we could touch her would have offered to do it, just because it's the right thing to do." That assessment is not shared by columnist George Vecsey:

> Would the Oakland A's have carried a sore-legged Kirk Gibson around the bases to complete his two-run homer that gave the Dodgers a 5–4 comeback victory in the opening game of the 1988 World Series? My guess is that if Gibson had crumpled in the dirt,

Tony La Russa (or Billy Martin or Leo Durocher or Earl Weaver or just about any manager) would have said, "Let him lie there."

Are they both right? And if so is it because, as Vecsey acknowledges, the stakes are much higher in a World Series game? Is the differential in stakes, as perceived by the contestants, great enough to justify a difference in outcome? *Cf.* JIM BOUTON, BALL FOUR 36–37 (20th anniv. ed. 1990) (saying that some high school games "were just as big to me as any major league game").

Putting aside whether everybody *would* have done as she did, is it nonetheless true that any opponent "who knew" that aiding Tucholsky around the bases was possible would or should have done it? Suppose, for example, that the umpires told Frederick, the Central Washington coach, "If you do nothing, they'll have to make a substitution at first, and it will just be a single. But I want to tell you that you have the option of offering to carry her around the bases, in which case she can be credited with a home run. It's entirely your choice." Would Frederick be fairly charged with bad sportsmanship had he chosen to instruct his players not to carry Tucholsky?

4.　Jesse Owens and Luz Long. Compare the two preceding cases with a famous incident from the 1936 Olympics, involving one of the greatest athletes of the twentieth century, Jesse Owens. Owens came to the 1936 Olympics— held in Hitler's Berlin—as the favorite in the broad jump, as it was then known, having set in 1935 a world record of 8.13 m. that would stand for a quarter century. His strongest competition figured to be Luz Long, a German law student who was the European record holder and who set a new Olympic record in the preliminary round. Owens had much more difficulty. He fouled on his first attempt and, rattled, he made an uncharacteristically poor jump on his second. If he fouled or failed to make the minimum distance of 7.15 m.— ordinarily no challenge for him—he would fail to make the finals. At that point, according to the story told by Owens in later years, Long came up to him and helped him out. Owens' renditions of the story varied to some extent. The essence, though, is that Long expressed empathy for Owens' psychological state and suggested that Owens make a mark well behind the bar to use as a guide for his take-off; the idea was that Owens would then be able to jump with confidence and easily achieve the minimum distance to qualify. In one rendition, Long actually laid down his towel for Owens to use as a guide, JESSE OWENS WITH PAUL NEIMARK, JESSE: THE MAN WHO OUTRAN HITLER 79–84 (1978); in another, Owens laid down his own towel. JESSE OWENS WITH PAUL NEIMARK, BLACKTHINK: MY LIFE AS A BLACK MAN AND A WHITE MAN 188–89 (1970); *see also* JESSE OWENS RETURNS TO BERLIN (1966) (documentary film narrated by Owens). Owens's last jump easily qualified him for the final. In that round, after a spirited competition, Owens won the gold and the silver went to Long, who greeted him warmly in front of Hitler and a full arena.

Though doubts have been raised, let's assume that the essence of the story is right. What might have motivated Long? Perhaps it was the fact that he knew that Owens was the greatest broad jumper in the world, and Long preferred to increase his chances of competing against Owens in the final round even at the expense of diminishing his chances of winning a gold medal. If so, where on the spectrum does Long's conduct lie, running from "That just defeats the point of competition and demeans the opponent," through "That was noble behavior, but we can't expect anybody but heroes to engage in it," to "This is the way athletes ought to act, even or especially elite athletes in championship competitions"? How would your answer change if instead of helping Owens avoid a foul in the preliminary round, in the middle of the final round he told Owens of an easily correctable technical flaw that was costing him distance? If you think the cases are different, why?

　　5.　*Sport and sportsmanship*. Recall the first topic in this book: what is sport? We observed then that figuring out what sport is might have implications for ethical or practical questions. Here's one possibility: the nature of sport informs the nature of sportsmanship. How might that be?

Recall the suggestion that it is a necessary condition of an activity being a sport that it exhibits "warranted seriousness." As explained earlier:

> This single condition has two components. First, there exists a recognizable community of participants whose members participate in the activity seriously, in the sense (roughly) of committing significant time and effort both in engaging in the activity and in training for it, as by seeking to improve their skills at it. That is, the activity is taken seriously by enough persons to constitute a community of serious participants. Second, this seriousness of engagement is warranted, not wholly misplaced. At a minimum . . ., an activity warrants being taken seriously if it develops and displays skills or qualities that qualify as human excellences—speed, strength, agility, hand-eye coordination, endurance, resilience, and so forth.

Berman, *Sport as a Thick Cluster Concept*, at 110. If that is so, then the virtue of sportsmanship might involve the disposition to reduce one's chances of winning in order to allow the particular excellences that the sport involves to be exhibited and to have their proper influence on the contest's outcome. That is, not every conduct that is generous to an opponent at personal cost counts as sportsmanship, but only self-abnegation that promotes the display and development of the particular human excellences that are necessary to make the activity a *sport* (and not merely a game or pastime).

　　On this view, Holtman and Wallace exhibited sportsmanship because hitting the ball over the fence is a signal excellence and, while baserunning often is too, no excellence is involved in being able to circle the bases after the batted ball has left the park—all that's required is that the batter touch the bases in order. Arsène Wenger exhibited sportsmanship. Jack Nicklaus did not. Putting under pressure is one of the excellences that golf tests, and Nicklaus relieved Jacklin of the obligation to execute that athletic challenge. (And what about Luz Long?)

That is not to say that Nicklaus was wrong to concede the putt, or that his concession wasn't praiseworthy. Perhaps it was; we have addressed some of the considerations in comment 1. But if so, it wasn't, on this view, by dint of displaying the virtue of sportsmanship. There are, after all, many different virtues. Perhaps his action was gallant or chivalrous or generous. But, according to this argument, it didn't embody the particular virtue that is sportsmanship.

Do you agree with this view? If not, why not? Could you defend a broader conception of sportsmanship? What, if anything, depends on the matter?

6. *Exploiting absent-mindedness: the forgotten chess clock.* Time is a critical element in competitive chess. In international chess matches, for example, each player must make the first 40 moves within two hours. Other competitions allow a shorter amount of time, either for a prescribed number of moves or for all the moves in the game. A player who runs out of time loses the game. Time is typically kept with a double-clock mechanism. As soon as a player moves, he presses a button on his clock, which stops his time running and starts his opponent's time. But suppose, as sometimes happens, that White makes a move and forgets to press the clock. Assuming, as is usually the case below elite levels, that there is no official monitoring the match, what, if anything, should Black do?

If Black points out White's absent-mindedness, or punches White's clock himself, so that he does not take advantage of White's error, we might consider that an exercise of good sportsmanship. Is that the ethically required course of conduct? If so, what standard should Black use for deciding when to intervene? Consider that until White presses the clock he *could* choose to make another move with the same piece—assuming another move with that piece is possible. (The usual rule is that once a player touches a piece he must make a move with that piece.)

If you do not believe that it is ethically imperative that Black take affirmative action to correct White's error, may Black affirmatively act in the other direction? Suppose, for example, that Black, having seen what appears to be White's move, decides quickly what his next move will be (once the clock is actually punched) but acts for an extended period as if he is having trouble deciding. So he leaves White sitting smugly, thinking that Black is willing to use a good bit of his remaining time before committing himself—but in fact it is White's time that is ticking away!

And if you think that Black need not, and perhaps should not, correct White's (apparent) error, but that Black ought not act affirmatively to expand on the consequences of that error, just what should Black do? Sit impassively staring into space? Stare at White's clock? Do something else?

7. *The spirit of curling.* The Rules of Curling promulgated by the World Curling Federation start by declaring "The Spirit of Curling":

> Curling is a game of skill and traditions. A shot well executed is a
> delight to see and so, too, it is a fine thing to observe the time-honored

traditions of curling being applied in the true spirit of the game. Curlers play to win but never to humble their opponents. A true curler would prefer to lose rather than win unfairly.

No curler ever deliberately breaks a rule of the game or any of its traditions. But, if a curler should do so inadvertently and be aware of it, he or she is the first to divulge the breach.

While the main objective of the game is to determine the relative skills of the players, the spirit of the game demands good sportsmanship, kindly feeling and honorable conduct.

This spirit should influence both the interpretation and application of the rules of the game and also the conduct of all participants on and off the ice.

Consider, in light of the Spirit of Curling, a famous incident from the 1988 Labatt Brier, the Canadian curling championship.

There are three types of throws in curling: (1) the draw, where the stone is intended to stop within the rings; (2) the hit, intended to remove the opponent's stone; and (3) the guards, which are left in front of the rings to protect the stones within the rings. For most of curling's five-centuries-long history, the hit was the poor stepchild: a curler would throw a hit when necessary to knock out an opponent's stone that was blocking the rings, but the emphasis was always on trying to throw accurate draws of your own, and not to knock your opponent's stones away. At the 1988 Brier, curler Pat Ryan embraced the hit. Choosing a defensive strategy over an offensive one, Ryan's team aimed with every shot to knock their opponents' stone away rather than to land their own stone in scoring position, thereby ensuring that the entire game would be determined by the hammer—the last shot—thrown by the skip. Opponents and fans alike hated Ryan's approach, complaining that it frustrated the many skills of the game and was painfully dull to watch. During a game that Ryan's team won 3–2 (the lowest scoring final game in Brier history), the crowd—a Canadian crowd, mind you—loudly chanted "bo-ring, bo-ring." The episode is engagingly recounted in *The Losers: Stone Cold* (Netflix release Mar. 1, 2019).

Did Pat Ryan violate the Spirit of Curling? Wasn't his strategy clearly a break in curling's traditions? If so, what follows? Does it matter that, in 1993, the World Curling Federation enacted a new rule (Rule 6) that protects the first three stones thrown by each team from being hit by the opponent, and that many curling players and fans believe that the game is more exciting and skillful now than it was before Ryan's innovation?

Consider too the controversy that arose at the 2018 Olympic women's curling competition in a match between Canada and Denmark when Danish player Julie Hoegh touched a moving stone thrown by a teammate when sweeping. This is known as "burning" a stone, and the rules provide that the non-offending team has the option to:

1)   remove the touched stone, and replace all stones that were displaced after the infraction to their positions prior to the violation taking place; or

2)   leave all stones where they came to rest; or

3)   place all stones where it reasonably considers the stones would have come to rest had the moving stone not been touched.

Rule 8(b)(i). Despite the formal availability of these three options, common practice clearly established that option (1) is disfavored, and that the non-offending team would elect option (2) if the burn didn't affect the speed or direction of the stone. Observers also agreed that Hoegh's touch of her team's stone was negligible and didn't affect its placement, as it had already come almost entirely to rest. Nonetheless, Canadian skip Rachel Homan chose option (1), removing the Danish stone, provoking an uproar even from fellow Canadian curlers. One member of the 1972 Canadian men's curling team thought it well established that "[i]f there's no change in the line of the rock and/or the speed of the rock, then you just let it run." Colleen Derworiz, *Curling has changed, say veteran players, after burned rock singes Canada's fortunes*, THE CANADIAN PRESS (Feb. 16, 2018). CBC Sports analyst and 1998 Olympic women's curling champion Joan McCusker criticized Homan's choice as "a rash move," adding that "They should have left it in play. It doesn't look good on you." *Bad burn: Rachel Homan criticized for poor curling etiquette*, CBC SPORTS (Feb. 16, 2018). Can there be much doubt that this was a violation of the Spirit of Curling? If so, why should it have been allowed?

8.   *The spirit of Aloha.* "Aloha," the common Hawaiian greeting, is a word with profound meaning. Often said to embrace love, affection, peace, compassion, and kindness, it is widely regarded as untranslatable into English. In 1986, the Hawaii legislature enacted the Aloha Spirit Law, which provides as follows:

(a)   "Aloha Spirit" is the coordination of mind and heart within each person. It brings each person to the self. Each person must think and emote good feelings to others. In the contemplation and presence of the life force, "Aloha", the following unuhi laula loa [acrostic] may be used:

"Akahai," meaning kindness to be expressed with tenderness;

"Lokahi," meaning unity, to be expressed with harmony;

"'Olu olu," meaning agreeable, to be expressed with pleasantness;

"Haahaa," meaning humility, to be expressed with modesty;

"Ahonui," meaning patience, to be expressed with perseverance.

These are traits of character that express the charm, warmth and sincerity of Hawaii's people. It was the working philosophy of native Hawaiians and was presented as a gift to the people of Hawaii.

"Aloha" is more than a word of greeting or farewell or a salutation. "Aloha" means mutual regard and affection and extends warmth in caring with no obligation in return. "Aloha" is the essence of relationships in which each person is important to every other person for collective existence. "Aloha" means to hear what is not said, to see what cannot be seen and to know the unknowable.

(b) In exercising their power on behalf of the people and in fulfillment of their responsibilities, obligations and service to the people, the legislature, governor, lieutenant governor, executive officers of each department, the chief justice, associate justices, and judges of the appellate, circuit, and district courts may contemplate and reside with the life force and give consideration to the "Aloha Spirit."

5 Hawaii Revised Statutes § 5–7.5.

Acknowledging that the law "is virtually impossible to enforce," Dana Viola, first deputy attorney general of Hawaii, nonetheless observed that "all citizens and government officials of Hawaii are obligated to conduct themselves in accordance with this law." Breena Kerr, *In Hawaii, being nice is the law,* BBC TRAVEL (Apr. 23, 2018). Is that correct? In what sense are they obligated? Is the Aloha Spirit any more or less enforceable than the spirit of curling?

3. CORRECTING OFFICIALS' ERRORS

A famous ad, sponsored by the Foundation for a Better Life, features a high school boys' basketball game between the Eagles in red and the Bears in white. With the score tied and only seconds remaining, two players lunge for an errant pass from a player on the Eagles. Calling the ball off the player in red, the referee signals possession for white, and the Bears call timeout. The player in white, Alex, jogs to the bench, and confesses sheepishly that he touched the ball last. His teammates berate him, and his coach grimaces. But Alex presses on—"I touched it. It's their ball"—and his coach indicates that Alex may tell the ref. As the Bears players run back onto the court, the coach yells to Alex. "Alex," he says, and pauses. "Good call." You can watch the ad here: https://tinyurl.com/y4t2zauj. (Are you sure that Alex did touch the ball? Could he have been mistaken?)

Now consider this dissenting view:

Sorry, Alex. Not so good call.

We're all for honesty, and I'd hug Alex if he were my son. But sports and life aren't nearly that simple. . . . Remember the "Hand of God" goal in the 1986 World Cup? If Maradona had told the official he touched the ball, he would have had to enter Argentina's Witness Protection Program.

Golfers are supposed to enforce their game's rules. In most other sports, officials officiate and players play. Both parties do

their best. If the refs fail to be perfect, it's not cheating to accept
their decision. . . .

Sports can teach great lessons, but I'd hate for Alex to feel
guilty for doing nothing wrong. . . . In a few years, Alex and
another guy are vying for the same job. The company awards it to
Alex even though he secretly believes the other guy deserves it
more.

What's he supposed to do, turn it down? I'd like to see him
explain that one to the wife and kids.

Honesty is the best policy, but sometimes life gives you a
break. There's nothing dishonest about taking it.

David Whitley, *Let's be Honest—In Sports, Like Life, Things Aren't Always
Black and White,* SPORTING NEWS, Apr. 25, 2011, at p. 67.

COMMENTS AND QUESTIONS

1. *"Sorry, Alex"?* Plainly, David Whitley is not a big fan of the
Foundation for a Better Life commercial, or of its hero, Alex. But what, exactly,
is Whitley's beef? On one hand, Whitley contends that "it's not cheating" to
accept a ref's decision even when you know it's wrong, and that "there's nothing
dishonest" about doing so. These are fairly modest claims, and possibly even
ones that the Foundation could agree with. The point of the ad need not be that
remaining silent in this context is wrongful or blameworthy. It could be much
more modest—say, that speaking up is virtuous or praiseworthy. Yet Whitley
could be read to maintain that even that is not true. That seems to be the
import of his gibe: "Sorry, Alex. Not so good call." Then again, Whitley says
that if Alex were his son, he'd hug him. So what is Whitley's point? Only that
Alex would not have acted badly had he stayed quiet, or (more strongly) that
Alex was somehow wrong to fess up—that what the ad presents as a virtue is
really a vice? Or is his point something else? How would you assess Alex's
behavior here? If you believe that Alex acted wrongfully, is that because he
owed a duty to his teammates not to unilaterally decline the referee's
inadvertent gift, or for some other reason?

2. *Beyond sports.* Consider the analogy Whitley offers from "real life."
Do you agree that it would be improper for you to turn down a promotion at
your job because you believe that another candidate was more deserving? If so,
do you also believe that, if a cashier or server gives you too much change, it
would be improper to return the extra money? Which do you think would be
harder to explain to your spouse and kids—returning the money or staying
silent? Which hypothetical case—"undeserved promotion" or "too much
change"—is more analogous to Alex's case? Is returning excess change to a
cashier like declining "Bank Error in Your Favor" in Monopoly?

3. *The Klose case.* In light of Whitley's comments about Maradona,
recall that Miroslav Klose admitted to an inadvertent handball in a league

game in Italy's Serie A. (See p. 500.) Klose's confession bears an unmistakable resemblance to Alex's, and Klose was roundly praised. Does this real-life incident support Alex, or is the Klose case not so close?

4. *Acts and omissions.* If you believe that competitors in officiated contests ought not to affirmatively deceive the officials but are under no obligation to correct what they know to be an official's misunderstanding, how would you assess the actions of German goalkeeper Manuel Neuer in a 2010 World Cup match against England? With Germany leading the Three Lions 2–1 in the round of 16, English midfielder Frank Lampard shot a ball that passed Neuer, hit the goal bar, landed inside the goal, and then jumped back into the field. Neuer quickly grabbed the ball and continued the game, as if the ball had not crossed the line. And indeed, the referee ruled that Lampard's ball had not passed the goal line and therefore did not constitute a goal for England, despite the fact that it clearly had. See p. 374.

After the game, Neuer admitted that he had seen that the ball landed within the goal, but tried to act "naturally" in order to deceive the referee. "I tried not to react to the referee and just concentrate on what was happening," he told reporters. I realised it was over the line and I think the way I carried on so quickly fooled the referee into thinking it was not over."[g] Did Neuer behave appropriately? Is there a difference between Neuer's conduct and Derek Jeter's behavior in inducing the homeplate umpire to mistakenly believe that he had been hit by a pitch (discussed pp. 492–496? Is there a difference between Neuer's conduct and pitch framing by catchers?

5. *The stronger claim.* If you take the more moderate position that Alex displayed praiseworthy good sportsmanship, but was not obligated to do as he did (and would not have been properly criticized had he remained mum), are there nonetheless times when one does have an obligation to make a call against oneself, or would be blameworthy for failing to do so? More broadly, when, if ever, is it condemnable bad sportsmanship to fail to exhibit praiseworthy good sportsmanship?

6. *Showing up the official?* Don Budge, the first man to win the tennis Grand Slam, told of an incident that occurred in his quarter-final match against Bunny Austin at Wimbledon in 1935. In the third set, while the match was close, Austin hit a good shot past Budge that the linesman called out. "[W]ith a certain martyr's flair," Budge intentionally hit Austin's next shot into the net, thinking this act was "the very hallmark of good sportsmanship." Budge won the match in four sets and then, to his surprise, Gottfried von Cramm of Germany, his prospective opponent in the semis, criticized him for unsportsmanlike conduct. Cramm told him:

> You made a great show of giving away a point because you felt the call had wronged Bunny. But is that your right? You made yourself an official, which you are not, and in improperly assuming this duty

---

[g]   *See, e.g.,* Matt Barlow, *Germany goalkeeper Manuel Neuer admits, 'Yes, I conned the referee,'* DAILY MAIL (June 28, 2010).

so that you could correct things your way, you managed to embarrass that poor linesman in front of 18,000 people.

DON BUDGE, DON BUDGE: A TENNIS MEMOIR 88–89 (1969). What do you think? Does your answer depend upon Budge's reasons or motives?

Do you think that the propriety of Budge's action depends upon the social context? In particular, is it significant that the criticism came from a German, and one who, though he was often at odds with the Nazi regime, played, and later fought, for it? The legal ethicists Monroe Freedman and Abbe Smith contend that this incident (which they place in a 1937 match) suggests that "there are political, social, and humanist values that are expressed in the American preference for a system in which there is relatively greater regard for the individual litigant and less for the bureaucratic decisionmaker." MONROE H. FREEDMAN & ABBE SMITH, UNDERSTANDING LAWYERS' ETHICS 40 (4th ed. 2010). What is the upshot of this observation?

Budge, for his part, reports that he was persuaded by Cramm and assured him that he "would never again be guilty of such misplaced charity"—and indeed that he began putting his new practice into place in his match against Cramm two days later. He expresses annoyance at Bill Tilden, who not only gave away points after bad calls in his favor but expected opponents to give away points after what Tilden thought were bad calls *against* him. And he says that when he turned pro he and Ellsworth Vines, another American, were each glad to find that both "played every shot exactly as it was called, without sympathy, and . . . never had a single argument on the whole tour." BUDGE, at 89–91.

Compare the following view:

A common misconception about sportsmanship is that the true sportsman respects the rulings of officials at all times. Wrong. Sometimes officials, being only human, make such glaring mistakes, or perpetrate such rank injustices, that their decisions need to be challenged. It is the players, and the bonds of respect between them, that constitute true sport: the man with the whistle is just an accessory.

MAX DAVIDSON, IT'S NOT THE WINNING THAT COUNTS: THE MOST INSPIRING MOMENTS OF SPORTING CHIVALRY 63 (2009). Is this sentiment admirable in principle but overly idealistic in a world in which one's opponents play by a different code? Or is it correct even in today's society? Or is it misguided even in principle? Or something else?

7. *Call your own, again?* Budge says that Cramm "was, simply, the greatest sportsman I ever encountered. There was no one even close to him." As an illustration, he presents an account of an incident, also in 1935, in which Cramm and his partner had appeared to win a Davis Cup match "until Cramm volunteered that the ball had illegally nicked his racket." The acknowledgment cost Germany the match. *Id.* at 9. How, if at all, is this conduct materially

distinguishable from the act of Budge's that Cramm criticized? Is it distinguishable from Alex's call?

Situations comparable to this one arise often in volleyball. Consider this account of his experiences from one player and coach:

> In volleyball, it has been customary for players to "call their own touches," telling the official that the opposing player's attack actually touched their finger tip while they were blocking, giving the point to the attacking side, when it was originally ruled "out" by the official. Often players will tell the official that they touched the net, granting the point to the opposing side. This practice becomes less common, the more competitive the level of sport, and it does not occur at the professional level. . . .
>
> I played high school volleyball on a team instructed to call both its own touches and its own nets. Our coach, who was tough, but whom we loved to play for, praised us for calling our own. The officials became habituated to this practice, as did most other teams in the league. After all, we were the gold standard of the league. We won the championship five out of six years in a row, losing fewer than ten matches in those six years. However, I also played Junior Olympic volleyball. The first time I called my own touch, our team captain, a future U.S. Olympian, looked at me sternly as if to say, "We don't do that here." I never saw players calling their own touches at the national tournaments. I returned to coach at my alma mater for ten years after only being away for three. The custom of calling your own touches was still lingering around, and our school participated. At this point, my former coach was coaching at another school in our league, and his team called their own as well. However, during my tenure as coach, we were the second best team in the league, not the first. We won one championship and placed second eight times, all to the same school. This school eventually stopped calling its touches. By the end of my tenure, only my former coach's team was calling theirs, and it seemed the custom was going the way of women riding horse back side-saddled. Its logic started seeming as absurd as that guiding Alex's.

Seth Vannatta, *Calling Your Own: Custom and Law in Sports Officiating* (unpublished manuscript, Sept. 9, 2011). What lesson do you draw from this account? Vannatta asks: "Could it be that the most dominant team in the league set the standard to be followed by others, and this largely formed the social context of the sport giving rise to its ethos?"

Ultimate, the team flying-disc sport also called Ultimate Frisbee, is, in most iterations, a self-refereed sport. The official rules of the World Flying Disc Federation (WFDF) provide that "only the player fouled may claim a foul," but also that "[i]f a breach is committed and not called, the player committing the breach should inform the opponent or their team." Rule 15.4, and Interpretation. Furthermore, Rule 1, "Spirit of the Game," provides generally that all players must "be truthful," and "only make a call where a breach is significant enough to make a difference to the outcome of the action." Rules 1.3.3, 1.3.8. If, after discussion, players cannot agree whether there was an infraction, or what would have occurred had an infraction not been committed, "the disc must be returned to the last non-disputed thrower." Rule 1.12. But increasingly in recent years, high-stakes games, including bracket play at major tournaments, feature "observers," who make some active calls, such as in or out, which players may (but rarely do) effectively overrule, but only to the detriment of their team. Players can also refer to observers questions of rules clarification or, more often, disagreements as to matters such as fouls. *See* USA Ultimate Observer Manual (modified 2020), https://tinyurl.com/yxtcrvxy; USA Ultimate Policy on Observers and Referees (adopted 2003), https://tinyurl.com/yy5s4oga (endorsing use of observers but not of referees; asserting that "[w]hile Observers can provide a neutral perspective for dispute resolution or calls of an objective nature, the responsibility for the integrity of Ultimate and the Spirit of the Game remains with the players"). The Premier Ultimate League, a new women's professional league, uses observers, but the American Ultimate Disc League, a men's professional league, uses ordinary referees. Why do you think the sport has drifted in the direction of relying on third parties? Do you think that good-faith self-refereeing is impossible, or unrealistic, at an elite level of competition? Do you think that adherence to the spirit of the game can survive the introduction of officials?

8. *When love means nothing.* In the decisive third set of a semifinal match at the 2003 French Open, Justine Henin-Hardenne raised her hand to indicate that she was not ready to receive a serve from her opponent, Serena Williams. Williams hit her serve softly into the net. But the chair umpire had not seen Henin-Hardenne's motion, and Williams was not awarded a first serve. Williams, who had been up a service break, lost the next four points and ultimately the match. Afterwards, she said that she was "a little disappointed" with Henin-Hardenne, and that "lying and fabricating is not fair." For her part, Henin-Hardenne said that "[t]he chair umpire is there to deal with these kind of situations," and that "[h]e didn't ask me anything." *She said, she said: Serena cries foul, but Henin-Hardenne offers no apology,* SPORTS ILLUSTRATED, June 6, 2003.

Is there a good reason why the chair umpire should not have asked Henin-Hardenne whether she had indicated that she wasn't ready for Williams's serve? If the umpire had asked, would Henin-Hardenne have been obligated to respond honestly? Should Henin-Hardenne have volunteered the truth even absent any questioning from the umpire? Was she guilty of bad sportsmanship, or did she merely fail to exhibit good sportsmanship? Note that a similar incident occurred in a fourth-round match at the same tournament four years later, with Maria Sharapova and Patty Schnyder replacing Henin-Hardenne and Williams, respectively. "It's tough playing tennis and being Mother Teresa at the same time," commented Sharapova about her failure to intervene. Greg Garber, *Gamesmanship is name of the game in tennis,* ESPN.com (July 31, 2007).

If you conclude that Henin-Hardenne and Sharapova acted badly in remaining mum, do you also conclude that Alex would have been guilty of bad sportsmanship had he not spoken up? Or are the cases distinguishable? Compare this rule from American tort law: an individual normally has no affirmative duty to protect another person from harm or injury; however, "[w]hen an actor's prior conduct, even though not tortious, creates a continuing risk of physical harm of a type characteristic of the conduct, the actor has a duty to exercise reasonable care to prevent or minimize the harm." Restatement (Third) Torts § 39.

9.   *Sportsmanship, professionalism in the law, and changing mores.* Many observers bemoan a decline in good sportsmanship. (For a striking image of sportsmanship from long ago, albeit not entirely representative, consider the English Corinthian Football Club, active from 1882 to 1939. Not only would the Corinthians, like the fictional basketball player Alex, correct referee errors in their favor, they also took an unconventional view toward penalty kicks: "if a penalty was awarded in their favour, they would deliberately miss it; if it was awarded against them, the Corinthian goalkeeper would stand aside and let the opposition score." DAVIDSON, IT'S NOT THE WINNING THAT COUNTS, at 61.) If there has in fact been a decline in sportsmanship, perhaps it is part of a broader social trend, exemplified as well, in the view of many, by a steep decline in the ideal of professionalism in the practice of law. *See, e.g.,* ANTHONY T. KRONMAN, THE LOST LAWYER: FAILING IDEALS OF THE LEGAL PROFESSION (1993); Warren E. Burger, *The Decline of Professionalism,* 63 FORDHAM L. REV. 949 (1995). As noted by one commentator, "the changing nature of society" may have had a deep impact on legal practice: "Some lawyers believe that the populace has become more cantankerous and litigious. Individuals are now more obstreperous when dealing with lawyers, judges, and governmental officials; are more insistent on filing unmeritorious litigation; and seem to prefer for their lawyers to engage in Rambo tactics." John F. Sutton, Jr., *Lawyers Today: Wise Professionals or Mere Skill Technicians,* 35 S. TEX. L. REV. 741, 750–51 (1994).

Consider, in this light, the following proposal that builds on Berman's suggestion, presented at p. 537, that sportsmanship is a particular virtue of athletic competition that aims to realize the excellences that a given sport facilitates and embodies even at the cost of reducing one's probability of winning in accordance with the formal rules. Similarly, professionalism in the law is a particular virtue of legal practice that aims to realize the excellences that a legal system is designed to secure (notably, but not exclusively, justice) even at the cost of reducing one's probability of winning in accordance with the rules.

More simply put, both sportsmanship in athletic competition and professionalism in law value central excellences that their respective domains of life serve and make possible even at the expense of victory in the zero-sum competitions that the respective domains structure. In both cases, these virtues can be contrasted both with gamesmanship, which is the virtue of pursuing victory in accordance with the formal rules without regard for other domain-specific excellences and values, and with cheating, which is the vice of pursuing victory by any means available. Is this an illuminating analogy? If not, why not? If so, does anything useful follow?

PART V

OUTSIDE THE LINES

■ ■ ■

This final part addresses two topics peripheral to the play of the game. Chapter 16 examines the growing tendency of sports leagues to regulate the off-field conduct of their athletes. Chapter 17 discusses record-keeping and related matters, such as eligibility for a sport's hall of fame.

CHAPTER 16

REGULATION OF OFF-FIELD CONDUCT

■ ■ ■

Many sports leagues have personal conduct policies, incorporated in their charters or adopted in collective bargaining agreements, that give the head of the league broad authority to punish conduct that puts the league in a bad light. (For one summary, see Janine Young Kim & Matthew J. Parlow, *Off-Court Misbehavior: Sports Leagues and Private Punishment*, 99 J. CRIM. L. & CRIMINOLOGY 573 (2009).) The progenitor of them all was the power given the first commissioner of baseball, Judge Kenesaw Mountain Landis, appointed after the 1919 Chicago "Black Sox" scandal, to investigate and punish any action he determined to be "detrimental to the best interest of the national game of baseball." Landis's successor, A.B. (Happy) Chandler invoked this power in suspending Leo Durocher, manager of the Brooklyn Dodgers, for one year in 1947, for an "accumulation of unpleasant incidents, in which he has been involved." *Text of the Decision by Commissioner Chandler*, N.Y. TIMES, Apr. 10, 1947, at 31. Among the unpleasantries said to motivate Chandler were "gambling debts, associations with known gamblers and nightlife figures, and a scandalous marriage with charges of adultery, bigamy, and contempt of court." Jeffrey Marlett, *The Suspension of Leo Durocher*, in THE TEAM THAT FOREVER CHANGED BASEBALL AND AMERICA: THE 1947 BROOKLYN DODGERS, SOCIETY FOR AMERICAN BASEBALL RESEARCH 50 (2012).

Section Article 8.13(A) of the NFL's Constitution and Bylaws provides that if, after notice and hearing, the Commissioner determines that any person connected with the League has committed "conduct detrimental to the welfare of the League or professional football," the Commissioner has power to suspend that person and impose a fine up to $500,000. The League's Personal Conduct Policy ("PCP") offers some elaboration. The 2016 version provides:

> It is a privilege to be part of the National Football League. **Everyone** who is part of the league must refrain from "conduct detrimental to the integrity of and public confidence in" the NFL. . . . Conduct by anyone in the league that is illegal, violent, dangerous, or irresponsible puts innocent victims at risk, damages the reputation of others in the game, and undercuts public respect and support for the NFL. We must endeavor at all times to be people of high character; we must show respect for others inside and outside our workplace; and we must strive to conduct ourselves in ways that favorably reflect on ourselves, our teams, the communities we represent, and the NFL.
>
> It is not enough simply to avoid being found guilty of a crime. We are all held to a higher standard and must conduct ourselves in a way that is responsible, promotes the values of the NFL, and is lawful. Players convicted of a crime or subject to a disposition of a criminal proceeding (as defined in this Policy) are subject to discipline. But even if the conduct does not result in a criminal conviction, players found to have engaged in any of the following conduct will be subject to discipline.

There follows a long, non-exclusive list that includes, among others, crimes of violence or dishonesty, sex offenses, drug-related crimes, cruelty to animals, crimes against law enforcement, and "[c]onduct that undermines or puts at risk the integrity of the NFL, NFL clubs, or NFL personnel." The list is long and broad enough to include most crimes that NFL players and other shareholders are likely to commit. (Few are suspected to have committed treason.) One may wonder why these crimes and not others—smuggling?—are listed. But the more difficult questions, perhaps, are these: What if there is plausible reason to believe that a player has committed a significant crime, but the player is not charged or is charged but not convicted? And what off-field misconduct that is *not* criminalized, if any, should the League prohibit and punish?

Consider these cases involving former or present NFL players:

- Ray Lewis, a linebacker for the Baltimore Ravens, was charged with murder in 2000 after an altercation of which he was a part led to the stabbing deaths of two men. Ultimately, at trial, Lewis negotiated a deal. He pled guilty to a misdemeanor charge of obstruction of justice, for having falsely told the police that he was not at the scene, and agreed to testify against his co-defendants (who ultimately were acquitted). Lewis was sentenced to one year of probation, and the League fined him $250,000, but he was not suspended. He was the MVP of the 2001 Super Bowl.

- Ray Rice, then a running back with the Baltimore Ravens, was charged with aggravated assault in 2014 after an altercation with his fiancée, Janay Palmer. A video made public shortly after the incident showed him dragging her out an elevator, apparently after knocking her out. The criminal charges were ultimately dropped with an agreement that the case would be dismissed if Rice satisfactorily completed an anger-management course, attended counseling sessions, and committed no further crimes. Commissioner Roger Goodell initially imposed a fine of one week's salary and a two-game suspension. This was met with a firestorm of criticism, that the punishment was too light, and Goodell announced that in the future the presumptive penalty for domestic violence for a first-time offender would be a six-game suspension. Then a video from inside the elevator became public; it showed Rice hitting Palmer on the head, knocking her out, and then attempting to lift her and dropping her. Goodell, claiming that this was newly discovered evidence and he had been misled, suspended Rice indefinitely. An arbitrator, however, concluded that Goodell knew the essential facts of the incident before first imposing a penalty, and so the increase was arbitrary. *In the Matter of Ray Rice*, Arbitration Decision (Barbara S. Jones 2014), https://tinyurl.com/y3dc6jut.

- In 2009, a civil suit accused Ben Roethlisberger, quarterback of the Pittsburgh Steelers, of sexual assault. The matter was ultimately resolved by a settlement, details of which were not made public. During the course of the proceedings, an affidavit filed by a friend of the plaintiff contended that the plaintiff had bragged about having had consensual sex with Roethlisberger. In 2010, police in Milledgeville, Georgia investigated a contention that Roethlisberger had sexually assaulted a woman in the women's restroom of a night club. Ultimately, the district attorney announced that he would not bring charges because he could not prove guilt beyond a reasonable doubt. The accuser had written a letter saying she no longer wanted to pursue criminal charges, because the personal experience would be too intrusive, but emphasizing that she was not recanting her accusation. Goodell suspended Roethlisberger for six games; ultimately, the suspension was reduced to four games.

COMMENTS AND QUESTIONS

1. PCPs and vagueness. Are broadly worded PCPs like the NFL's problematic or objectionable? If so, why? Consider the argument made by sports columnist Paula Duffy in response to the initial suspension of Roethlisberger. (Duffy quotes the League's Code of Conduct as it then stood and invokes Justice Potter Stewart's famous standard for assessing whether material is hard-core pornography):

> Under the NFL's Code of Conduct the only question that is relevant is if the behavior "promotes the values upon which the League is based", and oh yeah, it better be lawful. I'm as much an NFL junkie as the next person but I'll be darned if I know what values were chosen to base a football league on. Would I know it "when I see it"?

> Was the league based on the values of a traditional family structure? Adults producing children who were born within a marriage would likely fit that bill. How does the NFL look at its players who father children out of wedlock?

> We don't know, do we? No one has gotten suspended for having children by women with whom they don't live.

Paula Duffy, *NFL Personal Conduct Policy: Morality Legislation or Employee Code,* HUFFINGTON POST (June 21, 2010). Duffy mentions the cases of Tom Brady, a "league darling," and at the other end of the spectrum Antonio Cromartie, who had "seven children with women spread across five or six states." Duffy asks whether "the fact that Brady clearly didn't want to stick around to 'do the right thing' with his former lover promote[d] a league value," and whether Cromartie would violate league policy if he had his salary garnished for violating a court-ordered support agreement. And she wondered whether by using general phrases about values the NFL's rulemakers "really mean only misconduct that is brought to the attention of the public whose values the league thinks might be offended."

On one reading, Duffy's principal objection is that the relevant language is too vague, giving persons subject to the policy insufficient notice of what conduct would violate the policy. Is this how you read Duffy's piece? Is it a sound objection? Or are you persuaded by the following defense of the "conduct detrimental" language put forth by former NFL Commissioner Paul Tagliabue, in his ruling on the appeals brought by New Orleans Saints players to the suspensions levied by Commissioner Roger Goodell in connection with the 2009–11 scandal known as "bountygate"?

> There are vital reasons why all NFL-NFLPA Collective Bargaining Agreements since the 1970s have consistently given the Commissioner the exclusive and broad authority to decide what constitutes conduct detrimental. The integrity of and public confidence in the game of professional football are essential to the playing of the game itself and are critical to public interest in NFL football and to public respect for all those participating in NFL

football—owners, coaches, players, officials and executives. Equally important, the matters that can affect such integrity and public confidence evolve and change over time depending on both developments within and external to the League, and the parties to the CBAs have agreed not to operate with a static or frozen definition of conduct detrimental.

Paul Tagliabue, Final Decision on Appeal, *In the Matter of New Orleans Saints Pay-for-Performance/"Bounty,"* NFL.com (2012), https://tinyurl.com/yxanquym.

2.   *Overbreadth.* Are there other persuasive objections to PCPs like the NFL's? Consider the complaint that the policy governs conduct that is not the proper business of a sports league to police. If the first objection sounds in **vagueness**, this second sounds in **overbreadth**. (An overbroad norm covers things that, ideally, it wouldn't; a vague norm might encompass only the things that, in principle, it should, but gives suboptimal guidance to the norm's addressees and

Line-Drawing Problems

enforcers, thereby risking over- and under-deterrence and inviting excessive errors in application. See the discussion of rules and standards, pp. 95–100.) Do you agree with this complaint? Would it be an intolerable intrusion into personal liberty were the NFL to discipline players for fathering kids out of wedlock?

3.   *Slippery slopes.* Vagueness and overbreadth are distinct types of **line-drawing** difficulty or defect. A third distinct type is often called a **"slippery slope"** or **"camel's nose."** A norm that embodies this type of defect might be crisp (not vague) and on-target (not overbroad). The chief worry about norms that are claimed to reside on a slippery slope or embody a camel's nose (under the tent) is that they are likely to prove unstable—unusually ripe to be extended or supplemented in ways that would be objectionable even if the current norm isn't. For an insightful discussion, see FARNSWORTH, THE LEGAL ANALYST, at ch. 18 (with Eugene Volokh). Do PCPs present a slippery slope worry instead of, or in addition to, vagueness or overbreadth concerns? Why or why not?

4.   *Good for the gander?* In January 2019, Robert Kraft, owner of the New England Patriots, was captured on police surveillance video paying women working as massage therapists in Florida for manual and oral sex acts. As a result, Kraft was charged with two misdemeanor counts of soliciting prostitution, in violation of Florida law. Months later, a state judge threw out the video evidence as having been obtained on the strength of an overbroad warrant. *See* May Jeong, *"You Won't Believe What Happened": The Wild, Disturbing Saga of Robert Kraft's Visit to a Strip Mall Sex Spa,* VANITY FAIR, Nov. 2019. The state dropped the charges after losing its appeal. What consequences, if any, should the NFL impose on Kraft given this result? What if the state had won its appeal and Kraft had ultimately pled guilty or been convicted of one or both misdemeanors? If the basic facts are not in substantial

dispute, should it matter for purposes of league-imposed discipline whether the evidence was obtained in a manner that the criminal law, for its own purposes, deems objectionable? In 2018, Commissioner Goodell fined Jerry Richardson, then-owner of the Carolina Panthers, $2.75 million after Richardson faced credible accusations of mistreating female employees, and even though Richardson had not been criminally prosecuted or convicted. Are the Richardson and Kraft cases distinguishable?

5. *Bong hits 4 Michael*. Consider too the case of Michael Phelps. Six months after he won an unprecedented eight gold medals in swimming at the Beijing Olympics, Phelps was reprimanded and suspended from competition for three months by USA Swimming, his sport's governing body, for having been photographed smoking marijuana out of a water pipe at a party at the University of South Carolina. In a statement, USA Swimming explained, "We decided to send a strong message to Michael because he disappointed so many people, particularly the hundreds of thousands of USA Swimming member kids who look up to him as a role model and hero." Is it the proper business of an athletic federation to send messages to athletes concerning the propriety or desirability of their off-field conduct, when there is no serious contention that the conduct enhances performance in an illegitimate way?

Note that Kellogg's, one of Phelps's commercial sponsors, announced that as a result of his behavior it would not renew its contract with him. Surely Kellogg's, a private corporation with no obligation to Phelps beyond its then-current contract, was free not to renew. Given that, are there any grounds for concluding that USA Swimming acted beyond the scope of its authority? If you believe that Michael Phelps's recreational use of marijuana was properly subject to disciplinary action by USA Swimming, is it critical that such behavior was criminal? Would it have made a difference if Phelps had been caught smoking pot where it was legal to do so? If you believe that that is a critical distinction, do you also believe that athletic federations or sports leagues are without legitimate power to discipline athletes for making racist, sexist, anti-Semitic, or homophobic comments?

6. *Are sports leagues different?* Many employers, not only sports leagues, have adopted PCPs. Consider, accordingly, this response to the Duffy article, posted by one Huffington Post reader:

> This is a ludicrous article! The NFL and most corporations all have conduct policies and their employees all know what they include and what the penalties can be if said policies are violated. Our schools and universities also have these policies. There are consequences for bad behavior in the real world! The NFL is no more legislating morality than my company did when it said we couldn't bring guns to work or engage in sexual harassment!

Comment to Duffy, *NFL Personal Conduct Policy*. Do you agree, or might there be some reason why PCPs adopted by sports leagues are more troublesome than similarly worded policies adopted by single employers, either in the public or private sectors? Is it meaningful that antitrust law would usually prohibit all the employers in a single industry from agreeing to impose a single PCP, whereas sports leagues and federations are "the only game in town" for their athletes? Note too that, starting in the 2007 season, the Canadian Football League agreed with the NFL not to permit players suspended by the NFL to play in the CFL during the course of their suspensions. *CFL to Bar Suspended NFL Players*, CBC SPORTS, Nov. 19, 2006. Is this worrisome?

7. *Due process.* In addition to objections sounding in vagueness and overbreadth, many commentators have criticized PCPs for failing to provide persons disciplined under such policies with adequate procedural protections. The NFL's PCP provides, for example, that adverse rulings by the Commission can be appealed only to the Commissioner himself or to his designee. Is that a failure of due process? *See, e.g.,* David Sirotkin, *Disciplining the Disciplinary Systems in Professional Sports: An Attempt to Fix the Arbitrary and Overreaching Disciplinary Powers of Sports Commissioners,* 11 CARDOZO J. CONFLICT RESOL. 289 (2009).

8. *Gambling.* Since the Black Sox scandal of 1919, MLB has taken a rigorous stance against gambling on baseball. Anybody affiliated with a team or League who bets on "any baseball game in connection with which the bettor has no duty to perform" is rendered ineligible for one year, Major League Rule 21(d)(1), and if the bet is on a game in connection with which the bettor does have a duty to perform, then he "shall be declared permanently ineligible." Major League Rule 21(d)(2). A person on the ineligible list is not "eligible to play or associate with any Major or Minor League Club." Major League Rule 15(c)(1). These rules are well known throughout the sport. They have created little controversy—except with respect to Pete Rose.

Rose was indisputably a great baseball player. He is the all-time Major League hits leader, with 4,256 knocks spread across 24 seasons. He led the National League in batting three times and won three World Series rings. Remarkably, he played more than 500 games at each of five different positions. His intense style of play earned him the enduring nickname "Charlie Hustle." As his playing career wound down, he became manager of the team with which he had spent most of his career, the Cincinnati Reds. He had a winning record as manager over four seasons, but his career came to an abrupt end in 1989. After a league investigation into allegations that he had bet on baseball games, including Reds games, Rose agreed to accept permanent ineligibility and acknowledged that the Commissioner, A. Bartlett Giamatti, had "a factual basis to impose" that penalty. It appears that Rose, who continued to deny vehemently that he had bet on baseball, gained only one significant benefit from the agreement, avoidance of a formal determination that he had in fact done so. He did retain the right under Major League Rule 15(d) to apply for reinstatement.

And he has done so, repeatedly but to no avail. Giamatti died eight days after entering into the agreement, but each of the three succeeding Commissioners has declined to reinstate Rose—who, in 2004, finally acknowledged that he had bet on baseball and on the Reds (but never against them, he said). For all the years since 1989, this has meant that Rose could not manage, or perform any other role with a club, such as being a spring training instructor. (In recent years, the most salient consequence of the suspension has been that Rose, who was born in 1941, is ineligible for the Hall of Fame; we will consider the issues related to that aspect of the penalty separately, p. 572.)

At the time the penalty was imposed, was it justified? In thinking about this question, consider arguments based on the asserted benefits of (a) gaining *retribution* against Rose; (b) *incapacitation* of Rose, preventing him from betting on baseball while affiliated with a team; and (c) *deterrence* of Rose and others, inhibiting future violations of the Rules. What other considerations are relevant? Assuming that the penalty was justified when imposed, should Rose have been reinstated at any time since?[a] If you were the Commissioner, what more would you want to know before deciding? Would your answers change if it became clear that Rose had bet *against* the Reds? *How* clear would it have to be?

Which is a stronger basis for rendering Rose ineligible—that he gambled on baseball, and on his team, or that when he was in his 30s he had an ongoing sexual relationship with an underage girl, beginning (allegedly) when she was 14 or 15? Derek Hawkins, *Woman says she had sexual relationship with Pete Rose as an underage teen*, WASH. POST, Aug. 1, 2017.

Compare with the Rose case the NFL's handling of a gambling affair in April 1963. The Commissioner, Pete Rozelle, fined five Detroit Lions $2000 each for placing $50 bets on the previous season's championship game between the Green Bay Packers and the New York Giants. At the same time, Rozelle indefinitely suspended two top-flight stars, Paul Hornung of the Packers and Alex Karras of the Lions, for more sustained gambling, including on their own teams, and associations with gamblers. Both were reinstated eleven months later and continued their careers; Hornung was inducted into the NFL Hall of Fame in 1986, and Karras was elected in 2020.

9.   *Role models.* Broad league authority to police and penalize the off-field conduct of league athletes is sometimes defended, at least in part, on the ground that athletes are role models. Are they? What does this mean or entail? Consider the following view advanced by the philosopher Christopher Wellman:

> [I]t falls upon all of us to serve as appropriate role models, and so when I speak of celebrated athletes having a special responsibility, I mean only that [they] have *additional* moral reasons to act virtuously. Thus, I do not claim that [they] must necessarily behave *better* than others. In short, everyone has moral reasons to encourage

---

[a]   *See also, e.g.,* Rob Neyer, *Rethinking Pete Rose's Reinstatement*, FOX SPORTS.COM (Mar. 19, 2015) (arguing for a decision "that allows for the possible redemption of an old man while he might still enjoy it" and "that acknowledges our infinite fallibility, but also our infinite capacity for mercy and forgiveness"); Evan Caminker & Erwin Chemerinsky, *Pete Rose Has Done His Time*, N.Y. TIMES, Feb. 11, 2020 (noting a lawyers' petition to reinstate Rose).

virtue and discourage vice, but celebrated athletes have additional moral reasons to behave well.

[It is a mistake] to confuse those who *should* have influence with those who *do*. I agree that we would be a healthier society if more of us raised our children to emulate people who could write a graceful sentence, create a beautiful piece of artwork, or construct an elaborate and well-reasoned argument, but that is not the current state of affairs. Despite their being better suited for the job, these people do not have the influence [athletes] do, and so they do not have the extra moral reasons to behave well that [athletes] do. . . .

The relatively obscure professional athlete who is not emulated has no special responsibility, but the prominent amateur does. There is nothing intrinsic to athletics which requires its participants to be role models; were it not for the attention [they] happen to attract, [they] would have no special responsibilities.

Christopher Wellman, *Do Celebrated Athletes have Special Responsibilities to be Good Role Models? An Imagined Dialog between Charles Barkley and Karl Malone, in* SPORTS ETHICS: AN ANTHOLOGY 333 (Jan Boxill ed., 2003).

Randolph Feezell terms the position advanced by Wellman "exemplarism," and criticizes it in *Celebrated Athletes, Moral Exemplars, and Lusory Objects,* 32 J. PHIL. SPORT 20 (2005). Feezell's central objection is that it is redundant to say that celebrated athletes have *additional* reasons for acting virtuously, given that they already have moral reasons for doing so. But he worries that exemplarism has other defects, too. For one thing, because Wellman "admits, in the end, that celebrated athletes *are not* necessarily moral exemplars in the normative sense, although they are taken to be exemplars by people in our culture, especially children, there may be something dishonest or deceptive at the heart of the position." For another, the view "also appears to promote the false belief that being good at a practice entails being good overall or living a life whose perceived unity is worthy of being imitated."

After criticizing exemplarism on these and related grounds, Feezell has a suggestion:

Our sports heroes should be thought of more as imagined objects or fictional characters in a drama, whose character and exploits we admire within this illusory domain, rather than persons whose life outside of sports is exemplary, noteworthy, or even interesting. . . . We need know nothing of their life outside baseball to appreciate their play or encourage young players to learn from them and imitate their conduct within the world of baseball. . . .

Celebrated athletes are role models, not moral exemplars. They are lusory objects whose meaning and significance are internal to the world of the sport in which they excel. The major error of exemplarism is a confusion about the proper meaning of our sports heroes as lusory objects, inhabitants of a world set apart from the ordinary world by virtue of the conventions without which their heroic efforts would have no meaning or significance.

Id. at 31–32.

Do you find Feezell's criticisms of Wellman's position persuasive? Do you favor his proposal? Do you have a sense of how we could by act of will change how we think about our sports heroes? To what extent does resolution of this debate bear on the propriety of disciplinary action by sports leagues for the off-field conduct of their players? For coaches and other league officials who are *not* athletes?

CHAPTER 17

RECORDS, RECORD-KEEPING, AND HALLS OF FAME

■ ■ ■

"A trophy carries dust," says Olympian gold medalist gymnast Mary Lou Retton. "Memories last forever." Maybe so. How about records? They can't collect dust, they rarely last forever (though some do last longer than memories), and they hold for us a peculiar fascination. This Chapter concerns how and why we measure, evaluate, and recognize excellence in athletic performance and achievement. It has three Subchapters. Subchapter 17A concerns record-keeping basics. It examines the functions that the keeping of sports records serves and asks how record-keeping practices should be designed to best serve those functions. Subchapter 17B investigates whether and under what circumstances sport records should be revised in light of later developments. For example, the NCAA often strips teams of victories achieved on the playing field if it determines, even years after the fact, that a player on the team was ineligible. Is this a sensible practice? Subchapter 17C addresses considerations that should bear on an athlete's eligibility for sport-focused Halls of Fame.

A. RECORD-KEEPING BASICS

SHAYNA M. SIGMAN, ARE WE ALL DOPES? A BEHAVIORAL LAW AND ECONOMICS APPROACH TO LEGAL REGULATION OF DOPING IN SPORTS

19 MARQ. SPORTS L. REV. 125, 186–88 (2008)
© Marquette University, reprinted with permission

The motto of the Olympic Games, "Citrius, Altius, Fortius," means "Faster, Higher, Stronger." Records have long captivated the human imagination. People want to know who is the fastest, the strongest, who has done the most of anything, who represents the best of the best. Even for those who believe that winning is not everything, trying one's best is still a major component of athletic competition and participation. Anything less is somehow shirking a duty owed to oneself.

Record-keeping affords humanity the ability to measure established boundaries of achievement, aim to leap-frog them, set new limits, and demonstrate that even the seemingly impossible is attainable. The progress evinced within record-setting and record-breaking demonstrates the evolution of modern society, the triumph of body and spirit. Thus, athletic elite achievements themselves produce value in society.

The fascination with records is exemplified by the Guinness Book of World Records, a best-selling reference book (a record-setting book, even!) that has been translated and published around the globe at a rate that is perhaps only rivaled by the Bible. Nowhere is the significance of record-keeping more prominent than in sports. There is a tremendous amount of record-keeping and attention paid to statistics in sports, fueling not just the billion-dollar sports industry, but also the ever increasing in popularity sub-industry of fantasy leagues—which allow fans to focus on particular accomplishments and achievement of athletes independent from the performance of an existing sports team. Then there is the excitement and the attention surrounding record-breaking. Fans of sport debate which records are "unbreakable." The media focuses its attention on an athlete poised to break a significant record, and it is this possibility that keeps viewers on the edge of their seats. Yet not all record-breaking is equally captivating. . . .

Scholars have distinguished between different kinds of sport records. The most "pure" record occurs within a "standardized spatio-temporal framework." A "record sport" is one in which records can be measured in meters, seconds, or kilograms and are produced under identical or similar conditions. Weightlifting, running, or swimming all have the potential to be record sports. "Quasi-record sports" have standardized distances and timing requirements, but differences in venue or terrain can produce different results. Record sports, and even quasi-record sports, can be fascinating because they allow for the most precise determination of progress, evaluating who really is best, and what really is possible.

These two categories of sport records, however, exclude the vast majority of athletic competition. Any sport that is a competitive effort pitting one athlete or team against another cannot produce standardized records. Baseball, American football, futbol (soccer), basketball, hockey, tennis, and so many other sports all depend on the interaction of the competitors, e.g., offense vs. defense, player A draws a seed against player B, quality of a goaltender, and so forth. These sports do rely on quantifiable results—measuring goals, runs, baskets, touchdowns, points, and victories as well as other sub-components, such as aces, free-throw shots, or home-runs.

The lack of a standardized framework for judging performance does not deter record-keeping in these sports; on the contrary, it lends to robust debate seeking to compare athletes and teams despite the data limitations in doing so. Baseball is the sport that has generated the most sophisticated statistical forms of evaluating individuals in the context of team or both individuals and teams in the context of time. This is due both to a culture within baseball circles that reveres records and statistics as well as the ability to isolate performance, namely the one-on-one aspect of pitcher versus batter.

Some sports present an even greater hurdle for record-keeping and comparison, as they rely on a more significant element of judging to evaluate performance. Boxers, wrestlers, fencers, and martial artists may compete against one another, but without judges to score punches, hits landed, or take downs, there is no determination for victory. Gymnasts and figure skaters compete as individuals in standardized venues but receive their scores from a panel of judges.

While the nature of the records capable of being established might differ, given the right conditions, each form of elite sport is capable of demonstrating something about the limits and potential of humanity.

COMMENTS AND QUESTIONS

1. *Asymptotes.* Performances in record and quasi-record sports tend to improve asymptotically. They will continue to improve but in smaller and smaller increments, ever approaching, without quite reaching, an upper bound that marks the limits of human capacity. Take the 100m sprint, for example. As Sigman reports: "The fastest elite male athletes can run 100 meters in roughly 9.5 to 10 seconds. The fastest elite female athletes take between 10.5 to 11 seconds. No one expects to see male athletes post times under nine seconds or women under ten seconds. For thirty years, change has been measured by hundredths of a second. New records will be measured in thousandths of a second and beyond." Improvements in non-record sports are not asymptotic. To appreciate the difference, it might help to plot performances on a graph. Suppose that the x-axis represents time, and the y-axis represents performance. If you plotted the top ten performances every year for a century, what would the graph look like in record and quasi-record sports? What would it look like in non-record sports? Is there anything to be said in favor of one pattern of performance over the other?

2. *Plateaus.* When the limit of performance is defined by an asymptote, new records are always possible, though the margins of improvement will become increasingly small, and the time between records may become increasingly long. When the limit of performance is defined by a plateau, new records are foreclosed. That is the case in bowling, where the top possible score for a game—300—has been reached innumerable times and will never be exceeded; it is achieved by rolling strikes on 12 consecutive balls, the maximum number in a game. Is that a bug or a feature? If a bug, is it a big one? Can it be fixed? To preserve the possibility for record-breaking, many bowling governing bodies maintain records of performance in game blocks. For example, the current record for a 6-game block (the standard length of competition for qualifying rounds on the PBA Tour) recognized by the United States Bowling Congress is 1,705 (or just over 284 per game). UNITED STATES

BOWLING CONGRESS, https://www.bowl.com/records/. Is that a good solution to the problem of plateaus (if it *is* a problem)?

3. *Perfection.* A bowler throws a "perfect game" by bowling a strike—that is, knocking down all the pins on one ball—in each of the first nine rames, followed by three more in the tenth. A baseball pitcher throws a "perfect game" by completing an entire nine-inning game without allowing a single opposing batter on base. Through the 2020 season, 23 perfect games had been thrown in MLB history. Every perfect game in bowling is perfect in just the same way: twelve balls bowled, twelve strikes made. As far as the recorded events are concerned, all perfect games in bowling are identical. But that's not clearly true about perfect games in baseball, because the sport recognizes different ways to record outs. Would a truly perfect game be one in which the pitcher not only retires all 27 batters he faces—but strikes each one out? Or would it be more perfect to retire all 27 batters on just 27 pitches? (In his 1908 perfect game, Addie Joss struck out 3, and needed a mere 74 pitches to get the 27 outs. Matt Cain threw 51 more pitches, but struck out 11 more batters, in his 2012 perfect game. All else equal, was one performance better than the other?)

And why isn't there a perfect game for batters? Would that be a home run in every at bat? Sixteen players have hit four home runs in a single MLB game (and none has hit more than four), but only two of the sixteen—Rocky Colavito in 1959, and Carlos Delgado in 2003—accomplished that feat in only four at bats. See the Baseball Almanac records here: https://tinyurl.com/y5yecgr5. Are Colavito and Delgado the only two players who have achieved a perfect batter's game in MLB history? If not, is that because there is no such thing as a perfect game for batters, or because, although there is, this metric doesn't capture it? Is it relevant that both Colavito and Delgado batted in only 6 runs on their four homers, whereas Mark Whiten's four homers (1993) netted 12 RBIs? (Recall the discussion of perfect scores in judged sports, Subchapter 5E, pp. 164–168.)

4. *Peaks.* Peaks occur when circumstances in which records have been set change, and the new circumstances are much less conducive to superior performance. Frequently, the changed circumstances are changes in rules. An oft-given example is MLB's lowering of the pitching mound by five inches in 1969. And it was widely feared in swimming circles that FINA's 2009 decision to outlaw high-buoyancy suits (pp. 281–285) would produce a particularly steep peak. (See Subchapter 8A.) Are peaks (or cliffs) problems? Consider the following observations concerning the cognitive bias, known as "anchoring" or "focalism," in which people rely more heavily on a salient fact or piece of information than is warranted by that fact's relevance to the issue at hand:

> There are two different ways in which records and record-keeping are influenced by this cognitive bias. The first is the obsession with certain "targeted" numbers as marked signs of achievement, because of the symmetry or roundness of the number . . .
>
> The second, and more significant, effect of anchoring is that the record itself establishes a standard of what is truly remarkable or humanly possible. Subsequent performance is judged by how far

ahead—or behind—it falls from this record. Athletes, the media, and fans all anchor around existing records. As a matter of sports psychology, goal-setting, which is often linked to besting existing records, can spur greater results. There is a flipside—the negative psychological aspect—that limitations of what has been sometimes can prompt an athlete to question whether he or she can do any better.

This is also the reason that people care more about some records than others, and the "unbreakable" records garner special attention. A constantly moving and lowering record line might be interesting, but the record does not "stick" long enough for anchoring to happen.

Sigman, *Are We All Dopes?*, at 191–92.

Should a sports league or federation take any steps to mitigate problems produced by record peaks? For example, if it appears that a change in circumstances from time T1 to T2 caused a drop-off after a peak, should a league create and maintain a formally bifurcated set of records that separately collect pre-peak and post-peak performances? Should the league take affirmative steps to alter *other* contest-related circumstances to make T2 as performance-friendly as T1, on net? If so, how? Should it denote the records achieved during peak conditions with an asterisk? Would your answers to any of these questions be affected if it turns out that lowering the mound hampered pitcher performance very modestly, see George Resor, *The Height of the Hill*, THE HARDBALL TIMES (June 27, 2014), or that pre-2010 swimming records have not proven especially hardy?

5.   *Asterisks.* As just suggested, asterisks could perhaps be used to mitigate the anchoring effects of a record peak. For example, FINA could use asterisks (or another signaling device) to identify records achieved with a high-buoyancy suit. Asterisks can also be used, not to curb the effects of a peak, but to signify that any particular record is either more significant or less significant than might otherwise appear. In 1961, when Roger Maris hit 61 home runs to eclipse Babe Ruth's 1927 record of 60 round trippers, the American League was in the first year of expansion, to ten teams and a 162-game schedule. During the season, Commissioner Ford Frick ruled that if Ruth's record was not broken in the first 154 games of the season, there should be a special indication of that in record books. According to popular lore, MLB record books affixed an asterisk to Maris's new record; he got his 61st homer in the last game of the season. In fact, the record books did not contain an asterisk; rather, some books reported the record this way:

Most Home Runs, Season

61 Roger E. Maris, AL: NY, 1961 (162 G/S)

60 George H. Ruth, AL. NY, 1927.

On the 1961 chase to best Ruth's record, see PHIL PEPE, 1961*: THE INSIDE STORY OF THE MARIS-MANTLE HOME RUN CHASE (2011). According to the sports journalist Allen Barra, Major League Baseball had no official record book until the late 1990s, and while some books reported the home run record as indicated above, others did not. Allen Barra, *Roger Maris and the Myth of the Asterisk*, VILLAGE VOICE, June 27, 2011. But, official book or not, MLB evidently believed there were officially recognized records. In 1968, a special baseball records committee decided that no indication of season length should be given for single-season records, but the matter was not put to rest until MLB's Committee on Statistical Accuracy, chaired by Commissioner Fay Vincent, reached a similar conclusion in 1991. Murray Chass, *Maris's Feat Finally Recognized 30 Years After Hitting 61 Homers*, N.Y. TIMES, Sept. 5, 1991.

Was it appropriate for record books to editorialize in any way regarding the significance of Maris's new record for home runs in a season? If not, why not? Because lots of circumstances had changed between 1927 and 1961, and that while some (e.g., expansion and the longer season) favored Maris, others (e.g., the opening of Major League Baseball to Black ballplayers, night baseball, and increasing use of relief pitchers) disfavored him, thereby making it impossible to assess who faced more favorable circumstances on net? Or because, as a matter of principle, records should always be allowed to "speak for themselves"? Or for some other reason? If a main purpose of record-keeping—and possibly *the* main purpose—is to facilitate meaningful transtemporal comparisons, then how should performance-relevant differences in a competitive context be identified?

B. REVISING RECORDS

GREG BISHOP, N.C.A.A. PENALTIES ERASE WINS BUT NOT MEMORIES

The New York Times, August 1, 2011
© 2011 The New York Times Company, reprinted with permission

The University of Hawaii won a men's volleyball championship in 2002. Or did it? Coach John Calipari earned his 500th college basketball victory last season. Or did he?

For dozens of universities across collegiate sports, for the players who competed, for the officials who whistled fouls and for the fans who paid for tickets, those games happened. Yet technically, they did not.

Welcome to the fuzzy world of modern college athletics, where the N.C.A.A. often requires teams to vacate victories as punishment for rules violations. Rampant infractions have resulted in a post facto revision of record books across all sports.

This brand of punishment, although not entirely new, has been used by the N.C.A.A. with increasing frequency in recent years. Last month alone, the N.C.A.A. vacated the final three games of Georgia Tech's 2009 football season, including its conference championship, for using an ineligible player, and Ohio State offered to vacate each of its 2010 football victories, including its Big Ten Conference championship and Sugar Bowl victory, as a pre-emptive move before the N.C.A.A. issued its ruling on possible violations by the Buckeyes.

Whether the N.C.A.A.'s now preferred form of discipline is truly effective is a subject of some metaphysical debate.

As Ken Pomeroy, a college sports statistician, noted, University of Massachusetts men's basketball fans remember the team's 1996 Final Four appearance as the greatest sports moment in its history, and "they don't feel any different just because the N.C.A.A. says it doesn't exist."

Then again, John Infante, the author of the Bylaw Blog and the assistant compliance director at Colorado State, said: "If the whole point is to win, and those wins are taken away, it's significant. Even if you can't take away the memories."

Pomeroy said he thought forcing colleges to vacate victories was an appropriate punishment. But effective or not as a deterrent, it has created oddities, a degree of confusion, a vast world of asterisks and ambivalence.

If Ohio State vacates its 2010 football victories, does it still have a seven-game winning streak against archrival Michigan?

And consider Arizona and Southern California, who may or may not have squared off twice during the 2007–8 men's basketball season. Both universities were later found in violation of N.C.A.A. rules, and as part of their punishments, each had to vacate victories, including wins against each other. Because losses still count when wins are vacated, both teams finished their season series 0–1.

The N.C.A.A., in an effort to punish rule breakers who may have left— players to graduation, coaches to other jobs—effectively says that a game that happened did not happen.

"I know who won the games," said Kevin O'Neill, then the Arizona coach, now the coach at U.S.C. "But I don't understand the whole vacating thing, anyway."

In nine years spent on the N.C.A.A. Division I Committee on Infractions, Jo Potuto, now a law professor at Nebraska, said she often heard the same complaint: that most penalties, like taking away scholarships or banning universities from postseason play, did not affect the actual violators. In 2005 or 2006, Potuto said, the committee decided the most appropriate way to punish the departed was to vacate records.

"In a perfect world, the penalties would punish those who committed the violations," she said. "We don't live in a perfect world."

The shift elevated the most clerical of punishments. The N.C.A.A. removed such wins from its database. Colleges took down banners and changed media guides. Coaches lost victories from their win totals. The

N.C.A.A. argued that instead of rewriting history, it was simply, realistically, acknowledging it. (Even if, in the case of the 1996 N.C.A.A. men's basketball tournament, six teams vacated 15 of the 63 games played.)

The N.C.A.A. drew the line between vacating and forfeiting, which would retroactively reward victories to teams that had lost games and would require a rewriting of the record books. With vacated games, the statistics are still recorded but marked by an asterisk. Teams also vacate postseason losses, but usually not regular-season ones.

"I don't think it's confusing at all," Potuto said.

Some college basketball fans may not agree. Last season, when Kentucky toppled Florida in February, the university honored Calipari for his 500th victory, even if 42 vacated victories, including those in Final Four appearances at UMass and Memphis, left him short of that total in the technical sense. The Lexington Herald-Leader reported that the N.C.A.A. asked Kentucky to apologize publicly.

USA Today later called Calipari "the worldwide leader in Final Four asterisks," and when he guided Kentucky to the Final Four last season, it was technically his first appearance there; he had been there twice before. "I don't deal with that," Calipari said at the Final Four. "We've been here three times."

Some colleges have found that this type of vacation actually involves more work, as Tim Tessalone, the sports information director at U.S.C., discovered last year. After the N.C.A.A. ruled that Reggie Bush, the team's star running back, had accepted improper benefits from prospective agents, it vacated two of U.S.C.'s victories in 2004 and all 12 wins in 2005. At the end of that 2005 season, the Trojans lost to Texas in the national championship game. Or did they?

The N.C.A.A. ruling prompted a makeover of the team's media guide. Tessalone said the guide now contains about 100 asterisks, from series records to year-by-year records to any records set by Bush—so many, in fact, that U.S.C. officials joked about placing a giant asterisk on the cover.

Beyond that, all references at U.S.C. to Bush had to be removed. The university returned its copy of his Heisman Trophy, took down his jersey from display and even changed the wallpaper that featured Bush and other Trojans.

"We're not trying to erase history," Tessalone said. "We're trying to notate history. It's appropriate. And it's confusing. We had to vacate our appearance in the B.C.S. title game. In essence, we never lost to Texas."

———

When, if ever, is it appropriate for official records to be changed after the event? Consider the range of fact patterns discussed below.

COMMENTS AND QUESTIONS

1. *Cutting corners.* From 2013–15, Canadian triathlete Julie Miller was one of the dominant performers in her sport, winning her division (women, ages 40–44) in Ironman Canada 2013 and 2015, the 2014 Vancouver Triathlon, and the 2014 Long Course World Championships in Weihai, China. In time, though, competitors noticed that they saw more of Miller on the winners' podium than during the races. And a subsequent investigation concluded that Miller routinely skipped entire portions of the events in which she was entered. As a result, Ironman barred her indefinitely from its sanctioned races, and Triathlon Canada issued her a two-year suspension. In addition, she was retroactively disqualified from the races she had "won," and her records deleted.

Do you agree that it was proper for race organizers to expunge Miller's results from races completed months or years earlier? If not, do you believe that retroactive changes to results already recorded are *ever* appropriate? Under what circumstances, if not these? In thinking through this problem, consider the observation that, among the many ways to cheat in sports, "runners and long-distance competitors—marathoners, cyclists, triathletes— reserve a special circle of contempt, and feel a special sort of outrage, for athletes who deliberately cut courses, covering only part of the distance while claiming they covered it all." Sarah Lyall, *Swim. Bike. Cheat?*, NEW YORK TIMES, April 10, 2016, at SP1.

2. *Doing drugs.* The IOC drug tests all Olympic medalists. If testing reveals that a medalist used a proscribed PED, the IOC will delete the athlete's performance from all official records and request that the medal already awarded be returned. (The request is sometimes, but not always, complied with.) Is this proper? Are there any reasons to treat runners who "cut corners" by using illegal drugs any differently from those who "cut corners" by, well, cutting corners? Thanks to steady improvements in the methods for detecting PEDs in blood and urine samples, athletic federations are often able to determine years after the event that an athlete had doped. Should there be a statute of limitations to the revocation of medals and the rewriting of record books? If so, of what length?

Can you think of any reasons why a medal that is "stripped" (whether or not it is physically recovered) should not be reallocated to the next best-performing athlete in that competition?

3. *Fudging ages.* During the 2001 Little League World Series, a star was born. Pitcher Danny Almonte led his Bronx little league team to the U.S. Final. Along the way, he dominated opponents, pitching a perfect game, another no-hitter, and a one-hit shutout. Tom Friend, *Revenge of the Baseball Gods*, ESPN.com (Nov. 14, 2008).

Following Almonte's success and rise to superstardom, Sports Illustrated launched an investigation and found that Almonte was two years older than advertised, and thus two years too old to play in the Little League World Series—an eighth grader playing against sixth graders. Because Almonte's birth certificate was falsified, his Bronx Little League team was forced to forfeit all of its victories. Is this a proper result?

What if Almonte had been only one day older than the Little League limit? Should the team still be forced to forfeit each of its games? What if Almonte had been an occasional substitute on the team rather than its star player? If you believe that either of these variations should affect the outcome, do you conclude that the rules governing forfeiture should be crafted as standards rather than as rules? And what about the eligibility rules themselves? Should they be written as standards, not rules? If so, what should the standard be?

4. Stretching boundaries. Fourteen years after Almonte's exploits, Jackie Robinson West found the spotlight by becoming the first team with only African-American players to win the U.S. title at the Little League World Series. (They fell in the World Championship game to a team from Seoul, South Korea.) Within weeks of its victory, however, an investigation determined that Jackie Robinson West team officials had recruited players from outside of its district to play for the team. Worse, team officials created false boundary maps to demonstrate that certain players lived within the district. Erin Flynn, *Jackie Robinson West Title Stripped Due to Fraud, Cover-Up*, SPORTS ILLUSTRATED, Aug. 12, 2015. Is this case distinguishable from the Almonte case? Should different consequences attach?

5. Extending benefits. What sanctions are appropriate when college players receive benefits in violation of NCAA amateurism rules? (See Subchapter 7.A, pp. 238–241) Consider the case of the University of Michigan basketball team of the 1990s. The team achieved great success on the court, but a federal investigation later revealed that a booster, Ed Martin, had given a total of $616,000 to Chris Webber and three other players, before and during their time at Michigan. In 2002, the University (in an attempt to prevent worse punishment by the NCAA) imposed numerous penalties on itself, including disqualifying itself from post-season play for one year and going on probation for two years, returning to the NCAA $450,000 received for postseason play, vacating 113 regular-season and tournament victories, deleting the names of the players in questions from the University's playing records, and taking down the banners that had been hanging in Crisler Arena for the 1992 and 1993 Final Fours, the 1997 NIT title and the 1998 Big Ten tournament title. In 2003, the NCAA tacked on additional penalties: it added two years of probation, docked the school one scholarship from 2004–05 until 2007–08, and ordered the University to disassociate itself from the four players for a decade. (Initially, it also barred Michigan from postseason play for an additional year, but on an appeal by the University it reversed that decision.) *Michigan Forfeits Victories from Five Seasons*, ESPN.COM (Nov. 11, 2002); *University of Michigan basketball scandal*, WIKIPEDIA, https://tinyurl.com/y5k74jaf.

Consider each of the sanctions imposed by Michigan itself or by the NCAA. Whom do they actually punish? And whom should the NCAA be aiming to punish? What further information would you want in answering these questions?

6.   *Abetting felonies.* Jerry Sandusky was a highly regarded assistant coach for the Penn State football team, beginning in 1969. On his retirement in 1999, after 23 years as defensive coordinator, he was given special emeritus status, which included access to Penn State athletic facilities. Sandusky founded The Second Mile, a charitable organization for underprivileged children, and ran football camps on Penn State grounds. In 2011, he was indicted on 52 counts of sexual abuse of children. The next year he was convicted on 45 counts of sexual assault of ten victims between 1994 and 2009, though many experts believe that the abuse likely began in the 1970s and included many more victims. A subsequent independent investigation, commissioned by the Penn State Board of Trustees and undertaken by former FBI Director Louis Freeh, determined that Head Football Coach Joe Paterno, Athletic Director Tim Curley, and University President Graham Spanier had all known since 1998 of credible allegations of child abuse by Sandusky (many occurring in Penn State athletic facilities, before and after Sandusky's retirement), but had taken no meaningful steps to end the abuse or to bring Sandusky to justice. Instead, Penn State administration "empowered" Sandusky to continue to molest and sodomize young boys, displaying a "total disregard for the safety and welfare of Sandusky's child victims." As a result of the Freeh Report, the NCAA fined the University $60 million, imposed a four-year ban on postseason football play, reduced the number of football scholarships Penn State could award, and vacated all 112 wins that the football program had recorded from 1998 to 2011. Because Paterno had coached the team for all but one of the 112 wins over that period, this last sanction had the effect of dropping him from first to twelfth in career wins among NCAA football coaches. Thirty months later, the NCAA reinstated the 112 vacated wins, making Paterno, who died after Sandusky was indicted but before he was convicted, once again the most victorious coach in NCAA football history. What was the right response to this tragedy? Did the NCAA get things right the first time, or on reconsideration, or on neither occasion? Or on both? As compared to the Michigan basketball scandal, is there a better or worse argument for vacating wins in this case?

7.   *Oops?* Should an official record ever be changed as a result of later-discovered evidence that it had initially been measured or transcribed incorrectly, though due to no fault of the competitors affected? The question emerges as a coda to the independently fascinating story of the race for the 1910 American League batting title, and for the car—a Chalmers 30 touring sedan—that the Chalmers Motor Company had pledged as an accompanying prize.

By late summer, as Connie Mack's Philadelphia Athletics ran away with the pennant, only two men were left in contention for the batting title: the Cleveland Indians' 36-year-old superstar Nap Lajoie, and Ty Cobb, of the

Detroit Tigers, who though only 23 had won the last three titles. Their see-saw battle transfixed a baseball-loving public throughout September, even though following the state of play was severely hampered by the lack of standardization of scoring hits and errors, and the irregular and unreliable methods of score-reporting and record-keeping. Published batting statistics would often vary from newspaper to newspaper. Still, with two games to play, the general consensus of unofficial statistics showed Cobb with a comfortable lead over his rival, inducing him to sit out the games lest he lower his average by playing. On October 8, the final day of the season, while Cobb sat, Lajoie's Indians were in St. Louis for a doubleheader against the Browns. The *St. Louis Post Dispatch* reported that morning that Lajoie would have to go 7-for-8 to surpass Cobb, though everyone knew that was just an estimate, for the official statistics would await determination by American League Secretary Robert McRoy.

In the event, in 9 plate appearances, Lajoie registered 8 hits and a sacrifice bunt, the last six hits being bunt singles down the third baseline, where Red Corriden, a rookie and regular shortstop, was playing unusually deep. Most followers of the box scores believed that those eight hits were enough to give Lajoie the batting title. Yet fans and commentators worried that the Browns may have conspired to help the well-liked Lajoie surpass the generally loathed Cobb. League officials investigated. One week later, League President Ban Johnson cleared all parties of wrongdoing, accepting Corriden's explanation that he played deep on his own initiative, and that he did so both to respect Lajoie's power and due to his unfamiliarity with the position. In the same statement, Johnson announced McRoy's certified final batting statistics: Cobb—196 hits in 509 at bats, for an average, rounded to three digits, of .385; Lajoie—227 hits in 591 at bats, for an average of .384. Cobb was announced the AL batting champion, But in a show of good will, Chalmers announced it would award a Chalmers 30 to both men.

Seventy years later, a researcher looking through microfilm at the Baseball Hall of Fame discovered that league record keepers had mistakenly double counted a game on September 24, in which Cobb went 2 for 3 against the Boston Red Sox. As corrected, Cobb's record stands at 194 hits in 506 at bats—an average of .383339, almost a point lower than Lajoie.

Should Major League Baseball correct its official records to recognize Lajoie as the real batting champ for 1910? Should Ty Cobb's total hit count be reduced by two? If not, is that because too much time has elapsed? Or because it's inappropriate to revisit the records of *any* player unless it is done for *all* players? Or because Lajoie's 8-for-8 performance (or 9-for-9, because Johnson ruled that the sacrifice should have been recorded as a hit) in the season-ending doubleheader is itself too fishy? Or for other reasons? The compelling story is well told in RICK HUHN, THE CHALMERS RACE: TY COBB, NAPOLEON LAJOIE, AND THE CONTROVERSIAL 1910 BATTING TITLE THAT BECAME A NATIONAL OBSESSION (2014).

8.   *The standard of proof.* Before a record is expunged due to a competitor's malfeasance, what procedures should the record-keeping body be expected to follow? Most particularly, how confident must officials be that the relevant facts are as alleged before they retroactively alter a record? Is it enough that the decision maker believes that the facts are "more likely than not" to be true, or should "indisputable evidence" be required? Or something else? (Recall the discussions of standards of proof and review, at pp. 367–373 and 438–445.) *See Ryan Braun Apologizes for PED use,* ESPN.com (Aug. 23, 2013).

C. HALLS OF FAME

The National Baseball Hall of Fame opened in 1939, and since then Halls have been established in all other major North American sports; there are competing Halls in boxing. The Halls typically have exhibits devoted to the history of their respective sports, but the centerpiece is a section formally recognizing a limited number of outstanding participants in the sport—mainly players, but also coaches, officials, administrators, executives and others. Membership in a sport's Hall of Fame is at least arguably the greatest recognition a participant can receive for lifetime achievement, and so it inevitably raises numerous contentious issues.

COMMENTS AND QUESTIONS

1.   *Electors.* Who should choose members of a Hall? Journalists who cover the sport? (Might they play favorites?) Members of the Hall who have been inducted in prior years? (Might they be too reluctant to admit new inductees, for fear of cheapening the honor they have received? That suggestion has been made with respect to baseball's veterans committees.) Administrators? (Might they be too eager to admit new inductees, to generate business for the Hall?) Fans? (Might they be insufficiently knowledgeable?) A combination? (The International Tennis Hall of Fame now has a fan voting component. Li Na of China received the most fan votes in the first year; this gave her a 3% bonus added to her total in the Official Voting Group and helped her earn induction.) Others?

2.   *Minima and maxima.* The ground rules for the Selection Committee of the Pro Football Hall of Fame prescribe that each year it should select between four and eight new inductees. What are the pros and cons of such a rule?

3.   *Waiting periods and consideration limits.* Halls usually prescribe post-retirement waiting periods for players to be inducted—for example, five years in baseball and pro football, four years in basketball. Sometimes the same waiting period is applied to coaches as well, but an active basketball coach can be enshrined after 25 years of coaching. On the other hand, several active golfers have been admitted to the LPGA Tour Hall of Fame, and also to the World Golf Hall of Fame—but the current rules of the latter prescribe that

a golfer must be retired five years or at least 45 years old. Are waiting periods justified? If so, in what settings? If waiting periods are a good idea, should they be waivable? Note that the baseball writers waived the usual waiting period to vote Casey Stengel in less than a year after he retired as a manager at age 75.

If waiting periods cut an athlete's eligibility window from the front end, consideration limits or deadlines restrict the window from the back end. Baseball players are eligible for election to their Hall under the usual process of election by baseball writers until fifteen years after retirement, leaving them with a 10-year consideration window; after that, selection by a veterans' committee is still possible, but it is rarer. Is this justified? What are the relevant considerations?

4.   *Prescribed criteria.* Hall of Fame selection can generate endless debates about criteria for selection. Should a long career of very good and steady but not spectacular performance justify election to a Hall? (Think—or ask your grandparents to think—of Bill Mazeroski, who eventually made baseball's Hall.) How about a brief, sensational career shortened by injury. (Pete Reiser and Tony Conigliaro, neither of whom ever got close to Cooperstown, might be examples in baseball; Bo Jackson is an obvious example in football.) Should there be a minimum number of playing years?

Most Halls leave the criteria for selection rather loose and subjective. But there are exceptions. To be selected for the World Golf Hall of Fame, a golfer in the post-1980 era, male or female, must have won at least fifteen tournaments on one of the world's leading tours, or two majors. The LPGA Tour Hall of Fame has a point system for post-1998 players: In addition to having played for at least ten years and having won at least one major championship, the Vare Trophy (for lowest scoring average in a year), or Rolex Player of the Year honors, a player must have accumulated 27 points—one for each LPGA tournament win, and two for each major win, Vare Trophy, or Rolex honor earned. Do such criteria make sense for a golf Hall? Should other sports attempt to emulate them? (The International Tennis Hall of Fame has rigorous criteria for *automatic* inclusion on the ballot, but a player can be included, and selected, without meeting them.)

5.   *A thorny problem.* Recall that Pete Rose is on MLB's permanently ineligible list. By rules of baseball's Hall of Fame, this also renders him ineligible to be a member of the Hall. Assume for the purposes of argument that there remain good reasons to render Rose ineligible to associate with any team because of his gambling history. Does it follow that he should be ineligible to receive the honor of membership in his sport's Hall of Fame, which would have been a no-brainer if only his play on the field had been considered? Now assume that Rose should, after more than three decades in baseball purgatory, again be allowed to participate in the sport. Does it follow that, though he repeatedly violated a long-established rule meant to ensure the integrity of the sport, he should be given the honor of admittance to the Hall? Would your answers change if Rose had bet *against* his team?

6. Character more generally. Even apart from his gambling history, Rose has another problem. The Election Rules for the Hall of the Baseball Writers' Association of America (BBWA) provide: "Voting shall be based upon the player's record, playing ability, integrity, sportsmanship, character, and contributions to the team(s) on which the player played." Suppose Rose has been rendered eligible, you are a member of the BBWA voting on election to the Hall, and you have been persuaded that, as an adult, Rose did in fact knowingly have a continuing sexual relationship with a young girl (as has been alleged). How should that fact enter into your consideration?

Note that the Pro Football Hall of Fame has no comparable "character clause." Rather, only an individual's on-field achievements and contributions to the game matter for the purposes of Hall of Fame consideration. NFL Commissioner Roger Goodell disagrees with that policy. As Goodell has explained, "I do believe that it's more than just how you conduct yourself on the field. I believe very firmly that it's how you conduct yourself on and off the field as a member of the National Football League. That's part of your contribution to the game." Gregg Rosenthal, *Commissioner believes off-field conduct should be considered in Hall of Fame voting*, NBC SPORTS.COM (May 20, 2010). What do you think? Should Halls of Fame specify that "character" is relevant to inclusion, or that it isn't? Or should they say nothing at all, leaving the judgment up to its designated voters?

Jeff Idelson, the President of the Baseball Hall of Fame, has insisted that the BBWA's "character clause" is not intended to encompass all flaws of character. He explained, "Every voter has to determine what character means for them. It's meant to be a guide. It is meant to ask: 'Did this player respect the game? Did this player respect the uniform? Are you proud of this person in terms of how they conducted themselves with respect to the game?'" John McMurray, *Baseball Hall of Fame president Jeff Idelson talks character clause, PED users and ballot changes*, SPORTING NEWS.COM (Aug. 14, 2018). Is this a tenable middle-ground between two unacceptably extreme poles? How should it play out in Rose's case? Should a convicted serial killer be inducted into a Hall of Fame just so long as his stats are good enough? If he had already been inducted by the time his murderous history is uncovered, should he be expelled? If, notwithstanding Idelson's view, you think that statutory rape and murder are enough to keep a great player out of the Hall, or even cause expulsion, how about armed robbery? Tax evasion? Consider the cases of Duke Snider and Willie McCovey, two baseball Hall of Famers who repeatedly and knowingly failed to declare many thousands of dollars of memorabilia-related income.

7. The spitter and the Hall. What do you think Idelson would, or should, make of the presence in his Hall of a plaque for Gaylord Perry? Perry was a highly successful pitcher over 22 major league seasons, with 315 wins. But there is no doubt that, at least at times, he doctored the ball illegally. Take his word for it: In a book titled *Me and the Spitter: An Autobiographical Confession*, published in 1974, a little past the midpoint of his career, he wrote, "I reckon I tried everything on the old apple but salt and pepper and chocolate sauce topping. . . . Of course, I'm reformed now. I'm a pure law-abiding citizen." It may be that Perry benefited as much or more from batters' belief that he was doctoring, a belief he did nothing to dispel, as from the act itself. Not until his 21st season was he ever ejected from a game for throwing a spitter; he also received a 10-day suspension. In his first two years of eligibility for the Hall, Perry fell short, but not by much, of the 75% needed for induction and he cleared the bar, but not by much, in the third year. Were the electors justified in looking past Perry's breaking of the rules? If so, why?

8.   *The burden of proof.* Sammy Sosa was the fifth player in history to hit 600 home runs and he remains the only one to hit 60 or more homers in each of three seasons. He also has been dogged by the belief that his prolonged power surge was fueled by steroids. Over the first four years of his career, he hit one homer in every 38.9 plate appearances; from 1993 to the end, including even the twilight of his career, he hit one in every 14.83 PAs. In 2003, he— along with Alex Rodriguez, David Ortiz, Manny Ramirez, and 100 other MLB players—tested positive for banned PEDs; because these tests were conducted for informational purposes under the collective bargaining agreement, they carried no punishment, were supposed to remain anonymous, and were never confirmed. Sosa has consistently denied use of banned PEDs, and he never tested positive again. Suppose that you are an elector for baseball's Hall of Fame considering Sosa's case, and you conclude that he should be in the Hall unless he persistently used PEDs. To justify a No vote, how confident should you be that he did so? Sosa became eligible in 2013, but he only received 12.5% off the vote; since then, he has never gotten more than 14%.

9.   *How much of a taint?* To what extent does an act of misconduct, even though serious and game-related, taint an illustrious career that, for the most part, was achieved fair and square? Consider the following cases.

- Barry Bonds, among other distinctions, holds the career and single-season records for home runs; very probably, both were aided by steroid use. But early in his career, well before the time he is suspected of having begun to juice, Bonds won three MVP awards; he was an astonishing combination of power, speed, and defense. Roger Clemens was one of the most dominant pitchers of all time. He won seven Cy Young awards over his 24-year career. He also is suspected of extensive steroid use in the latter part of his career; like Bonds, he featured prominently in the Mitchell Report on steroid use in baseball. Like Sosa, Bonds and Clemens became eligible for the Hall in 2013. They each received well under 40% of the vote; those percentages have climbed to over 60%, but at this writing not yet to the 75% threshold needed for induction. Suppose again that you are an elector, and suppose also that you have satisfied yourself to a high degree of confidence that Clemens and Bonds were in fact steadily on the juice for years. Would you still feel justified in voting for them if you concluded that each had achieved Hall of Fame distinction early in his career, before ever touching steroids? How about on the ground that they played in an era in which many players were juiced, and they were still at the top of the heap? Would you be moved by an argument that denial of admission in their first several years of eligibility made a sufficient statement, and now it was time to recognize their achievements?

- Compare Bonds and Clemens with Robinson Canó, who was suspended by MLB for using PEDs in May 2018 and banned for 80 games. After he again tested positive in November 2020, the league suspended him without pay for the entire 2021 season. At the time of his second suspension, Canó's statistical profile was that of a Hall of Famer. Only eight second basemen have more hits than Canó, and they all have plaques in Cooperstown. However, many believe that this second suspension for PEDs will doom his prospects for election. As one Hall of Fame voting member explained: "My rule will be I'm not doing any judging unless a player was suspended after there was a testing system in place. So while I'd be a yes on Bonds and Clemens, I'm a no on Ramirez and Cano." Matt Snyder, *Robinson Cano's Hall of Fame fate has been sealed after his second PED suspension*, CBS SPORTS (Nov. 19, 2020). Indeed, although MLB has prohibited steroid use since 1991, it didn't institute drug testing until 2003. Does this voter's approach strike you as sound?

- Andy Pettitte, a pitcher who spent most of his career with the Yankees, admitted to having taken human growth hormone (HGH)—for two days, to promote healing while he was on the disabled list. He said he stopped because he was uncomfortable taking it. If you were an elector, and you concluded that Pettitte had in fact taken HGH, but only for the two days, and that it was a banned substance when he took it, what effect, if any, would it have on your vote?

- PEDs are not Sammy Sosa's only problem. During the 2003 season, in which he hit 40 homers, he served a seven-game suspension for using a corked bat. He contended that he had mistakenly gone to the plate with a bat he intended to use only for batting practice. His other bats were examined, and all were clean. What role, if any, should this incident play in considering his case?

- Vijay Singh was one of the greatest golfers of his generation. He won three majors, 34 PGA tournaments, and numerous other tournaments around the world. In 2004 and 2005, he interrupted Tiger Woods's prolonged period of dominance and had the world number 1 ranking for a total of 32 weeks. Two decades earlier, when he was 22, he was suspended indefinitely from the Asian Tour for taking off a stroke from his scorecard so he could make a tournament cut. Singh has said the incident was only a misunderstanding, but others have regarded it as blatant cheating. *See* John Garrity, *The Facts of the Matter: Revising Vijay Singh's History Only Obscures What He Has Accomplished,* SPORTS ILLUSTRATED, May 22, 2000. Should this incident have prevented Singh from being inducted into the World Golf Hall of Fame?

––––––––

Exercise 17C

You might not know that there is a national Trial Lawyer Hall of Fame, spearheaded by the National Trial Lawyers Association and its magazine, *The Trial Lawyer*, and housed since 2014 at the Temple University Beasley School of Law in Philadelphia. As of this writing, it honors just 69 inductees, from President John Adams and Supreme Court Justice Thurgood Marshall to Clarence Darrow and Johnnie Cochran. What do you think the rules for eligibility and induction should be? (The actual criteria for membership, and the nomination and selection process, are detailed here: https://tinyurl.com/y2qqasd7.)

ROSTER*

---

*   This index is modestly selective.

SUBJECT INDEX

References are to Pages

bold denotes names of individual sports and games;
n following page number denotes footnote